5th Workshop on Challenges and Applications of Automated Extraction of Socio-political Events from Text (CASE 2022)

Abu Dhabi, United Arab Emirates and Online
7-8 December 2022

ISBN: 978-1-7138-9105-5

Printed from e-media with permission by:

Curran Associates, Inc.
57 Morehouse Lane
Red Hook, NY 12571

Some format issues inherent in the e-media version may also appear in this print version.

Printed with permission by Curran Associates, Inc. (2024)

Association for Computational Linguistics
209 N. Eighth Street
Stroudsburg, Pennsylvania 18360

Phone: 1-570-476-8006
Fax: 1-570-476-0860

acl@aclweb.org

Additional copies of this publication are available from:

Curran Associates, Inc.
57 Morehouse Lane
Red Hook, NY 12571 USA
Phone: 845-758-0400
Fax: 845-758-2633
Email: curran@proceedings.com
Web: www.proceedings.com

CASE 2022

The 5th Workshop on Challenges and Applications of Automated Extraction of Socio-political Events from Text

Proceedings of the Workshop

December 7-8, 2022

Organizing Committee

Organizers

Ali Hürriyetoğlu, Koc University
Hristo Tanev, European Commission, Joint Research Centre
Vanni Zavarella, University of Cagliari, Italy
Erdem Yörük, Koc University
Reyyan Yeniterzi, Sabanci University
Osman Mutlu, Koc University
Fırat Duruşan, Koc University
Ali Safaya, Koc University
Bharathi Raja Chakravarthi, Insight SFI Centre for Data Analytics
Francielle Vargas, University of São Paulo
Farhana Ferdousi Liza, University of East Anglia
Milena Slavcheva, Bulgarian Academy of Sciences
Benjamin J. Radford, UNC Charlotte
Ritesh Kumar, Dr. Bhimrao Ambedkar University
Daniela Cialfi, The 'Gabriele d'Annunzio' University
Tiancheng Hu Hu, ETH Zürich
Niklas Stöhr, ETH Zürich
Fiona Anting Tan, National University of Singapore
Tadashi Nomoto, National Institute of Japanese Literature, Japan

Program Committee

Chairs

Hansi Hettiarachchi, Birmingham City University
Ali Hürriyetoğlu, KNAW
Tadashi Nomoto, National Institute of Japanese Literature
Fiona Anting Tan, Institute of Data Science, National University of Singapore

Program Committee

Fatih Beyhan, Sabancı University
Elizabeth Boschee, Information Sciences Institute
Tommaso Caselli, Rijksuniversiteit Groningen
Xingran Chen, University of Michigan
Daniela Cialfi, University of Studies Gabriele d'Annunzio
Martin Fajcik, Brno University of Technology
Andrew Halterman, Massachusetts Institute of Technology
Adeep Hande, Indiana University Bloomington
Tiancheng Hu, ETH Zurich
Zhuoqun Li, Institute of Software, Chinese Academy of Sciences
Pasquale Lisena, EURECOM
Arka Mitra, ETH Zurich
Roser Morante, UNED
Manolito Octaviano Jr., National University
Benjamin J. Radford, UNC Charlotte
Fabiana Rodrigues De Góes, University of São Paulo
Ali Safaya, Koç University
Ali Seyfi, The George Washington University
Milena Slavcheva, Institute of Information and Communication Technologies, Bulgarian Academy of Sciences
Niklas Stoehr, ETH Zurich
Surendrabikram Thapa, Virginia Tech
Paul Trust, University College Cork
Onur Uca, Department of Sociology, Mersin University
Francielle Vargas, University of São Paulo
Reyyan Yeniterzi, Sabanci University
Yongjun Zhang, Stony Brook University
Ge Zhang, University of Michigan
Juan Pablo Zuluaga-gomez, Idiap Research Institute

Keynote Talk: A total error approach to validating event data that is transparent, scalable, and practical to implement

Scott Althaus
University of Illinois Urbana-Champaign

Abstract: There are at least two reasonable ways to make your way toward where you want to go: looking down to carefully place one foot in front of the other, and looking up to focus on where you hope to arrive. Looking up beats looking down if there's a particular destination in mind, and for constructing valid event data that destination usually takes the form of high-quality human judgment. Yet many approaches to generating event data on protests and acts of political violence using fully-automated systems implicitly adopt a "looking down" approach by benchmarking validity as a series of incremental improvements over prior algorithmic efforts. And even those efforts that adopt a "looking up" approach often treat human-generated gold standard data as if it was prima facie valid, without ever testing or confirming the accuracy of this assumption. It stands to reason that if we want to automatically produce valid event data that approaches the validity of human judgment, then we also need to validate the human judgment tasks that provide the point of comparison. But because of obvious difficulties in implementing such a rigorous assessment within the time and budget constraints of typical research projects, this more rigorous double-validation approach is rarely attempted.

This presentation outlines a "looking up" approach for double-validating fully-automated event data developed by the Cline Center for Advanced Social Research at the University of Illinois Urbana-Champaign (USA), illustrates that approach with a test of the precision and recall for two widely-used event classification systems (the PETRARCH-2 coder used in Phoenix and TERRIER, as well as the BBN ACCENT coder used in W-ICEWS), and demonstrates the utility of the approach for developing fully-automated event data algorithms with levels of validity that approach the quality of human judgment.

The first part of the talk reviews the Cline Center's total error framework for identifying 19 types of error that can affect the validity of event data and addresses the challenge of applying a total error framework when authoritative ground truth about the actual distribution of relevant events is lacking (Althaus, Peyton, and Shalmon, 2022). We argue that carefully constructed gold standard datasets can effectively benchmark validity problems even in the absence of ground truth data about event populations. We propose that a strong validity assessment for event data should, at a minimum, possess three characteristics. First, there should be a standard describing ideal data; a gold standard that, in the best case, takes the form of ground truth. Second, there should be a direct "apples to apples" comparison of outputs from competing methods given identical input. Third, the test should use appropriate metrics for measuring agreement between the gold standard and data produced by competing approaches.

The second part of the talk presents the results of a validation exercise meeting all three criteria that is applied to two algorithmic event data pipelines: the Python Engine for Text Resolution and Related Coding Hierarchy (PETRARCH-2) and the BBN ACCENT event coder. It then reviews a recent Cline Center project that has built a fully-automated event coder which produces dramatic improvements in validity over both PETRARCH-2 and BBN ACCENT by leveraging the total error framework and a reliance on the double-validation approach using high-quality gold standard benchmark datasets.

Bio: Scott Althaus (https://pol.illinois.edu/directory/profile/salthaus): is Merriam Professor of Political Science, Professor of Communication, and Director of the Cline Center for Advanced Social Research at the University of Illinois Urbana-Champaign. He also has faculty appointments with the School of Information Sciences and the National Center for Supercomputing Applications. His work with the Cline Center applies text analytics methods and Artificial Intelligence algorithms to extract insights from millions of news stories in ways that produce new forms of knowledge that advance societal well-being around the world. His own research interests explore the communication processes that support political accountability in democratic societies and that empower political discontent in non-democratic societies. His interests focus on four areas of inquiry: (1) how journalists construct news coverage about public affairs, (2) how leaders attempt to shape news coverage for political advantage, (3) how citizens use news coverage for making sense of public affairs, and (4) how the opinions of citizens are communicated back to leaders. He has particular interests in popular support for war, data science methods for extreme-scale analysis of news coverage, cross-national comparative research on political communication, the psychology of information processing, and communication concepts in democratic theory. His current projects include using data mining methods to help journalists cover terrorist attacks in responsible ways, a solo-authored book manuscript to be published by Cambridge University Press about the dynamics of popular support for war in the United States, and a co-authored book manuscript (with Tamir Sheafer and Gadi Wolfsfeld) in press with Oxford University Press on understanding the role of media in supporting governmental accountability and increasing the government's responsiveness to citizen needs.

J. Craig Jenkins (https://sociology.osu.edu/people/jenkins.12) is Academy Professor Emeritus of Sociology at The Ohio State University. He directed the Mershon Center for International Security Studies from 2011 to 2015 and is now senior research scientist. Jenkins is author of more than 100 referred articles and book chapters, as well as author or editor of several books including The Politics of Insurgency: The Farm Worker's Movement of the 1960s (1986); The Politics of Social Protest: Comparative Perspectives on States and Social Movements, with Bert Klandermans (University of Minnesota Press, 1995); Identity Conflicts: Can Violence be Regulated?, with Esther Gottlieb (Transaction Publishers, 2007) and Handbook of Politics: State and Society in Global Perspective, with Kevin T. Leicht (Springer, 2010). He has received numerous awards, including the Robin M. Williams Jr. Award for Distinguished Contributions to Scholarship, Teaching and Service from the Section on Peace, War and Social Conflict of the American Sociological Association (2015), fellow of the American Association for the Advancement of Science (2009), Joan Huber Faculty Fellow (2003), chair of the Section on Committees of the American Sociological Association (1998-2000), chair of the Section on Political Sociology, ASA (1995-96), and chair of the Section on Collective Behavior and Social Movements, ASA (1994-95). He was elected to the Sociological Research Association in 1993 and was a national security fellow at the Mershon Center for International Security at Ohio State in 1988, a Mershon Center professor from 2003-06 and chair of the Sociology Department, 2006-2010. Jenkins has received numerous grants from funding agencies, including the National Science Foundation, National Endowment for Humanities and Russell Sage Foundation. In 2010-11, he received a Liev Eriksson Mobility Grant from the Norway Research Council. In 2011-12, Jenkins was a Fulbright Fellow to Norway and a visiting professor at the Peace Research Institute of Oslo (PRIO) in Oslo, Norway. In 2017, Jenkins and co-investigator Maciek Slomczynski received a $1.4 million grant from the National Science Foundation for a four-year project on "Survey Data Recycling: New Analytic Framework, Integrated Database and Tools for Cross-National Social, Behavioral and Economic Research." Jenkins has served as deputy editor of American Sociological Review (1986-1989), and on the editorial boards of Journal of Political and Military Sociology, International Studies Quarterly, Sociological Forum, and Sociological Quarterly.

Keynote Talk: Event Extraction in the Era of Large Language Models: Structure Induction and Multilingual Learning

Thien Huu Nguyen
University of Oregon

Abstract: Events such as protests, disease outbreaks, and natural disasters are prevalent in text from different languages and domains. Event Extraction (EE) is an important task of Information Extraction that aims to identify events and their structures in unstructured text. The last decade has witnessed significant progress for EE research, featuring deep learning and large language models as the state-of-the-art technologies. However, a key issue of existing EE methods involves modeling input text sequentially to solve each EE tasks separately, thus limiting the abilities to encode long text and capture various types of dependencies to improve EE performance. In this talk, I will present some of our recent efforts to address this issue where text structures are explicitly learned to realize important objects and their interactions to facilitate the predictions for EE.
In addition, current EE research still mainly focuses on a few popular languages, e.g., English, Chinese, Arabic, and Spanish, leaving many other languages unexplored for EE. In this talk, I will also introduce our current research focus on developing evaluation benchmarks and models to extend EE systems to multiple new languages, i.e., multilingual and cross-lingual learning for EE. Finally, I will highlight some research challenges that can be studied in future work for EE.

Bio: Thien Huu Nguyen (https://ix.cs.uoregon.edu/ thien/) is an assistant professor in the Department of Computer and Information Science at the University of Oregon. He obtained his Ph.D. in natural language processing (NLP) at New York University (working with Ralph Grishman) and did a postdoc at the University of Montreal (working with Yoshua Bengio). Thien's research areas involve information extraction, language grounding, and deep learning where he developed one of the first deep learning models for entity recognition, relation extraction, and event extraction. His current research explores multi-domain and multilingual NLP that aims to learn transferable representations to perform information extraction tasks over different domains and languages. Thien is the director of the NSF IUCRC Center for Big Learning (CBL) at the University of Oregon. His research has been supported by NSF, IARPA, Army Research Office, Adobe Research, and IBM Research.

Table of Contents

Program

Wednesday, December 7, 2022

09:00 - 18:30	*Day 1*
09:00 - 17:30	*Tutorials*
11:00 - 12:30	*Poster Session (S2)*
12:30 - 14:00	*Lunch Break (LB)*
14:00 - 15:30	*Afternoon Session (S3)*
15:30 - 16:00	*Afternoon Coffee Break (B2)*
16:00 - 17:30	*Afternoon Session (S4)*
17:30 - 18:30	*Keynote 1 Session (S5)*

Thursday, December 8, 2022

09:00 - 18:30	*Day 2*
09:00 - 17:30	*Tutorials*
11:00 - 12:30	*Poster Session (S2)*
12:30 - 14:00	*Lunch Break (LB)*
14:00 - 15:30	*Afternoon Session (S3)*
15:30 - 16:00	*Afternoon Coffee Break (B2)*
16:00 - 17:30	*Afternoon Session (S4)*
17:30 - 18:30	*Keynote 2 Session (S5)*

A Multi-Modal Dataset for Hate Speech Detection on Social Media: Case-study of Russia-Ukraine Conflict

Surendrabikram Thapa[1], Aditya Shah[1], Farhan Ahmad Jafri[2], Usman Naseem[3], Imran Razzak[4]
[1]Department of Computer Science, Virginia Tech, USA
[2]Department of Computer Science, Jamia Millia Islamia, India
[3]School of Computer Science, The University of Sydney, Australia
[4]School of Computer Science and Engineering, University of New South Wales, Australia
{sbt,aditya31}@vt.edu, farhanjafri88888@gmail.com
usman.naseem@sydney.edu.au, Imran.razzak@unsw.edu.au

Abstract

Hate speech consists of types of content (e.g. text, audio, image) that express derogatory sentiments and hate against certain people or groups of individuals. The internet, particularly social media and microblogging sites, have become an increasingly popular platform for expressing ideas and opinions. Hate speech is prevalent in both offline and online media. A substantial proportion of this kind of content is presented in different modalities (e.g. text, image, video). Taking into account that hate speech spreads quickly during political events, we present a novel multimodal dataset composed of 5680 text-image pairs of tweets data related to the Russia-Ukraine war and annotated with a binary class: "hate" or "no-hate" The baseline results show that multimodal resources are relevant to leverage the hateful information from different types of data. The baselines and dataset provided in this paper may boost researchers in direction of multimodal hate speech, mainly during serious conflicts such as war contexts.

1 Introduction

The internet has become an increasingly popular communication medium to express the views of people. People mostly express their opinions on various topics using social media, microblogging platforms, blogs, etc. With great internet penetration even in the rural parts of the world and ease of access to information in real-time, people mostly rely on social media platforms (Naseem et al., 2021). At times of political events and tension in any region, the users of such platforms become more active than usual and post their thoughts and updates regarding the issues. During the expression of such opinions and ideas, there can be mixed emotions. Some opinions lean towards supporting the people on the ground who are suffering in such political events whereas some opinions are about blaming each other, name-calling, exaggeration of information, etc (Dimitrov et al., 2021). In political situations pertaining to invasion, the situation becomes even worse. Social media sometimes get polarized into the ones supporting the invasion and the ones opposing the invasion. During such polarization, a lot of content can be found which uses extreme language, falsifies the information, and spreads hate. Such content when directed towards certain people or groups of individuals (race, gender, nationality) with the intent to show anger and hate is called hate speech (Parihar et al., 2021). While the legal definitions of hate speech vary from territory to territory, hate speech on the internet sphere is taken as hateful content on the internet that is directed toward certain individuals or groups of individuals. The Cambridge Dictionary defines hate speech as "public speech that expresses hate or encourages violence towards a person or group based on something such as race, religion, sex, or sexual orientation" (Miller and Brown, 2013).

On February 24, 2022, Russia started a full-scale invasion of Ukraine by land, sea, and air (Berninger et al., 2022). The world was again polarized into two, with one supporting the Russian invasion and the other opposing it. Many countries condemned the war, and sanctions were eventually imposed on Russia. With the development of these events, social media started getting active. People started to express their opinions related to the humanitarian crisis and economic crisis that was caused due to the invasion. Amid the healthy and respectful discourse and discussions, there was some hateful content targeted at various people (Figure 1).

Hate speech can bring serious consequences to society. Microblogging platforms and social media platforms put a lot of effort into managing the hateful content on their platforms. Mostly, the platforms use human mediators for the mediation of posts related to hate speech. Despite being an efficient method for regulating hate speech, it is not always possible for human mediators to flag

Proceedings of the 5th Workshop on Challenges and Applications of Automated Extraction of Socio-political Events from Text (CASE), pages 1 - 6
December 7-8, 2022

(a) Tweet with No Hate

(b) Tweet with Hate Speech

Figure 1: Examples of tweets with hate and no hate speech during Russia-Ukraine conflict

the posts provided that the volume of the hateful content becomes extremely high in situations of political events like an invasion. Thus, there has always been a need for an automated system to identify the contents related to hate speech. Our ***contributions*** can be summarized as follows:

- We construct and release new multi-modal data for identifying hate speech tasks on social media, consisting of 5,680 tweets (image-text pairs) labeled across binary labels.
- Our experimental analysis shows that both modalities (text and images) are important for the task.
- We experiment with several state-of-the-art textual, visual, and multi-modal models, which further confirm the importance of both modalities and the need for further research.

2 Related Works

Despite hate speech detection being a hard task, much research is being done to address hate speech on the internet. With advancements in the field of deep learning, there is a multitude of problems that are being solved by deep learning (Adhikari et al., 2022). Hate speech is one of the tasks that is being explored using deep learning techniques. Most of the research on hateful content is focused on leveraging the information from the textual content. Del Vigna et al. (2017) curated a dataset of 17,567 comments from Facebook posts and annotated for strong hate, weak hate, and no hate categories. The proposed long-short term memory (LSTM) (Hochreiter and Schmidhuber, 1997) and SVM models performed with an accuracy of 72.95% and 75.23% for hate and non-hate categories. Similarly, the accuracy of 64.61% and 60.50% were reported across all three categories. Similarly, Gambäck and Sikdar (2017) had proposed multiple CNN architectures in order to classify hate speech spanning across multiple classes, viz. racism, sexism, both (racism and sexism), and non-hate speech. The architecture with Word2Vec embeddings was able to achieve an F1-score of 0.7829. Calderón et al. (2020) did a slightly different task of hate speech classification by curating a dataset (1977 tweets) of the hate speech directed towards the immigrants in Spain and performing the task of topic modeling and meticulously studying linguistic cues of hate speech.

Apart from these, some research has been done on multi-modal hate speech detection. For instance, Shang et al. (2021) proposed Analogy-aware Offensive Meme Detection (AOMD) that was able to learn the implicit analogy from the multi-modal contents of the meme and detect the offensive analogy. The model that used ResNet50 (He et al., 2016) and Glove-based LSTM was able to achieve the accuracy of 69% and 72% for Gab and Reddit datasets. Similarly, Zhou et al. (2021) proposed a method that integrates the image captioning process into the memes detection process. The approach enhanced the cross-modality relationship and helped achieve AUROC as high as 78.86. For their study, they used the famous dataset from Hateful Memes Challenge (Kiela et al., 2020). Similarly, Dimitrov et al. (2021) presented a method to identify propaganda techniques in memes by leveraging the multi-modal information and classifying them into 22 propaganda techniques.

In recent days, the research relating to multimodal information has been growing (Sharma et al., 2022). Most microblogging sites allow users to post in various modalities like text, images, videos, etc. which add a dimension of research in addressing all the modalities. One modality often provides supplementary information to another modality which makes multimodal models more robust.

3 Datasets

3.1 Data Collection

The Russian invasion of Ukraine started on 22 February 2022. We started to crawl tweets from

Label	Annotation Instructions
Hate	A post (text or image or both) contains a hateful content such as personal attack, homophobic abuse, racial abuse, or attack on minority
No Hate	A post(text or image or both) reports the events or others' opinions objectively and contains no offensive or hateful content.

Table 1: Annotation instructions given to annotators.

22 February 2022 to 28 March 2022. Twitter API[1] was used to collect the tweets from the given time frame. We collected the tweets with certain list of keywords namely *ukraine*, *putin*, *russia*, *zelensky*, *kyiv*, *kiev*, *kremlin*, *ukrainian*, *nato*, *russian*, *soviet*, *moscow*, *kharkiv*, and *donbas*. The tweets for keywords *kharkiv*, and *donbas* were collected from 1 March 2022 whereas for all other keywords, tweets were collected starting from 22 February 2022. The tweets revolving around the Russia-Ukraine crisis had the above-mentioned keywords very frequently. Hence, the mentioned keywords were selected for our study. For filtering the tweets, we took the tweets which had media and were in the English language. We discarded the tweets which had media as videos or animations. Our dataset contains 5,680 labeled tweets that had image and text pairs with annotations.

3.2 Annotation

This subsection explains the annotation schema that we followed to label the dataset.

Instructions: The annotation of the data was done to label tweets into binary classes. The two categories, i.e., hate speech and no hate speech, were defined. Annotators were provided with the instructions, following which they assigned the labels to the tweets. If the annotators were not sure about the labels for any tweet, it was labeled as 'Non-Informative,' and such tweets were later dropped. Annotators were provided with posts that had tweets containing both image and text pairs. The images were named as the tweet ID in which they were present. The annotators thus looked into the image and text pairs for performing the annotation. Annotation instructions given to annotators are presented in Table 1. For a tweet to be labeled as hate speech, it needs to have at least one component that represents hate.

Annotations: There was a team of four male and female annotators with good fluency in the English language. All annotators had varying qualifications running from undergraduate to MS and Ph.D. degrees, including the highly experienced researchers in NLP research involving the data collection and establishment of benchmarks. This helped to frame clear instructions and ensure the quality of annotations. In the literature, it has been discussed that having a diverse range of annotators is useful to mitigate bias (Vargas et al., 2022). The annotators were volunteers and did not receive any remunerations. Since labeling tweets involving both text and image is challenging, we made the annotations go through three phases. In the first phase, we run a pilot annotation for 50 tweets to ensure that everyone understood the instructions. Each of the four members annotated the tweets. The instructions were revised to clarify that they addressed all the confusion that annotators had. In the second phase, all four annotators were made to annotate 200 tweets. The purpose of the second phase was to make sure that the instructions revised after the first stage were clear enough. In the third stage, a group discussion was done regarding the conflicts in annotation (Table 3). The instructions became apparent, and the annotators annotated all of the datasets. For example, Figure 1a shows that the text expresses solidarity with Ukraine. The image, which is the flag of Ukraine, also does not show any hate. Thus, the tweet is labeled as No Hate. Similarly, 1b shows the tweet in which the text shows hate towards the former president of the USA, Donald Trump. He does not belong to Siberia. The tweet text tries to demean Donald Trump by saying that he belongs to Siberia and he should be sent there. The image is also edited. It is demeaning and shows hate on multiple levels toward Donald Trump. Thus, this is labeled as hate speech.

Labels	No. of Tweets	Avg. char/ tweet	Avg word/ tweet
Hate	746	60.88	9.68
No Hate	4934	64.48	10.03

Table 2: Dataset statistics.

Dataset Statistics and Analysis: Our new multimodal dataset included 5680 tweets, with 746 (13.13%) tweets being labeled as 'hate speech' label whereas 4934 (86.87%) tweets are labeled as 'no hate' label (Table 2). The dataset statistics represent a true distribution in a real-world scenario

[1] https://developer.twitter.com/en/docs/twitter-api

Phase	Annotators	Kappa (κ)
Pilot Annotation	α_1 and α_2	0.57
	α_1 and α_3	0.50
	α_1 and α_4	0.62
	α_2 and α_3	0.53
	α_2 and α_4	0.63
	α_3 and α_4	0.51
Final Annotation	α_1 and α_2	0.87
	α_1 and α_3	0.90
	α_1 and α_4	0.89
	α_2 and α_3	0.89
	α_2 and α_4	0.88
	α_3 and α_4	0.90

Table 3: Cohen's Kappa (κ) for annotation during different Phases by four annotators

where many posts are neutral, and only some are related to hate speech.

4 Experimental Results

4.1 Baselines

We used various state-of-the-art unimodal and multimodal-based state-of-the-art methods to establish baselines. Below, we discuss each in detail.

4.1.1 Unimodal Models

For single modality-based models, we used the following unimodal methods:

- Unimodal-Text Only: For textual models, we used long-short term memory (LSTM) (Hochreiter and Schmidhuber, 1997), Bidirectional Encoder Representations (BERT) (Devlin et al., 2018) and optimized variant of BERT, i.e., RoBERTa (Liu et al., 2019).

- Unimodal-Image Only: For the image-based unimodal baseline methods, we used 3 pretrained convolutional networks based methods i.e., VGG-19 (Simonyan and Zisserman, 2014), ResNet (He et al., 2016) and DenseNet (Huang et al., 2017).

4.1.2 Multimodal Models

We used 3 multimodal models that have been widely used in previous similar studies. (1) We used (ResNet+BERT), where we pre-trained ResNet and BERT to train text and image and then fused the representations through the linear layer, (2) We also used VisualBERT (Li et al., 2019), a simple and flexible framework for modeling a broad range of vision-and-language tasks and (3) Besides, we have also used the current state-of-the-art model Contrastive Language-Image Pre-Training (CLIP) (Radford et al., 2021).

Modality	Model	Precision	Recall	F1-score
Textual	LSTM	0.74	0.86	0.79
	BERT	0.75	0.86	0.80
	RoBERTa	0.78	0.88	0.83
Visual	VGG-19	0.79	0.70	0.74
	ResNet	0.80	0.74	0.77
	DenseNet	0.82	0.72	0.77
Multimodal	ResNet+BERT	0.84	0.86	0.85
	VisualBERT	0.85	0.88	0.86
	CLIP	0.88	0.90	0.89

Table 4: Performance of different unimodal and multimodal algorithms on our dataset.

4.2 Experimental Settings

We used grid-search optimization to derive the optimal parameters of each baseline and used precision, recall, and F1-score as evaluation metrics.

4.3 Results

Table 4 show the results for the classification of hate and non-hate speech. We experimented with both unimodal and multimodal models. When only the text modality was used, the RoBERTa model performed the best with an F1-score of 0.83. Similarly, for the visual unimodal model, DenseNet and ResNet had a nearly equal performance with an F1-score of 0.77. Further, we can see that both multimodal models had better results than unimodal textual and visual models. The performance for the CLIP model is as high as 0.89 (F1-score). Based on our experiment, we observed that multi-modal models plays important role in detecting hateful content in comparison to uni-models.

5 Conclusion and Future Work

This paper presents a new multi-modal dataset for identifying hateful content on social media, consisting of 5,680 text-image pairs collected from Twitter, labeled across two labels. Experimental analysis of the presented dataset has shown that understanding both modalities is essential for detecting these techniques. It is confirmed in our experiments with several state-of-the-art multi-modal models. In future work, we plan to extend the dataset in size. We further plan to develop new multi-modal models tailored explicitly to hate-speech detection, aiming for a deeper understanding of the text and image relation. It would also be interesting to perform experiments in a direction that explores what social entities the given hate speech tweet targets.

Reproducibility: The dataset and resources for this work are available at our GitHub repository[2].

[2]https://github.com/therealthapa/emnlp-case2022

Ethical Considerations: The dataset does not contain direct identifiers. It contains tweet IDs. Tweet IDs can be used to retrieve the tweets. The tweet becomes unavailable if the user deletes the tweet. This gives the original author of the tweet full control over their content. All the tweets presented in the examples have been anonymized and obfuscated for user privacy and to avoid misuse. Thus, no ethical approval is required. The annotation is very subjective and hence we can expect some bias in the annotation. To address these issues, examples from various users and groups are collected, along with clear instructions for annotation. Due to excellent inter-annotator agreement (κ score), we are confident that annotation instructions are mostly valid.

Intended Use: We release our dataset in order to accelerate research into identifying hate speech at times of war on social media. We expect the dataset to be a valuable resource when used appropriately.

References

Surabhi Adhikari, Surendrabikram Thapa, Usman Naseem, Priyanka Singh, Huan Huo, Gnana Bharathy, and Mukesh Prasad. 2022. Exploiting linguistic information from nepali transcripts for early detection of alzheimer's disease using natural language processing and machine learning techniques. *International Journal of Human-Computer Studies*, 160:102761.

Marc Berninger, Florian Kiesel, and Sascha Kolaric. 2022. Should i stay or should i go? stock market reactions to companies' decisions in the wake of the russia-ukraine conflict. *Stock market reactions to companies' decisions in the wake of the Russia-Ukraine conflict (April 20, 2022)*.

Carlos Arcila Calderón, Gonzalo de la Vega, and David Blanco Herrero. 2020. Topic modeling and characterization of hate speech against immigrants on twitter around the emergence of a far-right party in spain. *Social Sciences*, 9(11):188.

Fabio Del Vigna, Andrea Cimino, Felice Dell'Orletta, Marinella Petrocchi, and Maurizio Tesconi. 2017. Hate me, hate me not: Hate speech detection on facebook. In *Proceedings of the First Italian Conference on Cybersecurity (ITASEC17)*, pages 86–95.

Jacob Devlin, Ming-Wei Chang, Kenton Lee, and Kristina Toutanova. 2018. Bert: Pre-training of deep bidirectional transformers for language understanding. *arXiv preprint arXiv:1810.04805*.

Dimitar Dimitrov, Bishr Bin Ali, Shaden Shaar, Firoj Alam, Fabrizio Silvestri, Hamed Firooz, Preslav Nakov, and Giovanni Da San Martino. 2021. Detecting propaganda techniques in memes. *arXiv preprint arXiv:2109.08013*.

Björn Gambäck and Utpal Kumar Sikdar. 2017. Using convolutional neural networks to classify hate-speech. In *Proceedings of the first workshop on abusive language online*, pages 85–90.

Kaiming He, Xiangyu Zhang, Shaoqing Ren, and Jian Sun. 2016. Deep residual learning for image recognition. In *Proceedings of the IEEE conference on computer vision and pattern recognition*, pages 770–778.

Sepp Hochreiter and Jürgen Schmidhuber. 1997. Long short-term memory. *Neural Computation*, 9(8):1735–1780.

Gao Huang, Zhuang Liu, Laurens Van Der Maaten, and Kilian Q Weinberger. 2017. Densely connected convolutional networks. In *Proceedings of the IEEE conference on computer vision and pattern recognition*, pages 4700–4708.

Douwe Kiela, Hamed Firooz, Aravind Mohan, Vedanuj Goswami, Amanpreet Singh, Pratik Ringshia, and Davide Testuggine. 2020. The hateful memes challenge: Detecting hate speech in multimodal memes. *Advances in Neural Information Processing Systems*, 33:2611–2624.

Liunian Harold Li, Mark Yatskar, Da Yin, Cho-Jui Hsieh, and Kai-Wei Chang. 2019. Visualbert: A simple and performant baseline for vision and language. *arXiv preprint arXiv:1908.03557*.

Yinhan Liu, Myle Ott, Naman Goyal, Jingfei Du, Mandar Joshi, Danqi Chen, Omer Levy, Mike Lewis, Luke Zettlemoyer, and Veselin Stoyanov. 2019. Roberta: A robustly optimized bert pretraining approach. *arXiv preprint arXiv:1907.11692*.

Jim E Miller and E Keith Brown. 2013. *The Cambridge dictionary of linguistics*. Cambridge University Press.

Usman Naseem, Imran Razzak, Matloob Khushi, Peter W Eklund, and Jinman Kim. 2021. Covidsenti: A large-scale benchmark twitter data set for covid-19 sentiment analysis. *IEEE Transactions on Computational Social Systems*, 8(4):1003–1015.

Anil Singh Parihar, Surendrabikram Thapa, and Sushruti Mishra. 2021. Hate speech detection using natural language processing: Applications and challenges. In *2021 5th International Conference on Trends in Electronics and Informatics (ICOEI)*, pages 1302–1308. IEEE.

Alec Radford, Jong Wook Kim, Chris Hallacy, Aditya Ramesh, Gabriel Goh, Sandhini Agarwal, Girish Sastry, Amanda Askell, Pamela Mishkin, Jack Clark, Gretchen Krueger, and Ilya Sutskever. 2021. Learning transferable visual models from natural language supervision. *CoRR*, abs/2103.00020.

Lanyu Shang, Yang Zhang, Yuheng Zha, Yingxi Chen, Christina Youn, and Dong Wang. 2021. Aomd: An analogy-aware approach to offensive meme detection on social media. *Information Processing & Management*, 58(5):102664.

Shivam Sharma, Firoj Alam, Md Akhtar, Dimitar Dimitrov, Giovanni Da San Martino, Hamed Firooz, Alon Halevy, Fabrizio Silvestri, Preslav Nakov, Tanmoy Chakraborty, et al. 2022. Detecting and understanding harmful memes: A survey. *arXiv preprint arXiv:2205.04274*.

Karen Simonyan and Andrew Zisserman. 2014. Very deep convolutional networks for large-scale image recognition. *arXiv preprint arXiv:1409.1556*.

Francielle Vargas, Isabelle Carvalho, Fabiana Rodrigues de Góes, Thiago Pardo, and Fabrício Benevenuto. 2022. Hatebr: A large expert annotated corpus of brazilian instagram comments for offensive language and hate speech detection. In *Proceedings of the Thirteenth Language Resources and Evaluation Conference*, pages 7174–7183.

Yi Zhou, Zhenhao Chen, and Huiyuan Yang. 2021. Multimodal learning for hateful memes detection. In *2021 IEEE International Conference on Multimedia & Expo Workshops (ICMEW)*, pages 1–6. IEEE.

EventGraph: Event Extraction as Semantic Graph Parsing

Huiling You,[1] **David Samuel,**[1] **Samia Touileb,**[2] and **Lilja Øvrelid**[1]
[1]University of Oslo
[2]University of Bergen
{huiliny, davisamu, liljao}@ifi.uio.no
samia.touileb@uib.no

Abstract

Event extraction involves the detection and extraction of both the event triggers and corresponding event arguments. Existing systems often decompose event extraction into multiple subtasks, without considering their possible interactions. In this paper, we propose EventGraph, a joint framework for event extraction, which encodes events as graphs. We represent event triggers and arguments as nodes in a semantic graph. Event extraction therefore becomes a graph parsing problem, which provides the following advantages: 1) performing event detection and argument extraction jointly; 2) detecting and extracting multiple events from a piece of text; and 3) capturing the complicated interaction between event arguments and triggers. Experimental results on ACE2005 show that our model is competitive to state-of-the-art systems and has substantially improved the results on argument extraction. Additionally, we create two new datasets from ACE2005 where we keep the entire text spans for event arguments, instead of just the head word(s). Our code and models are released as open-source.[1]

1 Introduction

Event extraction aims at extracting event-related information from unstructured texts into structured form (i.e. triggers and arguments), according to a predefined event ontology (Ahn, 2006; Doddington et al., 2004). In these types of ontologies, events are characterized by event triggers, and comprise a set of predefined argument types. Figure 1 shows an example of a sentence containing two events, an `Attack` event triggered by *"friendly-fire"* and a `Die` event triggered by *"died"*; the two events share the same arguments, but each plays a different role in the specific event. For instance, *"U.S."* is the `Agent` in the `Die` event, but plays the role of `Attacker` in the `Attack` event.

[1]https://github.com/huiling-y/EventGraph

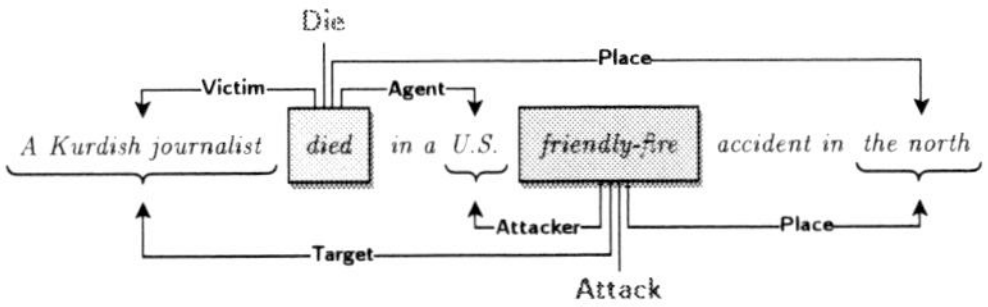

Figure 1: Example of an `Attack` and a `Die` events in the sentence *"A Kurdish journalist died in a U.S. friendly-fire accident in the north."*

As opposed to dividing event extraction into independent subtasks, we take advantage of recent advances in semantic dependency parsing (Dozat and Manning, 2018; Samuel and Straka, 2020) and develop an end-to-end event graph parser, dubbed EventGraph. We adopt intuitive graph encoding to represent the event mentions of a piece of text in a single event graph, and directly generate these event graphs from raw texts. We evaluate our EventGraph system on ACE2005 (LDC2006T06).[2] Our model achieves competitive results with state-of-the-art models, and substantially improves the results on event argument extraction. The main contributions of this work are:

1. We propose EventGraph, a text-to-event framework that solves event extraction as semantic graph parsing. The model does not rely on any language-specific features or event-specific ontology, so it can easily be applied to new languages and new datasets.
2. We design an intuitive graph encoding approach to represent event structures in a single event graph.
3. The versatility of our approach allows for an effortless decoding of full trigger and argument mentions. We create two novel and more challenging datasets from ACE2005, and provide corresponding benchmark results.

[2]https://catalog.ldc.upenn.edu/LDC2006T06

Proceedings of the 5th Workshop on Challenges and Applications of Automated Extraction of Socio-political Events from Text (CASE), pages 7 - 15
December 7-8, 2022 ©2022 Association for Computational Linguistics

2 Related work

Our work is closely related to two research directions, event extraction and semantic parsing.

Supervised event extraction is an established research area in NLP. There are different methods to obtain the structured information of an event, and the mainstream methods can be divided into: 1) classification-based methods: treat event extraction as several classification subtasks, and either solve them separately in a pipeline-based manner (Ji and Grishman, 2008; Li et al., 2013; Liu et al., 2020; Du and Cardie, 2020; Li et al., 2020) or jointly infer multiple subtasks (Yang and Mitchell, 2016; Nguyen et al., 2016; Liu et al., 2018; Wadden et al., 2019; Lin et al., 2020); 2) generation-based approaches: formulate event extraction as a sequence generation problem (Paolini et al., 2021; Lu et al., 2021; Li et al., 2021; Hsu et al., 2022); 3) prompt tuning methods: inspired by natural language understanding tasks, these approaches take advantage of "discrete prompts" (Shin et al., 2020; Gao et al., 2021; Li and Liang, 2021; Liu et al., 2022).

Meaning Representation Parsing has seen significant interest in recent years (Oepen et al., 2014, 2015, 2020). Unlike syntactic dependency representations, these semantic representations are crucially not trees, but rather general graphs, characterised by potentially having multiple entry points (*roots*) and not necessarily being connected, since not every token is a node in the graph. There has further been considerable progress in developing variants of both transition-based and graph-based dependency parsers capable of producing such semantic graphs (Hershcovich et al., 2017; Dozat and Manning, 2018; Samuel and Straka, 2020).

A recent and highly relevant development in the current context has been the application of semantic parsers to NLP tasks beyond meaning representation parsing. These approaches rely on the reformulation of task-specific representations to semantic dependency graphs. For example, Yu et al. (2020) exploit the parser of Dozat and Manning (2018) to predict spans of named entities, while Kurtz et al. (2020) phrase the task of negation resolution (Morante and Daelemans, 2012) as a graph parsing task with promising results. Recently, Barnes et al. (2021) proposed a dependency parsing approach to extract opinion tuples from text, dubbed Structured Sentiment Analysis, and a recent shared task dedicated to this task demonstrated the usefulness of graph parsing approaches to sentiment analysis (Barnes et al., 2022). Most similar to our work is the work by Samuel et al. (2022) which adapts the PERIN parser (Samuel and Straka, 2020) to parse directly from raw text into sentiment graphs.

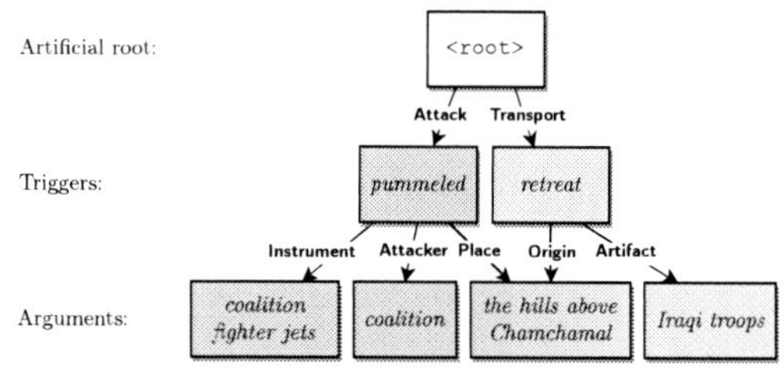

Figure 2: Event graph for the sentence *"That's because coalition fighter jets pummeled this Iraqi position on the hills above Chamchamal and Iraqi troops made a hasty retreat."*

3 Event graph representations

We adopt an efficient "labeled-edge" representation for event graph encoding within the scope of a sentence. Each node in an event graph corresponds to either an event trigger or an argument, which is anchored to a unique text span in a sentence, except for the top node, which is only a dummy node for every event graph. The edges are constrained only between the top node and an event trigger, or between an event trigger and an argument, with the corresponding edge label as an event type or argument role. The "labeled-edge" encoding has the ability to represent: 1) multiple event mentions; 2) nested structures (overlapping between arguments or trigger-argument); 3) multiple argument roles of a single argument. Taking the event graph from Figure 2 as example, the sentence contains two event mentions, which share the same argument *"the hills above Chamchamal"* but as different roles, and the argument *"coalition"* is nested inside the argument *"coalition fighter jets"*.

4 Event parsing

EventGraph is an adaptation of PERIN (Samuel and Straka, 2020), a general permutation-invariant framework for text-to-graph parsing. Given the "labeled-edge" encoding for event graphs, we create EventGraph by customizing the modules of PERIN as illustrated in Figure 3, which contains three classifiers to generate nodes, anchors, and edges, respectively. Each input sequence is processed by four modules of EventGraph to generate a final structured representation.

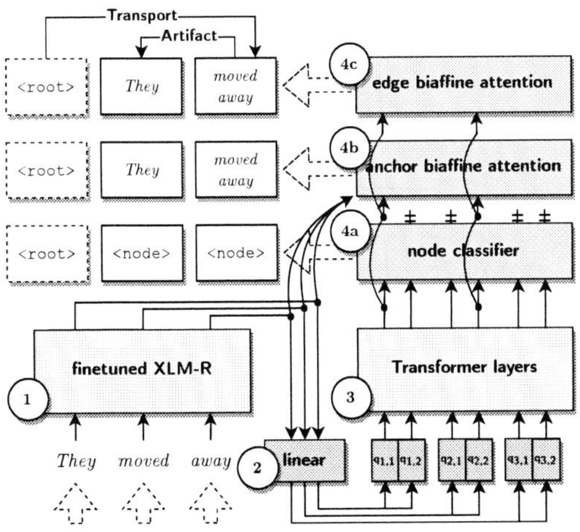

Figure 3: EventGraph architecture. 1) the input gets a contextualized representation, 2) queries are generated for every input token, 3) queries are further processed with a decoder to predict 4a) node presence, 4b) node anchors, and 4c) edge labels.

Encoder We use the large version of XLM-R (Conneau et al., 2020) as the encoder to obtain contextualized representations of the input sequence; each token gets a contextual embedding via a learned subword attention layer over the subwords.

Query generator We use a linear transformation layer to map each embebbed token onto n queries.

Decoder The decoder is a stack of Transformer encoder layers (Vaswani et al., 2017) without positional encoding, which is permutation-invariant (non-autoregressive); the decoder processes and augments the queries of each token by modelling the inter-dependencies between queries.

Parser head It consists of three classifiers: a) the **node classifier** is a linear classifier that predicts node presence by classifying the augmented queries of each token; since more than one query is generated for each token, a single token can produce more than one node; b) the **anchor biaffine classifier** (Dozat and Manning, 2017) uses deep biaffine attention between the augmented queries and contextual embeddings of each token to map the predicted nodes to surface tokens; c) the **edge biaffine classifier** uses two deep biaffine attention modules to process generated nodes and predict edge presence between a pair of nodes and the edge label.

Given a piece of text, EventGraph generates its corresponding graph, and it is effortless to extract the structured information of event mentions from the nodes and edges.[3]

5 Experimental setup

5.1 Datasets

We evaluate our system on the widely used benchmark dataset ACE2005[4] (LDC2006T06). The ACE2005 dataset contains 599 English documents annotated for several tasks, entities, values, relations, and events, with an event ontology of 33 event types, and 35 argument roles. Event arguments come from both entities and values. The annotation of an entity also includes its head word(s); for instance, from Table 1, entity "the Iraqi government's key center of power" has "center" as its head word. Following previous works (Wadden et al., 2019; Lin et al., 2020; Wang et al., 2019), we preprocess the dataset (details in Appendix B) and obtain the following configurations:

1. **ACE05-E**: Wadden et al. (2019) keep 22 event argument roles (excluding "time" and "value" event arguments), ignore events with multi-token trigger(s), and use only the head word(s) of event arguments.

2. **ACE05-E$^+$**: similar to Wadden et al. (2019), Lin et al. (2020) only use 22 event argument roles and keep only the head word(s) of event arguments, but keep events with multi-token trigger(s).

3. **ACE05-E^{++}**: we create a new dataset that keeps the full text spans for event triggers and event arguments, but also keep 22 argument roles for comparing with previous work.

4. **ACE05-E^{+++}**: we create another dataset that keeps all the 35 argument roles in ACE2005, with full text spans for event triggers and arguments.

Table 1 shows how an event mention is extracted in ACE05-E$^+$ and ACE05-E^{++}, and the same event is not present in ACE05-E. Although keeping the full text spans for arguments makes the task of argument extraction more difficult, we believe that the extracted events are more informative and self-contained.

[3]The tool for conversion between event mentions and event graphs is included in our codes.

[4]`https://catalog.ldc.upenn.edu/LDC2006T06`

	ACE05-E+	ACE05-E++
`Trigger`	*"push ahead"*	*"push ahead"*
`Destination`	*"center"*	*"the Iraqi government's key center of power"*
`Artifact`	*"forces"*	*"American forces"*

Table 1: A `Transport` event in "*Well, as American forces do push ahead toward the Iraqi government's key center of power, British forces are keeping up their work to the south of the Iraqi capital*", and corresponding extracted events in ACE05-E$^+$ and ACE05-E^{++}.

Dataset	Split	# Sentences	# Events	# Roles
ACE05-E	Train	17 172	4 202	4 859
	Dev	923	450	605
	Test	832	403	576
ACE05-E$^+$	Train	19 216	4 419	6 607
	Dev	901	468	759
	Test	676	424	689
ACE05-E^{++}	Train	15 603	4 416	6 513
	Dev	893	509	802
	Test	729	424	685
ACE05-E^{+++}	Train	15 603	4 416	7 844
	Dev	893	509	945
	Test	729	424	894

Table 2: Statistics of the preprocessed ACE2005 datasets.

Dataset	Triggers	Arguments		
	Avg. Len	Avg. Len	Single-token	Multi-token
ACE05-E	1.00	1.18	86.2%	13.8%
ACE05-E$^+$	1.06	1.17	88.0%	12.0%
ACE05-E^{++}	1.05	2.86	43.5%	56.5%
ACE05-E^{+++}	1.05	2.82	43.2%	56.8%

Table 3: Statistics of event triggers and arguments. We report the average lengths of triggers and arguments; for arguments, we also report the percentages of single-token and multi-token arguments.

5.2 Evaluation metric

We report Precision *P*, Recall *R*, and *F1* scores for each of the following evaluation criteria (Wadden et al., 2019; Lin et al., 2020):

- **Trigger classification (Trg-C)**: an event trigger is correctly predicted if its offsets and event type matches the gold trigger.
- **Argument classification (Arg-C)**: an event argument is correctly predicted if its offsets, argument role, and event type match the gold argument.

For argument classification, in order to have a better insight into our models' performance on multi-token arguments, we include another metric based on token-level span overlap for argument identification, instead of perfect match.

- **Token-level span overlap**: an event argument is correctly identified if its offsets have 80%[5] overlap (token-level) with the gold argument, and correctly predicted if its argument role and event type match the gold argument.

5.3 System comparisons

We compare EventGraph to the following event extraction systems: 1) DYGIE++ (Wadden et al., 2019): a span-based framework capturing both local and global contexts; 2) ONEIE (Lin et al., 2020): an end-to-end framework for general information extraction; 3) TEXT2EVENT (Lu et al., 2021): a generation-based model for sequence-to-event generation; 4) GTEE-DYNPREF (Liu et al., 2022): a template-based method for text-to-event generation.

5.4 Implementation details

Our code is built upon the official implementation of the PERIN parser (Samuel and Straka, 2020).[6] Details about our training setup and hyperparameter settings are given in Appendix A. For each dataset, we train 5 models with 5 different random seeds, and report the means and standard deviations of the corresponding results.

6 Results and discussion

In Table 4, we compare our results on ACE05-E and ACE05-E$^+$ with the previous systems. On both datasets, EventGraph achieves SOTA results on Arg-C over all metrics, with an improvement of 7 percentage points on ACE-E and more than 10 percentage points on ACE05-E$^+$ in *F1* scores. For Trg-C, despite not beating the SOTA systems, our results are still very competitive.

On the two new datasets that we created, EventGraph has achieved overall competitive results (Table 4). On ACE-E^{++}, despite having longer and more complicated arguments, EventGraph has generated comparable results to those of GTEE-DYNPREF (current SOTA) on ACE-E$^+$. On ACE-E^{+++}, even though the argument role set is expanded from 22 to 35 argument roles, the results of EventGraph on Arg-C remain stable.

[5]This metric only affects arguments longer than 5 tokens. Arguments containing fewer than 5 tokens are still evaluated with perfect match.

[6]`https://github.com/ufal/perin`

Model	Triggers (Trg-C)			Arguments (Arg-C)		
	P	R	F1	P	R	F1
Dataset: ACE05-E						
DYGIE++	——	——	69.7	——	——	48.8
ONEIE	——	——	**74.7**	——	——	56.8
GTEE-DYNPREF	63.7	**84.4**	72.6	49.0	64.8	55.8
EventGraph	**66.5**$^{\pm 0.7}$	71.0$^{\pm 0.9}$	68.6$^{\pm 0.7}$	**63.4**$^{\pm 2.7}$	**67.3**$^{\pm 2.0}$	**65.3**$^{\pm 2.2}$
Dataset: ACE05-E^{+}						
ONEIE	**72.1**	73.6	72.8	55.4	54.3	54.8
TEXT2EVENT	71.2	72.5	71.8	54.0	54.8	54.4
GTEE-DYNPREF	67.3	**83.0**	**74.3**	49.8	60.7	54.7
EventGraph	70.0$^{\pm 1.1}$	70.0$^{\pm 1.2}$	70.0$^{\pm 1.1}$	**64.5**$^{\pm 1.0}$	**66.4**$^{\pm 2.6}$	**65.4**$^{\pm 1.7}$
Dataset: ACE05-E^{++}						
EventGraph	72.9$^{\pm 1.3}$	75.2$^{\pm 1.9}$	74.0$^{\pm 1.5}$	57.3$^{\pm 0.8}$	59.9$^{\pm 1.2}$	58.6$^{\pm 0.9}$
Dataset: ACE05-E^{+++}						
EventGraph	72.4$^{\pm 0.7}$	75.9$^{\pm 1.0}$	74.0$^{\pm 0.7}$	56.9$^{\pm 0.6}$	58.2$^{\pm 0.9}$	57.5$^{\pm 0.6}$

Table 4: Results on ACE05-E, ACE05-E^{+}, ACE05-E^{++}, and ACE05-E^{+++}. We report the average performance of 5 runs with different random seeds, together with the standard deviations. For clarity, we bold the highest scores.

Results show that EventGraph performs well on joint modelling of event triggers and arguments, and benefits from longer text spans for event triggers and arguments. When the full text spans of arguments are used, the model receives more training signals, so it has more information in differentiating sentences containing events from those without, as shown in Table 6, and thus identifying event triggers, which is also shown by the increasing Trg-C scores from ACE-E and ACE-E^{+} to ACE-E^{++} and ACE-E^{+++}. For instance, as the example in Table 1 shows, "the Iraqi government's key center of power" is less ambiguous than mere "center". As shown in Table 3, the average argument length of ACE-E^{++} and ACE-E^{+++} is much longer, but the average trigger length is very similar across the four datasets; it is also evident that single-token arguments make up a large proportion of all arguments, even for ACE-E^{++} and ACE-E^{+++}, so there is a long tail in argument length distribution. For longer arguments, it is more difficult to obtain a perfect match with a gold argument, so we observe decreasing Arg-C scores when EventGraph is evaluated on ACE-E^{++} and ACE-E^{+++}.

To further look into our model's performance on identifying multi-token event arguments, especially those containing more than 5 tokens, we further report Arg-C scores based on token-level span overlap. As shown in Table 5, when we relax argument identification from perfect match to 80% token-level span overlap, the scores of Arg-C increase consistently, especially those of ACE-E^{++} and ACE-E^{+++}, now comparable to the results on ACE-E and ACE-E^{+}.

Dataset	Perfect Match			80% Span Overlap		
	P	R	F1	P	R	F1
ACE05-E	63.4$^{\pm 2.7}$	67.3$^{\pm 2.0}$	65.3$^{\pm 2.2}$	63.9$^{\pm 2.4}$	68.5$^{\pm 1.7}$	66.2$^{\pm 1.9}$
ACE05-E^{+}	64.5$^{\pm 1.0}$	66.4$^{\pm 2.6}$	65.4$^{\pm 1.7}$	65.1$^{\pm 0.9}$	67.8$^{\pm 2.5}$	66.4$^{\pm 1.5}$
ACE05-E^{++}	57.3$^{\pm 0.8}$	59.9$^{\pm 1.2}$	58.6$^{\pm 0.9}$	63.9$^{\pm 1.1}$	66.2$^{\pm 2.1}$	65.0$^{\pm 1.6}$
ACE05-E^{+++}	56.9$^{\pm 0.6}$	58.2$^{\pm 0.9}$	57.5$^{\pm 0.6}$	64.0$^{\pm 0.7}$	64.4$^{\pm 1.3}$	64.2$^{\pm 0.9}$

Table 5: Results of EventGraph on Arg-C, evaluated with perfect match and token-level span overlap.

ACE05-E	ACE05-E^{+}	ACE05-E^{++}	ACE05-E^{+++}
88.8$^{\pm 0.4}$	87.9$^{\pm 0.5}$	96.2$^{\pm 0.2}$	96.5$^{\pm 0.6}$

Table 6: Results of EventGraph correctly identifying the presence of event(s) in a sentence.

7 Conclusion

In this paper, we have proposed a new method for event extraction as semantic graph parsing. Our proposed EventGraph has achieved competitive results on ACE2005 for the task of event trigger classification, and obtained new state-of-the-art results for the task of argument role classification. We also provide a graph representation for better visualizing event mentions, and offer an efficient tool to facilitate graph conversion. We create two new datasets from ACE2005, with the full text spans for both triggers and arguments, and offer the corresponding benchmark results. We show that despite adding more and longer text sequences, EventGraph outperforms previous models tested on more restricted datasets. For future work, we would like to experiment with different pretrained language models, and carry out more detailed error analysis. Our codes and models are released as open-source.

Acknowledgements

This work was supported by industry partners and the Research Council of Norway with funding to *MediaFutures: Research Centre for Responsible Media Technology and Innovation*, through the centers for Research-based Innovation scheme, project number 309339.

References

David Ahn. 2006. The stages of event extraction. In *Proceedings of the Workshop on Annotating and Reasoning about Time and Events*, pages 1–8, Sydney, Australia. Association for Computational Linguistics.

Jeremy Barnes, Robin Kurtz, Stephan Oepen, Lilja Øvrelid, and Erik Velldal. 2021. Structured sentiment analysis as dependency graph parsing. In *Proceedings of the 59th Annual Meeting of the Association for*

Computational Linguistics and the 11th International Joint Conference on Natural Language Processing (Volume 1: Long Papers), pages 3387–3402, Online. Association for Computational Linguistics.

Jeremy Barnes, Laura Ana Maria Oberländer, Enrica Troiano, Andrey Kutuzov, Jan Buchmann, Rodrigo Agerri, Lilja Øvrelid, and Erik Velldal. 2022. Semeval-2022 task 10: Structured sentiment analysis. In *Proceedings of the 16th International Workshop on Semantic Evaluation (SemEval-2022), Seattle. Association for Computational Linguistics.*

Alexis Conneau, Kartikay Khandelwal, Naman Goyal, Vishrav Chaudhary, Guillaume Wenzek, Francisco Guzmán, Edouard Grave, Myle Ott, Luke Zettlemoyer, and Veselin Stoyanov. 2020. Unsupervised cross-lingual representation learning at scale. In *Proceedings of the 58th Annual Meeting of the Association for Computational Linguistics*, pages 8440–8451, Online. Association for Computational Linguistics.

George Doddington, Alexis Mitchell, Mark Przybocki, Lance Ramshaw, Stephanie Strassel, and Ralph Weischedel. 2004. The automatic content extraction (ACE) program – tasks, data, and evaluation. In *Proceedings of the Fourth International Conference on Language Resources and Evaluation (LREC'04)*, Lisbon, Portugal. European Language Resources Association (ELRA).

Timothy Dozat and Christopher D. Manning. 2017. Deep biaffine attention for neural dependency parsing. In *International Conference on Learning Representations*.

Timothy Dozat and Christopher D. Manning. 2018. Simpler but more accurate semantic dependency parsing. In *Proceedings of the 56th Annual Meeting of the Association for Computational Linguistics (Volume 2: Short Papers)*, pages 484–490, Melbourne, Australia. Association for Computational Linguistics.

Xinya Du and Claire Cardie. 2020. Event extraction by answering (almost) natural questions. In *Proceedings of the 2020 Conference on Empirical Methods in Natural Language Processing (EMNLP)*, pages 671–683, Online. Association for Computational Linguistics.

Tianyu Gao, Adam Fisch, and Danqi Chen. 2021. Making pre-trained language models better few-shot learners. In *Proceedings of the 59th Annual Meeting of the Association for Computational Linguistics and the 11th International Joint Conference on Natural Language Processing (Volume 1: Long Papers)*, pages 3816–3830, Online. Association for Computational Linguistics.

Daniel Hershcovich, Omri Abend, and Ari Rappoport. 2017. A transition-based directed acyclic graph parser for UCCA. In *Proceedings of the 55th Annual Meeting of the Association for Computational Linguistics (Volume 1: Long Papers)*, pages 1127–1138, Vancouver, Canada. Association for Computational Linguistics.

I-Hung Hsu, Kuan-Hao Huang, Elizabeth Boschee, Scott Miller, Prem Natarajan, Kai-Wei Chang, and Nanyun Peng. 2022. Degree: A data-efficient generative event extraction model. In *Proceedings of the 2022 Conference of the North American Chapter of the Association for Computational Linguistics (NAACL)*.

Heng Ji and Ralph Grishman. 2008. Refining event extraction through cross-document inference. In *Proceedings of ACL-08: HLT*, pages 254–262, Columbus, Ohio. Association for Computational Linguistics.

Robin Kurtz, Stephan Oepen, and Marco Kuhlmann. 2020. End-to-end negation resolution as graph parsing. In *Proceedings of the 16th International Conference on Parsing Technologies and the IWPT 2020 Shared Task on Parsing into Enhanced Universal Dependencies*, pages 14–24, Online. Association for Computational Linguistics.

Fayuan Li, Weihua Peng, Yuguang Chen, Quan Wang, Lu Pan, Yajuan Lyu, and Yong Zhu. 2020. Event extraction as multi-turn question answering. In *Findings of the Association for Computational Linguistics: EMNLP 2020*, pages 829–838, Online. Association for Computational Linguistics.

Qi Li, Heng Ji, and Liang Huang. 2013. Joint event extraction via structured prediction with global features. In *Proceedings of the 51st Annual Meeting of the Association for Computational Linguistics (Volume 1: Long Papers)*, pages 73–82, Sofia, Bulgaria. Association for Computational Linguistics.

Sha Li, Heng Ji, and Jiawei Han. 2021. Document-level event argument extraction by conditional generation. In *Proceedings of the 2021 Conference of the North American Chapter of the Association for Computational Linguistics: Human Language Technologies*, pages 894–908, Online. Association for Computational Linguistics.

Xiang Lisa Li and Percy Liang. 2021. Prefix-tuning: Optimizing continuous prompts for generation. In *Proceedings of the 59th Annual Meeting of the Association for Computational Linguistics and the 11th International Joint Conference on Natural Language Processing (Volume 1: Long Papers)*, pages 4582–4597, Online. Association for Computational Linguistics.

Ying Lin, Heng Ji, Fei Huang, and Lingfei Wu. 2020. A joint neural model for information extraction with global features. In *Proceedings of the 58th Annual Meeting of the Association for Computational Linguistics*, pages 7999–8009, Online. Association for Computational Linguistics.

Jian Liu, Yubo Chen, Kang Liu, Wei Bi, and Xiaojiang Liu. 2020. Event extraction as machine reading comprehension. In *Proceedings of the 2020 Conference on Empirical Methods in Natural Language Processing (EMNLP)*, pages 1641–1651, Online. Association for Computational Linguistics.

Xiao Liu, Heyan Huang, Ge Shi, and Bo Wang. 2022. Dynamic prefix-tuning for generative template-based event extraction. In *Proceedings of the 60th Annual Meeting of the Association for Computational Linguistics (Volume 1: Long Papers)*, pages 5216–5228, Dublin, Ireland. Association for Computational Linguistics.

Xiao Liu, Zhunchen Luo, and Heyan Huang. 2018. Jointly multiple events extraction via attention-based graph information aggregation. In *Proceedings of the 2018 Conference on Empirical Methods in Natural Language Processing*, pages 1247–1256, Brussels, Belgium. Association for Computational Linguistics.

Ilya Loshchilov and Frank Hutter. 2019. Decoupled weight decay regularization. In *7th International Conference on Learning Representations, ICLR 2019, New Orleans, LA, USA, May 6-9, 2019*. OpenReview.net.

Yaojie Lu, Hongyu Lin, Jin Xu, Xianpei Han, Jialong Tang, Annan Li, Le Sun, Meng Liao, and Shaoyi Chen. 2021. Text2Event: Controllable sequence-to-structure generation for end-to-end event extraction. In *Proceedings of the 59th Annual Meeting of the Association for Computational Linguistics and the 11th International Joint Conference on Natural Language Processing (Volume 1: Long Papers)*, pages 2795–2806, Online. Association for Computational Linguistics.

Roser Morante and Walter Daelemans. 2012. ConanDoyle-neg: Annotation of negation cues and their scope in Conan Doyle stories. In *Proceedings of the Eighth International Conference on Language Resources and Evaluation (LREC'12)*, pages 1563–1568, Istanbul, Turkey. European Language Resources Association (ELRA).

Thien Huu Nguyen, Kyunghyun Cho, and Ralph Grishman. 2016. Joint event extraction via recurrent neural networks. In *Proceedings of the 2016 Conference of the North American Chapter of the Association for Computational Linguistics: Human Language Technologies*, pages 300–309, San Diego, California. Association for Computational Linguistics.

Stephan Oepen, Omri Abend, Lasha Abzianidze, Johan Bos, Jan Hajic, Daniel Hershcovich, Bin Li, Tim O'Gorman, Nianwen Xue, and Daniel Zeman. 2020. MRP 2020: The second shared task on cross-framework and cross-lingual meaning representation parsing. In *Proceedings of the CoNLL 2020 Shared Task: Cross-Framework Meaning Representation Parsing*, pages 1–22, Online. Association for Computational Linguistics.

Stephan Oepen, Marco Kuhlmann, Yusuke Miyao, Daniel Zeman, Silvie Cinkova, Dan Flickinger, Jan Hajic, and Zdenka Uresova. 2015. SemEval 2015 Task 18: Broad-Coverage Semantic Dependency Parsing. *Proceedings of the 9th International Workshop on Semantic Evaluation (SemEval 2015)*, pages 915–926.

Stephan Oepen, Marco Kuhlmann, Yusuke Miyao, Daniel Zeman, Dan Flickinger, Jan Hajic, Angelina Ivanova, and Yi Zhang. 2014. SemEval 2014 Task 8: Broad-Coverage Semantic Dependency Parsing. *Proceedings of the 8th International Workshop on Semantic Evaluation (SemEval 2014)*, pages 63–72.

Giovanni Paolini, Ben Athiwaratkun, Jason Krone, Jie Ma, Alessandro Achille, RISHITA ANUBHAI, Cicero Nogueira dos Santos, Bing Xiang, and Stefano Soatto. 2021. Structured prediction as translation between augmented natural languages. In *International Conference on Learning Representations*.

David Samuel, Jeremy Barnes, Robin Kurtz, Stephan Oepen, Lilja Øvrelid, and Erik Velldal. 2022. Direct parsing to sentiment graphs. In *Proceedings of the 60th Annual Meeting of the Association for Computational Linguistics (Volume 2: Short Papers)*, pages 470–478, Dublin, Ireland. Association for Computational Linguistics.

David Samuel and Milan Straka. 2020. ÚFAL at MRP 2020: Permutation-invariant semantic parsing in PERIN. In *Proceedings of the CoNLL 2020 Shared Task: Cross-Framework Meaning Representation Parsing*, pages 53–64, Online. Association for Computational Linguistics.

Taylor Shin, Yasaman Razeghi, Robert L. Logan IV, Eric Wallace, and Sameer Singh. 2020. AutoPrompt: Eliciting Knowledge from Language Models with Automatically Generated Prompts. In *Proceedings of the 2020 Conference on Empirical Methods in Natural Language Processing (EMNLP)*, pages 4222–4235, Online. Association for Computational Linguistics.

Ashish Vaswani, Noam Shazeer, Niki Parmar, Jakob Uszkoreit, Llion Jones, Aidan N Gomez, Łukasz Kaiser, and Illia Polosukhin. 2017. Attention is all you need. *Advances in neural information processing systems*, 30.

David Wadden, Ulme Wennberg, Yi Luan, and Hannaneh Hajishirzi. 2019. Entity, relation, and event extraction with contextualized span representations. In *Proceedings of the 2019 Conference on Empirical Methods in Natural Language Processing and the 9th International Joint Conference on Natural Language Processing (EMNLP-IJCNLP)*, pages 5784–5789, Hong Kong, China. Association for Computational Linguistics.

Xiaozhi Wang, Ziqi Wang, Xu Han, Zhiyuan Liu, Juanzi Li, Peng Li, Maosong Sun, Jie Zhou, and Xiang Ren. 2019. HMEAE: Hierarchical modular event argument extraction. In *Proceedings of the 2019 Conference on Empirical Methods in Natural Language Processing and the 9th International Joint Conference on Natural Language Processing (EMNLP-IJCNLP)*, pages 5777–5783, Hong Kong, China. Association for Computational Linguistics.

Bishan Yang and Tom M. Mitchell. 2016. Joint extraction of events and entities within a document context.

In *Proceedings of the 2016 Conference of the North American Chapter of the Association for Computational Linguistics: Human Language Technologies*, pages 289–299, San Diego, California. Association for Computational Linguistics.

Juntao Yu, Bernd Bohnet, and Massimo Poesio. 2020. Named Entity Recognition as Dependency Parsing. In *Proceedings of the 58th Annual Meeting of the Association for Computational Linguistics*, pages 6470–6476, Online. Association for Computational Linguistics.

A Training details

We reuse the training settings from the original PERIN system (Samuel and Straka, 2020) whenever possible. The model weights are optimized with AdamW (Loshchilov and Hutter, 2019) following a warmed-up cosine learning rate schedule. We use a pre-trained multi-lingual XLM-R language model implemented by the HuggingFace `transformers` library.[7] The hyperparameter configuration is shown in Table 7, please consult it with our released code for context: `https://github.com/huiling-y/EventGraph`.

The training was done on a single Nvidia RTX3090 GPU, the runtimes and model sizes (including the fine-tuned language model backbone) for each dataset are given in Table 8.

Hyperparameter	EventGraph
batch_size	16
beta_2	0.98
decoder_learning_rate	1.0e-4
decoder_weight_decay	1.2e-6
dropout_transformer	0.25
dropout_transformer_attention	0.1
encoder	*"xlm-roberta-large"*
encoder_learning_rate	4.0e-6
encoder_weight_decay	0.1
epochs	180
hidden_size_anchor	256
hidden_size_edge_label	256
hidden_size_edge_presence	256
n_transformer_layers	3
query_length	2
warmup_steps	1 000

Table 7: Hyperparameter setting for our system, all four datasets use the same configuration.

Dataset	Runtime	Model size
ACE05-E	20:39 h	341.3 M
ACE05-E^{+}	21:59 h	341.3 M
ACE05-E^{++}	20:06 h	341.3 M
ACE05-E^{+++}	20:03 h	342.0 M

Table 8: The training times and model sizes (number of trainable weights) of all our experiments.

[7] `https://huggingface.co/docs/transformers/index`

B Data preprocessing

Data splits All datasets use the same splits[8] for train/dev/test. Out of the 599 documents, 529 documents are used for training, 30 documents for development, and 40 documents for testing.

ACE-E We use the preprocessing code[9] of Wadden et al. (2019) to obtain the dataset, and they use an older version (v2.0.18) of Spacy[10] for preprocessing.

ACE05-E^{+} We use the preprocessing code[11] (v0.4.8) of Lin et al. (2020) to obtain the dataset, and they use NLTK[12] for preprocessing.

ACE05-E^{++} and ACE05-E^{+++} We use the preprocessing code[13] of Wang et al. (2019) to obtain the two datasets, and they use Stanford CoreNLP[14] for preprocessing.

[8] `https://github.com/dwadden/dygiepp/tree/master/scripts/data/ace-event/event-split`

[9] `https://github.com/dwadden/dygiepp`

[10] `https://spacy.io/`

[11] `http://blender.cs.illinois.edu/software/oneie/`

[12] `https://www.nltk.org/`

[13] `https://github.com/thunlp/HMEAE`

[14] `https://stanfordnlp.github.io/CoreNLP/`

NLP4ITF @ Causal News Corpus 2022: Leveraging Linguistic Information for Event Causality Classification

Theresa Krumbiegel
Fraunhofer FKIE
Fraunhoferstraße 20
53343 Wachtberg
theresa.krumbiegel@fkie.fraunhofer.de

Sophie Decher
Fraunhofer FKIE
Fraunhoferstraße 20
53343 Wachtberg
sophie.decher@fkie.fraunhofer.de

Abstract

We present our submission to Subtask 1 of the CASE-2022 Shared Task 3: Event Causality Identification with Causal News Corpus as part of the 5th Workshop on Challenges and Applications of Automated Extraction of Sociopolitical Events from Text (CASE 2022) (Tan et al., 2022a). The task focuses on causal event classification on the sentence level and involves differentiating between sentences that include a cause-effect relation and sentences that do not. We approached this as a binary text classification task and experimented with multiple training sets augmented with additional linguistic information. Our best model was generated by training `roberta-base` on a combination of data from both Subtasks 1 and 2 with the addition of named entity annotations. During the development phase we achieved a macro F1 of 0.8641 with this model on the development set provided by the task organizers. When testing the model on the final test data, we achieved a macro F1 of 0.8516.

1 Introduction

Causal event classification can be categorized as a part of the Natural Language Processing (NLP) task of event extraction. When extracting event information from text, the general aim is to identify answers to the 5W1H questions (WHO, WHAT, WHEN, WHERE, WHY, HOW; Karaman et al., 2017). Some of the questions can be answered easily by means of open source NLP tools–a Named Entity Tagger can facilitate the extraction of locations (WHERE) and times or dates (WHEN), for example. However, some event information remains more difficult to identify reliably in texts, such as answers to WHY questions, which is also the type of question that causal event classification addresses. This task presents an opportunity to develop models that detect information about the reason behind a particular event. For this process, a binary classifier is used to determine whether a cause-effect relation is present in the input sentence. In an NLP pipeline, the output of such a classification process is often used as input for a span detection system, which identifies the particular cause and effect text spans in each causal sentence.

As described by Tan et al. (2022b), causality can be expressed either explicitly or implicitly. The authors illustrate this by providing the following examples:

(1) The treating doctors said Sangram lost around 5 kg due to the hunger strike.

(2) Dissatisfied with the package, workers staged an all-night sit-in.

Example 1 displays explicit causality, made apparent by the presence of the causal marker "due to". The organizers of the current shared task also refer to this marker as the *signal*. In contrast, the causal relation between the sit-in and worker dissatisfaction in Example 2 is implicit, as the sentence does not contain a causal marker.

In their survey of causal relation extraction in natural language texts, Yang et al. (2022) emphasize the potential of domain-specific pre-trained models in combination with graph-based models. They also stress the importance of leveraging linguistic information in order to identify both implicit and explicit causal relations. For this reason, the current study focuses primarily on experiments regarding the integration of linguistic information in the training data, to be used as input for the fine-tuning of pre-trained transformer models.

The remainder of this paper is structured as follows: Section 2 introduces the shared task and the dataset. In Section 3, we describe the training process, model configuration details, and the linguistic dataset alterations that we tested. Results are presented in Section 4 and discussed in Section 5, followed by concluding remarks and a summary of our findings in Section 6.

Proceedings of the 5th Workshop on Challenges and Applications of Automated Extraction of Socio-political Events from Text (CASE), pages 16 - 20
December 7-8, 2022 ©2022 Association for Computational Linguistics

2 Dataset and Task

The CASE-2022 Shared Task 3 on Event Causality Identification is divided into two subtasks. The data provided by the organizers stems from the Causal News Corpus, a collection of 3,559 English annotated event sentences from 869 news articles about protests (Tan et al., 2022b). The goal of Subtask 1 is to determine whether an event sentence contains a cause-effect relation. Subtask 2 is concerned with identifying the spans that correspond to cause, effect, or signal in each causal sentence. We developed and submitted models for the first of these two subtasks.

For the development phase, the task organizers provided a training dataset consisting of 2925 training instances. Sentences with the label 0 ($n = 1322$) did not contain a causal relation, while sentences with the label 1 included a causal relation and were in the majority ($n = 1603$). In addition, an unlabeled development set of 323 sentences was made available in order to allow for model testing via the CodaLab submission portal.

Preliminary exploratory analysis of the data provided for the development phase revealed an average inter-annotator agreement of 88.27% for causal sentences, while sentences labeled as containing no causal relation had an average agreement of 77.89%. Between 1 and 3 annotators labeled each sentence, coming to a consensus of 100% agreement for 70.31% ($n = 1127$) of the causal sentences but only 47.35% ($n = 626$) of the non-causal sentences.

For the test phase, the previously unlabeled development set was re-released with annotations so that it could be used as additional training data. An unlabeled test set of 311 previously unseen sentences was made available for the final testing and scoring process.

3 Methodology

We fine-tuned pre-trained language models (PLMs) on the training data and adjusted the model hyperparameters accordingly. We then tested four different methods of augmenting the training data with linguistic information and compared their efficacy.

3.1 Model settings

We used the Flair framework (Akbik et al., 2019) for model configuration and training. For the development phase, the original data was shuffled and divided into train, validate, and test sets (80/10/10). Using the `roberta-base` and `bert-base-cased` PLMs for comparison, we applied document embeddings to each sentence and fine-tuned the learning rate and batch size hyperparameters (Devlin et al., 2018; Liu et al., 2019). Weights were assigned to the different classes during training to account for the unbalanced distribution in the data with the help of the Scikit-learn `class_weight` parameter (Pedregosa et al., 2011). As the negative class was slightly underrepresented, it was assigned a proportionally higher weight.

3.2 Data Manipulation

In addition to adjusting model settings, we experimented with manipulating the model input and adding pertinent linguistic information during the development phase of the shared task. During the final testing phase, we retrained and tested our best model again using the additional data provided by the organizers. Regardless of the training data used, the test instances were always in the form of individual sentences, with no additional information added.

Baseline dataset In order to have a baseline for comparison, we used an unchanged version of the training data to fine-tune both the BERT and RoBERTa PLMs. This data consisted of individual sentences and corresponding binary labels (cf. Example 3).

(3) Some protesters attempted to fight back with fire extinguishers. 0

Flair NER We used the standard 4-class Flair NER model (pre-trained on the English CoNLL-03 task) to identify named entities of type **Person** (PER), **Location** (LOC), **Organization** (ORG), and **Miscellaneous** (MISC) in the training data, creating new training sets that contained all possible combinations of the four named entity classes. The identified text spans were replaced with the appropriate named entity tag (cf. Example 4).

(4) On Monday, the African National Congress condemned the shooting of Malunga, the Oshabeni branch chairman, and Chiliza, the branch secretary.

On Monday, the ORG condemned the shooting of PER, the LOC branch chairmain, and PER, the branch secretary.

AllenNLP The AllenNLP library was used to annotate the original training data with the semantic role labels ARG0 (proto-agent), ARG1 (proto-patient) and ARGM-CAU (cause clause) (Shi and Lin, 2019). The annotations were then added to the sentences as illustrated in Example 5.

(5) [ARG0: Mainland authorities] have launched [ARG1: a massive crackdown against terrorism] [ARGM-CAU: in wake of a string of violent attacks in the restive Xinjiang region and other cities on the mainland].

The starting point for the semantic role annotations was always the root of the sentence (e.g. the word "launched" in Example 5), which was determined with the help of the spaCy English dependency parser (Honnibal and Montani, 2017). The inclusion of explicit annotations for cause clauses in the training data seemed promising in the context of the given task. However, the AllenNLP model was only able to identify cause clauses in 1.6% of the training instances. We suspect that the model fails primarily at recognizing cause clauses in sentences that contain cause-effect relations only implicitly. Due to the small amount of annotations, we determined that this feature was not meaningful enough to improve classifier performance.

Cause-Effect-Signal Spans A further training dataset was created by adding information from the data provided for Subtask 2, which was identical to the Subtask 1 data, with the addition of Cause-Effect-Signal (CES) span annotations. All sentences from the negative class in the Subtask 1 data were added to the new training set without any annotations.

(6) <ARG1>They then decided to call off the protest</ARG1> <SIG0>as</SIG0> <ARG0>the police had ceded to their demand</ARG0> .

Sentences from the positive class were replaced with the corresponding annotated version from the Subtask 2 data (cf. Example 6). If the Subtask 2 data listed more than one possible annotation option for a sentence, the first option was selected.

NER & Cause-Effect-Signal Spans After creating the training set with Cause-Effect-Signal span annotations, we also used the 4-class Flair NER model to identify named entities and replaced the named entity text spans with the corresponding label (PER, LOC, ORG, MISC) in all training instances.

(7) <ARG1>Police took into custody fifteen activists</ARG1> <SIG0>for</SIG0> <ARG0>blocking the traffic in LOC</ARG0>.

Example 7 shows a training instance from the positive class containing both NER and Cause-Effect-Signal annotations. We experimented by including all possible combinations of named entity classes during training.

4 Results

4.1 Development phase

Models trained using `roberta-base` outperformed those trained with `bert-base-cased`. For this reason, we choose to focus on the models trained with the former architecture in the following pages. Regardless of the data used, the following hyperparameters worked best for all models: a batch size of 8, a learning rate of 3e-5, and the ADAM optimizer. The maximum number of epochs was set to 20, but training was terminated early if it became obvious that the model was overfitting the data, which could be observed as early as epoch 3.

Three of the four methods for adding linguistic information to the model input positively affected model performance: 1) Flair NER annotations; 2) Cause-Effect-Signal spans from the Subtask 2 data; or 3) a combination of both NER and Cause-Effect-Signal spans. When training models with data containing Flair NER annotations, we found that including only the PER and LOC classes (RoBERTa+PER+LOC) resulted in the best performance. When the training data contained both Cause-Effect-Signal spans and Flair NER classes, however, performance was better when only the PER class was included (RoBERTa+PER+CES).

The best performing model on the development set provided by the organizers was RoBERTa+PER+LOC with a macro F1 of 0.8802 (cf. Table 1). However, performance was inconsistent. When we tested the model on our self-

Model configuration	Precision	Recall	Macro F1
RoBERTa baseline	0.8256	0.9045	0.8633
RoBERTa+PER+LOC	0.8729	0.8876	0.8802*
RoBERTa+CES	0.8571	0.8427	0.8499
RoBERTa+PER+CES	0.8368	0.8933	0.8641

Table 1: Results of development phase scoring. Best performing model is marked with *.

Model configuration	Precision	Recall	Macro F1
BERT baseline (Tan et al., 2022a)	0.7801	0.8466	0.8120
LSTM baseline (Tan et al., 2022a)	0.7268	0.8466	0.7822
RoBERTa baseline	0.8000	0.9091	0.8511
RoBERTa+PER+LOC	0.7914	0.8409	0.8154
RoBERTa+CES	0.8239	0.8239	0.8239
RoBERTa+PER+CES	0.8245	0.8807	0.8516*
RoBERTa+PER+CES+FullDataset	0.8343	0.8580	0.8459

Table 2: Results of final test phase scoring. Best performing model is marked with *.

compiled test set during the training phase, the macro F1 score peaked at 0.8578, leading us to question the robustness of the model.

The RoBERTa baseline and the RoBERTa+PER+CES models performed similarly (macro F1 scores of 0.8633 and 0.8641, respectively) with regard to the development set and exhibited more robustness, i.e. the variance between development and self-compiled test set was comparatively small. The RoBERTa+CES model scored slightly lower than the other models with a macro F1 of 0.8499.

4.2 Test phase

Table 2 shows our results from the final testing phase of the shared task, as well as the baselines provided by the organizers. Hyperparameter settings used for development were kept constant for the final testing phase, as were the training datasets, with the exception of RoBERTa+PER+CES+FullDataset. This model was trained using the additional labeled data provided by the organizers for the final testing phase.

Models trained during the development phase consistently achieved lower macro F1 scores on the final testing data. The best model from the development phase (RoBERTa+PER+LOC) performed poorly with a macro F1 of 0.8154, supporting the idea that the model was not robust. The RoBERTa+PER+CES model achieved the highest macro F1 score of 0.8516, outperforming the RoBERTa baseline model by only 0.0005. Surprisingly, re-training this best model with the additional training data provided by the organizers did not improve model performance, resulting in a macro F1 score of only 0.8459.

5 Discussion

The discrepancies between the scores for the development and final testing phases call for a closer investigation of the model input and output. The results from the development phase suggest that model performance increases when training data includes linguistic information in the form of 1) named entity annotations for the PER and LOC classes, or 2) as a combination of both PER named entity annotations and Cause-Effect-Signal spans. Adding only Cause-Effect-Signal spans, however, appears to have had a negative impact on model test scores.

The fact that the RoBERTa+PER+LOC model outperformed the RoBERTa+PER+CES model also suggests that named entity information may prove more useful than Cause-Effect-Signal spans. It is frequently the case that named entities of type PER, i.e. proper nouns, have the semantic role of AGENT or PATIENT in a sentence. Replacing these nouns, along with location names, with named entity tags distills this important information and reduces the number of superfluous words in the data. We suggest that this creates a clearer pattern for the model, which in turn improves performance.

In the final test phase, however, only RoBERTa+PER+CES outperformed our established RoBERTa baseline by a small margin, while RoBERTa+PER+LOC and RoBERTa+CES had the lowest macro F1 scores. According to these results, it seems that adding linguistic information to the training data in the form of named entity annotations or Cause-Effect-Signal spans only leads to minute increases in model performance. It may be that our RoBERTa baseline model is able to extract this particular linguistic information on its own without the need for additional feature engineering. Further experimentation with linguistic features is needed in this area.

With only 2925 sentences, the size of the original amount of training data is also a potential factor that affected model performance. More training data would most likely increase model performance.

A closer investigation of the data revealed that some annotations also leave room for discussion, such as the sentence in Example 8:

(8) The house of a PDP MP was torched in south Kashmir. 1

The sentence is labeled as belonging to the positive class, but we were unable to identify a cause-effect relation. This shows that identifying causality can pose difficulties for expert human annotators. Such instances may negatively influence the detection of causal patterns during training.

Interestingly, re-training our best model with the additional training data in the final testing phase did not improve performance. Furthermore, the testing data used for evaluation in the development phase appears to consist of sentences from only two news articles. The data basis for development was accordingly very homogeneous and most likely did not provide an accurate representation of all possible articles that the model might need to classify in a real-world application. Optimization based on homogeneous data can lead to a preference for models that work well with that specific data but fail to generalize to more diverse data. The difference in model performance between the development and test phases might be evidence of this phenomenon.

6 Conclusion

Training data—including the source, domain, amount, and any added features—plays an important role when it comes to model optimization for NLP tasks, and the subfield of event causality is no exception. Our findings show that the generalizability of a model depends heavily on the quality and content of the model input. In our case, adding linguistic information to the training data only led to a minute increase in model performance as compared to our established RoBERTa baseline. It is possible that a larger training dataset would improve results. In addition, a larger, more diverse testing dataset is necessary in order to adequately evaluate the robustness of the model and predict its effectiveness for real-world applications. Future directions might also include a greater focus on strategies for the identification of implicit cause-effect relations.

References

Alan Akbik, Tanja Bergmann, Duncan Blythe, Kashif Rasul, Stefan Schweter, and Roland Vollgraf. 2019. FLAIR: An easy-to-use framework for state-of-the-art NLP. In *NAACL 2019, 2019 Annual Conference of the North American Chapter of the Association for Computational Linguistics (Demonstrations)*, pages 54–59.

Jacob Devlin, Ming-Wei Chang, Kenton Lee, and Kristina Toutanova. 2018. BERT: Pre-training of deep bidirectional transformers for language understanding. *CoRR*, abs/1810.04805.

Matthew Honnibal and Ines Montani. 2017. spaCy 2: Natural language understanding with Bloom embeddings, convolutional neural networks and incremental parsing.

Çağla Çığ Karaman, Serkan Yalıman, and Salih Atılay Oto. 2017. Event detection from social media: 5W1H analysis on big data. In *2017 25th Signal Processing and Communications Applications Conference (SIU)*, pages 1–4.

Yinhan Liu, Myle Ott, Naman Goyal, Jingfei Du, Mandar Joshi, Danqi Chen, Omer Levy, Mike Lewis, Luke Zettlemoyer, and Veselin Stoyanov. 2019. RoBERTa: A robustly optimized BERT pretraining approach.

Fabian Pedregosa, Gaël Varoquaux, Alexandre Gramfort, Vincent Michel, Bertrand Thirion, Olivier Grisel, Mathieu Blondel, Peter Prettenhofer, Ron Weiss, Vincent Dubourg, Jake Vanderplas, Alexandre Passos, David Cournapeau, Matthieu Brucher, Matthieu Perrot, and Édouard Duchesnay. 2011. Scikit-learn: Machine learning in Python. *Journal of Machine Learning Research*, 12:2825–2830.

Peng Shi and Jimmy Lin. 2019. Simple BERT models for relation extraction and semantic role labeling. *ArXiv*, abs/1904.05255.

Fiona Anting Tan, Ali Hürriyetoğlu, Tommaso Caselli, Nelleke Oostdijk, Hansi Hettiarachchi, Tadashi Nomoto, Onur Uca, and Farhana Ferdousi Liza. 2022a. Event causality identification with Causal News Corpus - Shared Task 3, CASE 2022. In *Proceedings of the 5th Workshop on Challenges and Applications of Automated Extraction of Socio-political Events from Text (CASE 2022)*, Online. Association for Computational Linguistics.

Fiona Anting Tan, Ali Hürriyetoğlu, Tommaso Caselli, Nelleke Oostdijk, Tadashi Nomoto, Hansi Hettiarachchi, Iqra Ameer, Onur Uca, Farhana Ferdousi Liza, and Tiancheng Hu. 2022b. The causal news corpus: Annotating causal relations in event sentences from news. In *Proceedings of the Language Resources and Evaluation Conference*, pages 2298–2310, Marseille, France. European Language Resources Association.

Jie Yang, Soyeon Caren Han, and Josiah Poon. 2022. A survey on extraction of causal relations from natural language text. *CoRR*, arXiv:2101.06426.

A Hybrid Knowledge and Transformer-Based Model for Event Detection with Automatic Self-Attention Threshold, Layer and Head Selection

Thierry Desot, Orphée De Clercq, and Veronique Hoste
LT[3], Language and Translation Technology Team
Ghent University, Groot-Brittanniëlaan 45, 9000 Gent, Belgium
{thierry.desot,orphee.declercq,veronique.hoste}@ugent.be

Abstract

Event and argument role detection are frequently conceived as separate tasks. In this work we conceive both processes as one task in a *hybrid* event detection approach. Its main component is based on *automatic keyword extraction* (AKE) using the self-attention mechanism of a *BERT* transformer model. As a bottleneck for AKE is defining the threshold of the attention values, we propose a novel method for *automatic self-attention threshold selection*. It is fueled by core event information, or simply the verb and its arguments as the backbone of an event. These are outputted by a knowledge-based syntactic parser. In a second step the event core is enriched with other semantically salient words provided by the transformer model. Furthermore, we propose an *automatic self-attention layer and head selection mechanism*, by analyzing which self-attention cells in the BERT transformer contribute most to the hybrid event detection and which linguistic tasks they represent. This approach was integrated in a pipeline event extraction approach and outperforms three state of the art multi-task event extraction methods.

1 Introduction

Event extraction, argument and semantic role detection are frequently conceived as separate tasks (Ji and Grishman, 2008; Gupta and Ji, 2009; Hong et al., 2011; Chen et al., 2015; Nguyen and Grishman, 2015; Liu et al., 2016a,b) where a *multi-word* event is first split into a verb as *single-word* event to process, after which its argument roles (subject, direct and indirect object(s)) and semantic roles (such as time and location) are extracted. These are typically trained in a multi-task setup for *event extraction*, which combines event span detection and classification. In this work, we tackle *multi-word* event extraction and conceive event span detection and argument extraction as *one task* in a hybrid knowledge and transformer-based event detection method. The verb, subject and object(s) (SVO) are first outputted by a knowledge-based syntactic parser and combined with *automatic keyword extraction* (AKE). In this latter step, the most relevant keywords in a sentence or most salient semantic information is selected, exploiting the attention mechanism of a transformer, i.e., *BERT* (Bidirectional Encoder Representations from Transformers) (Devlin et al., 2018). A bottleneck for AKE is defining the threshold of the attention values to take into account (Tang et al., 2019). Hence, we propose and outline a method for *automatic attention threshold selection* by exploiting the interaction between self-attention based AKE and rule-based event detection. As the main function of the rule-based component is to provide the necessary information for the automatic attention threshold mechanism, it targets only minimal event information, i.e., the core or backbone of the event or the verb and its SVO arguments. This allows the transformer's main component to complement it with other semantic roles and semantically salient information. However, the latter type of information is often essential to constitute the core meaning of the event. For example, omitting the adverb *"conditionally"* in the event *"He was conditionally released from detention."* changes its semantics and causes a misunderstanding of it. This kind of semantically salient information can only be provided by the transformer model, and not by the knowledge-based component in our hybrid model.

Our hybrid event detection mechanism is embedded in a *pipeline* event extraction approach that goes beyond short event spans: in a first step, event classification is applied to raw input sentences, whereas in a second step, the event span is detected. For a fair evaluation, we compare this approach with three event detection approaches as part of a multi-task event extraction method that jointly predicts event spans and classes. The main contributions of this paper are the following:

Proceedings of the 5th Workshop on Challenges and Applications of Automated Extraction of Socio-political Events from Text (CASE), pages 21 - 31
December 7-8, 2022

- To the best of our knowledge, this is the first work on hybrid event detection that conceives event span detection and argument extraction as one task. On top of that, AKE is integrated and combined with a novel automatic attention threshold selection mechanism.

- We also propose an automatic self-attention layer and head selection mechanism by investigating which layers and heads of the BERT transformer model contribute most to event detection, and which linguistic tasks they perform. Identifying such tasks in the transformer model can contribute to the creation of more domain-specific and tailor-made BERT models. Our methodology is language-independent. All experiments have been conducted on a Dutch corpus only, mainly because we did not find data in other languages with similar event *prominence* annotations (Section 3.1).

Our approach is positioned with respect to the state of the art in Section 2 and is presented in Sections 3 and 4. An overview of the data is given in Section 5. Section 6 presents the results of experiments, followed by a thorough analysis and discussion. The paper is concluded in Section 8.

2 Related Work

Knowledge-based event detection methods were initially based on ontologies (Frasincar et al., 2009; Schouten et al., 2010; Arendarenko and Kakkonen, 2012) or rule-sets (Valenzuela-Escárcega et al., 2015) which represent expert knowledge. These also include extracting candidate event words with part-of-speech tags (Mihalcea and Tarau, 2004), which can also satisfy predefined syntactic patterns (Nguyen and Phan, 2009). Statistical methods spot event spans using n-grams (Witten et al., 2005; Grineva et al., 2009), term frequency inverse document frequency (TF-IDF), word frequency and word co-occurrence (Kaur and Gupta, 2010).

Early supervised machine learning approaches recast event detection as a binary classification problem (Hasan and Ng, 2014) to decide whether an input word is part of an event or not. To that end, maximum entropy (Yih et al., 2006), support vector machines (SVM) (Lopez and Romary, 2010) and conditional random fields (CRF) (Zhang, 2008) were applied. As the event detection field initially concentrated on *fixed* event types using *single-word* or event spans with a short length (Mitamura et al., 2015), these supervised machine learning approaches have successfully used the ACE 2005 corpus (Walker et al., 2006) comprising *single-word* event span length annotations. With *feature engineering* approaches emerging, the scope became larger than a one-word event span (Patwardhan and Riloff, 2009). In Lefever and Hoste (2016) *multi-word* events in Dutch news text are detected using an SVM binary classifier combining lexical, syntactic and semantic features. These feature-based machine learning techniques, however, have been superseded by deep learning techniques which are able to learn hidden feature representations automatically from data. In Wang et al. (2017), a multi-word event detection approach using convolutional neural networks (CNN) outperforms an SVM approach. Spearheaded by their success in dealing with long-term dependencies in longer sequences, the LSTM (long short-term memory) and attention mechanism allow the decoder to learn which parts of the sequence should be attended to in an encoder-decoder architecture (Bahdanau et al., 2014; Luong et al., 2015), hence taking more context information into account. Zhao et al. (2018) presents a supervised *attention-based* RNN event detection approach that outperforms an RNN and CNN, both without attention mechanism.

Deep learning approaches that were in recent years combined with Word2Vec (Mikolov et al., 2013), GLoVe (Pennington et al., 2014) and fastText (Bojanowski et al., 2017) word embeddings have led to the rise of the *transformer architecture* (Vaswani et al., 2017). Its *contextual language models* have been successfully integrated in a range of NLP tasks using pre-trained contextual *BERT* (Bidirectional Encoder Representations from Transformers) word embeddings (Devlin et al., 2018). On top of that, the BERT model fully exploits the attention mechanism for multi-word event detection, which is illustrated in Mehta et al. (2020), where a multi-attention event detection tool, using BERT, fine-tuned on the Civil Unrest Gold Standard Report data (Ramakrishnan et al., 2014), outperforms a CNN. The *hybrid* target event detection method that is proposed here also fully benefits from the BERT multi-head self-attention, but is combined with subject, verb and object (*SVO*) information, as outputted by a knowledge-based syntactic parser.

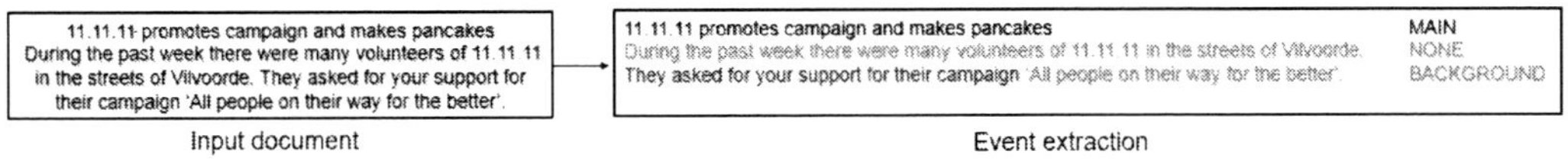

Figure 1: Example of EventDNA corpus event spans and Main, Background, None event prominence labels

3 Pipeline Event Extraction Approach

An event can be defined as the smallest extent of text that expresses its occurrence (Song et al., 2015) and is identified by a word or phrase called event *trigger, nugget, event span or mention*. Event mentions can be *single-word* event triggers that are usually (main) verbs, nouns, adjectives and adverbs. *Multi-word* event triggers can be consecutive tokens, complete sentences, or *discontinuous* when on top of the verb, its participants, or argument roles are also involved (Doddington et al., 2004). Our *hybrid* event detection approach targets *multi-word continuous event* spans. It goes *beyond* the scope of approaches tackling *single-word* events that are frequently using the ACE 2005 corpus (Section 2). Hence our models are trained on the (Dutch) EventDNA corpus, annotated with multi-word event spans and class labels (Section 5).

3.1 Event Prominence Classification

Our hybrid model is part of a pipeline event extraction model which comprises an event classifier and detection module. Event prominence classification was chosen, other than the typically used event type classification (Desot et al., 2021) that frequently fails to handle the variety of events expressed in real-world situations. To overcome this, we classify new information into *prominence* classes. Hence, the input sentence can be classified as `Main` event when it exhibits new information and, for example in a news context actually caused the reporter to write the article; or as `Background` event when it gives context or background to the `Main` event. Raw sentences without events are classified as `None` events. Figure 1 presents an example of an event span labeled as `Background` event, preceded by a `Main` and `None` event.

For event classification a transformer-based BERT model for the Dutch language, BERTje (de Vries et al., 2019) has been pre-trained on a dataset of 2.4 billion tokens from Wikipedia, Twente News Corpus (Ordelman et al., 2007) and SoNaR-500 (Oostdijk et al., 2013) with masked language modeling and next sentence prediction. BERTje has an architecture of 12 transformer blocks (bidirectional layers) and 12 self-attention heads and a hidden size of 768. This Dutch language model has been fine-tuned for sequence (event) classification on the raw sentences of the EventDNA data set (Section 5). Only output sentences with predicted `Main` prominence class or `Background` class are accepted as input for hybrid knowledge- and transformer-based event detection, whereas sentences predicted as `None` events are not further processed.

3.2 Knowledge and Transformer-Based Event Detection with Automatic Attention Threshold Selection

The main function of the rule-based part of our *hybrid* event detection approach is to provide the necessary information to the automatic attention threshold selection mechanism. Hence, the backbone of the event, i.e., the subject (`SUBJ`), (head) verb (`VERB`) and object (`OBJ`) information is outputted by a knowledge-based syntactic parser for the Dutch language, namely Alpino. This parser combines a rule-based head-driven phrase structure grammar (HPSG) with a lexicon of 100,000 entries and a part-of-speech (POS) tagger. On top of that, dependency parse trees are generated, which are disambiguated with a maximum entropy component (Van der Beek et al., 2002; Van Noord et al., 2006; Smessaert and Augustinus, 2010). For this parser, an F1 score of 91.14% has been reported on 1,400 manually annotated sentences from the Twente News corpus (Ordelman et al., 2007). Starting from these predicted tags a set of rules is then used to align them with the corresponding words.

In a next step, the syntactic output is the cornerstone of our automatic attention threshold selection mechanism. To this purpose, *automatic keyword extraction* (AKE) exploiting the attention mechanism of BERTje (Section 3.1) is used. Keywords are defined as the most relevant words in an event span (Sarracén and Rosso, 2021), and are extracted through attention weights obtained over the 12 x 12 transformer self-attention layers and heads from the BERTje model. In the study of Tang et al. (2019) only 10% of the words with the highest attention weights were kept as keywords. Initially, and in a similar vein, given a sequence of attention weights in $Att = (Att_1, ..., Att_n)$, in ascending weight value order, we identified the words above a certain threshold. We iteratively explored a range of threshold values between 0.1 and 0.9 per step of 0.1 to find an optimal threshold (0.25). This was only a preparatory step in order to estimate the feasibility of our approach, as such a *fixed* threshold percentage is arbitrary and not optimal over sentences with different lengths and data sets. Hence, we defined an *automatic* and *variable* threshold (Att_{thresh}) as the minimum value for the attention values to be selected. To this purpose the percentage (p) of subject, verb, object words ($\#SVO\_words$), as output from the previous step, in relation to the total number of words per sentence ($\#Sentence\_words$) was calculated as $p = \frac{\#SVO\_words * 100}{\#Sentence\_words}$. The threshold is the *lowest* attention weight in the range of the p percent of the top-ranked attention values per sentence, which we calculate using the $percentile$, $Att_{thresh} = percentile(Att, (100 - p))$. Finally, the resulting top-ranked attention values Att exceeding the threshold Att_{thresh} are selected (Att_{sel}), where $Att_{sel} = (Att_{thresh}, ..., Att_n)$. The subtokens of the words corresponding to these values are kept as keywords, discarding the special separator `[SEP]` and classification tokens `[CLS]`. The subtokens are then again concatenated into words. With the BERTje model, not all subtokens of a word have equal attention weights. In that case, we extracted the whole word as keyword if one of its subtokens passes the threshold. The resulting attention-based keywords are merged with the (*SVO*) combinations of the event detection module. Finally, the original word order is restored by aligning the merged words with the original input sentence. Figure 2 depicts the complete event detection process for the Dutch input sentence "(The company) XYZ moet extra personeelsleden vinden wegens uitval van werknemers."[1]

We want to emphasize that other argument roles, such as time and place on top of the SVO words, were not considered and are not outputted by the knowledge-based parser. In our initial experiments, these resulted in a too high percentage of selected words and too low threshold values, which led to an overgeneration of predicted event words. However, part of these semantic roles do occur in the semantically salient words predicted by the transformer model (Section 7).

3.3 Automatic Self-Attention Layer and Head Selection

Certain self-attention layers and heads of the transformer model exhibit linguistic notions, such as syntax and coreference (Vig, 2019; Vig and Belinkov, 2019; Clark et al., 2019). According to several studies (Goldberg, 2019; Hewitt and Manning, 2019; Jawahar et al., 2019; Vig and Belinkov, 2019) on the BERT transformer, attention follows syntactic *dependency* and subject-verb-object agreement most strongly in the *middle layers* of the BERT model. In order to automatically select the self-attention layer and head that contribute most to event detection performances, we exploit the interaction between the transformer and knowledge-based syntactic parser again and verify the number of SVO words predicted by the transformer model. We first apply our automatic threshold selection technique per self-attention transformer cell by calculating the attention values per isolated head per layer (Vig and Belinkov, 2019), for each of the 12 x 12 transformer cells (144 times) on the test data (Section 5). In a next step, per transformer matrix cell we calculate the percentage of overlap between selected event tokens with an attention value above the automatically selected threshold and between the knowledge-based predicted SVO words. We finally consider the self-attention layer and cell that output most SVO words, as exhibiting the linguistic notion of syntactic dependency. We verify if it improves event detection performance and analyse the behaviour of this layer in Section 7.

4 Baseline Multi-Task Event Extraction Approaches

We compare the target *pipeline* event extraction model (Section 3) with three baseline multi-task event extraction models. To the best of our knowledge, we are not aware of other baseline approaches applied to languages with a similar event *prominence* annotation scheme (Section 3.1). In the multi-task approach, event detection and classification tasks are performed simultaneously to benefit from their interplay (Li et al., 2013; Liu et al., 2017). The first model is an attention-based RNN model with LSTM from Liu and Lane (2016), with an encoder-decoder architecture. Its atten-

[1] English translation: *"(The company) XYZ has to find extra staff due to employee absence."*

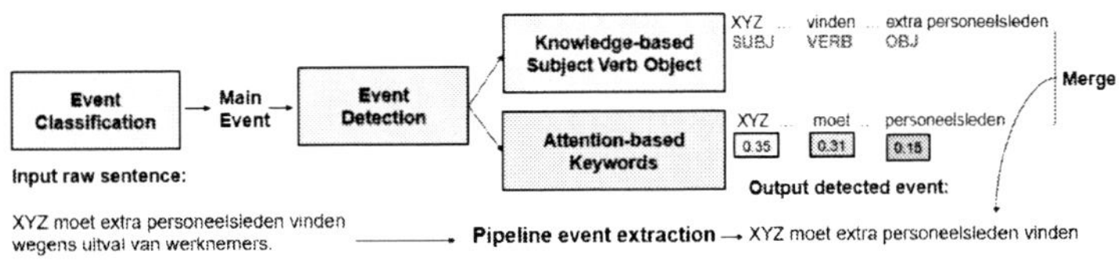

Figure 2: Overview of pipeline event extraction

Event span IOB labels:	**Event class:**
`B-EV I-EV I-EV I-EV I-EV O O O O`	Main
Raw input sentence	
`XYZ moet extra personeelsleden vinden wegens uitval van werknemers.`	

Table 1: Input raw sentence with event detection IOB labels and class

tion context vector provides information from parts of the input sequence that the classifier pays attention to. The second model is fine-tuned for combined event detection and classification on the same pre-trained BERTje model as our target approach (Section 3.1). For combining both tasks, given the input token sequence $x = (x_1, ..., x_T)$, the output hidden states of the BERTje model are $H = (h_1, ..., h_T)$. For event detection the final hidden states of $(h_2, ..., h_T)$ are fed into a softmax layer to classify over the detected event subtokens s. Based on the hidden state of the (first) special classification `[CLS]` token, denoted as h_1, the event y with weighted representations of query, key and value vectors W is predicted as,

$$y^s_n = softmax(W^s h_n + b^s), n \in 1 \ldots N \quad (1)$$

and the detected event sequence as $y^s = (y^s_1, ..., y^s_T)$ which are then jointly modeled as,

$$p(y^i, y^s|x)) = p(y^i|x) \prod_{n=1}^{N} p(y^s_n|x) \quad (2)$$

which maximizes the probability $p(y^i, y^s|x))$.

We finally added a CRF on top of the multi-task BERTje-based approach, resulting in our third baseline model where the joint BERT+CRF replaces the softmax classifier with CRF (Chen et al., 2019). The target event sequence is labeled in *IOB* format. Tokens at the *begin* of an event mention are labelled as *B-EV*, tokens *inside* the mention as *I-EV*, and tokens *outside* the mention as *O*. Table 1 includes the same example sentence as in Figure 2.

5 Data

Both event extraction approaches (Sections 3 and 4) were trained and tested using the event span and label annotations in the titles and lead paragraphs of the EventDNA corpus. This corpus comprises news articles and follows the *ERE* (Entities, Relations, Events) annotation standards (Song et al., 2015; Aguilar et al., 2014). For more detailed information about the corpus we refer the reader to Desot et al. (2021) which outlines event classification experiments, for validating the quality of the corpus and to Colruyt et al. (2019, accepted for publication) for the corpus design and annotations. A high number (32%) of event types in the EventDNA corpus do not correspond to the event types specified in the ERE-based EventDNA annotation protocol. Hence, event prominence classification was chosen, other than the typically used event type classification (Desot et al., 2021), as explained in Section 3.1 and Figure 1.

Events	#	Item	#
Main	4175	Vocab.	13050
Backgr.	3100	Tokens	88530
None	1792	Sentences	6813
Total	9069	Documents	1740

Table 2: Overview of EventDNA corpus statistics

The EventDNA data set comprises raw sentences with more than one event span. As a first step, only unique sentences with one event span were kept for our experiments. Table 2 exhibits information about the data set used for our experiments (Section 6), with an overview of the event prominence class distributions (first column). In order to train our models, the (6813) sentences of the data set were split into 80% train, 10% development (*Dev.*) and 10% held-out test partitions.

6 Experiments and Results

6.1 Baseline Multi-Task Event Extraction

The *raw sentences* in the training data set were used to train the baseline multi-task models and was automatically converted into *IOB* format (Section 4). The attention-based RNN model was trained for 10 epochs with a batch size of 10, using Adam optimizer, and with the number of LSTM cell units set as 128. Word embeddings of size 128 were randomly initialized. For fine-tuning the BERT-based models, optimal performances were obtained using the AdamW optimizer (Loshchilov and Hutter, 2017) with a learning rate of 1e-5 and a batch size of 10 instances during 10 epochs. The maximum sequence length is set to 82 tokens, which is the maximum sequence token length of the training data sentences. The special `[CLS]` (classification) token and `[SEP]` (separator) tokens were inserted.

Table 3 shows that the attention-based RNN model (*Att-RNN.*) is outperformed by the BERT-based models. The combined BERTje and CRF multi-task model (*BERTje+CRF*) outperforms the BERTje model without CRF (*BERTje*) for both event detection and classification. We compared event detection with (Table 3, *+class.*) and without (*-class.*) interaction with classification. Multi-task event detection benefits from the interaction between event classification and detection and outperforms event detection without the impact of event classification.

6.2 Target Pipeline Event Extraction

The target pipeline event extraction approach is composed of a BERTje-based *classifier* and a hybrid knowledge- and transformer attention-based *event detection* approach. Raw sentences that are classified as `Main` and `Background` events are fed to the hybrid event detection tool in order to identify the event span in the raw sentence. Similar parameters as used for the BERTje-based multi-task baseline models (Section 6.1) have been applied, except for a lower number (3) of epochs in order to obtain optimal performances. *Event prominence classification* performance on the test set is exhibited in Table 4, *Event class*, which outperforms classification of the baseline multi-task models (Table 3). As a next step, the sentences classified as `Main` or `Background` event, are fed to the hybrid *event detection* module that combines rule-based extraction of *SVO* words with self-attention based extraction of keywords. Performances in Table 4 are compared for:

- a fixed self-attention threshold (Section 3.2), *Fix. thresh.* of 0.25
- automatic self-attention threshold selection (Section 3.2), *Aut. thresh.*
- combined self-attention threshold, layer and head selection (Section 3.3), *Aut. thresh. + layer*.

These performances were calculated for raw sentence words, predicted as *inside*, *outside*, or in *initial* position of the gold standard annotated event spans of our data set. The model with a fixed threshold (*Fix. thresh.*) outperforms the second attention model with an automatically selected threshold (*Aut. thresh.*), although performances for the latter model are methodologically more fair. Performances on the gold standard event classes (*Fix. thresh. Gold.*) are slightly better compared to detection of events for the predicted event classes (*Fix. thresh. Pred.*). Best results however are shown for automatic threshold combined with self-attention layer and head selection (*Aut. thresh. + layer*) (layer 7, head 1). Event detection was also performed using attention-based keywords without knowledge-based predicted words (*Att.*) and vice versa (*SVO*). These results demonstrate that event detection performance increases, if knowledge- and attention-based event detection are combined.

7 Results Analysis and Discussion

In spite of the interaction between event classification and event detection, the multi-task baseline models could not outperform the classifier of the target pipeline model. On top of that, the pre-trained BERTje models of the BERT-based multi-task baseline models outperform the attention-based RNN multi-task model without BERT. This shows that a pre-trained BERT transformer model improves performances, when fine-tuning on a small data set. For event detection with automatic self-attention threshold selection, the target pipeline event extraction model did not outperform the BERT-based baseline models. However, combined with automatic self-attention layer and head selection, layer 7 and head 1 show the best event detection performances.

Hence, we analysed the latter result by correlating the order of transformer block layers and heads

Event extraction	Event classification			Event detection			Class
	Prec.	**Rec.**	**F1**	**Prec.**	**Rec.**	**F1**	**+/-**
Baseline multi-task models:							
Att.-RNN	0.52	0.54	0.52	0.60	0.61	0.60	+class
	-	-	-	0.58	0.59	0.58	-class
BERTje	0.60	0.61	0.60	0.66	0.65	0.65	+class
	-	-	-	0.65	0.64	0.64	-class
BERTje+CRF	0.61	0.62	0.61	0.66	0.67	0.66	+clas s
	-	-	-	0.65	0.65	0.65	-class

Table 3: Overview of baseline multi-task event extraction performances

Event extraction		Prec.	Rec.	F1
Event class.		0.69	0.68	**0.68**
Event det.				
Fix. thresh.	Gold.	0.83	0.57	0.65
	Pred.	0.79	0.58	0.64
Aut. thresh.		0.75	0.57	0.63
	SVO	0.70	0.51	0.57
	Att.	0.71	0.54	0.60
Aut. thresh. + layer		0.88	0.62	**0.71**

Table 4: Pipeline model event extraction performances

Correlation	Pearson	Spearman
Layer order	-0.30^{*}	-0.36^{*}
Head order	-0.13^{**}	-0.12^{**}
$^{*}p < 0.05$; $^{**}p > 0.05$		

Table 5: Layer/head order - event detection correlation

with event detection F1 scores. In a next step, attention attributions of the transformer model are visualised. Finally we check the impact on attention attribution stability by changing the word order of the input sentences.

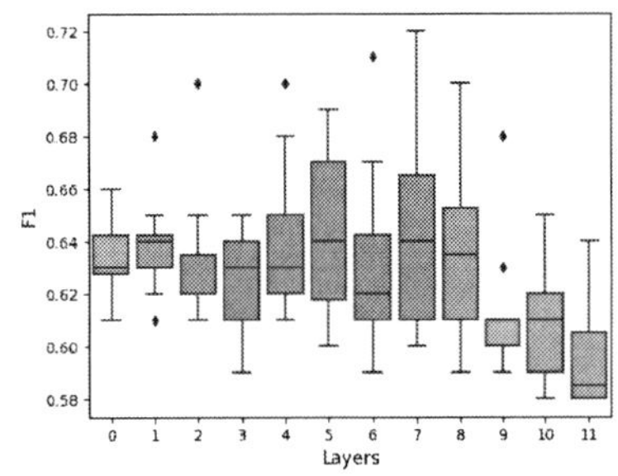

Figure 3: Transformer self-attention layer depth and hybrid target model event detection F1 scores

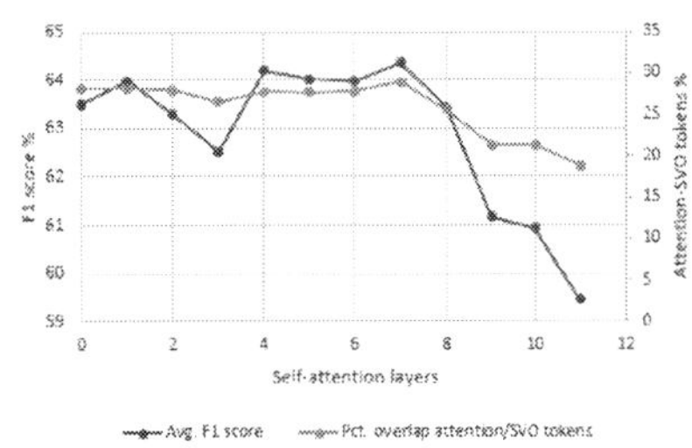

Figure 4: Hybrid event detection F1 score - overlap self-attention and knowledge-based model output SVO tokens per self-attention layer

7.1 Correlation between Transformer Layers, Heads and Event Detection Performances

Pearson's correlation coefficient was calculated, measuring the association strength between two variables and *Spearman's rank correlation* that measures correlations between two *ranked variables*. We use the p-value to determine if the resulting correlation coefficient is significant and whether or not to reject a null hypothesis. We reject the null hypothesis if the p-value is less than 0.05 ($p < 0.05$). Table 5 demonstrates *weak*, but *significant* ($p < 0.05$) negative Pearson and Spearman's rank correlations, -0.3 and -0.36 respectively, between event detection F1 scores and layer depth, unlike correlations between F1 scores and attention *heads*, which are not significant ($p > 0.05$). Figure 3 presents F1 scores (*F1*) averaged over the (12) heads per layer and shows a downward trend for F1 scores: maximum F1 score is obtained for middle *layer* 7 (0.71), whereas the minimum F1 scores are shown for the deepest layers 10 and 11. A similar trend is shown in Figure 4. It presents the percentages in overlap between the knowledge-based predicted SVO words and event tokens with an attention value above the automatically selected threshold (averaged over the 12 attention heads per layer), which we calculated for automatic self-attention layer and head selection (Section 3.3).

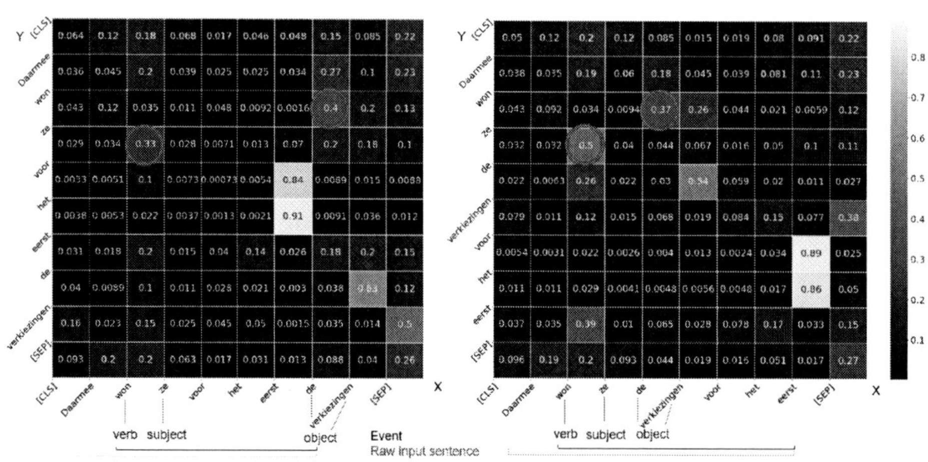

Figure 5: Self-attention values for SVO dependencies, layer 7 and head 1, without and with changed word order

The highest overlap is shown for layer 7, resulting in the best event detection *F1* scores (normalized to percentage). This indicates that layer 7 can be identified most with the notion of SVO dependencies. Furthermore, correlations in Table 5 show that layers are associated more with linguistic reasoning tasks than heads. This supports the hypothesis in the study of Hoover et al. (2019) that dependencies are probably encoded by a combination of heads rather than by a single head.

7.2 Attention Attribution and Stability

As attention follows SVO agreement most strongly in layer 7, head 1 of the BERTje model we visualise these attentions for the test set. For 100 randomly selected test sentences, with SVO attention values above the automatically selected threshold, we changed the word order (without changing the meaning). For the resulting sentences we found that for 61%, the same dependencies and words with most attention are preserved. This indicates a consistent behaviour of the BERTje model w.r.t. attention attributions. For the Dutch sentence *"And so she won the elections for the first time."*[2], the circles in the left attention heatmap matrix (Figure 5) mark intersections in cells with a high attention value that show a dependency between the `verb` (*"won"*) and `object` (*"de verkiezingen"*), and between the `subject` (*"ze"*) and the `verb` (*"won"*) with their corresponding words on the X and Y axis. Among the keywords with a weight > the threshold, the keyword with most attention (0.91) is *"eerst"*[3] in the collocation *"voor het eerst"* [4], a semantically very salient word in this context. *"voor het eerst"*, was moved to the end of the event (Figure 5, right heatmap), and has still the highest attention value (0.89), with the same SVO dependencies.

8 Conclusion and Future Work

This study outlines a pipeline hybrid knowledge- and transformer self-attention based event detection approach. It outperforms three state of the art multi-task baseline event extraction models. For keyword-based event detection, we solved the bottleneck of defining the threshold of the attention values to take into account. Automatic self-attention threshold, layer and head selection was applied, exploiting the interaction between a rule-based SVO (subject-verb-object) extraction and self-attention based automatic keyword extraction (AKE). Analysis of the BERTje transformer model shows that syntactic dependencies are most active in the middle layers and contribute most to event detection. We also found evidence for consistency of attention attributions of the transformer model. As a next step, the behaviour and stability of the surrounding layers, should be further investigated. Other data sets in Dutch or other languages can be used, comprising more than one event span per sentence.

Acknowledgements

This work was supported by Ghent University under grant BOFGOA2018000601.

[2]Original Dutch sentence: *"Daarmee won ze voor het eerst de verkiezingen."*

[3] *"first"*

[4] *"for the first time"*

References

Jacqueline Aguilar, Charley Beller, Paul McNamee, Benjamin Van Durme, Stephanie Strassel, Zhiyi Song, and Joe Ellis. 2014. A comparison of the events and relations across ace, ere, tac-kbp, and framenet annotation standards. In *Proceedings of the Second Workshop on EVENTS: Definition, Detection, Coreference, and Representation*, pages 45–53.

Ernest Arendarenko and Tuomo Kakkonen. 2012. Ontology-based information and event extraction for business intelligence. In *International Conference on Artificial Intelligence: Methodology, Systems, and Applications*, pages 89–102. Springer.

Dzmitry Bahdanau, Kyunghyun Cho, and Yoshua Bengio. 2014. Neural machine translation by jointly learning to align and translate. *arXiv preprint arXiv:1409.0473*.

Piotr Bojanowski, Edouard Grave, Armand Joulin, and Tomas Mikolov. 2017. Enriching word vectors with subword information. *Transactions of the Association for Computational Linguistics*, 5:135–146.

Qian Chen, Zhu Zhuo, and Wen Wang. 2019. Bert for joint intent classification and slot filling. *arXiv preprint arXiv:1902.10909*.

Yubo Chen, Liheng Xu, Kang Liu, Daojian Zeng, and Jun Zhao. 2015. Event extraction via dynamic multi-pooling convolutional neural networks. In *Proceedings of the 53rd Annual Meeting of the Association for Computational Linguistics and the 7th International Joint Conference on Natural Language Processing (Volume 1: Long Papers)*, pages 167–176.

Kevin Clark, Urvashi Khandelwal, Omer Levy, and Christopher D Manning. 2019. What does bert look at? an analysis of bert's attention. *arXiv preprint arXiv:1906.04341*.

Camiel Colruyt, Orhpée De Clercq, Thierry Desot, and Veronique Hoste. accepted for publication. Eventdna: a dataset for dutch news event extraction as a basis for news diversification. *Language Resources and Evaluation*.

Camiel Colruyt, Orphée De Clercq, and Véronique Hoste. 2019. Eventdna: guidelines for entities and events in dutch news texts (v1. 0). *LT3 Technical Report-LT3 19-01*.

Wietse de Vries, Andreas van Cranenburgh, Arianna Bisazza, Tommaso Caselli, Gertjan van Noord, and Malvina Nissim. 2019. Bertje: A dutch bert model. *arXiv preprint arXiv:1912.09582*.

Thierry Desot, Orphee De Clercq, and Veronique Hoste. 2021. Event prominence extraction combining a knowledge-based syntactic parser and a bert classifier for dutch. In *Proceedings of the International Conference on Recent Advances in Natural Language Processing (RANLP 2021)*, pages 346–357.

Jacob Devlin, Ming-Wei Chang, Kenton Lee, and Kristina Toutanova. 2018. Bert: Pre-training of deep bidirectional transformers for language understanding. *arXiv preprint arXiv:1810.04805*.

George R Doddington, Alexis Mitchell, Mark A Przybocki, Lance A Ramshaw, Stephanie M Strassel, and Ralph M Weischedel. 2004. The automatic content extraction (ace) program-tasks, data, and evaluation. In *Lrec*, volume 2, pages 837–840. Lisbon.

Flavius Frasincar, Jethro Borsje, and Leonard Levering. 2009. A semantic web-based approach for building personalized news services. *International Journal of E-Business Research (IJEBR)*, 5(3):35–53.

Yoav Goldberg. 2019. Assessing bert's syntactic abilities. *arXiv preprint arXiv:1901.05287*.

Maria Grineva, Maxim Grinev, and Dmitry Lizorkin. 2009. Extracting key terms from noisy and multi-theme documents. In *Proceedings of the 18th international conference on World wide web*, pages 661–670.

Prashant Gupta and Heng Ji. 2009. Predicting unknown time arguments based on cross-event propagation. In *Proceedings of the ACL-IJCNLP 2009 Conference Short Papers*, pages 369–372.

Kazi Saidul Hasan and Vincent Ng. 2014. Automatic keyphrase extraction: A survey of the state of the art. In *Proceedings of the 52nd Annual Meeting of the Association for Computational Linguistics (Volume 1: Long Papers)*, pages 1262–1273.

John Hewitt and Christopher D Manning. 2019. A structural probe for finding syntax in word representations. In *Proceedings of the 2019 Conference of the North American Chapter of the Association for Computational Linguistics: Human Language Technologies, Volume 1 (Long and Short Papers)*, pages 4129–4138.

Yu Hong, Jianfeng Zhang, Bin Ma, Jianmin Yao, Guodong Zhou, and Qiaoming Zhu. 2011. Using cross-entity inference to improve event extraction. In *Proceedings of the 49th annual meeting of the association for computational linguistics: human language technologies*, pages 1127–1136.

Benjamin Hoover, Hendrik Strobelt, and Sebastian Gehrmann. 2019. exbert: A visual analysis tool to explore learned representations in transformers models. *arXiv preprint arXiv:1910.05276*.

Ganesh Jawahar, Benoît Sagot, and Djamé Seddah. 2019. What does bert learn about the structure of language? In *ACL 2019-57th Annual Meeting of the Association for Computational Linguistics*.

Heng Ji and Ralph Grishman. 2008. Refining event extraction through cross-document inference. In *Proceedings of ACL-08: Hlt*, pages 254–262.

Jasmeen Kaur and Vishal Gupta. 2010. Effective approaches for extraction of keywords. *International Journal of Computer Science Issues (IJCSI)*, 7(6):144.

Els Lefever and Véronique Hoste. 2016. A classification-based approach to economic event detection in dutch news text. In *Proceedings of the Tenth International Conference on Language Resources and Evaluation (LREC'16)*, pages 330–335.

Qi Li, Heng Ji, and Liang Huang. 2013. Joint event extraction via structured prediction with global features. In *Proceedings of the 51st Annual Meeting of the Association for Computational Linguistics (Volume 1: Long Papers)*, pages 73–82.

Bing Liu and Ian Lane. 2016. Attention-based recurrent neural network models for joint intent detection and slot filling. *arXiv preprint arXiv:1609.01454*.

Shulin Liu, Yubo Chen, Shizhu He, Kang Liu, and Jun Zhao. 2016a. Leveraging framenet to improve automatic event detection. In *Proceedings of the 54th Annual Meeting of the Association for Computational Linguistics (Volume 1: Long Papers)*, pages 2134–2143.

Shulin Liu, Yubo Chen, Kang Liu, and Jun Zhao. 2017. Exploiting argument information to improve event detection via supervised attention mechanisms. In *Proceedings of the 55th Annual Meeting of the Association for Computational Linguistics (Volume 1: Long Papers)*, pages 1789–1798.

Shulin Liu, Kang Liu, Shizhu He, and Jun Zhao. 2016b. A probabilistic soft logic based approach to exploiting latent and global information in event classification. In *Thirtieth AAAI Conference on Artificial Intelligence*.

Patrice Lopez and Laurent Romary. 2010. Humb: Automatic key term extraction from scientific articles in grobid. In *SemEval 2010 Workshop*, pages 4–p.

Ilya Loshchilov and Frank Hutter. 2017. Decoupled weight decay regularization. *arXiv preprint arXiv:1711.05101*.

Minh-Thang Luong, Hieu Pham, and Christopher D Manning. 2015. Effective approaches to attention-based neural machine translation. *arXiv preprint arXiv:1508.04025*.

Sneha Mehta, Mohammad Raihanul Islam, Huzefa Rangwala, and Naren Ramakrishnan. 2020. Interpretable event detection and extraction using multi-aspect attention.

Rada Mihalcea and Paul Tarau. 2004. Textrank: Bringing order into text. In *Proceedings of the 2004 conference on empirical methods in natural language processing*, pages 404–411.

Tomas Mikolov, Kai Chen, Greg Corrado, and Jeffrey Dean. 2013. Efficient estimation of word representations in vector space. *arXiv preprint arXiv:1301.3781*.

Teruko Mitamura, Zhengzhong Liu, and Eduard H Hovy. 2015. Overview of tac kbp 2015 event nugget track. In *TAC*.

Chau Q Nguyen and Tuoi Thi Phan. 2009. An ontology-based approach for key phrase extraction. In *Proceedings of the ACL-IJCNLP 2009 Conference Short Papers*, pages 181–184.

Thien Huu Nguyen and Ralph Grishman. 2015. Event detection and domain adaptation with convolutional neural networks. In *Proceedings of the 53rd Annual Meeting of the Association for Computational Linguistics and the 7th International Joint Conference on Natural Language Processing (Volume 2: Short Papers)*, pages 365–371.

Nelleke Oostdijk, Martin Reynaert, Véronique Hoste, and Ineke Schuurman. 2013. The construction of a 500-million-word reference corpus of contemporary written dutch. In *Essential speech and language technology for Dutch*, pages 219–247. Springer, Berlin, Heidelberg.

Roeland Ordelman, Franciska de Jong, Arjan Van Hessen, and Hendri Hondorp. 2007. Twnc: a multifaceted dutch news corpus. *ELRA Newsletter*, 12(3/4):4–7.

Siddharth Patwardhan and Ellen Riloff. 2009. A unified model of phrasal and sentential evidence for information extraction. In *Proceedings of the 2009 Conference on Empirical Methods in Natural Language Processing*, pages 151–160.

Jeffrey Pennington, Richard Socher, and Christopher D Manning. 2014. Glove: Global vectors for word representation. In *Proceedings of the 2014 conference on empirical methods in natural language processing (EMNLP)*, pages 1532–1543.

Naren Ramakrishnan, Patrick Butler, Sathappan Muthiah, Nathan Self, Rupinder Khandpur, Parang Saraf, Wei Wang, Jose Cadena, Anil Vullikanti, Gizem Korkmaz, et al. 2014. 'beating the news' with embers: forecasting civil unrest using open source indicators. In *Proceedings of the 20th ACM SIGKDD international conference on Knowledge discovery and data mining*, pages 1799–1808.

Gretel Liz De la Peña Sarracén and Paolo Rosso. 2021. Offensive keyword extraction based on the attention mechanism of bert and the eigenvector centrality using a graph representation. *Personal and Ubiquitous Computing*, pages 1–13.

Kim Schouten, Philip Ruijgrok, Jethro Borsje, Flavius Frasincar, Leonard Levering, and Frederik Hogenboom. 2010. A semantic web-based approach for personalizing news. In *Proceedings of the 2010 ACM Symposium on Applied Computing*, pages 854–861.

Hans Smessaert and Liesbeth Augustinus. 2010. Nederbooms. *linguistics*, 2012.

Zhiyi Song, Ann Bies, Stephanie Strassel, Tom Riese, Justin Mott, Joe Ellis, Jonathan Wright, Seth Kulick, Neville Ryant, and Xiaoyi Ma. 2015. From light to rich ere: annotation of entities, relations, and events. In *Proceedings of the the 3rd Workshop on EVENTS: Definition, Detection, Coreference, and Representation*, pages 89–98.

Matthew Tang, Priyanka Gandhi, Md Ahsanul Kabir, Christopher Zou, Jordyn Blakey, and Xiao Luo. 2019. Progress notes classification and keyword extraction using attention-based deep learning models with bert. *arXiv preprint arXiv:1910.05786*.

Marco A Valenzuela-Escárcega, Gus Hahn-Powell, Mihai Surdeanu, and Thomas Hicks. 2015. A domain-independent rule-based framework for event extraction. In *Proceedings of ACL-IJCNLP 2015 System Demonstrations*, pages 127–132.

Leonoor Van der Beek, Gosse Bouma, Rob Malouf, and Gertjan Van Noord. 2002. The alpino dependency treebank. In *Computational linguistics in the netherlands 2001*, pages 8–22. Brill Rodopi.

Gertjan Van Noord et al. 2006. At last parsing is now operational. In *TALN06. Verbum Ex Machina. Actes de la 13e conference sur le traitement automatique des langues naturelles*, pages 20–42.

Ashish Vaswani, Noam Shazeer, Niki Parmar, Jakob Uszkoreit, Llion Jones, Aidan N Gomez, Lukasz Kaiser, and Illia Polosukhin. 2017. Attention is all you need. *arXiv preprint arXiv:1706.03762*.

Jesse Vig. 2019. A multiscale visualization of attention in the transformer model. *arXiv preprint arXiv:1906.05714*.

Jesse Vig and Yonatan Belinkov. 2019. Analyzing the structure of attention in a transformer language model. *arXiv preprint arXiv:1906.04284*.

Christopher Walker, Stephanie Strassel, Julie Medero, and Kazuaki Maeda. 2006. Ace 2005 multilingual training corpus. *Linguistic Data Consortium, Philadelphia*, 57:45.

Anran Wang, Jian Wang, Hongfei Lin, Jianhai Zhang, Zhihao Yang, and Kan Xu. 2017. A multiple distributed representation method based on neural network for biomedical event extraction. *BMC medical informatics and decision making*, 17(3):59–66.

Ian H Witten, Gordon W Paynter, Eibe Frank, Carl Gutwin, and Craig G Nevill-Manning. 2005. Kea: Practical automated keyphrase extraction. In *Design and Usability of Digital Libraries: Case Studies in the Asia Pacific*, pages 129–152. IGI global.

Wen-tau Yih, Joshua Goodman, and Vitor R Carvalho. 2006. Finding advertising keywords on web pages. In *Proceedings of the 15th international conference on World Wide Web*, pages 213–222.

Chengzhi Zhang. 2008. Automatic keyword extraction from documents using conditional random fields. *Journal of Computational Information Systems*, 4(3):1169–1180.

Yue Zhao, Xiaolong Jin, Yuanzhuo Wang, and Xueqi Cheng. 2018. Document embedding enhanced event detection with hierarchical and supervised attention. In *Proceedings of the 56th Annual Meeting of the Association for Computational Linguistics (Volume 2: Short Papers)*, pages 414–419.

Improving Zero-Shot Event Extraction via Sentence Simplification

Sneha Mehta* Independent San Francisco, CA USA snehamehta@twitter.com

Huzefa Rangwala George Mason University Fairfax, VA USA rangwala@gmu.edu

Naren Ramakrishnan Virginia Tech Arlington, VA USA naren@cs.vt.edu

Abstract

The success of sites such as ACLED and Our World in Data have demonstrated the massive utility of extracting events in structured formats from large volumes of textual data in the form of news, social media, blogs and discussion forums. Event extraction can provide a window into ongoing geopolitical crises and yield actionable intelligence.

In this work, we cast socio-political conflict event extraction as a machine reading comprehension (MRC) task. In this approach, extraction of socio-political actors and targets from a sentence is framed as an extractive question-answering problem conditioned on an event type. There are several advantages of using MRC for this task including the ability to leverage large pretrained multilingual language models and their ability to perform zero-shot extraction.

Moreover, we find that the problem of long-range dependencies, i.e., large lexical distance between trigger and argument words and the difficulty of processing syntactically complex sentences plague MRC-based approaches. To address this, we present a general approach to improve the performance of MRC-based event extraction by performing unsupervised sentence simplification guided by the MRC model itself. We evaluate our approach on the ICEWS geopolitical event extraction dataset, with specific attention to 'Actor' and 'Target' argument roles. We show how such context simplification can improve the performance of MRC-based event extraction by more than 5% for actor extraction and more than 10% for target extraction.

1 Introduction

With the proliferation of social media, microblogs and online news, we are able to gain a real-time understanding of events happening around the world. By ingesting large unstructured datasets and converting them into structured formats such as (actor, event, target) tuples we can make rapid progress in systems for event forecasting (Ramakrishnan et al., 2014), real-time event coding (Saraf and Ramakrishnan, 2016) or other applications that can grant organizations a strategic advantage. Historically, this has been enabled by efforts such as ICEWS[1] & GDELT[2]. These systems rely on event extraction technology to populate their knowledge bases. Fig. 1 gives an example of an event 'Bring lawsuit against' from the ICEWS dataset. Extraction involves identifying entities (businessman, employees) corresponding to argument roles 'Actor' and 'Target'. The *event* is triggered by the predicate 'sued' in the figure. Traditional event extraction technology relies on pattern-based approaches that

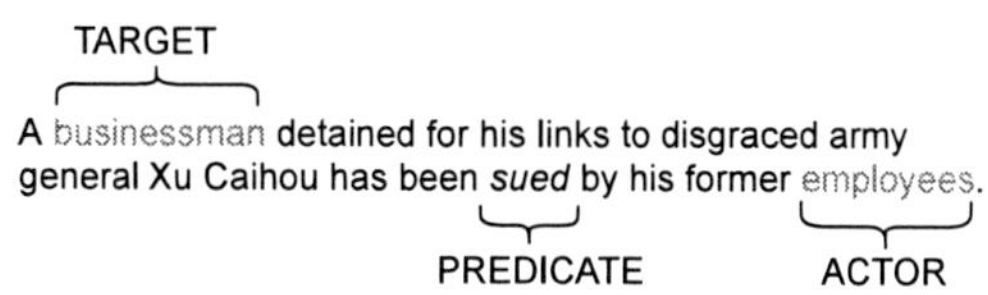

Figure 1: An example of an event of the type 'Bring lawsuit against' from the ICEWS dataset.

use handcrafted patterns designed to extract entities and events (Boschee et al., 2013). Even though pattern-based methods have high precision, they fail to work on unseen event types and with new event categories. Hence, there is a need to explore extraction methods that can extend beyond fixed domains and dictionaries. Modern approaches for event extraction (Chen et al., 2015; Nguyen et al., 2016; Wadden et al., 2019) rely on fine-grained annotations and suffer from data scarcity issues and error propagation due to pipeline systems.

With the success of large scale pretrained language models on machine reading comprehension (MRC) tasks (Devlin et al., 2019a; Liu et al., 2019; Huang

*Work was done when the author was a student at Virginia Tech

[1] https://dataverse.harvard.edu/dataverse/icews

[2] https://www.gdeltproject.org/

Proceedings of the 5th Workshop on Challenges and Applications of Automated Extraction of Socio-political Events from Text (CASE), pages 32 - 43
December 7-8, 2022

et al., 2018), a new paradigm for event extraction based on MRC has surfaced (Du and Cardie, 2020; Liu et al., 2020). In this approach, event argument extraction is posed as a span extraction problem from a context conditioned on a question for each argument. This approach is promising because it mitigates some of the issues faced by traditional approaches, such as relying on upstream systems to extract entities/triggers and hence sidestepping the error propagation problem in pipeline systems. It also gives rise to the possibility of zero-shot event extraction and hence the ability to extend to new domains which is traditionally hard due to difficulties in collecting high-quality labeled training data. However, MRC models struggle with long-range dependencies and syntactic complexities. For instance, Liu et al. (2020) observe that one typical error from their MRC-based extraction system is related to long-range dependency between an argument and a trigger, accounting for 23.4% errors on the ACE-2005 event dataset (Doddington et al., 2004) (here "long-range" denotes that the distance between a trigger and an argument is greater than or equal to 10 words). Du and Cardie (2020) observe that one of the failure modes of their extraction system is sentences with complex sentence structures containing multiple clauses, each with trigger and arguments. These observations make a promising case for complexity reduction or context simplification for MRC systems.

In this work, we pose the task of conflict event extraction as a reading comprehension task by generating QA-pairs per argument to be extracted. Then to mitigate the long-range dependency problem and to reduce the syntactic complexity we propose an unsupervised context simplification approach that is guided by a scoring function that incorporates syntactic fluency, simplicity and the confidence of an MRC model(§ 2) Our key contributions are:

1. Framing conflict event extraction as a machine reading comprehension task and exploration of context simplification to help mitigate the long-range dependency problem for MRC based event extraction (§ 2).

2. We empirically show that context simplification improves performance of MRC systems on zero-shot and in-domain training settings.

2 Methodology

Given that an event has been detected in a sentence, we focus on the problem of identifying the arguments of the detected event. For instance, in Fig. 1 the task is to identify the arguments 'Actor' and 'Target' of the event 'Bring lawsuit Against'. Corresponding to each event type, we first generate QA pairs corresponding to actor and target arguments. The QA generation procedure for the dataset used in this paper for evaluation is outlined in 4. Table 1 shows the generated QA-pair for the arguments Actor and Target for the event shown in Fig. 1.

Reading comprehension models can be brittle to subtle changes in context. They can be thrown-off by syntactic complexity, especially when the questions are not specific and do not include words overlapping with the context. Moreover, long range dependencies between the trigger/predicate and the argument are a leading source of error for MRC models applied to event extraction as described in section 1. For this purpose, we propose an **MRC**-guided **U**nsupervised **S**entence **S**implification algorithm (RUSS), that iteratively performs deletions and extractions from the context in search for a higher-scoring candidate. The score function incorporates components that ensure sentence fluency, information preservation and the confidence of the target MRC model. Fig. 2 gives an overview of the proposed approach.

Table 1: An example of a generated QA record for an event "Bring Lawsuit Against" from the ICEWS dataset shown in Fig. 1. The spans highlighted in red correspond to "Actor" and "Target" arguments of the event.

Sentence	A businessman detained for his links to disgraced army general Xu Caihou has been *sued* by his former employees.
Q-Actor	Who *sued* someone?
Q-Target	Who was *sued* by someone?

2.1 Sentence Simplification Algorithm

Given an input sentence s and a list of questions $\{q_1, ..., q_n\}$ corresponding to different arguments, our algorithm iteratively performs two operations on the sentence – deletion and extraction, in search for a higher-scoring sentence and outputs a candidate simplification c. For generating candidates, the algorithm first obtains the constituency parse tree of the context using a span-based constituency parser (Joshi et al., 2018). It then sequentially per-

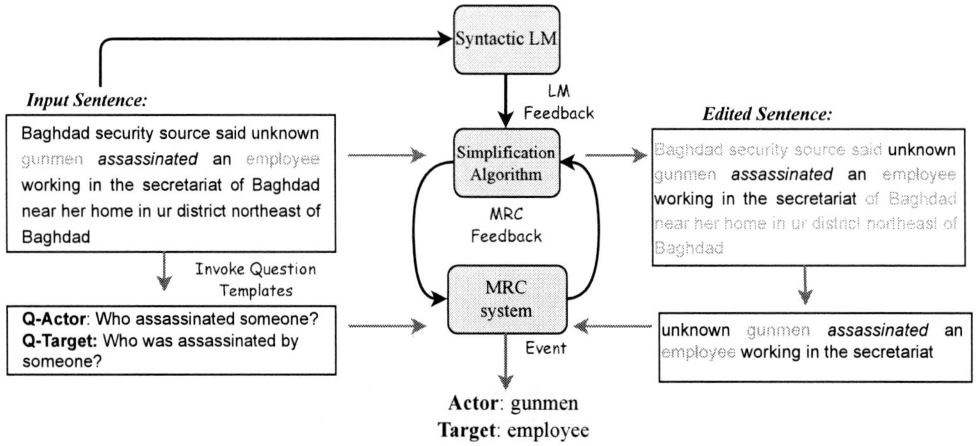

Figure 2: The RUSS sentence simplification approach.

forms two operations on the parse tree – deletion and extraction.

Deletion In this operation, the algorithm sequentially drops subtrees from the parse tree corresponding to different phrases. Note that the subtrees with the NP (Noun-Phrase) label are omitted because it is expected that many entities that form event arguments will be noun phrases and deleting them from the sentence would result in significant information loss.

Extraction This operation simply extracts a phrase, specifically corresponding to the the S and SBAR labels as the candidate sentence. This allows us to select different clauses in a sentence and remove remaining peripheral information.

These operations generate multiple candidates. Candidates with fewer than a threshold of t words are filtered out. We heuristically determine $t = 5$. From the remaining candidates, a highest-scoring candidate is chosen based on the score function described in the next section(§ 2.2). The algorithm terminates if the maximum score assigned to a candidate in the current iteration does not exceed the previous maximum score. The simplification algorithm RUSS is outlined as Algorithm 1 and the candidate generation algorithm is outlined as Algorithm 2 in Appendix.

2.2 Scoring Function

We score a candidate as a product of different scores corresponding to fluency, simplicity and its amenability to the downstream MRC model.

LM Score (ν_{lm}) This score is designed to measure the language fluency and structural simplicity of a candidate sentence. Instead of using LM-perplexity we use the syntactic log-odds ratio (SLOR) (Pauls and Klein, 2012; Carroll et al., 1999) score to measure the fluency. SLOR was also shown to be effective in simplification to enhance text readability (Kann et al., 2018; Kumar et al., 2020). Given a trained language model (LM) and a sentence s, SLOR is defined as

$$SLOR(s) = \frac{1}{|s|}(ln(P_{LM}(s)) - ln(P_U(s)) \quad (1)$$

where P_{LM} is the sentence probability given by the language model, $P_U(s) = \prod_{w \in s} P(w)$ is the product of the unigram probability of a word w in the sentence, and $|s|$ is the sentence length. SLOR essentially penalizes a plain LM's probability by unigram likelihood and the length. It ensures that the fluency score of a sentence is not penalized by the presence of rare words. A probabilistic language model (LM) is often used as an estimate of sentence fluency. In our work, instead of using a plain LM we use a syntax-aware LM, i.e., in addition to words, we use part-of-speech (POS) and dependency tags as inputs to the LM (Zhao et al., 2018). For a word w_i , the input to the syntax-aware LM is $[e(w_i); p(w_i); d(w_i)]$, where $e(w_i)$ is the word embedding, $p(w_i)$ is the POS tag embedding, and $d(w_i)$ is the dependency tag embedding. Note that our LM is trained on the original train corpus. Thus, the syntax-aware LM helps to identify candidates that are structurally ungrammatical.

Entity Score (ν_{entity}) Entities help identify the key information of a sentence and therefore are also useful in measuring meaning preservation. The desired argument roles are also entities. Thus, if any entity detected in the original sentence is omitted from a candidate the entity score for that candidate is 0, else it is set to 1.

Predicate Score (ν_{pred}) This score preserves the event predicates in a candidate. It checks if a candidate contains any predicate of interest corresponding to the event detected (Table 5). If it does not then ν_{pred} is set to 0, else it is set to 1.

MRC Score (ν_{rc}) Transformer-based MRC models can be brittle to subtle changes in context. To make the context robust to the MRC model this score allows us to control the complexity of context with respect to the confidence of the MRC model. It is computed separately for each role. Each argument of an event is a span in the context. $\nu_{{rc}^{r_i}_{role_i}}$ is the score of the best span in the context for the argument role i, where the score of a candidate span is defined as $ST_x + ET_y$ where $S \in R^H$ is a start vector and $E \in R^H$ is an end vector as defined in Devlin et al. (2019b). T_x and T_y are the final layer representations from the BERT model of the xth and y^{th} tokens in the context. Note that for a valid span, $y > x$. This score is computed separately for each argument role (Actor and Target in Example 1). The importance of the ith role can be controlled by the exponent r_i. The total contribution of each role is computed as the product of score corresponding to each role, given by $\prod \nu^{r_i}_{rc_{role_i}}$. The final score of a candidate c is computed as follows:

$$\nu(c) = \nu_{lm}(c)^a * \nu^b_{entity}(c) * \nu^c_{pred}(c) * \prod \nu^{r_i}_{rc_{role_i}}(c) \quad (2)$$

Note that b, c can be either 1 or 0 since ν_{entity} and ν_{pred} are binary. In later sections, we evaluate how the simplification can be controlled by varying the constants r_i's.

3 Datasets and Metrics

We evaluate RUSS on the ICEWS event dataset[3] (Halkia et al., 2020) from years 2013 to 2016. In this dataset, event data consists of coded interactions between socio-political actors (i.e., cooperative or hostile actions between individuals, groups, sectors and nation states) mapped to the CAMEO [4] ontology. We preprocess the ICEWS data to extract event triples consisting of a source actor, an event type (according to the CAMEO taxonomy of events), and a target actor. An ICEWS record contains an Event Sentence, Source and Target Names (Actor and Target) and Event Text amongst other metadata. However these Source and Target names are normalized, i.e. the exact Source and Target spans might not occur in Event Sentence. For e.g. a source name in an ICEWS record is "North Atlantic Treaty Organization" however, the event sentence contains its abbreviation "NATO". To retrieve the exact source and target names corresponding to spans that occur in the event sentence we perform denormalization by using the ICEWS actors and agents dictionaries[5] that contain aliases of different source and target entities. For the "NATO" example above, the actor dictionary contains the following aliases "North Atlantic Treaty Organization, NATO, North Atlantic Treaty Organisation". We resolve the source name to the alias that occurs within the sentence, which in this example is "NATO". We also remove country name from paranthesis of source and target names: $Citizen(Iraq) \rightarrow Citizen$ because of the format in which they occur in the dictionaries. After deduplication and cleaning of ICEWS data we obtain actor, event, target tuples for each event sentence. The next step is generating QA pairs for each tuple depending on the event type.

4 QA Dataset Generation

We first grouped the preprocessed ICEWS event records by event type. For each event type we identified a list of most common predicates (triggers) for that event type using a heuristic approach since trigger labels are not available in the ICEWS dataset. Using this approach we obtained a list of common predicates corresponding to event types and their CAMEO codes as shown in Table 5 in Appendix. For example, for 'Demonstrate or rally' event type the predicates identified are 'condemn', 'protest', 'demonstrate' and for 'Accuse' event type the predicates are 'blame', 'blaming', 'accused', 'alleged', 'accusing'. For each of the predicates identified for each event type we use one question template for each of the two argument roles Actor

[3] https://dataverse.harvard.edu/dataverse/icews

[4] https://parusanalytics.com/eventdata/data.dir/cameo.html

[5] https://dataverse.harvard.edu/dataset.xhtml?persistentId=doi:10.7910/DVN/28118

and Target. For the Actor role, the template used an active construction 'Who $predicate$ someone? and for the same event for the Target role the template used a passive construction – 'Who was $predicate$ by someone?'. This results in total 37,894 records for years 2013-2015 and 2,953 records for 2016 with a sentence and two questions one each for the Actor and Target roles and the Actor and Target names as their answers respectively distributed over 9 event types. The train/test distribution of the event records over the different event types is shown in Table 6. We will release the splits we used along with the generated questions, answers and span offsets for reproducibility.

4.1 Evaluation

We perform two-fold evaluation – 1) we evaluate the performance of an MRC system before and after simplification in a zero-shot setting; 2) In-Domain training: i.e. when we have labeled in-domain training data available, we investigate if simplification can help improve performance when the MRC system has been trained on in-domain data. In 1) we emulate a no-resource scenario, i.e. using the MRC system out-of-the-box in a target domain. We do not finetune a pretrained MRC model with the generated QA dataset. Rather, the aim is to assess the model performance in a zero-shot setting, without using any training data from the target domain whatsoever. We used the pretrained BERT model finetuned on the SQUAD 2.0 dataset (Rajpurkar et al., 2016) and use the predictor API provided here [6]. We further conduct follow-up analysis to study the controllability of simplification by performing ablation analysis and assessing model performance for different values of score component coefficients. For setting 1) we use the data from years 2013-2015 for evaluation and for 2) we use data from years 2013-2015 for train and 2016 for test. We extracted the best span(s) predicted and computed an exact match F1 score (Seo et al., 2017) matching the span against the ground truth answer.

5 Results & Discussion

The results of zero-shot extraction on the ICEWS dataset are outlined in Table 2. In the baselines used, simplification is performed with score function exponents for ν_{lm} as $a = 1.5$ and ν_{entity} as $b = 1$ held constant while varying c for ν_{pred}, r_1 for ν_{actor} and r_2 for ν_{target}. With no simplification we get F1 scores of 0.412 and 0.354 for actor and target roles respectively. For the most basic setting for simplification with $c = 0$, $r_1 = 1$ and $r_2 = 1$ scores improve by 4.6% for actor prediction to 0.431 and by 10.4% to 0.391 for target prediction respectively which shows that simplifying context can further improve a powerful model like BERT in a cross-domain zero-shot setting. For actor prediction, out of 37,894 records we find that for 10.99% records, F1 score improves after simplification, for 6.54% records F1 decreased after simplification and for the rest the score remained unchanged. For target prediction, for 17.4% records scores improve where as for 7.9% records the scores decreased and for the rest of the records, the scores remained unchanged. After introducing the predicate score ($c = 1$) we see that these improvements drop slightly. This is counter-intuitive, because one would expect model performance to improve when relevant predicates are present in the context. We attribute this behavior to the MRC model leveraging the language priors in the training data to predict the answers. For instance, the model could predict the subject of the predicate as an answer for 'Who' type of questions.

Next, we increase the coefficients of Actor and Target roles from 1 to 3. The reason why we choose an odd number for this exponent is because sometimes for bad candidates the RC scores can be negative and since all the scores are combined in a multiplicative way, raising a negative score to an even power would reverse the desired effect. Observing the results in rows 5 & 6 of Table 2 we can see that percentage of sentences with same scores before and after simplification have increased. We also observe that percentage of sentences for which scores decrease after simplification have also decreased for both actor (row 5) and target (row 6) respectively. We can conclude that by raising the coefficients of role specific scores we can make the simplification models more robust to inaccurate simplifications for those roles. We also observe, when $r_1 = 3$, we get the highest F1 for actor prediction, an improvement of 5.6% over no simplification and for $r_2 = 3$ we get an F1 on-par with the highest obtained in row 2. Our results clearly indicate the benefit of simplification over no simplification and also the gradual improvement in scores when the argument coefficients r_1, r_2 are

[6] https://docs.allennlp.org/models/v2.4.0/models/rc/predictors/transformer_qa/

Table 2: Results of zero-shot event extraction on the ICEWS dataset. ν_{lm} coefficient $a = 1.5$ and ν_{entity} coefficient $b = 1$ for all settings in which simplification is performed. $\Delta +ve$ indicates the % of records for which F1 improves after simplification, $\Delta -ve$ indicates the % of records for which F1 becomes worse after simplification and Δ same indicates the % of records for which F1 remains unchanged.

		Actor				Target			
	Method	F1	$\Delta +ve$	$\Delta -ve$	Δ same	F1	$\Delta +ve$	$\Delta -ve$	Δ same
1	No simplification	0.412	-	-	-	0.354	-	-	-
2	$c = 0, r_1 = 1, r_2 = 1$	0.431	**10.99%**	6.54 %	82.45%	0.391	**17.35%**	7.9%	74.9%
3	$c = 1, r_1 = 0, r_2 = 0$	0.429	10.81%	6.57 %	82.61%	0.390	16.54%	7.53%	75.93%
4	$c = 1, r_1 = 1, r_2 = 1$	0.424	10.5%	6.3 %	83.1%	0.387	16.29%	7.64%	76.05 %
5	$c = 1, r_1 = 3, r_2 = 0$	**0.435**	9.72%	**5.67%**	**84.6%**	0.391	16.89%	7.97%	75.12%
6	$c = 1, r_1 = 0, r_2 = 3$	0.427	10.54%	6.95%	82.5%	**0.391**	16.12%	**7.29%**	**76.59%**

varied from 0 to 3.

5.1 Long Range Dependencies

Mean length of the original sentences is 32 words where as mean length of the sentences after simplification is 22 words (row 2 setting). This indicates that simplification doesn't make sentences too short as is intuitive because cutting relevant information would harm the performance.

Next, we investigate if simplification has addressed the long-range dependency problem. We look at statistics concerning the distance between the predicate and its arguments (Actor and Target) for the setting $c = 0, r_1 = 1, r_2 = 1$, that is, when the predicate score(ν_{pred}) is not taken into account. As Table 2(row 2) indicates for 11% of the records performance increases after simplification for Actor and 17.35% for Target. We find that for those records the average distance between the predicate and its argument Actor is about 13 words and the average distance between the predicate and target in the simplified context is about 10 words. For the argument Target the average distance between the predicate and target is about 8 words for original and about 6 words for the simplified context.

We see that RUSS cuts about 3 words for Actor prediction and 2 words for Target prediction on average. We conclude that a certain percentage of improvement comes from cutting down the distance between the predicates and arguments hence mitigating the long-range dependency problem.

5.2 Qualitative Analysis

Table 3 lists some cases in which simplification helps MRC system perform better. In the first example, the proposed method deleted the word 'personally' from the original sentence (**Sentence**) to obtain the simplified sentence (**Simplified**) as shown in the Table. The question posed to RC model was "Who is being apologized to by someone" and the ground truth answer is "the opposition". For the original context the model extracts "Nawaz Sharif" as the answer which is the wrong, whereas after removing the adverb "personally", it gets the correct answer. Note, that this decreases the distance between the predicate *apologized* from its argument Nawaz Sharif. In the second example, RC model extracts the closest noun phrase "Xu Caihou" as answer which is incorrect. Simplification deletes the prepositional phrase "to disgraced army general Xu Caihou" aiding the RC model in extracting the correct answer. Note, that in this case it was especially important to delete the above phrase due to the inherent ambiguity of construction. This case also highlights the limitations of the current RC systems as the system was not able to successfully associate employees with businessman and predicted the noun-phrase closest to the predicate *sued*. In the third example, there was segmentation error in the ICEWS dataset and two sentences were strung together as seen in the Table. RUSS successfully deleted the unrelated sentence aiding the RC system in extracting the correct answer.

5.3 Error Analysis

From 6.54% records for which the score decreased after simplification for Actor prediction (row 2 of Table 2), for 39.5% records, the prediction using the original context is a substring of the prediction using the simplified context. This means that for some cases, both the original and the simplified context facilitate the correct answer, but the answer from the simplified context contains extra information for which it is penalized during F1 score computation. For example consider the context "baghdad security source said unknown gunmen assassinated an employee working in the secretariat

Table 3: Qualitative examples of zero-shot performance of RC model before and after simplifying the context using the proposed algorithm. Underlined words are ground truth answers, emphasized words are predicates(triggers) and strikethrough indicates that words were removed by the algorithm.

Question	Who is being apologized to by someone?
Sentence	Islamabad prime minister Nawaz Sharif personally *apologized* to the opposition today for what he called unfortunate comments made against PPP's Aitzaz Ahsan
Answer	Nawaz Sharif
Simplified	Islamabad prime minister Nawaz Sharif ~~personally~~ *apologized* to the opposition today for what he called unfortunate comments made against PPP's Aitzaz Ahsan
Answer	the opposition
Question	Who is being sued by someone?
Sentence	Scmp a businessman detained for his links to disgraced army general Xu Caihou has been *sued* by his former employees
Answer	Xu Caihou
Simplified	~~Scmp a~~ businessman detained for his links ~~to disgraced army general Xu Caihou~~ has been *sued* by his former employee
Answer	businessman
Question	Who is being accused of something?
Sentence	Thus after having attacked the two elected to his party ump Brice Hortefeux and Claude Goasguen it was accused of pressure and insults. Rachida Dati has *accused* Claude Goasguen to take to her because she had refused to sleep with him and this during an altercation proved by the Canard Enchan.
Answer	Rachida Dati
Simplified	~~Thus after having attacked the two elected to his party ump Brice Hortefeux and Claude Goasguen it was accused of pressure and insults.~~ Rachida Dati has *accused* Claude Goasguen ~~to take to her~~ because she had refused to sleep with him and this during an altercation proved by the Canard Enchan.
Answer	Claude Goasguen

of baghdad near her home in ur district northeast of baghdad" which after running the simplification algorithm is shortened to "~~in baghdad security source said~~ unknown gunmen assassinated an employee working in the secretariat ~~of baghdad near her home in ur district northeast of baghdad~~". (The strikethrough text represents the text deleted by the proposed algorithm.) For the question; "Who was assassinated by someone?" when presented with the original context the RC model extracts "an employee" whereas after removing the strikethrough text, RC model extracts "an employee working in the secretariat". The ground truth answer for this is "employee". As can be seen both answers are correct but the simplified contex is penalized for extra words. Interestingly, such cases also make up 48% of records for which performance improves after simplification, i.e. the prediction using the original context contains the answer but is longer and prediction using the simplified context is more precise. This is intuitive, since context becomes shorter and more precise after simplification and hence one expects RC models to extract more precise answers.

5.4 In-Domain Training

In sections 5.1- 5.3 we saw how RUSS improved performance in the zero-shot setting. In this section, we consider the scenario when we have labeled in-domain training data available and we wish to investigate if simplification can help improve performance when the MRC system has been trained on in-domain data. We benchmark three baselines. BiLSTM-CRF (Huang et al., 2015; Halkia et al., 2020), BertForQuestionAnswering model from the HuggingFace Transformers library[7] using BERT-base-cased model as our base model (BERT-RC), and use the same model after simplification by the RUSS algorithm (BERT-RC-Simple). For training we use the ICEWS dataset described above from years 2013-2015 and the year 2016 for testing.

BiLSTM-CRF For this baseline we convert the actor and target spans using the IOB labeling scheme into a sequence of tags. We use different tags for actor and targets (e.g. B-ACT, B-TARG). The problem becomes that of sequence labeling over the tokens of the sentence.

BERT-RC For this baseline, we use the sentence and QA-pairs for training. There are total 75,788 (37,894×2) examples for training and 5,906 (2,953×2) for test. We train all layers as opposed to just the classification layer as we observe a large

[7] https://huggingface.co/transformers/v4.9.2/model_doc/bert.html?highlight=bertforquestionanswering#bertforquestionanswering

improvement in the former case compared to the latter. We use an initial learning rate of 3e-5 and use early stopping with $patience = 5$ to find the best model. This model outputs span start and end scores for each token. All tokens between and including the tokens corresponding to max start and end scores are extracted as the predicted span.

BERT-RC-Simple Next, we use the RUSS algorithm to obtain simplifications of the test set and report the performance of BERT-RC on this simplified test set.

Table 4 indicates the performance of the model on the original test set. We report exact-match F1 for all baselines. It can be observed that BERT-RC performs better than BiLSTM-CRF. Context simplification brings about an additional improvement(1.4%) even on a model that's finetuned on in-domain data (BERT-RC-Simple).

Table 4: Table shows the performance of a BERT-base-uncased model finetuned on in-domain dataset. It can be seen that even after finetuning, RUSS approach improves model performance (BERT-RC-Simple).

Model	F1
BiLSTM-CRF	0.764
BERT-RC	0.776
BERT-RC-Simple	0.787

6 Related Work

Event extraction(EE) has been an active area of research in the past decade. In EE, supervised approaches usually rely on manually labeled training datasets and handcrafted ontologies. Li et al. (2013) utilize the annotated arguments and specific keyword triggers in text to develop an extractor. Supervised approaches have also been studied using dependency parsing by analyzing the event-argument relations and discourse of event interactions (McClosky et al., 2011). These approaches are usually limited by the availability of the fine-grained labeled data and required elaborately designed features. Recent work formulates event argument extraction as an MRC task. A major challenge with this approach is generating a dataset of QA pairs. Liu et al. (2020) propose a method combining template based and unsupervised machine translation for question generation. Du and Cardie (2020) follow a template approach and show that more natural the constructed questions better the event extraction performance. However, none of these methods directly aim to address the long-range dependency problem using simplification.

Automatic text simplification (ATS) systems aim to transform original texts into their lexically and syntactically simpler variants. The motivation for building the first ATS systems was to improve the performance of machine translation systems and other text processing tasks, e.g. parsing, information retrieval, and summarization (Chandrasekar et al., 1996). In the context of extraction, Zhang et. al. (Zhang et al., 2018) show that pruning dependency trees to remove irrelevant structures can improve relation extraction performance. Efforts have been made to incorporate syntactic dependencies into models in an effort to mitigate this problem 2016; 2018; 2020. Recently, Mehta et al. (2020) have used sentence simplification as a preprocessing step for improving machine translation. Edit-based simplification has been investigated to a great degree to improve the readability of the text (Kumar et al., 2020; Dong et al., 2019; Alva-Manchego et al., 2017). To the best of our knowledge this is the first work that studies sentence simplification for improving MRC-based event extraction.

7 Conclusion & Future Work

In this work, we motivated the need for MRC-based socio-political/conflict event extraction paradigm especially for zero-shot scenarios(§ 1). Next, we discussed the long-range dependency problem faced by event extraction systems. We proposed a simplification algorithm to reduce the syntactic complexity of the context aided by MRC-system feedback to address the problem(§ 2). Our results indicate that simplification can not only aid MRC systems in a zero-shot setting(§ 5.1- 5.3) but also when they're finetuned on in-domain data(§ 5.4).

In future work, we plan to scale our QA generation approach to improve coverage over more event types and languages. We can also make RUSS simplification more efficient by generating parallel training data for simplification using the RUSS method offline and train a simplification model using the generated data. In this way we can obtain guided simplifications via inference over a model.

Reproducibility: We release our code [8].

[8] `https://github.com/russ-event-extraction/russ_event_extraction`

References

Fernando Alva-Manchego, Joachim Bingel, Gustavo Paetzold, Carolina Scarton, and Lucia Specia. 2017. Learning how to simplify from explicit labeling of complex-simplified text pairs. In *Proceedings of the Eighth International Joint Conference on Natural Language Processing (Volume 1: Long Papers)*, pages 295–305, Taipei, Taiwan. Asian Federation of Natural Language Processing.

Elizabeth Boschee, Premkumar Natarajan, and Ralph Weischedel. 2013. *Automatic Extraction of Events from Open Source Text for Predictive Forecasting*, pages 51–67. Springer New York, New York, NY.

John Carroll, Guido Minnen, Darren Pearce, Yvonne Canning, Siobhan Devlin, and John Tait. 1999. Simplifying text for language-impaired readers. In *Ninth Conference of the European Chapter of the Association for Computational Linguistics*, pages 269–270, Bergen, Norway. Association for Computational Linguistics.

Raman Chandrasekar, Christine Doran, and Bangalore Srinivas. 1996. Motivations and methods for text simplification. In *Proceedings of the 16th conference on Computational linguistics-Volume 2*, pages 1041–1044. Association for Computational Linguistics.

Yubo Chen, Liheng Xu, Kang Liu, Daojian Zeng, and Jun Zhao. 2015. Event extraction via dynamic multi-pooling convolutional neural networks. In *Proceedings of the 53rd Annual Meeting of the Association for Computational Linguistics*, volume 1, pages 167–176.

Jacob Devlin, Ming-Wei Chang, Kenton Lee, and Kristina Toutanova. 2019a. Bert: Pre-training of deep bidirectional transformers for language understanding. In *NAACL-HLT*.

Jacob Devlin, Ming-Wei Chang, Kenton Lee, and Kristina Toutanova. 2019b. BERT: Pre-training of deep bidirectional transformers for language understanding. In *Proceedings of the 2019 Conference of the North American Chapter of the Association for Computational Linguistics: Human Language Technologies, Volume 1 (Long and Short Papers)*, pages 4171–4186, Minneapolis, Minnesota. Association for Computational Linguistics.

George Doddington, Alexis Mitchell, Mark Przybocki, Lance Ramshaw, Stephanie Strassel, and Ralph Weischedel. 2004. The automatic content extraction (ACE) program – tasks, data, and evaluation. In *LREC'04*, Lisbon, Portugal. European Language Resources Association (ELRA).

Yue Dong, Zichao Li, Mehdi Rezagholizadeh, and Jackie Chi Kit Cheung. 2019. EditNTS: An neural programmer-interpreter model for sentence simplification through explicit editing. In *Proceedings of the 57th Annual Meeting of the Association for Computational Linguistics*, pages 3393–3402, Florence, Italy. Association for Computational Linguistics.

Xinya Du and Claire Cardie. 2020. Event extraction by answering (almost) natural questions. In *Proceedings of the 2020 Conference on Empirical Methods in Natural Language Processing (EMNLP)*, pages 671–683, Online. Association for Computational Linguistics.

Matina Halkia, Stefano Ferri, Michail Papazoglou, Marie-Sophie Van Damme, and Dimitrios Thomakos. 2020. Conflict event modelling: Research experiment and event data limitations. In *Proceedings of the Workshop on Automated Extraction of Socio-political Events from News 2020*, pages 42–48, Marseille, France. European Language Resources Association (ELRA).

Lifu Huang, Heng Ji, Kyunghyun Cho, Ido Dagan, Sebastian Riedel, and Clare Voss. 2018. Zero-shot transfer learning for event extraction. In *Proceedings of the 56th Annual Meeting of the Association for Computational Linguistics (Volume 1: Long Papers)*, pages 2160–2170, Melbourne, Australia. Association for Computational Linguistics.

Zhiheng Huang, Wei Xu, and Kai Yu. 2015. Bidirectional LSTM-CRF models for sequence tagging. *CoRR*, abs/1508.01991.

Vidur Joshi, Matthew Peters, and Mark Hopkins. 2018. Extending a parser to distant domains using a few dozen partially annotated examples. In *Proceedings of the 56th Annual Meeting of the Association for Computational Linguistics (Volume 1: Long Papers)*, pages 1190–1199, Melbourne, Australia. Association for Computational Linguistics.

Katharina Kann, Sascha Rothe, and Katja Filippova. 2018. Sentence-level fluency evaluation: References help, but can be spared! In *Proceedings of the 22nd Conference on Computational Natural Language Learning*, pages 313–323, Brussels, Belgium. Association for Computational Linguistics.

Dhruv Kumar, Lili Mou, Lukasz Golab, and Olga Vechtomova. 2020. Iterative edit-based unsupervised sentence simplification. *arXiv preprint arXiv:2006.09639*.

Qi Li, Heng Ji, and Liang Huang. 2013. Joint event extraction via structured prediction with global features. In *Proceedings of the 51st Annual Meeting of the Association for Computational Linguistics (Volume 1: Long Papers)*, volume 1, pages 73–82.

Jian Liu, Yubo Chen, Kang Liu, Wei Bi, and Xiaojiang Liu. 2020. Event extraction as machine reading comprehension. In *Proceedings of the 2020 Conference on Empirical Methods in Natural Language Processing (EMNLP)*, pages 1641–1651, Online. Association for Computational Linguistics.

Xiao Liu, Zhunchen Luo, and Heyan Huang. 2018. Jointly multiple events extraction via attention-based graph information aggregation. In *Proceedings of the 2018 Conference on Empirical Methods in Natural Language Processing*, pages 1247–1256, Brussels, Belgium. Association for Computational Linguistics.

Yinhan Liu, Myle Ott, Naman Goyal, Jingfei Du, et al. 2019. Roberta: A robustly optimized bert pretraining approach. *arXiv preprint arXiv:1907.11692*.

Jie Ma, Shuai Wang, Rishita Anubhai, Miguel Ballesteros, and Yaser Al-Onaizan. 2020. Resource-enhanced neural model for event argument extraction. In *Findings of the Association for Computational Linguistics: EMNLP 2020*, pages 3554–3559, Online. Association for Computational Linguistics.

David McClosky, Mihai Surdeanu, and Christopher D Manning. 2011. Event extraction as dependency parsing. In *Proceedings of the 49th Annual Meeting of the Association for Computational Linguistics*, pages 1626–1635.

Sneha Mehta, Bahareh Azarnoush, Boris Chen, Avneesh Saluja, Vinith Misra, Ballav Bihani, and Ritwik Kumar. 2020. Simplify-then-translate: Automatic preprocessing for black-box machine translation.

Thien Huu Nguyen, Kyunghyun Cho, and Ralph Grishman. 2016. Joint event extraction via recurrent neural networks. In *Proceedings of the 2016 Conference of the North American Chapter of the Association for Computational Linguistics: Human Language Technologies*, pages 300–309, San Diego, California. Association for Computational Linguistics.

Adam Pauls and Dan Klein. 2012. Large-scale syntactic language modeling with treelets. In *Proceedings of the 50th Annual Meeting of the Association for Computational Linguistics (Volume 1: Long Papers)*, pages 959–968, Jeju Island, Korea. Association for Computational Linguistics.

Pranav Rajpurkar, Jian Zhang, Konstantin Lopyrev, and Percy Liang. 2016. SQuAD: 100,000+ questions for machine comprehension of text. In *Proceedings of the 2016 Conference on Empirical Methods in Natural Language Processing*, pages 2383–2392, Austin, Texas. Association for Computational Linguistics.

Naren Ramakrishnan, Patrick Butler, Sathappan Muthiah, Nathan Self, Rupinder Khandpur, Parang Saraf, Wei Wang, Jose Cadena, Anil Vullikanti, Gizem Korkmaz, Chris Kuhlman, Achla Marathe, Liang Zhao, Ting Hua, Feng Chen, Chang Tien Lu, Bert Huang, Aravind Srinivasan, Khoa Trinh, Lise Getoor, Graham Katz, Andy Doyle, Chris Ackermann, Ilya Zavorin, Jim Ford, Kristen Summers, Youssef Fayed, Jaime Arredondo, Dipak Gupta, and David Mares. 2014. 'beating the news' with embers: Forecasting civil unrest using open source indicators. In *Proceedings of the 20th ACM SIGKDD International Conference on Knowledge Discovery and Data Mining*, KDD '14, page 1799–1808, New York, NY, USA. Association for Computing Machinery.

Parang Saraf and Naren Ramakrishnan. 2016. Embers autogsr: Automated coding of civil unrest events. In *Proceedings of the 22Nd ACM SIGKDD International Conference on Knowledge Discovery and Data Mining*, pages 599–608.

Minjoon Seo, Aniruddha Kembhavi, Ali Farhadi, and Hannaneh Hajishirzi. 2017. Bidirectional attention flow for machine comprehension. *ArXiv*, abs/1611.01603.

Lei Sha, Jing Liu, Chin-Yew Lin, Sujian Li, Baobao Chang, and Zhifang Sui. 2016. RBPB: Regularization-based pattern balancing method for event extraction. In *Proceedings of the 54th Annual Meeting of the Association for Computational Linguistics (Volume 1: Long Papers)*, pages 1224–1234, Berlin, Germany. Association for Computational Linguistics.

David Wadden, Ulme Wennberg, Yi Luan, and Hannaneh Hajishirzi. 2019. Entity, relation, and event extraction with contextualized span representations. In *Proceedings of the 2019 Conference on Empirical Methods in Natural Language Processing and the 9th International Joint Conference on Natural Language Processing (EMNLP-IJCNLP)*, pages 5784–5789, Hong Kong, China. Association for Computational Linguistics.

Yuhao Zhang, Peng Qi, and Christopher D. Manning. 2018. Graph convolution over pruned dependency trees improves relation extraction. In *Proceedings of the 2018 Conference on Empirical Methods in Natural Language Processing*, pages 2205–2215, Brussels, Belgium. Association for Computational Linguistics.

Yang Zhao, Zhiyuan Luo, and Akiko Aizawa. 2018. A language model based evaluator for sentence compression. In *Proceedings of the 56th Annual Meeting of the Association for Computational Linguistics (Volume 2: Short Papers)*, pages 170–175.

A RUSS Algorithm

Algorithm 1: Sentence Simplification Algorithm – RUSS

```
Input: sentence := s, questions = {q_1, ..q_n}
Output: simplification := c
Function RUSS(s):
maxIter ← M
for iter ∈ maxIter do
    candidates ← generateCandidates(c)
    scores ← ∅
    maxScore ← 0
    for cand ∈ candidates do
        scores ←
          scores ∪ ν_lm^a * ν_entity^b * ν_pred^c * ∏ ν_rc_role_i^ri
    end
    currMax ← max(scores)
    if currMax > maxScore then
        maxScore ← currMax
        c ← candidates[argmax(scores)]
    end
end
return c
```

Algorithm 2: Candidate Generation Algorithm

```
Input: sentence := s
Output: candidates
Function generateCandidates(s):
parseTree ← getParseTree(s)
toRemove ← ∅
extractions ← ∅
candidates ← ∅
phraseTags ← getValidPhraseTags()
for pos ∈ parseTree.positions do
    if parseTree[pos] ∈ phraseTags then
        toRemove ←
          toRemove ∪ parseTree[pos].leaves
    end
    if pos.label ∈ [S, SBAR] then
        extractions ←
          extractions ∪ parseTree[pos].leaves
    end
end
for phrase ∈ toRemove do
    candidate ← s.replace(phrase, ∅)
    if candidate.length > t then
        candidates ← candidates ∪ candidate
    end
end
for phrase ∈ extractions do
    if phrase.length > t then
        candidates ← candidates ∪ candidate
    end
end
return candidates
```

A Training Details

For training the RUSS algorithm we used the TransformerQA model made available through the allennlp library predictors API [9]. Running the algorithm takes 5 hours on 1 CPU core and 1 GPU. However when parallelizing the computation across 5 cores that time can be brought down to 1 hour.

B Dataset Statistics

Table 6 outlines the distribution of different event types used in the ICEWS dataset used.

[9] https://github.com/allenai/allennlp-models/blob/main/allennlp_models/rc/models/transformer_qa.py

Table 5: Table lists the ICEWS event types used and their corresponding predicates that were identified for generating question templates.

Event Type	CAMEO Code	Predicates
Abduct, hijack, or take hostage	181	kidnapped, abducting, abducted, captured
Accuse	112	blame, blaming, accused, alleged, accusing
Apologize	55	apologize, apology
Assassinate	186	carried out assassination of, assassinate
Bring lawsuit against	115	is suing someone, sued, has sued, filed a suit against
Demonstrate or rally	141	condemn, protest, demonstrate
Arrest, detain, or charge with legal action	173	arrested, sentenced, detained, nabbed, captured, arresting, capture, jailed, routinely arrested, prosecuted, convicted
Use conventional military force	190	killed, shelled, combating, shells, strikes, strike, kill

Table 6: Table shows the distribution of event types in the ICEWS Train and Test datasets used.

Event Type	#Records Train	#Records Test
Abduct, hijack, or take hostage	3473	193
Accuse	8856	651
Apologize	181	11
Arrest, detain, or charge with legal action	9933	782
Assassinate	146	12
Bring lawsuit against	206	18
Demonstrate or rally	2890	175
Use conventional military force	12209	1111

SNU-Causality Lab @ Causal News Corpus 2022: Detecting Causality by Data Augmentation via Part-of-Speech tagging

Juhyeon Kim and **Yesong Choe** and **Sanghack Lee**
Graduate School of Data Science, Seoul National University, Seoul, South Korea, 08826
{kimjh9474,yesong,sanghack}@snu.ac.kr

Abstract

Finding causal relations in texts has been a challenge since it requires methods ranging from defining event ontologies to developing proper algorithmic approaches. In this paper, we developed a framework which classifies whether a given sentence contains a causal event. As our approach, we exploited an external corpus that has causal labels to overcome the small size of the original corpus (Causal News Corpus) provided by task organizers. Further, we employed a data augmentation technique utilizing Part-Of-Speech (POS) based on our observation that some parts of speech are more (or less) relevant to causality. Our approach especially improved the recall of detecting causal events in sentences.

1 Introduction

Nowadays, unprecedented amounts of data on social, political, and economic events offer a breakthrough potential for data-driven analytics. It drives and helps informed policy-making in the social and human sciences. Data of those humanities and social sciences cover a broad range of materials from structured numerical datasets to unstructured text data. An event is a specific occurrence of something that happens in a certain time and place involving humans. The events in texts can be understood in terms of causality, implies when one event, process, state, or object (namely, "cause") contributes to the production of another one (namely, "effect") where the cause is responsible for the effect.

Event-relating studies in the NLP have been growing, such as event extraction (EE), name entity recognition (NER), and relation extraction (RE). In particular, EE requires identifying the event, classifying event type and argument, and judging the argument role to collect knowledge about incidents found in texts (Li et al., 2021). Recent approaches to EE have taken advantage of dense features extractions by neural network models (Chen et al., 2015; Nguyen et al., 2016; Liu et al., 2018) as well as contextualized lexical representations from pre-trained language models (Wadden et al., 2019; Zhang et al., 2019).

However, there exist few studies regarding identifying or classifying events, especially based on causal relations. Phu and Nguyen (2021) studied Event Causality Identification (ECI) based on graph convolutional networks to learn document context-augmented representations for causality prediction between events. Cao et al. (2021) developed a model to learn a structure for event causality reasoning. Moreover, Man et al. (2022) introduced dependency path generation as a complementary task for ECI using causal label prediction.

In this study, we focus on causal event classification: whether a sentence contains any causal relation. Our framework employed both recent and traditional NLP techniques, which are pre-trained large language model (i.e., ELECTRA (Clark et al., 2020)) and POS tagging (Loper and Bird, 2002; Bird et al., 2009). To enhance the performance of detecting causality in each sentence, we attempted not only to concatenate another corpus that has causal labels but also to augment those corpora via POS tagging. With our base model, ELECTRA, those different combinations of datasets were compared to one another.

This paper is organized as follows. We first explore and examine the task and datasets. Based on the examination, we propose a new method in Section 3. We then present experimental results and discussion.

2 Task and Datasets

Causal event classification from natural language texts is a challenging open problem since causality in texts heavily relies on domain knowledge, which requires considerable human effort and time for annotating and feature engineering. In this study, as Subtask 1 of CASE-2022 Shared Task 3 (Tan

Proceedings of the 5th Workshop on Challenges and Applications of Automated Extraction of Socio-political Events from Text (CASE), pages 44 - 49
December 7-8, 2022 ©2022 Association for Computational Linguistics

et al., 2022a,b), we implemented causal event classification with large language pre-trained models.

The offered dataset is 'Causal News Corpus (CNC)' (Tan et al., 2022a). CNC contains sentences randomly sampled and refined from socio-political news. Each sentence in the dataset has a label, which represents whether it has a cause-effect relationship. This dataset was successfully used in Automated Extraction of Socio-political Events from News (AESPEN) at Language Resource and Evaluation Conference (LREC) in 2020 (Hürriyetoğlu et al., 2020) and Challenges and Applications of Automated Extraction of Socio-political Events from Text (CASE) in 2021 (Hürriyetoğlu et al., 2021). The number of training and validation data are 2925 and 323, respectively. Additionally, the organizers prepared the test set (which is only accessible through the task evaluation system) of size 311.

We additionally utilized an external dataset, 'SemEval-2010,' which was created for SemEval-2010 Task 8 (Hendrickx et al., 2019). The task was to classify semantic relations between pairs of nominals. One of the semantic relations is a causal relationship. Hence, we can directly infer whether a sentence in the dataset contains a causal relationship or not, allowing us to create another dataset to classify causality. `"The complication arose from the light irradiation."` is an example of a cause-effect labeled sentence from SemEval-2010. The training and test (used as validation) datasets contain 4450 and 786 sentences, respectively.

3 Methodology

CNC has a relatively small number of sentences to precisely detect whether any causal relation is contained in a sentence. Thus, we consider adding more sentences to CNC by (1) concatenating SemEval-2010 to CNC and (2) augmenting new sentences generated through POS tagging, which we will describe in the next section.

3.1 Data Augmentation via POS Tagging

A typical data augmentation is just attaching a new dataset to an existing original dataset. After augmentation, one may fine-tune the parameters of a model in hopes of improving performance of the model. Since a new dataset might come from a different distribution and features from the original one, it may negatively affect the performance. Hence, we propose to augment *causally relevant* information directly derived from the original datasets.

We argue that the causality in a sentence can be determined mainly by verbs and conjunctions, which is responsible for describing underlying causality, *not* nouns. That is, even if any nouns in a sentence are replaced with other nouns, a causal relation can still be preserved in the sentence. Consider `"There was a traffic jam as the taxi industry embarked on a protest"` for an example. Even if we eliminate the word `"traffic"`, the effect of `"protest"` is still `"jam"`. Regardless of the true meaning, there still exists a prominent causal relation. Hence, we proceed to exploit the following observation to devise our method: causal relationship is primarily captured by syntactic elements rather than semantics.

Against this background, we consider substituting words that are less likely to be related to causality (e.g., nouns, adjectives and adverbs) to their parts-of-speech, as depicted in Figure 1. This transformation preserves not only the original grammatical structure of the given sentence but also the underlying causality. Those newly transformed sentences were then concatenated to the original dataset for data augmentation.

One may consider replacing those words with any random words of the same POS as seen in *counterfactual augmentation* (Zmigrod et al., 2019). However, it could lead the model to learn wrong relationships since counterfactual sentences can cause spurious correlations with verbs or conjunctions. Thus, we just replaced those causally-irrelevant words with their corresponding POS tags.

3.2 Model

For our task, we initially considered three large pre-trained language models to construct a causal event classifier: Sentence-BERT, Span-BERT, and ELECTRA (ELECTRA-Base). We implemented the task with CNC for comparison among three models. Its result showed that ELECTRA outperformed other models. Therefore, we adopted our base model as ELECTRA. ELECTRA is trained via next sentence prediction similar to typical BERT models. Specifically, it learns through replaced token detection instead of masked language modeling. We conjecture that ELECTRA is effective especially for causal

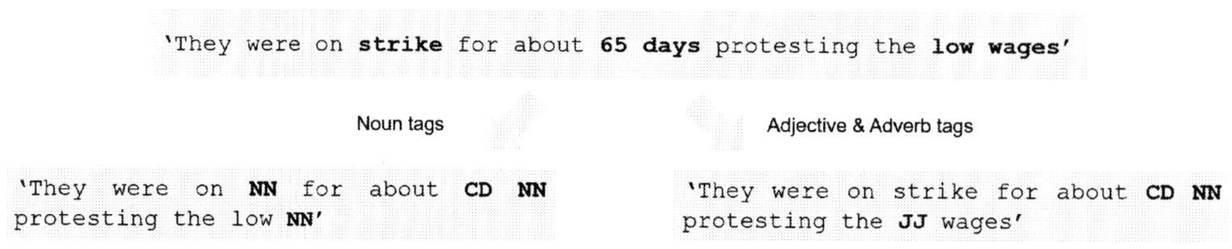

Figure 1: Examples of POS tag-based sentences: 'NN' is a noun tag, 'JJ' is an adjective tag, 'RB' is an adverb tag, and 'CD' is a cardinal number tag. We have those transformed sentences added to the original dataset(s) to create new datasets (3), (4), (5) and (6).

detection since the causality in a sentence can be changed with just a single, crucial word change (i.e., replaced to a POS tag).

3.3 Experimental Setup

In this section, we explain various datasets used to train different ELECTRA models and hyperparameters to train the models. To utilize SemEval-2010, we pre-processed SemEval-2010 to make it similar to CNC—"label" is 1 if there exists causality in the sentence and 0 otherwise. To implement POS-tag based data augmentation, we used NLTK (Loper and Bird, 2002). We simply mention 'noun-base X' for X dataset with noun replaced to NN. We similarly define for adj/adv-base. We created six different augmented datasets:

1. CNC (2925 sentences)
2. CNC + SemEval-2010 (7375)
3. CNC + noun-base CNC (5850)
4. CNC + adj/adv-base CNC (5850)
5. CNC + SemEval-2010 + noun-base SemEval-2010 (11825)
6. CNC + SemEval-2010 + adj/adv-base SemEval-2010 (11825)

While we initially constructed other combinations of datasets, those six are interesting to compare and discuss. We used the following metrics accuracy, precision, recall and (Micro) F_1 score to measure the performance of trained models.

We used following hyperparameters to train ELECTRA models across the above six datasets.[1] The batch size is set to 32, and the epoch is set to 20. Gradient clipping is performed to prevent gradients from exploding, and the highest gradient is set to 1. In the beginning, the learning rate is set to 2e-5 so that it could learn in large steps. As the epoch iterates, the learning rate decreases with cosine annealing for the model to converge gradually. The optimizer used is *AdamW* (Loshchilov and Hutter, 2017) with a weight decay and a L_2 regularization added. Cross-entropy is used as a loss function. All models were neatly fit into a *single* NVIDIA Tesla V100 (16GB) GPU and trained efficiently and effectively.

	(1)	(2)	(3)	(4)	(5)	(6)
Accuracy	0.849	0.841	0.855	0.849	0.852	**0.866**
Precision	0.865	0.865	0.838	0.838	0.865	**0.871**
Recall	0.871	0.859	**0.914**	0.901	0.882	0.908
F_1	0.866	0.862	0.874	0.868	0.874	**0.889**

Table 1: Performance of six models on the validation dataset where the models are trained on the datasets described in Section 3.3.

4 Results & Discussion

The performances of different datasets are compared (Table 1). Our results show that our proposed data augmentation method was effective.

4.1 Results

Our model trained on datasets with data augmentation achieved higher scores in all four measures. The recall increased remarkably: models with augmented datasets (3), (4) and (6) have the recall as 0.9 or above. While precision and recall are somewhat balanced across the models but precision is generally lower than recall. Due to the increase in recall, F_1 scores are all enhanced despite the increases in precision are negligible.

Compared to pure CNC (1), CNC with POS tag-base CNC (3, 4) produces better validation and test performances[2] than adding SemEval-2010 dataset (2) that also has causal labels but from a different distribution. Datasets (3) and (4) have recall above

[1] Our hyperparameters were not fully optimized in order to validate if our data augmentation method is effective so this is not for yielding the best of our model.

[2] Based on the performance reported in the leaderboard.

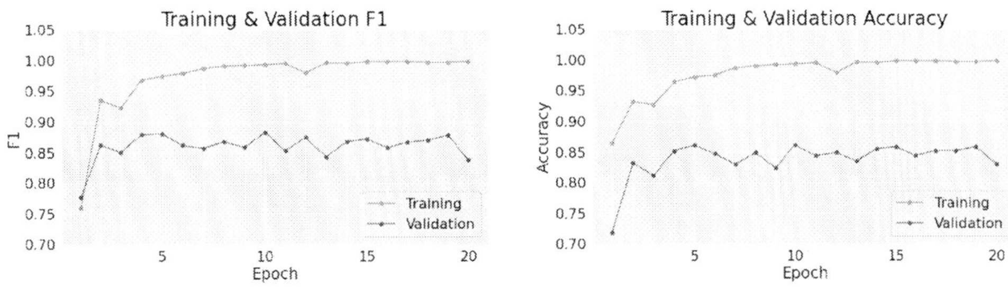

Figure 2: Training and validation F_1 scores (left) and accuracy (right) of dataset (6)

0.9, whereas dataset (2) has only 0.859.

Furthermore, dataset (6), which has SemEval-2010 and adj/adv-base SemEval-2010 added to the original CNC, achieved the highest F_1.

It is surprising given that adding SemEval-2010 *itself* (2) did not show improvements relative to (1). When it comes to the choice of POS tags to replace (noun (3, 5) vs. adj/adv (4, 6)), we do not have a consistent result to tell which tags are better to be replaced.

In Figure 2, we illustrate performance during training our model on (6). The accuracy and F_1 for the training dataset quickly reached 0.99 within 10 epochs in most of the experiments, and after it converges, the accuracies and F_1 scores were fluctuated slightly for the validation dataset.

Our model (6) was also evaluated with the test set through the task evaluation system. The model attained accuracy of 0.814, recall of 0.903, precision of 0.795, and F_1 of 0.848. The result is similar to what we have observed for the validation dataset.

4.2 Discussion

In this experiment, our model (6) trained with both SemEval-2010 and POS tag-base SemEval-2010 added to CNC attained the best performance in terms of accuracy and F_1 score. On account of the recall-precision trade-off, our results have higher recalls than precisions except for dataset (2). We think our model performs better with the sentences having causal relations since it seems to focus more on the features (e.g., embedding vectors) representing causality.

In the same vein, having a higher precision using the dataset with the SemEval-2010 added could be due to the more number of sentences having non-causal relations. Unlike other NLP corpora, not only the size of CNC is relatively small, but also there are not many causal-labeled datasets publicly available to additionally utilize. Furthermore, the ratio of the number of sentences that have causal relations to ones that do not is unbalanced (i.e., there is a way more number of sentences with no causal relations), so causal event classification is even more challenging. Thus, the data augmentation using POS tagging was effective and successful for this task. However, to increase the precision in the future, it is better to consider adjusting a threshold (i.e., decision boundary) for the results obtained through the current argmax function so that the model would not predict with certainty that causality exists when it truly did not.

We believe that our data augmentation method utilizing POS tagging can be generalizable and applicable to other learning methods. For instance, we found the benefit of the method for *prompt-based learning*, which allows the language model to be pre-trained on massive amounts of raw text to adapt to new scenarios with few or no labeled data (Liu et al., 2021). In our unreported experiment, we tried both original CNC sentences (i.e., dataset (1)) and their augmented one (i.e., dataset (3)) as prompt. Although both results were not as good as expected (i.e., the F_1 score is near 0.7), the result with having augmented dataset added had a higher recall, which corresponds to our results.

5 Conclusion

In this work, we proposed a framework that detects causal events from a sentence. In particular, because of the scarce number of sentences having causal relations, we devised a data augmentation strategy utilizing POS tags in place of causally irrelevant words. By augmenting the datasets, we indirectly increased the impact of verbs or conjunctions since causality relies on specific parts-of-speech in the context rather than the semantic meaning. The data augmentation strategy enhanced the performance of detecting causality especially in terms of recall and F_1. Given that the number of sentences having causal relations is small, detecting causality in those sentences is considered much more valuable than one in non-causal sentences.

Our contribution is that we provided an unconventional way of exploiting POS tags: previous studies using data augmentation via POS tagging *enhanced* the impact of specific words, such as informing proper nouns and word order for translation (Ding et al., 2020; Maimaiti et al., 2021). In contrast, we *weaken* the impact of specific words to indirectly improve the impact of other important words for detecting causality in sentences, such as verbs and conjunctions. By replacing those superfluous words with corresponding tags and adding those newly created sentences into the original corpus, our model outperformed those without data augmentation. This method can be a proper choice when adding new datasets is too expensive or there are few labeled datasets available.

References

Steven Bird, Ewan Klein, and Edward Loper. 2009. *Natural language processing with Python: analyzing text with the natural language toolkit*. O'Reilly Media, Inc.

Pengfei Cao, Xinyu Zuo, Yubo Chen, Kang Liu, Jun Zhao, Yuguang Chen, and Weihua Peng. 2021. Knowledge-enriched event causality identification via latent structure induction networks. In *Proceedings of the 59th Annual Meeting of the Association for Computational Linguistics and the 11th International Joint Conference on Natural Language Processing (Volume 1: Long Papers)*, pages 4862–4872.

Yubo Chen, Liheng Xu, Kang Liu, Daojian Zeng, and Jun Zhao. 2015. Event extraction via dynamic multi-pooling convolutional neural networks. In *Proceedings of the 53rd Annual Meeting of the Association for Computational Linguistics and the 7th International Joint Conference on Natural Language Processing (Volume 1: Long Papers)*, pages 167–176.

Kevin Clark, Minh-Thang Luong, Quoc V Le, and Christopher D Manning. 2020. Electra: Pre-training text encoders as discriminators rather than generators. *arXiv preprint arXiv:2003.10555*.

Bosheng Ding, Linlin Liu, Lidong Bing, Canasai Kruengkrai, Thien Hai Nguyen, Shafiq Joty, Luo Si, and Chunyan Miao. 2020. Daga: Data augmentation with a generation approach for low-resource tagging tasks. *arXiv preprint arXiv:2011.01549*.

Iris Hendrickx, Su Nam Kim, Zornitsa Kozareva, Preslav Nakov, Diarmuid O Séaghdha, Sebastian Padó, Marco Pennacchiotti, Lorenza Romano, and Stan Szpakowicz. 2019. Semeval-2010 task 8: Multi-way classification of semantic relations between pairs of nominals. *arXiv preprint arXiv:1911.10422*.

Ali Hürriyetoğlu, Hristo Tanev, Vanni Zavarella, Jakub Piskorski, Reyyan Yeniterzi, and Erdem Yörük. 2021. Challenges and applications of automated extraction of socio-political events from text (case 2021): Workshop and shared task report. *arXiv preprint arXiv:2108.07865*.

Ali Hürriyetoğlu, Vanni Zavarella, Hristo Tanev, Erdem Yörük, Ali Safaya, and Osman Mutlu. 2020. Automated extraction of socio-political events from news (aespen): Workshop and shared task report. *arXiv preprint arXiv:2005.06070*.

Qian Li, Jianxin Li, Jiawei Sheng, Shiyao Cui, Jia Wu, Yiming Hei, Hao Peng, Shu Guo, Lihong Wang, Amin Beheshti, et al. 2021. A compact survey on event extraction: Approaches and applications. *arXiv e-prints*, pages arXiv–2107.

Pengfei Liu, Weizhe Yuan, Jinlan Fu, Zhengbao Jiang, Hiroaki Hayashi, and Graham Neubig. 2021. Pre-train, prompt, and predict: A systematic survey of prompting methods in natural language processing. *arXiv preprint arXiv:2107.13586*.

Xiao Liu, Zhunchen Luo, and Heyan Huang. 2018. Jointly multiple events extraction via attention-based graph information aggregation. *arXiv preprint arXiv:1809.09078*.

Edward Loper and Steven Bird. 2002. Nltk: The natural language toolkit. *arXiv preprint cs/0205028*.

Ilya Loshchilov and Frank Hutter. 2017. Decoupled weight decay regularization. *arXiv preprint arXiv:1711.05101*.

Mieradilijiang Maimaiti, Yang Liu, Huanbo Luan, Zegao Pan, and Maosong Sun. 2021. Improving data augmentation for low-resource nmt guided by pos-tagging and paraphrase embedding. *Transactions on Asian and Low-Resource Language Information Processing*, 20(6):1–21.

Hieu Man, Minh Nguyen, and Thien Nguyen. 2022. Event causality identification via generation of important context words. In *Proceedings of the 11th Joint Conference on Lexical and Computational Semantics*, pages 323–330.

Thien Huu Nguyen, Kyunghyun Cho, and Ralph Grishman. 2016. Joint event extraction via recurrent neural networks. In *Proceedings of the 2016 Conference of the North American Chapter of the Association for Computational Linguistics: Human Language Technologies*, pages 300–309.

Minh Tran Phu and Thien Huu Nguyen. 2021. Graph convolutional networks for event causality identification with rich document-level structures. In *Proceedings of the 2021 Conference of the North American Chapter of the Association for Computational*

Linguistics: Human Language Technologies, pages 3480–3490.

Fiona Anting Tan, Ali Hürriyetoğlu, Tommaso Caselli, Nelleke Oostdijk, Tadashi Nomoto, Hansi Hettiarachchi, Iqra Ameer, Onur Uca, Farhana Ferdousi Liza, and Tiancheng Hu. 2022a. The causal news corpus: Annotating causal relations in event sentences from news. In *Proceedings of the Language Resources and Evaluation Conference*, pages 2298–2310, Marseille, France. European Language Resources Association.

Fiona Anting Tan, Ali Hürriyetoğlu, Tommaso Caselli, Nelleke Oostdijk, Hansi Hettiarachchi, Tadashi Nomoto, Onur Uca, and Farhana Ferdousi Liza. 2022b. Event causality identification with causal news corpus - shared task 3, CASE 2022. In *Proceedings of the 5th Workshop on Challenges and Applications of Automated Extraction of Socio-political Events from Text (CASE 2022)*, Online. Association for Computational Linguistics.

David Wadden, Ulme Wennberg, Yi Luan, and Hannaneh Hajishirzi. 2019. Entity, relation, and event extraction with contextualized span representations. *arXiv preprint arXiv:1909.03546*.

Tongtao Zhang, Heng Ji, and Avirup Sil. 2019. Joint entity and event extraction with generative adversarial imitation learning. *Data Intelligence*, 1(2):99–120.

Ran Zmigrod, Sabrina J Mielke, Hanna Wallach, and Ryan Cotterell. 2019. Counterfactual data augmentation for mitigating gender stereotypes in languages with rich morphology. *arXiv preprint arXiv:1906.04571*.

LTRC @ Causal News Corpus 2022: Extracting and Identifying Causal Elements using Adapters

Hiranmai Sri Adibhatla, Manish Shrivastava
Language Technologies Research Center, KCIS
IIIT Hyderabad, India
hiranmai.sri@research.iiit.ac.in,m.shrivastava@iiit.ac.in

Abstract

Causality detection and identification is centered on identifying semantic and cognitive connections in a sentence. In this paper, we describe the effort of team LTRC for Causal News Corpus - Event Causality Shared Task 2022 at the 5th Workshop on Challenges and Applications of Automated Extraction of Socio-political Events from Text (CASE 2022) (Tan et al., 2022a). The shared task consisted of two subtasks: 1) identifying if a sentence contains a causality relation, and 2) identifying spans of text that correspond to cause, effect and signals. We fine-tuned transformer-based models with adapters for both subtasks. Our best-performing models obtained a binary F1 score of 0.853 on held-out data for subtask 1 and a macro F1 score of 0.032 on held-out data for subtask 2. Our approach is ranked third in subtask 1 and fourth in subtask 2. The paper describes our experiments, solutions, and analysis in detail.

1 Introduction

A sizeable amount of text is generated every day due to increase in the amount of news available online from news portals and social media. Data available on social, political, and economics has the potential to revolutionise data-driven analysis (Barik et al., 2016). Causality identification and span detection (Do et al., 2011) is one such data-driven task. It is one of the many natural language processing (NLP) studies that attempts to address inference and comprehension. A causal relation is a semantic relationship between cause argument and effect argument such that the occurrence of one contributes to the occurrence of the other.

Cause is a span of text that results in the occurrence of an effect event. An effect is a span of text that is the consequence of the cause event and a signal is a span of text that binds both the cause and effect events. Together the study of cause and effect can help in understanding what agents contribute to the causes and the effects they create. Causality identification and span detection on climate science domain helps in analysing the rapid climate changes (Ionescu et al., 2020). Similarly analysis on financial domain news (Mariko et al., 2022) can help in improving trading strategies. Further examples include social, economic, and political sciences where the effects created by causes such as a change in policy can be identified over a period of time and analyzed.

Causal Text Mining have been shown to be beneficial for downstream tasks like summarization (Izumi et al., 2021; Hidey and McKeown, 2016), question answering and making inferences. Task 3 (Event causality identification) of CASE @ EMNLP 2022 (Tan et al., 2022a) aims at automatically identifying sentences that have a cause-effect event and extracting spans of text relating to cause, effect, and signal events. The shared Task 3 is divided into two sub-tasks:

Subtask 1: Causal Event Classification The first subtask identifies if a given event sentence contains any cause-effect.

Subtask 2: Cause-Effect-Signal Span Detection This subtask identifies the spans corresponding to cause and effect per sentence.

The causal news corpus (Tan et al., 2021, 2022b) comprises 3,559 event sentences, extracted from protest event news, that have been annotated with sequence labels on whether it contains causal relations or not. Subsequently, causal sentences are annotated with cause, effect, and signal spans. For both tasks, we use a Transformer-based model (Vaswani et al., 2017). We use adapters (Pfeiffer et al., 2020), a parameter-efficient fine-tuning method, in conjunction with a pre-trained model with strong language understanding and generation abilities (Liu et al., 2019). Recent research has shown that this method is robust to over-fitting in low-resource settings (He et al., 2021). In this way, the large pre-trained model RoBERTa, remains

Proceedings of the 5th Workshop on Challenges and Applications of Automated Extraction of Socio-political Events from Text (CASE), pages 50 - 55
December 7-8, 2022

	Labels		
	Causal	Non-causal	Total
Train	1603	1322	2925
Dev	178	145	323
Test	176	135	311
Total	1975	1602	3559

Table 1: Data split for sentences in subtask 1

frozen, and only small modules the model parameters are optimized. This effectively retains acquired knowledge in the pre-trained language model. The first task was treated as a binary classification task with a single label for the input sentence, while for the second task, label was predicted for each input word of the sentence.

2 System Description

2.1 Data

The data consists of English news in the socio-political and crisis context, extracted from Automated Extraction of Socio-political Events from News (AESPEN) in 2020 (Hürriyetoğlu et al., 2020) and Challenges and Applications of Automated Extraction of Socio-political Events from Text (CASE) in 2021 (Hürriyetoğlu et al., 2021) .

Figure 1 contains few annotated examples from the causal news corpus. The causes are highlighted in green, effects in purple and signals in cyan. Both cause and effect must be present in a same sentence to mark it as causal. The organizers made 3 datasets available for both the subtasks: *train, dev, and test*. Later UniCausal, a Causal Text Mining data (Tan et al., 2022c) was released to be used for both the subtasks. The labels for test data were not announced for both subtasks.

For subtask 1, around 869 news documents and 3559 English sentences were annotated with labels on whether they contained causal relations or not. Table 1 presents the sentence counts per data split.

For subtask 2, positive causal sentences from subtask 1 were retained and annotated with cause-effect-signal spans. From the total positive sentences, 180 sentences were annotated and there could be multiple relations per sentence. The data splits were: 130 train and 13 development.

After combining the causal news corpus and UniCausal corpus, the total number of unique samples on adding train and dev datasets are 6767 for subtask 1 and 1249 for subtask 2. We used 20% of the combined dataset for validation.

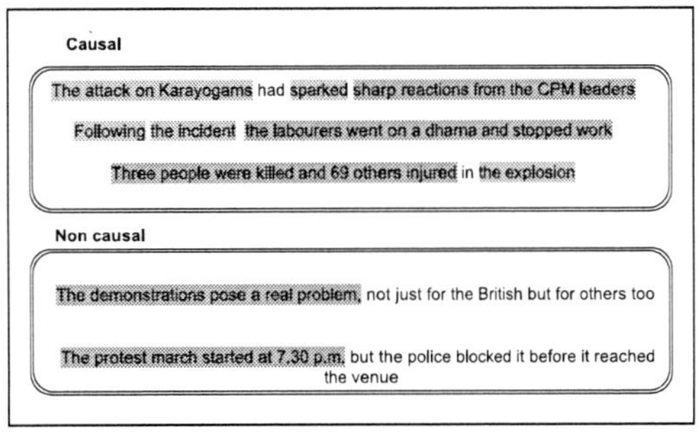

Figure 1: Annotated examples from Causal News Corpus. Causes are in highlighted in green, Effects in purple and Signals in cyan.

2.2 Solutions

Transformer based language models models (Vaswani et al., 2017) that have been pre-trained on massive amounts of text data and then fine-tuned on target tasks have resulted in significant advances in NLP (Liu, 2019; Yang et al., 2019), with state-of-the-art results across the board. However, models like BERT (Devlin et al., 2019) and RoBERTa (Liu et al., 2019) have millions of parameters, making sharing and distributing fully fine-tuned models for each individual downstream task prohibitively expensive.

Adapters (Pfeiffer et al., 2020), which consist of only a small set of newly introduced parameters at each transformer layer, are a lightweight alternative to full model fine-tuning. Because of their modularity and compact size, adapters overcome several limitations associated with full model fine-tuning: they are parameter-efficient, they speed up training iterations, and they are shareable and composable. Furthermore, adapters typically outperform state-of-the-art full fine-tuning (Rücklé et al., 2020).

2.2.1 Subtask 1

Three transformers-based language models (Vaswani et al., 2017) were considered for the subtask 1 and fine-tuned on the causal news corpus dataset. The models experimented are BART (large) (Lewis et al., 2020), RoBERTa (base and large) (Delobelle et al., 2020) with an additional linear layer on top, RoBERTa (base and large) with adapter (Pfeiffer et al., 2020) and a classification head. Adapters are small learnt bottleneck layers inserted within each layer of a pre-trained model to avoid full fine-tuning of the entire model. The adapters framework enables them to be small, and scalable, particularly in low resource scenarios. It freezes all weights of the pre-trained model so only the adapter weights are updated during training. It activates the adapter and the prediction head such that both are used in every forward pass. As NLP tasks become more complex and necessitate knowledge that is not readily available in a pre-trained model (Ruder et al., 2019), adapters will provide a plethora of additional sources of relevant information that can be easily combined in a modular and efficient manner. We added a task-specific layer which is a classification head adapter. RoBERTa with classification adapter head and a linear layer added on top of RoBERTa (base) performed better than the BART-large model.

2.2.2 Subtask 2

Subtask 2 was modeled as a token classification task in the lines of named entity recognition (Li et al., 2020; Nadeau and Sekine, 2007) and parts-of-speech tagging (Schmid, 1994; Voutilainen, 2003). Each token of the cause effect sentence should be labeled as either cause, effect, signal or other. In the annotated data shared, span of text for cause was between ARG0 opening and closing tags, span of text for effect was between ARG1 closing and opening tags and span of text corresponding to signal enclosed between SIG0 opening and closing tags. The labeled annotations were pre-processed to be written in the Inside-Outside-Beginning (IOB) format (Ramshaw and Marcus, 1999) to aid in the identification of the sequences during inference. BertForTokenClassification model from BERT (base) (Devlin et al., 2019) was used for obtaining the contextual embeddings for the token and trained to predict the most probable label sequence. Since we saw a slight boost in performance on using adapters, we added a adapter head to RoBERTa (base) to predict the label sequence. In spite of using IOB format and contextual embeddings of BERT in modelling the problem as token labelling task, inference of predicted labels is difficult. A limitation that the model has is, that it can make an incorrect prediction in the middle of a cause/effect sequence or predict a cause/effect token in the middle of O tags. Few heuristics were employed to address the issue:

1. If a cause or effect sequence has a length lower than 2, it is ignored.

2. If a token is being preceded by a beginning-tag[1] and followed by either 'O' (for other) or the inside-tag [2], then the label is changed to its corresponding inside-tag.

3. If a token is predicted as (other) 'O', the sequence length of 'O' is less than 2, and is surrounded by beginning and inside tags of a single kind, then the label is changed to its corresponding inside-tag.

4. If a token is predicted as a beginning or inside tag of a kind, the whole sequence length is less than 2 and is surrounded by beginning and inside tags of another category, then the current category is changed to match the surrounding labels.

3 Evaluation

3.1 Experimental Setup

We fine-tune pre-trained transformers: BERT, BART and RoBERTa provided by huggingface [3]. The maximum sequence length for base models was 256 and for 512 for large model. The learning rate was 1e-4 and the models were fine tuned for 10 epochs for subtask 1 and 20 epochs for subtask 2. Adam optimizer was used with a dropout of 0.2 in each transformer layers. The train and validation batch sizes are 8 and 4 respectively.

3.2 Results

Model	R	P	F1
BART-large	0.85	0.81	0.84
RoBERTa-large+Adapter	0.82	0.84	0.83
RoBERTa-base+Adapter	**0.87**	**0.86**	**0.87**
RoBERTa-base+linear layer	0.86	0.83	0.84
Baseline	0.86	0.80	0.83

Table 2: Performance on Devset for subtask 1

Model	R	P	F1
BERT+Adapter	**0.056**	**0.023**	**0.032**
Baseline	0.003	0.009	0.005

Table 3: Performance on Devset for subtask 2

Table 2 shows the performance of our transformer based models for subtask 1 on the dev data

[1]The beginning-tags could be B-E for effect, B-C for cause and B-S for signal

[2]The inside-tags could be I-E for effect, I-C for cause and I-S for signal

[3]https://huggingface.co/docs/transformers

set. All the transformer variants have surpassed the baseline scores. RoBERTa (base) with adapters was our best-performing model. The slight improvement in precision and F1 scores for RoBERTa (base) with adapters over RoBERTa base with linear layer could be because, in the adapters framework, the adapters are added within each transformer layer while in the other approach, the linear layer is added to the output of the last layer of RoBERTa.

Table 3 shows the results obtained by using adapter on BERT (base). the predictions were post edited employing the heuristics discussed above. The results have improved marginally over the baseline model.

3.3 Error Analysis

While reviewing and analyzing the errors made by our models, we discovered few patterns where the models failed. Table 4 shows a few samples that were misclassified for subtask 1. We observed that the model fails to identify effects and causes that are not explicit. For the first example in Table 4, the effect is *"attracted a motley crowd"* and the cause *"the one-day fast"*. The cause phrase contains polysemous word *"fast"*, that could be misleading. In the second example *"raining bombs"* is a simile and in NLP tasks similies, idioms and proverbs have always been tough to comprehend. The model fails to identify phrases with length of less than four words without signal words. To check this further, we reordered the phrases in the second example and added a signal. The modified sentence we tested our model on was *"Mondal was hit by one of the bombs because both sides were raining bombs on each other, Murshidabad district magistrate Pervez Ahmed Siddiqui said"*. This sample does not change the meaning of the original sentence, but is reorganised and the conjunction is changed from a joining conjunction ('and') to a causal one ('because') and the model could classify the modified sentence as a causal sentence. False positives were also observed, the third and fourth examples contained an event or action, but the cause is not explicitly mentioned in the sentences. These incorrect predictions are a result of frequently encountering similar sentence structures in causal sentences. Longer sentences, having multiple clauses were also misclassified as causal sentences even when they are missing a cause of effect for the same reason.

Errors in subtask 2 were mainly because of incorrect and inconsistent predictions of cause and effect. The number of samples containing signals are very few in the dataset and therefore not well generalised by the model. As observed in Table 5, either the complete sequence is not predicted, or few tokens in the middle are incorrectly predicted.

4 Conclusion and Future Work

With the rapid growth in information from news portals, automated solutions to analyse data and draw inferences from the data play a pivotal role. Our solution for the both the subtasks involved adding an adapter layer which improves the performance by avoiding full fine-tuning of the entire model and instead adding additional newly initialized weights at every layer of the transformer which are trained during fine-tuning. Though the solutions work well, they could be further improved by using an ensemble model for subtask 1 and by adding an LSTM (Hochreiter and Schmidhuber, 1997) and CRF (Ye et al., 2009; Huang et al., 2015; Huang and Xu, 2015) on top of the contextual embeddings layer for proper alignment of tokens and labels for subtask 2.

In our experiments on the causal news corpus and on analyzing the misclassified samples we feel that the models for both subtasks can also benefit from having extra syntactic and semantic information. For subtask 1, verbs and signal arguments like conjunctions play a major role in determining if the sentence is causal or non-causal. Similarly for subtask 2, having part-of-speech tags information for all the tokens along with contextual embedding from BERT might work well. The current models have good contextual representations, but appending them with an extra embedding of the main verbs, conjunctions and parts-of-speech tags might steer the task inference in a better direction.

References

Biswanath Barik, Erwin Marsi, and Pinar Øzturk. 2016. Event causality extraction from natural science literature.

Pieter Delobelle, Thomas Winters, and Bettina Berendt. 2020. RobBERT: a Dutch RoBERTa-based Language Model. In *Findings of the Association for Computational Linguistics: EMNLP 2020*, pages 3255–3265, Online. Association for Computational Linguistics.

Samples	Actual Label	Predicted Label
The one-day fast attracted a "motley crowd" according to Sumitra M. Gautama, a teacher with the Krishnamurthi Foundation of India (KFI)	1	0
Both sides were raining bombs on each other and Mondal was hit by one of the bombs , Murshidabad district magistrate Pervez Ahmed Siddiqui said .	1	0
Another 'TP' issue may also leave a blot on the CPM , as public opinion is heavily pitted against the assault made upon former diplomat T P Srinivasan by SFI activists	0	1
The police did not grant a permit for the march – the second time authorities have rejected a protest request – following a ban on the Saturday rally in Yuen Long	0	1

Table 4: Misclassified samples of subtask 1

Samples	Predicted Cause	Actual Cause	Predicted Effect	Actual Effect
The treating doctors said Sangram lost around lost around 5 kg due to the hunger strike.	due to the hunger strike	due to the hunger strike	The treating doctors said Sangram lost around 5 kg	Sangram lost around 5 kg
The Sadtu protest was a call for the resignation of Motshekga and her director general Bobby Soobrayan.	resignation of Motshekga	the resignation of Motshekga and her director general Bobby Soobrayan	The Sadtu protest was a call	The Sadtu protest
Troops also killed two militants making infiltration bids in Gurez sector today.	making infiltration bids in Gurez sector	making infiltration bids in Gurez sector today	Troops ('also' predicted as 'O') killed two militants	Troops also killed two militants

Table 5: Misclassified samples of subtask 2

Jacob Devlin, Ming-Wei Chang, Kenton Lee, and Kristina Toutanova. 2019. BERT: Pre-training of deep bidirectional transformers for language understanding. In *Proceedings of the 2019 Conference of the North American Chapter of the Association for Computational Linguistics: Human Language Technologies, Volume 1 (Long and Short Papers)*, pages 4171–4186, Minneapolis, Minnesota. Association for Computational Linguistics.

Quang Do, Yee Seng Chan, and Dan Roth. 2011. Minimally supervised event causality identification. In *Proceedings of the 2011 Conference on Empirical Methods in Natural Language Processing*, pages 294–303.

Ruidan He, Linlin Liu, Hai Ye, Qingyu Tan, Bosheng Ding, Liying Cheng, Jiawei Low, Lidong Bing, and Luo Si. 2021. On the effectiveness of adapter-based tuning for pretrained language model adaptation. In *Proceedings of the 59th Annual Meeting of the Association for Computational Linguistics and the 11th International Joint Conference on Natural Language Processing (Volume 1: Long Papers)*, pages 2208–2222, Online. Association for Computational Linguistics.

Christopher Hidey and Kathy McKeown. 2016. Identifying causal relations using parallel Wikipedia articles. In *Proceedings of the 54th Annual Meeting of the Association for Computational Linguistics (Volume 1: Long Papers)*, pages 1424–1433, Berlin, Germany. Association for Computational Linguistics.

Sepp Hochreiter and Jürgen Schmidhuber. 1997. Long short-term memory. *Neural computation*, 9(8):1735–1780.

Zhiheng Huang and Wei Xu. 2015. Kai yu. *Bidirectional LSTM-CRF models for sequence tagging. CoRR, abs/1508.01991.*

Zhiheng Huang, Wei Xu, and Kai Yu. 2015. Bidirectional lstm-crf models for sequence tagging. *arXiv preprint arXiv:1508.01991.*

Ali Hürriyetoğlu, Ali, Hristo Tanev, Vanni Zavarella, Jakub Piskorski, Reyyan Yeniterzi, and Erdem Yörük. 2021. Challenges and applications of automated extraction of socio-political events from text (case 2021): Workshop and shared task report. *arXiv preprint arXiv:2108.07865.*

Ali Hürriyetoğlu, Ali, Vanni Zavarella, Hristo Tanev, Erdem Yörük, Ali Safaya, and Osman Mutlu. 2020. Automated extraction of socio-political events from news (aespen): Workshop and shared task report. *arXiv preprint arXiv:2005.06070.*

Marius Ionescu, Andrei-Marius Avram, George-Andrei Dima, Dumitru-Clementin Cercel, and Mihai Dascalu. 2020. UPB at FinCausal-2020, tasks 1 & 2: Causality analysis in financial documents using pretrained language models. In *Proceedings of the 1st Joint Workshop on Financial Narrative Processing and MultiLing Financial Summarisation*, pages 55–59, Barcelona, Spain (Online). COLING.

Kiyoshi Izumi, Hitomi Sano, and Hiroki Sakaji. 2021. Economic causal-chain search and economic indicator prediction using textual data. In *Proceedings of the 3rd Financial Narrative Processing Workshop*, pages 19–25, Lancaster, United Kingdom. Association for Computational Linguistics.

Mike Lewis, Yinhan Liu, Naman Goyal, Marjan Ghazvininejad, Abdelrahman Mohamed, Omer Levy, Veselin Stoyanov, and Luke Zettlemoyer. 2020. BART: Denoising sequence-to-sequence pre-training for natural language generation, translation, and comprehension. In *Proceedings of the 58th Annual Meeting of the Association for Computational Linguistics*, pages 7871–7880, Online. Association for Computational Linguistics.

Jing Li, Aixin Sun, Jianglei Han, and Chenliang Li. 2020. A survey on deep learning for named entity recognition. *IEEE Transactions on Knowledge and Data Engineering*, 34(1):50–70.

Yang Liu. 2019. Fine-tune bert for extractive summarization. *arXiv preprint arXiv:1903.10318*.

Yinhan Liu, Myle Ott, Naman Goyal, Jingfei Du, Mandar Joshi, Danqi Chen, Omer Levy, Mike Lewis, Luke Zettlemoyer, and Veselin Stoyanov. 2019. Roberta: A robustly optimized bert pretraining approach. *arXiv preprint arXiv:1907.11692*.

Dominique Mariko, Hanna Abi Akl, Kim Trottier, and Mahmoud El-Haj. 2022. The financial causality extraction shared task (fincausal 2022). In *Proceedings of the 4th Financial Narrative Processing Workshop@ LREC2022*, pages 105–107.

David Nadeau and Satoshi Sekine. 2007. A survey of named entity recognition and classification. *Lingvisticae Investigationes*, 30(1):3–26.

Jonas Pfeiffer, Andreas Rücklé, Clifton Poth, Aishwarya Kamath, Ivan Vulić, Sebastian Ruder, Kyunghyun Cho, and Iryna Gurevych. 2020. Adapterhub: A framework for adapting transformers. *arXiv preprint arXiv:2007.07779*.

Lance A Ramshaw and Mitchell P Marcus. 1999. Text chunking using transformation-based learning. In *Natural language processing using very large corpora*, pages 157–176. Springer.

Andreas Rücklé, Gregor Geigle, Max Glockner, Tilman Beck, Jonas Pfeiffer, Nils Reimers, and Iryna Gurevych. 2020. Adapterdrop: On the efficiency of adapters in transformers. *arXiv preprint arXiv:2010.11918*.

Sebastian Ruder, Matthew E Peters, Swabha Swayamdipta, and Thomas Wolf. 2019. Transfer learning in natural language processing. In *Proceedings of the 2019 conference of the North American chapter of the association for computational linguistics: Tutorials*, pages 15–18.

Helmut Schmid. 1994. Part-of-speech tagging with neural networks. *arXiv preprint cmp-lg/9410018*.

Fiona Anting Tan, Devamanyu Hazarika, See-Kiong Ng, Soujanya Poria, and Roger Zimmermann. 2021. Causal augmentation for causal sentence classification. In *Proceedings of the First Workshop on Causal Inference and NLP*, pages 1–20, Punta Cana, Dominican Republic. Association for Computational Linguistics.

Fiona Anting Tan, Hansi Hettiarachchi, Ali Hürriyetoğlu, Tommaso Caselli, Onur Uca, Farhana Ferdousi Liza, and Nelleke Oostdijk. 2022a. Event causality identification with causal news corpus - shared task 3, CASE 2022. In *Proceedings of the 5th Workshop on Challenges and Applications of Automated Extraction of Socio-political Events from Text (CASE 2022)*, Online. Association for Computational Linguistics.

Fiona Anting Tan, Ali Hürriyetoğlu, Tommaso Caselli, Nelleke Oostdijk, Tadashi Nomoto, Hansi Hettiarachchi, Iqra Ameer, Onur Uca, Farhana Ferdousi Liza, and Tiancheng Hu. 2022b. The causal news corpus: Annotating causal relations in event sentences from news. In *Proceedings of the Thirteenth Language Resources and Evaluation Conference*, pages 2298–2310, Marseille, France. European Language Resources Association.

Fiona Anting Tan, Xinyu Zuo, and See-Kiong Ng. 2022c. Unicausal: Unified benchmark and model for causal text mining.

Ashish Vaswani, Noam Shazeer, Niki Parmar, Jakob Uszkoreit, Llion Jones, Aidan N Gomez, Łukasz Kaiser, and Illia Polosukhin. 2017. Attention is all you need. *Advances in neural information processing systems*, 30.

Atro Voutilainen. 2003. *Part-of-speech tagging*, volume 219. The Oxford handbook of computational linguistics.

Wei Yang, Yuqing Xie, Aileen Lin, Xingyu Li, Luchen Tan, Kun Xiong, Ming Li, and Jimmy Lin. 2019. End-to-end open-domain question answering with bertserini. *arXiv preprint arXiv:1902.01718*.

Nan Ye, Wee Lee, Hai Chieu, and Dan Wu. 2009. Conditional random fields with high-order features for sequence labeling. *Advances in neural information processing systems*, 22.

Cross-modal Transfer Between Vision and Language for Protest Detection

Ria Raj * [1,2] **Kajsa Andreasson** * [1,2] **Tobias Norlund**[1,2]
Richard Johansson[1,3] **Aron Lagerberg**[2]
[1]Department of Computer Science and Engineering, Chalmers University of Technology,
[2]Recorded Future, [3]University of Gothenburg
{firstname.lastname}@recordedfuture.com,
richard.johansson@gu.se

Abstract

Most of today's systems for socio-political event detection are text-based, while an increasing amount of information published on the web is multi-modal. We seek to bridge this gap by proposing a method that utilizes existing annotated unimodal data to perform event detection in another data modality, zero-shot. Specifically, we focus on protest detection in text and images, and show that a pretrained vision-and-language alignment model (CLIP) can be leveraged towards this end. In particular, our results suggest that annotated protest *text* data can act supplementarily for detecting protests in images, but significant transfer is demonstrated in the opposite direction as well.

1 Introduction

Information published on the web, and in particular social media, has become a crucial source for understanding the world and how it develops. Systems for the automatic detection and extraction of socio-political events are an important tool for processing this stream of information at scale. Traditionally, these systems are primarily designed to process information in the form of text, but with the growing use of multimedia content (such as images and video) on the web and social media especially, there is a great potential for extending the analysis to additional data modalities as well (Joo and Steinert-Threlkeld, 2018). A question is however how this can be done in the most efficient manner, and whether existing data in one modality can be reused for extending analysis to another.

In this work, we take a focused look at the task of *protest detection*, and investigate whether data from different modalities can act both *supplementarily* as well as *complementarily* for this task. We do so by seeking to answer the following research questions:

RQ1 To which extent can the performance of a unimodal protest detection model transfer from one modality to another?

RQ2 Can unimodal detection of protests be improved by using a multi-modal protest detection model?

Considering the natural way text and images complement each other, the hypothesis is that a multi-modal model trained on both text and images would have a broader understanding of the concept of protests.

The investigation has been carried out by combining two existing open datasets for protest event detection, namely the textual CLEF 2019 Protest News dataset (Hürriyetoğlu et al., 2019) and the UCLA Protest Image dataset (Won et al., 2017).

Our contributions are:

1. We propose a modality-agnostic setup for socio-political event detection, where annotated data in one modality can be leveraged to detect the same event in another modality.
2. We demonstrate significant zero-shot protest detection performance when applying a model on a modality not observed during training.
3. Whereas we show protest text and image data to act supplementarily, our results do not support the hypothesis that the data can act complementarily to the same degree.

2 Datasets

We took use of two open-source datasets: the UCLA Protest Image dataset (Won et al., 2017) for images and CLEF 2019 Protest News (Hürriyetoğlu et al., 2019) for texts. The UCLA dataset consists of a training set of 32,612 images and a test set of 8,154. In our experiments we only consider the binary protest/not protest prediction task. Meanwhile, for the Protest News dataset we only

*Equal contribution.

Proceedings of the 5th Workshop on Challenges and Applications of Automated Extraction of Socio-political Events from Text (CASE), pages 56 - 60
December 7-8, 2022 ©2022 Association for Computational Linguistics

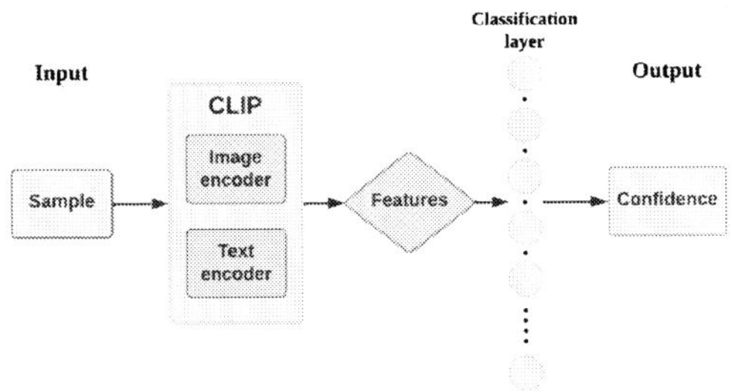

Figure 1: Our model setup. A sample is fed through its respective CLIP encoder and the resulting feature vector is fed through a classification layer that outputs a binary prediction score.

consider the binary sentence-level classification task in English. It comprises 22,825 sentences in total, retrieved from news articles, which was split into a training and test set with a 75-25 ratio.

3 Experiments

We begin by exploring RQ1, that is, whether text and image representations can be interchanged in the task of protest detection. In practice, this would mean that a classifier trained on protest *images* is tested on protest *texts*, and vice versa. This is made possible by using a pretrained encoder that is able to represent both modalities in a common feature space. We denote such experiments as *cross-modal*, where training and test data are of different modalities, meaning zero-shot classification. The extent to which this capability can be transferred between modalities can then be evaluated by comparing to a *unimodal* baseline, which essentially means we train and test on the same modality. To get a lower bound we also compare against a random classifier baseline. In all experiments we evaluate using the AUC-PR metric.

To adress RQ2, we consider the case where training data for both text and images are available and investigate whether these datasets can synergistically complement each other. Specifically, we explore training a model jointly on the Protest News and UCLA datasets, but evaluate on each modality separately, similarly to the above experiments. We denote this experiment *multi-modal*, because it is trained on both modalities. This experiment is implemented by combining sentences and images in each training batch. To make use of all the image data, each batch contained 65% images and the remaining 35% sentences. These results can then be also compared to the unimodal baselines explained above.

	Model			
Test set	IM	TXT	MM	Random
Image	**0.962**	0.687	0.957	0.290
Text	0.458	**0.734**	0.707	0.187

Table 1: AUC-PR scores for the models trained on different regimes, when testing over the different modalities.

4 Model

CLIP (Radford et al., 2021) was used to generate feature representations of each text and image in the datasets. CLIP is a pretrained visual-and-language model that has been trained to align text and images in a common feature space where samples containing similar textual or visual concepts are pulled together while nonsimilar concepts are pushed apart. Models like CLIP are suitable for the investigation in this work since it should create similar feature representations of protests regardless of the modality. While little information is provided about the pretraining data of CLIP, we hypothesize news, including protests, to be represented to some extent. In such case, the representations of CLIP should be somewhat aligned for this type of data. The features generated by CLIP were used as input to a linear classification layer, which was trained to classify text or image samples as protest or non-protest. This is visualized in Figure 1. We train only the linear classification layer weights, and keep the pretrained CLIP weights frozen during training. This is to be able to swap the encoder at test time in the cross-modal experiments.

The training was done on three different datasets, as described in Section 2, resulting in three trained classifiers: one trained on the pure image dataset (henceforth refered to as IM), one on the pure text dataset (henceforth refered to as TXT) and a third trained jointly on both, i.e. the multi-modal mixed dataset (henceforth refered to as MM).

For IM, the learning rate (LR) was set to 0.01, and for both TXT and MM it was set to 0.001. The LR-scheduler for IM and TXT was a lambda decay, with $\lambda = 0.95$, and none for MM. In addition to these hyperparameters, the Adam optimizer and batch size of 128 were used for all three models.

(a) IM model score: 0.99
TXT model score: 0.91
MM model score: 0.98
Label: protest

(b) IM model score: 0.99
TXT model score: 0.21
MM model score: 0.92
Label: protest

(c) IM model score: 0.097
TXT model score: 0.96
MM model score: 0.43
Label: protest

(d) IM model score: 0.0052
TXT model score: 0.51
MM model score: 0.097
Label: not protest

Figure 2: Three randomly chosen positive examples and one negative from the UCLA test data along with the three models' prediction scores. Subfigure 2a shows an example when the scores of the IM and TXT models coincide and Subfigure 2b when the IM model scores high, but the TXT model does not. Subfigure 2c shows an example in which the TXT model scores high and the IM model does not and Subfigure 2d shows a negative (i.e. not protest) example.

5 Results and Discussion

As seen from Table 1, the image and text baselines both perform better than their cross-modal counterparts, where the models are tested on the opposite modality than they are trained on. However, the cross-modal performance is significantly better than the random baseline, which indicates that the protest detection ability indeed can be transferred between modalities to some extent. One interesting result is that the TXT model performs almost equally well on images compared to when testing on text. This indicates that the TXT model's understanding of protests can almost fully be transferred to images, since the performance between the modalities only differs by a score of ~ 0.05. In contrast, the performance of the IM model decreases by more than half when testing on text compared to images. Considering these two outcomes, it seems reasonable to conclude that training a classifier on texts provides a more general understanding of protests, which can be transferred to images, while training on images gives the model a way of interpreting protests that cannot be found to the same extent in the texts used for testing.

When comparing the unimodal baselines, it is clear that the IM model performs much better with an AUC-PR score of 0.962 compared to the TXT baseline of 0.734. This could be a consequence of the image data being more homogenous in terms of how they represent protests. This also follows the reasoning above: that the texts contain a wider range of representations of protests.

An aspect that would be interesting to further investigate is which characteristics in the data that are significant for the separate models when classifying protests, by carrying out an even more thorough data analysis. When inspecting some samples that the IM model scores high on, see Figure 2, many of them contains concepts such as banners and placards, full-body humans, roads and cities as well as buildings. As for the text-model, some words that often occured in samples that recieved high scores include protest, traffic, roads, bodies of power (ie. government, police), bomb, students, injured, crowd. Neither the list of visual concepts or words are exhaustive, but they could give an

Fragment	P_{IM}	P_{MM}	P_{TXT}	Label
"Taxi operators marching in protest against the government's taxi recapitalisation scheme reached the Union Buildings in Pretoria on Friday."	0.87	0.82	0.93	protest
"(SUBS: Pics will be available later on www.sapapics.co.za) South African rape laws still blame the survivor of rape, People Opposing Woman Abuse (Powa) said on Friday at a protest outside the Johannesburg High Court."	0.85	0.77	0.63	protest
"Workers at the company's Zondereinde mine, near Amandelbult in Limpopo, went on strike on November 3."	0.30	0.67	0.87	protest

Table 2: Three randomly chosen positive examples from the Protest News test data. The first row shows an example for which both IM and TXT give high scores of it being a protest. The second row shows an example that recieves high scores from IM, but not from TXT. The last row shows an example that recieves a high score from TXT, but not from IM.

indication of what the models recognize when identifying protests. These lists also show that different aspects of protests are captured in the data due to the nature of the modalities and the sources of the data, which could be an aspect that affects the performance. Figure 2d shows one image with a negative label that recieves low scores from the IM model, despite the fact that it pictures a crowd. It does however lack placards and several of the other characteristics that are described above as possible factors that trigger the IM model to give high scores. The TXT model on the other hand, gives an intermediate score which indicates that the model is inferior at distinguishing between casual, friendly crowds and protest related crowds in images. This behaviour is seen for multiple similar samples that aren't displayed here.

When it comes to the case of the multi-modal (MM) model we see two things. Firstly, when comparing performance to the unimodal baselines it is clear that the MM model performs slightly worse in both cases. When testing on images, the difference in performance is $\sim$0.013, whereas for text $\sim$0.034. In contrast to our hypothesis, this indicates that training on both modalities does *not* provide the model with a broader understanding of the concept of protests, and consequently the performance on unimodal test sets is not improved. We speculate this is partly due to the fact that texts and images come from different source types (mainstream news vs social media), whereas CLIP has been trained to align text and image pairs from the *same source*. There is a possibility that the results would be different if the data used for testing was collected from a wider range of sources than the data used for training, since new data sources may represent protest in slightly different ways.

What one does see however, is that when comparing the MM model to both the IM and TXT models in the cross-modal set up, the MM model performs noticeably better. This is an indication that the multi-modal model in fact learns a representation of protests that succesfully incorporates information from both modalities.

6 Related work

Our work is a contribution to the field of event detection, that is, identifying mentions of whether a certain event has occurred. Early data-driven approaches to this task based on machine learning relied heavily on hand-designed lexical and syntactic features e.g. (Li et al., 2013; Patwardhan and Riloff, 2007). However, since then approaches based on deep learning indicate better performance can be achieved using less feature engineering by training on "raw" (textual) data (Nguyen et al., 2016; Chen et al., 2015; Boros, 2018). Specifically for the extraction and detection of socio-political events such as protests, some recent works have taken a pure visual approach. For example, Joo and Steinert-Threlkeld (2018) demonstrated that a visual analysis can contribute protest related features that might be harder to extract from pure text, such as violence, crowd size as well as demographic composition. Won et al. (2017) further investigated the ability to extract protest related information from images, where the UCLA Protest Image dataset is presented along with experiments for the detection of protests and related attributes.

Previous works taking a multi-modal approach to socio-political event detection also exist. Petkos et al. (2012) used a clustering method of textual as well as visual features to discover events in social media data. Qian et al. (2015) proposed a boosted multi-modal extension to LDA for training a supervised event classification model. More recently, Zhang and Pan (2019) take a deep learning approach to the detection of collective action events based on text and potentially an image from social media posts in China. Similarly to CLIP, they use a late-fusion dual encoder for the processing of text and image modalities.

Our work differs in that we investigate using non-parallel data, e.g. where protest texts and images are labeled and classified individually. We also differ in that we use data from different sources (images from social media and text from mainstream news), as well as using state-of-the-art pretrained visual-and-language representations.

7 Conclusions

From the results and discussion carried out, we can conclude that the performance of a unimodal protest detection model trained on text can transfer almost fully to do zero-shot classification of protests in images. This means that a protest classifier trained on texts can be used directly on images without any further training or fine-tuning involved, and without significant decrease in performance. The benefit of this would naturally be that an image protest classifier can be put in use without the need of annotating any image data. On the other hand, we observe that the transfer from images to text implies a loss of performance while it is still significant compared to the random baseline. Furthermore, the investigation shows that multi-modal training for protest detection can be used almost interchangeably to a unimodaly trained model, as performance does not differ substantially.

Ethical statement

Socio-political analysis is important for understanding society at large, and to be able to report on how it develops. It is however of utmost importance that the development of tools and methods is performed with ethical considerations in mind. For example, risks include misuse for large scale surveillance by authoritarian regimes as well as discriminatory performance against minorities due to hidden system biases.

The underlying data used for training protest detection models will inevitably contain spurious correlations that the model might learn to base a protest/not protest decision on. For text based detection, this could be names of organizations, geographical locations or other entities prominent in protests occuring when the data was collected. For image based detection, visual traits such as the etnicity of individual protestors might also be a source of bias.

While these aspects of the model were not explicitly addressed by our research questions in this work, they are important to investigate further as a prerequisite for application of these systems.

Acknowledgements

This work was partially supported by the Wallenberg AI, Autonomous Systems and Software Program (WASP) funded by the Knut and Alice Wallenberg Foundation.

References

Emanuela Boros. 2018. *Neural methods for event extraction*. Ph.D. thesis, Université Paris Saclay (COmUE).

Yubo Chen, Liheng Xu, Kang Liu, Daojian Zeng, and Jun Zhao. 2015. Event extraction via dynamic multi-pooling convolutional neural networks. In *Proceedings of the 53rd Annual Meeting of the Association for Computational Linguistics and the 7th International Joint Conference on Natural Language Processing (Volume 1: Long Papers)*, pages 167–176, Beijing, China. Association for Computational Linguistics.

Ali Hürriyetoğlu, Erdem Yörük, Deniz Yüret, Çağrı Yoltar, Burak Gürel, Fırat Duruşan, Osman Mutlu, and Arda Akdemir. 2019. Overview of clef 2019 lab protestnews: Extracting protests from news in a cross-context setting. In *Experimental IR Meets Multilinguality, Multimodality, and Interaction*, pages 425–432, Cham. Springer International Publishing.

Jungseock Joo and Zachary C. Steinert-Threlkeld. 2018. Image as data: Automated visual content analysis for political science.

Qi Li, Heng Ji, and Liang Huang. 2013. Joint event extraction via structured prediction with global features. In *Proceedings of the 51st Annual Meeting of the Association for Computational Linguistics (Volume 1: Long Papers)*, pages 73–82, Sofia, Bulgaria. Association for Computational Linguistics.

Thien Huu Nguyen, Kyunghyun Cho, and Ralph Grishman. 2016. Joint event extraction via recurrent neural networks. In *Proceedings of the 2016 Conference of the North American Chapter of the Association for Computational Linguistics: Human Language Technologies*, pages 300–309, San Diego, California. Association for Computational Linguistics.

Siddharth Patwardhan and Ellen Riloff. 2007. Effective information extraction with semantic affinity patterns and relevant regions. In *Proceedings of the 2007 Joint Conference on Empirical Methods in Natural Language Processing and Computational Natural Language Learning (EMNLP-CoNLL)*, pages 717–727.

Georgios Petkos, Symeon Papadopoulos, and Yiannis Kompatsiaris. 2012. Social event detection using multimodal clustering and integrating supervisory signals. In *Proceedings of the 2nd ACM International Conference on Multimedia Retrieval*, ICMR '12, New York, NY, USA. Association for Computing Machinery.

Shengsheng Qian, Tianzhu Zhang, Changsheng Xu, and M. Shamim Hossain. 2015. Social event classification via boosted multimodal supervised latent dirichlet allocation. *ACM Trans. Multimedia Comput. Commun. Appl.*, 11(2).

Alec Radford, Jong Wook Kim, Chris Hallacy, Aditya Ramesh, Gabriel Goh, Sandhini Agarwal, Girish Sastry, Amanda Askell, Pamela Mishkin, Jack Clark, Gretchen Krueger, and Ilya Sutskever. 2021. Learning transferable visual models from natural language supervision.

Donghyeon Won, Zachary C. Steinert-Threlkeld, and Jungseock Joo. 2017. Protest activity detection and perceived violence estimation from social media images.

Han Zhang and Jennifer Pan. 2019. Casm: A deep-learning approach for identifying collective action events with text and image data from social media. *Sociological Methodology*, 49(1):1–57.

IDIAPers @ Causal News Corpus 2022: Efficient Causal Relation Identification Through a Prompt-based Few-shot Approach

Sergio Burdisso[*,1,2], **Juan Zuluaga-Gomez**[1,3], **Esaú Villatoro-Tello**[1,5], **Martin Fajcik**[1,4]
Muskaan Singh[1], **Pavel Smrz**[4], **Petr Motlicek**[1]
[1]Idiap Research Institute, Martigny, Switzerland
[2]Universidad Nacional de San Luis (UNSL), San Luis, Argentina
[3]Ecole Polytechnique Fédérale de Lausanne, Switzerland
[4]Brno University of Technology, Brno, Czech Republic
[5]Universidad Autónoma Metropolitana Unidad Cuajimalpa, Mexico City, Mexico
[*]*corresponding author: sergio.burdisso@idiap.ch*

Abstract

In this paper, we describe our participation in the subtask 1 of CASE-2022, Event Causality Identification with Casual News Corpus. We address the Causal Relation Identification (CRI) task by exploiting a set of simple yet complementary techniques for fine-tuning language models (LMs) on a small number of annotated examples (i.e., a *few-shot* configuration). We follow a prompt-based prediction approach for fine-tuning LMs in which the CRI task is treated as a masked language modeling problem (MLM). This approach allows LMs natively pre-trained on MLM problems to directly generate textual responses to CRI-specific prompts. We compare the performance of this method against ensemble techniques trained on the entire dataset. Our best-performing submission was fine-tuned with only 256 instances per class, 15.7% of the all available data, and yet obtained the second-best precision (0.82), third-best accuracy (0.82), and an F1-score (0.85) very close to what was reported by the winner team (0.86).[1]

1 Introduction

Causal relation identification aims to predict whether or not there exists a cause-effect relation between a pair of events mentioned in a given text. For example, in the sentence *"Protests spread to 15 towns and resulted in the destruction of property"*, the automatic causal identification system must be able to realize that there is cause-effect relation between the events *"protest"* and *"destruction"*.

Hence, understanding causal relations within a text is an essential aspect of natural language processing (NLP) and understanding (NLU) (Ayyanar et al., 2019a; Li et al., 2021; Tan et al., 2022c). Once the causal information is identified within a text, such knowledge becomes beneficial for many other downstream NLP tasks, e.g., Information Extraction, Question Answering, Text Summarization (Ayyanar et al., 2019a; Man et al., 2022). However, due to the ambiguity and diversity in written documents, causality identification is not easy and remains a challenging problem.

The Event Causality Identification with Causal News Corpus (CASE-2022) shared task (Tan et al., 2022b) addresses this problem on a recently created corpus named the Causal News Corpus (CNC) (Tan et al., 2022a). Contrary to previous existing causality corpora, the CNC dataset, manually annotated by experts, incorporates a broader set of causal linguistic constructions, i.e., not only limited to explicit constructions, resulting in a more challenging dataset.

In this paper, we describe our followed methodology for addressing the causal event classification shared task (subtask 1) during the CASE-2022 competition (Tan et al., 2022b).[2] Our primary method, based on a *few-shot* configuration, follows a prompt-based approach for fine-tuning the language model (LM). The intuitive idea of this approach is to allow the LM to directly auto-complete natural language prompts. Following this technique, we leverage the LM's knowledge and let it decide the correct label of the input sequence. Additionally, we evaluate the performance of ensemble techniques trained using the entire dataset available. Our results demonstrate that our few-shot, prompt-based, fine-tuning approach can generalize well even when using as few as 256 samples per class for training, outperforming ensemble techniques trained with the entire dataset, as well as most of other teams' submissions.

The rest of the paper is organized as follows.

[1]Code available at https://github.com/idiap/cncsharedtask.

[2]We refer the reader to our standalone publication (Fajcik et al., 2022) to know our results for subtask 2.

Proceedings of the 5th Workshop on Challenges and Applications of Automated Extraction of Socio-political Events from Text (CASE), pages 61 - 69
December 7-8, 2022

Section 2 describes relevant related work, Section 3 describes the components of our main method, namely the prompt-based approach. Section 4 describes the experimental setup, i.e., datasets, additional baselines, experiments configuration and obtained results. Finally, Section 5 depicts our main conclusions and future work directions.

2 Related Work

Previous work on causal relation identification varies from knowledge-based to deep neural network approaches (Deep-NN). Knowledge-based systems rely on linguistic patterns extracted using an exhaustive exploration of the data, where lexico-semantic and syntactic analysis lead to the identification of relevant structures and keywords that depict the presence of a causal relation in the text (Garcia, 1997; Khoo et al., 2000). Although interpretable, these methods require a lot of human effort to generate relevant patterns and result in models that are not readily applicable in different domains.

Statistical machine learning (ML) approaches leave to the selected algorithm to find patterns in the data on the basis of the manual annotation. Traditionally, using different NLP tools, it is possible to compute various features for a given collection and apply any ML pipeline to train a causality relation classifier, e.g., (Rutherford and Xue, 2014; Hidey and McKeown, 2016). However, one main disadvantage of these techniques is the language dependency and error propagation of the NLP tools, e.g., syntactic parsers.

Finally, recent approaches based on Deep-NN have become popular, given their powerful representation learning ability. Typical approaches include convolutional neural networks (Ayyanar et al., 2019b), long short-term memory networks (Li et al., 2021), and pre-trained transformer-based LMs such as BERT (Devlin et al., 2019), where following a standard fine-tuning approach makes possible the detection of causality relations (Tan et al., 2022c; Khetan et al., 2022; Fajcik et al., 2020). Normally, these methods involve high computational costs and large amounts of labeled data. However, in this work, we show that pre-trained LMs can still be effective even when fine-tuned with very few instances.

Contrary to previous work, we evaluate the effectiveness of very recent prompt-based prediction approaches under a *few-shot* configuration for causal relation identification.

3 Prompt-Based Approach

In the "pre-train, prompt, and predict" paradigm, unlike the standard "pre-train and fine-tune" paradigm, instead of adapting pre-trained LMs to downstream tasks via objective engineering,[3] downstream tasks are reformulated to look more like those solved during the LM pre-training phase (Liu et al., 2021). More precisely, prompt-based prediction treats the downstream task as a masked language modeling problem, where the model directly generates a textual response (referred to as a *label word*) to a given prompt defined by a task-specific *template* (Gao et al., 2021). For instance, when identifying the sentiment of a movie review like "I love this movie." we may continue with "Overall, it was a `[MASK]` movie." and ask the LM to fill the mask with a sentiment-bearing word. In this example, the original input text x ("I love this movie.") is modified using the *template* "`[x]` Overall, it was a `[MASK]` movie." into a textual string prompt x' in which the mask will be filled with a *label word*. Some examples of *label words* for this example could be "fantastic" or "boring".

In the case of classification tasks, in addition to defining a set of possible *label words*, it is necessary to define a mapping between each one and the actual output labels. For instance, if labels $+$ and $-$ refer to positive and negative sentiment, respectively, "fantastic" in previous example could be mapped to output label $+$, and "boring" to $-$.

Formally, let $\mathcal{L}$ be a pre-trained language model, $f_t(x)$ a function that converts the input x into a prompt by instantiating template t which contains one `[MASK]` token, $mask$. Let $word : \mathcal{Y} \rightarrow \mathcal{W}$ be a mapping from the task label space, $\mathcal{Y}$, to the *label words* set, $\mathcal{W}$. Then, the classification task is converted to a *masked language modeling* (MLM) task in which the probability of predicting class $y \in \mathcal{Y}$ is modeled as:

$$p(y|x) = p(mask = word(y)|f_t(x)) = \\ = \frac{exp(\mathbf{w}_{word(y)} \cdot \mathbf{h}_{mask})}{\sum_{y' \in \mathcal{Y}} exp(\mathbf{w}_{word(y')} \cdot \mathbf{h}_{mask})}, \quad (1)$$

where $\mathbf{h}_{mask}$ is the hidden vector of `[MASK]` and $\mathbf{w}_v$ denotes the vector encoding word v. Note that

[3] *Objective engineering* referes to both the pre-training and fine-tuning stages of LMs (Liu et al., 2021).

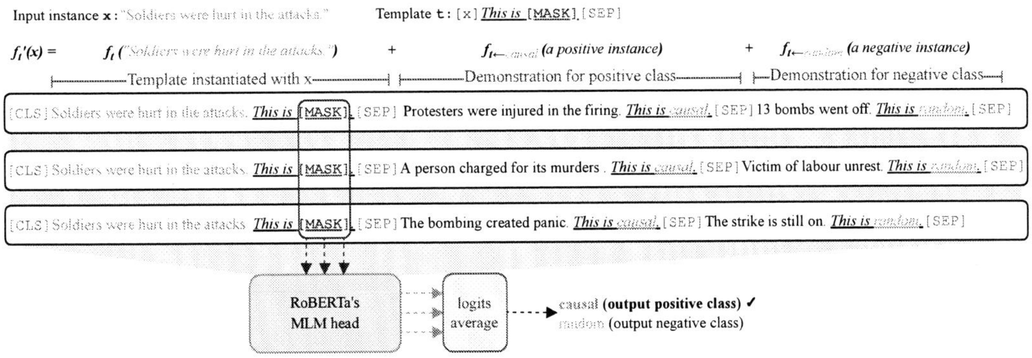

Figure 1: Augmented prompt-based classification for causality identification task. First, the input instance $x =$ *"Soldiers were hurt in the attacks"* is converted into three different input prompts by applying $f_t'(x)$ three times. Then, these three prompts are given to a RoBERTa model, and one logit vector is obtained for each. These vectors are then averaged, and the word with the highest score, *"causal"*, is selected. Finally, this word is mapped to its corresponding class, and x is classified as positive. Note that, in this example, we have the following word-to-class label mapping $word(positive) =$ *"causal"* and $word(negative) =$ *"random"*.

when fine-tuning $\mathcal{L}$ to minimize the cross-entropy loss, the pre-trained weights $\mathbf{w}_v$ are re-used, and there's no need to introduce any new parameter. On the contrary, with standard fine-tuning a task-specific head, $softmax(\mathbf{W}_o\mathbf{h}_{[\texttt{CLS}]})$, has to be added, with new task-specific learnable parameters $\mathbf{W}_o \in \mathbb{R}^{|\mathcal{Y}|\times d}$, which increases the gap between pre-training and fine-tuning.

Hereafter we will refer to the "causal" and "non-causal" classes as "positive" $(+)$ and "negative" $(-)$ respectively. In addition, and following previous work by Gao et al. (2021), we append one answered prompt for each class to the input prompt as *demonstrations*.[4] More precisely, let $\mathcal{Y} = \{+, -\}$ be the set of labels for the binary causality identification task, let $t \leftarrow v$ be the template t in which its `[MASK]` token has been filled with word v, and $w^y = word(y)$ the *word label* for class $y \in \mathcal{Y}$, then we redefine $f_t(x)$ in Equation 1 as $f_t'(x)$ defined as:

$$f_t'(x) = f_t(x) \parallel f_{t\leftarrow w^+}(x^+) \parallel f_{t\leftarrow w^-}(x^-) \quad (2)$$

where $\parallel$ is the string concatenation operator, and x^y is an instance of class y randomly sampled from the training set. Figure 1, depicts an example of three different input prompts are shown by applying $f_t'(x)$ three times to the input instance x.

Classification process: the process is illustrated in Figure 1. First, the input instance x is converted into d different input prompts by applying $f_t'(x)$, d times. Then, each input prompt is given to the LM to obtain d logit vectors holding the word scores for the mask in each prompt. A simple ensemble scheme is then applied by averaging all d logit vectors, and the *word label* with the highest score is selected, which is finally mapped to its corresponding class y using mapping $word(y)$.

Training and model selection: for developing our prompt-based models, we performed a simplified version of the process described in previous work by Gao et al. (2021). Namely, we carried out the following six steps:

Step 1: we created a new training set, τ_k, by extracting k instances per class from the original train partition, and used the remaining $2925 - 2 \times k$ instances as a large evaluation set δ_{T-k} (dataset stats are given in Table 2).

Step 2: in order to add *demonstrations* to a given input x (see Equation 1), we uniformly sampled x^- and x^+ from the top-50% most similar instances in τ_k.[5] To do so, we pre-computed the sentence embeddings of training instances using a pre-trained SBERT (Reimers and Gurevych, 2019) model, and cosine distance was used as a similarity metric.

Step 3: using *"causal"* and *"random"* as *word labels*,[6] the next step was to generate candidate

[4]These *demonstrations* (Gao et al., 2021) are used to demonstrate the LM, in-context, how it should provide the answer to the input prompt.

[5]We tested different percentages, however 50% was the best-performing one.

[6]We performed some simple preliminary tests using different words like "coincidence", "choice", "causal", "cause", with few trivial hand-crafted templates (e.g. "`[x]` *It was* `[MASK]`"), from which "random" and "casual" where selected.

Submission	Precision		Recall		Accuracy		F1-Score	
	dev	*test*	*dev*	*test*	*dev*	*test*	*dev*	*test*
Ensemble-10m	**88.46**	82.78	90.45	84.66	**88.26**	81.35	**89.44**	83.70
Prompt-256	85.49	**82.80**	**92.70**	87.50	87.30	**82.64**	88.95	**85.08**
Prompt-356e	82.72	80.41	88.76	**88.64**	83.60	81.35	85.63	84.32
Prompt-1000	84.56	81.08	91.57	85.22	86.07	80.39	87.87	83.10
Ensemble-8p	86.10	81.15	90.44	88.07	86.69	81.67	88.22	84.47

Table 1: Official performance metrics in percentages (%) from the selected methods in dev and test partitions of the Causal News Corpus.

templates automatically using T5. First, each training instance x of class y in τ_k was converted to "`[x]`<P>$word(y)$<S>" where <P> and <S> are T5 mask tokens, and used a 100 wide beam search to decode multiple template candidates by filling <P> and <S> tokens.

Step 4: next step was sorting all 100 final candidate templates by F1 score. However, since this is a time-consuming step, a subset of the evaluation set was used by sampling 256 unique positive and negative instances from δ_{T-k}. Note that no fine-tuning is used at this point, just the out-of-the-box pre-trained LM.

Step 5: we selected the top-10 best-performing templates as final candidates. For each candidate template we fine-tuned the LM as a MLM task (see Equation 1) on the training set, τ_k, evaluating it on the complete evaluation set, δ_{T-k}.

Step 6: finally, the model with the best F1 score on the official dev set was selected as a candidate for submission —we also checked that the F1 score on δ_{T-k} was among the first ones too (if not first). Note that in this step we're evaluating the model on unseen data since the official dev set is being used as an unofficial test set.

The above process was repeated varying the number k of training instances, with $k = 256$, 356, 512, and 1000;[7] the number d of input prompts to ensemble during classification stage, with d from 1 to 9; and using RoBERTa (large and base), and DeBERTa V3 (base) as pre-trained LMs. In step 5, models were fine-tuned for a maximum of 1000 steps using AdamW (Loshchilov and Hutter, 2019) optimizer (β_1=0.9, β_2=0.999, ϵ=1e−8) with a learning rate of γ=1e−5 with no weight decay (λ=0). Models were evaluated every 100 steps and check-pointed when new best F1 scores were obtained.

[7]Inspired by evidence showing a performance saturation when $k = 256$ (Figure 3 in Gao et al. (2021)), compared to standard fine-tuning on the entire dataset, we decided to start from this value.

Label	Train	Dev	Test	Total
Causal	1603	178	176	1957
Non-causal	1322	145	135	1602
Total:	2925	323	311	**3559**

Table 2: Number of positive (causal) and negative (non-causal) instances in the *train, dev,* and *test* sets of the shared task. We refer the interested reader to (Tan et al., 2022b) to know more details about the data and the labeling process.

4 Results & Discussion

In this section we provide the details of the employed dataset, a set of additional experiments based on recent ensemble techniques, and the final configuration of our submitted runs to the subtask 1 of CASE 2022.

4.1 Dataset

As mentioned earlier, the main goal of subtask 1 of CASE-2022 is to classify whether or not a given sentence contains a *cause-effect* relation. Thus, systems have to be able to predict *Causal* or *Non-causal* labels per sentence. Table 2 contains a few statistics regarding the distribution of the classes in the *train, dev*, and *test* partitions.

4.2 Ensemble-based Approach

We also performed several ensembles of different fine-tuned LMs to increase the generalization and compensate for the overfitting of the models. We followed the approach described in Fajcik et al. (2019), called *TOP-N* fusion. In this formulation, we first define a *set* of M pre-trained LMs, varying the training seed. *TOP-N* fusion starts by choosing one uniformly random model from the *set*, which is added to the ensemble. Next, it randomly shuffles the rest of the models and tries adding them into the ensemble once, as long as the F1 score improves. Each time a model is added to the ensemble, its performance gets measured. The model would stay in the ensemble only and only if it improved the overall performance. This aims at an iterative optimization of the ensemble's F1 score by averaging the output probabilities. As the selection process is stochastic, we repeat the process N=10000 times. We construct a new ensemble for each iteration, independently of the previous ones. Finally, we select the best performing ensemble for submission. Further details are given in Appendix B (Figure 2).

4.3 Official Submissions

Next, we describe each one of our submissions:

Ensemble-10m: ensemble model described in subsection 4.2 with 10 final models obtained from a set of 150 initial ones (50 fine-tuned *bert-base-cased*, *roberta-base*, and *deberta-v3-base* models).

Prompt-256: prompt-based *roberta-large* model with k=256 training instances per class, d=3 input prompts to ensemble during classification stage; and template t = "`[x]` *This is not* `[MASK]`".

Prompt-1000: The same previous model but with t = "`[x]` *There were no* `[MASK]`*ities in this*", k=1000, and d=1.

Ensemble-8p: ensemble model described in subsection 4.2 with 8 final models obtained from the top-50 best performing prompt-based models as the initial set.

Prompt-356e: three prompt-base models trained with k=356 instances. The first two models have the same template as *Prompt-1000* but with d=2 and 3, respectively. The third one uses the template t = "`[x]` *The incident is not* `[MASK]`" with d=1.[8] Finally, a simple majority voting ensemble among these three models generates the output.

4.4 Results

Table 1 shows the official results, both in dev and test partitions, for our five submissions. As expected, the ensemble of several LMs (Ensemble-10m) was able to obtain outstanding performance across several metrics during the validation phase (i.e., dev partition[9]). However, the performance dropped significantly in the test partition (F1= 89.44 $\rightarrow$ F1= 83.70). On the contrary, our prompt-based approach trained on 256 instances per class (Prompt-256) could generalize better on the test partition. Such submission obtained 2nd place in terms of precision (82.80%), 3rd in accuracy (82.64%), and 5th in F1 (85.08%) —the best F1 was 86.19%. However, the main advantage of our approach is that it allows the LM to be trained in a few-shot setting, making it harder for the model to overfit the data. Moreover, most of the available data can be kept and used for measuring the generalization power of the model instead. For instance, our best-performing model (Prompt-256) was fine-tuned only on 15.7% of all available data,[10] allowing the remaining 84.3% to be used for evaluation and model selection (74.3% as evaluation set and 10% as our own test set). Therefore, model selection choice is more robust since the risk of performance drop on unseen data, such as the official test set, is expected to be lower.

5 Conclusions

This paper describes our participation in the CASE-2022 subtask 1. Our proposed approach uses a few-shot configuration in which a prompt-based model is fine-tuned using *only 256 instances* per class and yet was able to obtain remarkable results among all 16 participant teams. The comparison against traditional fine-tuning techniques, ensemble approaches, as well as the other participating models, show the potential of the proposed approach for better generalizing the posed task.

For future work, we plan to perform further ablation studies when we have access to test set ground truth labels. For instance, measuring the dev-to-test performance drop in relation to k or the robustness against different training and demonstration sampling given a fixed k.

Acknowledgements

This work was supported by CRiTERIA, an EU project, funded under the Horizon 2020 programme, grant agreement no. 101021866 and the Ministry of Education, Youth and Sports of the Czech Republic through the e-INFRA CZ (ID:90140). Esaú Villatoro-Tello, was supported partially by Idiap, SNI CONACyT, and UAM-Cuajimalpa Mexico.

[8] Note that these prompts, as well as previous ones, were automatically generated as described in section 3.

[9] We further performed a 5-cvf experiment on six different architectures, see the results on Table 3 in Appendix A.

[10] i.e. train + dev sets in Table 2

References

Raja Ayyanar, George Koomullil, and Hariharan Ramasangu. 2019a. Causal relation classification using convolutional neural networks and grammar tags. In *2019 IEEE 16th India Council International Conference (INDICON)*, pages 1–3. IEEE.

Raja Ayyanar, George Koomullil, and Hariharan Ramasangu. 2019b. Causal relation classification using convolutional neural networks and grammar tags. In *2019 IEEE 16th India Council International Conference (INDICON)*, pages 1–3.

Jacob Devlin, Ming-Wei Chang, Kenton Lee, and Kristina Toutanova. 2019. BERT: Pre-training of deep bidirectional transformers for language understanding. In *Proceedings of the 2019 Conference of the North American Chapter of the Association for Computational Linguistics: Human Language Technologies, Volume 1 (Long and Short Papers)*, pages 4171–4186, Minneapolis, Minnesota. Association for Computational Linguistics.

Martin Fajcik, Josef Jon, Martin Docekal, and Pavel Smrz. 2020. BUT-FIT at SemEval-2020 task 5: Automatic detection of counterfactual statements with deep pre-trained language representation models. In *Proceedings of the Fourteenth Workshop on Semantic Evaluation*, pages 437–444, Barcelona (online). International Committee for Computational Linguistics.

Martin Fajcik, Muskaan Singh, Juan Zuluaga-Gomez, Esaú Villatoro-Tello, Sergio Burdisso, Petr Motlicek, and Pavel Smrz. 2022. Idiapers @ causal news corpus 2022: Extracting cause-effect-signal triplets via pre-trained autoregressive language model. In *The 5th Workshop on Challenges and Applications of Automated Extraction of Socio-political Events from Text (CASE @ EMNLP 2022)*. Association for Computational Linguistics.

Martin Fajcik, Pavel Smrz, and Lukas Burget. 2019. BUT-FIT at SemEval-2019 task 7: Determining the rumour stance with pre-trained deep bidirectional transformers. In *Proceedings of the 13th International Workshop on Semantic Evaluation*, pages 1097–1104, Minneapolis, Minnesota, USA. Association for Computational Linguistics.

Tianyu Gao, Adam Fisch, and Danqi Chen. 2021. Making pre-trained language models better few-shot learners. In *Proceedings of the 59th Annual Meeting of the Association for Computational Linguistics and the 11th International Joint Conference on Natural Language Processing (Volume 1: Long Papers)*, pages 3816–3830, Online. Association for Computational Linguistics.

Daniela Garcia. 1997. Coatis, an nlp system to locate expressions of actions connected by causality links. In *Knowledge Acquisition, Modeling and Management*, pages 347–352, Berlin, Heidelberg. Springer Berlin Heidelberg.

Pengcheng He, Jianfeng Gao, and Weizhu Chen. 2021a. Debertav3: Improving deberta using electra-style pre-training with gradient-disentangled embedding sharing. *ArXiv preprint*, abs/2111.09543.

Pengcheng He, Xiaodong Liu, Jianfeng Gao, and Weizhu Chen. 2021b. Deberta: decoding-enhanced bert with disentangled attention. In *9th International Conference on Learning Representations, ICLR 2021, Virtual Event, Austria, May 3-7, 2021*. OpenReview.net.

Dan Hendrycks and Kevin Gimpel. 2016. Gaussian error linear units (gelus). *ArXiv preprint*, abs/1606.08415.

Christopher Hidey and Kathy McKeown. 2016. Identifying causal relations using parallel Wikipedia articles. In *Proceedings of the 54th Annual Meeting of the Association for Computational Linguistics (Volume 1: Long Papers)*, pages 1424–1433, Berlin, Germany. Association for Computational Linguistics.

Vivek Khetan, Roshni Ramnani, Mayuresh Anand, Subhashis Sengupta, and Andrew E. Fano. 2022. Causal bert: Language models for causality detection between events expressed in text. In *Intelligent Computing*, pages 965–980, Cham. Springer International Publishing.

Christopher S. G. Khoo, Syin Chan, and Yun Niu. 2000. Extracting causal knowledge from a medical database using graphical patterns. In *Proceedings of the 38th Annual Meeting of the Association for Computational Linguistics*, pages 336–343, Hong Kong. Association for Computational Linguistics.

Mike Lewis, Yinhan Liu, Naman Goyal, Marjan Ghazvininejad, Abdelrahman Mohamed, Omer Levy, Veselin Stoyanov, and Luke Zettlemoyer. 2020. BART: Denoising sequence-to-sequence pre-training for natural language generation, translation, and comprehension. In *Proceedings of the 58th Annual Meeting of the Association for Computational Linguistics*, pages 7871–7880, Online. Association for Computational Linguistics.

Quentin Lhoest, Albert Villanova del Moral, Yacine Jernite, Abhishek Thakur, Patrick von Platen, Suraj Patil, Julien Chaumond, Mariama Drame, Julien Plu, Lewis Tunstall, Joe Davison, Mario Šaško, Gunjan Chhablani, Bhavitvya Malik, Simon Brandeis, Teven Le Scao, Victor Sanh, Canwen Xu, Nicolas Patry, Angelina McMillan-Major, Philipp Schmid, Sylvain Gugger, Clément Delangue, Théo Matussière, Lysandre Debut, Stas Bekman, Pierric Cistac, Thibault Goehringer, Victor Mustar, François Lagunas, Alexander Rush, and Thomas Wolf. 2021. Datasets: A community library for natural language processing. In *Proceedings of the 2021 Conference on Empirical Methods in Natural Language Processing: System Demonstrations*, pages 175–184, Online and Punta Cana, Dominican Republic. Association for Computational Linguistics.

Zhaoning Li, Qi Li, Xiaotian Zou, and Jiangtao Ren. 2021. Causality extraction based on self-attentive bilstm-crf with transferred embeddings. *Neurocomputing*, 423:207–219.

Pengfei Liu, Weizhe Yuan, Jinlan Fu, Zhengbao Jiang, Hiroaki Hayashi, and Graham Neubig. 2021. Pre-train, prompt, and predict: A systematic survey of prompting methods in natural language processing. *ArXiv preprint*, abs/2107.13586.

Yinhan Liu, Myle Ott, Naman Goyal, Jingfei Du, Mandar Joshi, Danqi Chen, Omer Levy, Mike Lewis, Luke Zettlemoyer, and Veselin Stoyanov. 2019. Roberta: A robustly optimized bert pretraining approach. *ArXiv preprint*, abs/1907.11692.

Ilya Loshchilov and Frank Hutter. 2019. Decoupled weight decay regularization. In *7th International Conference on Learning Representations, ICLR 2019, New Orleans, LA, USA, May 6-9, 2019*. OpenReview.net.

Hieu Man, Minh Nguyen, and Thien Nguyen. 2022. Event causality identification via generation of important context words. In *Proceedings of the 11th Joint Conference on Lexical and Computational Semantics*, pages 323–330, Seattle, Washington. Association for Computational Linguistics.

Nils Reimers and Iryna Gurevych. 2019. Sentence-BERT: Sentence embeddings using Siamese BERT-networks. In *Proceedings of the 2019 Conference on Empirical Methods in Natural Language Processing and the 9th International Joint Conference on Natural Language Processing (EMNLP-IJCNLP)*, pages 3982–3992, Hong Kong, China. Association for Computational Linguistics.

Attapol Rutherford and Nianwen Xue. 2014. Discovering implicit discourse relations through brown cluster pair representation and coreference patterns. In *Proceedings of the 14th Conference of the European Chapter of the Association for Computational Linguistics*, pages 645–654, Gothenburg, Sweden. Association for Computational Linguistics.

Victor Sanh, Lysandre Debut, Julien Chaumond, and Thomas Wolf. 2019. Distilbert, a distilled version of bert: smaller, faster, cheaper and lighter. *ArXiv preprint*, abs/1910.01108.

Fiona Anting Tan, Ali Hürriyetoğlu, Tommaso Caselli, Nelleke Oostdijk, Tadashi Nomoto, Hansi Hettiarachchi, Iqra Ameer, Onur Uca, Farhana Ferdousi Liza, and Tiancheng Hu. 2022a. The causal news corpus: Annotating causal relations in event sentences from news. In *Proceedings of the Thirteenth Language Resources and Evaluation Conference*, pages 2298–2310, Marseille, France. European Language Resources Association.

Fiona Anting Tan, Ali Hürriyetoğlu, Tommaso Caselli, Nelleke Oostdijk, Hansi Hettiarachchi, Tadashi Nomoto, Onur Uca, and Farhana Ferdousi Liza. 2022b. Event causality identification with causal news corpus - shared task 3, CASE 2022. In *Proceedings of the 5th Workshop on Challenges and Applications of Automated Extraction of Socio-political Events from Text (CASE 2022)*, Online. Association for Computational Linguistics.

Fiona Anting Tan, Xinyu Zuo, and See-Kiong Ng. 2022c. Unicausal: Unified benchmark and model for causal text mining. *ArXiv preprint*, abs/2208.09163.

Thomas Wolf, Lysandre Debut, Victor Sanh, Julien Chaumond, Clement Delangue, Anthony Moi, Pierric Cistac, Tim Rault, Remi Louf, Morgan Funtowicz, Joe Davison, Sam Shleifer, Patrick von Platen, Clara Ma, Yacine Jernite, Julien Plu, Canwen Xu, Teven Le Scao, Sylvain Gugger, Mariama Drame, Quentin Lhoest, and Alexander Rush. 2020. Transformers: State-of-the-art natural language processing. In *Proceedings of the 2020 Conference on Empirical Methods in Natural Language Processing: System Demonstrations*, pages 38–45, Online. Association for Computational Linguistics.

A Baseline results

We performed standard cross-entropy fine-tuning on six different pre-trained LMs (see first column in Table 3) to produce baselines. We perform 5-fold cross-validation for each architecture following the partitions proposed in Tan et al. (2022a). Each system is fine-tuned on the sequence classification task to discriminate between casual and non-causal text input sequences. We report the mean and standard deviation (mean $\pm$ std) on the official development set over several metrics, see Table 3.

During experimentation, we use the same learning rate of $\gamma = 5\text{e}{-5}$ with a linear learning rate scheduler. Dropout is set to $dp = 0.1$ for the attention and hidden layers, while Gaussian Error Linear Units (GELU) is used as activation function (Hendrycks and Gimpel, 2016). We fine-tune each model with an effective batch size of 32 for 50 epochs with AdamW (Loshchilov and Hutter, 2019) optimizer (β_1=0.9, β_2=0.999, ϵ=1e$-$8). We noted that *deberta-v3-base* performed systematically better in all metrics as shown in Table 3.

B Ensembling

We compose ensembles before submission to leaderboard in two manners. `Ensembling-type-1` and `Ensembling-type-2`:

- `Ensembling-type-1`: we define a *set* of models, which contains only baseline LMs fine-tuned on the sequence classification task (see Table 3). We fine-tune 50 LMs for each architecture from first column of Table 3. Next, we run our *TOP-N* fusion algorithm (see subsection 4.2) with the *set* of models previously defined. The model submitted with `Ensembling-type-1` is **Ensemble-10m**, reporting its performance in Table 1.

- `Ensembling-type-2`, we define a *set* of models containing prompt-based LMs. We select the top models for leaderboard submission. The overall process for ensembling is illustrated in Figure 2. Even though the figure only depicts our first approach (explained above), we perform exactly the same with the prompt-based models explained in section 3. The model submitted with `Ensembling-type-2` is **Ensemble-8p**, reporting its performance in Table 1.

Details about the ensemble: we select the best ensembles based on its F1-score performance on the dev set. For example, in Table 4 we list the performance of the `Ensembling-type-1` system (i.e., **Ensemble-10m**) we used for our submission in the leaderboard.

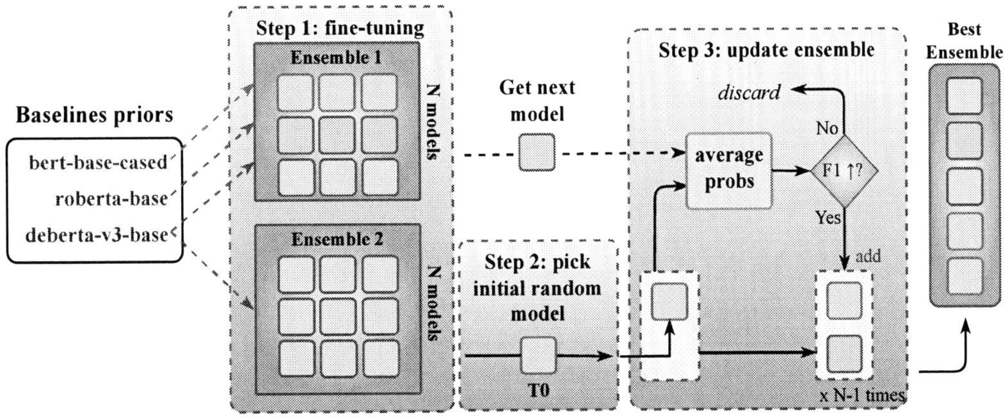

Figure 2: Our proposed method to ensemble N fine-tuned LMs, based on Fajcik et al. (2019) approach. We fine-tune several LMs by modifying only the training seed. Our implementation uses the sequence classification task from HuggingFace toolkit (Wolf et al., 2020; Lhoest et al., 2021).

Model	Precision	Recall	Accuracy	F1-score	Reference
`bert-base-cased`	83.52 $\pm$ 1.01	87.88 $\pm$ 3.08	79.68 $\pm$ 1.83	81.03 $\pm$ 1.20	(Devlin et al., 2019)
`bart-base`	84.21 $\pm$ 0.88	87.80 $\pm$ 2.26	80.99 $\pm$ 2.19	81.98 $\pm$ 0.95	(Lewis et al., 2020)
`roberta-base`	85.13 $\pm$ 1.11	87.86 $\pm$ 2.41	82.66 $\pm$ 2.35	83.21 $\pm$ 1.10	(Liu et al., 2019)
`distilroberta-base`	84.41 $\pm$ 1.20	88.05 $\pm$ 1.69	81.12 $\pm$ 2.09	82.22 $\pm$ 1.12	(Sanh et al., 2019)
`deberta-base`	82.67 $\pm$ 2.76	85.74 $\pm$ 2.72	80.32 $\pm$ 6.49	80.31 $\pm$ 3.44	(He et al., 2021b)
`deberta-v3-base`	**85.87 $\pm$ 1.18**	**88.88 $\pm$ 1.74**	**83.18 $\pm$ 3.16**	**84.00 $\pm$ 1.18**	(He et al., 2021a)

Table 3: Mean and standard deviation (mean $\pm$ std) of different metrics on the dev set using a 5-fold cross validation scheme on the CNC dataset. We report results for six different architectures of pre-trained LMs.

Model	F1-score (%)
`bert-base-cased`	85.15
`roberta-base`	86.76
`deberta-v3-base`	89.69
Ensemble-10m†	**89.7**

Table 4: Obtained F1-scores on the *dev* partition of subtask 1 of the Causal News Corpus. Results depict the top performance of three models that belong to the ***Ensemble-10m*** configuration. The last row corresponds to an ensemble model composed of ten independent LMs, namely, six *deberta-v3-base*, two *bert-base-cased*, and two *roberta-base*. More details about the ensemble construction are described in subsection 4.2 and Fajcik et al. (2019).

IDIAPers @ Causal News Corpus 2022: Extracting Cause-Effect-Signal Triplets via Pre-trained Autoregressive Language Model

Martin Fajcik[*, 1, 2], **Muskaan Singh**[1], **Juan Zuluaga-Gomez**[1,3], **Esaú Villatoro-Tello**[1,4], **Sergio Burdisso**[1,5], **Petr Motlicek**[1, 2], **Pavel Smrz**[2]

[1]Idiap Research Institute, Martigny, Switzerland
[2]Brno University of Technology, Brno, Czech Republic
[3]Ecole Polytechnique Fédérale de Lausanne, Switzerland
[4]Universidad Autónoma Metropolitana Unidad Cuajimalpa, Mexico City, Mexico
[5]Universidad Nacional de San Luis (UNSL), San Luis, Argentina
corresponding author: martin.fajcik@vut.cz

Abstract

In this paper, we describe our shared task submissions for Subtask 2 in CASE-2022, Event Causality Identification with Casual News Corpus. The challenge focused on the automatic detection of all cause-effect-signal spans present in the sentence from news-media. We detect cause-effect-signal spans in a sentence using T5 — a pre-trained autoregressive language model. We iteratively identify all cause-effect-signal span triplets, always conditioning the prediction of the next triplet on the previously predicted ones. To predict the triplet itself, we consider different causal relationships such as *cause→effect→signal*. Each triplet component is generated via a language model conditioned on the sentence, the previous parts of the current triplet, and previously predicted triplets. Despite training on an extremely small dataset of 160 samples, our approach achieved competitive performance, being placed second in the competition. Furthermore, we show that assuming either *cause→effect* or *effect→cause* order achieves similar results.[1]

1 Introduction

Causality links the relationship between two arguments — cause and effect (Barik et al., 2016). Figure 1 shows examples extracted from the Causal News Corpus (CNC) (Tan et al., 2022b). *Cause* clauses appear in yellow, *Effect* in green, and *Signals* in pink; hereafter referred to as CES triplets. As shown in the example, *"the bombing created panic among villagers"*, illustrates that the event "bombing" caused the event "panic among villagers" termed as *effect*. The linkage among the cause and effect, i.e., the word "created", is termed as *signal* and can be expressed explicitly or implicitly.

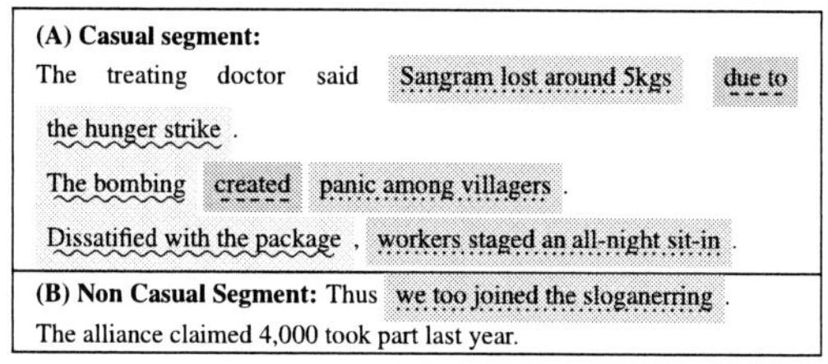

Figure 1: Examples from the Causal News Corpus, causes are in yellow, effects in green, and signals in pink. If a sentence has both — cause and effect — it is referred to as casual (A), otherwise, as non-casual (B).

Automatically detecting and extracting causality relations plays a vital role in many natural language processing (NLP) works to tackle inference and understanding (Dunietz et al., 2020; Fajcik et al., 2020; Jo et al., 2021; Feder et al., 2021a). It has applications in various down-streaming NLP tasks, namely, causal question-answering generation, explaining social media behavior, political phenomena, effective education, and gender bias in the research community (Tan et al., 2014; Wood-Doughty et al., 2018; Sridhar and Getoor, 2019; Veitch et al., 2020; Zhang et al., 2020; Feder et al., 2021b).

In this paper, we describe our methodology for CASE-2022 cause-effect-signal span detection shared task (Subtask 2). Overall, our main contributions are listed below:

1. We show that cause-effect-signal spans can be extracted by a simple pre-trained generative seq2seq model trained on just 160 instances.

2. We develop a method for extracting all causal triplets from the sentence in an iterative manner.

3. We investigate how language models deal with

[1]Code at https://github.com/idiap/cncsharedtask.

Proceedings of the 5th Workshop on Challenges and Applications of Automated Extraction of Socio-political Events from Text (CASE), pages 70 - 78
December 7-8, 2022 ©2022 Association for Computational Linguistics

the causal order of the cause and effect spans to answer the research question *"should cause be identified first, and only then effect, or vice-versa?"*.

4. We show that an efficient F1 best-substring matching algorithm, known for question answering, can be applied to deal with rare cases when a language model (LM) does not generate part of the input sequence.

2 Related Work

The problem of causality extraction from text is a challenging task as it requires semantic understanding and contextual knowledge. There were many attempts in the domain of linguistics for corpora creation for event extraction but with limited size such as CausalTimeBank (CTB) (Mirza et al., 2014) from news with 318 pairs, CaTeRS (Mostafazadeh et al., 2016) from short stories with 488 casual links, EventStoryLine (Caselli and Vossen, 2017) from online news articles with 1,770 casual event pairs, semantic relation corpora PDTB-3 (Webber et al., 2019) with over 7, 000 causal relations and CNC corpus (Tan et al., 2022b,c) with 1,957 casual events with multiple event pairs. Compared to previous datasets, CNC differs by focusing on event sentences, accepting arguments which does not need to form a clause, and not limiting itself to pre-defined list of connectives, but instead including causal examples in more varied linguistic constructions. The previous work in this domain can be broadly classified into knowledge-based approaches, statistical ML, and deep-learning-based approaches. The knowledge-based approach uses linguistic patterns by predefining hand-crafted or keywords (Garcia et al., 1997; Khoo et al., 2000; Radinsky et al., 2012; Beamer et al., 2008; Girju et al., 2009; Ittoo and Bouma, 2013; Kang et al., 2014; Khoo et al., 1998; Bui et al., 2010).

Statistical techniques (Girju, 2003; Do et al., 2011) rely on building probabilistic models over features extracted via third-party NLP tools such as Wordnet (Miller, 1994). Deep-learning techniques map words and features into low-dimensional dense vectors, which may alleviate the feature sparsity problem. The most frequent used sequence to sequence models are feed-forward network (Ponti and Korhonen, 2017), long short-term memory networks (Kruengkrai et al., 2017; Dasgupta et al., 2018; Martínez-Cámara et al., 2017) convolutional neural networks (Jin et al., 2020; Kruengkrai et al., 2017; Wang et al., 2016), recurrent neural networks (Yao et al., 2019), gated recurrent units (Chen et al., 2016) which embed semantic and syntactic information in local consecutive word sequences (Yao et al., 2019). Later unsupervised training model such as BERT (Devlin et al., 2018; Sun et al., 2019), RoBERTa (Becquin, 2020), graph convolution network (Zhang et al., 2018), graph attention networks and joint model for entity relation extraction (Li et al., 2017; Wang and Lu, 2020; Zhao et al., 2021; Bekoulis et al., 2018).

In this work, we base our model on T5 (Raffel et al., 2020), a sequence-to-sequence transformer model, pre-trained on a mixture of denoising objective and 25 supervised tasks such as machine translation, linguistic acceptability, abstractive summarization or question answering. The unsupervised denoising objective randomly replaces spans of the input with different mask tokens, and generates contents of these masked spans prefixed with these special mask tokens. Furthermore, our work shares similarities with pointer-network (Vinyals et al., 2015) based generative framework for various NER subtasks introduced by Yan et al. (2021). Contrastively, our work is more adapted to low-resource scenarios, as no extra parameters were added to our system, at the cost of errors, which can happen in the postprocessing matching step.

3 Problem Description

CASE-2022 shared task challenge (Tan et al., 2022a) aimed for event causality identification, and extraction in casual news corpus (Tan et al., 2022b). It comprised of two subtasks, namely casual event classification (Subtask 1) and cause-effect-signal span detection (Subtask 2)[2]. Subtask 2 aims on extracting the spans corresponding to cause-effect-signal (CES) triplets, as shown in Figure 1. We trained a generative seq2seq model to address this challenge and extracted the CES triplets using an iterative procedure (see Section 4.1).

The dataset statistics are presented in Table 1. The number of total sentences is given by the column *#Sentences*, whereas a total number of CES triplets is in column *#Relations*. Column *#Signals* shows how many signal annotations were present in the total number of CES triplets.

[2]We participated in both subtasks, but report on Subtask 2 in this paper. For Subtask 1, we refer reader to our standalone publication (Burdisso et al., 2022).

Split	#Sentences	#Relations	#Signals
Train	160	183	118 (64%)
Dev	15	18	10 (56%)
Test	89	119	98 (82%)

Table 1: Dataset statistics. See text for details.

4 Methodology

4.1 Language Model Training

We utilize T5 (Raffel et al., 2020), a pre-trained autoregressive transformer-based language model trained on a mixture of unsupervised and supervised tasks that require language understanding. The model is conditioned $n \times 3$ times for each example, as there can be n CES triplets in one sentence (up to $n = 4$ triplets in training data). Each time, we condition the language model 3 times for every example and its corresponding CES triplet, generating a different triplet component (cause, effect, and signal) to learn to generate the entire CES triplet. As these triplets are unordered, we uniformly sample a random path among them (e.g., 2-3-1-4, for sample with four triplets) during training. We only train with as many triplets, as available in the training data. We now describe the input format, further illustrated in Appendix B.

Firstly, the model's encoder is conditioned with sentence tokens `<sentence>` followed by the history of already generated CES triplets for this example (empty if there was none) as

```
<sentence> _history : <history>.
```

The history is always prepended with `_history:` tokens. The content of the history are the already generated triplets. Each part of the triplet is prepended with its corresponding `_cause:`, or `_effect:`, or `_signal:` sequence. Concurrently, model's decoder is prefixed with `_cause:` sequence. In this case, the probability of cause sequence is maximized.

Secondly, the model is conditioned with sentence tokens `<sentence>` and cause tokens `<cause>`, prepended with `_cause:` token as

```
<sentence> _cause : <cause>
_history : <history>.
```

This time, the decoder is prompted with `_effect:` prefix, and the probability of effect sequence is maximized.

Thirdly, the model is conditioned with sentence tokens `<sentence>`, cause tokens `<cause>`, and effect tokens `<effect>` with `_effect:` token prepended as

```
<sentence> _cause : <cause> _effect
: <effect> _history : <history>.
```

Analogically, decoder is prompted with `_signal:` prefix and probability of signal sequence is maximized. As the signal might not always be part of the CES triplet, we let the model generate `_empty` token in these cases.

4.2 Experimental Details

We use cross-entropy (CE) loss to train the T5. We firstly average CE loss over tokens, then over inputs per example (for all CES triplets), and then across mini-batch. We use greedy search to generate the sequences. In inference time, we always generate 4 CES triplets for each sentence, as that is the maximum we observed in the training data.

As we don't constrain the decoding, the generated sequence does not have to match certain sub-string in the input. However, the extractive task requires inserting tags around a cause, effect, or signal span inside the input sentence. Therefore we map the generated sequences back to the input sentence via F1 matching. In particular, for each generated sequence, we find the most similar substring in the input, where the similarity is measured via token-level F1 score. We utilize an efficient F1 matching technique, which prunes out a significant part of the search space, presented in the Appendix C.1 of Fajcik et al. (2021)[3]. We base our implementation on PyTorch (Paszke et al., 2019), Transformers (Wolf et al., 2020) libraries and use AdamW (Loshchilov and Hutter, 2017) for optimization. We tune hyperparameters via HyperOpt (Bergstra et al., 2015) and report the exact hyperparameters in Appendix A.

4.3 Evaluation Metrics

In this section, we describe the metrics we used to evaluate the system.

F1: F1 score was the official main evaluation metric in the challenge. It is computed over B, and I tags in sequence following the BIO tagging scheme for every example and every CES triplet component separately, using `seqeval`[4]. The F1 is then

[3]Implemented at https://shorturl.at/kxEVW.

[4]https://github.com/chakki-works/seqeval.

System	CE	Cause	Effect	Signal	Overall
Baseline	-	-	-	-	2.2
T5-NoHistory	.181	-	-	-	67.7±2
T5-ECS	.168	75.9±5	71.3±4	76.1±5	73,5±2
T5-CES	.183	81.0±4	67.8±2	66.7±5	73.0±2
T5-CES$_{LARGE}$	.159	73.5±8	74.1±4	77.2±7	74.8±2

Table 2: Main results, in terms of Cross-Entropy (CE) and F1, with ± standard deviations on dev data.

averaged firstly across dataset examples, obtaining F1 for each component (*Cause F1*, *Effect F1*, *Signal F1*). *Overall F1* is computed as a weighted average of component examples by their frequency.

CE: is an average token cross-entropy, computed as described in Section 4.2.

ES Acc: is an empty-signal accuracy, i.e., an accuracy of the model predicting no signal span in the CES triplet when given golden cause and effect.

4.4 Baseline Model

As a baseline model, we used the CASE-2022 organizers' provided model for Subtask 2: a random generator that uniformly samples a cause, effect, and signal spans[5] from the sentence. This baseline guarantees the cause and the effect do not overlap.

5 Results & Discussion

We now report the results obtained from averaging at least ten measured performances from 10 checkpoints trained with different seeds[6]. We studied 4 different variants of our system. System T5-CES is our vanilla model described in 4.1, based on T5-base. System T5-CES$_{LARGE}$ is the same model based on T5-large. Unlike T5-CES, system T5-ECS reverses the generation order by generating the first effect and cause, followed by the signal (assuming causal order *effect→cause→signal*, hence the suffix ECS). Lastly, we studied the effect of conditioning the model on the history of already generated triplets. We remove the history from the input at all times in training and predict the four identical CES triplets for each example in test time. Our ablated results are available in Table 2.

Firstly, the model with no history at input performs significantly worse, validating our hypothesis that the model can learn to decrease the probability of the triplets already contained within the input, even from just 160 samples. Secondly, we observed a general trend that *in the Cause F1 T5-CES outperforms T5-ECS* and *in Effect F1, T5-ECS outperforms T5-CES*. This leads to the hypothesis that whichever part of the triplet, cause or effect, is generated first, the language model performs better in its case. Thirdly, we observed that the large model achieved the best results on average. It also achieved our best single-checkpoint performance on the dev set (78.3 Overall F1). However, given the sample size of the dev set, the differences between T5-CES, T5-ECS, and T5-CES$_{LARGE}$ can hardly be deemed significant.

[5]Available at https://shorturl.at/msY04.

[6]Dev set predictions from our best t5-base model are available at https://shorturl.at/bjVZ9.

System	Dev F1	Dev$_1$ F1	Dev$_2$ F1	Dev ES Acc	Test F1
T5-ECS	77.7	80.9	71.1	82	43.4
T5-CES$_{LARGE}$	78.3	77.4	80.0	70	43.7
T5-CES	77.5	79.6	73.3	70	**48.8**

Table 3: Top checkpoints submitted to the leaderboard.

Next we present our results on the test set in Table 3. We submitted checkpoints with the best overall F1 score on the dev set (Dev F1) to the leaderboard while varying the model types. We observed a significant drop in performance on the test data. As the annotation on the test data is not released at the time of writing, the causes of this performance drop remain unknown. We hypothesize it could have been caused by a covariate shift in the test data, as supported by #Signals statistics in Table 1.

Additionally, we include extra statistics (Dev$_0$ F1, Dev$_1$ F1, Dev ES Acc) for our best checkpoints. We expected the performance on the dev subset with two triplets (Dev$_2$ F1) per example to be worse than on the dev subset with one triplet per sentence (Dev$_1$ F1). Performance-wise this does not always seem to be the case. Upon manual analysis, we found that the model often failed in the second round of triplet extraction. We found 2 LM hallucinations out of 18 dev samples in the second generation round.

6 Inference Speed

Measuring the inference speed on test set, we used Intel i5-based 2080Ti GPU workstation. The inference of 4 CES triplets without postprocessing per 1 sentence example took 1.46 seconds on average. The postprocessing runtime was negligible, taking 0.025 seconds per sentence example on average.

7 Conclusion

In this work, we have analyzed our CASE-2022 2nd place submissions on Subtask 2. We showed that a generative model could extract cause-effect-signal triplets at the competitive level using just 160 annotated samples. We investigated causal assumptions about the generation order of cause and effect to answer the research question *"should cause be identified first, and only then effect, or vice-versa?"* and found that while the Overall F1 won't change significantly, whichever component was generated first achieved better performance on average (Cause first achieved better Cause-F1, and Effect first Effect-F1 respectively). Finally, we showed the F1 difference between the dev subset with 1 or 2 causal triplets per sentence is negligible.

Acknowledgements

This work was supported by CRiTERIA, an EU project, funded under the Horizon 2020 programme, grant agreement no. 101021866 and the Ministry of Education, Youth and Sports of the Czech Republic through the e-INFRA CZ (ID:90140). Esaú Villatoro-Tello, was supported partially by Idiap, SNI CONACyT, and UAM-Cuajimalpa Mexico.

References

Biswanath Barik, Erwin Marsi, and Pinar Øzturk. 2016. Event causality extraction from natural science literature.

Brandon Beamer, Alla Rozovskaya, and Roxana Girju. 2008. Automatic semantic relation extraction with multiple boundary generation. In *AAAI*, pages 824–829.

Guillaume Becquin. 2020. Gbe at fincausal 2020, task 2: span-based causality extraction for financial documents. In *Proceedings of the 1st Joint Workshop on Financial Narrative Processing and MultiLing Financial Summarisation*, pages 40–44.

Giannis Bekoulis, Johannes Deleu, Thomas Demeester, and Chris Develder. 2018. Adversarial training for multi-context joint entity and relation extraction. *arXiv preprint arXiv:1808.06876*.

James Bergstra, Brent Komer, Chris Eliasmith, Dan Yamins, and David D Cox. 2015. Hyperopt: a python library for model selection and hyperparameter optimization. *Computational Science & Discovery*, 8(1):014008.

Quoc-Chinh Bui, Breanndán Ó Nualláin, Charles A Boucher, and Peter Sloot. 2010. Extracting causal relations on hiv drug resistance from literature. *BMC bioinformatics*, 11(1):1–11.

Sergio Burdisso, Juan Zuluaga-Gomez, Martin Fajcik, Esaú Villatoro-Tello, Muskaan Singh, Petr Motlicek, and Pavel Smrz. 2022. IDIAPers @ causal news corpus 2022: Efficient causal relation identification through a prompt-based few-shot approach. In *The 5th Workshop on Challenges and Applications of Automated Extraction of Socio-political Events from Text (CASE @ EMNLP 2022)*. Association for Computational Linguistics.

Tommaso Caselli and Piek Vossen. 2017. The event storyline corpus: A new benchmark for causal and temporal relation extraction. In *Proceedings of the Events and Stories in the News Workshop*, pages 77–86.

Jifan Chen, Qi Zhang, Pengfei Liu, Xipeng Qiu, and Xuan-Jing Huang. 2016. Implicit discourse relation detection via a deep architecture with gated relevance network. In *Proceedings of the 54th Annual Meeting of the Association for Computational Linguistics (Volume 1: Long Papers)*, pages 1726–1735.

Tirthankar Dasgupta, Rupsa Saha, Lipika Dey, and Abir Naskar. 2018. Automatic extraction of causal relations from text using linguistically informed deep neural networks. In *Proceedings of the 19th Annual SIGdial Meeting on Discourse and Dialogue*, pages 306–316.

Jacob Devlin, Ming-Wei Chang, Kenton Lee, and Kristina Toutanova. 2018. Bert: Pre-training of deep bidirectional transformers for language understanding. *arXiv preprint arXiv:1810.04805*.

Quang Do, Yee Seng Chan, and Dan Roth. 2011. Minimally supervised event causality identification. In *Proceedings of the 2011 Conference on Empirical Methods in Natural Language Processing*, pages 294–303.

Jesse Dunietz, Gregory Burnham, Akash Bharadwaj, Owen Rambow, Jennifer Chu-Carroll, and David Ferrucci. 2020. To test machine comprehension, start by defining comprehension. *arXiv preprint arXiv:2005.01525*.

Martin Fajcik, Martin Docekal, Karel Ondrej, and Pavel Smrz. 2021. R2-D2: A modular baseline for open-domain question answering. In *Findings of the Association for Computational Linguistics: EMNLP 2021*, pages 854–870, Punta Cana, Dominican Republic. Association for Computational Linguistics.

Martin Fajcik, Josef Jon, Martin Docekal, and Pavel Smrz. 2020. BUT-FIT at SemEval-2020 task 5: Automatic detection of counterfactual statements with deep pre-trained language representation models. In *Proceedings of the Fourteenth Workshop on Semantic Evaluation*, pages 437–444, Barcelona (online). International Committee for Computational Linguistics.

Amir Feder, Katherine A Keith, Emaad Manzoor, Reid Pryzant, Dhanya Sridhar, Zach Wood-Doughty, Jacob Eisenstein, Justin Grimmer, Roi Reichart, Margaret E Roberts, et al. 2021a. Causal inference in natural language processing: Estimation, prediction, interpretation and beyond. *arXiv preprint arXiv:2109.00725*.

Amir Feder, Nadav Oved, Uri Shalit, and Roi Reichart. 2021b. Causalm: Causal model explanation through counterfactual language models. *Computational Linguistics*, 47(2):333–386.

Daniela Garcia et al. 1997. Coatis, an nlp system to locate expressions of actions connected by causality links. In *International Conference on Knowledge Engineering and Knowledge Management*, pages 347–352. Springer.

Roxana Girju. 2003. Automatic detection of causal relations for question answering. In *Proceedings of the ACL 2003 workshop on Multilingual summarization and question answering*, pages 76–83.

Roxana Girju, Preslav Nakov, Vivi Nastase, Stan Szpakowicz, Peter Turney, and Deniz Yuret. 2009. Classification of semantic relations between nominals. *Language Resources and Evaluation*, 43(2):105–121.

Ashwin Ittoo and Gosse Bouma. 2013. Minimally-supervised learning of domain-specific causal relations using an open-domain corpus as knowledge base. *Data & Knowledge Engineering*, 88:142–163.

Xianxian Jin, Xinzhi Wang, Xiangfeng Luo, Subin Huang, and Shengwei Gu. 2020. Inter-sentence and implicit causality extraction from chinese corpus. In *Pacific-Asia Conference on Knowledge Discovery and Data Mining*, pages 739–751. Springer.

Yohan Jo, Seojin Bang, Chris Reed, and Eduard Hovy. 2021. Classifying argumentative relations using logical mechanisms and argumentation schemes. *Transactions of the Association for Computational Linguistics*, 9:721–739.

Ning Kang, Bharat Singh, Chinh Bui, Zubair Afzal, Erik M van Mulligen, and Jan A Kors. 2014. Knowledge-based extraction of adverse drug events from biomedical text. *BMC bioinformatics*, 15(1):1–8.

Christopher SG Khoo, Syin Chan, and Yun Niu. 2000. Extracting causal knowledge from a medical database using graphical patterns. In *Proceedings of the 38th annual meeting of the association for computational linguistics*, pages 336–343.

Christopher SG Khoo, Jaklin Kornfilt, Robert N Oddy, and Sung Hyon Myaeng. 1998. Automatic extraction of cause-effect information from newspaper text without knowledge-based inferencing. *Literary and Linguistic Computing*, 13(4):177–186.

Canasai Kruengkrai, Kentaro Torisawa, Chikara Hashimoto, Julien Kloetzer, Jong-Hoon Oh, and Masahiro Tanaka. 2017. Improving event causality recognition with multiple background knowledge sources using multi-column convolutional neural networks. In *Proceedings of the AAAI Conference on Artificial Intelligence*, volume 31.

Fei Li, Meishan Zhang, Guohong Fu, and Donghong Ji. 2017. A neural joint model for entity and relation extraction from biomedical text. *BMC bioinformatics*, 18(1):1–11.

Ilya Loshchilov and Frank Hutter. 2017. Decoupled weight decay regularization. *arXiv preprint arXiv:1711.05101*.

Eugenio Martínez-Cámara, Vered Shwartz, Iryna Gurevych, and Ido Dagan. 2017. Neural disambiguation of causal lexical markers based on context. In *IWCS 2017—12th International Conference on Computational Semantics—Short papers*.

George A. Miller. 1994. WordNet: A lexical database for English. In *Human Language Technology: Proceedings of a Workshop held at Plainsboro, New Jersey, March 8-11, 1994*.

Paramita Mirza, Rachele Sprugnoli, Sara Tonelli, and Manuela Speranza. 2014. Annotating causality in the tempeval-3 corpus. In *Proceedings of the EACL 2014 Workshop on Computational Approaches to Causality in Language (CAtoCL)*, pages 10–19.

Nasrin Mostafazadeh, Alyson Grealish, Nathanael Chambers, James Allen, and Lucy Vanderwende. 2016. Caters: Causal and temporal relation scheme for semantic annotation of event structures. In *Proceedings of the Fourth Workshop on Events*, pages 51–61.

Adam Paszke, Sam Gross, Francisco Massa, Adam Lerer, James Bradbury, Gregory Chanan, Trevor Killeen, Zeming Lin, Natalia Gimelshein, Luca Antiga, Alban Desmaison, Andreas Kopf, Edward Yang, Zachary DeVito, Martin Raison, Alykhan Tejani, Sasank Chilamkurthy, Benoit Steiner, Lu Fang, Junjie Bai, and Soumith Chintala. 2019. Pytorch: An imperative style, high-performance deep learning library. In H. Wallach, H. Larochelle, A. Beygelzimer, F. d'Alché-Buc, E. Fox, and R. Garnett, editors, *Advances in Neural Information Processing Systems 32*, pages 8024–8035. Curran Associates, Inc.

Edoardo Ponti and Anna-Leena Korhonen. 2017. Event-related features in feedforward neural networks contribute to identifying implicit causal relations in discourse.

Kira Radinsky, Sagie Davidovich, and Shaul Markovitch. 2012. Learning causality for news events prediction. In *Proceedings of the 21st international conference on World Wide Web*, pages 909–918.

Colin Raffel, Noam Shazeer, Adam Roberts, Katherine Lee, Sharan Narang, Michael Matena, Yanqi Zhou, Wei Li, Peter J Liu, et al. 2020. Exploring the limits of transfer learning with a unified text-to-text transformer. *J. Mach. Learn. Res.*, 21(140):1–67.

Dhanya Sridhar and Lise Getoor. 2019. Estimating causal effects of tone in online debates. *arXiv preprint arXiv:1906.04177*.

Cong Sun, Zhihao Yang, Ling Luo, Lei Wang, Yin Zhang, Hongfei Lin, and Jian Wang. 2019. A deep learning approach with deep contextualized word representations for chemical–protein interaction extraction from biomedical literature. *IEEE Access*, 7:151034–151046.

Chenhao Tan, Lillian Lee, and Bo Pang. 2014. The effect of wording on message propagation: Topic- and author-controlled natural experiments on twitter. *arXiv preprint arXiv:1405.1438*.

Fiona Anting Tan, Ali Hürriyetoğlu, Tommaso Caselli, Nelleke Oostdijk, Hansi Hettiarachchi, Tadashi Nomoto, Onur Uca, and Farhana Ferdousi Liza. 2022a. Event causality identification with causal news corpus - shared task 3, CASE 2022. In *Proceedings of the 5th Workshop on Challenges and Applications of Automated Extraction of Socio-political Events from Text (CASE 2022)*, Online. Association for Computational Linguistics.

Fiona Anting Tan, Ali Hürriyetoğlu, Tommaso Caselli, Nelleke Oostdijk, Tadashi Nomoto, Hansi Hettiarachchi, Iqra Ameer, Onur Uca, Farhana Ferdousi Liza, and Tiancheng Hu. 2022b. The causal news corpus: Annotating causal relations in event sentences from news. In *Proceedings of the Language Resources and Evaluation Conference*, pages 2298–2310, Marseille, France. European Language Resources Association.

Fiona Anting Tan, Xinyu Zuo, and See-Kiong Ng. 2022c. Unicausal: Unified benchmark and model for causal text mining.

Victor Veitch, Dhanya Sridhar, and David Blei. 2020. Adapting text embeddings for causal inference. In *Conference on Uncertainty in Artificial Intelligence*, pages 919–928. PMLR.

Oriol Vinyals, Meire Fortunato, and Navdeep Jaitly. 2015. Pointer networks. *Advances in neural information processing systems*, 28.

Jue Wang and Wei Lu. 2020. Two are better than one: Joint entity and relation extraction with table-sequence encoders. *arXiv preprint arXiv:2010.03851*.

Linlin Wang, Zhu Cao, Gerard De Melo, and Zhiyuan Liu. 2016. Relation classification via multi-level attention cnns. In *Proceedings of the 54th Annual Meeting of the Association for Computational Linguistics (Volume 1: Long Papers)*, pages 1298–1307.

Bonnie Webber, Rashmi Prasad, Alan Lee, and Aravind Joshi. 2019. The penn discourse treebank 3.0 annotation manual. *Philadelphia, University of Pennsylvania*, 35:108.

Thomas Wolf, Lysandre Debut, Victor Sanh, Julien Chaumond, Clement Delangue, Anthony Moi, Pierric Cistac, Tim Rault, Remi Louf, Morgan Funtowicz, Joe Davison, Sam Shleifer, Patrick von Platen, Clara Ma, Yacine Jernite, Julien Plu, Canwen Xu, Teven Le Scao, Sylvain Gugger, Mariama Drame, Quentin Lhoest, and Alexander Rush. 2020. Transformers: State-of-the-art natural language processing. In *Proceedings of the 2020 Conference on Empirical Methods in Natural Language Processing: System Demonstrations*, pages 38–45, Online. Association for Computational Linguistics.

Zach Wood-Doughty, Ilya Shpitser, and Mark Dredze. 2018. Challenges of using text classifiers for causal inference. In *Proceedings of the Conference on Empirical Methods in Natural Language Processing. Conference on Empirical Methods in Natural Language Processing*, volume 2018, page 4586. NIH Public Access.

Hang Yan, Tao Gui, Junqi Dai, Qipeng Guo, Zheng Zhang, and Xipeng Qiu. 2021. A unified generative framework for various ner subtasks. In *Proceedings of the 59th Annual Meeting of the Association for Computational Linguistics and the 11th International Joint Conference on Natural Language Processing (Volume 1: Long Papers)*, pages 5808–5822.

Liang Yao, Chengsheng Mao, and Yuan Luo. 2019. Graph convolutional networks for text classification. In *Proceedings of the AAAI conference on artificial intelligence*, volume 33, pages 7370–7377.

Justine Zhang, Sendhil Mullainathan, and Cristian Danescu-Niculescu-Mizil. 2020. Quantifying the causal effects of conversational tendencies. *Proceedings of the ACM on Human-Computer Interaction*, 4(CSCW2):1–24.

Yuhao Zhang, Peng Qi, and Christopher D Manning. 2018. Graph convolution over pruned dependency trees improves relation extraction. *arXiv preprint arXiv:1809.10185*.

Shan Zhao, Minghao Hu, Zhiping Cai, and Fang Liu. 2021. Modeling dense cross-modal interactions for joint entity-relation extraction. In *Proceedings of the Twenty-Ninth International Conference on International Joint Conferences on Artificial Intelligence*, pages 4032–4038.

Hyperparameter	Value
learning rate	.0002
hidden dropout	.1436
attention dropout	.4719
weight decay	.0214
minibatch size	8
warmup proportion	.1570
scheduler	constant (no lr decrease)
max steps	10,000
max gradient norm	1

Table 4: Hyperparameter setting used in this work.

A Hyperparameters

In Table 4, we report the exact hyperparameters used when fine-tuning T5. Warmup proportion, weight decay, and dropouts are in the (0,1) range (for instance, .4719 means 47.19%).

B Example of Inputs

The input format and label format for a single training example, a sentence with 2 CES triplets, are illustrated in Figure. 2.

ENCODER INPUT: _" _I _think _independent _film _producers _have _the _responsibility _to _document _what _mainstream _media _failed _to _report _on . _" _But _on _the _ e ve _of _the _protest s _ ' _second _anniversary _ , _Chan _claims _all _of _Hong _Kong _ ' _ s _major _cinema s _are _refus ing _to _show _his _film _ , _the _result _ , _ he _suspect s _ , _of _creep ing _self - censor ship _as _businesses _shy _away _from _off ending _Beijing _ . **_history :**
DECODER PREFIX: **_cause :**
DECODER TARGET: **_cause :** _businesses _shy _away _from _off ending _Beijing

ENCODER INPUT: _" _I _think _independent _film _producers _have _the _responsibility _to _document _what _mainstream _media _failed _to _report _on . _" _But _on _the _ e ve _of _the _protest s _ ' _second _anniversary _ , _Chan _claims _all _of _Hong _Kong _ ' _ s _major _cinema s _are _refus ing _to _show _his _film _ , _the _result _ , _ he _suspect s _ , _of _creep ing _self - censor ship _as _businesses _shy _away _from _off ending _Beijing _ . **_cause :** business e s _shy _away _from _off ending _Beijing **_history :**
DECODER PREFIX: **_effect :**
DECODER TARGET: **_effect :** _creep ing _self - censor ship

ENCODER INPUT: _" _I _think _independent _film _producers _have _the _responsibility _to _document _what _mainstream _media _failed _to _report _on . _" _But _on _the _ e ve _of _the _protest s _ ' _second _anniversary _ , _Chan _claims _all _of _Hong _Kong _ ' _ s _major _cinema s _are _refus ing _to _show _his _film _ , _the _result _ , _ he _suspect s _ , _of _creep ing _self - censor ship _as _businesses _shy _away _from _off ending _Beijing _ . **_cause :** business e s _shy _away _from _off ending _Beijing **_effect :** cre e ping _self - censor ship **_history :**
DECODER PREFIX: **_signal :**
DECODER TARGET: **_signal :** _as

ENCODER INPUT: _" _I _think _independent _film _producers _have _the _responsibility _to _document _what _mainstream _media _failed _to _report _on . _" _But _on _the _ e ve _of _the _protest s _ ' _second _anniversary _ , _Chan _claims _all _of _Hong _Kong _ ' _ s _major _cinema s _are _refus ing _to _show _his _film _ , _the _result _ , _ he _suspect s _ , _of _creep ing _self - censor ship _as _businesses _shy _away _from _off ending _Beijing _ . **_history : _cause :** _businesses _shy _away _from _off ending _Beijing **_effect :** _creep ing _self - censor ship **_signal :** _as
DECODER PREFIX: **_cause :**
DECODER TARGET: **_cause :** _creep ing _self - censor ship

ENCODER INPUT: _" _I _think _independent _film _producers _have _the _responsibility _to _document _what _mainstream _media _failed _to _report _on . _" _But _on _the _ e ve _of _the _protest s _ ' _second _anniversary _ , _Chan _claims _all _of _Hong _Kong _ ' _ s _major _cinema s _are _refus ing _to _show _his _film _ , _the _result _ , _ he _suspect s _ , _of _creep ing _self - censor ship _as _businesses _shy _away _from _off ending _Beijing _ . **_cause :** cre e ping _self - censor ship **_history : _cause :** _businesses _shy _away _from _off ending _Beijing **_effect :** _creep ing _self - censor ship **_signal :** _as
DECODER PREFIX: **_effect :**
DECODER TARGET: **_effect :** _all _of _Hong _Kong _ ' _ s _major _cinema s _are _refus ing _to _show _his _film

ENCODER INPUT: _" _I _think _independent _film _producers _have _the _responsibility _to _document _what _mainstream _media _failed _to _report _on . _" _But _on _the _ e ve _of _the _protest s _ ' _second _anniversary _ , _Chan _claims _all _of _Hong _Kong _ ' _ s _major _cinema s _are _refus ing _to _show _his _film _ , _the _result _ , _ he _suspect s _ , _of _creep ing _self - censor ship _as _businesses _shy _away _from _off ending _Beijing _ . **_cause :** cre e ping _self - censor ship **_effect :** all _of _Hong _Kong _ ' _ s _major _cinema s _are _refus ing _to _show _his _film **_history : _cause :** _businesses _shy _away _from _off ending _Beijing **_effect :** _creep ing _self - censor ship **_signal :** _as
DECODER PREFIX: **_signal :**
DECODER TARGET: **_signal :** _the _result _ , _ he _suspect s _ , _of

Figure 2: Example of tokenized inputs for a sentence with two annotated CES triplets. Phrases "ENCODER INPUT". "DECODER PREFIX" and "DECODER TARGET" are not parts of the input, and are included for illustrative purposes only. Special sequences (`_cause:`, `_effect:`, `_signal:`, `_history:`) used between concatenated parts of the input are in bold.

NoisyAnnot@ Causal News Corpus 2022: Causality Detection using Multiple Annotation Decisions

Quynh Anh Nguyen[1, 2] **Arka Mitra**[2]
[1] University of Milan [2] ETH Zürich
quynguyen@ethz.ch, amitra@ethz.ch

Abstract

The paper describes the work that has been submitted to the 5th workshop on Challenges and Applications of Automated Extraction of socio-political events from text (CASE 2022). The work is associated with Subtask 1 of Shared Task 3 that aims to detect causality in protest news corpus. The authors used different large language models with customized cross-entropy loss functions that exploit annotation information. The experiments showed that *bert-based-uncased* with refined cross-entropy outperformed the others, achieving a F1 score of 0.8501 on the Causal News Corpus dataset.

1 Introduction

A causal relationship in a sentence implies an underlying semantic dependency between the two main clauses. The clauses in these sentences are generally connected by markers which can have different parts of tags in the sentence. Moreover, the markers can be either implicit or explicit and for these reasons, one cannot rely on regex or dictionary-based systems. Thus, there is a need to investigate the context of the sentences. For the given task, we exploited different large language models that provide a contextual representation of sentences to tackle causality detection.

Shared task 3 in CASE-2022 (Tan et al., 2022a) aims for causality detection in news corpus, which can be structured as a text classification problem with binary labels. Pre-trained transformer-based models (Vaswani et al., 2017) have shown success on tackling a wide range of NLP tasks including text generation, text classification, etc. The authors look into inter-annotation agreements and number of experts and how they can be included in the loss to improve the performance of the pre-trained models.

The main contributions of the paper are as follows:

1. Extensive experimentation with different large language models.
2. Incorporation of additional annotation information, i.e inter-annotation agreement and the number of annotators, to the loss.

The remaining paper is formulated as follows: Section 2 reviews the related work, section 3 describes the dataset on which the work has been done, section 4 discusses the methodology used in the paper, the following section discusses the results and provides an ablation of the various loss functions introduced and finally, section 6 concludes the paper and suggests future works.

2 Related Work

Multiple annotations on a single sample reduce the chances of the labelling to be incorrect or bias being incorporated into the dataset (Snow et al., 2008). Including multiple annotators also leads to disagreement among the labels that have been provided by them. The final or gold annotation is then usually determined by majority voting (Sabou et al., 2014) or by using the label of an "expert" (Waseem and Hovy, 2016). There are also different methodologies which do not use majority voting to select the "ground truth".

Expectation Maximization algorithm has been used to account for the annotator error (Dawid and Skene, 1979). Entropy metrics have been developed to identify the performance of the annotators(Waterhouse, 2012; Hovy et al., 2013; Gordon et al., 2021). Multi-task learning is also used to deal with disagreement in the labels (Fornaciari et al., 2021; Liu et al., 2019; Cohn and Specia, 2013; Davani et al., 2022). There are methods which include the annotation disagreement into the loss function for part of speech tagging (Plank et al., 2014; Prabhakaran et al., 2012) on SVMs and perceptron model. The present work considers the inter-annotator agreement as well as the number

Proceedings of the 5th Workshop on Challenges and Applications of Automated Extraction of Socio-political Events from Text (CASE), pages 79 - 84
December 7-8, 2022

of annotators into the loss function for any model. The work also compares the performance when the annotators who disagree with the majority voting has been ignored.

3 Dataset

The Causal News Corpus dataset (Tan et al., 2022b) consists of 3,559 event sentences extracted from protest event news. Each sample in the dataset contains the text, the corresponding label, the number of experts who annotated the label and the degree of agreement among the experts. Figure 1 shows a sample from the provided training set. The training data is fairly balanced, containing 1603 sentences with a causal structure and 1322 sentences without a causal structure. Also, the number of causal and non-causal sentences in the validation set does not differ significantly. Finally, 311 news articles have been used as test set for evaluation.

```
{'index': 'train_01_10',
 'text': "The farmworkers ' strike
resumed on Tuesday when their demands
were not met .",
 'label': 1,
 'agreement': 1.0,
 'num_votes': 3,
 'sample_set': 'train_01'}
```

Figure 1: A datapoint from the provided training data.

Besides the binary labels, the Causal News Corpus dataset also provides additional information regarding the number of experts who labeled the sentence and the percentage of agreement between them. Figure 1 shows that the number of experts who annotated the text *"The farmworkers'strike resumed on Tuesday when their demands were not met."* is 3 (num_votes = 3). Also, all of the experts labeled the sentence to be causal so the agreement is 1.0 (100% agreement) and the label is 1. In case only one of three experts assigned label 1 to the previous text, the three predictors `num_votes`, `agreement`, `label` would now become 3, $\frac{2}{3}$, 0 respectively. In this paper, the authors exploit this information to give the model more prior and thus potentially improve the model's performance, which has been described in more detail in section 4.

4 Methodology

The section discusses the pipeline, the different types of loss functions that were implemented, and the experimental details that have been used in the third shared task for CASE 2022 (Tan et al., 2022a).

4.1 Pipeline

The authors finetuned large language models with different loss functions to tackle Subtask 1 in Shared Task 3 of CASE@EMNLP-2022, causality detection in a given sentence. The problem can be reformulated as a binary classification where the model predicts whether the sentence is causal or not. Since contextual awareness plays an essential role in handling this specific task, the authors used several transformer-based models, namely, BERT (Devlin et al., 2019), FinBERT (Liu et al., 2020), XLNET (Yang et al., 2019) and RoBERTa (Zhuang et al., 2021).

The given sentence is first tokenized by a tokenizer from the corresponding pretrained model architecture provided by HuggingFace (Wolf et al., 2020). The vector output from the tokenization stage is then fed as input to the model. The most informative token is the classification token ([CLS]), which is a special token that can be used as a sentence representation. The [CLS] token is then passed through a feed-forward network to generate logits. The softmax over the logits gives us the probability of whether the sentence is causal or not. For each model, the authors experimented with cross-entropy loss and proposed two loss functions described in detail in subsection 4.2.

4.2 Loss Functions

Cross Entropy Loss The loss of the classification task can be represented by a simple cross-entropy loss, as shown in Equation 1:

$$L = \frac{1}{M}\sum_{i=1}^{M}(-y_i^{true}log(y_i^{pred}) - (1-y_i^{true})log(1-y_i^{pred})) \quad (1)$$

where y_i^{true} and y_i^{pred} denote the true label and the predicted label for the ith input in a batch of M sentences.

Noisy Cross Entropy Loss The dataset not only provides the standard information about {`text`, `label`}, but also contains the information about the number of experts who annotated the sentence's label, and proportion of agreement between them. The authors have considered the annotation by each of the experts to be the true label for the sentence. For a sentence with n expert annotations (`num_votes` $= n$) and r percent of agreement (`agreement` $= r$), the loss for each sentence can be written as shown in Equation 2.

$$L = \begin{cases} (-rlog(y^{pred}) \\ -(1-r)log(1-y^{pred})), & \text{if } y^{true} = 1, \\ (-(1-r)log(y^{pred}) \\ -rlog(1-y^{pred})), & \text{if } y^{true} = 0. \end{cases} \tag{2}$$

The equations can be combined and the loss for a batch of M sentences can be rewritten as:

$$\begin{aligned} L = & \frac{1}{\sum_{i=1}^{M} n_i} \sum_{i=1}^{M} (-y_i^{true} n_i (r_i log(y_i^{pred}) \\ & + (1-r_i) log(1-y_i^{pred})) \\ & - (1-y_i^{true}) n_i (r_i log(1-y_i^{pred}) \\ & + (1-r_i) log(y_i^{pred}))) \end{aligned} \tag{3}$$

.

The different annotations from all the experts has been considered, adding more information to the model. Equation 3 takes the n votes from the different experts into account, out of which $n \times r$ times it is assigned the correct label, and the incorrect label has been used the other $n \times (1-r)$ times. If the labels from the different experts are taken directly, there will be conflicts in the labels when the experts disagree. Considering the loss for one sentence when the true label is 1, the derivative of the loss is shown in Equation 4. Figure 2 shows that the loss is minimized when y^{pred} is equal to r and its minima shifts from 1 to 0 as the level of agreement decreases when the true label is 1. A similar profile is obtained when the true label is considered to be 0. The formulation pushes the solution to a distribution where the ideal output is not a one-hot encoding, which is similar to the label smoothing method. Label smoothing was initially proposed by Szegedy et al. (Szegedy et al., 2016) to improve the performance of the Inception architecture on the ImageNet dataset (Deng et al., 2009). In label-smoothing, the ground truth sent to the model is not encoded as a one-hot representation. Since there are conflicts in the annotations and the loss considers all of the noisy data, it has been referred as noisy cross-entropy loss.

$$\frac{\partial L}{\partial y^{pred}} = \frac{y^{pred} - r}{y^{pred}(1-y^{pred})} \tag{4}$$

Refined Cross Entropy Loss The ideal output of the model should be close to the ground truth label. Thus, a modification to loss function should be done to improve the performance. The error occurs when the annotators who have not agreed for a particular label have also been taken into consideration. The number of experts who provided the correct label can also be an important signal to the model. If a sentence has been given a label by a more significant number of experts, the model should be penalized more if the sentence is misclassified. The new loss, over a batch of M sentences, can thus be written as :

$$\begin{aligned} L = & \frac{1}{\sum_{i=1}^{M} n_i r_i} \sum_{i=1}^{M} (-y_i^{true} n_i r_i log(y_i^{pred}) \\ & - (1-y_i^{true}) n_i r_i log(1-y_i^{pred})) \end{aligned} \tag{5}$$

.

The number of causal and non-causal sentences is almost the same and there is no significant class imbalance. The authors have thus not considered weight penalization to the class with the higher number of samples.

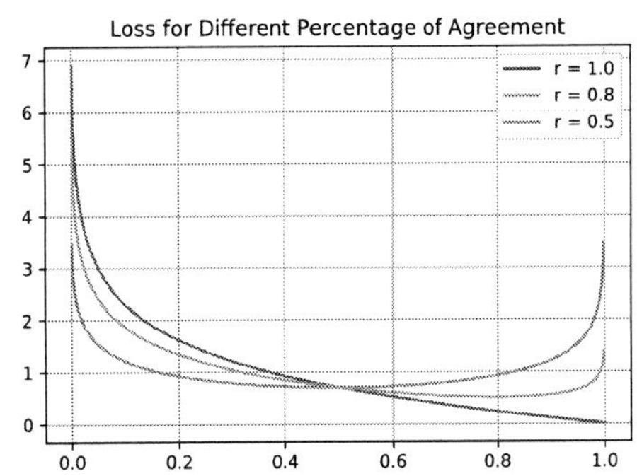

Figure 2: Loss for noisy cross-entropy

4.3 Experimental Details

The experiments have been performed in PyTorch (Paszke et al., 2019) and the authors used the HuggingFace (Wolf et al., 2020) library to generate the pipeline for the different experiments. Each model has been trained for 10 epochs with a learning rate of 5×10^{-5} and a seed of 42 for reproducibility. Various models have been considered and trained with the same set of hyperparameters. The code is made publicly available on Github [1].

[1] `https://github.com/jyanqa/case-2022-causual-event`

Model name	Cross Entropy	Noisy Cross Entropy	Refined Cross Entropy
bert-based-cased (Devlin et al., 2019)	**0.8251**	0.8225	0.8235
bert-base-uncased (Devlin et al., 2019)	0.8283	0.8313	**0.8501**
bert-large-cased (Devlin et al., 2019)	0.7105	**0.7549**	0.7105
xlnet-based-cased (Yang et al., 2019)	0.7953	**0.8216**	0.8199
roberta-base (Zhuang et al., 2021)	0.8279	0.8279	**0.8280**

Table 1: Evaluation of models on different loss functions. The best F1 score of each model is marked in bold.

5 Results and Discussion

In this section, the results of the different models and the different losses are discussed.

Table 1 shows the evaluation of the different models on the validation set. Performances of four in five models, excepting the *bert-base-uncased* case, are enhanced by leveraging the modified cross-entropy loss. In fact, the F1 scores of four models are significantly increasing when we replaced vanilla cross-entropy loss with noisy cross-entropy loss and refined cross-entropy loss. Specifically, model fine-tuned from *bert-base-uncased* investigating Refined cross-entropy loss function yields the best performance in all experimented models with F1 score of 0.8501. On the other hand, *bert-base-cased* is the only pretrained model that does not benefit from customized cross-entropy losses. Adapting vanilla cross-entropy function on *bert-base-cased* model results in its best F1 scores of 0.8251.

The models with noisy and refined cross-entropy loss utilizes the annotated information and thus performs better. The noisy cross-entropy loss is similar to restricting the highest probability output that a model can predict. However, in almost all cases, the degree of agreement was either 1 or $\frac{2}{3}$. In general, the smooth labelling has a value in the range of 0.9 to 1. Different contradicting annotations of labels might make the model face difficulties in learning and yielding an accurate prediction for each sentence. The refined cross-entropy solely considers the labels that do not contradict each other, thus it performs the best.

Moreover, the experiments show that *roberta-based* models achieve lower performance compared to BERT-based models, especially *bert-base-uncased* models. The model pretrained on *bert-large-cased* has been fine-tuned for only one epoch due to computation limitations. Their F1 scores are worse than those of *bert-base-cased* and *bert-base-uncased* models. *bert-base* models result in better performance, as compared to models fine-tuned on *roberta-base*. The reason could be that RoBERTa-based models had not been trained on next sentence prediction (NSP) while BERT-based models were. Causality detection can benefit from NSP. A sentence can be considered to be two relevant clauses that are joined by a causal effect. Thus, knowing if the clauses are relevant or not benefits the task of causality detection.

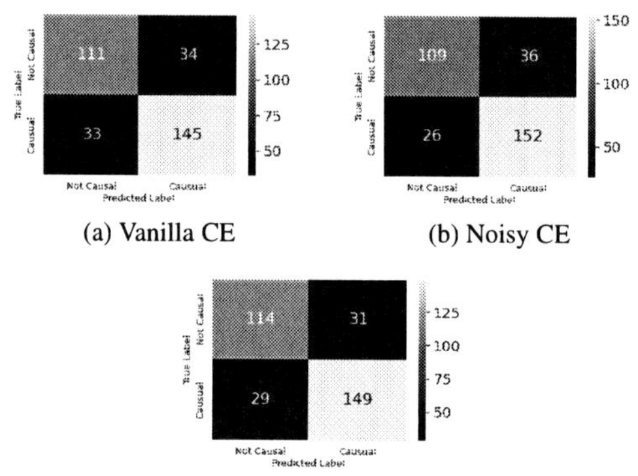

(a) Vanilla CE

(b) Noisy CE

(c) Refined CE

Figure 3: Confusion matrix for the different losses

Figure 3 shows the confusion matrix resulting from *bert-base-uncased* models which result the best F1 scores in all implemented models. Models are generally good at predicting non-causal sentences regardless of the loss function used. In fact, true negatives and true positives are always the highest measures compared to the others. On the other hand, there is a clear trend in the number of true positives when we shift the loss function from vanilla to noisy and refined cross-entropy. In particular, the model yields 145 true positives and is improved to 152 and 149 true positives when we replaced vanilla cross-entropy loss with noisy and refined cross-entropy loss function.

6 Conclusion

This paper presents our work on detecting causal effect relationships in news corpus by fine-tuning Transformers-based models and adapting multiple loss functions. The experiments showed that considering annotation information using customized loss functions significantly improved the model performance in four out of five experimented models. Besides, the experiments show that BERT outperformed RoBERTa, which can be attributed to the fact that RoBERTa is not trained on NSP. Last but not least, the *bert-base-uncased* obtained the best performance amongst all 15 models with an F1-score of 0.8501 in validation set and 84.930 in the test set using the refined cross-entropy loss that takes account of the annotation information presented in the dataset.

The authors plan to look into exploiting the uncertainty of the annotator's information and parameterizing the loss function to further enhance the model's performance.

References

Trevor Cohn and Lucia Specia. 2013. Modelling annotator bias with multi-task gaussian processes: An application to machine translation quality estimation. In *ACL*.

Aida Mostafazadeh Davani, Mark D'iaz, and Vinodkumar Prabhakaran. 2022. Dealing with disagreements: Looking beyond the majority vote in subjective annotations. *Transactions of the Association for Computational Linguistics*, 10:92–110.

A. Philip Dawid and Allan Skene. 1979. Maximum likelihood estimation of observer error-rates using the em algorithm. *Journal of The Royal Statistical Society Series C-applied Statistics*, 28:20–28.

Jia Deng, Wei Dong, Richard Socher, Li-Jia Li, K. Li, and Li Fei-Fei. 2009. Imagenet: A large-scale hierarchical image database. *2009 IEEE Conference on Computer Vision and Pattern Recognition*, pages 248–255.

Jacob Devlin, Ming-Wei Chang, Kenton Lee, and Kristina Toutanova. 2019. BERT: Pre-training of deep bidirectional transformers for language understanding. In *Proceedings of the 2019 Conference of the North American Chapter of the Association for Computational Linguistics: Human Language Technologies, Volume 1 (Long and Short Papers)*, pages 4171–4186, Minneapolis, Minnesota. Association for Computational Linguistics.

Tommaso Fornaciari, Alexandra Uma, Silviu Paun, Barbara Plank, Dirk Hovy, and Massimo Poesio. 2021. Beyond black & white: Leveraging annotator disagreement via soft-label multi-task learning. In *NAACL*.

Mitchell L. Gordon, Kaitlyn Zhou, Kayur Patel, Tatsunori B. Hashimoto, and Michael S. Bernstein. 2021. The disagreement deconvolution: Bringing machine learning performance metrics in line with reality. *Proceedings of the 2021 CHI Conference on Human Factors in Computing Systems*.

Dirk Hovy, Taylor Berg-Kirkpatrick, Ashish Vaswani, and Eduard H. Hovy. 2013. Learning whom to trust with mace. In *NAACL*.

Xiaodong Liu, Pengcheng He, Weizhu Chen, and Jianfeng Gao. 2019. Multi-task deep neural networks for natural language understanding. In *ACL*.

Zhuang Liu, Degen Huang, Kaiyu Huang, Zhuang Li, and Jun Zhao. 2020. Finbert: A pre-trained financial language representation model for financial text mining. In *IJCAI*.

Adam Paszke, Sam Gross, Francisco Massa, Adam Lerer, James Bradbury, Gregory Chanan, Trevor Killeen, Zeming Lin, Natalia Gimelshein, Luca Antiga, Alban Desmaison, Andreas Kopf, Edward Yang, Zachary DeVito, Martin Raison, Alykhan Tejani, Sasank Chilamkurthy, Benoit Steiner, Lu Fang, Junjie Bai, and Soumith Chintala. 2019. Pytorch: An imperative style, high-performance deep learning library. In *Advances in Neural Information Processing Systems 32*, pages 8024–8035. Curran Associates, Inc.

Barbara Plank, Dirk Hovy, and Anders Søgaard. 2014. Learning part-of-speech taggers with inter-annotator agreement loss. In *EACL*.

Vinodkumar Prabhakaran, Michael Bloodgood, Mona T. Diab, B. Dorr, Lori S. Levin, Christine D. Piatko, Owen Rambow, and Benjamin Van Durme. 2012. Statistical modality tagging from rule-based annotations and crowdsourcing. In *ExProM@ACL*.

Marta Sabou, Kalina Bontcheva, Leon Derczynski, and Arno Scharl. 2014. Corpus annotation through crowdsourcing: Towards best practice guidelines. In *LREC*.

Rion Snow, Brendan T. O'Connor, Dan Jurafsky, and A. Ng. 2008. Cheap and fast – but is it good? evaluating non-expert annotations for natural language tasks. In *EMNLP*.

Christian Szegedy, Vincent Vanhoucke, Sergey Ioffe, Jon Shlens, and Zbigniew Wojna. 2016. Rethinking the inception architecture for computer vision. In *2016 IEEE Conference on Computer Vision and Pattern Recognition (CVPR)*, pages 2818–2826.

Fiona Anting Tan, Ali Hürriyetoğlu, Tommaso Caselli, Nelleke Oostdijk, Hansi Hettiarachchi, Tadashi Nomoto, Onur Uca, and Farhana Ferdousi Liza. 2022a. Event causality identification with causal news corpus - shared task 3, CASE 2022. In *Proceedings of the 5th Workshop on Challenges and Applications of Automated Extraction of Socio-political Events from Text (CASE 2022)*, Online. Association for Computational Linguistics.

Fiona Anting Tan, Ali Hürriyetoğlu, Tommaso Caselli, Nelleke Oostdijk, Tadashi Nomoto, Hansi Hettiarachchi, Iqra Ameer, Onur Uca, Farhana Ferdousi Liza, and Tiancheng Hu. 2022b. The causal news corpus: Annotating causal relations in event sentences from news. In *Proceedings of the Language Resources and Evaluation Conference*, pages 2298–2310, Marseille, France. European Language Resources Association.

Ashish Vaswani, Noam Shazeer, Niki Parmar, Jakob Uszkoreit, Llion Jones, Aidan N Gomez, Ł ukasz Kaiser, and Illia Polosukhin. 2017. Attention is all you need. In *Advances in Neural Information Processing Systems*, volume 30. Curran Associates, Inc.

Zeerak Waseem and Dirk Hovy. 2016. Hateful symbols or hateful people? predictive features for hate speech detection on twitter. In *NAACL*.

Tamsyn P. Waterhouse. 2012. Pay by the bit: an information-theoretic metric for collective human judgment. *Proceedings of the 2013 conference on Computer supported cooperative work.*

Thomas Wolf, Lysandre Debut, Victor Sanh, Julien Chaumond, Clement Delangue, Anthony Moi, Pierric Cistac, Tim Rault, Remi Louf, Morgan Funtowicz, Joe Davison, Sam Shleifer, Patrick von Platen, Clara Ma, Yacine Jernite, Julien Plu, Canwen Xu, Teven Le Scao, Sylvain Gugger, Mariama Drame, Quentin Lhoest, and Alexander Rush. 2020. Transformers: State-of-the-art natural language processing. In *Proceedings of the 2020 Conference on Empirical Methods in Natural Language Processing: System Demonstrations*, pages 38–45, Online. Association for Computational Linguistics.

Zhilin Yang, Zihang Dai, Yiming Yang, Jaime G. Carbonell, Ruslan Salakhutdinov, and Quoc V. Le. 2019. Xlnet: Generalized autoregressive pretraining for language understanding. In *NeurIPS*.

Liu Zhuang, Lin Wayne, Shi Ya, and Zhao Jun. 2021. A robustly optimized BERT pre-training approach with post-training. In *Proceedings of the 20th Chinese National Conference on Computational Linguistics*, pages 1218–1227, Huhhot, China. Chinese Information Processing Society of China.

GGNN@Causal News Corpus 2022: Gated Graph Neural Networks for Event Causality Identification from Social-Political News Articles

Paul Trust
University College Cork
Cork, Ireland

Rosane Minghim
University College Cork
Cork, Ireland

Kadusabe Provia
Worldquant University
Louisiana, USA

Evangelos Millos
Dalhousie University
Halifax, Canada

Abstract

The discovery of causality mentions from text is a core cognitive concept and appears in many natural language processing (NLP) applications. In this paper, we study the task of Event Causality Identification (ECI) from social-political news. The aim of the task is to detect causal relationships between event mention pairs in text. Although deep learning models have recently achieved a state-of-the-art performance on many tasks and applications in NLP, most of them still fail to capture rich semantic and syntactic structures within sentences which is key for causality classification. We present a solution for causal event detection from social-political news that captures semantic and syntactic information based on gated graph neural networks (GGNN) and contextualized language embeddings. Experimental results show that our proposed method outperforms the baseline model (BERT (Bidirectional Embeddings from Transformers) in terms of $f1-$score and accuracy.

1 Introduction

Causality is a core cognitive concept and appears in many natural language processing (NLP) tasks. We can define causality in generic terms as a semantic relationship between two arguments known as cause and effect. The occurrence of one argument (cause argument) causes the occurrence of the other (effect argument) (Feder et al., 2021; Tan et al., 2022b).

Event Causality Identification (ECI) is a task that identifies causal relationships between events from a given text (Zuo et al., 2021). To understand how documents containing causal relationships are identified, we present a sample of 5 sentences highlighting causes, effects and causal-markers leading to the rationale for classifying different documents in Figure 1 . Let us take an example of two sentences; Sentence 1: "The protests spread to 15 other towns and resulted in two death and the destruction of property" and sentence 5: "The properties including houses, banks were destroyed" as shown in Figure 1. Sentence 1 is causal and sentence 5 is non-causal. The first sentence is regraded as causal because it has the cause (in blue color) and effect (in green color) linked by a causal-marker (in red color) unlike the 5-th sentence which only has the effect.

Figure 1: Examples of different text statements indicating whether they contain causal relationships or not. The causal markers are in red color, causes are in blue color and effects are in green color

In general, an expression is regarded as non-causal if any of the following conditions are satisfied; (1) the reader is unable to construct a "why" question regarding the effect, (2) the cause does not precede the effect in time, (3) the effect is equally likely to occur or not without the cause and (4) the cause and effect can be swapped without change in meaning (Tan et al., 2022b).

Event Causality Identification has been actively studied in information retrieval with deep learning as the dominant approach delivering state-of-the-art performance (Chen et al., 2015; Lai et al., 2020; Zuo et al., 2021). BERT (Devlin et al., 2019) has been utilized for automatic event causality detection on the Causal News Corpus (a dataset used in this study) (Tan et al., 2022b,a). The challenge with deep learning models is that they represent documents as a sequence of tokens either using

Proceedings of the 5th Workshop on Challenges and Applications of Automated Extraction of Socio-political Events from Text (CASE), pages 85 - 90
December 7-8, 2022

the traditional count based methods or embedding based methods yet the task of causality detection requires understanding rich structures and reasoning within a sentence. The main contribution of this work is the use of the gated graph neural networks (GGNN) initialized with contextualized language representations on the task of causal event detection from social-political news.

2 Related Work and Background

In this section, we highlight some of the related work and background information relevant to our proposed methodology.

2.1 Document Representations

The nature in which words are represented directly influences the performance of models trained using them on downstream tasks. Traditionally, documents were represented using bag of word approaches that base on co-occurrence statistics of terms within documents (Salton et al., 1975). The key challenge with this approach is that it does not easily capture semantic relationships among words. An alternative approach to bag of words is word embeddings (Mikolov et al., 2013). Word embeddings represent words as real-valued vectors rather than counts capturing semantic and syntactic information. Word embeddings are classified into static word embeddings and contextualized word embeddings.

Static word embeddings obtain stand-alone representations of words without considering the context in which these words are used . Popular models in this category are Word2Vec models (Skip-gram and CBOW (Continuous bag of Words)) (Mikolov et al., 2013). Skip-gram uses center words to predict contextual words while CBOW uses contextual words to predict central words. GloVe (Global Vectors for Word Representation) (Pennington et al., 2014) is a log bi-linear regression model which leverages co-occurrence statistics of the corpus to represent documents. Contextual embeddings such ELMO (Peters et al., 2018) (Embeddings from Language Models) and BERT move beyond global representations like Word2Vec and assign each word a representation basing on its context hence achieving a better performance compared to static word embeddings.

2.2 Graph Neural Networks

Deep learning models especially those based on the recent transformer architecture have become dominant strategies for NLP tasks because of their impressive performance. One of the most popular transformer models is BERT (Devlin et al., 2019; Vaswani et al., 2017). BERT is a language representation model that pre-trains deep bi-directional representations from unlabeled text by jointly conditioning on both left and right contexts in all layers. It is pre-trained with two objectives: masked language modeling and next sentence prediction using the bookcorpus (800 million words) and English wikepedia (2,500 million words).

Despite the impressive performance, transformer models represent documents as a sequence of tokens which is a limitation for some NLP problems that can be naturally expressed with a graph structure. There is now a growing interest to perform deep learning on graphs using graph neural networks. Graph neural networks exploit the global features in text representations learning by aggregating information from neighbors through edges. Convolutional neural networks were first extended to handle graphs for text classification (Defferrard et al., 2016). Graph Neural Networks have since been extended to other architectures like Recurrent Neural Networks and Gated Recurrent Unit (Wu et al., 2021). In our work, we apply models graph neural networks in an application context for event causality classification from social-political news.

2.3 Event Causality Identification

The task of event causality detection from text is a semantically challenging task since it involves understanding the complex structure, relationships and dependencies within text. Traditional methods have used lexical and syntactical patterns (Hashimoto, 2019; Gao et al., 2019), co-occurrence statistics of events (Hu et al., 2017), causality markers like "due" and "because" (Hidey and McKeown, 2016) and temporal semantics of events (Ning et al., 2018). Our proposed model uses GGNN to automatically extract and induce more abstract representations.

Advanced deep learning methods based on the transformer architecture (Vaswani et al., 2017) like BERT (Bidirectional Embeddings from Transformers) (Devlin et al., 2019) have also been applied for this task (Al-Garadi et al., 2022; Nan et al., 2020). Even-though these models have achieved good per-

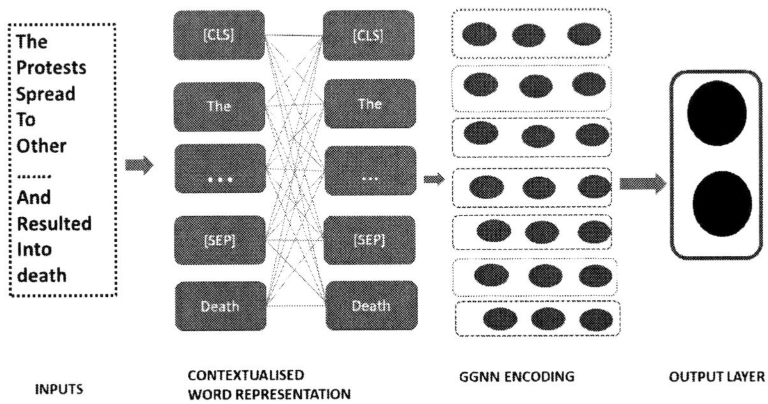

Figure 2: We first obtain contextualized embeddings of the news articles which we use to build a graph representation. A gated graph neural encoder (GGNN) and recurrent neural network decoder were used for graph neural network encoding. Finally, a fully connected neural networks was used for Event Causality Identification binary classification task

formance on event causality detection, they represent text as sequences which may not be sufficient to capture the long dependencies that are required for this event causality detection task.

Graph neural networks which extract rich structures and represent text as graph have also been explored. Graph convolutional Network (GCN) have been proposed for document level event causality detection that captures inter-sentence event mention pairs (Tran Phu and Nguyen, 2021).

Our model is different from such related work in that we use a gated graph neural network on a novel dataset; Causal News Corpus where such models have not yet as of writing the paper not explored (Tan et al., 2022b).

3 Methodology

In this section, we describe our proposed methodology for the task of Event Causality Identification from social-political news.

3.1 Document Representation

Formally, let us denote a corpus of N documents we would like to classify as $D = \{x_i, y_i\}^N$ where x_i is the i-th document with a co-responding label $y_i \in Y$ for $Y \in \{1, ..., K\}$. Each document $x_i \in D$ is represented by a sequence of words $\{w_1, ..., w_{nt}\}(w_i \in v)$ where nt is the number of words in document x_i and v is the vocabulary size.

We encode words $w_i \in x_i$ into a continuous vector representation using contextualized language representations produced by BERT (Devlin et al., 2019). Each document x_i in the corpus is represented in one token sequence which may contain a single sentence or a pair of sentences. The first token of every sequence is always a special classification token ([CLS]) and different sentences are separated by a special token ([SEP]). Documents are represented as follows [[CLS],$w_1, ...w_n$,[SEP],w_t,[SEP]] for an input into pre-trained BERT. We concatenate vectors of the top layers of the pre-trained BERT to obtain continuous vector representations of each word denoted as $E = \{e_i, ...e_n\}$. The embedding vectors in E are fed into a bidirectional LSTM (Hochreiter and Schmidhuber, 1997) (Long Short Term Memory) to produce a sequence of hidden vectors $h^0 = \{h_n^0, ..., h_n^0\}$ that will be used as initialization to the graph encoder (Wu et al., 2021).

3.2 Gated Graph Neural Encoder

After representing each word in the corpus C with a corresponding word embedding, we build a graph representation of all documents in the corpus and their associated dependencies. To apply our encoder, we represent our documents as $G = (V, E)$, where V indicates a set consisting of different word embeddings for each word in the vocabulary and E indicates a set of edges (relationships) formed between documents.

We use a Gated Graph Neural network (GGNN) which is a modification of the vanilla Graph Neural Network by adding Gated Recurrent Unit filters (Chung et al., 2014). Our GGNN encoder consists of L stacked GGNN layers operating over a sequence of hidden vectors at the $i-$th layer $h^{(i)}$. The hidden vector h_i^l at the $l-$th layer is computed by averaging the hidden vectors of neighboring nodes x_i at the $(l-1)-$th layer: Gated Recurrent Unit (GRU) is used to update node embeddings by incorporating the aggregated information taking into consideration of edge type and edge direction:

$$\begin{aligned} h_i^{(0)} &= [x_i^T, 0]^T \\ a_i^{(l)} &= A_{i:}^T [h_i^{(l-1)}, ..., h_n^{(l-1)}]^T \\ h_i^{(l)} &= GRU(a_i^{(l)}, h_l^{(l-1)}) \end{aligned} \quad (1)$$

where $A \in \mathcal{R}$ is a matrix determining how nodes in the graph are communicating with each other, x_i are the initial node features, $a_i^{(l)}$ is the aggregation of information from different nodes and $h_i^{(l)}$ is the $i-$th hidden state at the $l-$th layer.

3.3 Recurrent Neural Network Decoder

The graph-level embeddings C obtained by the Graph Encoder are fed into a sequence decoder as heuristic information. In the decoding stage, an embedding layer is used to embed all the previous sequences. We used graph embedding C and sequence embedding e^t at time step t using a recurrent neural network:

$$\begin{aligned} h^t &= RNN(Concat(e^{(t)}, C), h^{(t-1)}) \\ y_t &= FC(e^{(t)}, h^{(t)}, C) \end{aligned}$$

where $h^{(t)}$ represents hidden state at time step t, $FC(.)$ represents fully connected layer and we initialize the hidden state with global graph representation C i.e $h^{(0)} = C$.

4 Experimental Results

4.1 Data

The dataset used for experiments in this paper was provided by the organizers of the shared task on Causal Event Classification organized at 5th Workshop on Challenges and Applications of Automated Extraction of Socio-political Events from Text (CASE) at EMNLP 2022. The training data consists of 2925 news articles, validation set contained 323 news articles and test data consisted of 311 news articles (Tan et al., 2022b,a).

4.2 Experimental Setup

We conduct experiments with pre-trained BERT (Devlin et al., 2019) and gated graph neural networks . Experiments are done with 50 epochs, max length of 512, batch size of 50 and the learning rate was set at 0.0005. The final submissions are evaluated using $f1$-score. Transformers are implemented using hugging-face transformer library (Wolf et al., 2020) and graph neural networks were implemented using graph4nlp library (Wu et al., 2021). Our code implementation can be found on the this link (`https://github.com/TrustPaul/ggnn.git`).

4.3 Discussion

Model	f1	Accuracy
BERT (Baseline)	80.06	81.11
GGNN-W2V	81.01	75.23
GGNN-B(Ours)	**84.78**	**84.52**

Table 1: $f1-$score and accuracy on the development set of the baseline model (BERT (Bidirectional Embeddings from Transformers) and our proposed model (GGNN(Gated Graph Neural Network (Li et al., 2016; Devlin et al., 2019; Tan et al., 2022b))

Experimental results demonstrate that the performance of our proposed method (GGNN-B) compared to the baseline method that uses BERT (Devlin et al., 2019; Tan et al., 2022b) proposed by Tan et al.,(2022) as shown in Table 1. Our method improves over the baseline in terms of precision (84.78% versus 80.06%), f1 (86.19 versus 83.47%) and accuracy (84.52% versus 81.11). However fine-tuned BERT outperforms GGNN-W2V (83.47% against 76.19%) in terms of f1-score, a gated neural network of the same architecture as GGNN-B but with the graph constructed with Word2Vec embeddings.

Model	f1	Accuracy
BERT (Baseline)	78.01	77.81
GGNN-W2V	75.72	72.03
GGCN-B(Ours)	**81.67**	**80.06**

Table 2: $f1-$score and accuracy on the test set of the baseline model (BERT (Bidirectional Embeddings from Transformers) and our proposed model (GGNN(Gated Graph Neural Network (Li et al., 2016; Devlin et al., 2019; Tan et al., 2022b))

Experimental results on the test set demonstrate that our proposed method GGNN-B achieves an accuracy of 80.06% compared to an accuracy of 77.81% achieved by the baseline model (BERT). GGNN-B (our model) achieves a better f1-score compared to the baseline (82.58% against 81.12%) but BERT outperforms the same graph neural network architecture initialized with Word2Vec embeddings (Mikolov et al., 2013).

We hypothesize that the performance difference observed between our model which is based on graph neural networks and the baseline model based on only BERT is due to the superiority of graphs in representing complex structures required for understanding causal relationship against BERT that represents text as sequences. The fact that BERT outperforms Graph Neural networks when initialized with Word2Vec reinforces the role played by graph initialization of graph neural networks on performance and also demonstrates the advantages of contextualized embeddings extracted by BERT to downstream tasks over static embeddings extracted by Word2Vec.

5 Conclusion

In this work, we propose a novel deep learning approach for event causality detection from social-political news articles. Our proposed approach use gated graph neural networks and contextualized language representations which represent text documents as a graph and model complex semantic relationships ideal for causality detection. Experimental results reveal that our proposed model improves performance over the baseline comparison model (BERT) in terms of accuracy (80.06% versus 77.81%) and $f1-$score (82.58% versus 81.12%).

6 Acknowledgements

We thank Science Foundation Ireland (SFI) Center for Research Training in Advanced Networks and Future communications at University College Cork for funding this research and Irish Centre for High-End Computing (ICHEC) for providing access to computing power for running some of our experiments.

References

Mohammed Ali Al-Garadi, Sangmi Kim, Yuting Guo, Elise Warren, Yuan-Chi Yang, Sahithi Lakamana, and Abeed Sarker. 2022. Natural language model for automatic identification of intimate partner violence reports from twitter. *Array*, page 100217.

Yubo Chen, Liheng Xu, Kang Liu, Daojian Zeng, and Jun Zhao. 2015. Event extraction via dynamic multi-pooling convolutional neural networks. In *Proceedings of the 53rd Annual Meeting of the Association for Computational Linguistics and the 7th International Joint Conference on Natural Language Processing (Volume 1: Long Papers)*, pages 167–176, Beijing, China. Association for Computational Linguistics.

Junyoung Chung, Caglar Gulcehre, KyungHyun Cho, and Yoshua Bengio. 2014. Empirical evaluation of gated recurrent neural networks on sequence modeling. *arXiv preprint arXiv:1412.3555*.

Michaël Defferrard, Xavier Bresson, and Pierre Vandergheynst. 2016. Convolutional neural networks on graphs with fast localized spectral filtering. *Advances in neural information processing systems*, 29.

Jacob Devlin, Ming-Wei Chang, Kenton Lee, and Kristina Toutanova. 2019. BERT: Pre-training of deep bidirectional transformers for language understanding. In *Proceedings of the 2019 Conference of the North American Chapter of the Association for Computational Linguistics: Human Language Technologies, Volume 1 (Long and Short Papers)*, pages 4171–4186, Minneapolis, Minnesota. Association for Computational Linguistics.

Amir Feder, Katherine A Keith, Emaad Manzoor, Reid Pryzant, Dhanya Sridhar, Zach Wood-Doughty, Jacob Eisenstein, Justin Grimmer, Roi Reichart, Margaret E Roberts, et al. 2021. Causal inference in natural language processing: Estimation. *Prediction, Interpretation and Beyond.*

Lei Gao, Prafulla Kumar Choubey, and Ruihong Huang. 2019. Modeling document-level causal structures for event causal relation identification. In *Proceedings of the 2019 Conference of the North American Chapter of the Association for Computational Linguistics: Human Language Technologies, Volume 1 (Long and Short Papers)*, pages 1808–1817, Minneapolis, Minnesota. Association for Computational Linguistics.

Chikara Hashimoto. 2019. Weakly supervised multilingual causality extraction from Wikipedia. In *Proceedings of the 2019 Conference on Empirical Methods in Natural Language Processing and the 9th International Joint Conference on Natural Language Processing (EMNLP-IJCNLP)*, pages 2988–2999, Hong Kong, China. Association for Computational Linguistics.

Christopher Hidey and Kathy McKeown. 2016. Identifying causal relations using parallel Wikipedia articles. In *Proceedings of the 54th Annual Meeting of the Association for Computational Linguistics (Volume 1: Long Papers)*, pages 1424–1433, Berlin, Germany. Association for Computational Linguistics.

Sepp Hochreiter and Jürgen Schmidhuber. 1997. Long short-term memory. *Neural computation*, 9(8):1735–1780.

Zhichao Hu, Elahe Rahimtoroghi, and Marilyn Walker. 2017. Inference of fine-grained event causality from blogs and films. In *Proceedings of the Events and Stories in the News Workshop*, pages 52–58, Vancouver, Canada. Association for Computational Linguistics.

Viet Dac Lai, Tuan Ngo Nguyen, and Thien Huu Nguyen. 2020. Event detection: Gate diversity and syntactic importance scores for graph convolution neural networks. In *Proceedings of the 2020 Conference on Empirical Methods in Natural Language Processing (EMNLP)*, pages 5405–5411, Online. Association for Computational Linguistics.

Yujia Li, Daniel Tarlow, Marc Brockschmidt, and Richard S. Zemel. 2016. Gated graph sequence neural networks. In *4th International Conference on Learning Representations, ICLR 2016, San Juan, Puerto Rico, May 2-4, 2016, Conference Track Proceedings*.

Tomás Mikolov, Kai Chen, Greg Corrado, and Jeffrey Dean. 2013. Efficient estimation of word representations in vector space. In *1st International Conference on Learning Representations, ICLR 2013, Scottsdale, Arizona, USA, May 2-4, 2013, Workshop Track Proceedings*.

Guoshun Nan, Zhijiang Guo, Ivan Sekulic, and Wei Lu. 2020. Reasoning with latent structure refinement for document-level relation extraction. In *Proceedings of the 58th Annual Meeting of the Association for Computational Linguistics*, pages 1546–1557, Online. Association for Computational Linguistics.

Qiang Ning, Zhili Feng, Hao Wu, and Dan Roth. 2018. Joint reasoning for temporal and causal relations. In *Proceedings of the 56th Annual Meeting of the Association for Computational Linguistics (Volume 1: Long Papers)*, pages 2278–2288, Melbourne, Australia. Association for Computational Linguistics.

Jeffrey Pennington, Richard Socher, and Christopher Manning. 2014. GloVe: Global vectors for word representation. In *Proceedings of the 2014 Conference on Empirical Methods in Natural Language Processing (EMNLP)*, pages 1532–1543, Doha, Qatar. Association for Computational Linguistics.

Matthew E. Peters, Mark Neumann, Mohit Iyyer, Matt Gardner, Christopher Clark, Kenton Lee, and Luke Zettlemoyer. 2018. Deep contextualized word representations. In *Proceedings of the 2018 Conference of the North American Chapter of the Association for Computational Linguistics: Human Language Technologies, Volume 1 (Long Papers)*, pages 2227–2237, New Orleans, Louisiana. Association for Computational Linguistics.

Gerard Salton, Anita Wong, and Chung-Shu Yang. 1975. A vector space model for automatic indexing. *Communications of the ACM*, 18(11):613–620.

Fiona Anting Tan, Hansi Hettiarachchi, Ali Hürriyetoğlu, Tommaso Caselli, Onur Uca, Farhana Ferdousi Liza, and Nelleke Oostdijk. 2022a. Event causality identification with causal news corpus - shared task 3, CASE 2022. In *Proceedings of the 5th Workshop on Challenges and Applications of Automated Extraction of Socio-political Events from Text (CASE 2022)*, Online. Association for Computational Linguistics.

Fiona Anting Tan, Ali Hürriyetoğlu, Tommaso Caselli, Nelleke Oostdijk, Tadashi Nomoto, Hansi Hettiarachchi, Iqra Ameer, Onur Uca, Farhana Ferdousi Liza, and Tiancheng Hu. 2022b. The causal news corpus: Annotating causal relations in event sentences from news. In *Proceedings of the Language Resources and Evaluation Conference*, pages 2298–2310, Marseille, France. European Language Resources Association.

Minh Tran Phu and Thien Huu Nguyen. 2021. Graph convolutional networks for event causality identification with rich document-level structures. In *Proceedings of the 2021 Conference of the North American Chapter of the Association for Computational Linguistics: Human Language Technologies*, pages 3480–3490, Online. Association for Computational Linguistics.

Ashish Vaswani, Noam Shazeer, Niki Parmar, Jakob Uszkoreit, Llion Jones, Aidan N Gomez, Łukasz Kaiser, and Illia Polosukhin. 2017. Attention is all you need. *Advances in neural information processing systems*, 30.

Thomas Wolf, Lysandre Debut, Victor Sanh, Julien Chaumond, Clement Delangue, Anthony Moi, Pierric Cistac, Tim Rault, Remi Louf, Morgan Funtowicz, Joe Davison, Sam Shleifer, Patrick von Platen, Clara Ma, Yacine Jernite, Julien Plu, Canwen Xu, Teven Le Scao, Sylvain Gugger, Mariama Drame, Quentin Lhoest, and Alexander Rush. 2020. Transformers: State-of-the-art natural language processing. In *Proceedings of the 2020 Conference on Empirical Methods in Natural Language Processing: System Demonstrations*, pages 38–45, Online. Association for Computational Linguistics.

Lingfei Wu, Yu Chen, Heng Ji, and Yunyao Li. 2021. Deep learning on graphs for natural language processing. In *Proceedings of the 2021 Conference of the North American Chapter of the Association for Computational Linguistics: Human Language Technologies: Tutorials*, pages 11–14, Online. Association for Computational Linguistics.

Xinyu Zuo, Pengfei Cao, Yubo Chen, Kang Liu, Jun Zhao, Weihua Peng, and Yuguang Chen. 2021. Improving event causality identification via self-supervised representation learning on external causal statement. In *Findings of the Association for Computational Linguistics: ACL-IJCNLP 2021*, pages 2162–2172, Online. Association for Computational Linguistics.

1Cademy @ Causal News Corpus 2022: Leveraging Self-Training in Causality Classification of Socio-Political Event Data

Adam Nik[2 4*], **Ge Zhang**[1 2 3*], **Xingran Chen**[3], **Mingyu Li**[2 3], **Jie Fu**[† 1]
[1] Beijing Academy of Artificial Intelligence, China
[2] 1Cademy Community, USA
[3] University of Michigan Ann Arbor, USA
[4] Carleton College, USA
fujie AT baai.ac.cn

Abstract

This paper details our participation in the Challenges and Applications of Automated Extraction of Socio-political Events from Text (CASE) workshop @ EMNLP 2022, where we take part in Subtask 1 of Shared Task 3 (Tan et al., 2022a). We approach the given task of event causality detection by proposing a self-training pipeline that follows a teacher-student classifier method. More specifically, we initially train a teacher model on the true, original task data, and use that teacher model to self-label data to be used in the training of a separate student model for the final task prediction. We test how restricting the number of positive or negative self-labeled examples in the self-training process affects classification performance. Our final results show that using self-training produces a comprehensive performance improvement across all models and self-labeled training sets tested within the task of event causality sequence classification. On top of that, we find that self-training performance did not diminish even when restricting either positive/negative examples used in training. Our code is be publicly available at https://github.com/Gzhang-umich/1CademyTeamOfCASE.

1 Introduction

Task 1 of the CASE workshop @ EMNLP 2022 works to identify and classify event causality in socio-political event (SPE) data, with subtask 1 being a binary classification of causality. In other words, participants are tasked with answering: Does an event sentence contain cause-effect meaning? The workshop provides data from Causal News Corpus (CNC) (Tan et al., 2022b) for training and evaluation of the subtask. Causality itself aims to identify a semantic relationship between two events where one event (the cause) is responsible for the production of the other event (the effect). Utilizing the CNC dataset serves as a benchmark for participants to evaluate the ability of a given model or process to identify causality in event data.

We approach the problem of causality sequence classification by applying self-training (Ouali et al., 2020; Van Engelen and Hoos, 2020; Triguero et al., 2015) as a means to improve the performance of language models in this task. The goal of self-training is to generate proxy labels for previously unlabeled data to enhance the learning process. The self-training process works by iteratively labeling previously unpredicted data, and then using the new pseudo-labels as truthful labels in the next training stage. The intuition behind self-training comes from the fact that it can pseudo-expand the training space to basically an unlimited size in a very cheap manner, as no hand-labeling is required in the process.

Additionally, we run supplementary experiments to test the effectiveness of self-training against various transformer-based data augmentation techniques (Feng et al., 2021) and separate multi-task learning approaches (Caruana, 1997) that we originally designed for the competition. The description and results of these additional experiments can be found in the Appendix.

In summary, our main contributions are as follows.

1) We propose a self-training pipeline for the task of causality detection in SPE data for the purposes of competing in Subtask 1 of Shared Task 3 of the CASE workshop @ EMNLP 2022. Our best model achieved 0.8135 accuracy and a 0.8398 F_1 score on the competition's test set.

2) We evaluate our self-training pipeline with collected self-labeled datasets of highly positive samples, highly negative samples, and even distributed positive and negative samples. We show that using self-labeled datasets improves performance across

* The two authors contributed equally to this work.
† Corresponding Author

Proceedings of the 5th Workshop on Challenges and Applications of Automated Extraction of Socio-political Events from Text (CASE), pages 91 - 99
December 7-8, 2022 ©2022 Association for Computational Linguistics

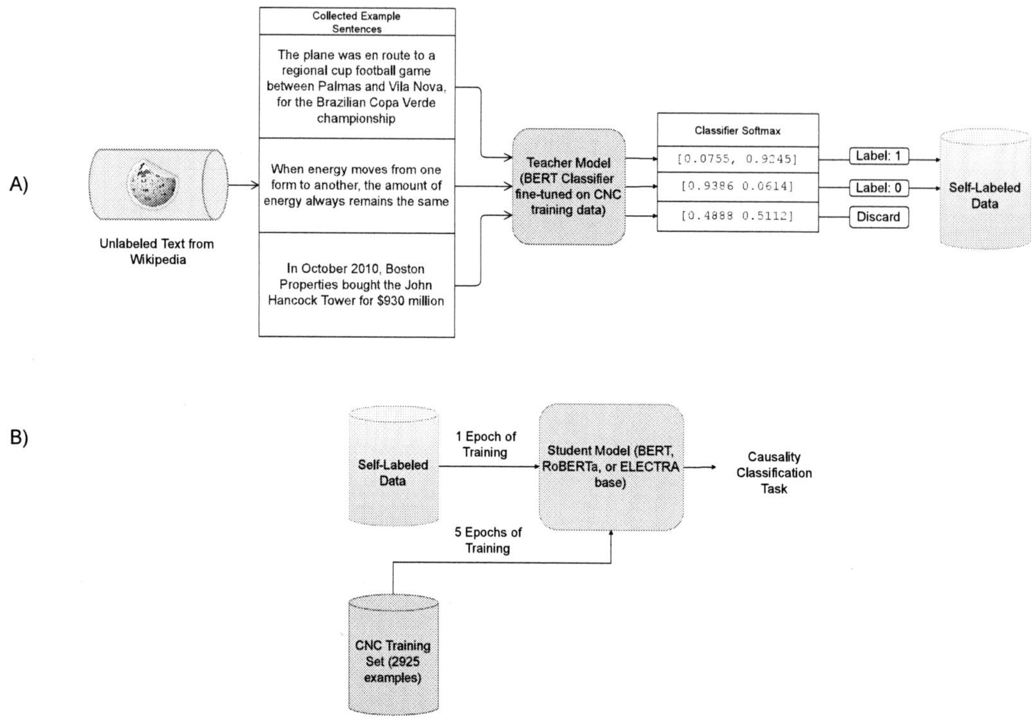

Figure 1: A) Self-training pipeline with Teacher Model. B) We use the self-labeled examples as part of the training when training in Student Models for the task of causality classification

the board on all tested models, and that the performance increase provided by self-training did not significantly change based on the ratio of positive to negative self-labeled samples used in training.

For all implementations of our code, we use the HuggingFace Transformers library (Wolf et al., 2020) (version 4.21.2) and all models are built using PyTorch (Paszke et al., 2019) (version 1.12.1).

Organization. As for how the rest of the paper is outlined, §2 describes the data used in the training, evaluation, and final testing of our models, §3 recounts the procedures used in our self-training approach, §4 discusses our findings, and §5 wraps up the paper with our final remarks and ideas for future direction.

2 Data

2.1 Causal News Corpus

The CNC dataset (Tan et al., 2022b) is a corpus of 3,559 event sentences from protest event news labeled on whether a given sentence contains causal relations or not. The data of the CNC comes from two workshops focused on mining socio-political data: Automated Extraction of Socio-political Events from News (AESPEN) (Hürriyetoğlu et al., 2020) in 2020 and the CASE 2021 workshop @ ACL-IJCNLP (Hürriyetoğlu et al., 2021). For the purposes of subtask 1, the data is split into a training set of 2925 examples, a development set of 323 examples, and a final test set of 311 examples that is used as an evaluation benchmark for the competition.

2.2 Self-labeled Training Data

Sample sentences used in the self-labeling phase of self-training are gathered from 205,328 articles on Wikipedia. The Wikipedia dataset is built from the Wikipedia dump [1] and is available as on HuggingFace Dataset library (Lhoest et al., 2021). We use the 20220301.simple training split to generate our self-labeled examples.

3 Methodology

In this section, we review the methods we used in our approach to the sequence causality classification subtask.

[1]https://dumps.wikimedia.org

3.1 Self-Training

We follow a similar teacher-student pipeline as Yalniz et al., 2019 that includes using a teacher model to generate a new labeled dataset $\mathcal{D}'$ from the original dataset $\mathcal{D}$ and then training a new student model on both the new labeled dataset $\mathcal{D}'$ and the original dataset $\mathcal{D}$. We use the training split provided of 2925 CNC samples (Tan et al., 2022b) as the original dataset $\mathcal{D}$, and fine-tune a BERT base-cased model (Devlin et al., 2019) for sequence classification, which serves as our teacher model. Figure 1a shows the full pipeline from Wikipedia data collection to saving self-labeled samples. These self-labeled examples are used as training data for the separate student models later in the experimentation process, as shown in Figure 1b.

3.1.1 Data Preprocessing

To preprocess Wikipedia data (§ 2.2), we first split the articles into individual sentences and discarded all sentences of less than 50 characters and more than 500 characters. To self-label the sentences, we feed the sentences into the teacher model and keep all examples with a softmax classifier over a predetermined threshold $\mathcal{T}$. For the purposes of our experiments, we choose a $\mathcal{T}$ of 0.9. In total, we collect a pool of 77,748 positive (causal) examples and 77,940 negative (non-causal) examples. The large total number of examples collected for this data pool is done to minimize the overlap of examples between the later created self-labeled training splits.

3.1.2 Training Splits

From the pools of self-labeled Wikipedia examples, we collect 5 different training sets, all with the size of 10,000 samples but with varying ratios of positive to negative self-labeled examples. We collect sets with positive to negative proportions of 1:3, 1:1, and 3:1 (that is, for a positive to negative proportion of 1:3, we include 2,500 self-labeled positive examples in the training set and 7,500 negative samples). We design this set-up to test how the different polarity proportions of self-labeled data used in training affect not only overall model accuracy, but also if there is a discrepancy between model precision and recall with the varying polarity splits. We chose a training split size of 10,000 examples as we notice that self-training performance does not continue to improve with training with splits larger than this [2]. When formulating each set, we randomly reshuffle the positive and negative self-labeled sets and chose the first s and t positive and negative samples for a training set that require s positive examples and t negative examples. From there, we combine the s positives and the t negatives and again shuffle the concatenated training set.

3.1.3 Fine-tuning on Self-labeled data

For each self-labeled dataset, we fine-tune a classifier—which serves as our student model—on one epoch of the self-labeled dataset and then five epochs of the CNC provided training data. The predictions generated after the final epoch of training are used for evaluation. We run our experiments with student classifiers built on BERT base-cased (Devlin et al., 2019), RoBERTa base (Liu et al., 2019), and Google ELECTRA-base-discriminator (Clark et al., 2016) pre-trained models.

3.2 Transformer-based Data Augmentation and Multi-task Learning

In our participation of the CASE workshop, we also explore both Transformer-based data augmentation and multi-task learning as a means to improve performance on causality classification. While our both of these approaches are out-performed by our self-training approaches and thus are not the main focus of this paper, we still find significant results with these methods and implement both a Transformer-based data augmentation technique and a multi-task architecture that comprehensively outperform the baseline classifier for the given task. The full methodology and experimentation of our Transformer-based data augmentation and multi-task learning approaches are available in the Appendix.

4 Experiments and Results

4.1 Experiment Set up

In our experimentation setup, we test all three backbone models (BERT, RoBERTa, and Google ELECTRA Discriminator) with both the self-training pipeline and a simple fine-tuning process that only uses the provided CNC training set that served as the baseline. In the baseline experiments, the classifiers are trained solely on five epochs of the CNC training data. We conduct five trials of each setup, each trial having a randomly initialized seed. We

[2]Observed in our initial internal testing phase

Baseline Training vs. Self-Training Results							
			Accuracy	F1	Recall	Precision	MCC
Baseline Training (simple fine-tuning, no self-training)	BERT		0.8204	0.8394	0.8516	0.8276	0.6363
	RoBERTa		0.8390	0.8543	0.8561	0.8525	0.6745
	Google ELECTRA Discriminator		0.8365	0.8535	0.8640	0.8432	0.6689
		Ratio of Positive to Negative Self-Labeled Examples used in training	Accuracy	F1	Recall	Precision	MCC
Self-Training	BERT	1:3	0.8380	0.8531	0.8539	0.8525	0.6726
		1:1	0.8225	0.8377	0.8315	0.8468	0.6425
		3:1	0.8380	0.8526	0.8502	0.8552	0.6728
	RoBERTa	1:3	0.8576	0.8715	**0.8764**	0.8671	0.7123
		1:1	**0.8586**	0.8711	0.8670	**0.8755**	**0.7149**
		3:1	**0.8586**	**0.8719**	0.8727	0.8711	0.7142
	Google ELECTRA Discriminator	1:3	0.8400	0.8579	**0.8764**	0.8415	0.6760
		1:1	0.8524	0.8665	0.8689	0.8641	0.7016
		3:1	0.8421	0.8580	0.8652	0.8510	0.6806

Table 1: Results of the evaluating the CNC development set on both simple fine-tuning with only CNC training data (top) and fine-tuning classifiers on training sets of self-labeled data in addition to CNC training data (bottom). **Bold** indicates highest performance across all splits and model types, underline indicates the highest performance of the specific model type.

use the CNC development set as our testing benchmark due to the limited number of allowed workshop testing phase submissions.

4.2 Classifier Set up

In our experiments, we run all trials on a Tesla V100-SXM2-16GB GPU device. We use an AdamW optimizer with β_1 = 0.9, β_2 = 0.999, a learning rate of $5e - 5$, and a linear decay rate. Finally, all experiments are run with a batch size of 8.

4.3 Findings

Table 1 displays the results from our experiments, which include the averages of 5 trials for each setup. From the table, we can see that every self-training setup outperforms the baseline classifier in terms of accuracy, with an average accuracy improvement of 1.33% across all models and polarity splits. Furthermore, for all but one self-training set-up, there is an improvement of the F_1 score from the baseline, with an average improvement of 0.011.

Other key takeaways from our results are that 1) there is very little overall performance degradation across the polarity splits (1:3, 1:1, 3:1) in the self-labeled datasets (only the BERT model shows a range of F1 scores above 0.01) and 2) there is low discrepancy between recall and precision among the splits (only the 1:3 split with an ELECTRA backbone shows a recall-precision discrepancy > 0.015.)

4.4 Competition Results

Our best-performing prediction set of the final competition testing comes from a RoBERTa classifier trained on a self-labeled training set with a polarity ratio of 1:1. The results of our all of our competition submissions [3] are shown in Table 2. All of our competition submissions comprehensively outperform the provided baseline, and our best overall performing submission achieve competition rankings of 6th in accuracy, 10th in F1, 7th in recall, 7th in precision, and 10th in MCC.

5 Conclusion and Discussion

This paper explores how training a classifier on self-labeled data can improve the performance of sequence classification tasks. In our case, we examine the effect of self-training on the task of event causality in socio-political event data as part of Subtask 1 of Shared Task 3 of the CASE workshop @ EMNLP 2022.

Our results show that training a classifier on self-labeled data using a teacher-student approach comprehensively improves task performance. Furthermore, we find that performance improvement from self-training did not differ significantly between self-labeled training sets with varying levels of example polarity. This indicates that the model is capable of reaping the full benefits of self-training despite having limited access to positive or negative samples. One thing that could help explain this is our relatively high threshold $\mathcal{T}$ of 0.9 which determines whether or not to keep an example during the

[3]Workshop competition limited participants to five submissions for the testing phase

Competition Results (CNC Test Set)						
	Ratio of Positive to Negative Self-Labeled Examples	Accuracy	F1	Recall	Precision	MCC
RoBERTa	1:3	0.8071	0.8256	0.8068	0.8452	0.6108
	1:1	**0.8135**	**0.8398**	**0.8636**	0.8172	0.6185
	3:1	0.7974	0.8215	0.8239	0.8192	0.5873
ELECTRA	1:1	**0.8135**	0.8324	0.8181	**0.8471**	**0.6228**
	3:1	0.7942	0.8107	0.7784	0.8457	0.5886
Provided Competition Baseline (BERT baseline model)		0.7781	0.8120	0.8466	0.7801	0.5452

Table 2: Results of competition submissions on CNC test set. **Bold** indicates highest performer.

initial self-labeled process. Further research should explore whether a lower $\mathcal{T}$ could alter the benefits of self-training, especially when self-labeled examples would have a higher chance of being incorrectly labeled.

Next, given that our self-labeled examples are gathered from an assortment of articles from Wikipedia, it should be well noted that the benefits of self-training are apparent even when the self-labeled examples are not domain specific to the original labeled data. We decide to use Wikipedia as the source of our self-labeled examples as we view it as a more accessible source with far greater amounts available unlabeled data. Thus, our findings indicate that performance improvements from self-training work with non-domain specific data, which alleviates us from the restriction of confining our self-labeled data to the single domain of the original labeled data.

Finally, one more aspect of our experiments that should be further explored is the classifier's actual dependence on the self-labeled data versus the originally provided training data. In our setup, we choose to train our models on one epoch of self-labeled data and then on five epochs of the original training data in order to prioritize the true labeled training data. We believe that it would be worthwhile to explore training classifiers with a higher training priority on the self-labeled data, or even to test the performance of classifiers trained solely on the self-labeled data, without the original true data.

Acknowledgments

The work for this study is supported by the National Key R&D Program of China (2020AAA0105200) and the Sam '75 and Meg Woodside Fund for Career Exploration provided through Carleton College.

References

Rich Caruana. 1997. Multitask learning. *Machine learning*, 28(1):41–75.

Kevin Clark, Minh-Thang Luong, Quoc V Le, and Christopher D Manning. 2016. Electra: Pre-training text encoders as discriminators rather than generators. *ELECTRA*, 85:90.

Jacob Devlin, Ming-Wei Chang, Kenton Lee, and Kristina Toutanova. 2019. BERT: Pre-training of deep bidirectional transformers for language understanding. In *Proceedings of the 2019 Conference of the North American Chapter of the Association for Computational Linguistics: Human Language Technologies, Volume 1 (Long and Short Papers)*, pages 4171–4186, Minneapolis, Minnesota. Association for Computational Linguistics.

Steven Y Feng, Varun Gangal, Jason Wei, Sarath Chandar, Soroush Vosoughi, Teruko Mitamura, and Eduard Hovy. 2021. A survey of data augmentation approaches for nlp. In *Findings of the Association for Computational Linguistics: ACL-IJCNLP 2021*, pages 968–988.

Pengxin Guo, Feiyang Ye, and Yu Zhang. 2021. Safe multi-task learning. *arXiv preprint arXiv:2111.10601*.

Ali Hürriyetoğlu, Hristo Tanev, Vanni Zavarella, Jakub Piskorski, Reyyan Yeniterzi, Osman Mutlu, Deniz Yuret, and Aline Villavicencio. 2021. Challenges and applications of automated extraction of socio-political events from text (CASE 2021): Workshop and shared task report. In *Proceedings of the 4th Workshop on Challenges and Applications of Automated Extraction of Socio-political Events from Text (CASE 2021)*, pages 1–9, Online. Association for Computational Linguistics.

Ali Hürriyetoğlu, Vanni Zavarella, Hristo Tanev, Erdem Yörük, Ali Safaya, and Osman Mutlu. 2020. Automated extraction of socio-political events from news (AESPEN): Workshop and shared task report. In *Proceedings of the Workshop on Automated Extraction of Socio-political Events from News 2020*, pages 1–6, Marseille, France. European Language Resources Association (ELRA).

Quentin Lhoest, Albert Villanova del Moral, Yacine Jernite, Abhishek Thakur, Patrick von Platen, Suraj Patil, Julien Chaumond, Mariama Drame, Julien Plu, Lewis Tunstall, Joe Davison, Mario Šaško, Gunjan Chhablani, Bhavitvya Malik, Simon Brandeis, Teven Le Scao, Victor Sanh, Canwen Xu, Nicolas Patry, Angelina McMillan-Major, Philipp Schmid, Sylvain Gugger, Clément Delangue, Théo Matussière, Lysandre Debut, Stas Bekman, Pierric Cistac, Thibault Goehringer, Victor Mustar, François Lagunas, Alexander Rush, and Thomas Wolf. 2021. Datasets: A community library for natural language processing. In *Proceedings of the 2021 Conference on Empirical Methods in Natural Language Processing: System Demonstrations*, pages 175–184, Online and Punta Cana, Dominican Republic. Association for Computational Linguistics.

Yinhan Liu, Myle Ott, Naman Goyal, Jingfei Du, Mandar Joshi, Danqi Chen, Omer Levy, Mike Lewis, Luke Zettlemoyer, and Veselin Stoyanov. 2019. Roberta: A robustly optimized bert pretraining approach. *arXiv preprint arXiv:1907.11692*.

Andrei Mikheev, Marc Moens, and Claire Grover. 1999. Named entity recognition without gazetteers. In *Ninth Conference of the European Chapter of the Association for Computational Linguistics*, pages 1–8.

Behrang Mohit. 2014. Named entity recognition. In *Natural language processing of semitic languages*, pages 221–245. Springer.

Nathan Ng, Kyra Yee, Alexei Baevski, Myle Ott, Michael Auli, and Sergey Edunov. 2019. Facebook fair's wmt19 news translation task submission. In *Proceedings of the Fourth Conference on Machine Translation (Volume 2: Shared Task Papers, Day 1)*, pages 314–319.

Yassine Ouali, Céline Hudelot, and Myriam Tami. 2020. An overview of deep semi-supervised learning. *arXiv preprint arXiv:2006.05278*.

Adam Paszke, Sam Gross, Francisco Massa, Adam Lerer, James Bradbury, Gregory Chanan, Trevor Killeen, Zeming Lin, Natalia Gimelshein, Luca Antiga, Alban Desmaison, Andreas Kopf, Edward Yang, Zachary DeVito, Martin Raison, Alykhan Tejani, Sasank Chilamkurthy, Benoit Steiner, Lu Fang, Junjie Bai, and Soumith Chintala. 2019. Pytorch: An imperative style, high-performance deep learning library. In H. Wallach, H. Larochelle, A. Beygelzimer, F. d'Alché-Buc, E. Fox, and R. Garnett, editors, *Advances in Neural Information Processing Systems 32*, pages 8024–8035. Curran Associates, Inc.

Clionadh Raleigh, Andrew Linke, Håvard Hegre, and Joakim Karlsen. 2010. Introducing acled: an armed conflict location and event dataset: special data feature. *Journal of peace research*, 47(5):651–660.

Sebastian Ruder. 2017. An overview of multi-task learning in deep neural networks. *arXiv preprint arXiv:1706.05098*.

Fiona Anting Tan, Ali Hürriyetoğlu, Tommaso Caselli, Nelleke Oostdijk, Hansi Hettiarachchi, Tadashi Nomoto, Onur Uca, and Farhana Ferdousi Liza. 2022a. Event causality identification with causal news corpus - shared task 3, CASE 2022. In *Proceedings of the 5th Workshop on Challenges and Applications of Automated Extraction of Socio-political Events from Text (CASE 2022)*, Online. Association for Computational Linguistics.

Fiona Anting Tan, Ali Hürriyetoğlu, Tommaso Caselli, Nelleke Oostdijk, Tadashi Nomoto, Hansi Hettiarachchi, Iqra Ameer, Onur Uca, Farhana Ferdousi Liza, and Tiancheng Hu. 2022b. The causal news corpus: Annotating causal relations in event sentences from news. In *Proceedings of the Language Resources and Evaluation Conference*, pages 2298–2310, Marseille, France. European Language Resources Association.

Isaac Triguero, Salvador García, and Francisco Herrera. 2015. Self-labeled techniques for semi-supervised learning: Taxonomy, software and empirical study. *Knowl. Inf. Syst.*, 42(2):245–284.

Jesper E Van Engelen and Holger H Hoos. 2020. A survey on semi-supervised learning. *Machine Learning*, 109(2):373–440.

Alex Wang, Amanpreet Singh, Julian Michael, Felix Hill, Omer Levy, and Samuel Bowman. 2018. Glue: A multi-task benchmark and analysis platform for natural language understanding. In *Proceedings of the 2018 EMNLP Workshop BlackboxNLP: Analyzing and Interpreting Neural Networks for NLP*, pages 353–355.

Thomas Wolf, Lysandre Debut, Victor Sanh, Julien Chaumond, Clement Delangue, Anthony Moi, Pierric Cistac, Tim Rault, Rémi Louf, Morgan Funtowicz, Joe Davison, Sam Shleifer, Patrick von Platen, Clara Ma, Yacine Jernite, Julien Plu, Canwen Xu, Teven Le Scao, Sylvain Gugger, Mariama Drame, Quentin Lhoest, and Alexander M. Rush. 2020. Transformers: State-of-the-art natural language processing. In *Proceedings of the 2020 Conference on Empirical Methods in Natural Language Processing: System Demonstrations*, pages 38–45, Online. Association for Computational Linguistics.

I Zeki Yalniz, Hervé Jégou, Kan Chen, Manohar Paluri, and Dhruv Mahajan. 2019. Billion-scale semi-supervised learning for image classification. *arXiv preprint arXiv:1905.00546*.

Yu Zhang and Qiang Yang. 2021. A survey on multi-task learning. *IEEE Transactions on Knowledge and Data Engineering*.

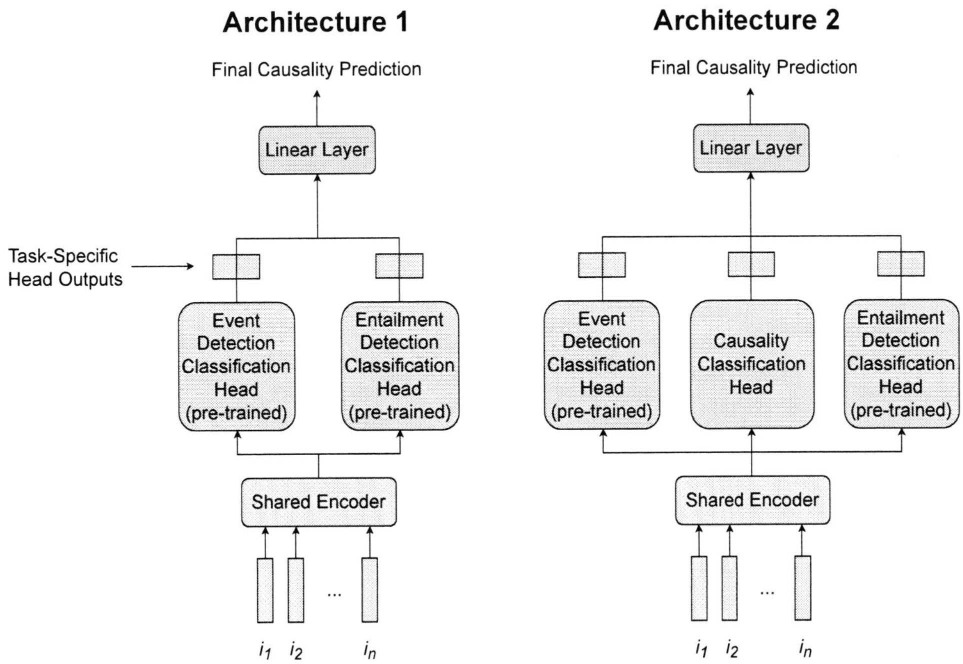

Figure 2: Multi-task learning architectures used in supplementary testing.

6 Appendix

Here, we outline the supplementary experimentation we conducted to compare our self-training results with other methods we explored in the CASE event causality competition. These methods include a few popular transformer-based textual data augmentation techniques and two multi-task learning-based classifier architectures.

6.1 Transformer-based Data Augmentation

In general, data augmentation—within the context of textual data—works by altering a given labeled example and attaching the label of the original example to the augmented one. Each of the transformer-based data augmentation techniques is considered with the same goal of increasing the training data space to improve the model performance on the task of causality classification. We use the CNC training split of 2925 as the original data to be augmented in our experiments.

6.1.1 Sequence to Sequence Data Augmentation

Sequence-to-sequence text augmentation works by taking the sentence of the original example (all of our data examples are English examples), translating the sentence into a foreign language, and then finally translating the rendered sentence back to the original language. This works by altering some words or clusters of words in a sentence while preserving the original structure and semantics. For the purposes of our experiments, we use two foreign languages to augment the data, German and Russian, using HuggingFace's ported versions of the Facebook FAIR's WMT19 News Translation Task Submission (Ng et al., 2019). The sequence-to-sequence augmented training set has 8,775 examples; 2,925 from the original training set and 5,850 augmented examples.

6.1.2 Random Fill-mask Data Augmentation

In random fill-mask augmentation, we first randomly select a word from the original. From there, we replace the selected word with a masking token and use the new sentence with masking as input to a pre-trained RoBERTa fill-mask language model (Liu et al., 2019) to select the three most likely fill-mask options for the masked word. With the three selected substitutions for the masked word, we create three new sentences by replacing each respective substitution with the original masked word and keeping the original label of the sentence with the new augmented examples. The final random fill-mask augmented set has 11,700 total samples.

6.1.3 NER Fill-Mask Data Augmentation

The NER fill-mask data augmentation functions in a similar fashion to the random fill-mask data augmentation, but instead of selecting a single random word to replace, we make substitutions to any named entities identified by Named Entity Recognition (NER) (Mikheev et al., 1999; Mohit, 2014). Specifically, we use the EntityRecognizer module from spaCy [4] to identify which tokens in a sentence corresponded to named entities. For each example sentence from the original training data that contained named entities, we create three augmented sentences by substituting the best unused fill-mask option for each named entity in the text. The final NER augmented dataset has 10,443 example sentences in total.

6.2 Multi-Task Learning Approaches

Multi-task learning (MTL) (Caruana, 1997; Zhang and Yang, 2021; Ruder, 2017) is a paradigm of machine learning that improves the performance of a model in a given task by leveraging simultaneous learning of other distinct but related tasks. Our MTL architectures learn the distinct tasks of entailment classification (binary classification of whether the meaning of one sentence can be inferred from another sentence) and event detection (whether a sentence contains information about a socio-political event), then combine the prior knowledge of those two tasks to help supplement the classifier's prediction to the task of causality classification.

6.2.1 MTL Datasets

We used two distinct datasets for the multi-task learning of entailment detection and event detection.

Entailment Detection Dataset We evaluate using the Recognizing Textual Entailment (RTE) task provided in the GLUE Benchmark (Wang et al., 2018) for the entailment detection task. In training, we used the given training set that consisted of 2490 examples. Each example from the RTE dataset consisted of two sentences and a binary label on whether or not one of the two sentences holds logical entailment to the other. To better fit the structure of the other data, we concatenated the two provided sentences into a single text to be used as input into the models.

Event Detection Dataset In order to learn the task of event detection, we used data provided in the second shared task of CASE @ ACL-IJCNLP 2021 (Hürriyetoğlu et al., 2021), which provided data to the object of sentence-level event classification. The data provided from subtask 2 of CASE 2021 included 1023 examples sentences of socio-political events, labeled using the Armed Conflict Location & Event Data Project (ACLED) (Raleigh et al., 2010) event taxonomy, which consists of 25 fine-grained event subtypes. These 1023 example sentences are concatenated with 720 non-event-specific English sentences to create an event detection dataset, with all sentences coming from the event classification receiving a label of '1', denoting that the sentence contained information about an event.

6.2.2 MTL Pre-training

Prior to fine-tuning our models for the task of causality classification, we train a shared encoder (Guo et al., 2021)-a RoBERTa pre-trained model-on the separate tasks of event detection and entailment detection by fine-tuning the shared encoder on the respective datasets for each task. We fine-tune three epochs for both tasks.

6.2.3 MTL Architectures

We experiment with two similar but different architectures in MTL testing. In both architectures, we first simultaneously fine-tune a classifier on the two tasks of entailment detection and event detection. Because we have distinct datasets for each respective task, we implement this by using the shared encoder approach, where model parameters are hard-shared and each task has its own task-specific classification head.

The distinction between our two MTL architectures comes from how we choose to combine prior knowledge. The architectures we build are shown in Figure 2. Both architectures include task-specific classification heads for the tasks of entailment detection and event detection. The distinction between the two architectures comes in where Architecture no. 2 also includes a causality-specific classification head; the outputs of all three task heads are combined and inputted into a final linear layer to output the final logits prediction. Architecture no. 1 omits the causality-specific classification head and simply combines the outputs of the entailment detection and event detection heads before the linear layer.

[4]https://spacy.io/

Supplementary Experiments Results							
		Accuracy	F1	Recall	Precision	MCC
Baseline		0.8390	0.8543	0.8561	0.8525	0.6745
Self-Training (1:1 polarity)		**0.8586**	**0.8711**	**0.8670**	**0.8755**	**0.7149**
Transformer-based Data Augmentations	Sequence to Sequence	0.8235	0.8430	**0.8596**	0.8270	0.6424
	Random Fill-Mask	**0.8406**	**0.8562**	**0.8574**	**0.8556**	**0.6778**
	NER Fill-Mask	**0.8452**	**0.8571**	0.8427	**0.8721**	**0.6888**
Multi-Task Learning	Architecture 1	**0.8498**	**0.8655**	**0.8764**	**0.8548**	**0.6960**
	Architecture 2	0.8313	0.8489	**0.8596**	0.8385	0.6583

Table 3: Results from supplementary testing done on CNC development set. All runs use a RoBERTa backbone model. The baseline and self-training results are taken from the main experiments of the paper. **Bold** indicates outperforming the baseline.

AdamW Optimizer w/ Linear Decay	
β_1	0.9
β_2	0.999
Per device batch size	8

Table 4: Classifier hyperparameter settings.

6.3 Supplementary Experiments and Results

6.3.1 Set up

For the supplementary experiments, we follow the same setup as in the main study to maintain consistency. Thus, models trained on a transformer-augmented dataset are trained on five epochs of the respective dataset, and each MTL architecture is trained on five epochs of the CNC training set. The evaluations are calculated on the predictions made after the final epoch of training. Likewise, we use the same hyperparameter setup as the main experiments, meaning that we run all trials on a Tesla V100-SXM2-16GB GPU device. Hyperparameters are listed in Table 4. For purposes of the supplementary experiments, we run all trials using a RoBERTa backbone.

6.3.2 Results

Table 3 displays the results of our supplementary tests. Consistent with the main study, the results are the averages over five trials for each of the setups on the CNC development set. Between the transformer-augmented experiments, the random fill-mask and NER fill-mask experiments outperformed the baseline in terms of both accuracy and F_1 score. Similarly, Architecture no. 1 of the MTL approaches also outperformed the baseline in terms of accuracy and F_1.

6.3.3 Discussion

We include the supplementary experiments to **1)** show how our self-training results compared to popular state-of-the-art data augmentation techniques using contemporary NLP, and **2)** propose the multi-task learning architectures we originally developed for the Subtask 1 of the competition. Although the final results of the MTL approaches did not reach the same level of performance as the self-training approaches and therefore did not belong in the main paper, we believe the MTL experiments and results are still notable and worth mentioning for further investigation.

1Cademy @ Causal News Corpus 2022: Enhance Causal Span Detection via Beam-Search-based Position Selector

Xingran Chen[3*], Ge Zhang[1 2 3*], Adam Nik[2 4], Mingyu Li[2 3], Jie Fu[† 1]
[1] Beijing Academy of Artificial Intelligence, China
[2] 1Cademy Community, USA
[3] University of Michigan Ann Arbor, USA
[4] Carleton College, USA
`fujie AT baai.ac.cn`

Abstract

In this paper, we present our approach and empirical observations for Cause-Effect Signal Span Detection—Subtask 2 of Shared task 3 (Tan et al., 2022a) at CASE 2022. The shared task aims to extract the cause, effect, and signal spans from a given causal sentence. We model the task as a reading comprehension (RC) problem and apply a token-level RC-based span prediction paradigm to the task as the baseline. We explore different training objectives to fine-tune the model, as well as data augmentation (DA) tricks based on the language model (LM) for performance improvement. Additionally, we propose an efficient beam-search post-processing strategy to due with the drawbacks of span detection to obtain a further performance gain. Our approach achieves an average F_1 score of 54.15 and ranks 1st in the CASE competition. Our code is available at `https://github.com/Gzhang-umich/1CademyTeamOfCASE`.

1 Introduction

Event extraction has long been a challenging and popular area for natural language processing (NLP) researchers. There are known classic benchmarks, including ACE-2005 (Christopher et al., 2005) and ERE (Song et al., 2015). In recent years, more and more interesting corpora about event detection and extraction have emerged based on different specific source corpora, including biomedical literature (Kim et al., 2003), scientific knowledge resources (Jain et al., 2020), Wiki (Li et al., 2021), and trade-related news (Zhou et al., 2021). In sharp contrast, Cause-Effect Signal Span Detection aims to extract the cause, effect, and signal spans from sentences that have cause-effect relations. Cause-Effect Signal Span Detection is an innovative and important event detection/extraction task that assists in understanding causal relationships from comprehensive sentence samples.

As a new corpus with great potential in event extraction challenges, the Causal News Corpus (CNC) (Tan et al., 2022b) contains socio-political event (SPE) text data with annotated causal spans. The CNC event extraction challenge[1] is the first Cause-Effect Signal Span Detection challenge on a social political news corpus. The challenge itself provides a limited number of annotated samples for supervision, making it more difficult compared to other challenging event extraction tasks. The exploration of causality in news data and the detection of corresponding spans is helpful in reading comprehensive language expressions, making CNC attractive to NLP researchers.

In this paper, we describe our RC-based model with a carefully designed post-processing strategy. We also conduct ablation studies to analyze the influence of both different training objectives and different hyper-parameter settings of the post-processing strategy on our model. In addition, we apply an LM-based data augmentation strategy to further better performance gains, given the low-resource challenge. Our approach improves performance by a large margin in Cause-Effect Signal Span Detection compared to any other competitors.

The main contributions of our paper are as follow:

- We propose an RC-based model with an original post-processing strategy.
- We achieve state-of-the-art performance on the new Cause-Effect Signal Span Detection competition on the CNC.
- We apply an LM-based data augmentation technique to the challenge and prove its positive effect on the challenge of low resources.

[*] The two authors contributed equally to this work.
[†] Corresponding Author

[1] `https://github.com/tanfiona/CausalNewsCorpus`

Proceedings of the 5th Workshop on Challenges and Applications of Automated Extraction of Socio-political Events from Text (CASE), pages 100 - 105
December 7-8, 2022 ©2022 Association for Computational Linguistics

Table 1: Dataset statistics. Avg. Signal represents the average number of Signal spans in each split of dataset.

	Train	Valid	Test	Total
# Sentences	160	15	89	264
# Relations	183	18	119	320
Avg. Signal	0.67	0.56	0.82	0.72

2 Causal News Corpus

The corpus we used in our model training and evaluation is the CNC dataset (Tan et al., 2022b). This dataset is built on the extraction of social-political events from News (AESPEN) (Hürriyetoğlu et al., 2020) in 2020 and the CASE 2021 workshop @ ACL-IJCNLP (Hürriyetoğlu et al., 2021). Each sample in the dataset is annotated with causal labels, that is, whether a sentence contains a causal event. Furthermore, some sentences are annotated with the span of the specific Cause and Effect of a causal event, as well as the signal markers that imply the causality. The spans are labeled by <ARG0>, <ARG1>, and <SIG> annotations to represent the cause, effect, and causal signal in the sentence, respectively. Note that it is possible to have multiple annotations for the same sentence in the dataset if the sentence contains multiple casual relationships of events. The dataset statistics are shown in Table 1.

3 Methodology

In this section, we describe in detail the methodology we used in the task. To begin, we introduce the baseline model established from a pre-trained language model for the task. Next, a beam-search-based post-processing method is introduced to solve the overlap span detection problem in the baseline model. To address the problem that not all examples have signal markers within the sentence, we propose training a signal classifier to determine whether we need to find the signal span of the target test sample. Finally, a pre-trained paraphrasing model is applied for data augmentation.

3.1 Baseline

To solve the task, we first fine-tune the pre-trained language model based on the reading comprehension training fashion proposed by BERT (Devlin et al., 2019). Specifically, assume that we need to predict a span within sentence $x = \{t_1, ..., t_n\}$, where t_i is the ith token of sentence x. We can obtain a contextualized representation h_i of t_i using the pre-trained language model:

Algorithm 1 beam-search-based span selector

Input: $P_{s_c}, P_{e_c}, P_{s_{ef}}, P_{e_{ef}}, n, k, m.$
Output: $H = \{(s_1, e_1, s_2, e_2, t_i = CBeforeE/CAfterE) : i \leq m\}$

CBeforeE = $\{p^i_{s_c} + p^j_{e_{ef}} : 1 \leq i, j \leq n\}$.
CAfterE = $\{p^i_{s_{ef}} + p^j_{e_c} : 1 \leq i, j \leq n\}$.
Find position pairs with Top-k largest score from both CBeforeE and CAfterE.
Denote the gotten position pairs set as $PS = \{(sp_i, ep_i, t_i = CBeforeE/CAfterE) : sp_i \leq ep_i\}$. t_i implies whether the pair is retrieved from CBeforeE or CAfterE.
Initialize a min heap H.
for $ps_p = (sp_p, ep_p, t_p)$ in PS **do**
  if $t_p = CBeforeE$ **then**
    Find the position pair (i, j) with the largest $p^i_{e_c} + p^j_{s_{ef}}$, which satisfies $sp_p \leq i \leq j \leq ep_p$.
    Calculate $sc_{(sp_p,i,j,ep_p)} = p^{sp_p}_{s_c} + p^i_{e_c} + p^j_{s_{ef}} + p^{ep_p}_{e_{ef}}$.
  else
    Find the position pair (i, j) with the largest $p^i_{e_{ef}} + p^j_{s_c}$, which satisfies $sp_p \leq i \leq j \leq ep_p$.
    Calculate $sc_{(sp_p,i,j,ep_p)} = p^{sp_p}_{s_{ef}} + p^i_{e_{ef}} + p^j_{s_c} + p^{ep_p}_{e_c}$.
  Push $\{(sp_p, i, j, ep_p), t_p, sc_{(sp_p,i,j,ep_p)}\}$ into H.
  if $len(H) > m$ **then**
    $heappop(H)$ based on $sc_{(sp_p,i,j,ep_p)}$.
return H

$$H = \{h_1, ..., h_n\} = BERT(x) \quad (1)$$

Next, we define two parameterized vectors: $v_s, v_e \in R^d$ to calculate the probability that the ith token is the start / end position:

$$P_s = \{p_s^{(1)}, ..., p_s^{(n)}\} = Softmax(v_s^T H) \quad (2)$$

$$P_e = \{p_e^{(1)}, ..., p_e^{(n)}\} = Softmax(v_e^T H) \quad (3)$$

We select the positions with maximum probability as the prediction of the model:

$$s = \underset{1 \leq i \leq n}{\text{argmax}}\, p_s^{(i)}, \quad (4)$$

$$e = \underset{1 \leq j \leq n}{\text{argmax}}\, p_e^{(j)}, \quad (5)$$

where s, e represent the predicted start/end position, respectively.

The prediction of the spans of cause, effect, and signal are all similar to the span prediction task described above. For convenience, we will denote the start/end position of cause, effect, and signal as $s_c, e_c, s_{ef}, e_{ef}, s_{sig}, e_{sig}$, respectively, to specify which span we are detecting. Therefore, the training objective is to maximize the probability of ground-truth positions in the model.

3.2 Beam-search-based Span Selector

The proposed baseline model has two drawbacks. First, it is possible that the end position is right before the start position. Second, it is possible to generate spans that overlap each other, which is not allowed in the challenge. Thus, we need to introduce constraints in post-processing to ensure that: 1) the predicted end position must be after the start position of the same span, and 2) the predicted spans of cause and effect do not overlap with each other. In this sub-section, we describe our modified beam search-based algorithm to address the overlapping issue. The beam search algorithm is widely used to find the most possible output with tractable memory and time usage in text generation tasks (Xie, 2017). In reading comprehension or question answering, it is also used to introduce constraint information (Hu et al., 2019), and therefore encourage more accurate predictions. Given a paragraph with length n, we can calculate $P_{s_c} = \{p_{s_c}^{(1)}, ..., p_{s_c}^{(n)}\}$ based on the process introduced in § 3.1. Similarly, we can calculate P_{e_c}, $P_{s_{ef}}$, and $P_{e_{ef}}$ accordingly. Formally, given the input probability vectors P_{s_c}, P_{e_c}, $P_{s_{ef}}$, $P_{e_{ef}}$, a hyper-parameter m denoting the requested answer number, and a hyper-parameter k denoting the beam search size, the span selector is expected to output position pairs s_c, e_c, s_{ef} and e_{ef}. We describe the span selector in detail in Algorithm 1. We denote the proposed span selector as **BSS**. It should be noted that the proposed BSS post-processing algorithm can also generate multiple predictions for cases containing multiple causal relations. For example, we could change the hyperparameter m to retrieve the prediction of cause/effect spans combinations with the top-m highest scores as our predictions of multiple causal relations. For the signal span, we always use the span with the highest score as our prediction (if it presents).

3.3 Signal Classifier

We observe that some samples do not have signal markers (spans) within the sentence even while the baseline model predicts s_{sig}, e_{sig} for each target sample. Therefore, we propose to train a classifier to address this issue. Specifically, we first automatically annotate training samples based on whether signal markers appear within the samples. Then, we fine-tune the pre-trained language model to train a binary classifier. Note that we can share the language model parameters between signal classifier and span detection, i.e. we optimize both training objectives during our fine-tuning process. In addition, we can also train a signal classifier with a separate language model. In our experiments, we apply the two methods separately and compare their effectiveness.

3.4 Data Augmentation with Pre-trained Paraphrasing Model

Considering that only 183 training samples are available for subtask 2, it is important to introduce the data augmentation trick to increase the size of the training dataset. Therefore, in this work, we propose using language models to paraphrase the existing data. Specifically, we use a PEGASUS model (Zhang et al., 2020) fine-tuned for paraphrasing [2] to re-write the phrases of Cause, Effect in each sample. For example, for a training sample "*<ARG1>The farmworkers ' strike resumed on Tuesday</ARG1> when <ARG0>their demands were not met</ARG0>*.", we paraphrase the cause and effect spans within the sample, then obtain the augmented sample "*<ARG1>On Tuesday, the farmworkers resumed their strike</ARG1> when <ARG0>their demands weren't met</ARG0>*.". In this case, the semantic meaning of the original sentence is preserved. Hence, the annotation of the original sample is still reasonable and can continue to be used in the augmented sample. In our implementation, n new phrases were generated for each span. Namely that each sample will end up with n^2 augmented samples. We denote the trick as **DA**.

4 Experiments

In this section, we present the experimental details of training the model and discuss the performance of our proposed approach.

4.1 Experimental Details

In our experiment, we use Albert (Lan et al., 2019) as our LM backbone. We perform hyper-parameter searching to find the best hyper-parameter setting. Specifically, we select the learning rate l

[2]We directly use fine-tuned checkpoint in https://huggingface.co/tuner007/pegasus_paraphrase

Table 2: Experimental results and related ablation study on subtask 2. The evaluation metric of all the results is F_1. Note that n represents the hyper-parameter of data augmentation described in § 3.4.

Methods	Cause	Effect	Signal	Overall
Baseline	77.8	66.7	53.5	68.2
Baseline-NER	57.8	57.4	10.8	47.4
Baseline + DA ($n = 2$)	72.2	77.8	60.9.	71.9
Baseline + BSS + DA ($n = 2$)	77.8	**83.3**	60.9	74.1
Baseline + ES + DA ($n = 2$)	72.2	77.8	76.7	75.4
Baseline + JS + DA ($n = 2$)	72.2	72.2	71.3	69.8
Baseline + BSS + ES + DA ($n = 2$)	77.8	**83.3**	76.7	77.5
Baseline + BSS + ES + DA ($n = 3$)	**83.3**	77.8	**80.0**	**80.4**

from $\{1e-5, 2e-5, 5e-5\}$, batch size b from $\{1, 2, 4, 8, 16, 32\}$. We fine-tune the pre-trained model for 30 epochs, and select the checkpoint with the best performance on the development set to conduct evaluation on the test set. Our implementation is based on `Huggingface` (Wolf et al., 2019).

In terms of the signal classifier, we consider two settings: 1) We fine-tune the signal classifier in conjunction with the main training objective as described in § 3.3. We denote this approach as **Joint Sig. (JS)**; 2) We additionally fine-tune a language model to specifically decide whether to predict the span of Signal. We denote this approach by **Extra Sig. (ES)**

We also include another implementation of the baseline recommended by the organizers, where the fine-tuning process is carried out in the end-to-end fashion of Named Entity Recognition (NER). We denote this baseline by **Baseline-NER**.

4.2 Main Results and Ablation Study

Here, we present and discuss the experimental results of our best-performing method for this task, together with the corresponding ablation study. Note that all results are evaluated on the dev set, due to the inaccessibility of the test dataset. We present the score of different approaches F_1 on all three span detection in Table 2.

The results clearly show that the reading comprehension style of the training significantly improves the effectiveness of the approach. We can also observe that it is better to apply the reading comprehension training fashion than token-level tagging for the causal span detection task. Regarding our proposed approaches, the LM-based paraphrasing data augmentation technique improves the performance of the approach by a large margin compared to the baseline. The improvement is consistent, that is, there is an improvement in the prediction of all types of spans. In addition, our proposed BSS post-processing algorithm further improves our approach. However, it can be seen that the improvement of the approach by BSS mainly comes from the prediction of cause and effect. This is reasonable because the algorithm does not post-process the predictions of Signal. As for the signal classifier, both ES and JS make an improvement, which comes mainly from the better prediction of Signal. However, note that the improvement in ES is larger. We conjecture that it might be because of a new training objective introduced by JS, which is harmful to the proposed approach to learning to predict the spans better. Finally, we mix all of the approaches together with our approach and ended up with the best performance. Here, we also compared the impact of data augmentation at different scales. Specifically, we compare the results when $n = 2$ ($4\times$ dataset size) with $n = 3$ ($9\times$ dataset size). We find that higher data augmentation sizes lead to better results in the validation dataset.

4.3 Case Study of Data Augmentation

In this subsection, we provide a case study on the effectiveness of data augmentation proposed in the system. The comparisons between generated texts and the original texts are shown in Table 3.

From the results, the expressions in the data-augmented texts are more diverse while remaining semantically consistent with the original sentence. Furthermore, the data-augmented texts are competitive with the original in terms of fluency and grammatical correctness.

Table 3: Case Study of Data Augmentation. Note that we generate two sentences for Cause and Effect, respectively. Therefore, there are in total 4 outcomes sentences via combinations.

Ori.	<ARG1>The farmworkers ' strike resumed on Tuesday</ARG1>when <ARG0>their demands were not met</ARG0>
DA	<ARG1>On Tuesday, the farmworkers resumed their strike</ARG1>when <ARG0>their demands weren't met</ARG0>. <ARG1>On Tuesday, the farmworkers resumed their strike</ARG1>when <ARG0>their demands didn't get met</ARG0>. <ARG1>On Tuesday, the farmworkers went on strike</ARG1>when <ARG0>their demands weren't met</ARG0>. <ARG1>On Tuesday, the farmworkers went on strike</ARG1>when <ARG0>their demands didn't get met</ARG0>.

Table 4: Overall performance of the proposed approach on the test set. The numbers in parentheses represent the rankings.

Final Competition Results	
Recall	0.5387 (1)
Precision	0.5509 (2)
F1	0.5415 (1)
Accuracy	0.4315 (1)

4.4 Competition Result

We reveal and discuss the final results of our proposed approach competition on a test set. The results are shown in Table 4.

As shown in the table, our proposed approach achieves state-of-the-art results in 3 out of 4 evaluation metrics on subtask 2. This shows the excellent performance of the proposed approach in solving the task of causal spans detection.

5 Conclusion

This paper introduces a reading comprehension-based method, an original post-processing strategy, and an LM-based data augmentation trick for the new Cause-Effect Signal Span Detection competition. We compare the RC-based method with the NER-based one and prove that the RC-based method gets an observing performance gain compared to the NER-based one. We provide experimental results and ablation studies of our beam-search-based Span Selector and LM-based data augmentation tricks to analyze their efficiency and prove their compatibility with other tricks. Our approach achieves state-of-the-art performance in the new competition.

Acknowledgements

This study was supported by the National Key R&D Program of China (2020AAA0105200).

References

Walker Christopher, Strassel Stephanie, Medero Julie, and Maeda Kazuaki. 2005. Ace 2005 multilingual training corpus.

Jacob Devlin, Ming-Wei Chang, Kenton Lee, and Kristina Toutanova. 2019. BERT: Pre-training of deep bidirectional transformers for language understanding. In *Proceedings of the 2019 Conference of the North American Chapter of the Association for Computational Linguistics: Human Language Technologies, Volume 1 (Long and Short Papers)*, pages 4171–4186, Minneapolis, Minnesota. Association for Computational Linguistics.

Minghao Hu, Yuxing Peng, Zhen Huang, and Dongsheng Li. 2019. A multi-type multi-span network for reading comprehension that requires discrete reasoning. *arXiv preprint arXiv:1908.05514*.

Ali Hürriyetoğlu, Hristo Tanev, Vanni Zavarella, Jakub Piskorski, Reyyan Yeniterzi, Osman Mutlu, Deniz Yuret, and Aline Villavicencio. 2021. Challenges and applications of automated extraction of socio-political events from text (CASE 2021): Workshop and shared task report. In *Proceedings of the 4th Workshop on Challenges and Applications of Automated Extraction of Socio-political Events from Text (CASE 2021)*, pages 1–9, Online. Association for Computational Linguistics.

Ali Hürriyetoğlu, Vanni Zavarella, Hristo Tanev, Erdem Yörük, Ali Safaya, and Osman Mutlu. 2020. Automated extraction of socio-political events from news (AESPEN): Workshop and shared task report. In *Proceedings of the Workshop on Automated Extraction of Socio-political Events from News 2020*, pages 1–6, Marseille, France. European Language Resources Association (ELRA).

Sarthak Jain, Madeleine van Zuylen, Hannaneh Hajishirzi, and Iz Beltagy. 2020. SciREX: A challenge dataset for document-level information extraction. In *Proceedings of the 58th Annual Meeting of the Association for Computational Linguistics*, pages 7506–7516, Online. Association for Computational Linguistics.

J-D Kim, Tomoko Ohta, Yuka Tateisi, and Jun'ichi Tsujii. 2003. Genia corpus—a semantically annotated corpus for bio-textmining. *Bioinformatics*, 19(suppl_1):i180–i182.

Zhenzhong Lan, Mingda Chen, Sebastian Goodman, Kevin Gimpel, Piyush Sharma, and Radu Soricut.

2019. Albert: A lite bert for self-supervised learning of language representations. In *International Conference on Learning Representations*.

Sha Li, Heng Ji, and Jiawei Han. 2021. Document-level event argument extraction by conditional generation. In *Proceedings of the 2021 Conference of the North American Chapter of the Association for Computational Linguistics: Human Language Technologies*, pages 894–908, Online. Association for Computational Linguistics.

Zhiyi Song, Ann Bies, Stephanie Strassel, Tom Riese, Justin Mott, Joe Ellis, Jonathan Wright, Seth Kulick, Neville Ryant, and Xiaoyi Ma. 2015. From light to rich ERE: Annotation of entities, relations, and events. In *Proceedings of the The 3rd Workshop on EVENTS: Definition, Detection, Coreference, and Representation*, pages 89–98, Denver, Colorado. Association for Computational Linguistics.

Fiona Anting Tan, Hansi Hettiarachchi, Ali Hürriyetoğlu, Tommaso Caselli, Onur Uca, Farhana Ferdousi Liza, and Nelleke Oostdijk. 2022a. Event causality identification with causal news corpus - shared task 3, CASE 2022. In *Proceedings of the 5th Workshop on Challenges and Applications of Automated Extraction of Socio-political Events from Text (CASE 2022)*, Online. Association for Computational Linguistics.

Fiona Anting Tan, Ali Hürriyetoğlu, Tommaso Caselli, Nelleke Oostdijk, Tadashi Nomoto, Hansi Hettiarachchi, Iqra Ameer, Onur Uca, Farhana Ferdousi Liza, and Tiancheng Hu. 2022b. The causal news corpus: Annotating causal relations in event sentences from news.

Thomas Wolf, Lysandre Debut, Victor Sanh, Julien Chaumond, Clement Delangue, Anthony Moi, Pierric Cistac, Tim Rault, Rémi Louf, Morgan Funtowicz, et al. 2019. Huggingface's transformers: State-of-the-art natural language processing. *arXiv preprint arXiv:1910.03771*.

Ziang Xie. 2017. Neural text generation: A practical guide. *arXiv preprint arXiv:1711.09534*.

Jingqing Zhang, Yao Zhao, Mohammad Saleh, and Peter Liu. 2020. Pegasus: Pre-training with extracted gap-sentences for abstractive summarization. In *International Conference on Machine Learning*, pages 11328–11339. PMLR.

Zhihan Zhou, Liqian Ma, and Han Liu. 2021. Trade the event: Corporate events detection for news-based event-driven trading. In *Findings of the Association for Computational Linguistics: ACL-IJCNLP 2021*, pages 2114–2124, Online. Association for Computational Linguistics.

Hybrid Knowledge Engineering Leveraging a Robust ML Framework to Produce an Assassination Dataset

Abigail Sticha and **Ernesto Verdeja** and **Paul Brenner**
University of Notre Dame
Notre Dame, IN 46556
{asticha, everdeja, paul.r.brenner}@nd.edu

Abstract

Social and political researchers require robust event datasets to conduct data-driven analysis, an example being the need for trigger event datasets to analyze under what conditions and in what patterns certain trigger-type events increase the probability of mass killings. Fortunately, NLP and ML can be leveraged to create these robust datasets. In this paper we (i) outline a robust ML framework that prioritizes understandability through visualizations and generalizability through the ability to implement different ML algorithms, (ii) perform a comparative analysis of these ML tools within the framework for the coup trigger, (iii) leverage our ML framework along with a unique combination of NLP tools, such as NER and knowledge graphs, to produce a dataset for the the assassination trigger, and (iv) make this comprehensive, consolidated, and cohesive assassination dataset publicly available to provide temporal data for understanding political violence as well as training data for further socio-political research.

1 Introduction

Peace and conflict researchers have identified several large-scale structural conditions that make state-led mass killings more likely, such as ongoing political instability or histories of state violence against vulnerable groups (Verdeja, 2016). However, the timing of mass killing onset is less understood. Burley et al. (2020) identifies nine potential triggering events for state mass killings, such as coups and assassinations, but before socio-political researchers can conduct systematic analysis to examine whether, and if so when, certain patterns of trigger-type events actually increase the probability of mass killings, it is necessary for political researchers to obtain political event datasets for each of these potential triggering events.

Processing the massive amount of information in available data in order to create socio-policial event (SPE) datasets for events such as the triggers described above takes extensive time, money, and human power. Fortunately, natural language processing (NLP) and related machine learning (ML) tools can be harnessed to classify the rapidly growing, but often poorly structured and unlabeled, data as to whether they contain an event or not. ML classification tools have been increasing combined with other NLP tools such as Named Entity Recognition (NER) and Knowledge Graphs (KGs) to engineer these datasets. Although these ML and NLP tools have become more robust, it is important for the AI research community to acknowledge that each tool comes with limitations and a scope of use. With this in mind, our project seeks to uniquely leverage a combination of these tools in order to mitigate their drawbacks to create an SPE dataset.

The most cited challenge for political event extraction is small labeled training datasets (Büyüköz et al., 2020; Ramrakhiyani et al., 2021; Caselli et al., 2021) which become an issue when working with ML classification algorithms. Therefore, our first task is to provide a clear, efficient, and accessible machine learning framework that future social scientists may utilize when implementing NLP-focused algorithms to classify large quantities of text documents given a small labeled training dataset. We prioritize a framework that is reproducible, understandable, and generalizable by both including essential visualizations of the input data and results and structuring the framework in such a way that fellow researchers can implement different ML algorithms, such as support vector machines (SVMs) or bidirectional encoder representations from transformers (BERT). We demonstrate that different ML algorithms are most suitable for a given optimization problem by performing a thorough comparative analysis of these different ML algorithms for the coup trigger in the process of refining our framework.

After explaining our ML framework, we demon-

Proceedings of the 5th Workshop on Challenges and Applications of Automated Extraction of Socio-political Events from Text (CASE), pages 106 - 116
December 7-8, 2022 ©2022 Association for Computational Linguistics

strate how we implement this framework to create a dataset for a new trigger: assassinations. We describe the process of deciding which ML tool to implement within the framework and subsequently leverage our robust ML framework along with a combination of additional NLP tools, such as NER and KGs, to create the SPE dataset. By mitigating the drawbacks and uniting the strengths of both machine-based and human-centric approaches we create the most comprehensive (targeting all known assassination events), consolidated (a single dataset solely focused on assassination events), and cohesive (easily filterable and readable) assassinations dataset to provide temporal data for understanding political violence as well as training data for further socio-political research [1].

2 Related Work

2.1 Existing Assassinations Datasets

To date, there is no dataset created with the sole intent of targeting all global assassinations of leadership figures. There are pre-existing datasets that either include assassination events as a small portion of the data entries or small scale case studies focusing on specific assassination events in a given country. Nevertheless, there are two previously existing dataset that we explored for assassination events: (1) the Archigos dataset (Goemans et al., 2009) and (2) the Global Terrorism Database (GTD) (LaFree and Dugan, 2007).

Created in 2009, Archigos serves primarily as a data set of political leaders in 188 countries from 1875 to 2015 and has 1,287 entries in its latest version (4.1). Each entry contains the political leader's name, age, gender, term start date and end date, and fate a year after leaving office. The GTD is more comprehensive, as it contains over 200,000 terrorism event entries from 171 countries in the years 1970 to 2019. This data was retrieved from approximately four million global news articles. Each entry contains the date, location, weapons used, target, number of casualties, and group or individuals responsible; but unfortunately, often includes a position description (i.e. mayor) as opposed to the name for the assassination target ('target1' column in dataset)

[1]Upon the completion of the blind review process our dataset will be released publicly at the conference through our university curation system.

2.2 Existing Tools for SPE Extraction

Although no comprehensive assassination dataset is available, building robust SPE databases is not a new task of interest and the tools used to create these databases have varied. Many of these more established databases, as well as some newer databases, are manually coded by humans (Raleigh et al., 2010; Gleditsch et al., 2002; Kriesi et al., 2020). These human in the loop projects require full-time permanent employees and extensive support and funding due to the large amount of data to code. For example, Gleditsch et al. (2002) staff processes nearly 50,000 news items and other reports yearly. To mitigate these challenges, many SPE projects have relied on automated event coders like KEDS (Schrodt et al., 1994) or PETRARCH (Schrodt et al., 2014) to record political events (Leetaru and Schrodt, 2013; Halterman et al., 2017). Although these tools provide increased automation, they produce further challenges, such as bias due to human-curated dictionaries, the inability for replication, and issues with aggregating multiple reports into a single event (Rød and Weidmann, 2013). Therefore, many SPE projects have shifted focus to new ML frameworks.

Some projects leverage a hybrid approach of human coding and ML such as Nardulli et al. (2015) to curate a Social, Political and Economic Event Database and Pavlick et al. (2016) to curate a gun violence database. Other projects focus strictly on ML, such as using BERT-based models to extract protest events (Caselli et al., 2021; Celik et al., 2021; Hanna, 2017; Büyüköz et al., 2020). Researchers have also incorporated NER and pre-existing databases along with the ML tools to perform distant supervision such as Reschke et al. (2014) to create a plane crashes database and Keith et al. (2017) to create a police killings dataset. Finally, KGs have been leveraged by Rudnik et al. (2019) to create an event search engine and other researchers have began combining ML and KG for engineering datasets (Guo et al., 2020; Subasic et al., 2019) but to our knowledge there are no examples of this specific combination in the SPE domain.

These hybrid ML methodologies either rely on the availability of many trained human readers, large training datasets, or structured and dense existing datasets for distant supervision. Our project, on the other hand, is focused on minimizing human labor, leveraging a small training dataset, and building off incomplete datasets and therefore calls for a novel hybrid approach to dataset engineering that leverages a ML framework for small training sets, NER, KGs, and human-centric approaches.

2.3 Choosing a ML Tool

Researches have implemented traditional ML tools, such as SVMs, K-nearest neighbor, Decision Trees, and Naive Bayes for text classification. From these tools, we selected SVMs as the baseline for our project based on background research that shows that SVMs often outperform other text machine learning tools due to their "simple structure, complete theory, high adaptability, global optimization, short training time, and good generalization performance" (Liu et al., 2010; Gayathri and Marimuthu, 2013; Kwok, 1998; Wright et al., 2013). We also experimented with neural network architecture such as CNNs, RNNs, and LSTMs, but whereas SVMs are equipped to train on smaller datasets (Díaz Rodríguez et al., 2004; Gao and Sun, 2010; Zhang et al., 2008), these models require larger training sets than were available [2].

Newer NLP neural network tools include word embedding tools such as word2vec (Mikolov et al., 2013) and transformers (Vaswani et al., 2017) such as BERT (Devlin et al., 2019). BERT is a transformer based NLP tool that was pre-trained through masked language modeling and next sentence prediction tasks using 3.3 Billion words total with 2.5B from Wikipedia and 0.8B from BooksCorpus (Devlin et al., 2019). The model can be fine-tuned using labeled text for different downstream NLP tasks, such a classification (González-Carvajal and Garrido-Merchán, 2020). Since this is such a powerful and efficient model, there have been countless variants of BERT which can be viewed on the Huggingface library (Wolf et al., 2020). In this study we will focus on 1) BERT-base, a smaller version of the BERT model released by Google, which we will refer to as our 'BERT model' and 2) Longformer, a BERT-based model that aims to handle inputs of longer length by using segment-level recurrence mechanisms to capture information from all the tokens of a document (Beltagy et al., 2020). With Longformer each document can be represented by up to 4,096 tokens, as opposed to 512 for BERT, so we hoped leveraging Longformer would rescue information from our long text inputs that was potentially lost when implementing BERT.

There have been several studies comparing SVMs and pre-trained BERT models for SPE extraction. Olsson et al. (2020); Büyüköz et al. (2020) find that BERT-based models outperform tradition ML algorithms while Piskorski and Jacquet (2020) finds that tf-idf-weighted character n-gram SVM models outperform BERT-based models. It is important to note that Olsson et al. (2020); Büyüköz et al. (2020) and other SPE projects that focus solely on pre-trained models, such as Caselli et al. (2021); Celik et al. (2021), have significantly larger training sets available than our project.

2.4 Wikidata

Knowledge graphs leverage graph structure to represent data where edges capture the relations between entities within the data which allows researchers to extract knowledge, such as events, from the structure (Hogan et al., 2021). The KG that we leverage is Wikidata, which contains over 96 million data items that are expressed through property-value pairs, so each item can have many different properties associated with it. Vrandečić and Krötzsch (2014) discuss some of the applications of Wikidata, including browsing and querying the data it contains. Wikidata also provides an interface for access as a directed labeled graph using the RDF data model and SPARQL query language [3]. Some of the most cited issues with large knowledge graphs like Wikidata include "maintaining their coverage, correctness, and freshness" (Hur et al., 2021), challenges that will be mitigated through our hybrid engineering approach.

3 A Robust ML Framework

3.1 Dataset for Refining Framework: Coups

In order to refine a robust machine learning framework and highlight challenges along the way we chose to focus on one trigger, namely coups. We chose this trigger because it had the highest overlap in classification by humans at the time with an intercoder reliability score of 87.50% agreement. The coup data consists of the English-translated text of news articles retrieved via LexisNexis queries based on several search parameters: a date filter from 1989-2017, a source filter for our list of 20 sources, and keywords, such as 'coup' and 'over-

[2]Models only reached scores of 66.4% (CNN), 76.3% (RNN), and 61.8% (LSTM) with validation losses stagnating above 50 percent or rising dramatically during training for coups

[3]https://query.wikidata.org

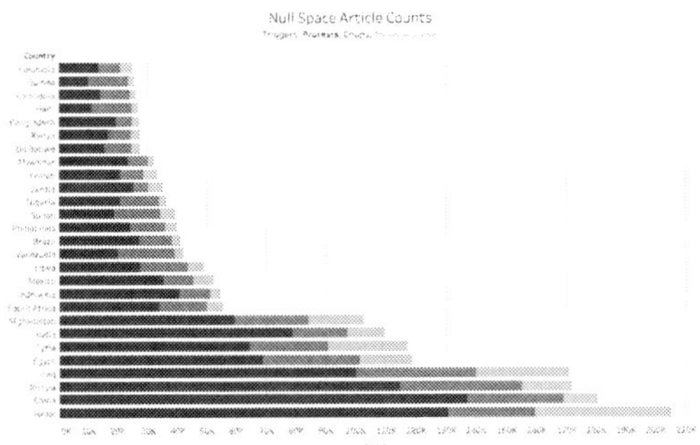

Figure 1: Article counts for countries that comprise >1% of the total articles pulled down across each trigger.

throw', based on trigger definition[4]. The corpus that we hope to classify contains 647,989 unclassified articles. This large magnitude of queried articles (Fig 1), even for a trigger with high intercoder scores and simple keywords, highlights the importance of defining the event of focus with amazing clarity to enable a precise query. In addition to the unclassified dataset, we used a training set consisting of 551 articles (117 positive and 434 negative) retrieved in the same manner and labeled by a team of researchers trained to identify articles that qualify as a coup event.

3.2 Event Coding with PETRARCH

In the beginning stages of the project we leveraged the PETRARCH (Schrodt et al., 2014) event coding software to search for specific key word associations that are defined within a custom definition file fed to the PETRARCH software. These dictionary files are unique to a given trigger and follow the CAMEO standard for political event extraction (Gerner et al., 2002). We employed the trigger coding definitions from Burley et al. (2020) which included the specific key words for coups. During the dictionary creation process, we found that creating new dictionaries for each refinement of a search is labor intensive and risks added bias. This motivated us to shift towards newer machine learning methods to develop an inference engine to gather articles that fit our trigger definitions.

3.3 Classification with SVMs

Our overall ML framework (Fig 2) is split into two phases: the development phase and the production phase. The development phase involves training,

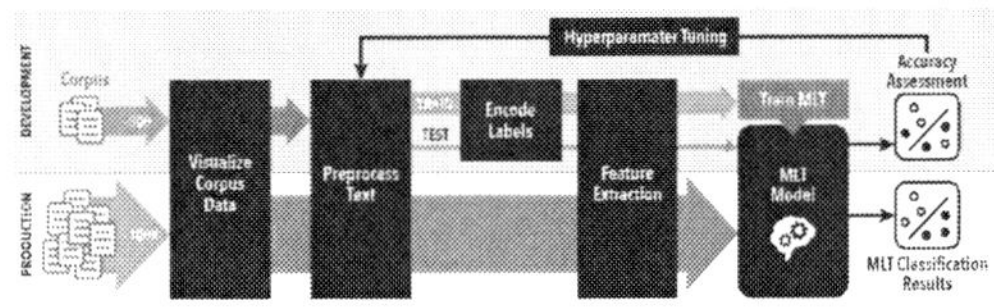

Figure 2: ML framework for article classification.

testing, and iteratively tuning the machine learning algorithm which allows each model to 'learn' the patterns in the data that separate an instance of a potential trigger versus a non-trigger. Once a model is sufficiently optimized, we classify our larger, unlabeled data set in the production phase.

Our SVM workflow script was initially modeled off of a concise text classification example written by Gungit Bedi (Bedi, 2019). The workflow begins with robust visualizations of the data, as these can aid in understanding the textual relationships from which the machine learning algorithms will produce insights. Next, the text is preprocessed: blank rows removed, text lowercased, stopwords removed, and text tokenized and lemmatized. After these steps, and once the labels are encoded, the processed text is transformed into a numerical vector that can be understood and utilized in the SVM algorithm. The tf-idf vectorizer builds a vocabulary by transforming the articles into a tf-idf-weighted document-term sparse matrix of size (n_articles, m_features). Within the matrix, a higher tf-idf value denotes a stronger relationship between a term and the document in which it appears (Lilleberg et al., 2015). Finally, both the encoded labels and text vectors are inputted into the SVM model where the model trains and learns from the data. After finding optimal training hyperparameters via a grid-search, we ultimately set the training percentage = 80%, C-value = 1, and kernel type = linear.

3.4 Classification with BERT and Longformer

The framework for training our BERT and Longformer is the same as Figure (2), making our pipeline understandable and reproducible. The scripts for BERT and Longformer are based on a tutorial provided by Venelin Valkov (Valkov, 2020). We decided to train the Longformer in addition to BERT due to the high percentage of articles over the 512 token limit for BERT (Fig 3).

The BERT-based preprocessing begins similarly to our SVM as the data is imported and blank rows are removed. Conveniently, the Hugging-

[4]Please contact authors for robust trigger definitions and associated keyword

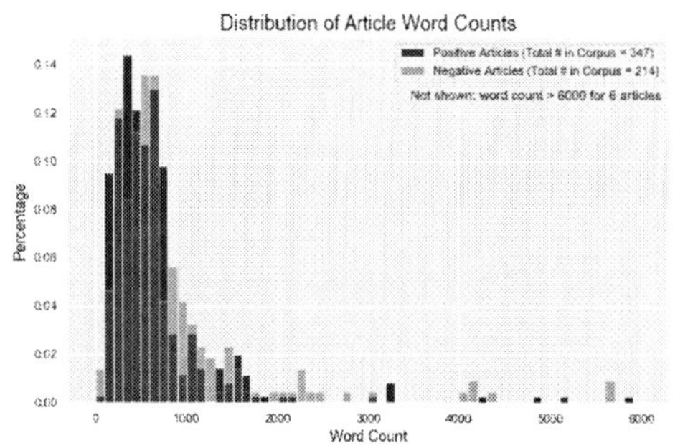

Figure 3: Distribution of training word counts by class.

Face Library provides tokenizers for each model which pre-process the text. Under the hood, these tokenizers lowercases all words and decomposes the input into individual words. More precisely, the BERT tokenizer decomposes inputs into word-pieces (Wordpiece tokenization) while the Longformer tokenizer decomposes words via byte-pair encoding. Since the BERT model uses the original text data to gain understanding of long-term dependencies between words, vectorizing with tf-idf is unnecessary. Rather, the tokenizer simply transforms the tokens to their corresponding integer ids. There are several special tokens added to each input, such as [PAD] which is added to the end of inputs to make each entry the same length, but all other tokens are integer IDs given to each word based on the WordPiece embeddings vocabulary. These input IDs, along with an attention mask are passed to each of the BERT-based models.

The training of the BERT model is more abstract than the SVM. The BERT and Longformer pre-trained weights were downloaded from the pretrained models named 'bert-base-uncased' and 'allenai/longformer-base-4096' on the HuggingFace library, respectively. Then a dropout layer and a final linear layer for classification was added to each of these models. We closely followed the original BERT hyperparameters in our script, specifically, sparse categorical cross-entropy as the loss function, ADAM for the optimization algorithm, a batch size of 6, a learning rate of 2e-5, and 50 epochs. A maximum token length of 512 was used for the BERT model and a length of 1,250 was used for the Longformer model (based on counts in Fig 3) which reduces long inputs down to this maximum length for each model and leaves out remaining tokens.

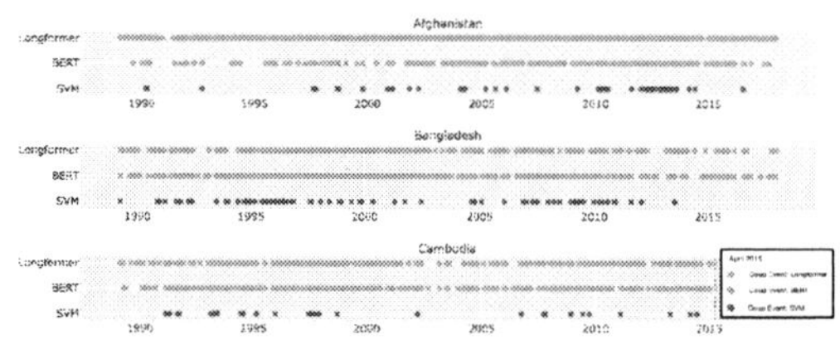

Figure 4: Timeline of articles describing coup events for a subset of countries as classified by each model.

Table 1: Acccuracy Comparison of SVM, BERT, and Longformer Models

	SVM	BERT	Longformer
Number of Positive Coups	28,552	74,871	73,580
Accuracy Score	96.39	96.34	91.67
Precision Score	98.0	95.0	92.0
Human Validation Score	78.93	78.05	77.56

3.5 Comparative Analysis of Models

We used the trained SVM kernels, BERT, and Longformer models to classify the 647,989 unlabeled coup articles and performed a comparative analysis of the results. We created Fig 4 to visualize the classified data and quickly identify differences in how each of the model classify different articles.

Number of Articles Classified as a Coup Event Figure 4 highlights the issue that all models seem to over-specify articles as positive coups (a high false positive rate), shown by the deceiving appearance of constant coup events occurring in each country across 1989-2017. Therefore, we record the total number of articles classified as a coup event (Fig 1, row 1). Evidently, the SVM outperformed BERT and Longformer in terms of refraining from over-specifying articles as coups.

Accuracy Score on Test Data - We compared the predicted labels on the test data to their correct labels (Fig 1, row 2). These scores were extremely promising given our small training dataset.

Precision on Test Data - We produced confusion matrices and classification reports which output precision, recall, and F1 scores. Precision was the most important metric for our project due to the problem of false positives and preference for Type II errors over Type I errors. Maximizing precision minimizes false positive errors. The precision of each model are shown in row 3 of Table 1.

Accuracy Score on Subset of Human Validation Data - A subset of the classification results were validated/coded by the political science researchers. There were 622 articles in this subset, 15 labeled "yes" by the human coders and 607 la-

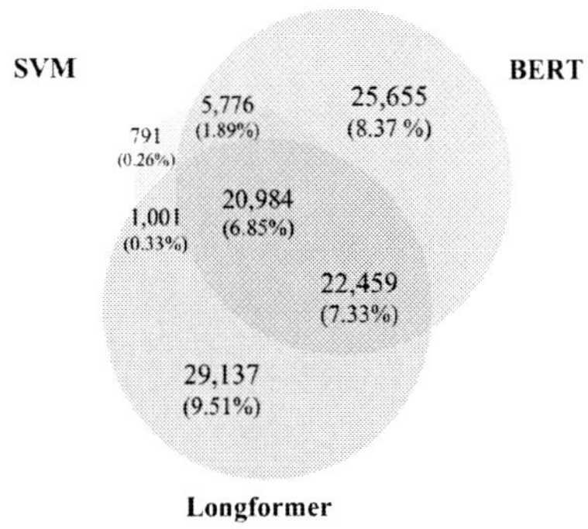

Figure 5: Overlap in model predictions of positively-classified coup articles

beled "no." We compared these labels to the labels that each model gave to these same 622 articles. These percentages are given in row 3 of Table 1.

Similarity Percentage Between Models In addition to statistical accuracies, it is also useful to analyze the similarities between our 3 models. Specifically, we focused on reporting the overlap of the positive coup articles as shown in Figure 5. We found a 93.72% overlap between SVM and BERT, 59.04% between BERT and Longformer, and 77% between SVM and Longformer. We also found that the "yes" articles could be further decreased from 28,552 to 20,984 articles by taking the overlap of SVM, BERT, and Longformer results where all agree on a positive classification (as opposed to focusing on the SVM classified coup events.)

Resource Restraints The SVM model showed no time or resource restraints. The BERT-based models, on the other hand, took 15 times longer to train than the SVM, and required a GPU for training. Additionally, the batch sizes for both BERT-based models could not exceed the size of 6 due to memory constraints.

Interpretability The SVM proved more interpretable than the BERT-based algorithms. We were able to visualize the most significant tokens for classification as measured by tf-idf scores (Fig 6). We also used a dimensionality reduction algorithm, UMAP (McInnes et al., 2020) to reduce each tf-idf document vector to 2-dimensional vectors and plot these vectors. In the resulting plot the 'yes' and 'no', or coup and non-coup, articles are roughly clustered together (Fig 7). The line added to the figure to separate these two clusters is a hypothetical representation of the SVM. These types of tangible representations are not as readily available for the BERT-based models due to their complexity and

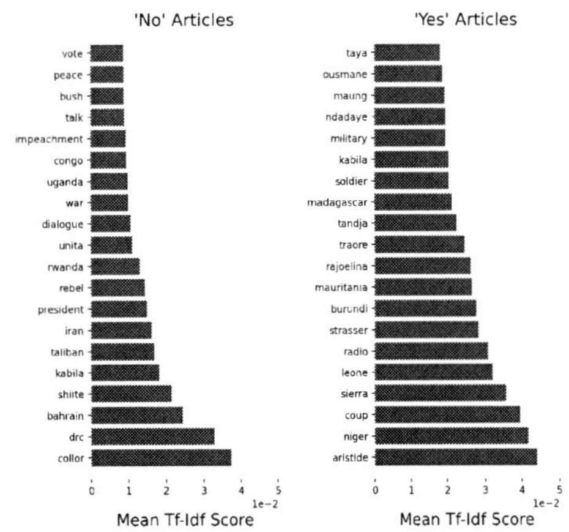

Figure 6: The most significant tokens towards classification of the training set, measured by tf-idf score.

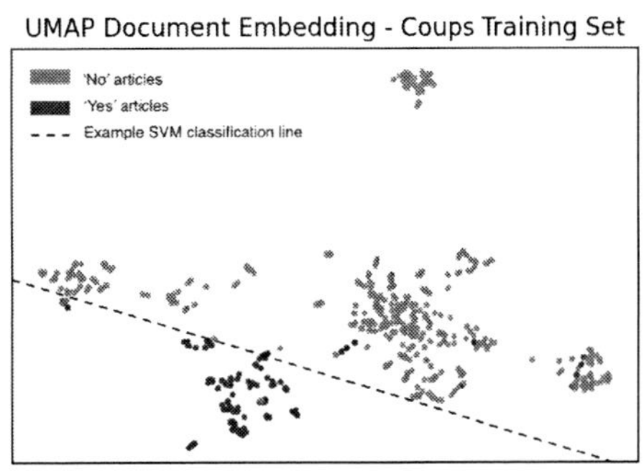

Figure 7: 2D projection of the training set documents with an example SVM classification line.

the pre-trained aspects.

4 Hybrid Knowledge Engineering to Create a SPE Dataset: Assassinations

After refining our ML framework, our next step was to implement the framework on one of SPE of interest in order to create the desired dataset. We switched to assassination events to create our SPE dataset because we saw a lack of assassination datasets in literature (Section 2.1) and assassinations are the most clearly defined trigger[5] for the triggers laid out in (Burley et al., 2020) with one keyword ('assassination'). We leveraged our flushed out machine learning pipeline, along with existing assassination datasets, KGs, and NER to enhance our new assassinations dataset (Fig 8).

[5]Please contact authors for robust trigger definitions and associated keyword

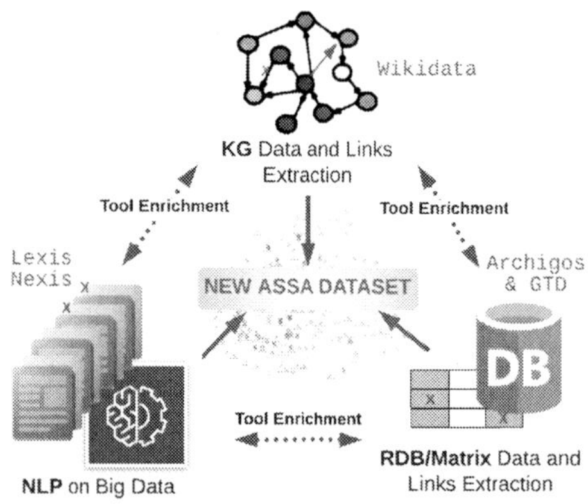

Figure 8: Methodology for linking disparate datasets to build a robust assassinations dataset.

4.1 Existing Assassination Datasets

The Archigos and GTD datasets were the initial contribution to our new assassination dataset. Of the 1,287 entries in the Archigos dataset, 22 of them had "irregular" exits from political office and a post tenure fate marked as "death" with their death year also being the same as their final year of office. It is important to note that natural deaths are marked as regular exits from office, meaning that these irregular exits are actually assassinations.

The GTD contains 6,064 assassination events over the same period of time but includes far more assassinations than simply those of well-known political leaders. The three largest categories for assassinated individuals includes government officials, private citizens, and police. Overall, the GTD contains 6,064 assassinations where 4,442 are successful (target is killed) and 1,622 are unsuccessful (target is not killed).

4.2 Linking in Wikidata

Neither existing database was comprehensive in nature, namely Archigos contained very few assassinations and GTD did not always contain names of the assassinated. We therefore turned to Wikidata to create a stronger baseline for our dataset. For initial exploration of Wikidata, we queried for assassination events, political murders, and deliberate murders using the SPARQL interface. Filters were constructed for the dates ranges and countries of interest, generating 77 results, of which only 55 had a victim associated with them in Wikidata.

After querying for events, we queried for victims. We queried for 3 different properties shown in Fig 9: (1) Instance of human (Q5), (2) Date of

```
SELECT ?item ?itemLabel ?deathdate ?countryLabel WHERE {
  VALUES ?country {wd:Q889 wd:Q916 wd:Q398 wd:Q902 wd:Q225 wd:Q155 wd:Q967 wd:Q424 wd:Q1009
  ?item wdt:P31 wd:Q5 ;
        wdt:P106 wd:Q82955 ;
        wdt:P1196 wd:Q149086 ;
        wdt:P27 ?country ;
        wdt:P570 ?deathdate .
  BIND(YEAR(?deathdate) as ?date) FILTER(?date <= 2017 && ?date >= 1970)
  SERVICE wikibase:label { bd:serviceParam wikibase:language "[AUTO_LANGUAGE],en". }
}
```

Figure 9: SPARQL Query to retrieve Wikidata entries.

death (P570) between 1970 and 2017, (3) Manner of death of homicide (Q149086). This resulted in 4,765 individuals. Politician was the most frequent occupation, with 736 individuals, followed by journalist, but there was a large decrease in the frequency of subsequent occupations. We ultimately decided to move forward with just the politician and journalist entries, which gave us 953 victims. Note that these were successful assassinations as the Wikidata methodology does not allow for querying attempted assassinations.

Once we recorded the individual Wikidata "Q" identifiers for the assassination victims, we retrieved the data about each victim using the *qwikidata*[6] library that populates a python dictionary for each Wikidata entity. This allowed us to filter for 5 attributes about the victim: (1) Name, (2) Death Date, (3) Occupation (i.e. politician), (4) Position Held (i.e. Prime Minister of Israel), and (5) Country of Citizenship. Once these Wikidata identifiers were retrieved, we again utilized *qwikidata* to get the Wikidata label strings associated with these entities to populate our dataset.

4.3 Leveraging our ML Framework

To complete our dataset we implemented our ML framework to identify and record all assassination events found in our assassination news data which was pulled with the same LexisNexis query as coups but used assassination keywords. The unclassified corpus consisted of 169,637 unique entries and our training set consisted of 165 humanly labeled articles (76 positive and 89 negative). We trained an SVM, BERT, and Longformer models with our framework since it was necessary to evaluate all models before choosing one or a combination of the models. Both BERT and Longformer performed poorly, with accuracy scores of 64% and 44%, and showed extreme cases of overfitting. The SVM reached an accuracy score of 72.67% which was sufficient considering the human readers only reached 75% in intercoder reliability checks. These

[6]qwikidata: `https://qwikidata.readthedocs.io/en/stable/index.html`

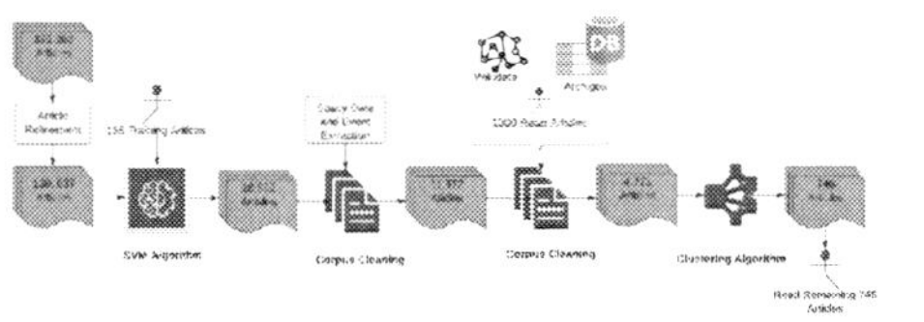

Figure 10: Pipeline for reducing the number of articles read by human readers.

Data Source	LexisNexis NLP	Wikidata	GTD	Archigos
Original # of Data Entries	169,637	Over 97 million	200,000	1,287
Number of ASSA Events	621	954	6,064	22
Unique ASSA Events	523	837	5,921	7
Information Extracted				
Successful Assassination	X	X	X	X
Attempted Assassinations	X		X	
Name	\	\	\	X
Date	X	X	X	X
Country	X	\	X	X
Position	X	X	X	X
Unique Identifier	X	X	X	X

Figure 11: Dataset Summary (For each tool, a given information category was extracted for either all (X), the majority (\), or none (blank) of the extracted events)

results, along with the high accuracy and precision, smaller number of 'yes' articles, lower resource restraints, and better interpretability shown in Section 3.5, resulted in the use of SVMs to classify the assassination articles.

The trained SVM classified 28,532 articles as assassination events. Similar to Section 3.5, the large magnitude of positively classified assassination articles was a limitation to our ML methodology. So, although ML was leveraged to reduce the number of human read articles, we were still left with nearly 30,000 articles to read through. To rectify this, NER and clustering algorithms were used so reduce the number of human read articles without the need for a larger training dataset (Fig 10).

We first explored SpaCy to refine our assassination event extraction by uploading a pre-trained English pipeline (Honnibal and Montani, 2017) and extracting all names and dates from each positively classified article. This did not assist us in directly identifying assassination events due to the length, complexity, and quantity of names in each article, but during this process, we pinpointed 3 ways to further clean the positively labeled articles: (1) removed articles with text extraction errors (articles with less than 25 words), (2) removed articles with no extracted names, and (3) removed any articles that were nearly duplicates of another by dropping articles that were published within 1 week of another article that had the same subset of extracted names. After this, 11,572 articles remained.

Next, a team of political scientists read 1,000 articles from our original positively labeled articles. The readers classified these articles and recorded all identified assassination events. Based on these events, Wikidata, and Archigos, we removed all articles that contained the person's name of already recorded events. This produced a corpus of 4,771 articles. Next, we clustered articles based on year published and country mentioned in the article and randomly selected one article from each cluster since many articles from a country published in the same year reference the same assassination. Readers read through the remaining 746 articles.

5 Results: The Assassination Dataset

By uniting the strengths of each tool within our hybrid approach we created an assassination dataset with 7,457 assassination events. For each entry we collected available information on Name, Date, Country, Position, and Success status (successful vs. attempted) of each assassination event along with the unique identifiers from the source(s) it was identified from. Figure 11 highlights the unique information and number of assassination events contributed by each tools. This shows that despite each method's limitations, ambiguous event definitions for humans, incomplete datasets, missing Wikidata properties, and small training datasets for ML, it is evident that each tool benefited the dataset. Existing databases provided a starting point for our dataset, Wikidata enhanced our repository, and the ML pipeline allows us to extract assassination events from 169,637 articles with only a 165 article training set.

6 Conclusion & Future Work

We have contributed to ongoing SPE research by providing a robust ML framework for small training datasets, performing a comparative analysis of ML tools, presenting a novel hybrid knowledge engineering approach to curate a dataset, and releasing our comprehensive, consolidated, and cohesive assassination dataset which will provide temporal data for understanding political violence as well as training data for further socio-political research. Although our framework and hybrid knowledge engineering approach will not perfectly transfer for every SPE dataset curation task, our focus on understandability visualizations, replicable frameworks, and explanation of challenges will allow future researches to incorporate our work for a variety of SPE extraction tasks. In future work, we hope to apply the knowledge engineering approach, encompassing our ML framework, to the remaining triggers of interest while continuing to improve and automate our ML framework.

7 Acknowledgments

The authors would like to thank Timothy Burley, Sophia Henn, Steven Broussard, Ian Havenaar, Angela Chessler, Dr. Patrick Regan, and Dr. Charles Vardeman for their contributions.

References

Gunjit Bedi. 2019. Simple guide to text classification(nlp) using svm and naive bayes with python. Medium.

Iz Beltagy, Matthew E. Peters, and Arman Cohan. 2020. Longformer: The long-document transformer.

Timothy Burley, Lorissa Humble, Charles Sleeper, Abigail Sticha, Angela Chesler, Patrick Regan, Ernesto Verdeja, and Paul Brenner. 2020. Nlp workflows for computational social science: Understanding triggers of state-led mass killings. In *Practice and Experience in Advanced Research Computing*, pages 152–159.

Berfu Büyüköz, Ali Hürriyetoğlu, and Arzucan Özgür. 2020. Analyzing ELMo and DistilBERT on socio-political news classification. In *Proceedings of the Workshop on Automated Extraction of Socio-political Events from News 2020*, pages 9–18, Marseille, France. European Language Resources Association (ELRA).

Tommaso Caselli, Osman Mutlu, Angelo Basile, and Ali Hürriyetoğlu. 2021. Protest-er: Retraining bert for protest event extraction. In *Proceedings of the 4th Workshop on Challenges and Applications of Automated Extraction of Socio-political Events from Text (CASE 2021)*, pages 12–19.

Furkan Celik, Tuğberk Dalkılıç, Fatih Beyhan, and Reyyan Yeniterzi. 2021. Su-nlp at case 2021 task 1: Protest news detection for english. In *Proceedings of the 4th Workshop on Challenges and Applications of Automated Extraction of Socio-political Events from Text (CASE 2021)*, pages 131–137.

Jacob Devlin, Ming-Wei Chang, Kenton Lee, and Kristina Toutanova. 2019. Bert: Pre-training of deep bidirectional transformers for language understanding.

Susana Irene Díaz Rodríguez, José Ranilla Pastor, Elena Montañés Roces, Javier Fernández, and Elías Fernández-Combarro Álvarez. 2004. Improving performance of text categorization by combining filtering and support vector machines. *Journal of the American Society for Information Science and Technology, 55 (7)*.

Ya Gao and Shiliang Sun. 2010. An empirical evaluation of linear and nonlinear kernels for text classification using support vector machines. In *2010 seventh international conference on fuzzy systems and knowledge discovery*, volume 4, pages 1502–1505. IEEE.

K Gayathri and A Marimuthu. 2013. Text document pre-processing with the knn for classification using the svm. In *2013 7th International Conference on Intelligent Systems and Control (ISCO)*, pages 453–457. IEEE.

Deborah J Gerner, Philip A Schrodt, Omur Yilmaz, and Rajaa Abu-Jabr. 2002. The creation of cameo (conflict and mediation event observations): An event data framework for a post cold war world. In *annual meeting of the American Political Science Association*, volume 29.

Nils Petter Gleditsch, Peter Wallensteen, Mikael Eriksson, Margareta Sollenberg, and Håvard Strand. 2002. Armed conflict 1946-2001: A new dataset. *Journal of peace research*, 39(5):615–637.

Henk E Goemans, Kristian Skrede Gleditsch, and Giacomo Chiozza. 2009. Introducing archigos: A dataset of political leaders. *Journal of Peace research*, 46(2):269–283.

Santiago González-Carvajal and Eduardo C Garrido-Merchán. 2020. Comparing bert against traditional machine learning text classification. *arXiv preprint arXiv:2005.13012*.

Kaihao Guo, Tianpei Jiang, and Haipeng Zhang. 2020. Knowledge graph enhanced event extraction in financial documents. In *2020 IEEE International Conference on Big Data (Big Data)*, pages 1322–1329. IEEE.

Andrew Halterman, Jill Irvine, Manar Landis, Phanindra Jalla, Yan Liang, Christan Grant, and Mohiuddin Solaimani. 2017. Adaptive scalable pipelines for political event data generation. In *2017 IEEE International Conference on Big Data (Big Data)*, pages 2879–2883. IEEE.

Alex Hanna. 2017. Mpeds: Automating the generation of protest event data.

Aidan Hogan, Eva Blomqvist, Michael Cochez, Claudia d'Amato, Gerard De Melo, Claudio Gutierrez, Sabrina Kirrane, José Emilio Labra Gayo, Roberto Navigli, Sebastian Neumaier, et al. 2021. Knowledge graphs. *ACM Computing Surveys (CSUR)*, 54(4):1–37.

Matthew Honnibal and Ines Montani. 2017. spaCy 2: Natural language understanding with Bloom embeddings, convolutional neural networks and incremental parsing. To appear.

Ali Hur, Naeem Janjua, and Mohiuddin Ahmed. 2021. A survey on state-of-the-art techniques for knowledge graphs construction and challenges ahead. In *2021 IEEE Fourth International Conference on Artificial Intelligence and Knowledge Engineering (AIKE)*, pages 99–103. IEEE.

Katherine A Keith, Abram Handler, Michael Pinkham, Cara Magliozzi, Joshua McDuffie, and Brendan O'Connor. 2017. Identifying civilians killed by police with distantly supervised entity-event extraction. *arXiv preprint arXiv:1707.07086*.

Hanspeter Kriesi, Edgar Grande, Swen Hutter, Argyrios Altiparmakis, Endre Borbáth, S Bornschier, B Bremer, M Dolezal, T Frey, T Gessler, et al. 2020. Poldem-national election campaign dataset.

James Tin-Yau Kwok. 1998. Automated text categorization using support vector machine. In *In Proceedings of the International Conference on Neural Information Processing (ICONIP*. Citeseer.

Gary LaFree and Laura Dugan. 2007. Introducing the global terrorism database. *Terrorism and political violence*, 19(2):181–204.

Kalev Leetaru and Philip A Schrodt. 2013. Gdelt: Global data on events, location, and tone, 1979–2012. In *ISA annual convention*, volume 2, pages 1–49. Citeseer.

Joseph Lilleberg, Yun Zhu, and Yanqing Zhang. 2015. Support vector machines and word2vec for text classification with semantic features. In *2015 IEEE 14th International Conference on Cognitive Informatics & Cognitive Computing (ICCI* CC)*, pages 136–140. IEEE.

Zhijie Liu, Xueqiang Lv, Kun Liu, and Shuicai Shi. 2010. Study on svm compared with the other text classification methods. In *2010 Second international workshop on education technology and computer science*, volume 1, pages 219–222. IEEE.

Leland McInnes, John Healy, and James Melville. 2020. Umap: Uniform manifold approximation and projection for dimension reduction.

Tomas Mikolov, Ilya Sutskever, Kai Chen, Greg Corrado, and Jeffrey Dean. 2013. Distributed representations of words and phrases and their compositionality.

Peter F Nardulli, Scott L Althaus, and Matthew Hayes. 2015. A progressive supervised-learning approach to generating rich civil strife data. *Sociological methodology*, 45(1):148–183.

Fredrik Olsson, Magnus Sahlgren, Fehmi Ben Abdesslem, Ariel Ekgren, and Kristine Eck. 2020. Text categorization for conflict event annotation. In *Proceedings of the Workshop on Automated Extraction of Socio-political Events from News 2020*, pages 19–25.

Ellie Pavlick, Heng Ji, Xiaoman Pan, and Chris Callison-Burch. 2016. The gun violence database: A new task and data set for nlp. In *Proceedings of the 2016 Conference on Empirical Methods in Natural Language Processing*, pages 1018–1024.

Jakub Piskorski and Guillaume Jacquet. 2020. Tf-idf character n-grams versus word embedding-based models for fine-grained event classification: a preliminary study. In *Proceedings of the Workshop on Automated Extraction of Socio-political Events from News 2020*, pages 26–34.

Clionadh Raleigh, Andrew Linke, Håvard Hegre, and Joakim Karlsen. 2010. Introducing acled: an armed conflict location and event dataset: special data feature. *Journal of peace research*, 47(5):651–660.

Nitin Ramrakhiyani, Swapnil Hingmire, Sangameshwar Patil, Alok Kumar, and Girish Palshikar. 2021. Extracting events from industrial incident reports. In *Proceedings of the 4th Workshop on Challenges and Applications of Automated Extraction of Socio-political Events from Text (CASE 2021)*, pages 58–67.

Kevin Reschke, Martin Jankowiak, Mihai Surdeanu, Christopher D Manning, and Dan Jurafsky. 2014. Event extraction using distant supervision. In *Proceedings of the Ninth International Conference on Language Resources and Evaluation (LREC'14)*, pages 4527–4531.

Espen Geelmuyden Rød and Nils B Weidmann. 2013. Protesting dictatorship: The mass mobilization in autocracies database. Technical report, Citeseer.

Charlotte Rudnik, Thibault Ehrhart, Olivier Ferret, Denis Teyssou, Raphaël Troncy, and Xavier Tannier. 2019. Searching news articles using an event knowledge graph leveraged by wikidata. In *Companion proceedings of the 2019 world wide web conference*, pages 1232–1239.

Philip A Schrodt, John Beieler, and Muhammed Idris. 2014. Three'sa charm?: Open event data coding with el: Diablo, petrarch, and the open event data alliance. In *ISA Annual Convention*. Citeseer.

Philip A Schrodt, Shannon G Davis, and Judith L Weddle. 1994. Political science: Keds—a program for the machine coding of event data. *Social Science Computer Review*, 12(4):561–587.

Pero Subasic, Hongfeng Yin, and Xiao Lin. 2019. Building knowledge base through deep learning relation extraction and wikidata. In *AAAI Spring Symposium: Combining Machine Learning with Knowledge Engineering*.

Venelin Valkov. 2020. Text classification | sentiment analysis with bert using huggingface, pytorch and python tutorial. YouTube.

Ashish Vaswani, Noam Shazeer, Niki Parmar, Jakob Uszkoreit, Llion Jones, Aidan N. Gomez, Lukasz Kaiser, and Illia Polosukhin. 2017. Attention is all you need.

Ernesto Verdeja. 2016. Predicting genocide and mass atrocities. *Genocide Studies and Prevention: An International Journal*, 9(3):5.

Denny Vrandečić and Markus Krötzsch. 2014. Wikidata: a free collaborative knowledgebase. *Communications of the ACM*, 57(10):78–85.

Thomas Wolf, Lysandre Debut, Victor Sanh, Julien Chaumond, Clement Delangue, Anthony Moi, Pierric Cistac, Tim Rault, Rémi Louf, Morgan Funtowicz, Joe Davison, Sam Shleifer, Patrick von Platen, Clara Ma, Yacine Jernite, Julien Plu, Canwen Xu, Teven Le Scao, Sylvain Gugger, Mariama Drame, Quentin Lhoest, and Alexander M. Rush. 2020. Transformers: State-of-the-art natural language processing. In *Proceedings of the 2020 Conference on Empirical Methods in Natural Language Processing: System Demonstrations*, pages 38–45, Online. Association for Computational Linguistics.

Adam Wright, Allison B McCoy, Stanislav Henkin, Abhivyakti Kale, and Dean F Sittig. 2013. Use of a support vector machine for categorizing free-text notes: assessment of accuracy across two institutions. *Journal of the American Medical Informatics Association*, 20(5):887–890.

Wen Zhang, Taketoshi Yoshida, and Xijin Tang. 2008. Text classification based on multi-word with support vector machine. *Knowledge-Based Systems*, 21(8):879–886.

Political Event Coding as Text-to-Text Sequence Generation

Yaoyao Dai and **Benjamin J. Radford**
University of North Carolina at Charlotte
benjamin.radford@uncc.edu

Andrew Halterman
Michigan State University
halterm3@msu.edu

Abstract

We report on the current status of an effort to produce political event data from unstructured text via a Transformer language model. Compelled by the current lack of publicly available and up-to-date event coding software, we seek to train a model that can produce structured political event records at the sentence level. Our approach differs from previous efforts in that we conceptualize this task as one of text-to-text sequence generation. We motivate this choice by outlining desirable properties of text generation models for the needs of event coding. To overcome the lack of sufficient training data, we also describe a method for generating synthetic text and event record pairs that we use to fit our model.

1 Introduction

Political event records that are automatically derived from text are an important source of structured data for researchers in social science. Existing approaches to generating event data often rely on dictionary methods, which are brittle and go obsolete, or classifiers trained on hand-labeled text that required large amounts of expensive data. This paper introduces a new proof of concept model for generating structured event data from news text that does not require dictionaries or hand-labeled document. We generate synthetic news stories using a novel combination of rules based generation and a paraphrasing model and train a text-to-text Transformer to produce event records from text. When evaluated on synthetic test data, the model correctly identifies high-level event types 83% of the time and reaches accuracies of 63% and 56.9% on the source and target actors, respectively. The article concludes with a brief real-world evaluation and a discussion of the model's limitations.

1.1 Political Event Data

Political event data describe who did what to whom and, usually, where and when that action occurred. While the actors and actions themselves are derived directly from source texts, locations and times are often determined via the textual metadata. Therefore, the core component of political event data is the source actor, target actor, action three-tuple.

Precisely what actors and actions are included in an event dataset varies; some tend to be specific to certain classes of events while others seek to capture the full range of politically-relevant interactions. Examples of the latter include the Global Database of Events, Language, and Tone (GDELT)[1], the Integrated Crisis Early Warning System (ICEWS)[2], and the various Phoenix datasets.[3]

1.2 Generating Event Data

Historically political event data have been made by hand (Azar, 1980; McClelland, 2006), by rules-based software tools (Schrodt, 1998, 2001, 2011; Schrodt et al., 2014; Norris et al., 2017), and via machine learning. Rules based software typically relies on large hand-curated dictionaries to perform pattern matching. These dictionaries will conform to a predetermined event ontology like that defined by CAMEO, the Conflict and Mediation Event Observations (Schrodt, 2012). Neural networks have been used in conjunction with PETRARCH, one rules based coding software, to generate event data by (Radford, 2021a) and to classify events into quad-class categories by (Beieler, 2016). Recently, workshops like ProtestNews at CLEF 2019, AESPEN at LREC 2020, and CASE have prompted even more work on machine learning approaches to coding event data from text (Hürriyetoğlu et al., 2020; Hürriyetoğlu et al., 2020;

[1] https://gdeltproject.org
[2] https://dataverse.harvard.edu/dataverse/icews
[3] https://clinecenter.illinois.edu/project/machine-generated-event-data-projects/phoenix-data

Proceedings of the 5th Workshop on Challenges and Applications of Automated Extraction of Socio-political Events from Text (CASE), pages 117 - 123
December 7-8, 2022

Hürriyetoğlu, 2021). Transformer models were used for zero-shot classification of previously unseen event types and for cross-context and multilingual protest detection (Haneczok et al., 2021; Barker et al., 2021; Kent and Krumbiegel, 2021; Radford, 2021b). These zero-shot methods rely primarily on textual entailment formulations of the event data coding task (Yin et al., 2019).

2 Methodology

2.1 Training Data

The ideal training data for our model would be a dataset of source texts and their associated coded events, produced by an existing event coder. However, due to copyright restrictions, there are no publicly available large scale event datasets that include event's associated source texts. We therefore propose generating synthetic news stories from coded events. The use of synthetic text is growing in political science (Halterman, 2022), but we introduce a novel technique using a combination of rule-based generation and a paraphrase model to generate synthetic text that contains the content we require. To generate positive examples, we generate synthetic stories through a rule-based process. We parse the CAMEO and Petrarch dictionaries available from the Open Event Data Alliance and piece together pseudo-sentences by substituting random actors, agents, and word synonyms in the placeholders denoted within the CAMEO verbs dictionary.

To ensure that our model learns to refrain from returning coded events when no event is reported, we also include negative samples, drawn randomly from sentences published in the *New York Times* (NYT) between 1970 and 2022 and assumed to have no event present.[4] From these two sources, we draw 4.08 million samples (4,000,000 training, 40,000 validation, and 40,000 test set) with a ratio of 39 positive to 1 negative. One sample represents approximately a single sentence.

Because the heuristic approach to generating positive examples often results in bizarre, poorly-formed, and repetitive sentences, we post-process 50% of all samples (positive and negative) by running them through a Transformer model for paraphrase generation.[5] This model attempts to output a sentence that is not identical to, but semantically similar to, an input sentence. The paraphraser is set by default to produce a sentence of no more than 30 tokens in length.[6] Unfortunately, this induces a bias in our model towards coding shorter and simpler sentences than are typical for new text and we intend to adjust the paraphraser parameters in future iterations.[7] Our target values are comma-delimited three-tuples of action category, source actor, and target actor. An example of a raw synthetic story, a paraphrased story, and the associated event code is given below.

Raw synthetic story: "Ministries For Public Health And Social Welfare Rossija said could beat Jibouti within Unmanned Aircraft."

Paraphrased text: "Rossija said that he could beat Jibouti with Unmanned Aircraft".[8]

Event record: 138 (Threaten with military force), RUSGOVHLH (Russian government healthcare), DJIMIL (Djibouti military).

In the raw synthetic story, the randomly-drawn actors are "Ministries for Public Health and Social Welfare Rossija," and "Jibouti," the verb phrase is "[SOURCE ACTOR] said could [VERB] [TARGET ACTOR]," the verb is "beat," and "Unmanned Aircraft" is a synonym for "aircraft." "Within" is one of a set of available random prepositions.

To minimize the leakage of actors or phrases from the training set into the (out-of-sample) validation or test sets, we partition the dictionaries prior to generating synthetic samples. Specifically, we partition the NYT sentences, verb phrases, agents, countries, and actors into their own training, validation, and test sets prior to constructing our three respective data partitions. We then construct synthetic samples for each of the training, validation, and test sets by sampling only from those words and phrases found in the corresponding partitions

[4]It is likely that these sentences from the NYT contain a small number of relevant socio-political events. We have not attempted to remove these false negatives from the corpus and therefore admit that the negative examples in our training data likely contain a small proportion of errors.

[5]`https://huggingface.co/ramsrigouthamg/t5_sentence_paraphraser`

[6]This is likely too short and we recommend longer maximum sequence lengths be used in future work. However, producing longer paraphrased sentences requires greater computational resources or computation time than were available for this study. We therefore leave the paraphraser set to the default 30 tokens maximum output.

[7]An open-ended text generation model like GPT-2, applied after the paraphraser, could expand the paraphrase in such a way that results better simulate the target distribution of news texts (Radford et al., 2019).

[8]It is possible that the paraphraser model changes the content of some texts such that they no longer correspond to the codes associated with their original associated synthetic event records. Nonetheless, paraphrase-based data augmentation is becoming common in NLP applications (Kumar et al., 2019; Corbeil and Abdi Ghavidel, 2020; Beddiar et al., 2021).

of dictionaries. Synsets, words that are effectively synonyms of one another, are not partitioned in such a way.

2.2 Model

Text-to-Text Transfer Transformer (T5) is a language model tailored for text generation (Raffel et al., 2020). It comes in a variety of sizes, of which we select T5-Base version 1.1 with 250m parameters. T5 was trained on a variety of natural language tasks, distinguished by prepending a keyword describing the task to the input ("context") to the model. We fine tune T5 on our synthetic dataset for a single epoch with a learning rate of 5.6×10^{-6} and all other hyperparameters held at their default values. We decode our output using the default configuration for T5 in HuggingFace's pipeline (greedy search).[9] Alternative configurations may lead to different output values.

Continuing with the example from Section 2.1, the input to our model would be the Sentencepiece-tokenized version of either the raw synthetic story or the paraphrased story, drawn with equal probability (50% each) (Kudo and Richardson, 2018). The desired output of the model is the comma-delimited, semicolon-terminated event record "138, RUSGOVHLH, DJIMIL;".

3 Results

This section provides descriptions of our results in two experimental settings: an out-of-sample test set evaluation using data generated via the same process as the training data and an out-of-distribution case study using a small sample of real world news text.

3.1 Within Distribution Performance

We evaluate the test set accuracy of the model on the event category, actor coding, and exact match accuracy on the full event triple. At the coarser level of 20 event types, the model achieves 83.4% accuracy and reaches 77.8% accuracy for the full set of 295 fine-grained action codes. Source and target actor exact match accuracy are 63% and 56.9%, respectively. Because actors are represented by sets of three-character sub codes, we can compute the precision, recall, and F1-score of these sub codes. We find values of 0.73, 0.78, and 0.75, respectively. Evaluating against the complete event record, our model achieves 30.7% exact match accuracy in the test set.

The model only fails to code events for 15 input samples that contain events and erroneously codes events for 53 samples that should not contain events, corresponding to an F1-score of 0.999. These scores likely reflect the differences in samples generated by our synthetic process versus those drawn from the NYT more so than they do strong model performance. Overall, we find these results promising but acknowledge that synthetic data often fail to sufficiently mimic their real world targets. For this reason, we turn now to a small case study with real world data that are representative of data that would typically be used in event coding applications.

3.2 Real World Performance

While we reserve a full real-world evaluation of our neural event coder for a follow-up paper, here we demonstrate its use in a very short case study: the top ten articles on the Associated Press's World page as retrieved on September 6, 2022. We first attempt to code the introductory sentence from each of the ten articles to no success: not a single sentence produced an event. However, as we noted before, these sentences are far longer and more complex than those generated by our heuristic process. If we first use the paraphraser model to paraphrase these sentences such that they better resemble the distribution of the training data, we find three events.[10] Furthermore, if we code the headlines rather than the introductory sentences, six out of the ten produce event data records. See Table 1 for the headlines and coded events. Most of the event records produced from headlines are at least partially correct. The verb codes correspond to "make pessimistic comment," "threaten with military force," "express intent to cooperate militarily," "praise or endorse," "investigate," and "reduce relations," in order. Example 2 ("UN agency calls for safety zone around Ukraine nuclear plant") was correctly coded as 0256 "appeal for de-escalation of military engagement" when using the paraphrased introductory sentence but incorrectly coded as a threat when using the headline. While the actor countries tend to match those described in the headlines, the model is ambitious about inferring unstated actor affiliations. For instance, in example 9, the target actor ("cabinet") is incorrectly assumed

[9] `https://huggingface.co/docs/transformers/main_classes/pipelines`

[10] Sentences, paraphrases, and events given in the Appendix.

Headline	Headline Event
1. New UK leader vows to tackle energy crisis, ailing economy	012 (Statement), GBR, NGOENV
2. UN agency calls for safety zone around Ukraine nuclear plant	138 (Threaten), IGOUNODEV, UKRUNR
3. EXPLAINER: Why Truss went to Scotland to become UK leader	–
4. US: Russia to buy rockets, artillery shells from North Korea	0312:0312 (Intent to cooperate), RUS, PRK
5. Rallies show Pakistan's ex-PM Khan remains political force	051 (Diplomatic cooperation), NGOHRI, PAKOPP
6. 'This is it, folks': Boris Johnson bids an ambiguous goodbye	–
7. Fears high as Canadian police search for stabbing suspect	090 (Investigate), CAN, CAN
8. UN: Tribal clashes in Sudan kill 380 in Jan.-Aug. period	–
9. Chile's Boric shakes up cabinet after constitution loss	160 (Reduce relations), CHL, HRVGOV
10. Tension rises as Turkey, Greece voice festering grievances	–

Table 1: World section headlines from the AP on September 6, 2022 and associated predicted event records. Top-level CAMEO action categories are given in parentheses; specific action codes can be found in the CAMEO codebook (Schrodt, 2012).

by the model to be the Herzegovina government. However, sometimes these assumptions are warranted: the model correctly identifies "Pakistan's ex-PM Khan" as a Pakistani opposition figure. In fact, inspection of the CAMEO actors dictionary reveals that Imran Khan is not ever coded as PAKOPP in the dictionary and therefore cannot be coded as such in the training data–this label is inferred by the model entirely out-of-sample.

4 Conclusion

Text-to-text is a flexible modeling task that is amenable to complicated output data types. Using multiple classification heads is an alternative method for event coding text via large language model, but it offers less flexibility for future improvements. For example, a text-to-text model can be trained to generate an arbitrary number of events from a single input text.[11] A more traditional classification-based approach is suitable for coding only up to a predefined number of events. We also appreciate that the open-ended nature of text output means that we do not need to generate all possible actor combinations prior to training as we would in a multiclass classification setup. The text-to-text model can simply append actor codes to one another as necessary, even if it has not previously seen a sample with the particular given combination.

We leave a more formal evaluation of our methodology and model to a follow-up paper in which we plan to employ expert human annotators to generate comparable event data against which we can benchmark our model. Nonetheless, we believe the results presented here are promising for future development of text-to-text models for political event data coding.

4.1 Limitations

We regret that we cannot distribute the entirety of our datasets due to copyright issues. A portion of our samples are drawn from a corpus derived from the *New York Times* and we therefore lack the ability to redistribute them. We do make available the samples generated via our heuristic and paraphrase approach, though. In future iterations of this work, we plan to replace the NYT derived data with samples drawn from open sources.[12]

Our actor resolution step is also limited by our reliance on the existing CAMEO dictionaries and the world knowledge built into T5. Without access to an external data set such as Wikipedia, our accuracy for obscure political entities or people whose roles change frequently will be limited.

Our model exhibits a strange sensitivity to punctuation, especially periods. The model appears to more readily code events when the sentence in question does not end with a period. We have been unable to identify a source of this bias in our training data.

We append a semicolon to the end of every event record. In our next version of this model, we will train on paragraph-length texts and allow the model to output an arbitrary number of semicolon-delimited event records per input example.

We hope to compare our model's performance

[11] We have preliminary work in which we generate up to four events per input paragraph.

[12] For example, we are considering *Voice of America* and Common Crawl as substitute text sources.

directly with that of Petrarch or TABARI. Unfortunately, this will require a functional instance of the software in question which we do not currently possess.

4.2 Broader Impacts

Political event coding software has been publicly available for decades now, as have been the dictionaries of actors and verb phrases that they require. As such, we do not believe that our work poses any additional risk for misuse. Furthermore, we rely on a synthetic data generation technique that allows us to train our model with limited access to real-world text data that may contain sensitive information or reflect undesirable societal biases. As always, we implore others interested in our work to not use it for evil.

References

Edward E. Azar. 1980. The Conflict and Peace Data Bank (COPDAB) Project. *The Journal of Conflict Resolution*, 24(1):143–152.

Ken Barker, Parul Awasthy, Jian Ni, and Radu Florian. 2021. IBM MNLP IE at CASE 2021 task 2: NLI reranking for zero-shot text classification. In *Proceedings of the 4th Workshop on Challenges and Applications of Automated Extraction of Socio-political Events from Text (CASE 2021)*, pages 193–202, Online. Association for Computational Linguistics.

Djamila Romaissa Beddiar, Md Saroar Jahan, and Mourad Oussalah. 2021. Data expansion using back translation and paraphrasing for hate speech detection. *Online Social Networks and Media*, 24:100153.

John Beieler. 2016. Generating politically-relevant event data. In *Proceedings of the First Workshop on NLP and Computational Social Science*, pages 37–42, Austin, Texas. Association for Computational Linguistics.

Jean-Philippe Corbeil and Hadi Abdi Ghavidel. 2020. Bet: A backtranslation approach for easy data augmentation in transformer-based paraphrase identification context. *arXiv preprint*.

Andrew Halterman. 2022. Synthetically generated text for supervised text analysis. *PolMeth conference paper*.

Jacek Haneczok, Guillaume Jacquet, Jakub Piskorski, and Nicolas Stefanovitch. 2021. Fine-grained event classification in news-like text snippets - shared task 2, CASE 2021. In *Proceedings of the 4th Workshop on Challenges and Applications of Automated Extraction of Socio-political Events from Text (CASE 2021)*, pages 179–192, Online. Association for Computational Linguistics.

Ali Hürriyetoğlu, editor. 2021. *Proceedings of the 4th Workshop on Challenges and Applications of Automated Extraction of Socio-political Events from Text (CASE 2021)*. Association for Computational Linguistics, Online.

Ali Hürriyetoğlu, Vanni Zavarella, Hristo Tanev, Erdem Yörük, Ali Safaya, and Osman Mutlu. 2020. Automated extraction of socio-political events from news (AESPEN): Workshop and shared task report. In *Proceedings of the Workshop on Automated Extraction of Socio-political Events from News 2020*, pages 1–6, Marseille, France. European Language Resources Association (ELRA).

Ali Hürriyetoğlu, Erdem Yörük, Deniz Yüret, Çağrı Yoltar, Burak Gürel, Fırat Duruşan, Osman Mutlu, and Arda Akdemir. 2020. Overview of clef 2019 lab protestnews: Extracting protests from news in a cross-context setting.

Samantha Kent and Theresa Krumbiegel. 2021. CASE 2021 task 2 socio-political fine-grained event classification using fine-tuned RoBERTa document embeddings. In *Proceedings of the 4th Workshop on Challenges and Applications of Automated Extraction of Socio-political Events from Text (CASE 2021)*, pages 208–217, Online. Association for Computational Linguistics.

Taku Kudo and John Richardson. 2018. SentencePiece: A simple and language independent subword tokenizer and detokenizer for neural text processing. In *Proceedings of the 2018 Conference on Empirical Methods in Natural Language Processing: System Demonstrations*, pages 66–71, Brussels, Belgium. Association for Computational Linguistics.

Ashutosh Kumar, Satwik Bhattamishra, Manik Bhandari, and Partha Talukdar. 2019. Submodular optimization-based diverse paraphrasing and its effectiveness in data augmentation. In *Proceedings of the 2019 Conference of the North American Chapter of the Association for Computational Linguistics: Human Language Technologies, Volume 1 (Long and Short Papers)*, pages 3609–3619, Minneapolis, Minnesota. Association for Computational Linguistics.

Charles McClelland. 2006. World Event/Interaction Survey (WEIS) Project, 1966-1978. *Inter-university Consortium for Political and Social Research [Distributor]*.

Clayton Norris, Philip Schrodt, and John Beieler. 2017. Petrarch2: Another event coding program. *Journal of Open Source Software*, 2(9):133.

Alec Radford, Jeff Wu, Rewon Child, David Luan, Dario Amodei, and Ilya Sutskever. 2019. Language models are unsupervised multitask learners.

Benjamin J. Radford. 2021a. Automated dictionary generation for political event coding. *Political Science Research and Methods*, 9(1):157–171.

Benjamin J. Radford. 2021b. CASE 2021 task 2: Zero-shot classification of fine-grained sociopolitical events with transformer models. In *Proceedings of the 4th Workshop on Challenges and Applications of Automated Extraction of Socio-political Events from Text (CASE 2021)*, pages 203–207, Online. Association for Computational Linguistics.

Colin Raffel, Noam Shazeer, Adam Roberts, Katherine Lee, Sharan Narang, Michael Matena, Yanqi Zhou, Wei Li, and Peter J. Liu. 2020. Exploring the limits of transfer learning with a unified text-to-text transformer. *Journal of Machine Learning Research*, 21(140):1–67.

Philip A. Schrodt. 1998. KEDS: Kansas Event Data System V 1.0.

Philip A. Schrodt. 2001. Automated Coding of International Event Data Using Sparse Parsing Techniques.

Philip A. Schrodt. 2011. TABARI: Textual Analysis by Augmented Replacement Instructions V. 0.7.6.

Philip A. Schrodt. 2012. CAMEO Conflict and Mediation Event Observations Event and Actor Codebook.

Philip A. Schrodt, John Beieler, and Muhammed Idris. 2014. Three's a Charm?: Open Event Data Coding with EL:DIABLO, PETRARCH, and the Open Event Data Alliance.

Wenpeng Yin, Jamaal Hay, and Dan Roth. 2019. Benchmarking Zero-shot Text Classification: Datasets, Evaluation and Entailment Approach. *Proceedings of the 2019 Conference on Empirical Methods in Natural Language Processing and the 9th International Joint Conference on Natural Language Processing*, pages 3914–3923.

A Appendix

Below are the headlines, introductory paragraphs, and automatically paraphrased paragraphs drawn from the Associated Press World section.

Example 1

Headline: New UK leader vows to tackle energy crisis, ailing economy

First paragraph: "Liz Truss became U.K. prime minister on Tuesday and immediately faced up to the enormous tasks ahead of her: curbing soaring prices, boosting the economy, easing labor unrest and fixing a national health care system burdened by long waiting lists and staff shortages."

Paraphrase: "Liz Truss became the Prime Minister of the United Kingdom on Tuesday and immediately faced the"

Example 2

Headline: UN agency calls for safety zone around Ukraine nuclear plant

First paragraph: "The U.N. atomic watchdog agency urged Russia and Ukraine on Tuesday to establish a "nuclear safety and security protection zone" around the Zaporizhzhia power plant amid mounting fears the fighting could trigger a catastrophe in a country still scarred by the Chernobyl disaster."

Paraphrase: "the United Nations nuclear watchdog group urged Russia and Ukraine to establish a "n"

Paraphrase code: `(0256, IGOUNOKID, RUS)`

Example 3

Headline: EXPLAINER: Why Truss went to Scotland to become UK leader

First paragraph: "Liz Truss, a onetime accountant who has served in Parliament for the past 12 years, became Britain's prime minister on Tuesday after Queen Elizabeth II formally asked her to form a government."

Paraphrase: "Liz Truss, a one-time accountant who has served in Parliament for the"

Example 4

Headline: US: Russia to buy rockets, artillery shells from North Korea

First paragraph: "The Russian Ministry of Defense is in the process of purchasing millions of rockets and artillery shells from North Korea for its ongoing fight in Ukraine, according to a newly downgraded U.S. intelligence finding."

Paraphrase: "according to a recently downgraded US intelligence report, the Russian Ministry of Defense is in"

Example 5

Headline: Rallies show Pakistan's ex-PM Khan remains political force

First paragraph: "Since he was toppled by parliament five months ago, former Prime Minister Imran Khan has demonstrated his popularity with rallies that have drawn huge crowds and signaled to his rivals that he remains a considerable political force."

Paraphrase: "former Prime Minister Imran Khan has resurrected his popularity since being deposed"

Paraphrase code: `(051, ELI, PAKGOV)`

Example 6

Headline: 'This is it, folks': Boris Johnson bids an ambiguous goodbye

First paragraph: "Boris Johnson's term as British leader was a mix of high drama and low disgrace. But he left office Tuesday with a casual shrug of a farewell: "Well, this is it, folks.""

Paraphrase: "Boris Johnson's term as British leader was a mix of high drama and low"

Example 7

Headline: Fears high as Canadian police search for stabbing suspect

First paragraph: "Fears ran high Tuesday on an Indigenous reserve in the Canadian province of Saskatchewan after police warned that the suspect in a deadly stabbing rampage over the weekend might be nearby and officers surrounded a house with guns drawn."

Paraphrase: "fear erupted on an Indigenous reserve in the Canadian province of Saskatchewan on Tuesday,"

Paraphrase code: `(012, CAN, CVL)`

Example 8

Headline: UN: Tribal clashes in Sudan kill 380 in Jan.-Aug. period

First paragraph: "Around 380 people were killed in tribal clashes in Sudan between January and August, most of them in the conflict-wracked Darfur region, the U.N. said Tuesday."

Paraphrase: "380 people were killed in tribal clashes in Sudan between January and August, the bulk"

Example 9

Headline: Chile's Boric shakes up cabinet after constitution loss

First paragraph: "Chile's President Gabriel Boric shook up his cabinet Tuesday in an effort to relaunch his government less than 48 hours after he was dealt a resounding blow when citizens overwhelmingly rejected a new progressive constitution he had championed."

Paraphrase: "Chile's President Gabriel Boric shook up his cabinet Tuesday in an attempt to"

Example 10

Headline: Tension rises as Turkey, Greece voice festering grievances

First paragraph: "Troubled relations between regional rivals Turkey and Greece worsened Tuesday, with Turkey's president doubling down on a thinly veiled invasion threat and Athens responding that it's ready to defend its sovereignty."

Paraphrase: "tensions between regional rivals Turkey and Greece worsened on Tuesday, with Turkey"

Zero-Shot Ranking Socio-Political Texts with Transformer Language Models to Reduce Close Reading Time

Kiymet Akdemir
Boğaziçi University
kiymet.akdemir@boun.edu.tr

Ali Hürriyetoğlu
KNAW Humanities Cluster DHLab
ali.hurriyetoglu@dh.huc.knaw.nl

Abstract

We approach the classification problem as an entailment problem and apply zero-shot ranking to socio-political texts. Documents that are ranked at the top can be considered positively classified documents and this reduces the close reading time for the information extraction process. We use Transformer Language Models to get the entailment probabilities and investigate different types of queries. We find that DeBERTa achieves higher mean average precision scores than RoBERTa and when declarative form of the class label is used as a query, it outperforms dictionary definition of the class label. We show that one can reduce the close reading time by taking some percentage of the ranked documents that the percentage depends on how much recall they want to achieve. However, our findings also show that percentage of the documents that should be read increases as the topic gets broader.

1 Introduction

For the information retrieval process positively labeled documents in a dataset are important and should not be missed, therefore achieving high recall is extremely important. However, there is generally a large number of documents that are relevant or not to the concerned topic and doing close reading for all documents and annotating them requires lots of time and resources (Hürriyetoğlu et al., 2016; Hürriyetoğlu et al., 2017). Therefore, ranking documents according to relevance to the investigated class may help to reduce close reading time and decrease the likelihood of missing critical information.

Baeza-Yates and Ribeiro-Neto (1999) propose ranking documents in decreasing order of being relevant to a given query to accelerate the information retrieval process. Halterman et al. (2021) apply this method with Natural Language Understanding (NLU) models for binary classification problems using the entailment probabilities of a document and a declarative form of the label. Therefore, to catch a high percentage of positively labeled documents, reading some percentage of documents would be enough since documents that are relevant would be at the top with a high probability. However, their dataset India Police Events focuses on a relatively specific task in information retrieval that is police actions like killing, arresting, failing to intervene, etc. Besides, they apply this method at the sentence level and as they also stated their model suffers from understanding multi-sentence context that increases the false negative rate.

We apply this approach to ProtestNews dataset (Hürriyetoğlu et al., 2021) along with the India Police Events dataset (Halterman et al., 2021) and investigate whether sentence level evaluation or document level evaluation ranks positive documents at the higher level measured by different evaluation metrics. We further investigate whether using the dictionary definition of a class or the declarative form of a class for the query performs this task better. We compare two NLU models DeBERTa-Large-MNLI (He et al., 2020) and RoBERTa-Large-MNLI (Liu et al., 2019) in terms of recall and mean average precision.

We present the related work in Section 2. Next, we introduce two datasets we used in our experiments in Section 3. Then we explain our methodology and list all queries used in this work in Section 4. We detail our experiments for both datasets and present results in Section 5. Finally, we conclude this work in Section 6 and state what can be done as future work in Section 7.

2 Related Work

Protest Event Detection Protest event extraction holds an important place in political social sciences and detection of protest events is generally the first step of the extraction. Due to the cost of manual event extraction, besides the presence of digital news articles and enhancing machine learning

Proceedings of the 5th Workshop on Challenges and Applications of Automated Extraction of Socio-political Events from Text (CASE), pages 124 - 132
December 7-8, 2022 ©2022 Association for Computational Linguistics

methods; automated event extraction comes into play.

Hanna (2017) presents MPEDS, an automated system for protest event extraction that contains an ensemble of shallow machine learning classifiers (SVM, SGD and Logistic Regression) to detect protest-related documents. Caselli et al. (2021) proposes Domain Adaptive Retraining for Transformer Language Models and shows that further training BERT with domain-specific dataset improves the performance. They present PROTEST-ER by retraining pre-trained BERT with protest related data from TREC Washington Post Corpus. Wiedemann et al. (2022) classifies protest related documents in German local news using Pretrained Language Models. They attempt to improve performance and generalizability by eliminating protest-unrelated sentences with keyword search and also by masking named entities with the idea of models may overfit on data by recognizing actors, organizatons and places.

Elsafoury (2019) focuses on both protest events and police actions i.e. protest repression events in Twitter with Machine Learning models with the claim of news articles suffer from bias, censorship and duplication. Won et al. (2017) detects and analyze protest events in geotagged tweets and associated images with Convolutional Neural Networks.

Ranking Documents with Transformer Language Models Yates et al. (2021) presents a comprehensive survey of how BERT (Devlin et al., 2019) works, ranking documents with BERT, retrieve and rerank approach with monoBERT, ranking metrics, etc. One of the most remarkable works in the survey is monoBERT and duoBERT, a multistage ranking approach with transformer language models proposed by Nogueira et al. (2019). The first stage retrieves the candidate documents with BM25 by treating the query as a bag of words and later, documents are reranked with their relevance score with BERT. DuoBERT also takes into account one document being more relevant than the other at a third stage. However, we rank the documents with a language model at one stage.

Halterman et al. (2021) rank documents with RoBERTa-Large-MNLI (Liu et al., 2019) on sentence level by being relevant to a police activity. Yet sentence level evaluation does not take into consideration the relationship between the sentences. Moreover, the task of extracting police events is a relatively specific topic in political event extraction. We apply this method with different document sizes and test on datasets in different topic specificities.

Transformer Language Models DeBERTa and RoBERTa DeBERTa-Large-MNLI (DLM) (He et al., 2020) and RoBERTa-Large-MNLI (RLM) (Liu et al., 2019) are pre-trained language models that improve BERT. Both models are pre-trained on Wikipedia (English Wikipedia dump3; 12GB), BookCorpus (6GB), OPENWEBTEXT (38GB), and STORIES (a subset of CommonCrawl (31GB) and fine-tuned for MNLI task. RLM has a token limitation of 512 whereas DLM has a limitation of theoretically 24,528. We limit the inputs to 512 tokens for both models to be able to compare them fairly. Ye and Manoharan (2021) find that DLM achieves a better performance in different sentence similarity tasks with respect to RLM and BERT. He et al. (2020) also show that DeBERTa outperforms RoBERTa in a variety of NLP tasks even when DeBERTa is trained on half of the training data. Therefore, we use DLM and compare it with RLM for our task.

Transferring Question Answering to Entailment Problem Khot et al. (2018) and Demszky et al. (2018) transfer the question answering problem to the entailment problem by forming the question into a declarative form. Clark et al. (2019) transfer yes/no question answering to entailment problem by training supervised models on entailment datasets and treating entailment probabilities as the probability of the answer being yes. They also use pre-trained ELMo, BERT, and OpenAI GPT as unsupervised models and show that fine-tuning BERT on entailment dataset MultiNLI boosts the performance. The problem of any binary classification can be also transferred to an entailment problem similar to the yes/no question answering, by considering the probability of entailment as the probability of data belonging to the positive class.

3 Data

We carried out the experiments on two different datasets: India Police Events dataset[1] (Halterman et al., 2021) and the ProtestNews dataset of the workshop CASE @ ACL-IJCNLP 2021[2] (Hürriyetoğlu et al., 2021).

[1]Data and code are provided at `https://github.com/slanglab/IndiaPoliceEvents`.

[2]Information and data are provided at `https://github.com/emerging-welfare/case-2021-shared-task`.

Event type	Question
kill	Did police kill someone?
arrest	Did police arrest someone?
fail	Did police fail to intervene?
force	Did police use force or violence?
any action	Did police do anything?

Table 1: Question form of each event type.

Event type	Positive Documents
kill	50 (3.98%)
arrest	128 (10.17%)
fail	114 (9.05%)
force	90 (7.15%)
any action	457 (36.24%)

Table 2: Number of positive documents for each event class (India Police Events Dataset).

India Police Events dataset includes 1,257 articles about the Indian state Gujarat from The Times of India and from March 2002. The articles are in English and contain 21,391 sentences in total. Each sentence is classified into 5 different labels regarding police activity: kill, arrest, fail, force, and any action. Question form of the each event type is given in Table 1. A document belongs to a class if any of its sentences belongs to that class. Table 2 illustrates the number of positive documents and the proportion of the positive documents for each event class. Note that one document may belong to one class, several classes or none of them.

ProtestNews dataset includes local news articles of countries India, China, Argentina, and Brazil. These articles are in English, Spanish, Portuguese, and Hindi. For this work, we have only used English articles. There are 9,327 English documents but to equalize data sizes with the India Police Events Dataset we randomly selected 1,257 articles among those. Documents that contain past or ongoing protest events are labeled as positive (Duruşan et al., 2022). Number and proportion of positive documents are given in Table 3.

Dataset	Positive Documents
ProtestNews Dataset	1,912 (20.51%)
ProtestNews Subset	268 (21.32 %)

Table 3: Number of positive documents for ProtestNews Dataset and its subset.

4 Method

First, the probability of entailment for each document and a query is calculated with NLU models from Huggingface[3], and documents are ranked by the decreasing probability of being relevant to the query. Thus we expect the documents that are more relevant are ranked at the top.

Entailment probabilities are evaluated on both sentence and document levels. At sentence level evaluation, entailment probabilities of sentences in a document with the given query are calculated and the largest probability among the sentences is considered as the probability of the document being relevant. For the document level evaluation since RLM is limited to 512 tokens, we divided documents into parts such that each part does not exceed 512 tokens. Similar to the sentence-level approach, probabilities of each part are calculated and the one with the largest probability is considered as the probability of the document. After getting the probabilities for all documents, they are ranked in the decreasing probability.

We compare the results by checking how much recall is achieved when a specified proportion of data is read from the ranked documents following Halterman et. al. (2021) and also by calculating the mean average precision. We release our code publicly[4].

4.1 Models

We focused on the performances of two multilingual NLU models that are RLM[5] (Liu et al., 2019) and DLM[6] (He et al., 2020) which are pre-trained on the same datasets (Wikipedia and BookCorpus). We conduct experiments with both models and compare the results.

4.2 Queries

We have experimented with different types of queries: definitional queries, extended definitional queries and declarative queries.

We used the Cambridge Dictionary[7] and form the definitional queries by using the definitions of the class name (protest, kill, arrest, etc.). Annota-

[3] http://huggingface.co

[4] https://github.com/kiymetakdemir/zero-shot-entailment-ranking

[5] https://huggingface.co/roberta-large-mnli

[6] https://huggingface.co/microsoft/deberta-large-mnli

[7] https://dictionary.cambridge.org

Query type	Query
Declarative query	There is a protest.
Definitional query	There is a strong complaint expressing disagreement, disapproval, or opposition. (definition of protest[9])
Social protest definition (Annotation Manual)	Individuals, groups, or organizations voice their objections, oppositions, demands or grievances to a person or institution of authority.
Contentious politics event definition (Annotation Manual)	There is a politically motivated collective action event.
'protest' + definitional query	Protest, there is a strong complaint expressing disagreement, disapproval, or opposition.
Protest definition + opposition definition	There is a strong complaint expressing disagreement, disapproval, or opposition. Disagreement with something, often by speaking or fighting against it, or (esp. in politics) the people or group who are not in power. (definition of opposition[10])
Protest definition + disapproval definition	There is a strong complaint expressing disagreement, disapproval, or opposition. The feeling of having a negative opinion of someone or something. (definition of disapproval[11])

Table 4: Queries used for the ProtestNews dataset.

Event type	Declarative query	Definitional query
kill	Police killed someone.	Police caused someone or something to die. (definition of kill[12])
arrest	Police arrested someone.	Police used legal authority to catch and take someone to a place where the person may be accused of a crime. (definition of arrest[13])
fail	Police failed to intervene.	Police failed to have an effect. (definition of act[14])
force	Police used violence.	Police used actions or words that are intended to hurt people. (definition of violence[15])
any action	Police did something.	Police have an effect. (definition of act)

Table 5: Queries for the India Police Events dataset.

tion manual may possibly be a good resource to find the definition of the investigated class. For this reason, we also experimented with definitions from Annotation Manual[8] (Duruşan et al., 2022). On the other hand, a declarative query is a sentence that simply describes the class. For instance, we use "There is a protest." as the declarative query for the ProtestNews dataset. For the India Police Events dataset, we use declarative queries proposed by Halterman et al. (2021).

We also extended protest dictionary definition by concatenating it with the definitions of words that pass in the query (see last 3 rows in Table 4). In one of the queries, the 'protest' word is added to the beginning of the protest definition. In the other one, definition of opposition is concatenated with the protest definition. In the third one, definitions of protest and definition of disapproval are concatenated and used as a query. Note that we used the definitions of opposition and disapproval since they occur in the protest definition. All queries used for both datasets are listed in Table 4 and 5.

5 Experiments & Results

ProtestNews Dataset is tested with declarative queries, definitional queries and extended definitions on models DLM and RLM and results are presented in Figure 1a for the sentence level evalu-

[8] https://github.com/emerging-welfare/general_info/tree/master/annotation-manuals

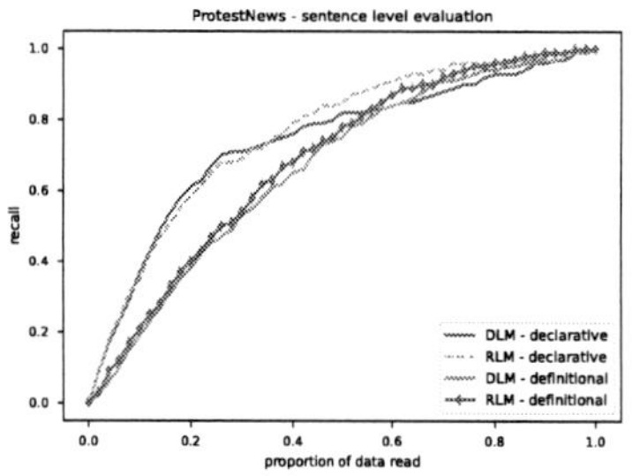

(a) Sentence level evaluation.

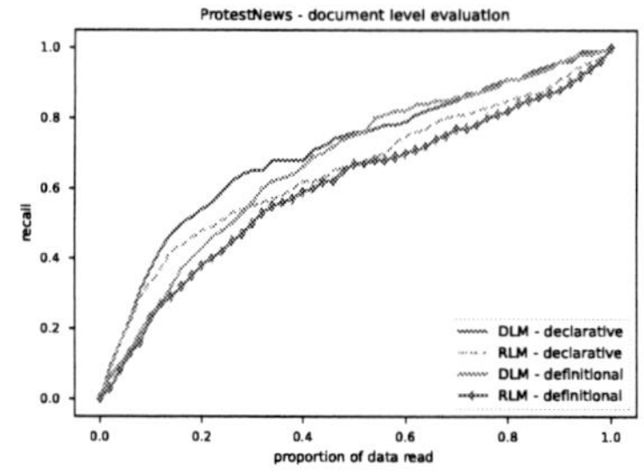

(b) Document level evaluation.

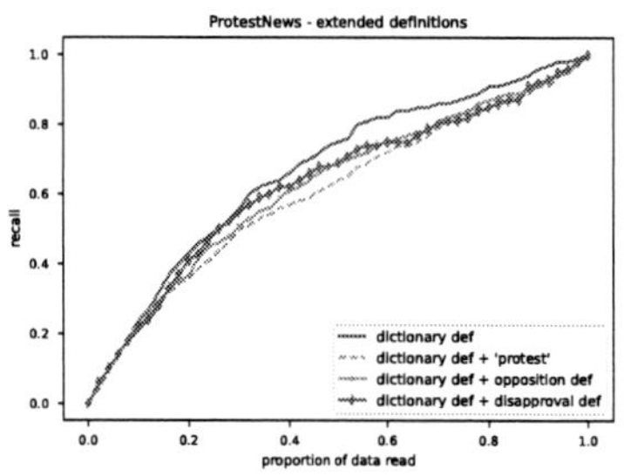

(c) Extended definitions.

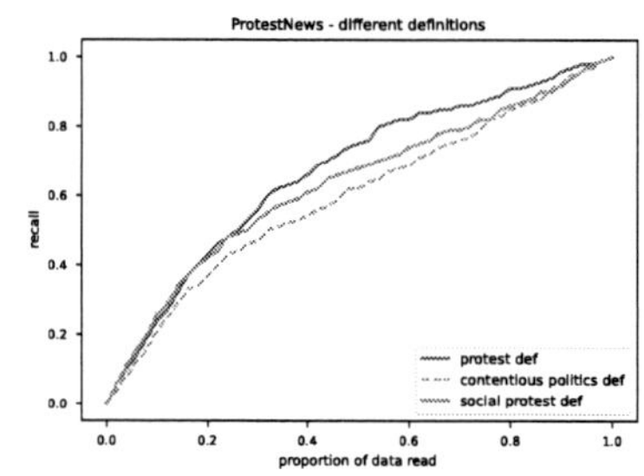

(d) Different definitions.

Figure 1: ProtestNews dataset tested on two models: RLM and DLM.

ation. The x-axis represents what percentage of the data is read and the y-axis represents how much recall is achieved at that stage. One can investigate what percentage of the data should be read to achieve a specified recall. We see that both models yield similar results when the same query is given but positive documents are accumulated at more top with the declarative query compared to the definitional query.

For document level evaluation, Figure 1b illustrates the comparison of the models. DLM achieves higher recall scores than RLM, however, the query type does not affect the performance of the model at the document level significantly.

We compare the extended and Annotation Manual definitions at document level using the DLM model since the DLM achieves higher recall compared to RLM at the document level as in Figure 1b. However, from Figure 1c we see that extending the protest definition performs slightly worse than using the only dictionary definition. Also, Annotation Manual definitions do not perform better than the dictionary definition as we see from Figure 1d.

India Police Events Dataset is tested with declarative and definitional queries on RLM and DLM as in ProtestNews dataset. For all event types, we see from Figure 2 and Figure 3 that DLM with declarative query gives the best result that is positive documents are accumulated at more top-level, whereas RLM with a definitional query stays behind other combinations of model and queries.

Mean Average Precision (mAP) is calculated for each ranking and reported in Table 6. Query and document length combination that gives the highest mAP is marked in bold for each dataset and event type.

For the ProtestNews dataset we observe that using models DLM or RLM, and document lengths do not differ significantly. Whereas using a declarative query gives much better mAP than the definitional query. For the India Police Events dataset for all event types DLM and declarative query with the sentence level evaluation yield the highest score rather than the definitional or document level evaluation. Besides, note that there is a large difference with the other combinations. For example for event type force, sentence level evaluation with DLM and the declarative query gives 0.91 mAP whereas document level evaluation with RLM and the definitional query yields 0.11 mAP.

As the topic gets broader, we see that performance gets worse in Table 6. For instance, kill is a more

		ProtestNews	India Police Events				
		-	kill	arrest	fail	force	any action
DLM	decl-sent	0.64	**0.96**	**0.94**	**0.65**	**0.91**	**0.89**
DLM	decl-doc	0.60	0.80	0.75	0.25	0.75	0.80
DLM	def-sent	0.35	0.89	0.63	0.47	0.71	0.69
DLM	def-doc	0.41	0.62	0.42	0.21	0.21	0.65
RLM	decl-sent	**0.65**	0.55	0.91	0.34	0.66	0.42
RLM	decl-doc	0.51	0.18	0.44	0.18	0.27	0.36
RLM	def-sent	0.38	0.36	0.26	0.23	0.18	0.38
RLM	def-doc	0.34	0.11	0.15	0.16	0.11	0.37

Table 6: mAP scores for DLM and RLM models with different document lengths and queries.

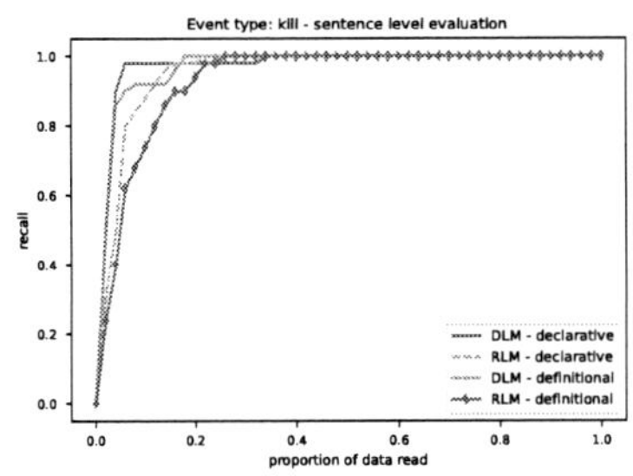

(a) kill

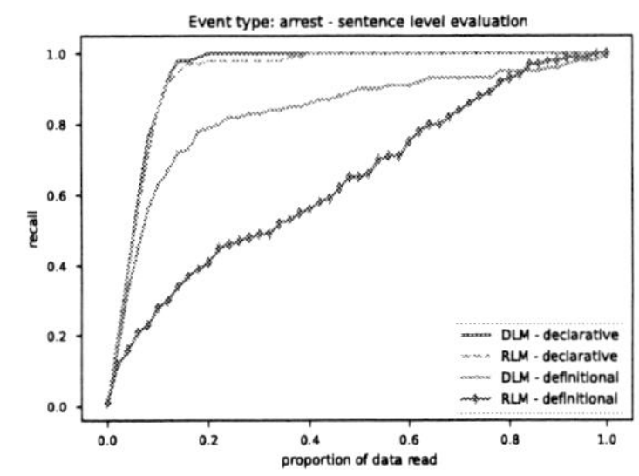

(b) arrest

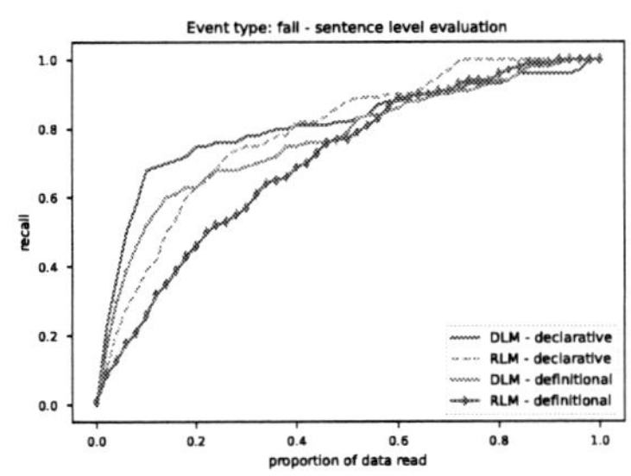

(c) fail

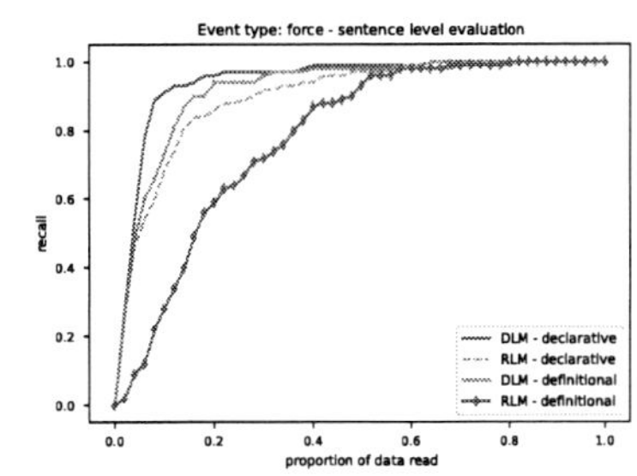

(d) force

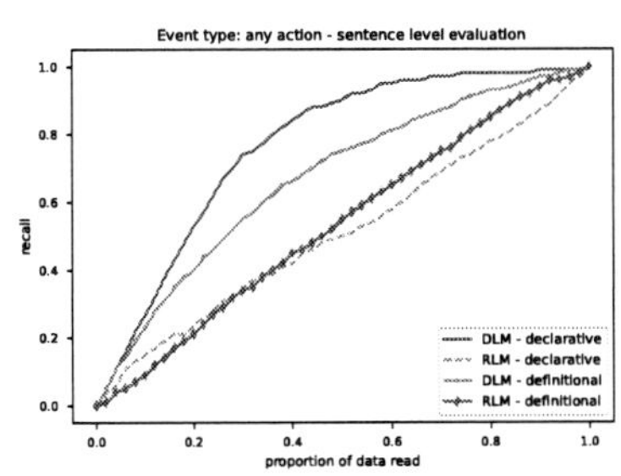

(e) any action

Figure 2: India Police Events dataset sentence level evaluation tested on RLM and DLM.

specific topic than any action since any action event type also includes kill events. When 20% of the data read, 90% recall is achieved for event type kill, on the other hand, even 60% recall is not reached for any action.

We take the average sentence and document level mAP scores for each model and present in Table 7. For ProtestNews dataset, sentence or document

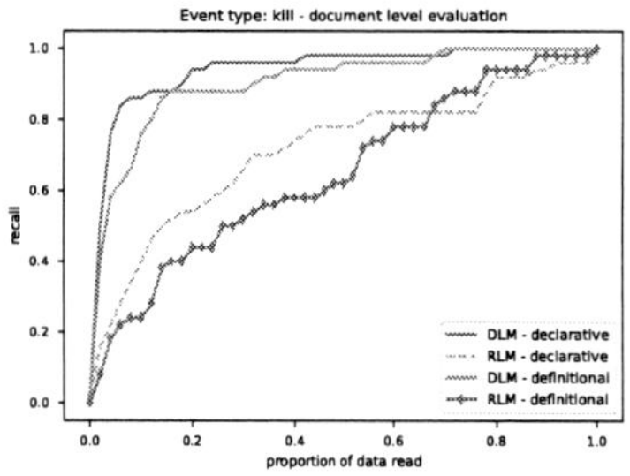

(a) kill

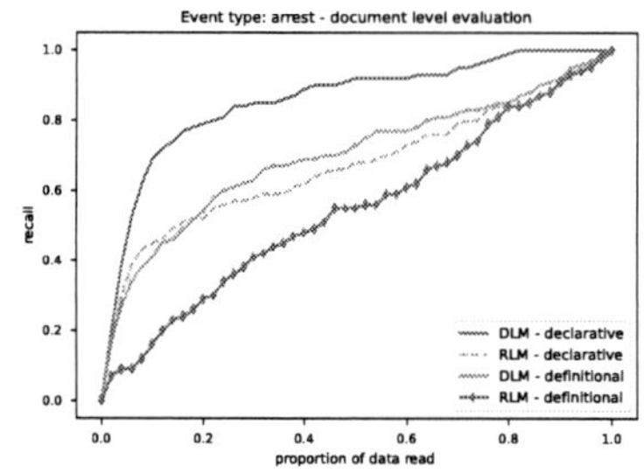

(b) arrest

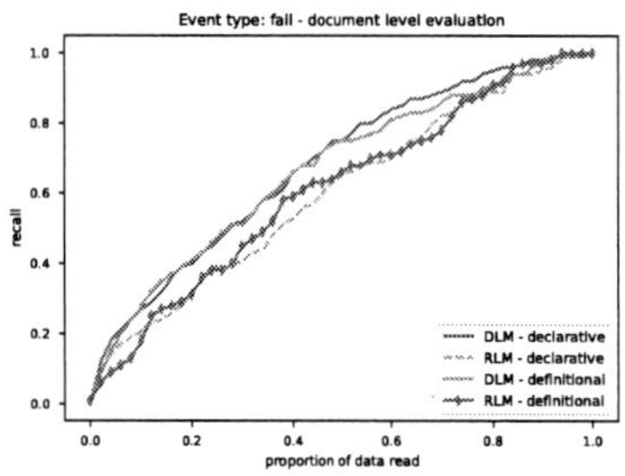

(c) fail

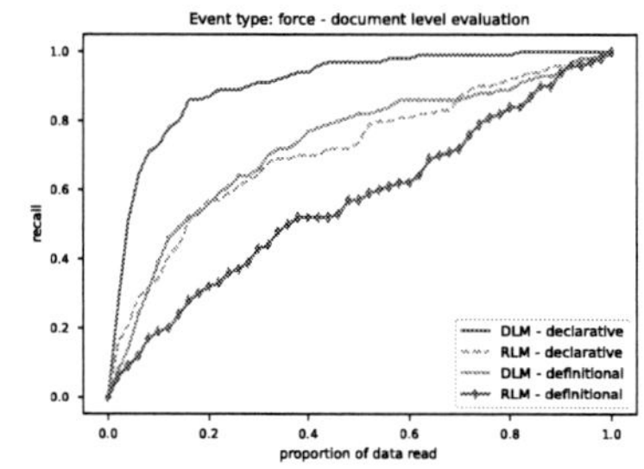

(d) force

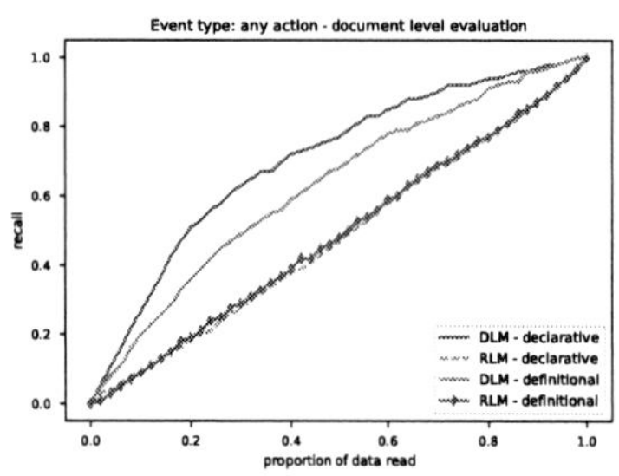

(e) any action

Figure 3: India Police Events dataset document level evaluation tested on RLM and DLM.

level does not differ in mAP when DLM is used. However, for India Police Events dataset sentence level evaluation achieves much higher mAP than document level evaluation (0.24 mAP increase for DLM and 0.21 increase for RLM). For both sentence and document level, DLM reaches higher mAP than RLM.

	ProtestNews		India Police Events	
	DLM	RLM	DLM	RLM
sent	**0.50**	**0.52**	**0.77**	**0.43**
doc	**0.50**	0.42	0.53	0.22

Table 7: Average mAP on ProtestNews and India Police Events Dataset for all event types.

6 Conclusion

We investigate the performances of two Transformer Language Models (DLM and RLM), different query types (declarative and definitional) in different document lengths (document and sen-

[9] https://dictionary.cambridge.org/dictionary/english/protest

[10] https://dictionary.cambridge.org/dictionary/english/opposition

[11] https://dictionary.cambridge.org/dictionary/english/disapproval

[12] https://dictionary.cambridge.org/dictionary/english/kill

[13] https://dictionary.cambridge.org/dictionary/english/arrest

[14] https://dictionary.cambridge.org/dictionary/english/act

[15] https://dictionary.cambridge.org/dictionary/english/violence

tence level). Our experiments that conclude DLM achieves higher mAP scores than RLM are consistent with the findings of Ye and Manoharan (2021) and He et al. (2020). In general, we find that the combination of DLM with a declarative query in sentence level outperforms other combinations in mAP score. However, scores decrease as the topic or event type gets broader where protest events can be considered broader than specific police actions.

7 Future Work

We plan to analyze results more for example by considering subcategories of protest events for the ProtestNews dataset. Future work can extend this work to a different political event classification dataset and further investigate the association between the broadness of the topic and metric scores. Experiments in languages other than English are also left as future work.

References

Ricardo A. Baeza-Yates and Berthier A. Ribeiro-Neto. 1999. *Modern Information Retrieval*. ACM Press / Addison-Wesley.

Tommaso Caselli, Osman Mutlu, Angelo Basile, and Ali Hürriyetoğlu. 2021. PROTEST-ER: Retraining BERT for protest event extraction. In *Proceedings of the 4th Workshop on Challenges and Applications of Automated Extraction of Socio-political Events from Text (CASE 2021)*, pages 12–19, Online. Association for Computational Linguistics.

Christopher Clark, Kenton Lee, Ming-Wei Chang, Tom Kwiatkowski, Michael Collins, and Kristina Toutanova. 2019. BoolQ: Exploring the surprising difficulty of natural yes/no questions. In *Proceedings of the 2019 Conference of the North American Chapter of the Association for Computational Linguistics: Human Language Technologies, Volume 1 (Long and Short Papers)*, pages 2924–2936, Minneapolis, Minnesota. Association for Computational Linguistics.

Dorottya Demszky, Kelvin Guu, and Percy Liang. 2018. Transforming question answering datasets into natural language inference datasets.

Jacob Devlin, Ming-Wei Chang, Kenton Lee, and Kristina Toutanova. 2019. BERT: Pre-training of deep bidirectional transformers for language understanding. In *Proceedings of the 2019 Conference of the North American Chapter of the Association for Computational Linguistics: Human Language Technologies, Volume 1 (Long and Short Papers)*, pages 4171–4186, Minneapolis, Minnesota. Association for Computational Linguistics.

Fırat Duruşan, Ali Hürriyetoğlu, Erdem Yörük, Osman Mutlu, Çağrı Yoltar, Burak Gürel, and Alvaro Comin. 2022. Global contentious politics database (glocon) annotation manuals.

Fatma Elsafoury. 2019. *Detecting protest repression incidents from tweets*. Ph.D. thesis, University of Glasgow.

Andrew Halterman, Katherine Keith, Sheikh Sarwar, and Brendan O'Connor. 2021. Corpus-level evaluation for event QA: The IndiaPoliceEvents corpus covering the 2002 Gujarat violence. In *Findings of the Association for Computational Linguistics: ACL-IJCNLP 2021*, pages 4240–4253, Online. Association for Computational Linguistics.

Alex Hanna. 2017. Mpeds: Automating the generation of protest event data.

Pengcheng He, Xiaodong Liu, Jianfeng Gao, and Weizhu Chen. 2020. Deberta: Decoding-enhanced bert with disentangled attention.

Ali Hürriyetoğlu, Osman Mutlu, Erdem Yörük, Farhana Ferdousi Liza, Ritesh Kumar, and Shyam Ratan. 2021. Multilingual protest news detection - shared task 1, CASE 2021. In *Proceedings of the 4th Workshop on Challenges and Applications of Automated Extraction of Socio-political Events from Text (CASE 2021)*, pages 79–91, Online. Association for Computational Linguistics.

Ali Hürriyetoğlu, Nelleke Oostdijk, Mustafa Erkan Başar, and Antal van den Bosch. 2017. *Supporting Experts to Handle Tweet Collections About Significant Events*, pages 138–141. Springer International Publishing, Cham.

Ali Hürriyetoğlu, Christian Gudehus, Nelleke Oostdijk, and Antal van den Bosch. 2016. Relevancer: Finding and labeling relevant information in tweet collections. In *Social Informatics - 8th International Conference, SocInfo 2016, Bellevue, WA, USA, November 11-14, 2016, Proceedings, Part II*, volume 10047 of *Lecture Notes in Computer Science*, pages 210–224.

Tushar Khot, Ashish Sabharwal, and Peter Clark. 2018. Scitail: A textual entailment dataset from science question answering. *Proceedings of the AAAI Conference on Artificial Intelligence*, 32(1).

Yinhan Liu, Myle Ott, Naman Goyal, Jingfei Du, Mandar Joshi, Danqi Chen, Omer Levy, Mike Lewis, Luke Zettlemoyer, and Veselin Stoyanov. 2019. Roberta: A robustly optimized bert pretraining approach.

Rodrigo Nogueira, Wei Yang, Kyunghyun Cho, and Jimmy J. Lin. 2019. Multi-stage document ranking with bert. *ArXiv*, abs/1910.14424.

Gregor Wiedemann, Jan Matti Dollbaum, Sebastian Haunss, Priska Daphi, and Larissa Daria Meier. 2022. A generalized approach to protest event detection in German local news. In *Proceedings of the Thirteenth Language Resources and Evaluation Conference*, pages 3883–3891, Marseille, France. European Language Resources Association.

Donghyeon Won, Zachary C Steinert-Threlkeld, and Jungseock Joo. 2017. Protest activity detection and perceived violence estimation from social media images. In *Proceedings of the 25th ACM international conference on Multimedia*, pages 786–794.

Andrew Yates, Rodrigo Nogueira, and Jimmy Lin. 2021. Pretrained transformers for text ranking: Bert and beyond. In *Proceedings of the 44th International ACM SIGIR Conference on Research and Development in Information Retrieval*, SIGIR '21, page 2666–2668, New York, NY, USA. Association for Computing Machinery.

Xinfeng Ye and Sathiamoorthy Manoharan. 2021. Performance comparison of automated essay graders based on various language models. In *2021 IEEE International Conference on Computing (ICOCO)*, pages 152–157.

SPOCK @ Causal News Corpus 2022: Cause-Effect-Signal Span Detection Using Span-Based and Sequence Tagging Models

Anik Saha Alex Gittens Bulent Yener
Rensselaer Polytechnic Institute
{sahaa, gittea}@rpi.edu, yener@cs.rpi.edu

Oktie Hassanzadeh Jian Ni Kavitha Srinivas
IBM Research
{nij, hassanzadeh}@us.ibm.com, kavitha.srinivas@ibm.com

Abstract

Understanding causal relationship is an importance part of natural language processing. We address the causal information extraction problem with different neural models built on top of pre-trained transformer-based language models for identifying Cause, Effect and Signal spans, from news data sets. We use the Causal News Corpus subtask 2 training data set to train span-based and sequence tagging models. Our span-based model based on pre-trained BERT base weights achieves an F1 score of 47.48 on the test set with an accuracy score of 36.87 and obtained 3rd place in the Causal News Corpus 2022 shared task.

1 Introduction

Subtask 2 of the the Causal News Corpus shared task at the CASE-22 (Workshop on Challenges and Applications of Automated Extraction of Socio-political Events from Text) addresses the causal information extraction problem (Tan et al., 2022). The goal of this task is to detect the spans of text in an input sentence that represent cause-effect pairs and, if extant, to also detect the text spans that "signal" this causal relationship. Figure 3 shows a sample from the data set. Simple examples of such signal spans are *result in*, *lead to*, and *due to*. In other cases, the causal relationship is implicit and it is important to understand the meaning of the whole sentence to detect causality. The Causal News Corpus data set contains sentences with both implicit and explicit causal relationship, so for this task, language understanding is an essential step. We adopt different pre-trained language models to develop our system owing to their tremendous success in natural language understanding tasks.

In this paper, we train and evaluate the performance of span-based and sequence tagging neural network models for the Cause-Effect-Signal Span Detection task. Our team name SPOCK (SPan and sequence based mOdels for Causal Knowledge) for the Causal News Corpus 2022 shared task is inspired by these model architectures. We trained a span-based (Eberts and Ulges, 2019) causality extraction system[1] by fine tuning the BERT-Base (Devlin et al., 2018) model. This model resulted in an F1 score of 47.48 and Accuracy score of 36.87. This was our best performing model compared to the ensemble of sequence tagging models based on the BIO scheme using the BERT-base and RoBERTa-large (Liu et al., 2019) language models.

2 Dataset and Task

We use the data sets from Causal News Corpus 2022 in our experiments. The sentences in this data set are collected from news sources containing event mentions. There are two subtasks in this challenge: subtask 1 is Causal Event Classification, where the goal is to determine if a sentence expresses a cause-effect relationship; subtask 2 is Cause, Effect and Signal Span Detection, where the goal is to identify the span of words in a sentence corresponding to a cause, effect, or signal (a span indicating the existence of a causal relation). This paper documents two approaches towards subtask 2. The training and dev set from subtask 2 are used for the training and evaluation of our models. In the final submission to the challenge, the trained models were used to obtain predictions on the test set.

This data set contains labels for Cause, Effect and Signal spans in a sentence whereas other commonly used data sets for causal relation extraction only contain labels for Cause and Effect. Further, it is possible for the Signal spans to overlap with the Cause or Effect spans. In some examples, the Signal words are not a contiguous span, i.e. words in different parts of the sentence are tagged as Signal. Data set statistics for subtask 2 are shown in Table 1.

[1] code for SpERT model available in https://github.com/aniksh/spert-causalnewscorpus

Proceedings of the 5th Workshop on Challenges and Applications of Automated Extraction of Socio-political Events from Text (CASE), pages 133 - 137
December 7-8, 2022 ©2022 Association for Computational Linguistics

Data Split	Size
Train	180
Dev	323
Test	311

Table 1: Data set statistics

Each example in the training and dev sets is labeled with a single pair of Cause and Effect span. Some sentences contain multiple cause-effect pairs; each pair comprises a separate example, so that each example has a single cause and effect pair. Not all sentences in the data set contain a signal span. In some examples, the signal span overlaps with the cause or effect span. We show some examples in Figure 1.

3 Methodology

We experimented with two types of neural models for the Causal News Corpus 2022 challenge.

3.1 Span-based Model

We introduced this model in our submission (Saha et al., 2022) to the FinCausal 2022 challenge. The span-based model takes a sequence of tokens as input and predicts the Cause and Effect spans in the sentence by classifying a list of candidate spans of words. The list of candidate spans is generated by selecting all possible spans of words in the sentence up to a maximum span length. This model is based on SpERT (Eberts and Ulges, 2019) that classifies each span into 4 classes (Cause, Effect, Signal or None).

The input to the span classifier is a span embedding which takes the output layer embeddings from the *BERT-base* model. We split the words in a sentence with HuggingFace's *BertTokenizer* function (Wolf et al., 2019) to feed the pre-trained BERT model. We convert the annotations in the Causal News Corpus data set to Cause, Effect and Signal span labels for the span-based models.

The span-based model takes in a list of spans and builds an embedding for each span by using a max-pooling operation over the BERT output embeddings of the word pieces in that span. A context embedding is added to the span representation by concatenating the output layer embedding from BERT corresponding to the CLS token. The width of the span is included in the span representation by concatenating a span width embedding. The span-width embeddings are stored in a look-up table with a row for each unique span length of a cause or effect in the training data set. The embedding for a given span is thus the concatenation of the CLS token embedding, the width embedding, and a max-pool of the token embeddings in the span.

$$\mathbf{e}(s) = e_{CLS} \circ w_{k+1} \circ f(\mathbf{e}_i, \mathbf{e}_{i+1}, \ldots \mathbf{e}_{i+k})$$

where $\mathbf{e}(s)$ is the span embedding, e_{CLS} is the CLS token embedding, w_n is the width embedding for a span of size n and $\mathbf{e}_i$ the embedding for i-th token. A softmax layer is used on top of a linear classifier to convert the span embeddings into probabilities over 4 classes.

$$y_s = \text{softmax}(W_s \cdot \mathbf{e}(s) + b_s)$$

where W_s is the weight of the linear classifier and b_s is the bias of the linear classifier.

The cross-entropy loss is used to train the span classifier in this model. Spans are classified as either Cause, Effect, Signal, or None. Consider, for instance, the process of selecting a single Cause span. First we drop from consideration all spans whose probability of being a Cause are smaller than a threshold t. If there is no span left after applying the threshold, we predict there is no Cause in the sentence. Otherwise we take the Cause to be the span that achieves

$$\max_{s \in S} p_s$$

where S is the set of spans after dropping all spans below the threshold and all spans whose highest probability class is None, and p_s is the predicted probability for span s to be labeled as a Cause. Similar rules are used to identify the single Effect and Signal span.

Since the data set only contains positive labels for Cause, Effect and Signal spans, we generate negative examples by randomly sampling spans of words from the input sentence and labeling those as None. The negative span samples are selected from a list of all possible spans in the sentence up to the maximum span length from before. At inference time, a list of candidate spans is generated up to this maximum span size. We explain the span selection process in Appendix A. Since we predict Cause and Effect from a list of overlapping spans, the predicted Cause and Effect might possibly overlap but we did not face this problem as the span representation for overlapping spans are very similar.

<ARG1>Four students appeared in court on Monday</ARG1> <SIG0>for</SIG0> <ARG0>allegedly removing street signs</ARG0> .

Four	students	appeared	in	court	on	Monday	for	allegedly	removing	street	signs	.
B-E	I-E	I-E	I-E	I-E	I-E	I-E	O	B-C	I-C	I-C	I-C	O
O	O	O	O	O	O	O	B-S	O	O	O	O	O

<ARG1>The workers had embarked on a wildcat strike</ARG1> <ARG0><SIG0>demanding</SIG0> better working conditions</ARG0> .

The	workers	had	embarked	on	a	wildcat	strike	demanding	better	working	conditions	.
B-E	I-E	I-E	I-E	I-E	I-E	I-E	I-E	B-C	I-C	I-C	I-C	O
O	O	O	O	O	O	O	O	B-S	O	O	O	O

Figure 1: Examples with Cause, Effect and Signal span labels from the Causal News Corpus 2022 data set. The input text is labeled with ARG0, ARG1 and SIG0 labels. These are converted to the BIO tags for Cause-Effect and Signal as shown in different lines. The second example has overlapping Cause-Effect and Signal tags.

Model	Dev Set				Test Set			
	P	R	F1	Acc	P	R	F1	Acc
Baseline (Random)	2.17	2.17	2.17	20.84	0.30	0.89	0.45	21.94
Ensemble Tagging Model (BERT-base)	53.26	43.48	46.88	46.45	35.20	23.51	27.44	31.36
Ensemble Tagging Model (RoBERTa-large)	66.30	54.35	58.47	49.65	51.58	38.09	42.52	35.92
Span-based Model	56.52	72.16	62.62	44.71	57.62	43.75	47.48	36.87

Table 2: Precision (P), Recall (R), F1 and Accuracy score (Acc) of different sequence tagging models and the span-based model on the dev and test set.

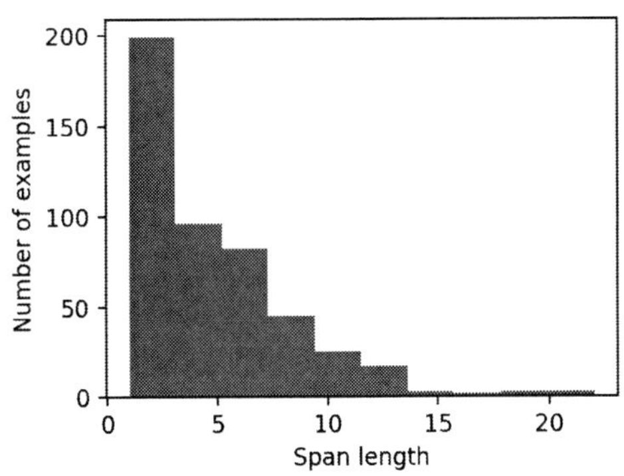

Figure 2: Span length distribution of the training set

The maximum span size is a hyperparameter for this model, chosen based on the distribution of the size of labeled Cause and Effect spans in the data set. Figure 2 plots the distribution of span sizes of all types in the training set. From our initial experiments, we found the 99-percentile span size from the training data to work well.

3.2 Sequence Tagging Models

This is a standard sequence tagging model that classifies each token in the sentence with BIO-style tags. The input text is tokenized with Huggingface tokenizers. For an input sequence, each token is assigned one of the following tags: {B-Cause, I-Cause, B-Effect, I-Effect, O}, where "B" stands for "Beginning", "I" for "Inside", and "O" for "Outside". Since this data set contains Signal span labels which overlap with the Cause and Effect labels we cannot represent these spans within a single sequence of BIO-style tags. To address the overlapping span problem, we introduce a separate set of tags for the Signal span. Figure 1 shows such an example with the BIO tags.

We experiment with both BERT-base and RoBERTa-large (Liu et al., 2019) as the encoder for the input sentence. The BERT-base model has 12 transformer layers with a token embedding dimension of 768 while the RoBERTa-large models has 24 layers with an embedding dimension of 1024. We add a 2-layer MLP to the output embeddings from the encoder to classify each token in the sentence. Since we have two sets of sequence tags, we train one MLP for detecting the Cause-Effect spans and another for detecting the Signal spans. These token classifiers share the same embedding representation. There are two cross-entropy loss functions for the two types of labels. We take a sum of these two loss functions as the total loss for the model. We fine-tune the pre-trained model weights and train the MLP parameters from scratch. We use the dev set performance to select the hyperparameters.

We take an ensemble approach to reduce the influence of randomness in the training on the final model performance. Specifically, we use majority voting to aggregate the token-level predictions on the test set from 11 different models trained with 11 different random seeds (0,10,20,... 100).

3.3 Training

We selected the hyperparameters by using the dev set performance as validation score and selecting the model with the highest F1 score. All models described here were trained on NVIDIA Tesla V100 gpus. We set the maximum span size to 20 as it covers 99% of the training data spans. The models are trained for 40 epochs with a learning rate of $5e^{-5}$. The number of negative samples per true label for the span classifier is set to 10.

4 Results

Span-based Model

The span-based model has a multi-class span classifier that predicts a score for each of the 4 classes. During inference, we filter all spans classified as None i.e. not a Cause, Effect or Signal. We assume the test data set might contain both causal and non-causal sentences, so we use a threshold ($t = 0.3$) on the predicted probability to filter spans which belong to a specific class (Cause or Effect). After thresholding, we select the span with the highest probability in each class.

This model achieves an F1 score of 47.48 and an Accuracy score of 36.87; it places 3rd in the shared task in terms of F1 score. It has the highest precision (57.62) among the submitted systems but low recall (43.75) value. We believe this model can achieve a higher score if we add a mechanism to predict multiple cause-effect pairs instead of a single cause-effect pairs.

Sequence Tagging Model

The sequence tagging model predicts both Cause-Effect and Signal tags to address the cases where these spans overlap. Since the model has a token-level classifier, it is possible that the predicted tags can form multiple spans for the same class. To convert the predicted token tags to span predictions, we take the first sequence of tokens in the sentence tagged in a class to be the single span for that class. We utilize only the class prediction to form the spans; in particular, either the 'B' or 'I' tags signals the start of a predicted span. The span prediction ends when the model predicts a different class for the next token or the sentence ends. We apply majority voting on the tags predicted for each tokens over 11 models trained with different random seeds. The ensemble method helps to reduce errors but we do not add any constraints to predict consecutive tokens. The RoBERTa-large model has 12% higher F1 score compared to the BERT-base model but it is lower than the Span-based model by about 4%.

Model	Text
Ground Truth	The treating doctors said San-gram lost around 5 kg due to the hunger strike .
BERT-base (Ensemble)	The treating doctors said San-gram lost around 5 kg due to the hunger strike .
RoBERTa-large (Ensemble)	The treating doctors said San-gram lost around 5 kg due to the hunger strike .
Span-based Model	The treating doctors said San-gram lost around 5 kg due to the hunger strike .

Figure 3: Sample predictions from the span-based model and the sequence tagging model. Yellow for Cause, Cyan for Effect, Red for Signal

Sample Prediction

We show the predictions from the sequence tagging and span-based models for the same input sentence in Figure 3. All 3 models label the same words as the Signal and the Cause spans. The BERT-base model predicts the wrong Effect span by selecting the phrase "treating doctors". The Cause-Effect span predictions from the RoBERTa-large model and the span-based models are the same. Since this sentence has a simple structure, it is relatively easier for these neural models to predict the Cause, Effect and Signal spans. The similarity in predictions from the span-based and the RoBERTa-large is also reflected in the results in Table 2 where these models have a small difference in F1 score.

5 Conclusion

In this paper, we adopt two approaches towards solving the Cause-Effect-Signal Detection task for participating in the subtask 2 of the Causal News

Corpus 2022 challenge. The span-based model outperforms the ensemble of sequence tagging models in both the dev set and the blind test set. In future work, we would like to adapt the models to predict multiple cause-effect pairs for a sentence. We will also focus on addressing the lack of large labeled data sets for this tasks by utilizing semi-supervised domain adaptation or generalization techniques.

References

Jacob Devlin, Ming-Wei Chang, Kenton Lee, and Kristina Toutanova. 2018. Bert: Pre-training of deep bidirectional transformers for language understanding. *arXiv preprint arXiv:1810.04805*.

Markus Eberts and Adrian Ulges. 2019. Span-based joint entity and relation extraction with transformer pre-training. *arXiv preprint arXiv:1909.07755*.

Yinhan Liu, Myle Ott, Naman Goyal, Jingfei Du, Mandar Joshi, Danqi Chen, Omer Levy, Mike Lewis, Luke Zettlemoyer, and Veselin Stoyanov. 2019. RoBERTa: A robustly optimized BERT pretraining approach. *arXiv preprint arXiv:1907.11692*.

Anik Saha, Jian Ni, Oktie Hassanzadeh, Alex Gittens, Kavitha Srinivas, and Bulent Yener. 2022. Spock at fincausal 2022: Causal information extraction using span-based and sequence tagging models. In *Proceedings of the 4th Financial Narrative Processing Workshop@ LREC*, pages 108–111.

Fiona Anting Tan, Ali Hürriyetoğlu, Tommaso Caselli, Nelleke Oostdijk, Hansi Hettiarachchi, Tadashi Nomoto, Onur Uca, and Farhana Ferdousi Liza. 2022. Event causality identification with causal news corpus - shared task 3, CASE 2022. In *Proceedings of the 5th Workshop on Challenges and Applications of Automated Extraction of Socio-political Events from Text (CASE 2022)*, Online. Association for Computational Linguistics.

Thomas Wolf, Lysandre Debut, Victor Sanh, Julien Chaumond, Clement Delangue, Anthony Moi, Pierric Cistac, Tim Rault, Rémi Louf, Morgan Funtowicz, et al. 2019. HuggingFace's transformers: State-of-the-art natural language processing. *arXiv preprint arXiv:1910.03771*.

A Span Selection

The span selection procedure is explained here with an example sentence. For the sentence, *The treating doctors said Sangram lost around 5 kg due to the hunger strike .* with a maximum span size of 5, we list all possible spans from size 1 to 5. We slide a window of a certain span size over the sentence to get all possible spans. For span size 3, the list of spans in this sentence would be - *[The, treating, doctors], [treating, doctors, said]* ... *[hunger, strike, .]*. So for each span size 1, 2, 3, 4, 5 we list all possible spans in the sentence to form the set of candidate spans.

Training. We select 10 negative samples randomly from each sentence during training. **Prediction.** To predict a Cause or Effect span, we need to list all possible spans from a sentence. So we classify all spans upto a maximum span size during inference.

CSECU-DSG @ Causal News Corpus 2022: Fusion of RoBERTa Transformers Variants for Causal Event Classification

Abdul Aziz, Md. Akram Hossain, and Abu Nowshed Chy
Department of Computer Science and Engineering
University of Chittagong, Chattogram-4331, Bangladesh
{aziz.abdul.cu, akram.hossain.cse.cu}@gmail.com,
and nowshed@cu.ac.bd

Abstract

Identifying cause-effect relationships in sentences is one of the formidable tasks to tackle the challenges of inference and understanding of natural language. However, the diversity of word semantics and sentence structure makes it challenging to determine the causal relationship effectively. To address these challenges, CASE-2022 shared task 3 introduced a task focusing on event causality identification with causal news corpus. This paper presents our participation in this task, especially in subtask 1 which is the causal event classification task. To tackle the task challenge, we propose a unified neural model through exploiting two fine-tuned transformer models including RoBERTa and Twitter-RoBERTa. We perform score fusion through combining the prediction scores of each component model using weighted arithmetic mean to generate the probability score for class label identification. The experimental results showed that our proposed method achieved the top performance (ranked 1st) among the participants' systems.

1 Introduction

Causality is a fundamental cognitive concept that frequently emerges in various natural language processing (NLP) works. It mostly focuses on the challenges of inference and understanding of the natural language. In general, a causal relation is a semantic relationship between two arguments known as cause and effect, where the occurrence of one (cause argument) incurs the occurrence of the other (effect argument). Such causal relation plays an important role in various contemporary NLP tasks including document-summarization, event prediction from text, scene and story generation, question-answering (Q/A), product recommendation based on user comments, and other textual entailments (Yu et al., 2022; Yang et al., 2022).

**The first two authors have equal contributions.

To address the challenges of event causality identification in texts, Tan et al. (Tan et al., 2022a) introduced a shared task at the CASE-2022 workshop. The task is composed of two subtasks including a causal event classification task (subtask1) and a cause-effect-signal span detection task (subtask 2). However, we only participated in the causal event classification task (subtask1), where given a text a system needs to determine whether it contains a cause-event meaning or not. To demonstrate a clear view of the task definition, we articulate a few examples from subtask 1 in Table 1.

Sentence	Label
The farmworkers ' strike resumed on Tuesday when their demands were not met	1
He said he was about 100 metres away when he witnessed the attack .	0

Table 1: Example of subtask 1. Here, label 1 means Causal and 0 means Non-Causal.

Prior work on event causality identification has mostly employed semi-supervised methods (Rink et al., 2010; Mirza, 2014; Aziz et al., 2020) based on features (e.g. psycho-linguistic, syntactic, semantic, etc.) or supervised methods (Gordeev et al., 2020; Ionescu et al., 2020) based on transformers model (e.g. BERT, RoBERTa, DistilBERT, etc.). However, transformer-based methods obtained more competitive results (Mariko et al., 2020), although those methods have some limitations in the fusion technique. In order to overcome this limitation, we proposed a RoBERTa-based unified method where we utilise the weighted average fusion technique.

We organize the rest of the paper as follows: Section 2 describes our proposed system in the CASE-2022 causal event classification task whereas, in

Proceedings of the 5th Workshop on Challenges and Applications of Automated Extraction of Socio-political Events from Text (CASE), pages 138 - 142
December 7-8, 2022

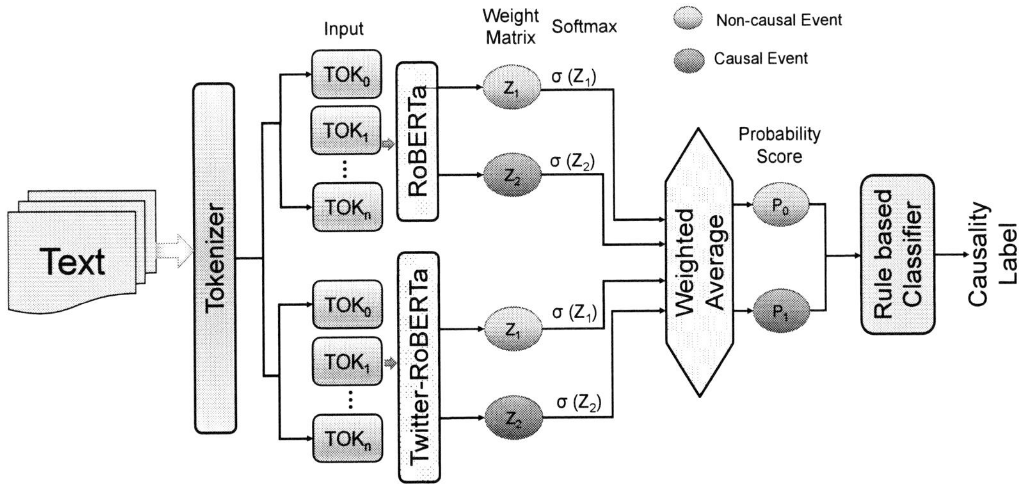

Figure 1: Our proposed model for the causal event classification task.

Section 3, we present our system design with parameter settings and conduct the results and performance analysis. Finally, we conclude with some future directions in Section 4.

2 Proposed Framework

In this section, we describe our proposed approach for the event causality identification task. Our goal is to exploit the inherent semantics of the sentence to identify whether the event sentence contains any cause-effect meaning. The overview of our proposed framework is depicted in Figure 1.

Given an input text, we employ two transformer models including RoBERTa (Liu et al., 2019) and one of its variants Twitter_RoBERTa (Barbieri et al., 2020) to extract the diverse contextual features. Such feature representation better captures the inherent semantics of the text. Later, a linear feed-forward layer is utilized in each model to estimate the probability score of each class. Finally, for the effective fusion of the scores, we take the weighted arithmetic mean of the prediction scores of these models. A class that contains the highest probability scores is considered as the final label.

2.1 Transformer Models

RoBERTa (Liu et al., 2019) stands for robustly optimized BERT pre-training approach. RoBERTa has the same architecture as BERT, but it eliminates the next sentence prediction (NSP) objective used in BERT during pre-training. Besides, it trained on longer sequences with much larger mini-batches and learning rates. Instead of using static masking like BERT, RoBERTa utilizes dynamic masking that is employed every time a text sequence is fed to the model. Therefore, the model encodes the several versions of the same sentence with masks on different positions. It helps the model to capture the inherent semantics of the text.

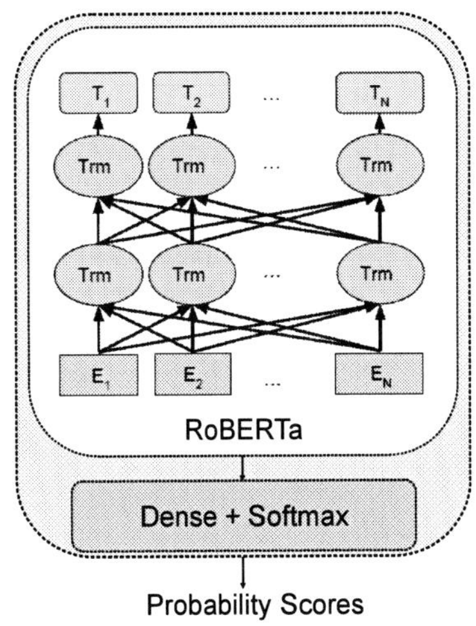

Figure 2: RoBERTa model.

We also employ the Twitter_RoBERTa (Barbieri et al., 2020), a RoBERTa-base model trained on 58M tweets, described and evaluated in the TweetEval benchmark. In our proposed framework, we use RoBERTa along with its Twitter variants to capture the diverse semantic features effectively. Here, we use the HuggingFace's implementation of the *roberta-base* model (Wolf et al., 2019). It is composed of 12-layers (i.e. transformer block), the dimension of hidden size is 768, the number of the self-attention head is 12, and contains 125M parameters. In Figure 2, we demonstrate an overview of the setup of RoBERTa transformer model to obtain the prediction score of each text.

2.2 Fusion of Transformer Models

In the NLP domain, it is usually a common practice to fuse multiple models to enhance the performance of individual models or tackle the limitations of models. In our proposed framework, we also employ a fusion strategy to combine the effectiveness of RoBERTa and Twitter_RoBERTa transformer models. We estimate a unified probability score for each class through fusing the prediction scores generated from each model. For the score fusion, we employ the weighted arithmetic mean of these two scores. Finally, based on the highest probability score, we determine the final label for a given text. The estimation is computed as follows:

$$f(x_i, y_i) = \begin{cases} 0, & \text{if } W_0 > W_1 \\ 1, & \text{otherwise} \end{cases}$$

$$W_i = \frac{x_i * R + y_i * T}{R + T} \quad (1)$$

x_i and y_i correspond to the RoBERTa and Twitter-RoBERTa probability score, where R and T represent their weight respectively. W_i (i.e. i = {0, 1}) is the unified probability score for each class.

3 Experiment and Evaluation

3.1 Dataset Description

The organizers used the Causal News Corpus (CNC) (Tan et al., 2022b), a benchmark dataset published in LREC-2022 to evaluate the performance of the participants' systems at the CASE-2022 event causality shared task (Subtask 1). The dataset statistics are summarized in Table 2.

Category	Causal	Non-Causal	Total
Train	1603	1322	2925
Dev	178	145	323
Test	176	135	311
Total	1957	1602	3559

Table 2: The statistics of causal news corpus used in event causality shared task in CASE-2022.

The dataset comprises of 3559 event sentences where 2925, 323, and 311 samples are used for the train, dev, and test phases. Each sentence is annotated with binary labels (Causal: 1 and Non-Causal: 0) which indicates whether there is a causal relationship available in a sentence or not.

3.2 Experimental Settings

We now describe the details of our experimental settings and the hyper-parameter settings with fine-tuning strategy that we have employed to design our proposed CSECU-DSG system for the CASE-2022 event causality identification shared task.

Parameter	Optimal Value
Learning rate	3e-5
Max-len	128
Epoch	5
Batch size	16
Manual seed	4

Table 3: Model settings for CASE-2022 event causality identification shared task (subtask 1).

In our CSECU-DSG system, we utilize two state-of-the-art Huggingface transformer models with fine-tuning, including RoBERTa and Twitter-RoBERTa. We use simpletransformers API (Rajapakse, 2019) to implement our system. We use the train and development data during the model training phase. We used the CUDA-enabled GPU and set the manual seed = 4 to generate reproducible results. We obtained the optimal parameter settings of our proposed model based on the performance of the development set which articulated in Table 3 and we used the default settings for the other parameters.

To generate the unified prediction, we fuse the probability score of RoBERTa and Twitter-RoBERTa based classification model as described in Section 2.2. To select the optimal weight as defined in Equation 1, we swept the parameter value of R and T between $\{0.1, ..., 0.9\}$ and conduct some experiments on training data. Based on the experimental results, we choose the weight $R = 0.6$ for RoBERTa and weight $T = 0.4$ for Twitter-RoBERTa model.

3.3 Evaluation Measures

To evaluate the participants' system at the CASE-2022 event causality identification shared task (sub-

https://huggingface.co/roberta-base

https://huggingface.co/cardiffnlp/twitter-roberta-base-sentiment

Team (Rank)	Recall	Precision	F1-score	Accuracy	MCC
CSECU-DSG (1st)	0.8864	0.8387	0.8619	0.8392	0.6714
Participants system performance on subtask 1					
Arguably (2nd)	0.9148	0.8131	0.8610	0.8328	0.6602
hiranmai (3rd)	0.8864	0.8211	0.8525	0.8264	0.6451
NLP4ITF (4th)	0.8807	0.8245	0.8516	0.8264	0.6449
IDIAPers (6th)	0.8750	0.8280	0.8508	0.8264	0.6449
LXPER AI Research (9th)	0.8636	0.8261	0.8444	0.8199	0.6318
Innovators (15th)	0.7898	0.7202	0.7534	0.7074	0.3981
Baseline	0.8466	0.7801	0.8120	0.7781	0.5452

Table 4: Comparative results with other selected participants (Subtask 1).

Method	Recall	Precision	F1-score	Accuracy	MCC
CSECU-DSG	0.8864	0.8387	0.8619	0.8392	0.6714
Performance of individual model					
RoBERTa	0.8807	0.8245	0.8516	0.8264	0.6449
Twitter-RoBERTa	0.8409	0.8087	0.8245	0.7974	0.5858

Table 5: Performance analysis of individual model used in our proposed CSECU-DSG system (Subtask 1).

task 1) (Tan et al., 2022a), the organizers employed standard evaluation metrics including recall, precision, F1-score, accuracy, and Matthews correlation coefficient (MCC) (Matthews, 1975). However, the F1 score is considered as the primary evaluation metric for subtask 1 and systems performances were ranked based on this score.

3.4 Results and Analysis

In this section, we analyze the performance of our proposed CSECU-DSG system in the CASE-2022 event causality identification shared task (subtask 1). The comparative results of our proposed CSECU-DSG system along with other top-performing systems (Tan et al., 2022a) in subtask 1 are presented in Table 4. Following the benchmark of CASE-2022 event causality identification subtask 1, participants' systems are ranked based on the primary evaluation metric F1 score.

At first, we presented the performance of our proposed CSECU-DSG system. We also presented the performance of top-ranked participating systems and the baseline used in subtask 1. Here, we see that our proposed method obtained the highest score in terms of the primary evaluation metric F1 score compared to the other top-performing systems. This deduces the superiority and effectiveness of our proposed system for the event causality identification task.

In our proposed CSECU-DSG system, we perform the effective fusion of two state-of-the-art RoBERTa transformer models. However, to validate the performance of our used fusion strategy, we conduct individual experiments using each transformer models to estimate the effect of each model used in our proposed system. The summarized experimental results regarding this are presented in Table 5.

From the results, it can be observed that RoBERTa based model performed better compared to the Twitter-RoBERTa model when considering individual model performances. However, combining two models prediction scores by using weighted arithmetic mean improved the performance. It shows that the fusion strategy improves the $\sim$1% performance compared to the RoBERTa model and improves the $\sim$4% performance compared to the Twitter-RoBERTa model in terms of the primary evaluation measure F1 score. This validates the importance of our fusion strategy.

4 Conclusion and Future Directions

In this paper, we present an approach to identify the cause-effect relation in texts by exploiting RoBERTa variants with an effective fusion strategy. Experimental results demonstrated the efficacy of our fusion strategy of the two SOTA transformers model which helped us to obtain the best result in subtask 1.

In the future, we intend to explore other indicators of textual causal relations for further improvement. Especially, a graph-based neural model may exploit complex dependency patterns of cause-effect relations from text more effectively.

References

Abdul Aziz, Afrin Sultana, Md Akram Hossain, Nabila Ayman, and Abu Nowshed Chy. 2020. Feature fusion with hand-crafted and transfer learning embeddings for cause-effect relation extraction. In *FIRE (Working Notes)*, pages 756–764.

Francesco Barbieri, Jose Camacho-Collados, Luis Espinosa Anke, and Leonardo Neves. 2020. Tweeteval: Unified benchmark and comparative evaluation for tweet classification. In *Findings of the Association for Computational Linguistics: EMNLP 2020*, pages 1644–1650.

Denis Gordeev, Adis Davletov, Alexey Rey, and Nikolay Arefyev. 2020. Liori at the fincausal 2020 shared task. In *Proceedings of the 1st Joint Workshop on Financial Narrative Processing and MultiLing Financial Summarisation*, pages 45–49.

Marius Ionescu, Andrei-Marius Avram, George-Andrei Dima, Dumitru-Clementin Cercel, and Mihai Dascalu. 2020. Upb at fincausal-2020, tasks 1 & 2: Causality analysis in financial documents using pretrained language models. In *Proceedings of the 1st Joint Workshop on Financial Narrative Processing and MultiLing Financial Summarisation*, pages 55–59.

Yinhan Liu, Myle Ott, Naman Goyal, Jingfei Du, Mandar Joshi, Danqi Chen, Omer Levy, Mike Lewis, Luke Zettlemoyer, and Veselin Stoyanov. 2019. Roberta: A robustly optimized bert pretraining approach. *arXiv preprint arXiv:1907.11692*.

Dominique Mariko, Hanna Abi Akl, Estelle Labidurie, Stephane Durfort, Hugues De Mazancourt, and Mahmoud El-Haj. 2020. The financial document causality detection shared task (fincausal 2020). In *Proceedings of the 1st Joint Workshop on Financial Narrative Processing and MultiLing Financial Summarisation*, pages 23–32.

Brian W Matthews. 1975. Comparison of the predicted and observed secondary structure of t4 phage lysozyme. *Biochimica et Biophysica Acta (BBA)-Protein Structure*, 405(2):442–451.

Paramita Mirza. 2014. Extracting temporal and causal relations between events. In *Proceedings of the ACL 2014 Student Research Workshop*, pages 10–17.

T. C. Rajapakse. 2019. Simple Transformers. `https://github.com/ThilinaRajapakse/simpletransformers`.

Bryan Rink, Cosmin Adrian Bejan, and Sanda Harabagiu. 2010. Learning textual graph patterns to detect causal event relations. In *Twenty-Third International FLAIRS Conference*.

Fiona Anting Tan, Ali Hürriyetoğlu, Tommaso Caselli, Nelleke Oostdijk, Hansi Hettiarachchi, Tadashi Nomoto, Onur Uca, and Farhana Ferdousi Liza. 2022a. Event causality identification with causal news corpus - shared task 3, CASE 2022. In *Proceedings of the 5th Workshop on Challenges and Applications of Automated Extraction of Socio-political Events from Text (CASE 2022)*, Online. Association for Computational Linguistics.

Fiona Anting Tan, Ali Hürriyetoğlu, Tommaso Caselli, Nelleke Oostdijk, Tadashi Nomoto, Hansi Hettiarachchi, Iqra Ameer, Onur Uca, Farhana Ferdousi Liza, and Tiancheng Hu. 2022b. The causal news corpus: Annotating causal relations in event sentences from news. In *Proceedings of the Language Resources and Evaluation Conference*, pages 2298–2310, Marseille, France. European Language Resources Association.

Thomas Wolf, Lysandre Debut, Victor Sanh, Julien Chaumond, Clement Delangue, Anthony Moi, Pierric Cistac, Tim Rault, Rémi Louf, Morgan Funtowicz, et al. 2019. HuggingFace's Transformers: State-of-the-art Natural Language Processing. *arXiv preprint arXiv:1910.03771*.

Jie Yang, Soyeon Caren Han, and Josiah Poon. 2022. A survey on extraction of causal relations from natural language text. *Knowledge and Information Systems*, pages 1–26.

Xiaoxiao Yu, Xinzhi Wang, Xiangfeng Luo, and Jianqi Gao. 2022. Multi-scale event causality extraction via simultaneous knowledge-attention and convolutional neural network. *Expert Systems*, 39(5):e12952.

ARGUABLY @ Causal News Corpus 2022: Contextually Augmented Language Models for Event Causality Identification

Guneet Singh Kohli
Thapar University, Patiala, India
guneetsk99@gmail.com

Prabsimran Kaur
Thapar University, Patiala, India
pkaur_be18@thapar.edu

Jatin Bedi
Thapar University, Patiala, India
jatin.bedi@thapar.edu

Abstract

Causal (a cause-effect relationship between two arguments) has become integral to various NLP domains such as question answering, summarization, and event prediction. To understand causality in detail, Event Causality Identification with Causal News Corpus (CASE-2022) has organized shared tasks. This paper defines our participation in Subtask 1, which focuses on classifying event causality. We used sentence level augmentation based on contextualized word embeddings of distillBERT to construct new data. This data was then trained using two approaches. The first technique used the DeBERTa language model, and the second used the RoBERTa language model in combination with cross attention. We obtained the second-best F1 score (0.8610) in the competition with Contextually Augmented DeBERTa model.

1 Introduction

Causality is a cause-effect relationship between two arguments, events, processes, states, or objects in which the occurrence of one (cause) is partly responsible for the occurrence of the other (effect) (Barik et al., 2016). A few instances of this cause-effect relationship are illustrated in Figure 1, which were extracted from the Causal News Corpus (CNC) (Tan et al., 2022a). The first instance comprises a causal relation between the phrase "allegedly being involved in the blast" (cause) and "Two more youths were arrested later," indicating that the youths were arrested because they were accused of being involved in the bomb blast. The word "for" indicates that this relationship is causal. Similarly, other words can be used for indication, as seen in the case of the second instance where "over" is the signal word. There are also cases where the causal relation is explicit and does not have a word to signal the causality, as can be seen in the third instance. For the sentences that do not have causality, they are either missing the effect or the cause argument missing (as illustrated by the fifth instance), or both.

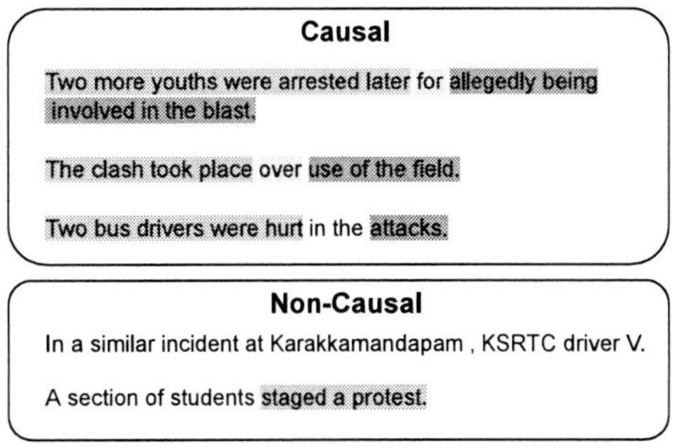

Figure 1: The cause, signal of causality, and effect are highlighted using the red, yellow, and green colors respectively. Any sentence that comprises of only cause or only effect is not considered as causal.

Causality is often used in Natural Language Processing (NLP) tasks that address Natural language inference and understanding (Jo et al., 2021; Dunietz et al., 2020; Feder et al., 2021). The information retrieved from the detection of causal relations can be used for various NLP tasks like Causal Question Answering and Generation applications (Dalal et al., 2021; Hassanzadeh et al., 2019; Stasaski et al., 2021), and Event prediction (Radinsky et al., 2012). However, identifying and extracting a causal relationship is challenging as it requires significant semantic knowledge.

This paper describes our participation in the Event Causality Identification with Causal News Corpus (CASE-2022), the third shared task of the CASE 2022 (Tan et al., 2022b). Under this task, there are two subtasks, and this paper describes an approach for subtask 1. We have used the following methods to classify causal events:

- We used sentence level augmentation based on contextualized word embeddings of distillBERT to construct new data.
- The training of this data is done using two approaches. The first technique used the De-

Proceedings of the 5th Workshop on Challenges and Applications of Automated Extraction of Socio-political Events from Text (CASE), pages 143 - 148
December 7-8, 2022 ©2022 Association for Computational Linguistics

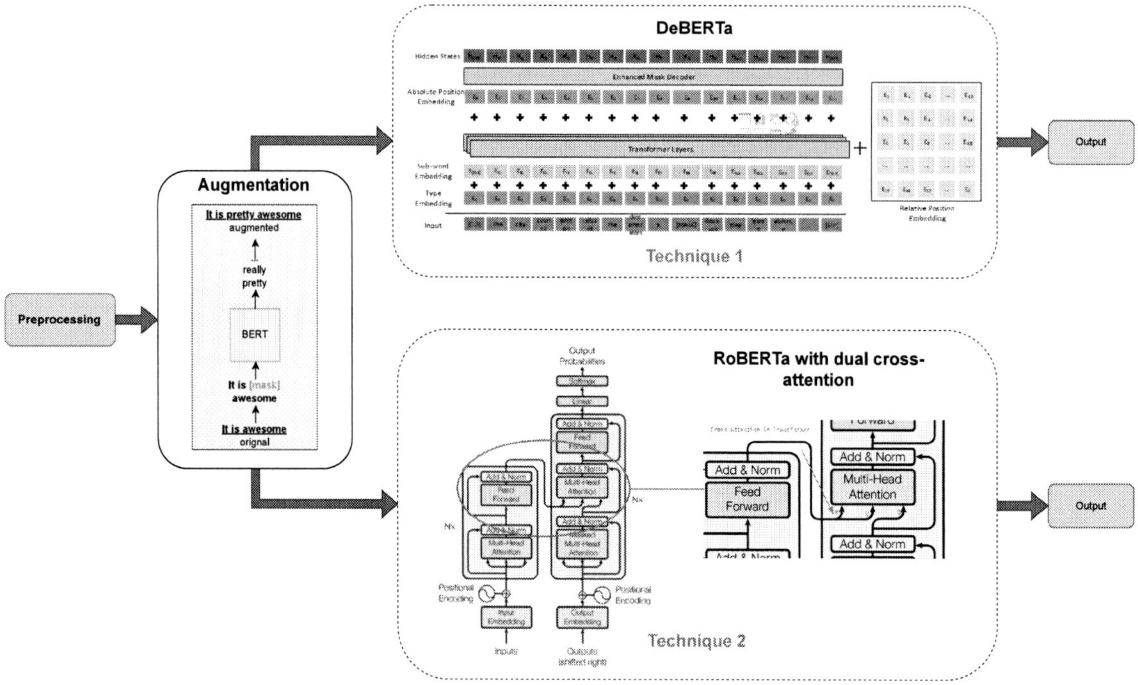

Figure 2: Architecture of the proposed pipeline. The initial part of the pipeline is same for both the techniques. Note that we illustrate the Encoder portion of RoBERTa with dual cross attention. The other components of RoBERTa architecture were not refactored for any changes

BERTa language model, and the second used the RoBERTa language model in combination with cross-attention.

The aim of the task and the details of data is explained in Section 2. Section 3 gives a detailed overview of the method used for the binary classification. The results obtained, it's analysis and the experimental setup is described in Section 4.

2 Task & Data Description

Event Causality Identification Shared Task aims at tackling inference and understanding by organizing two subtasks: a) Causal Event Classification and b) Cause-Effect-Signal Span Detection. Our team participated in the first subtask, which required the participants to classify the given text into "0" (non-causal) and "1"(causal). The dataset provided in the task was the Causal News Corpus (CNC) deals with event causality in the news. The CNC dataset builds upon the following datasets: Automated Extraction of Socio-political Events from News (AESPEN) in 2020 (Hürriyetoğlu et al., 2020b,a) and Challenges and Applications of Automated Extraction of Socio-political Events from Text (CASE) in 2021 (Hürriyetoğlu et al., 2021a,b). The data in

Label	Train	Dev
0	1322	145
1	1603	178

Table 1: Data distribution for the CNC database.

CNC is based on random samples that have been collected from a total of 869 news documents. The corpus comprises 3,559 data samples, out of which 2925 data points were provided for training, 323 data points were provided for the development set, and the remaining 311 samples were used as the test set.

3 Methodology

This section gives an exhaustive overview of the proposed pipeline. Section 3.1 provides the details of the preprocessing performed on the given dataset. Section 3.2 describes the augmentation technique used on the data. Section 3.3 discusses the transformer models and techniques used to train the data.

Orignal	Augmented	Label
The protests spread to 15 other towns and resulted in two deaths and the destruction of property .	the protests **had** spread **quickly** to 15 other towns and **resulted ultimately in** two **premature** deaths **locally** and **essentially** the destruction of property.	1
The protests spread to 15 other towns and resulted in two deaths and the destruction of property .	the protests spread **out** to **over** 15 other **other** towns **offshore and territory** resulted in two **workers** deaths and the destruction of property	1
The demonstrations pose a real problem , not just for the British but for others too.	the demonstrations pose **considered a serious** real **negativ**e problem, **affecting** not just **resentment** for the british but for others all too.	0
The demonstrations pose a real problem , not just for the British but for others too.	the demonstrations **allegedly** pose **potentially** a real **world** problem, not just **perhaps** for **interested** the british but for **important** others too.	0

Table 2: Illustration of the contextual augmentation performed by our proposed methodology. The words that are added or changed in the original sentence have been highlighted.

Model	Recall	Precision	F1	Accuracy	MCC
Top Performing	0.8864	0.8387	0.8619	0.8392	0.6714
Proposed Model	**0.9148**	**0.8131**	**0.8610**	**0.8328**	**0.6602**
Average Score	0.8686	0.7838	0.8233	0.7870	0.5619

Table 3: Comparison of the proposed model with the top performing model and the average results of all the models on the leaderboard. The proposed model refers to our best-performing model DeBERTa trained on augmented data.

3.1 Data Pre-Processing

The quality of data highly impacts the performance of any machine learning or deep learning model. However, the raw data present is unstructured. It comprises noise, punctuations, special symbols, and unusual texts that might affect the feature selection process of the model, causing it to underperform. Thus a basic preprocessing involving the tokenization of the sentences into words, conversion of the words into lowercase, and removal of stopwords (the, an, a) and punctuations was done using the NLTK library (Loper and Bird, 2002).

3.2 Augmentation

Models like BERT and RoBERTa comprise millions of parameters that require a considerable amount of data to generalize and obtain meaningful results. However, the dataset provided to the participants has only 2925 data points, which is insufficient to train these heavy models. Thus, data augmentation, a technique of applying transformation on the original labeled data to construct new data , was used on the training data to reduce overfitting. NLPaug tool[1], a well-known library that can perform three types of augmentations: Character level, Word Level, and Sentence Level was used for augmentation in our pipeline. For this task, we used sentence-level augmentation based on contextualized word embeddings of distillBERT. NLPaug also allows you to perform various actions like 'Insertion' and 'Substitution' operations. Our technique utilizes the Insertion operation, which randomly picks a position in the sentence and inserts in that position a word that best fits the local context. It was ensured that the causality of the dataset was not changed during the augmentation process as can be seen in Table 2. Contextualized word embeddings provide these words chosen for insertion.

3.3 Modeling

A transformer-based approach is used to perform Event Causality Identification. The training was done using DeBERTa (He et al., 2020) and dual Cross attention RoBERTa (Liu et al., 2019). A detailed explanation of their architecture is given in this Section. The architecture of the pipeline is illustrated in Figure 2.

3.3.1 DeBERTa

Decoding-enhanced BERT with Disentangled Attention (DeBERTa) is an enhanced version of the

[1]urlhttps://github.com/makcedward/nlpaug.

BERT and RoBERTa. It differs from BERT in two aspects. The first is the disentangled self-attention mechanism, which involves using two vectors to encode the content and position rather than a single vector to address these embeddings. This helps the model naturally encode the word position information, which conventional transformers lack. The second is Enhanced Mask Decoder (EMD), a technique that performs masked token prediction in model pre-training using absolute positions in the decoding layer, unlike BERT, which uses relative position. This helps DeBERTa obtain better accuracy since the words' syntactic roles depend highly on their absolute positions in a sentence.

3.3.2 Dual Cross attention RoBERTa

Robustly Optimized BERT-Pretraining Approach (RoBERTa) is an extension of BERT. Similar to BERT, data is passed through RoBERTa in the form of sequences. However, before passing these sequences, they are tokenized into words, the sequences are masked, a [CLS] token is added to the beginning of the first sentence, and a [SEP] is added after each sequence to indicate the end. Three embeddings, namely, token, sentence, and positional, are attached to each token. Once the encoding is done, these sentences are passed through the transformer.

RoBERTa differs from BERT in the aspect of token masking. BERT used a static masking technique while pretraining, in which each sequence was masked in 10 different patterns. The training data was further trained for 40 epochs indicating that each sequence was trained for the same masking pattern four times. Unlike BERT, RoBERTa was trained using a dynamic masking technique where a new masking pattern is generated every time a sequence is fed into the model. This helps create a more generalised model.

In the proposed pipeline, we used two layers of cross-attention while training RoBERTa to enhance the overall performance. In contrast to the conventionally used self-attention technique, which takes a single embedding sequence as input, the cross-attention combines two different asymmetrical sequences of identical dimensions. One of the sequences serves as a query input, while the other as a key and value input.

4 Results and Discussion

4.1 Comparative Analysis

In this section we present a detailed comparison of our best submission with other submissions present on the leaderboard.The comparitive study can be observed in Table 3. Our system ranked 2nd overall with F1 Score of 0.8610. The following results were obtained with **DeBERTa trained on Augmented data with Token length of 450**. The contextualized word embedding augmentation with distillBERT helped DeBERTa be more robust and handle the test data well. The best performing system of the task had F1 score of 0.0009 greater than our submission. Our system reports the highest Recall of 0.9148 across the leaderboard. The high recall is a direct indicator of high quality of augmented data we had produced for the task. In comparison to the average scores calculated from the leaderboard our system had 4.5% higher F1 score, 5.3% higher recall and 5.819% higher accuracy.

4.2 Experimental Setup

We trained the language models on Tesla-T4 16 GB GPU. For training, we kept the batch size as four and configured the AdamW optimizer with the learning rate of 1e-05. We fine-tuned the language models with a token length of 450 and trained the data up to 3 epochs.

4.3 Analysis of Experiments

This section discusses the results and performance of our models, DeBERTa and Dual Cross Attention RoBERTa, as illustrated in Table 4. The core idea was the introduction of contextual augmentation using fine-tuned distillBert. The use of contextual embedding helped maintain the causality of the sentence that was necessary for the scope of the task. The increase in the data significantly impacted the performance of the proposed approaches. DeBERTa fine-tuned on augmented data yielded an F1 score of 0.8610 [our best performing system], an improvement of 3.5% from the unaugmented data version. For Dual Cross Attention RoBERTa, using augmented data brought about a gain of 2.6%.

DeBERTa uses disentangled attention which computes the attention weight of a word pair as a sum of four attention scores using disentangled matrices on their contents and positions as content-to-content, content-to-position, position-to-content, and position-to-position.

Model	Recall	Precision	F1	Accuracy	MCC
RoBERTa [Naive] unaugmented,Token length:450	**0.9261**	0.7477	0.8274	0.7813	0.5615
RoBERTa [Dual Cross Attn] unaugmented,Token length:450	0.8806	0.7868	0.8311	0.7974	0.5858
RoBERTa [Dual Cross Attn] augmented,Token length:450	0.8977	0.8061	0.8494	0.8199	0.6327
DeBERTa unaugmented,Token length:450	0.8863	0.7839	0.8320	0.7974	0.5862
DeBERTa augmentated,Token length:450	0.9148	**0.8131**	**0.8610**	**0.8328**	**0.6602**

Table 4: Results of the models experimented on. The Best Performing System has been highlighted.

Text	Gold	Predicted
Rath interacted with the affected farmers who were yet to get compensation despite repeated agitation over the issue .	0	1
Another ' TP ' issue may also leave a blot on the CPM , as public opinion is heavily pitted against the assault made upon former diplomat T P Srinivasan by SFI activists .	0	1
Police said fighting broke out in Charbatan area in Murshidabad constituency even as the results were being declared .	0	0
Some protesters attempted to fight back with fire extinguishers.	0	0
The one-day fast attracted a " motley crowd " according to Sumitra M. Gautama, a teacher with the Krishnamurthi Foundation of India (KFI)	1	0
Both sides were raining bombs on each other and Mondal was hit by one of the bombs , " Murshidabad district magistrate Pervez Ahmed Siddiqui said .	1	0
SI Gopal Mondal , who was part of the police team that rushed to the spot , was killed by a crude bomb explosion .	1	1
The workers had embarked on a wildcat strike demanding better working conditions .	1	1

Table 5: Behavioural Analysis of our best performing model (DeBERTa with augmentation) on the validation set.

The position-to-content term is impactful since the attention weight of a word pair depends not only on their contents but on their relative positions, which is calculated by the content-to-position and position-to-content terms. The causality of a sentence is highly sensitive to the positioning of words in the sentence, and thus DeBERTa uses the position-to-content weights to capture the underlying semantics of the causality.

We used dual cross attention in RoBERTa by generating two embedding representation of an instance and calculating the attention weights for generating the attention filters. The improvements in the results can be observed in Table 4.

4.4 Quantitative analysis

This section discusses the quantitative analysis of the labels predicted by our best model on the validation set. Table 5 illustrates a few instances from the validation dataset along with the original and predicted labels. The first two instances demonstrate the cases where the model failed to understand the semantic meaning of words like "affected," "issue," and "against" and interpreted the immediate sense rather than trying to understand what the sentence as a whole means.

The fifth and sixth instance demonstrates the model's inability to distinguish the cause and effect portions of the sentence. "The one-day fast attracted a motley crowd " was considered the cause and thus could not find any effect, thus predicting this sentence to be non-causal. Similarly, the model did not identify "was hit by one of the bombs" as the effect for the sixth instance. Instances three, four, seven, and eight, demonstrate the cases where the model successfully understood the semantics and identified the cause-effect relations.

5 Conclusion

In this paper we propose Contextual Embedding Augmented DeBERTa and Dual Cross Attention RoBERTa to identify event causality. Our approach yielded an F1 score of 0.8610 which was the second best system throughout the shared task. We study the behaviour of both the models in augmented and unaugmented settings to derive proper understanding about the impact of our complete pipeline. In future, experimenting with other language models and extensive hyperparameter tuning through Neural Architectural Search will be an ideal path to follow. The augmentation was successful in maintaining its causality nature. This acts as a fine way of up sampling low resource tasks which lack adequate data.

References

Biswanath Barik, Erwin Marsi, and Pinar Øzturk. 2016. Event causality extraction from natural science literature.

Dhairya Dalal, Mihael Arcan, and Paul Buitelaar. 2021. Enhancing multiple-choice question answering with causal knowledge. In *Proceedings of Deep Learning Inside Out (DeeLIO): The 2nd Workshop on Knowledge Extraction and Integration for Deep Learning Architectures*, pages 70–80.

Jesse Dunietz, Gregory Burnham, Akash Bharadwaj, Owen Rambow, Jennifer Chu-Carroll, and David Ferrucci. 2020. To test machine comprehension, start by defining comprehension. *arXiv preprint arXiv:2005.01525*.

Amir Feder, Katherine A Keith, Emaad Manzoor, Reid Pryzant, Dhanya Sridhar, Zach Wood-Doughty, Jacob Eisenstein, Justin Grimmer, Roi Reichart, Margaret E Roberts, et al. 2021. Causal inference in natural language processing: Estimation, prediction, interpretation and beyond. *arXiv preprint arXiv:2109.00725*.

Oktie Hassanzadeh, Debarun Bhattacharjya, Mark Feblowitz, Kavitha Srinivas, Michael Perrone, Shirin Sohrabi, and Michael Katz. 2019. Answering binary causal questions through large-scale text mining: An evaluation using cause-effect pairs from human experts. In *IJCAI*, pages 5003–5009.

Pengcheng He, Xiaodong Liu, Jianfeng Gao, and Weizhu Chen. 2020. Deberta: Decoding-enhanced bert with disentangled attention. *arXiv preprint arXiv:2006.03654*.

Ali Hürriyetoğlu, Osman Mutlu, Erdem Yörük, Farhana Ferdousi Liza, Ritesh Kumar, and Shyam Ratan. 2021a. Multilingual protest news detection-shared task 1, case 2021. In *Proceedings of the 4th Workshop on Challenges and Applications of Automated Extraction of Socio-political Events from Text (CASE 2021)*, pages 79–91.

Ali Hürriyetoğlu, Hristo Tanev, Vanni Zavarella, Jakub Piskorski, Reyyan Yeniterzi, and Erdem Yörük. 2021b. Challenges and applications of automated extraction of socio-political events from text (case 2021): Workshop and shared task report. *arXiv preprint arXiv:2108.07865*.

Ali Hürriyetoğlu, Erdem Yörük, Vanni Zavarella, and Hristo Tanev. 2020a. Proceedings of the workshop on automated extraction of socio-political events from news 2020. In *Proceedings of the Workshop on Automated Extraction of Socio-political Events from News 2020*.

Ali Hürriyetoğlu, Vanni Zavarella, Hristo Tanev, Erdem Yörük, Ali Safaya, and Osman Mutlu. 2020b. Automated extraction of socio-political events from news (aespen): Workshop and shared task report. *arXiv preprint arXiv:2005.06070*.

Yohan Jo, Seojin Bang, Chris Reed, and Eduard Hovy. 2021. Classifying argumentative relations using logical mechanisms and argumentation schemes. *Transactions of the Association for Computational Linguistics*, 9:721–739.

Yinhan Liu, Myle Ott, Naman Goyal, Jingfei Du, Mandar Joshi, Danqi Chen, Omer Levy, Mike Lewis, Luke Zettlemoyer, and Veselin Stoyanov. 2019. Roberta: A robustly optimized bert pretraining approach. *arXiv preprint arXiv:1907.11692*.

Edward Loper and Steven Bird. 2002. Nltk: The natural language toolkit. *arXiv preprint cs/0205028*.

Kira Radinsky, Sagie Davidovich, and Shaul Markovitch. 2012. Learning causality for news events prediction. In *Proceedings of the 21st international conference on World Wide Web*, pages 909–918.

Katherine Stasaski, Manav Rathod, Tony Tu, Yunfang Xiao, and Marti A Hearst. 2021. Automatically generating cause-and-effect questions from passages. In *Proceedings of the 16th Workshop on Innovative Use of NLP for Building Educational Applications*, pages 158–170.

Fiona Anting Tan, Ali Hürriyetoğlu, Tommaso Caselli, Nelleke Oostdijk, Tadashi Nomoto, Hansi Hettiarachchi, Iqra Ameer, Onur Uca, Farhana Ferdousi Liza, and Tiancheng Hu. 2022a. The causal news corpus: Annotating causal relations in event sentences from news. *arXiv preprint arXiv:2204.11714*.

Fiona Anting Tan, Ali Hürriyetoğlu, Tommaso Caselli, Nelleke Oostdijk, Hansi Hettiarachchi, Tadashi Nomoto, Onur Uca, and Farhana Ferdousi Liza. 2022b. Event causality identification with causal news corpus - shared task 3, CASE 2022. In *Proceedings of the 5th Workshop on Challenges and Applications of Automated Extraction of Socio-political Events from Text (CASE 2022)*, Online. Association for Computational Linguistics.

ClassBases at CASE-2022 Multilingual Protest Event Detection Tasks: Multilingual Protest News Detection and Automatically Replicating Manually Created Event Datasets

Peratham Wiriyathammabhum
peratham.bkk@gmail.com

Abstract

In this report, we describe our ClassBases submissions to a shared task on multilingual protest event detection. For the multilingual protest news detection, we participated in subtask-1, subtask-2, and subtask-4, which are document classification, sentence classification, and token classification. In subtask-1, we compare XLM-RoBERTa-base, mLUKE-base, and XLM-RoBERTa-large on finetuning in a sequential classification setting. We always use a combination of the training data from every language provided to train our multilingual models. We found that larger models seem to work better and entity knowledge helps but at a non-negligible cost. For subtask-2, we only submitted an mLUKE-base system for sentence classification. For subtask-4, we only submitted an XLM-RoBERTa-base for token classification system for sequence labeling. For automatically replicating manually created event datasets, we participated in COVID-related protest events from the New York Times news corpus. We created a system to process the crawled data into a dataset of protest events.

1 Introduction

A shared task on multilingual protest event detection at CASE-2022 is the second installment from the previous event at CASE-2021 about socio-political and crisis events detection (Hürriyetoğlu et al., 2021; Hürriyetoğlu et al., 2021). The shared task focuses on protest events where people complain, put their objections, or display their unwillingness to a course of action whether that action is from an authority or a government (Merriam-Webster, 2022).

As in the previous installment, this shared task organizes the automated multilingual protest event detection pipeline into multiple subsequent steps at different granularity levels as four subtasks, document classification, sentence classification, event sentence coreference identification, and event extraction. Moreover, the shared task contains many languages in many different magnitudes of data sizes, from ten thousand data points to hundreds of data points to no data points. In other words, many settings are varying from full training to low-resource training to few-shot learning to zero-shot learning.

- The first subtask, *document classification*, tries to classify whether a given document, a piece of news, or an article, contains any information about a past or an ongoing socio-political protest event. The shared task provides a full training setting for English, Spanish and Portuguese on a scale of thousands of data points. Then, there is a zero-shot training setting for Hindi, Turkish, Urdu, and Mandarin.
- The second subtask, *sentence classification*, classifies whether a given sentence from a document contains any information about a past or an ongoing socio-political protest event. The shared task provides a full training setting for English, Spanish and Portuguese on the scale of ten thousand data points for English and thousands of data points for Spanish and Portuguese.
- The third subtask, *event sentence coreference identification*, tries to group sentences, from the same document, containing socio-political events from the same stories together. There are hundreds of training instances for English and around twenty training instances for Spanish and Portuguese.
- The fourth subtask, *event extraction*, extracts event entity spans, triggers, and arguments, from event sentences within the same story.

We participate in the first, second, and fourth subtasks. We build our system solutions upon

Proceedings of the 5th Workshop on Challenges and Applications of Automated Extraction of Socio-political Events from Text (CASE), pages 149 - 154
December 7-8, 2022 ©2022 Association for Computational Linguistics

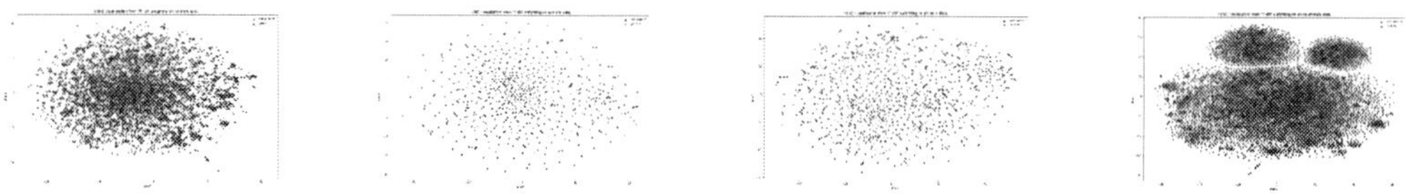

(a) English (en) (b) Spanish (es) (c) Portuguese (pt) (d) en-es-pt concatenated

Figure 1: **The distribution of tf-idf weighted subtask1 training set document data visualized using t-SNE (Van der Maaten and Hinton, 2008). The blue dots have no protest event, and the orange dots have some protest events.**

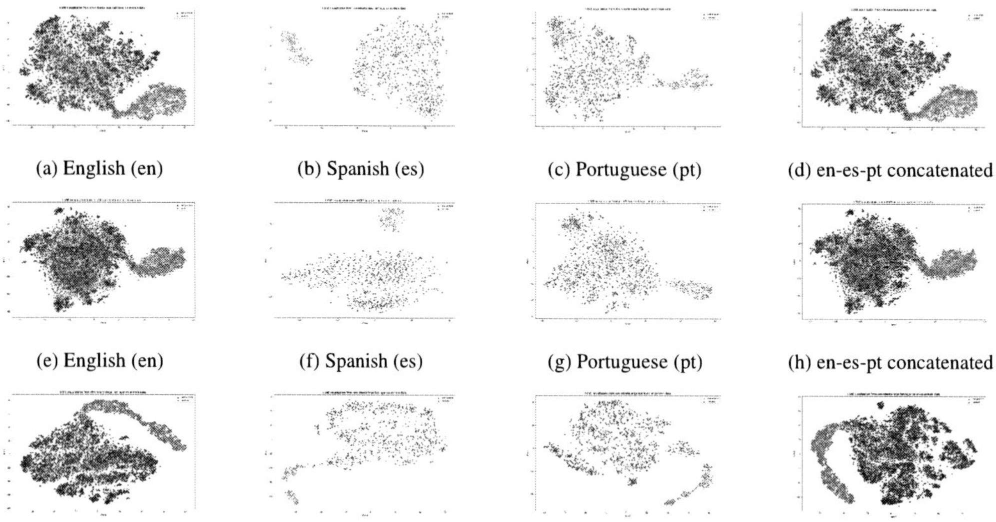

(a) English (en) (b) Spanish (es) (c) Portuguese (pt) (d) en-es-pt concatenated

(e) English (en) (f) Spanish (es) (g) Portuguese (pt) (h) en-es-pt concatenated

(i) English (en) (j) Spanish (es) (k) Portuguese (pt) (l) en-es-pt concatenated

Figure 2: **The distribution of subtask1 training set document features extracted by averaging over the sequence dimension of the last layer from our finetuned XLM-RoBERTa-base (the first row), mLUKE-base (the second row), and XLM-RoBERTa-large (the third row) visualized using t-SNE (Van der Maaten and Hinton, 2008). The blue dots have no protest event, and the orange dots have some protest events.**

Huggingface's multilingual transformer language models (Wolf et al., 2020), specifically, XLM-RoBERTa language models (Conneau et al., 2020) and mLUKE multilingual transformer language models with entity embedding (Ri et al., 2022). We also participated in creating COVID-related protest event datasets from the New York Times news corpus (Zavarella and Tanev, 2022). The codes for our systems are open-sourced and available at our GitHub repository[1].

2 Models

As in the IBM MNLP team report (Awasthy et al., 2021), whose systems top-scored in most subtasks of the previous CASE-2021, we consider XLM-RoBERTa language models (XLM-R) (Conneau et al., 2020) trained on the concatenation of the data from all languages available from the shared task. XLM-RoBERTa built upon the RoBERTa language model (Liu et al., 2019) and multilingual pretrained on 2.5 TB of filtered CommonCrawl data consisting of 100 languages. By pretraining jointly across many multiple languages, hopefully, the model can transfer information across languages. However, the paper indicates the *curse of multilinguality* trade-off where we can scale the number of languages up to the point that the model performance for low-resource languages starts to degrade. Still, XLM-RoBERTa seems not to suffer from this trade-off yet by increasing the model capacity and performing very well on many benchmarks.

We also consider mLUKE, a multilingual transformer language model with entity embeddings, (Ri et al., 2022). The mLUKE language model is

[1] `https://github.com/perathambkk/case_shared_task_emnlp2022`

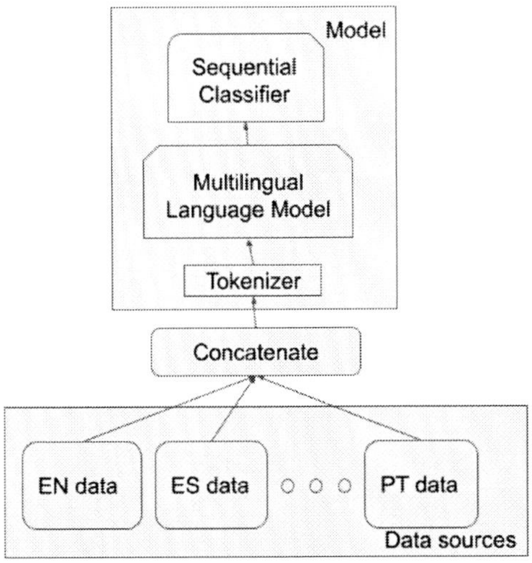

Figure 3: **The architecture of our systems. We concatenated data from all languages and randomly sample them into batches. The batches are inputs to our models. The model part consists of a tokenizer, a multilingual language model, and a sequential classifier, all are from the Huggingface's library (Wolf et al., 2020). For subtask4, we replace a sequential classifier with a token classifier.**

also based on XLM-RoBERTa but has an optional entity embedding set for downstream tasks and was pretrained on 24 languages using Wikipedia. The entity embeddings are cross-lingual mappings of entities learned from Wikipedia. The language model part was pretrained as a masked language model and the entity embedding part was pretrained in a masked entity prediction task. Despite the performance gains on entity-related downstream tasks, a major limitation of incorporating entity embeddings is the large memory footprint. That is, using only an mLUKE-base model requires about the same GPU memory as an XLM-RoBERTa-large model.

3 Experimental Results

All of our experiments were done in the Google Colab setting on NVIDIA Tesla T4 GPUs. We used the batch size in the range of $16 - 36$ and the learning rate for an AdamW optimizer (Loshchilov and Hutter, 2018) in the set of $\{2.5e-5, 5e-5\}$ for all experiments. We considered a linear annealing scheduler. Also, adding a warm-up step does not make any difference so we set the warm-up step to zero in all experiments.

Except otherwise stated, we concatenated the given training data in all languages as our combined training set for every subtask. We also employed the early stopping with zero patience training strategy schema (Prechelt, 1998; Bengio, 2012). We varied the training epoch until the training metric saturated with manual monitoring, and then stopped right at the end of that epoch. However, we mostly tried with one or two candidate numbers of training epochs since training large language models takes a few hours and Gooogle's Colab GPU time just runs out.

3.1 Document Classification

We trained XLM-RoBERTa-base, XLM-RoBERTa-large, and mLUKE-base as sequence classifiers for document classification. The models classify whether a given document contains any protest events or not as a binary classification task. The input document is truncated to the maximum length of 150. Then, the truncated document is fed into a transformer language model with a softmax layer on top which outputs logits for binary classifications. We trained XLM-RoBERTa-base for 12 epochs, mLUKE-base for 15 epochs, and XLM-RoBERTa-large for 5 epochs, respectively. We used the batch size of 36 for base models, XLM-RoBERTa-base and mLUKE-base, and we used the batch size of 16 for our large model, XLM-RoBERTa-large.

The experimental results in Table 1 suggest that a small model (XLM-RoBERTa-base) does not perform well in general. However, adding entity knowledge makes a small model (mLUKE-base) performs much better typically at a cost except in Hindi where mLUKE-base might be trained on less number of languages and does not perform well in the zero-shot setting. Still, a larger language model (XLM-RoBERTa-large) performs best most of the time. Surprisingly, our XLM-RoBERTa-large submissions perform better than the best submissions from the previous year in Portuguese and Hindi using only a single model and without any external data. In the previous CASE-21, the best Portuguese submission uses an ensemble and the best Hindi submission uses some external data so it is not a zero-shot setting.

We visualized the tf-idf weighted training data in Figure 1 using t-SNE (Van der Maaten and Hinton, 2008; Wattenberg et al., 2016). The scatter plots show the inseparability of the class data, and the concatenated data plot in Figure 1(d) shows that the data in each language are in different regions.

Table 1: Test macro F1-scores of our models in subtask1: Document Classification 2021 test data. (The numbers in subscript are submission rankings on the leaderboard from our best submissions. The symbol † denotes the result is better than the previous CASE-21 best submission.)

Model	en	pt	es	hi
XLM-R-base	79.82	79.55	68.70	79.35
mLUKE-base	79.91	80.02	72.93	75.77
XLM-R-large	$\mathbf{82.30_4}$	$\mathbf{85.39_2}$†	$\mathbf{73.48_4}$	$\mathbf{80.77_1}$†
CASE-21 best (Hürriyetoğlu et al., 2021)	84.55	84.00	77.27	78.77

Table 2: Test macro F1-scores of our models in subtask1: Document Classification 2021+2022 test data. (The numbers in subscript are submission rankings on the leaderboard from our best submissions.)

Model	en	pt	es	hi	tr	ur	zh
mLUKE-base	77.35	74.67	$\mathbf{69.25_6}$	69.54	$\mathbf{78.57_5}$	67.91	73.79
XLM-R-large	$\mathbf{78.50_6}$	$\mathbf{77.11_5}$	66.86	$\mathbf{80.78_1}$	75.66	$\mathbf{75.72_5}$	$\mathbf{77.16_5}$

However, the visualization of the XLM-RoBERTa-base, mLUKE-base, and XLM-RoBERTa-large features shows that the finetuned multilingual language models cram the data from various languages into the same space by their class information. The plots in the same row from Figure 2 are all the same shapes.

This year, the shared task organizers provide a new test set that contains more data and more languages (Hürriyetoğlu et al., 2022). There are Turkish, Urdu, and Mandarin test data in addition to the existing English, Portuguese, Spanish, and Hindi. We also tested our models in this setting where Hindi, Turkish, Urdu, and Mandarin were tested in zero-shot settings. We compare mLUKE-base and XLM-RoBERTa-large in Table 2. From the results, mLUKE-base works better in Spanish and Turkish while XLM-RoBERTa-large works best for the remaining languages. The results are not consistent for zero-shot setting languages, however, XLM-RoBERTa-large works better 3 out of 4 cases. Also, in the low-resource settings, mLUKE-base works better in Spanish while XLM-RoBERTa-large works better in Portuguese.

3.2 Sentence Classification

We trained XLM-RoBERTa-large and mLUKE-base as sequence classifiers for sentence classification. Similar to document classification, we set the maximum sentence length to 150 and fed a sentence to a transformer language model with a softmax layer on top. In this subtask, we trained each model for 2.30 hours. We trained mLUKE-base for 15 epochs with a batch size of 36 and XLM-RoBERTa-large for 6 epochs with a batch size of 30 (a batch size of 10 with a gradient accumulation step of 3.). We observed that mLUKE-base was converged but XLM-RoBERTa-large was just fitted to a degree given the same resource.

Table 3: Test macro F1-scores of our models in subtask1: Sentence Classification 2021 test data. (The numbers in subscript are submission rankings on the leaderboard from our best submissions. The best results from the previous year are from (Hürriyetoğlu et al., 2021).)

Model	en	pt	es
mLUKE-base	79.65	$\mathbf{86.83_3}$	$\mathbf{87.10_4}$
XLM-R-large	$\mathbf{81.12_4}$	85.39	84.62
CASE-21 best	85.32	88.47	88.61

The experimental results in Table 3 suggest that mLUKE-base works better in low-resource languages, Portuguese and Spanish, while XLM-RoBERTa-large works better in English despite being undertrained. Our submissions are not better than the previous year's best results in this subtask.

3.3 Event Extraction

We only trained an XLM-RoBERTa-base model for token classification. We split the data into training and validation using the ratio of 0.2. However, there are so few Portuguese and Spanish data and XLM-RoBERTa-base does not have enough capacity so it does not perform well in our experiments as shown in Table 4, sadly.

We speculate that some training strategy, which does not require data partitioning, and larger language models will perform better in this subtask.

Table 4: Test CoNLL F1-scores of our models in subtask4: Event Extraction. (The numbers in subscript are submission rankings on the leaderboard.)

Model	en	pt	es
XLM-R-base	46.88_5	12.53_5	37.10_5

3.4 Automatically Replicating Manually Created Event Datasets

In this task (Zavarella and Tanev, 2022), event detection systems are going to be evaluated on their spatio-temporal pattern extraction performance. Similar to the previous shared task installment on Black Lives Matter (Giorgi et al., 2021), this year's target event is COVID-related protests in the US spanning three months (July 27, 2020 through October 27, 2020). We adopt our components from last year's report.

To begin with, we used the trained XLM-RoBERTa-large from subtask1 to classify the news using a concatenation of its news title and news abstract to see whether it contains any protest events or not. If the classifier outputs positive (logits were thresholded at 0.9), we ran a SpaCy named entity recognizer (Honnibal et al., 2020) on the textual concatenation to get spans with location tags ('GPE'). Then, those spans were concatenated into a query string which we used a geocoder library[2] to geocode using the Bing Maps REST Services API[3]. We used the provided dates from the date column as outputs given the filtered ids. Finally, we created a row for each filtered id containing five tuples, which are the id, the date, the city, the region or state, and the country.

4 Conclusions

This report describes our systems for a shared task on multilingual protest event detection at CASE-2022. We compared a small multilingual language model (XLM-RoBERTa-base), a knowledge-based multilingual model (mLUKE-base), and a large multilingual language model (XLM-RoBERTa-large). From all experimental results, we observed consistent outperforms from XLM-RoBERTa-large over smaller language models, XLM-RoBERTa-base, and mLUKE-base. Therefore, we concluded that language model capacity matters a lot for multilingual tasks. Also, we observed that mLUKE-base mostly outperforms XLM-RoBERTa-large. Hence, incorporating entity knowledge helps improve performance but with a nonnegligible computational cost. From our visualizations, we found that our finetuned multilingual language models cram data from various languages into the same space by their class information.

[2]https://geocoder.readthedocs.io/

[3]https://learn.microsoft.com/en-us/bingmaps/rest-services/

Limitations

This report is like a class assignment, given our work progress depicted here. We only compared several multilingual language models and implemented some basic systems to solve the tasks.

The authors are self-affiliated and do not represent any entities. The authors also participated in the shared task under many severe unattended local personal criminal events in their home countries. There might be some unintentional errors and physical limitations based on these unlawful interruptions. Even at the times of drafting this report, the authors suffer from unknown toxin flumes spraying into their places. We want to participate in the shared task because it is fun and educational. We apologize for any errors in this report. We tried our best.

Ethics Statement

Scientific work published at EMNLP 2022 must comply with the ACL Ethics Policy. We, the authors, intend the uses of our systems for peace and social good only. No harm. To see and alleviate people dangers, pains, and angers, detecting these socio-political and crisis events is meant to be helpful and savior for all, not the other way around.

Acknowledgments

We would like to thank the reviewers for their constructive feedback.

References

Parul Awasthy, Jian Ni, Ken Barker, and Radu Florian. 2021. IBM MNLP IE at CASE 2021 task 1: Multigranular and multilingual event detection on protest news. In *Proceedings of the 4th Workshop on Challenges and Applications of Automated Extraction of Socio-political Events from Text (CASE 2021)*, pages 138–146, Online. Association for Computational Linguistics.

Yoshua Bengio. 2012. Practical recommendations for gradient-based training of deep architectures. In *Neural networks: Tricks of the trade*, pages 437–478. Springer.

Alexis Conneau, Kartikay Khandelwal, Naman Goyal, Vishrav Chaudhary, Guillaume Wenzek, Francisco Guzmán, Edouard Grave, Myle Ott, Luke Zettlemoyer, and Veselin Stoyanov. 2020. Unsupervised cross-lingual representation learning at scale. In *Proceedings of the 58th Annual Meeting of the Association for Computational Linguistics*, pages 8440–8451, Online. Association for Computational Linguistics.

Salvatore Giorgi, Vanni Zavarella, Hristo Tanev, Nicolas Stefanovitch, Sy Hwang, Hansi Hettiarachchi, Tharindu Ranasinghe, Vivek Kalyan, Paul Tan, Shaun Tan, Martin Andrews, Tiancheng Hu, Niklas Stoehr, Francesco Ignazio Re, Daniel Vegh, Dennis Atzenhofer, Brenda Curtis, and Ali Hürriyetoğlu. 2021. Discovering black lives matter events in the United States: Shared task 3, CASE 2021. In *Proceedings of the 4th Workshop on Challenges and Applications of Automated Extraction of Socio-political Events from Text (CASE 2021)*, pages 218–227, Online. Association for Computational Linguistics.

Matthew Honnibal, Ines Montani, Sofie Van Landeghem, and Adriane Boyd. 2020. spacy: Industrial-strength natural language processing in python.

Ali Hürriyetoğlu, Osman Mutlu, Fırat Duruşan, Onur Uca, Alaeddin Selçuk Gürel, Benjamin Radford, Yaoyao Dai, Hansi Hettiarachchi, Niklas Stoehr, Tadashi Nomoto, Milena Slavcheva, Francielle Vargas, Aaqib Javid, Fatih Beyhan, and Erdem Yörük. 2022. Extended multilingual protest news detection - shared task 1, case 2021 and 2022. In *Proceedings of the 5th Workshop on Challenges and Applications of Automated Extraction of Socio-political Events from Text (CASE 2022)*, online. Association for Computational Linguistics (ACL).

Ali Hürriyetoğlu, Osman Mutlu, Erdem Yörük, Farhana Ferdousi Liza, Ritesh Kumar, and Shyam Ratan. 2021. Multilingual protest news detection - shared task 1, CASE 2021. In *Proceedings of the 4th Workshop on Challenges and Applications of Automated Extraction of Socio-political Events from Text (CASE 2021)*, pages 79–91, Online. Association for Computational Linguistics.

Ali Hürriyetoğlu, Erdem Yörük, Osman Mutlu, Fırat Duruşan, Çağrı Yoltar, Deniz Yüret, and Burak Gürel. 2021. Cross-Context News Corpus for Protest Event-Related Knowledge Base Construction. *Data Intelligence*, pages 1–28.

Yinhan Liu, Myle Ott, Naman Goyal, Jingfei Du, Mandar Joshi, Danqi Chen, Omer Levy, Mike Lewis, Luke Zettlemoyer, and Veselin Stoyanov. 2019. Roberta: A robustly optimized bert pretraining approach. *arXiv preprint arXiv:1907.11692*.

Ilya Loshchilov and Frank Hutter. 2018. Decoupled weight decay regularization. In *International Conference on Learning Representations*.

Merriam-Webster. 2022. Protest. In *Merriam-Webster.com dictionary*.

Lutz Prechelt. 1998. Early stopping-but when? In *Neural Networks: Tricks of the trade*, pages 55–69. Springer.

Ryokan Ri, Ikuya Yamada, and Yoshimasa Tsuruoka. 2022. mLUKE: The power of entity representations in multilingual pretrained language models. In *Proceedings of the 60th Annual Meeting of the Association for Computational Linguistics (Volume 1: Long Papers)*, pages 7316–7330, Dublin, Ireland. Association for Computational Linguistics.

Laurens Van der Maaten and Geoffrey Hinton. 2008. Visualizing data using t-sne. *Journal of machine learning research*, 9(11).

Martin Wattenberg, Fernanda Viégas, and Ian Johnson. 2016. How to use t-sne effectively. *Distill*.

Thomas Wolf, Lysandre Debut, Victor Sanh, Julien Chaumond, Clement Delangue, Anthony Moi, Pierric Cistac, Tim Rault, Remi Louf, Morgan Funtowicz, Joe Davison, Sam Shleifer, Patrick von Platen, Clara Ma, Yacine Jernite, Julien Plu, Canwen Xu, Teven Le Scao, Sylvain Gugger, Mariama Drame, Quentin Lhoest, and Alexander Rush. 2020. Transformers: State-of-the-art natural language processing. In *Proceedings of the 2020 Conference on Empirical Methods in Natural Language Processing: System Demonstrations*, pages 38–45, Online. Association for Computational Linguistics.

Vanni Zavarella and Hristo Tanev. 2022. Tracking covid-19 protest events in the united states: Database replication, case 2022. In *Proceedings of the 5th Workshop on Challenges and Applications of Automated Extraction of Socio-political Events from Text (CASE 2022)*, online. Association for Computational Linguistics (ACL).

EventGraph at CASE 2021 Task 1: A General Graph-based Approach to Protest Event Extraction

Huiling You,[1] **David Samuel,**[1] **Samia Touileb,**[2] and **Lilja Øvrelid**[1]
[1]University of Oslo
[2]University of Bergen
{huiliny, davisamu, liljao}@ifi.uio.no
samia.touileb@uib.no

Abstract

This paper presents our submission to the 2022 edition of the CASE 2021 shared task 1, subtask 4. The EventGraph system adapts an end-to-end, graph-based semantic parser to the task of Protest Event Extraction and more specifically subtask 4 on event trigger and argument extraction. We experiment with various graphs, encoding the events as either "labeled-edge" or "node-centric" graphs. We show that the "node-centric" approach yields best results overall, performing well across the three languages of the task, namely English, Spanish, and Portuguese. EventGraph is ranked 3rd for English and Portuguese, and 4th for Spanish. Our code is available at: `https://github.com/huiling-y/eventgraph_at_case`

1 Introduction

The automated extraction of socio-political event information from text constitutes an important NLP task, with a number of application areas for social scientists, policy makers, etc. The task involves analysis at different levels of granularity: document-level, sentence-level, and the fine-grained extraction of event triggers and arguments within a sentence. The CASE 2022 Shared Task 1 on Multilingual Protest Event Detection extends the 2021 shared task (Hürriyetoğlu et al., 2021a) with additional data in the evaluation phase and features four subtasks: (i) document classification, (ii) sentence classification, (iii) event sentence co-reference, and (iv) event extraction.

The task of event extraction involves the detection of explicit event triggers and corresponding arguments in text. Current classification-based approaches to the task typically model the task as a pipeline of classifiers (Ji and Grishman, 2008; Li et al., 2013; Liu et al., 2020; Du and Cardie, 2020; Li et al., 2020) or using joint modeling approaches (Yang and Mitchell, 2016; Nguyen et al., 2016; Liu et al., 2018; Wadden et al., 2019; Lin et al., 2020).

In this paper, we present the EventGraph system and its application to Task 1 Subtask 4 in the 2022 edition of the CASE 2021 shared task. EventGraph is a joint framework for event extraction, which encodes events as graphs and solves event extraction as semantic graph parsing. We show that it is beneficial to model the relation between event triggers and arguments and approach event extraction via structured prediction instead of sequence labelling. Our system performs well on the three languages, achieving competitive results and consistently ranked among the top four systems.

In the following, we briefly describe the data supplied by the shared task organizers and present Subtask 4 in some more detail. We then go on to present an overview of the EventGraph system focusing on the encoding of the data to semantic graphs and the model architecture. We experiment with several different graph encodings and provide a more detailed analysis of the results.

2 Data and task

Our contribution is to subtask 4, which falls under shared task 1 – the detection and extraction of socio-political and crisis events. While most subtasks of shared task 1 have sentence-level annotations, subtask 4 has been annotated at the token-level while providing the annotators the document-level contexts. Subtask 4 focuses on the extraction of event triggers and event arguments related to contentious politics and riots (Hürriyetoğlu et al., 2021a). This subtask has been previously approached as a sequence labeling problem combining various methods of fine-tuning pre-trained language models (Hürriyetoğlu et al., 2021a).

The data supplied for Subtask 4 is identical to that of the 2021 edition of the task, as presented in Hürriyetoğlu et al. (2021a). The data is part of the multilingual extension of the GLOCON dataset (Hürriyetoğlu et al., 2021b) with data from English, Portuguese, and Spanish. The source of the

Proceedings of the 5th Workshop on Challenges and Applications of Automated Extraction of Socio-political Events from Text (CASE), pages 155 - 160
December 7-8, 2022 ©2022 Association for Computational Linguistics

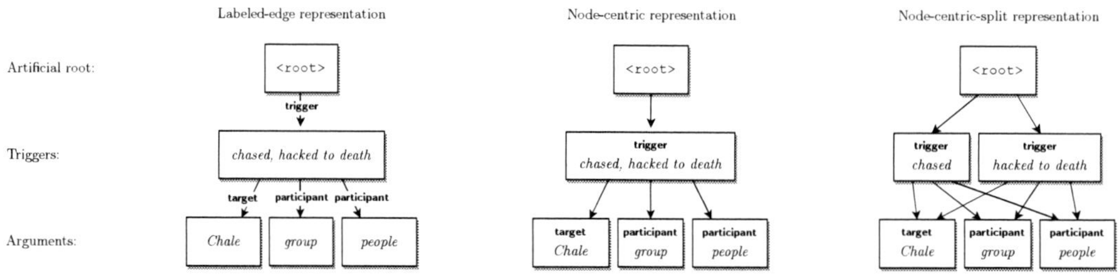

Figure 1: Graph representations of sentence *"Chale was allegedly chased by a group of about 30 people and was hacked to death with pangas, axes and spears."*

data is protest event coverage in news articles from specific countries: China and South Africa (English), Brazil (Portuguese), and Argentina (Spanish). The data has been doubly annotated by graduate students in political science with token-level information regarding event triggers and arguments. Hürriyetoğlu et al. (2021a) reports the token level inter-annotator agreement to be between 0.35 and 0.60. Disagreements between annotators were subsequently resolved by an annotation supervisor. Table 1 shows the number of news articles for each of the languages in the task, distributed over the training and test sets. This clearly shows that the majority of the data is in English with only a fraction of articles in Portuguese and Spanish.

Relevant statistics for the different event component annotations for Subtask 4 are presented in Table 1 detailing the number of triggers, participants, and various other types of argument components, such as place, target, organizer, etc. Once again, the table also illustrates the comparative imbalance in data across the three languages.

	English	**Portuguese**	**Spanish**
train	732 (2,925)	29 (78)	29 (91)
dev	76 (323)	4 (9)	1 (15)
test	179 (311)	50 (190)	50 (192)
trigger	4,595	122	157
participant	2,663	73	88
place	1,570	61	15
target	1,470	32	64
organizer	1,261	19	25
etime	1,209	41	40
fname	1,201	48	49

Table 1: **Top**: Number of articles (sentences) for the different languages in Subtask 4 (Hürriyetoğlu et al., 2021a). About 10 percent (in terms of sentences) of the official training data is used as the development split. **Bottom**: Counts for the different event components in Subtask 4 training data for English, Portuguese, and Spanish (Hürriyetoğlu et al., 2021a).

3 System overview

We use our system, EventGraph, that adapts an end-to-end graph-based semantic parser to solve the task of extracting socio-political events. In what follows, we give more details about the graph representation and the model architecture of our system.

3.1 Graph representations

We represent each sentence as an event graph, which contains event trigger(s) and arguments as nodes. In an event graph, edges are constrained between the trigger(s) and the corresponding arguments. However, since our system can take as input graphs in a general sense the precise graph representation that works best for this task must be determined empirically. We here explore two different graph encoding methods, where the labels for triggers and arguments are represented either as edge labels or node labels, namely "labeled-edge" and "node-centric". Since sentences in the data may contain information about several events with arguments shared across these, we also experiment with a version of the "node-centric" approach where multiple triggers give rise to separate nodes in the graph. The intuition behind this is that it is easier for the model to predict a node anchoring to a single span than to several disjoint spans.

- **Labeled-edge**: labels for event trigger(s) and arguments are represented as edge labels; multiple triggers are merged into one node, as shown by the first graph of Figure 1.
- **Node-centric**: labels for event trigger(s) and arguments are represented as node labels;

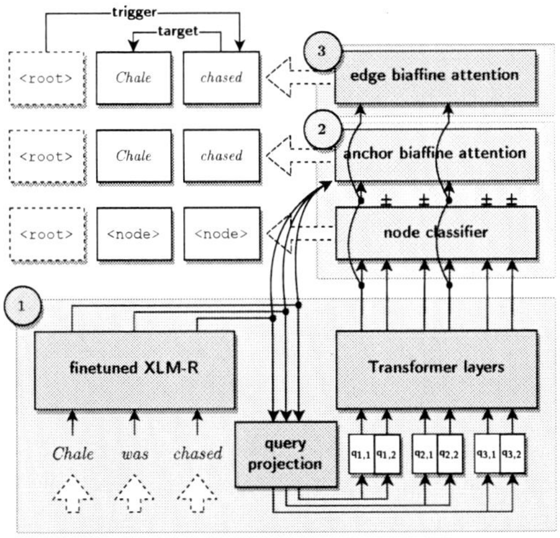

Figure 2: EventGraph architecture. 1) the input gets a contextualized representation from **the sentence encoding** module, 2) graph nodes are decoded by **the node prediction** module and 3) connected by **the edge prediction** module. The given example is for "label-edge" event graph parsing.

there is always a single node for trigger(s), as shown by the second graph of Figure 1.

- **Node-centric-split**: node labels denote trigger(s) and argument roles; multiple triggers are represented in different nodes, as shown by the third graph of Figure 1.

3.2 Model architecture

Our model is built upon a winning framework (Samuel and Straka, 2020) from a previous meaning representation parsing shared task (Oepen et al., 2020). The model contains customizable components for predicting nodes and edges, thus generating event graphs for different graph representations. We introduce each component of the model as following (Figure 2):

Sentence encoding Each token of an input sentence obtains a contextualized embedding from a pretrained language model, the large version of XLM-R (Conneau et al., 2020) in our implementation. These embeddings are mapped onto latent queries by a linear transformation layer, and processed by a stack of Transformer layers (Vaswani et al., 2017) to model the dependencies between queries.

Node prediction A node-presence classifier processes the queries and predicts nodes by classifying each query. An anchor biaffine classifier (Dozat and Manning, 2017) creates anchors from the nodes to surface strings via deep biaffine attention between the queries and the contextual embeddings.

Edge prediction With predicted nodes, two biaffine classifiers are used to construct the edges between nodes: one classifier predicts the presence of edge between a pair of nodes and the other predicts the corresponding edge label.

The graph generated for each input sentence contains the extracted event components. We then convert the labels to BIO format.

4 Experimental setup

Data We use all the official training data to train our final model, without using any additional data. During development time, we set aside about 10 percent of the training data for development. A breakdown of the number of articles and sentences in train and dev are provided in Table 1.

Joint training We train our model on the training data of all three languages and test on the official test data. As shown in Table 1, the training data for Portuguese and Spanish makes only a small portion of all training data, which leads to few-shot learning for these two languages.

Implementation details We use the large version of XLM-R via HuggingFace `transformers` library (Wolf et al., 2020). All models were trained with a single Nvidia RTX3090 GPU.

Evaluation metrics The evaluation metric is a macro F_1 score for individual languages. The predicted event-annotated texts are in BIO format, and the scores are calculated with a python implementation[1] of the `conlleval` evaluation script used in CoNLL-2000 Shared Task (Tjong Kim Sang and Buchholz, 2000), where precision, recall and F_1 scores are calculated for predicted spans against the gold spans and there is no dependency between event arguments and triggers.

Submitted systems We submitted three models as listed in Table 3.

5 Results and discussion

We summarize the results of our systems on the official test data in Table 3. All scores are obtained by submitting our test predictions to the shared

[1] https://github.com/sighsmile/conlleval

Language	System	trigger	target	Place	Participant	Organizer	fname	etime	all
En		*457*	*134*	*118*	*293*	*131*	*129*	*121*	
	Label-edge	82.48	56.29	75.44	74.62	74.52	50.42	77.06	73.46
	Node-centric	84.21	62.09	74.89	76.42	75.46	54.31	81.22	75.85
	Node-centric-split	84.62	52.88	75.11	73.75	74.91	52.28	78.97	73.92
Es		*28*	*5*	*5*	*7*	*4*	*7*	*5*	
	Label-edge	66.67	60.00	100.00	100.00	66.67	71.43	80.00	73.85
	Node-centric	65.62	72.73	100.00	100.00	80.00	76.92	80.00	75.76
	Node-centric-split	71.19	54.55	100.00	100.00	66.67	85.71	60	75.59
Pr		*11*	*7*	*3*	*5*	*2*	*2*	*5*	
	Labeled-edge	83.33	71.43	75.00	90.91	66.67	100.00	66.67	78.87
	Node-centric	88.00	61.54	66.67	90.91	100.00	100.00	66.67	79.45
	Node-centric-split	91.67	71.43	50	90.91	100.00	66.67	100.00	83.78

Table 2: Detailed F_1 scores of our systems on the development data with different graph representations. We also add the number of each event component to better compare the distribution of components against the scores.

System	Language	Macro F_1
Labeled-edge	English	73.12
	Spanish	64.02
	Portuguese	69.62
Node-centric	English	74.02
	Spanish	64.16
	Portuguese	70.73
Node-centric-split	English	74.76_3
	Spanish	64.49_4
	Portuguese	71.72_3
Winning systems	English	77.46_1
	Spanish	69.87_1
	Portuguese	74.57_1

Table 3: Results of our systems on the official test data with different graph representations. We also include the winning system results from the shared task leaderboard. Subscripts indicate the ranking on the leaderboard, so we only add corresponding ranking to our best-performing system.

task.[2] Results show that "node-centric" systems generate better results than "label-edge" systems, and it is more beneficial to keep multiple event triggers as separate nodes. In terms of languages, all models perform best on English, which is unsurprising, since the training data consists mostly of English. However, the results on Portuguese are consistently better than those of Spanish, signaling English might be a better transfer language for Portuguese than for Spanish.

Compared with other participating systems, in particular the winning systems,[2] as shown in Table 3, our results are still competitive. We rank 3rd for English and Portuguese, and 4th for Spanish; our best results are achieved by a single system. For English and Portuguese, our results are very close to the winning results, which are achieved by different participating systems.

[2]`https://codalab.lisn.upsaclay.fr/competitions/7126`, accessed on September 29, 2022.

Argument	System	P	R	$F1$
fname	Labeled-edge	47.62	53.57	50.42
	Node-centric	52.50	56.25	54.31
	Node-centric-split	48.84	56.25	52.28
target	Labeled-edge	60.28	52.80	56.29
	Node-centric	65.52	59.01	62.09
	Node-centric-split	58.21	48.45	52.88

Table 4: Detailed Precision, Recall, and $F1$ scores of `fname` and `target` arguments for English developmentset.

5.1 Error analysis on development data

Since the gold data for the test set is not available to task participants, we are not able to perform more detailed error analysis. Hence, to have more insights into our models' performance, we provide some error analysis on the development data (as described in Table 1). As previously mentioned, during our model development phase, we did not use all the official training data for training, but set aside small set for validation (about 10%).

As shown in Table 2, over all event components, `target` and `fname` arguments are more difficult to extract than others, with the scores substantially lower across different languages and models. In general, our models perform best in `trigger` extraction, partly because the number of triggers is much larger than event arguments for all datasets.

We further look at `target` and `fname` prediction scores of the English development set. As shown in Table 4, for `fname`, our systems tend to over-predict, with consistently lower precision scores; by manually going through our systems' predictions, we find many labeled chunks of `fname` are actually non-event components. For `target`, our systems tend to under-predict, with consistently higher precision scores; we also find that our systems would predict a longer span, for instance "former diplomat" as opposed to "diplomat", which is the gold span, and sometimes our systems confuse `organizer` and `participant` with `target`, by wrongly labelling the corresponding span as `target`.

6 Conclusion

In this paper we have presented the EventGraph system for event extraction and its application to the CASE 2022 shared task on Multilingual Protest Event Detection. EventGraph solves the task as a graph parsing problem hence we experiment with different ways of encoding the event data as general graphs, contrasting a so-called "labeled-edge" and "node-centric" approach. Our results indicate that the "node-centric" approach is beneficial for this task and furthermore that the separation in the graph of nodes belonging to different events in the same sentence proves useful. A more detailed analysis of the development results indicates that our system performs well in trigger identification, however struggles in the identification of `target` and `fname` arguments.

Acknowledgments

This research was supported by industry partners and the Research Council of Norway with funding to *MediaFutures: Research Centre for Responsible Media Technology and Innovation*, through the Centres for Research-based Innovation scheme, project number 309339.

References

Alexis Conneau, Kartikay Khandelwal, Naman Goyal, Vishrav Chaudhary, Guillaume Wenzek, Francisco Guzmán, Edouard Grave, Myle Ott, Luke Zettlemoyer, and Veselin Stoyanov. 2020. Unsupervised cross-lingual representation learning at scale. In *Proceedings of the 58th Annual Meeting of the Association for Computational Linguistics*, pages 8440–8451, Online. Association for Computational Linguistics. 3

Timothy Dozat and Christopher D. Manning. 2017. Deep biaffine attention for neural dependency parsing. In *International Conference on Learning Representations*. 3

Xinya Du and Claire Cardie. 2020. Event extraction by answering (almost) natural questions. In *Proceedings of the 2020 Conference on Empirical Methods in Natural Language Processing (EMNLP)*, pages 671–683, Online. Association for Computational Linguistics. 1

Ali Hürriyetoğlu, Osman Mutlu, Erdem Yörük, Farhana Ferdousi Liza, Ritesh Kumar, and Shyam Ratan. 2021a. Multilingual protest news detection - shared task 1, CASE 2021. In *Proceedings of the 4th Workshop on Challenges and Applications of Automated Extraction of Socio-political Events from Text (CASE 2021)*, pages 79–91, Online. Association for Computational Linguistics. 1, 2

Ali Hürriyetoğlu, Erdem Yörük, Osman Mutlu, Fırat Duruşan, Çağrı Yoltar, Deniz Yüret, and Burak Gürel. 2021b. Cross-context news corpus for protest event-related knowledge base construction. *Data Intelligence*, 3(2):308–335. 1

Heng Ji and Ralph Grishman. 2008. Refining event extraction through cross-document inference. In *Proceedings of ACL-08: HLT*, pages 254–262, Columbus, Ohio. Association for Computational Linguistics. 1

Fayuan Li, Weihua Peng, Yuguang Chen, Quan Wang, Lu Pan, Yajuan Lyu, and Yong Zhu. 2020. Event extraction as multi-turn question answering. In *Findings of the Association for Computational Linguistics: EMNLP 2020*, pages 829–838, Online. Association for Computational Linguistics. 1

Qi Li, Heng Ji, and Liang Huang. 2013. Joint event extraction via structured prediction with global features. In *Proceedings of the 51st Annual Meeting of the Association for Computational Linguistics (Volume 1: Long Papers)*, pages 73–82, Sofia, Bulgaria. Association for Computational Linguistics. 1

Ying Lin, Heng Ji, Fei Huang, and Lingfei Wu. 2020. A joint neural model for information extraction with global features. In *Proceedings of the 58th Annual Meeting of the Association for Computational Linguistics*, pages 7999–8009, Online. Association for Computational Linguistics. 1

Jian Liu, Yubo Chen, Kang Liu, Wei Bi, and Xiaojiang Liu. 2020. Event extraction as machine reading comprehension. In *Proceedings of the 2020 Conference on Empirical Methods in Natural Language Processing (EMNLP)*, pages 1641–1651, Online. Association for Computational Linguistics. 1

Xiao Liu, Zhunchen Luo, and Heyan Huang. 2018. Jointly multiple events extraction via attention-based graph information aggregation. In *Proceedings of the 2018 Conference on Empirical Methods in Natural*

Language Processing, pages 1247–1256, Brussels, Belgium. Association for Computational Linguistics. 1

Thien Huu Nguyen, Kyunghyun Cho, and Ralph Grishman. 2016. Joint event extraction via recurrent neural networks. In *Proceedings of the 2016 Conference of the North American Chapter of the Association for Computational Linguistics: Human Language Technologies*, pages 300–309, San Diego, California. Association for Computational Linguistics. 1

Stephan Oepen, Omri Abend, Lasha Abzianidze, Johan Bos, Jan Hajic, Daniel Hershcovich, Bin Li, Tim O'Gorman, Nianwen Xue, and Daniel Zeman. 2020. MRP 2020: The second shared task on cross-framework and cross-lingual meaning representation parsing. In *Proceedings of the CoNLL 2020 Shared Task: Cross-Framework Meaning Representation Parsing*, pages 1–22, Online. Association for Computational Linguistics. 3

David Samuel and Milan Straka. 2020. ÚFAL at MRP 2020: Permutation-invariant semantic parsing in PERIN. In *Proceedings of the CoNLL 2020 Shared Task: Cross-Framework Meaning Representation Parsing*, pages 53–64, Online. Association for Computational Linguistics. 3

Erik F. Tjong Kim Sang and Sabine Buchholz. 2000. Introduction to the CoNLL-2000 shared task chunking. In *Fourth Conference on Computational Natural Language Learning and the Second Learning Language in Logic Workshop*. 3

Ashish Vaswani, Noam Shazeer, Niki Parmar, Jakob Uszkoreit, Llion Jones, Aidan N Gomez, Łukasz Kaiser, and Illia Polosukhin. 2017. Attention is all you need. *Advances in neural information processing systems*, 30. 3

David Wadden, Ulme Wennberg, Yi Luan, and Hannaneh Hajishirzi. 2019. Entity, relation, and event extraction with contextualized span representations. In *Proceedings of the 2019 Conference on Empirical Methods in Natural Language Processing and the 9th International Joint Conference on Natural Language Processing (EMNLP-IJCNLP)*, pages 5784–5789, Hong Kong, China. Association for Computational Linguistics. 1

Thomas Wolf, Lysandre Debut, Victor Sanh, Julien Chaumond, Clement Delangue, Anthony Moi, Pierric Cistac, Tim Rault, Remi Louf, Morgan Funtowicz, Joe Davison, Sam Shleifer, Patrick von Platen, Clara Ma, Yacine Jernite, Julien Plu, Canwen Xu, Teven Le Scao, Sylvain Gugger, Mariama Drame, Quentin Lhoest, and Alexander Rush. 2020. Transformers: State-of-the-art natural language processing. In *Proceedings of the 2020 Conference on Empirical Methods in Natural Language Processing: System Demonstrations*, pages 38–45, Online. Association for Computational Linguistics. 3

Bishan Yang and Tom M. Mitchell. 2016. Joint extraction of events and entities within a document context. In *Proceedings of the 2016 Conference of the North American Chapter of the Association for Computational Linguistics: Human Language Technologies*, pages 289–299, San Diego, California. Association for Computational Linguistics. 1

NSUT-NLP at CASE 2022 Task 1: Multilingual Protest Event Detection using Transformer-based Models

Manan Suri, Krish Chopra, Adwita Arora
Netaji Subhas University of Technology, New Delhi
{manan.suri.ug20, krish.ug20, adwita.ug20} @nsut.ac.in

Abstract

Event detection, specifically in the socio-political domain, has posed a long-standing challenge to researchers in the NLP domain. Therefore, the creation of automated techniques that perform classification of the large amounts of accessible data on the Internet becomes imperative. This paper is a summary of the efforts we made in participating in Task 1 of CASE 2022. We use state-of-art multilingual BERT (mBERT) with further fine-tuning to perform document classification in English, Portuguese, Spanish, Urdu, Hindi, Turkish and Mandarin. In the document classification subtask, we were able to achieve F1 scores of 0.8062, 0.6445, 0.7302, 0.5671, 0.6555, 0.7545 and 0.6702 in English, Spanish, Portuguese, Hindi, Urdu, Mandarin and Turkish respectively achieving a rank of 5 in English and 7 on the remaining language tasks.

1 Introduction

Protests exist as a natural way for citizens of a nation to show their dissatisfaction with decisions taken by the respective governments or authorities (Neogi et al., 2021). The sentiment prevalent in such events and the reaction by various parties to these events provide the basis for carrying out many studies in the sociopolitical field, such as the public opinion about the event that was the cause for the protest, how much freedom the protesters were afforded as a measure of the democracy in the nation, and so on. With the advancement of technology, there has also been an exponential rise in the use of social networks as a medium for exchanging information across the globe, with global events and their inner nuances being available to the public at large. However, extracting valuable insights from such events on a national or global scale is a daunting task if done manually (Carothers and Youngs, 2015). Even if we leverage automated techniques for the process, there are numerous challenges faced while working on multilingual data (Hershcovich et al., 2022). Hence, there exists an incentive to automate the task of processing protest news from multiple locations and in multiple languages and to create an NLP system that could be generalized for the task of detecting protest news. Task 1 of CASE 2022 (Hürriyetoğlu et al., 2022a) aims at working on multilingual protest news corpora, with Subtask 1 working towards the binary classification of news reports, where if a document reports on an event that has happened or is ongoing, it is marked as relevant, otherwise it is considered irrelevant.

Our approach revolves around the use of state-of-art Pre-Trained Language Models (PLMs) and finetuning them to perform the task we require. We leverage the `bert-base-multilingual-cased` (Devlin et al., 2018) that was trained in over 104 languages to tackle the multilingual task. We fine-tune it for protest news detection. Since most of the training datasets had a bias toward the negative class, we augmented the datasets by translating positive samples from other language datasets and hence improving the balance between the positive and negative class to prevent our model from being biased towards the negative class. Furthermore, the lack of samples in Portuguese and Spanish presents us with a few-shot learning scenario, which we tackle by augmenting these datasets with samples from the English dataset translated into the respective languages. For languages with no training datasets (Urdu, Turkish, Mandarin and Hindi), we created training datasets by translating the English corpus.

The rest of the paper is organised as follows: We begin by laying out the past literature and work done in the field of protest event detection in Section 2 followed by the description of the task at hand and the data given to us in Section 3. In Section 4, we describe the techniques we employed, namely data augmentation and the model we used, multilingual BERT (mBERT). The experimental

Proceedings of the 5th Workshop on Challenges and Applications of Automated Extraction of Socio-political Events from Text (CASE), pages 161 - 168
December 7-8, 2022 ©2022 Association for Computational Linguistics

setup for our system is described in Section 5 and the results on the test set are mentioned and analysed in Section 6. Finally, in Section 7, we draw a conclusion to our work and go over prospective directions for additional research.

2 Related Work

Protest detection and allied fields have drawn a lot of attention from researchers in the NLP domain. MAVEN (Wang et al., 2020) and CySecED (Trong et al., 2020) are annotated datasets in the English language created for the purposes of event detection. ACE 2005 (Walker, Christopher et al., 2006) and TempEval-2 (Verhagen et al., 2010) are multilingual datasets where ACE 2005 covers English, Arabic, and Chinese and TempEval-2 covers Chinese, English, French, Italian, Korean and Spanish. MINION (Veyseh et al., 2022) is another multilingual ED dataset covering 8 different languages (English, Spanish, Portuguese, Polish, Turkish, Hindi, Japanese and Korean). MMCHIVED (Steinert-Threlkeld and Joo, 2022) is another dataset containing multimodal data like text and images compiled from social media regarding Chile and Venezuela protests. There have also been region-specific case studies, such as detection of protest events in Turkey 2013 (Elsafoury, 2020) and protest analysis in Greece over the last twenty years through the scope of Computational Social Science (Papanikolaou and Papageorgiou, 2020). Previously event detection has also been researched upon by researchers participating in the Task 1 of CASE 2021 (Hürriyetoğlu et al., 2021). Teams which participated in the task earlier have used multilingual pre-trained language models (Re et al., 2021; Awasthy et al., 2021a; Gürel and Emin, 2021) which is similar to the approach used by our system.

3 Background

3.1 Task

Event Detection aims at extracting event triggers (in the forms of singular nouns or verbs or even full sentences sometimes) and classifying the triggers into the type of event they belong to (Awasthy et al., 2021b). The main challenge of this task comes from the fact there exists a many-to-many relationship between the trigger and event type, i.e. the same event can be represented by various event triggers and the same expression can represent different events in different contexts (Feng et al., 2016). The CASE 2022 workshop (Hürriyetoğlu et al., 2022a) focuses on protest news event detection. In this paper, we aim to tackle Shared Task 1: Multilingual Protest News Detection, specifically Subtask 1.

Subtask 1 - Document Classification is a binary classification task on the document-level (news article) where we classify an event as positive if the event actually occurred or is ongoing. Scheduled events, rumors, and speculations are considered as irrelevant and hence marked as negative.

The task we deal with is a binary classification task where we classify documents that pertain to ongoing or already occurred events as positive samples. Events that are merely rumors, scheduled to take place in future or speculations are marked as negative samples.

The task is multilingual, as we have training data consisting of English, Portuguese, and Spanish Languages for both training and evaluation of the model. The Portuguese and Spanish datasets present us with a few-shot scenario to the dearth of data compared to the English data set. At the same time, Hindi, Mandarin, Turkish and Urdu evaluation sets present a zero-shot setting to evaluate our model.

The metric used for the evaluation of the results produced by the model is the Macro-F1 score. It provides a balance between Precision and Recall of the model, by taking a harmonic mean of both metrics.

$$F_1 = \frac{2 \times Precision \times Recall}{Precision + Recall}$$

3.2 Data

Language	Split	Subtask 1
English	Train	9,324
	Test	3,871
Spanish	Train	1,000
	Test	671
Portuguese	Train	1,487
	Test	671
Hindi	Test only	268
Urdu	Test only	299
Turkish	Test only	300
Mandarin	Test only	300

Table 1: Distribution of samples in respective datasets for the given languages

	English	Spanish	Portuguese
Characters	1067.37	932.87	635.25
Tokens	199.74	177.35	116.03

Table 2: Analysis of the average number of characters and tokens in the respective training sets for English, Spanish, and Portuguese.

The data for this task has been created and annotated using the methods described in Hürriyetoğlu et al. (2022b). While the task is multilingual, there isn't an even distribution of data for all languages, with the English corpus having more data than both Portuguese and Spanish. Also, some languages to be evaluated do not have any training data (a zero-shot learning problem), namely Hindi, Turkish, Urdu and Mandarin. The distribution of data is given in Table 1 as shown.

The distribution of labels for training data for subtask 1 is as follows: The positive sample ratio for Subtask-1 is 0.205 for English dataset, 0.131 for Spanish dataset and 0.132 for Portuguese.

This highlights that the data is skewed towards the negative class for all languages. It is natural to tackle this bias problem so that our model does not align itself too much with one class, which would lead to its performance suffering in a more balanced scenario.

The number of characters in each training dataset is shown in Table 2. One would believe that a longer sentence gives the model more context to work with and therefore produces better results; however, a longer text also runs the risk of confusing the model with interference from mixed signals (Çelik et al., 2021). The number of tokens in each language dataset is also shown.

Another thing to note is the low amount of training data in the case of Portuguese and Spanish, and the complete lack of it in the case of Hindi, Urdu, Mandarin and Turkish. We attempt to alleviate this problem by translating the English corpus examples into the respective language and training on this augmented dataset.

4 System Overview

4.1 Data Augmentation

Data augmentation refers to the set of techniques to increase the quantity and diversity of data points in a data-set without collecting new data. The purpose of data augmentation in our system was as follows:

- **Class Imbalance:** In the English, Spanish and Portuguese datasets provided by the organizers, the ratio of the positive samples was 0.205, 0.131 and 0.132 for Subtask 1. Therefore to provide enough diversity of samples of the positive class, data augmentation was required
- **Lack of Training Data:** Spanish and Portuguese had limited training data compared to English. For Hindi, Urdu, Mandarin and Turkish, no training data was available. Therefore to create an appropriately large dataset, data augmentation is used.

The technique used for data augmentation in our system leverages the availability of three linguistically different datasets. We translated various combinations of positive and negative samples from the three available datasets of English, Spanish and Portuguese

Our augmentation strategy can be understood by Fig 1. The process is described below:

1. **English** The final training set consisted of the original English dataset along with positive samples of Spanish and Portuguese datasets translated into English.
2. **Spanish** The final training set consisted of the original Spanish dataset along with the English dataset (both positive and negative samples), Portuguese dataset translated into Spanish.
3. **Portuguese** The final training set consisted of the original Portuguese dataset along with the English dataset (both positive and negative samples), Spanish dataset translated into Spanish
4. **Hindi, Urdu, Mandarin and Turkish** The training datasets for Hindi, Urdu, Mandarin and Turkish were created by translating the final English dataset into the respective languages.

Table 3 displays the size and final data distribution of the respective train datasets after data augmentation.

4.2 Finetuning Pretrained MultiModal BERT

Pre-training in NLP refers to moulding a large collection of unannotated text input into general-purpose language representations. It is useful as it

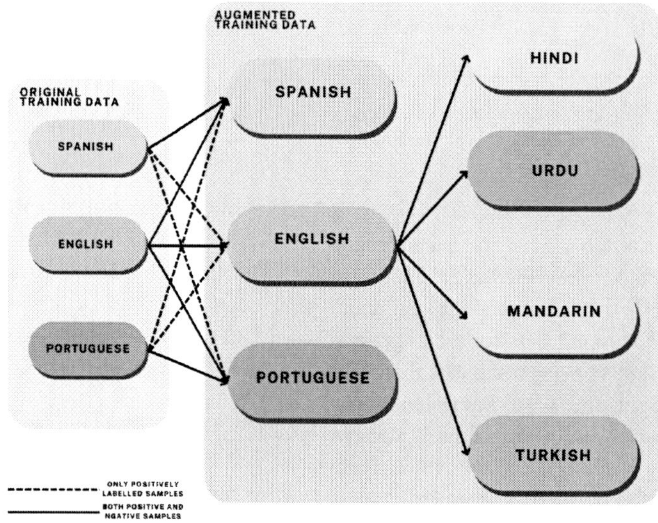

Figure 1: Data augmentation using translation. In the given diagram, each directed edge represents translation from a source language to a target language. The graph represents the combination of datasets used during translation to achieve the final augmented training sets.

Language(s)	Label 0	Label 1	Total
English, Hindi, Urdu, Mandarin and Turkish	2240	7412	9652
Spanish	2240	8281	10521
Portuguese	2240	8702	10942

Table 3: Distribution of labels in the respective training set after data augmentation.

prevents having to start from scratch when training a new model for downstream tasks. Because it offers a stronger model initialization, pre-training improves generalization performance and aids in convergence on downstream tasks. Pretraining can be considered a form of regularization that avoids overfitting on smaller datasets with relatively few human-annotated examples. On many NLP tasks, pre-training models followed by fine-tuning them for downstream tasks, have demonstrated good performance (Erhan et al., 2010).

The model used in our system is based on the BERT architecture. Bidirectional Encoder Representations from Transformers (BERT) (Devlin et al., 2019) is a transformer-based (Vaswani et al., 2017) pre-trained language model that was created with the objective of fine-tuning a pre-trained model yields better performance. The pretraining phase of BERT includes two tasks. Firstly, Masked Language Modeling (MLM) is where certain words are randomly masked in a sequence. About 15% of the words in a sequence are masked. The model then attempts to predict the masked words. Secondly, Next Sentence Prediction (NSP), where the model has an additional loss function, NSP loss, indicates if the second sequence follows the first one. Around 50% of the inputs are a pair, and they randomly chose the other 50.

Our system uses a multimodal BERT (mBERT) specifically, `bert-base-multilingual-cased` which has been trained on 104 languages with the largest Wikipedia content. Since the size of Wikipedias for different languages varies, exponentially smoothed weighting of the data is performed to under-sample resource-rich languages and over-sample low-resource languages. The model has 12 layers of transformer blocks with 768 hidden dimensions conditioned on 12 self-attention heads. In total, the model has 110M trained parameters.

Preprocessing involves splitting the input document into tokens and generating a compatible in-

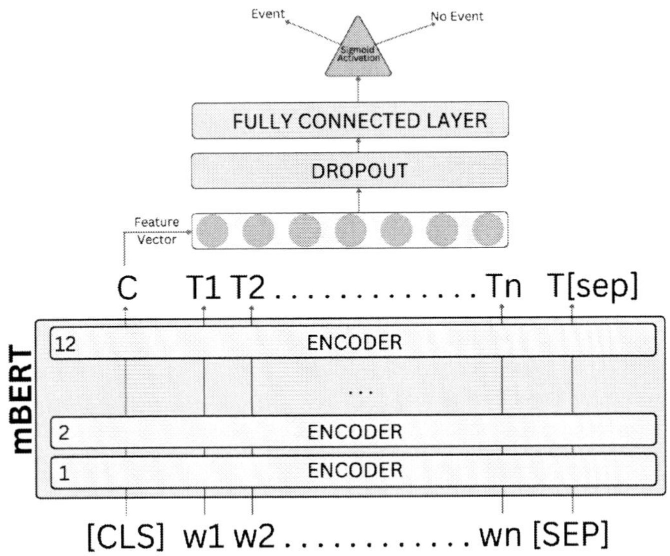

Figure 2: Diagrammatic representation of the model used for the system.

put sequence. Considering that different languages have different vocabularies, the model uses a shared 110k WordPiece vocabulary. For Mandarin texts, a whitespace is inserted around every character before applying the WordPiece tokenizer, making the Mandarin input character tokenized. For other languages, lower casing and accent removal is the first step. This is followed by punctuation splitting and finally whitespace tokenization. Special tokens, [CLS] used to indicate the beginning of the input, [SEP] used to indicate the end of a sequence and [PAD] used for padding sequences to max-length are inserted into the tokenized sequence. Fine-tuning of the model involved stacking a dense layer on top of the BERT output. The dense layer is stacked with a dropout layer. The final layer of the model consists of two neurons with sigmoid activation to predict the binary labels.The features of the [CLS] token are used for classification. A benchmark of 0.62 was used to classify a sample as positive. Fig 2 summarises the model architecture used by our system.

5 Experimental Set-up

The models were developed on Keras[1] (Chollet et al., 2015), and implemented using the transformers library by HuggingFace[2] (Wolf et al., 2019). The model used is `bert-base-multilingual-cased` [3]. We use the AutoTokenizer [4] offered by HuggingFace's transformers library to tokenize our inputs. We experimented with learning rates of 1e-5, 3e-5 and 5e-5 for all models, finding the best results at 3e-5. For all the models, we fixed the max length parameter at 512 tokens and the batch size parameter to 6. The finetuning for the models was performed on Google Colab GPU. We trained each model for 3-4 epochs and found the best results at 4 epochs. The dropout rate during fine-tuning is 0.2. We used the Adam (Kingma and Ba, 2014) optimizer from Keras. The loss function used is binary cross-entropy. The translation was performed using the Google Translation library in Python `googletrans(v3.1.0a0)` [5].

6 Results and Discussion

Table 4 demonstrates the results of our system on the test set for the respective languages. One common pitfall of the system across languages is that it performs better on the majority class and fails to identify the minority class correctly. Our hypothesis is that this happens because despite data augmentation increasing the count of samples, the dataset is still imbalanced. The quality of aug-

[1]https://keras.io/

[2]https://huggingface.co/docs/transformers/index

[3]https://huggingface.co/bert-base-multilingual-cased

[4]https://huggingface.co/transformers/v3.0.2/model_doc/auto.html#autotokenizer

[5]https://pypi.org/project/googletrans/

mented samples depends on the performance of the translation engine which is a decisive factor in our system. Furthermore, we believe that a task like protest event detection involves nuanced references and linguistic nuances may get lost during translation, even more so when the datasets for Hindi, Urdu, Mandarin and Turkish are generated through two cycles of translation.

Our model seems to have performed better on the English dataset indicating that the multilingual BERT has a better contextualizing ability for the *Lingua Franca*, English. The preprocessing process involves removal of accents which might be detrimental to performance of many languages which heavily rely on accents such as Hindi, Urdu, Turkish and Spanish. For example, in Turkish ı and i (non -dotted and dotted) are very different vowels with the phonetic sounds (as in cycle - sīkl) and ē (as in easy - ēzē).

Language	Macro F1 Score
English	0.8062
Spanish	0.6445
Portuguese	0.7302
Hindi	0.5671
Urdu	0.6555
Mandarin	0.7545
Turkish	0.6702

Table 4: The results on the given test set for each of the respective languages given by our system. The metric for evaluation is the Macro F1 score.

7 Conclusion and Future Work

The amounts of publicly available data on the Internet, especially social networks, desire for skillful analysis for the purposes of protest detection. This becomes especially imperative because of the significance of protests in the social, political and economic domains. Our submission in Task 1 of CASE 2022 demonstrated the effective use of Pretrained Language Models (PLMs), specifically multilingual BERT (mBERT) in the binary classification of documents into events or not events. We were also successful in tackling the dearth in training data and class imbalance using data augmentation. We have been able to achieve F1 scores of 0.8062, 0.6445, 0.7302, 0.5671, 0.6555, 0.7545 and 0.6702 in English, Spanish, Portuguese, Hindi, Urdu, Mandarin, and Turkish respectively. In the future, we can deal with class imbalance using class weighing (Suri, 2022). We would also like to experiment with cross-lingual finetuning on a multilingual model by training in one language and testing in another language. We would like to extend this work by using language specific PLMs rather than a multilingual model.

References

Parul Awasthy, Jian Ni, Ken Barker, and Radu Florian. 2021a. IBM MNLP IE at CASE 2021 task 1: Multi-granular and multilingual event detection on protest news. In *Proceedings of the 4th Workshop on Challenges and Applications of Automated Extraction of Socio-political Events from Text (CASE 2021)*, pages 138–146, Online. Association for Computational Linguistics.

Parul Awasthy, Jian Ni, Ken Barker, and Radu Florian. 2021b. IBM MNLP IE at CASE 2021 task 1: Multi-granular and multilingual event detection on protest news. In *Proceedings of the 4th Workshop on Challenges and Applications of Automated Extraction of Socio-political Events from Text (CASE 2021)*, pages 138–146, Online. Association for Computational Linguistics.

Thomas Carothers and Richard. Youngs. 2015. The complexities of global protests.

Furkan Çelik, Tuğberk Dalkılıç, Fatih Beyhan, and Reyyan Yeniterzi. 2021. SU-NLP at CASE 2021 task 1: Protest news detection for English. In *Proceedings of the 4th Workshop on Challenges and Applications of Automated Extraction of Socio-political Events from Text (CASE 2021)*, pages 131–137, Online. Association for Computational Linguistics.

Francois Chollet et al. 2015. Keras.

Jacob Devlin, Ming-Wei Chang, Kenton Lee, and Kristina Toutanova. 2018. Bert: Pre-training of deep bidirectional transformers for language understanding.

Jacob Devlin, Ming-Wei Chang, Kenton Lee, and Kristina Toutanova. 2019. BERT: Pre-training of deep bidirectional transformers for language understanding. In *Proceedings of the 2019 Conference of the North American Chapter of the Association for Computational Linguistics: Human Language Technologies, Volume 1 (Long and Short Papers)*, pages 4171–4186, Minneapolis, Minnesota. Association for Computational Linguistics.

Fatma Elsafoury. 2020. Teargas, water cannons and twitter: A case study on detecting protest repression events in turkey 2013. In *Text2story@ ecir*.

Dumitru Erhan, Yoshua Bengio, Aaron Courville, Pierre-Antoine Manzagol, Pascal Vincent, and Samy Bengio. 2010. Why does unsupervised pre-training help deep learning? *Journal of Machine Learning Research*, pages 625–660.

Xiaocheng Feng, Lifu Huang, Duyu Tang, Heng Ji, Bing Qin, and Ting Liu. 2016. A language-independent neural network for event detection. In *Proceedings of the 54th Annual Meeting of the Association for Computational Linguistics (Volume 2: Short Papers)*, pages 66–71, Berlin, Germany. Association for Computational Linguistics.

Alaeddin Gürel and Emre Emin. 2021. ALEM at CASE 2021 task 1: Multilingual text classification on news articles. In *Proceedings of the 4th Workshop on Challenges and Applications of Automated Extraction of Socio-political Events from Text (CASE 2021)*, pages 147–151, Online. Association for Computational Linguistics.

Daniel Hershcovich, Stella Frank, Heather Lent, Miryam de Lhoneux, Mostafa Abdou, Stephanie Brandl, Emanuele Bugliarello, Laura Cabello Piqueras, Ilias Chalkidis, Ruixiang Cui, Constanza Fierro, Katerina Margatina, Phillip Rust, and Anders Søgaard. 2022. Challenges and strategies in cross-cultural nlp.

Ali Hürriyetoğlu, Osman Mutlu, Fırat Duruşan, Onur Uca, Alaeddin Selçuk Gürel, Benjamin Radford, Yaoyao Dai, Hansi Hettiarachchi, Niklas Stoehr, Tadashi Nomoto, Milena Slavcheva, Francielle Vargas, Aaqib Javid, Fatih Beyhan, and Erdem Yörük. 2022a. Extended multilingual protest news detection - shared task 1, case 2021 and 2022. In *Proceedings of the 5th Workshop on Challenges and Applications of Automated Extraction of Socio-political Events from Text (CASE 2022)*, online. Association for Computational Linguistics (ACL).

Ali Hürriyetoğlu, Osman Mutlu, Farhana Ferdousi Liza, Erdem Yörük, Ritesh Kumar, and Shyam Ratan. 2021. Multilingual protest news detection - shared task 1, case 2021. In *Proceedings of the 4th Workshop on Challenges and Applications of Automated Extraction of Socio-political Events from Text (CASE 2021)*, online. Association for Computational Linguistics (ACL).

Ali Hürriyetoğlu, Hristo Tanev, Vanni Zavarella, Reyyan Yeniterzi, Osman Mutlu, and Erdem Yörük. 2022b. Challenges and applications of automated extraction of socio-political events from text (case 2022): Workshop and shared task report. In *Proceedings of the 4th Workshop on Challenges and Applications of Automated Extraction of Socio-political Events from Text (CASE 2022)*, online. Association for Computational Linguistics (ACL).

Diederik Kingma and Jimmy Ba. 2014. Adam: A method for stochastic optimization. *International Conference on Learning Representations*.

Ashwin Sanjay Neogi, Kirti Anilkumar Garg, Ram Krishn Mishra, and Yogesh K Dwivedi. 2021. Sentiment analysis and classification of indian farmers' protest using twitter data. *International Journal of Information Management Data Insights*, 1(2):100019.

Konstantina Papanikolaou and Harris Papageorgiou. 2020. Protest event analysis: A longitudinal analysis for greece. In *Proceedings of the Workshop on Automated Extraction of Socio-political Events from News 2020*, pages 57–62.

Francesco Re, Daniel Vegh, Dennis Atzenhofer, and Niklas Stoehr. 2021. Team "DaDeFrNi" at CASE 2021 task 1: Document and sentence classification for protest event detection. In *Proceedings of the 4th Workshop on Challenges and Applications of Automated Extraction of Socio-political Events from Text (CASE 2021)*, pages 171–178, Online. Association for Computational Linguistics.

Zachary Steinert-Threlkeld and Jungseock Joo. 2022. Mmchived: Multimodal chile and venezuela protest event data. *Proceedings of the International AAAI Conference on Web and Social Media*, 16(1):1332–1341.

Manan Suri. 2022. PiCkLe at SemEval-2022 task 4: Boosting pre-trained language models with task specific metadata and cost sensitive learning. In *Proceedings of the 16th International Workshop on Semantic Evaluation (SemEval-2022)*, pages 464–472, Seattle, United States. Association for Computational Linguistics.

Hieu Man Duc Trong, Duc-Trong Le, Amir Pouran Ben Veyseh, Thut Nguyn, and Thien Huu Nguyen. 2020. Introducing a new dataset for event detection in cybersecurity texts. In *Proceedings of the 2020 Conference on Empirical Methods in Natural Language Processing (EMNLP)*, pages 5381–5390.

Ashish Vaswani, Noam Shazeer, Niki Parmar, Jakob Uszkoreit, Llion Jones, Aidan N. Gomez, Lukasz Kaiser, and Illia Polosukhin. 2017. Attention is all you need. *CoRR*, abs/1706.03762.

Marc Verhagen, Roser Saurí, Tommaso Caselli, and James Pustejovsky. 2010. SemEval-2010 task 13: TempEval-2. In *Proceedings of the 5th International Workshop on Semantic Evaluation*, pages 57–62, Uppsala, Sweden. Association for Computational Linguistics.

Amir Pouran Ben Veyseh, Minh Van Nguyen, Franck Dernoncourt, and Thien Nguyen. 2022. Minion: a large-scale and diverse dataset for multilingual event detection. In *Proceedings of the 2022 Conference of the North American Chapter of the Association for Computational Linguistics: Human Language Technologies*, pages 2286–2299.

Walker, Christopher, Strassel, Stephanie, Medero, Julie, and Maeda, Kazuaki. 2006. Ace 2005 multilingual training corpus.

Xiaozhi Wang, Ziqi Wang, Xu Han, Wangyi Jiang, Rong Han, Zhiyuan Liu, Juanzi Li, Peng Li, Yankai Lin, and Jie Zhou. 2020. Maven: A massive general domain event detection dataset. *arXiv preprint arXiv:2004.13590*.

Thomas Wolf, Lysandre Debut, Victor Sanh, Julien Chaumond, Clement Delangue, Anthony Moi, Pierric Cistac, Tim Rault, Rémi Louf, Morgan Funtowicz, and Jamie Brew. 2019. Huggingface's transformers: State-of-the-art natural language processing. *CoRR*, abs/1910.03771.

CamPros at CASE 2022 Task 1: Transformer-based Multilingual Protest News Detection

Kumari Neha[†] **Mrinal Anand**[†] **Tushar Mohan**[†]
Arun Balaji Buduru[†] **Ponnurangam Kumaraguru**[‡]
[†]Indraprastha Institute of Information Technology, Delhi
[‡]International Institute of Information Technology, Hyderabad
{nehak,mrinal20222,tushar19393,arunb}@iiitd.ac.in
{pk.guru}@iiit.ac.in

Abstract

Socio-political protests often lead to grave consequences when they occur. The early detection of such protests is very important for taking early precautionary measures. However, the main shortcoming of protest event detection is the scarcity of sufficient training data for specific language categories, which makes it difficult to train data-hungry deep learning models effectively. Therefore, cross-lingual and zero-shot learning models are needed to detect events in various low-resource languages. This paper proposes a multi-lingual cross-document level event detection approach using pre-trained transformer models developed for Shared Task 1 at CASE 2022. The shared task constituted four subtasks for event detection at different granularity levels, i.e., document level to token level, spread over multiple languages (English, Spanish, Portuguese, Turkish, Urdu, and Mandarin). Our system achieves an average F_1 score of 0.73 for document-level event detection tasks. Our approach secured 2nd position for the Hindi language in subtask 1 with an F_1 score of 0.80. While for Spanish, we secure 4th position with an F_1 score of 0.69. Our code is available at `https://github.com/nehapspathak/campros/`.

1 Introduction

The recent technological advancement has led to a continuous flow of information among users in online and offline ecosystems. Users' information may cover various social and political factors, often constituting information related to political violence, crisis, and protests, among others. The automatic detection of such socio-political protests/crisis events from news and social media has become crucial from a peaceful society perspective (Hürriyetoğlu et al., 2020, 2021). Not only does the early detection of such event helps in the deployment of early interventions, but it also helps understand people's perception of a socio-political event.

Event detection aims to identify and extract pertinent data from a text about specific categories of events. It is a crucial information extraction task that unearths and collects information about current and historical occurrences concealed in vast amounts of textual data. The CASE 2022 workshop focuses on detecting socio-political and crisis events in a multi-lingual setting at different granularity levels. This paper focuses on developing models and systems for "Multilingual Protest News Detection - Shared Task 1". In shared task 1, there are 4 subtasks. The aim of subtask 1 is to detect whether a news article contains event information. The news articles are in the form of documents. Hence the subtask looks at whether a given document contains event information. The second subtask focuses on detecting a sentence containing information about a past or ongoing event. The third task focuses on event sentence coreference identification, such as which event sentences in subtask 2 belong to the same event. The fourth and final subtask focuses on event extraction and aims to identify the event triggers and their arguments. We present our proposed system for subtask 1 in this paper.

Researchers have focused on Event extraction from various aspects in the past (Yadav et al., 2021; Lai et al., 2021a). The task presented by (Hürriyetoğlu et al., 2020) focused on event sentence co-reference identification. In the CASE 2021 socio-political and crisis event detection, the training dataset consisted of English, Spanish and Portuguese, while the test data were from English, Spanish, Portuguese, and Hindi (Hürriyetoğlu et al., 2021). In CASE 2022, however, new languages are introduced for multilingual document-level event detection. The workshop allows participants to create models for various subtasks and contrast related approaches. Subtask 1 consists of documents from English, Spanish, and Portuguese for training. For testing, the documents are available

Proceedings of the 5th Workshop on Challenges and Applications of Automated Extraction of Socio-political Events from Text (CASE), pages 169 - 174
December 7-8, 2022 ©2022 Association for Computational Linguistics

in a zero-shot setting, including languages from low-resource languages; Hindi, Turkish, Urdu, and Mandarin. Identifying crisis and socio-political protest detection in a multi-lingual setting makes the Task very complex.

Our work mainly focuses on document-level (subtask 1) event detection in a multilingual setting. Our approach is based on pretrained transformer models and different learning strategies for making predictions. Since the tasks are designed for protests in a multilingual setting, we do not perform language-level pre-processing on our dataset. Our submission for subtask 1 achieved 2nd position in zero-shot Hindi document-level event detection.

The rest of the paper is organized as follows. Section 2 describes the Related literature. The details of the Task and dataset are presented in Section 3. The proposed approach and experimental setup are described in Section 4. Results are described in Section 5, followed by Conclusion in Section 6. We intend to make our code public for further use by the community.

2 Related Work

In natural language processing (NLP), Event detection is a task that detects event triggers/mentions (i.e., the key terms that drive or express an event) and categorizes them into predefined event types (Lai et al., 2021b). The early detection of ongoing and past events exploited feature-based approaches to detect events (Li et al., 2013). However, the early data-driven (Hogenboom et al., 2011), knowledge-driven, and rule-based approaches missed the semantic relationship in the data (Danilova and Popova, 2014). Other early approaches for event detection include machine learning models such as SVM and decision trees (Schrodt et al., 2014). The recent deep learning approaches proposed in the literature (Ahmad et al., 2020) improve event detection; nonetheless, they are not generalizable for low-resource languages. To address the data scarcity problem for low-resource languages, researchers have recently used the pre-trained language model GPT-2 to generate training samples (Veyseh et al., 2021a).

Another less-discovered approach in the Event detection task is Cross-Lingual event detection which proposes model creation for effective performance over different languages (Guzman-Nateras et al., 2022). The work presented in (Lai et al., 2021b) utilizes knowledge from open-domain word sense disambiguation to transfer knowledge into few-shot learning models for Event detection, such that the model can generalize to new event types. To perform Event detection at the document level, the work in (Veyseh et al., 2021b) proposes a dynamic selection of relevant sentences in a document to create improved representation learning. Targeting the issues with scarce availability of low-resource languages, the CASE 2021 subtask introduced the multi-lingual crisis event detection dataset, which focuses on the zero-shot and few-shot detection of protest and crisis event (Hürriyetoğlu et al., 2021).

Language	**Label 1**	**Label 0**	**Total**
English (En)	$1,912$	$7,412$	$9,324$
Spanish (Es)	131	869	$1,000$
Portuguese (pt)	197	$1,290$	$1,487$

Table 1: Training Data available for training for Shared Task 1, subtask 1: Document-level crisis event prediction.

Language	**Documents**
English	$3,871$
Hindi	268
Mandarin	300
Spanish	400
Portuguese	671
Turkish	300
Urdu	299

Table 2: Test Data for testing for Shared Task 1, subtask 1: Document-level crisis event prediction.

3 Data

The dataset used in CASE 2022 has been created in the process presented in (Hürriyetoğlu et al., 2022). For subtask 1, the new data contains documents with and without protest events. The data provided for training are highly imbalanced and provided for only 3 languages. The testing data contains 7 languages, with documents from additional 4 languages apart from training data. Table 1 provides the details of the training data provided in the shared task. Table 2 presents the test data for the Task. Given that no training data is present for Hindi, Mandarin, Turkish and Urdu, the task of document event detection becomes a zero-shot classification problem.

Language	Model	macro-F1
English	mBERT+Softmax	0.76
	XLM-Roberta+LSTM	0.74
	XLM-Roberta+Sigmoid	**0.77**
	XLM-Roberta+Sigmoid (U)	0.72
Spanish	**mBERT+Softmax**	**0.69**
	XLM-Roberta+LSTM	0.63
	XLM-Roberta+Sigmoid	0.64
	XLM-Roberta+Sigmoid (U)	0.63
Portuguese	mBERT+Softmax	0.68
	XLM-Roberta+LSTM	0.71
	XLM-Roberta+Sigmoid	**0.76**
	XLM-Roberta+Sigmoid (U)	0.72

Table 3: Test results for English, Spanish and Portuguese documents, as reported in the shared task. The training data were present for the above 3 languages. U represents a model with under-sampled data.

3.1 Data proprocessing

Since we experiment with mBERT (cased) and other sentence-based embeddings, we do not lowercase our document corpus before training. We also do not conduct language-specific pre-processing to keep the preprocessing step language agnostic. However, we removed any URLs, and a single occurrence replaced repeated symbols. We also removed any extra spaces present in the data.

4 Methodology

The transformer-based models have recently gained success in various multilingual NLP tasks such as offensive content detection (Arango et al., 2022) and various zero-shot cross-lingual tasks (Kuo and Chen, 2022). We experiment with different multilingual models and analyze how the different models perform on the downstream task of document classification in subtask 1. We design the document classification problem as a sequence classification problem (Hettiarachchi et al., 2021; Gürel and Emin, 2021).

In our approach, we use different transformer models including XLM-Roberta (Conneau et al., 2020), mBERT (Devlin et al., 2018) and encoder-decoder based LASER (Artetxe and Schwenk, 2019) to generate embedding from the documents. We experiment with different layers on top of the multi-lingual sentence embedding. Our preliminary analysis found that transformer-based XLM-Roberta with a sigmoid layer outperformed other models in the macro-F1 score. Therefore, in our approach, we propose the XLM-Roberta model with a sigmoid classification layer for event prediction. XLM-Roberta is pre-trained on unlabeled Wikipedia text and CommonCrawl Corpus of 100 languages. The XLM-Roberta has a vocabulary size of $25,000$ and uses SentencePiece tokenizer (Kudo and Richardson, 2018). We fine-tuned the model for our task with the training data provided. The training data was highly imbalanced. However, oversampling and under-sampling methods did not provide any marginal improvement in the model's output as per our experiments.

4.1 XLM-Roberta Based Document Classification Models

XLM-Roberta belongs to an unsupervised representation learning framework as it does not use cross-lingual resources (Conneau et al., 2020). XLM-Roberta has L = 12 transformers, with H = 768 attention heads with A = 12, and 270M parameters. The maximum token size for input for XLM-Roberta is 512 tokens. The token size of 512 is less for creating document-level creation, as a lot of information might not be captured. However, breaking the sentences into 512-length tokens might lead to an incorrect labeling process for different sentence splits (Gürel and Emin, 2021). Due to the limitation of our system, our final approach uses a 256-length token for document embedding creation. The learning rate was $2.75e^{-05}$, the batch size for training was 32, and the training was done for 20 epochs. The total training time taken for the XLM-Robert-based model was approximately 2 hours. Since we use the Sigmoid layer on the top of XLM-Roberta, the final decision boundary for 0/1 was taken based on the probability of 0.6 for

Language	Model	macro-F1
Hindi	mBERT+Softmax	0.71
	XLM-Roberta+LSTM	0.75
	XLM-Roberta+Sigmoid	**0.80**
	XLM-Roberta+Sigmoid (U)	0.77
Turkish	mBERT+Softmax	0.69
	XLM-Roberta+LSTM	0.70
	XLM-Roberta+Sigmoid	**0.74**
	XLM-Roberta+Sigmoid (U)	0.69
Urdu	mBERT+Softmax	0.67
	XLM-Roberta+LSTM	0.72
	XLM-Roberta+Sigmoid	0.71
	XLM-Roberta+Sigmoid (U)	**0.73**
Mandarin	**mBERT+Softmax**	**0.75**
	XLM-Roberta+LSTM	0.71
	XLM-Roberta+Sigmoid	0.75
	XLM-Roberta+Sigmoid (U)	0.73

Table 4: Test results for Hindi, Mandarin, Turkish and Urdu documents, as reported in the shared task. Training data was not provided for the above language. Hence classification is done in a zero-shot setting.

all cases.

4.2 Experimental setup

For training all models, we use the Nvidia RTX 3090 GPU system with an installed Cuda version of 11.3. For training, we combined the training data from the 3 languages, English, Spanish, and Portuguese, as shown in Table 1. We performed at a 90:10 split for training and testing, respectively. The split was done randomly but stayed the same for all the experiments with models to obtain the result on the same set of datasets. The score we demonstrated for document-level classification was the F1-macro metric, which was selected as an evaluation metric for our models. We performed experiments with different epoch numbers and batch sizes with the same experimental setup.

4.3 Baselines

We experimented with different multilingual models such as XLM-Roberta (Conneau et al., 2020), mBERT (Devlin et al., 2018) and LASER (Artetxe and Schwenk, 2019) to obtain predictions. The performance for LASER was the worst in our case. Hence, we do not report the results from LASER-based models.

XLM-Roberta+Softmax (under-sampling): In this approach, before feeding the data into the model, we under-sample the majority class (i.e., a class with label 0 representing a no-event class) such that we have an equal number of documents for both label 0 and label 1 class. We under-sample the training data constituting the combination of documents from all the 3 languages. After this, we split the data into the ratio of 90:10 and fed it to the model with XLM-Roberta with softmax as the classification layer. The number of epochs for training is set to 20, and the batch size is taken as 32.

XLM-Roberta+LSTM: After we have created embedding using XLM-Roberta, we feed the embedding into long short-term memory (LSTM) layers to train the model. We use the sigmoid layer for the classification of events.

mBERT+Softmax: We also tried mBERT to create embedding, which is the multilingual BERT embedding for our experiment. The BERT tokenizer is based on wordpiece tokenizer. We used softmax as a classification layer and trained the model.

5 Results

In this section, we demonstrate and elaborate on the results from different models for each language. Table 3 shows the result for English, Spanish and Portuguese language, for which we had training data available. The best model for English came out to be XLM-Roberta+Sigmoid model, with a macro-F1 score of 0.77. The second best model for English was mBERT+Softmax model, with a macro-

F1 score of 0.76. While XLM-Roberta+LSTM showed macro-F1 score of 0.74, the undersampled majority class for XLM-Roberta+Sigmoid produced the worst result, with a macro-F1 score of 0.72. For Spanish, however, our proposed framework of XLM-Roberta+Sigmoid model was outperformed by mBERT+Softmax, with macro-F1 of 0.69. XLM-Roberta+Sigmoid remained the second best model with macro-F1 score of 0.64. The result for XLM-Roberta+LSTM and undersampled XLM-Roberta+Sigmoid came as 0.63. In Portuguese, our proposed framework outperformed all other baselines, with macro-F1 score of 0.76. The second best model for Portuguese was undersampled XLM-Roberta+Sigmoid, with macro-F1 score of 0.72. The macro-F1 score for XLM-Roberta+LSTM came as 0.71, while mBERT+Softmax performed worst for the Portuguese document classification task. Hence, we found that XLM-Roberta with the Sigmoid layer outperformed for English and Portuguese tasks; however, the best model for Spanish was multilingual BERT with the softmax layer.

Table 4 presents the results for the zero-shot classification for the respective languages. Our best model, the XLM-Roberta+Sigmoid model, obtained a macro-F1 score of 0.80 for Hindi and secured 2nd in the shared task. The second best model for zero-shot Hindi document classification was undersampled XLM-Roberta+Sigmoid with a macro-F1 score of 0.77. The macro-F1 score for XLM-Roberta+LSTM model was 0.75. We found that for Hindi, mBERT+Softmax produced the worst results, with macro-F1 score of 0.71. For Turkish, the best model also came out as XLM-Roberta+Sigmoid, with macro-F1 as 0.74. Among the baselines, the XLM-Roberta+LSTM model produced a macro-F1 score of 0.70, while the macro-F1 score for both mBERT+Softmax and undersampled XLM-Roberta+Sigmoid came as 0.69. For the Urdu language, XLM-Roberta+LSTM marginally outperformed the proposed model, with a macro-F1 score of 0.72. The macro-F1 score for the proposed XLM-Roberta+Sigmoid came as 0.71. The worst model for Urdu was mBERT+Softmax, with a macro-F1 score of 0.67. In contrast, the best model for the Urdu language was the undersampled XLM-Roberta+Sigmoid model with a macro-F1 score of 0.73. For Mandarin, however, the best F1-score was obtained from both the mBERT+Softmax model and the proposed XLM-Roberta+Sigmoid model, with a marginal difference on the macro-F1 score of 0.75. The undersampled XLM-Roberta+Sigmoid produced a macro-F1 score of 0.73, while the XLM-Roberta+LSTM model produced a macro-F1 score of 0.71.

6 Conclusion

This paper describes our approaches for CASE@EMNLP 2022: Shared Task on Socio-political and Crisis Events Detection in multilingual settings. We explored various multilingual and zero-shot approaches and showed results across the languages in subtask 1. We propose XLM-Roberta with a Sigmoid layer for classifying crisis events in zero-shot and low-resource language settings. Our system achieved an average F1 score of 0.73. Among the given languages, our proposed approach was able to secure 2nd place in the Hindi document event classification task. While comparing with our approach, the multilingual Bert with softmax layer obtained better results for Spanish and Mandarin, with the result for Spanish securing the 4th spot in the shared task.

Acknowledgements

Thank you to the Precog Research Group for giving us constructive feedback, the IIIT Delhi and IIIT Hyderabad IT support teams for their assistance, and anonymous reviewers for their constructive feedback.

References

Faizan Ahmad, Ahmed Abbasi, Brent Kitchens, Donald A Adjeroh, and Daniel Zeng. 2020. Deep learning for adverse event detection from web search. *IEEE Transactions on Knowledge and Data Engineering*.

Aymé Arango, Jorge Pérez, Bárbara Poblete, Valentina Proust, and Magdalena Saldaña. 2022. Multilingual resources for offensive language detection. *WOAH 2022*, page 122.

Mikel Artetxe and Holger Schwenk. 2019. Massively multilingual sentence embeddings for zero-shot cross-lingual transfer and beyond. *Transactions of the Association for Computational Linguistics*, 7:597–610.

Alexis Conneau, Kartikay Khandelwal, Naman Goyal, Vishrav Chaudhary, Guillaume Wenzek, Francisco Guzmán, Edouard Grave, Myle Ott, Luke Zettlemoyer, and Veselin Stoyanov. 2020. Unsupervised cross-lingual representation learning at scale. In *Proceedings of the 58th Annual Meeting of the Association for Computational Linguistics*, pages 8440–8451, Online. Association for Computational Linguistics.

Vera Danilova and Svetlana Popova. 2014. Socio-political event extraction using a rule-based approach. In *OTM Confederated International Conferences" On the Move to Meaningful Internet Systems"*, pages 537–546. Springer.

Jacob Devlin, Ming-Wei Chang, Kenton Lee, and Kristina Toutanova. 2018. Bert: Pre-training of deep bidirectional transformers for language understanding. *arXiv preprint arXiv:1810.04805*.

Alaeddin Gürel and Emre Emin. 2021. Alem at case 2021 task 1: Multilingual text classification on news articles. In *Proceedings of the 4th Workshop on Challenges and Applications of Automated Extraction of Socio-political Events from Text (CASE 2021)*, pages 147–151.

Luis Guzman-Nateras, Minh Van Nguyen, and Thien Nguyen. 2022. Cross-lingual event detection via optimized adversarial training. In *Proceedings of the 2022 Conference of the North American Chapter of the Association for Computational Linguistics: Human Language Technologies*, pages 5588–5599.

Hansi Hettiarachchi, Mariam Adedoyin-Olowe, Jagdev Bhogal, and Mohamed Medhat Gaber. 2021. Daai at case 2021 task 1: Transformer-based multilingual socio-political and crisis event detection. In *Proceedings of the 4th Workshop on Challenges and Applications of Automated Extraction of Socio-political Events from Text (CASE 2021)*, pages 120–130.

Frederik Hogenboom, Flavius Frasincar, Uzay Kaymak, and Franciska De Jong. 2011. An overview of event extraction from text. *DeRiVE@ ISWC*, pages 48–57.

Ali Hürriyetoğlu, Osman Mutlu, Fırat Duruşan, Onur Uca, Alaeddin Selçuk Gürel, Benjamin Radford, Yaoyao Dai, Hansi Hettiarachchi, Niklas Stoehr, Tadashi Nomoto, Milena Slavcheva, Francielle Vargas, Aaqib Javid, Fatih Beyhan, and Erdem Yörük. 2022. Extended multilingual protest news detection - shared task 1, case 2021 and 2022. In *Proceedings of the 5th Workshop on Challenges and Applications of Automated Extraction of Socio-political Events from Text (CASE 2022)*, online. Association for Computational Linguistics (ACL).

Ali Hürriyetoğlu, Osman Mutlu, Erdem Yörük, Farhana Ferdousi Liza, Ritesh Kumar, and Shyam Ratan. 2021. Multilingual protest news detection - shared task 1, CASE 2021. In *Proceedings of the 4th Workshop on Challenges and Applications of Automated Extraction of Socio-political Events from Text (CASE 2021)*, pages 79–91, Online. Association for Computational Linguistics.

Ali Hürriyetoğlu, Vanni Zavarella, Hristo Tanev, Erdem Yörük, Ali Safaya, and Osman Mutlu. 2020. Automated extraction of socio-political events from news (aespen): Workshop and shared task report. In *Proceedings of the Workshop on Automated Extraction of Socio-political Events from News 2020*, pages 1–6.

Taku Kudo and John Richardson. 2018. Sentencepiece: A simple and language independent subword tokenizer and detokenizer for neural text processing. In *Proceedings of the 2018 Conference on Empirical Methods in Natural Language Processing: System Demonstrations*, pages 66–71.

Chia-Chih Kuo and Kuan-Yu Chen. 2022. Toward zero-shot and zero-resource multilingual question answering. *IEEE Access*.

Viet Dac Lai, Minh Van Nguyen, Heidi Kaufman, and Thien Huu Nguyen. 2021a. Event extraction from historical texts: A new dataset for black rebellions. In *Findings of the Association for Computational Linguistics: ACL-IJCNLP 2021*, pages 2390–2400, Online. Association for Computational Linguistics.

Viet Dac Lai, Minh Van Nguyen, Thien Huu Nguyen, and Franck Dernoncourt. 2021b. Graph learning regularization and transfer learning for few-shot event detection. In *Proceedings of the 44th International ACM SIGIR Conference on Research and Development in Information Retrieval*, pages 2172–2176.

Qi Li, Heng Ji, and Liang Huang. 2013. Joint event extraction via structured prediction with global features. In *Proceedings of the 51st Annual Meeting of the Association for Computational Linguistics (Volume 1: Long Papers)*, pages 73–82.

Philip A Schrodt, John Beieler, and Muhammed Idris. 2014. Three'sa charm?: Open event data coding with el: Diablo, petrarch, and the open event data alliance. In *ISA Annual Convention*. Citeseer.

Amir Pouran Ben Veyseh, Viet Lai, Franck Dernoncourt, and Thien Huu Nguyen. 2021a. Unleash gpt-2 power for event detection. In *Proceedings of the 59th Annual Meeting of the Association for Computational Linguistics and the 11th International Joint Conference on Natural Language Processing (Volume 1: Long Papers)*, pages 6271–6282.

Amir Pouran Ben Veyseh, Minh Van Nguyen, Nghia Ngo Trung, Bonan Min, and Thien Huu Nguyen. 2021b. Modeling document-level context for event detection via important context selection. In *Proceedings of the 2021 Conference on Empirical Methods in Natural Language Processing*, pages 5403–5413.

Nishant Yadav, Nicholas Monath, Rico Angell, and Andrew McCallum. 2021. Event and entity coreference using trees to encode uncertainty in joint decisions. In *Proceedings of the Fourth Workshop on Computational Models of Reference, Anaphora and Coreference*, pages 100–110, Punta Cana, Dominican Republic. Association for Computational Linguistics.

ARC-NLP at CASE 2022 Task 1: Ensemble Learning for Multilingual Protest Event Detection

Umitcan Sahin, Oguzhan Ozcelik, Izzet Emre Kucukkaya, Cagri Toraman
{ucsahin, ogozcelik, ekucukkaya, ctoraman}@aselsan.com.tr
Aselsan Research Center, Ankara, Turkey

Abstract

Automated socio-political protest event detection is a challenging task when multiple languages are considered. In CASE 2022 Task 1, we propose ensemble learning methods for multilingual protest event detection in four subtasks with different granularity levels from document-level to entity-level. We develop an ensemble of fine-tuned Transformer-based language models, along with a post-processing step to regularize the predictions of our ensembles. Our approach places the first place in 6 out of 16 leaderboards organized in seven languages including English, Mandarin, and Turkish.

1 Introduction

Socio-political protest events are organized to protest against various decision and policy makers. An example is the social movement of Arab Springs and Internet hacktivism. The detection of socio-political protest events in news articles is a challenging task when news are reported in multiple languages.

The shared task of Multilingual Protest News Detection (Hürriyetoğlu et al., 2022; Hürriyetoğlu et al., 2020), organized in the workshop of Challenges and Applications of Automated Extraction of Socio-political Events from Text (CASE) that is held at the 2022 Conference on Empirical Methods in Natural Language Processing (EMNLP), targets automated detection of protest events considering language generalization of the event information collection systems. The shared task includes four subtasks:

Subtask 1, Protest Document Classification: The subtask aims to detect if news articles contain past or ongoing protest events. There are three source languages; English, Spanish, and Portuguese. In addition, there are seven target languages including English, Turkish, and Mandarin. The granularity of classification is document-level. The prediction output is binary (protest exists or not).

Subtask 2, Protest Sentence Classification: The subtask aims to detect if the news sentences contain protest events. There are three source and target languages; English, Spanish, and Portuguese. The granularity of classification is sentence-level. The prediction output is binary.

Subtask 3, Protest Event Sentence Coreference Identification: The subtask aims to identify which protest sentences are about the same event. There are three source and target languages; English, Spanish, and Portuguese. The granularity of grouping is sentence-level. The prediction output is clusters of protest event sentences.

Subtask 4, Protest Event Extraction: The subtask aims to extract or label protest entity spans such as triggers and participants. There are three source and target languages; English, Spanish, and Portuguese. The granularity of classification is word span-level. The prediction output is entity labels.

The ARC-NLP team participated in all subtasks of Multilingual Protest News Detection. Our main approach for all subtasks is based on two factors. First, we utilize Transformer-based language models that are pretrained on specific languages, e.g. RoBERTa (Liu et al., 2019), and also multilingual corpus, e.g. mDeBERTa (He et al., 2021a). Second, we apply ensemble learning and post-processing methods to obtain better and smoother predictions, considering that large language models are stochastic (Bender et al., 2021). Besides, we apply customized methods for each subtask according to the subtask's definition and requirements. Our approach places the first place in 6 out of 16 leaderboards organized in seven languages including English, Mandarın, and Turkish. In the following sections, we present our detailed solutions and leaderboard results for all subtasks of multilingual protest event detection.

Proceedings of the 5th Workshop on Challenges and Applications of Automated Extraction of Socio-political Events from Text (CASE), pages 175 - 183
December 7-8, 2022

Language	Train	Test
English (EN)	9,324	3,871
Spanish (ES)	1,000	400
Portuguese (PR)	1,487	671
Hindi (HI)	-	268
Turkish (TR)	-	300
Mandarin (MA)	-	300
Urdu (UR)	-	299

Table 1: The number of instances in **Subtask 1.**

2 Subtask 1: Protest Document Classification

2.1 Dataset

The dataset in Subtask 1 consists of news documents collected in various languages, and corresponding protest labels (positive or negative). The collection and annotation processes are described in (Hürriyetoğlu et al., 2021) for the 2021 data, and in (Hürriyetoğlu et al., 2020) for the 2022 data. The number of instances is given for 2022 in Table 1. While English, Spanish, and Portuguese have training samples that are labeled, the other languages only have unlabeled test samples (i.e. zero-shot evaluation). In Subtask 1, the class labels are unbalanced, that is, there are more negative samples (no past or ongoing event in document) than positive ones.

2.2 Methods

We focus on ensemble learning of multilingual or monolingual language models. We also use data processing techniques, such as data translation to improve our models further. In Table 2, we share our best performing three submissions for each language for Subtask 1 (S1), which are based on four methods[1]:

Ensemble of multilingual language models (S1-multi): English, Spanish, and Portuguese have labeled data that can be used in training models, but not other languages. Therefore, we combine the labeled samples from English, Spanish, and Portuguese to construct the training data (i.e., source). We rely on a Transformer-based multilingual model, namely mDeBERTa (He et al., 2021c), which is the multilingual version of DeBERTa. It is pre-trained with the 2.5T CC100 multilingual dataset. In Subtask 1, we use the mDeBERTa V3 base model that has 12 layers and a hidden size of 768. We use the HuggingFace's Pytorch implementation of this model (He et al., 2021b), the corresponding tokenizer with max length 512, extra padding and truncation. We set epoch number to 5 and use constant learning rate $2e-5$.

We train five *split* mDeBERTa models, each with 80% of the training data randomly selected from the entire training data with replacement. Furthermore, we train a single *full* mDeBERTa model using the entire training data. While **S1-multi-5** in Table 2 uses the predictions of the five split models, **S1-multi-6** uses the predictions of the five split models and one full model together. Moreover, we follow two approaches to ensemble the models' predictions into final test labels. First, we take the majority voting of the five split models, called **M1**. Second, we compute the average softmax probabilities of the five split models and one full model for each class in test samples, called **M2**. The classes with the highest probabilities are selected for final test labels.

Ensemble of monolingual language models (S1-mono): We use Transformer-based monolingual models, namely RoBERTa (Liu et al., 2019) and DeBERTa (He et al., 2021c) for English[2], BETO (Cañete et al., 2020) for Spanish, and BERTimbau (Souza et al., 2020) for Portuguese. All monolingual models are their base versions, and HuggingFace's Pytorch implementations are used. We fine-tune these models with the samples from their respective languages for document classification. Other notations (ensemble size, majority method, and hyperparameters) are the same as in multilingual models.

Ensemble of monolingual language models with Target Translation (S1-mono-TT): For zero-shot evaluation, we translate each target test language with no training instances (Spanish, Hindi, Turkish, Mandarin, and Urdu) to a source language (English) using Google's translation[3]. **mono-TT-5** in Table 2 consists of five DeBERTa models (trained with 80% of train data). The predictions are computed from the translated test data and ensembled together using M1 majority voting. In addition, **mono-TT-6** consists of five DeBERTa models and one full DeBERTa model whose predictions are computed on the translated test data using M2 majority voting. We use the same hyperparameters and settings as in previous setups.

[1]We did not submit all versions of the following methods for each language. Instead, we submitted best performing three models in our internal experiments for each language.

[2]We mostly observe that DeBERTa and mDeBERTa have better performances than RoBERTa and XLM-R in our internal experiments.

[3]https://translate.google.com

Method	Target Lang.	Train data (Source)	Backbone Models	Majority	Score
S1-mono-5	EN	EN	RoBERTa (x5 split)	M1	**80.74**
S1-mono-6		EN	RoBERTa (x5 split + x1 full)	M2	80.67
S1-multi-6		EN+ES+PR	mDeBERTa (x5 split + x1 full)	M2	80.03
S1-multi-5	PR	EN+ES+PR	mDeBERTa (x5 split)	M1	**79.85**
S1-multi-6		EN+ES+PR	mDeBERTa (x5 split + x1 full)	M2	78.73
S1-mono-6		PR	BERTimbau (x5 split + x1 full)	M2	77.96
S1-mono-TT-6	ES_{trans}^{EN}	EN	DeBERTa (x5 split + x1 full)	M2	**69.44**
S1-mono-6	ES	ES	BETO (x5 split + x1 full)	M2	68.75
S1-multi-6		EN+ES+PR	mDeBERTa (x5 split + x1 full)	M2	67.74
S1-multi-5	HI	EN+ES+PR	mDeBERTa (x5 split)	M1	**80.08**
S1-multi-6		EN+ES+PR	mDeBERTa (x5 split + x1 full)	M2	78.96
S1-mono-TT-6	HI_{trans}^{EN}	EN	DeBERTa (x5 split + x1 full)	M2	75.63
S1-mono-ST-6	TR	EN_{trans}^{TR}	BERTurk-128k (x5 split + x1 full)	M2	**84.06**
S1-mono-ST-5			BERTurk-128k (x5 split)	M1	83.27
S1-mono-TT-6	TR_{trans}^{EN}	EN	DeBERTa (x5 split + x1 full)	M2	82.89
S1-mono-TT-5	MA_{trans}^{EN}	EN	DeBERTa (x5 split)	M1	**83.39**
S1-mono-TT-6		EN	DeBERTa (x5 split + x1 full)	M2	83.23
S1-multi-6	MA	EN+ES+PR	mDeBERTa (x5 split + x1 full)	M2	83.06
S1-mono-TT-5	UR_{trans}^{EN}	EN	DeBERTa (x5 split)	M1	**77.99**
S1-mono-TT-6		EN	DeBERTa (x5 split + x1 full)	M2	77.48
S1-multi-6	UR	EN+ES+PR	mDeBERTa (x5 split + x1 full)	M2	76.15

Table 2: Our submitted models for **Subtask 1 (S1), Document Classification**. $\mathrm{L1}_{trans}^{L_2}$ means that language L_1 is translated to language L_2. Split models are trained with randomly selected 80% of the train data and full models with all train data. Highest F1-macro scores are given in bold.

Ensemble of monolingual language models with Source Translation (S1-mono-ST): We translate a source language (English training samples) to a target language with no training data (Turkish) using Google's translation tool. We use Transformer-based monolingual BERTurk[4], which is trained with translated Turkish data. **mono-ST-5** in Table 2 consist of five split BERTurk models (trained with 80% of the training data) and final test labels are computed on the original Turkish test data using M1 majority voting. Similarly, **mono-ST-6** consists of five split BERTurk models and one full BERTurk model (trained with the entire training data) together, and final test labels are computed on the original Turkish test data using M2 majority voting. We use the same hyper-parameter and tokenizer settings as in previous setups.

2.3 Leaderboard Results

Our best performing model for each language in Subtask 1 is given in Table 3 along with best competitor scores in 2022 and our rankings. We rank the first place in Turkish and Mandarin, second place in Portuguese, and third place in Urdu.

[4]https://huggingface.co/dbmdz/bert-base-turkish-128k-cased

3 Subtask 2: Protest Sentence Classification

3.1 Dataset

The dataset in Subtask 2 consists of news sentences and corresponding protest labels (positive or negative) in English, Spanish, and Portuguese. The collection and annotations are described in (Hürriyetoğlu et al., 2021) for the 2021 data. There is no new data provided in 2022. The number of examples for each language are given in Table 4. The problem of unbalanced class label distributions is also present in this task.

3.2 Methods

We mainly focus on multilingual and monolingual language models as in Subtask 1. In Table 5, we share our best performing two methods for each language for Subtask 2 (S2), which are based on two methods[5]:

Ensemble of multilingual language models (S2-multi): We combine the labeled instances from English, Spanish, and Portuguese to construct the training data (source). We utilize multilingual language models, namely mDeBERTa (He et al., 2021c), in the subtask. We use the corresponding tokenizer with max length 128, extra padding and truncation. We set epoch number to 5 and use

[5]We follow a similar approach to Subtask 1 in our internal experiments for Subtask 2.

Lang.	Method	Our score	Best Competitor Score 2022	Rank 2022
EN	S1-mono-5	80.74	**82.49**	4
PR	S1-multi-5	79.85	**80.07**	2
ES	S1-mono-TT-6	69.44	**74.96**	5
HI	S1-multi-5	80.08	**80.78**	4
TR	S1-mono-ST-6	**84.06**	82.91	1
MA	S1-mono-TT-5	**83.39**	83.06	1
UR	S1-mono-TT-5	77.99	**79.71**	3

Table 3: The 2022 leaderboard scores for **Subtask 1, Document Classification**.

Language	Train	Test
English (EN)	22,825	1,290
Spanish (ES)	2,741	686
Portuguese (PR)	1,182	1,445

Table 4: The number of instances in **Subtask 2**.

constant learning rate $2e-5$ throughout the training. We train five *split* mDeBERTa models, each with 80% of the training data randomly selected from the entire training data with replacement. Furthermore, we train a single *full* mDeBERTa model using the entire training data. While *S2-multi-5* uses the predictions of the five split models, *S2-multi-6* uses the predictions of the five split models and one full model together. The meanings of M1 and M2 are also the same as in Subtask 1.

Ensemble of monolingual language models (S2-mono): Our second method utilizes monolingual language models. In Subtask 2, we use RoBERTa (Liu et al., 2019) for English. The model is the base version. We use HuggingFace's pytorch implementation, the corresponding tokenizers with max length 128, extra padding and truncation. We set epoch number to 10 and use constant learning rate $2e-5$. *S2-mono-6* includes five split models (trained with the 80% of training data) and one full model (trained with the entire training data) together, whose predictions are ensembled using the M2 majority voting.

3.3 Leaderboard Results

Our best performing model for each language in Subtask 2 is reported in Table 6 along with best competitor scores in both 2021 and 2022, and our rankings. We rank the third place in English and Spanish in 2022.

4 Subtask 3: Event Sentence Coreference Identification

4.1 Dataset

The dataset in Subtask 3 consists of news sentences and corresponding clusters in three different languages (English, Spanish, and Portuguese). The statistics of the dataset are given in Table 7. The numbers of instances are smaller than those of previous subtasks. The number of instances in English is significantly higher than those of other languages. The number of clusters also varies in the dataset.

4.2 Methods

Our approach for Subtask 3 is based on ensemble learning of hierarchical clustering. In order to cluster the sentences, we calculate the distance between two sentences, and then feed this distance score to a hierarchical clustering algorithm.

We construct pairs of sentences from the dataset by labeling them according to existing clustering labels. For instance, assume that there are three sentences with numbers 20, 21, and 22 in two clusters as [[20],[21, 22]]. We then construct the sentence pairs (21, 22) as positive, and (20, 21) and (20, 22) as negative pairs. We calculate the Cosine distance similarity between these sentence pairs for obtaining training instances. The training of sentence pairs is a binary classification task (positive or negative) with binary cross-entropy loss. The output softmax probability is used as distance score.

After training and obtaining a distance similarity model, we apply hierarchical or agglomerative clustering algorithm using the distance scores. For linking two clusters, we use single linkage, where the distance between nearest points in two clusters is considered.

Based on this clustering approach, we apply ensemble learning as in previous subtasks. Since there are very small number of training instances in Spanish and Portuguese training datasets, we exploit translating target languages to English, and merging the instances of all languages in multilingual models. In Table 8, we share our best performing submissions for each language for Subtask 3 (S3), which are based on four methods[6]:

[6] We also tried different methods such as BERTopic (Grootendorst, 2022) and SBERT (Reimers and Gurevych, 2019),

Method	Target Lang.	Train data (Source)	Backbone Models	Majority	Score
S2-multi-6	EN	EN+ES+PR	mDeBERTa (x5 split + x1 full)	M2	**83.77**
S2-mono-6		EN	RoBERTa (x5 split + x1 full)	M2	80.68
S2-multi-5	PR	EN+ES+PR	mDeBERTa (x5 split)	M1	**86.53**
S2-multi-6		EN+ES+PR	mDeBERTa (x5 split + x1 full)	M2	86.11
S2-multi-6	ES	EN+ES+PR	mDeBERTa (x5 split + x1 full)	M2	**87.20**
S2-multi-5		EN+ES+PR	mDeBERTa (x5 split)	M1	85.16

Table 5: Our submitted models for **Subtask 2 (S2), Sentence Classification**. Split models are trained with randomly selected 80% of the train data and full models with all train data. Highest F1-macro scores are given in bold.

Lang.	Method	Our score	Best Competitor Score		Rank	
			2021	2022	2021	2022
EN	S2-multi-6	83.77	85.32(Hu and Stoehr, 2021)	**85.93**	3	3
PR	S2-multi-5	86.53	88.47(Awasthy et al., 2021)	**89.67**	4	4
ES	S2-multi-6	87.20	88.61(Awasthy et al., 2021)	**88.78**	2	3

Table 6: The 2021 and 2022 leaderboard scores for **Subtask 2, Sentence Classification**.

Language	Train	Test
English (EN)	596	100
Spanish (ES)	21	40
Portuguese (PR)	11	40

Table 7: The number of instances in **Subtask 3.**

Multilingual language model with hierarchical clustering (S3-multi-1): We merge the original instances from English, Spanish, and Portuguese to construct the training data. We apply distance model and hierarchical clustering as explained above. For distance model, we rely on a Transformer-based multilingual model, namely XLM-R (Conneau et al., 2020). In Subtask 3 (S3), we train only a single (1) multilingual model without using ensembles (*S3-multi-1*). We use the XLM-R base model that has 12 layers and a hidden size of 768. We use the HuggingFace's Pytorch implementation of this model (He et al., 2021b), the corresponding tokenizer with max length 512, extra padding and truncation. We set epoch number to 20 and use constant learning rate $2e-5$. We use the SciPy implementation for hierarchical clustering. We set the hierarchical clustering threshold as 0.65.

Ensemble of monolingual language models with hierarchical clustering and Source Translation (S3-mono-ST): We translate Spanish and Portuguese to English, and then merge all instances. The test data is also translated to English. We apply distance model and hierarchical clustering as explained above. For distance model, we train a monolingual language model, namely RoBERTa (Liu et al., 2019). We use the RoBERTa base model that has 12 layers and a hidden size of 768. The hyperparameters and other settings are the same as in the previous method.

We train five *split* RoBERTa models, each with 80% of the training data randomly selected from the entire training data with replacement. Furthermore, we train a single *full* RoBERTa model using the entire training data. **S3-mono-ST-6** in Table 8 uses the predictions of the five split models and one full model together. Moreover, we apply the following approach to ensemble the models' predictions into final test labels. The algorithm we are using is based on the getting connected components on a graph after getting rid of the low probability connections. To do so, the binary similarity matrix that is symmetric is calculated based on the pairs in clusters for each clustering model. After that, we get element-wise average of the similarity matrices to get a single matrix of probabilities. A pre-determined threshold (0.60) is then applied to remove the low probability scores, so that we obtain a final similarity matrix that contains binary decisions for sentence pairs.

Ensemble of monolingual language models with hierarchical clustering and Target Translated (S3-mono-TT): We use only English instances for training a monolingual language model. However, we translate the target languages (Spanish and Portuguese) to English, since they have very small number of training instances. We apply distance model and hierarchical clustering as explained above. For distance model, we train RoBERTa (Liu et al., 2019) base model. The hyperparameters and other settings are the same as in the previous

however we did not achieve better performances. We did not submit all versions of the reported methods for each language. Instead, we submitted best performing models in our internal experiments for each language.

Method	Target Lang.	Train data	Backbone Models	Score
S3-multi-1	EN	EN + ES + PR	XLM-RoBERTa Base	79.44
S3-mono-ST-6	EN	EN + ES^{EN}_{trans} + PR^{EN}_{trans}	RoBERTa (x5 split + x1 full)	84.24
S3-mono-TT-6	EN	EN	RoBERTa (x5 split +x1 full)	84.26
S3-mono-TT-16	EN	EN	RoBERTa (3x5 split (15) + x1 full)	**85.11**
S3-multi-1	ES	EN + ES + PR	XLM-RoBERTa Base	82.68
S3-mono-ST-6	ES^{EN}_{trans}	EN + ES^{EN}_{trans} + PR^{EN}_{trans}	RoBERTa (x5 split + x1 full)	**85.25**
S3-mono-TT-6	ES^{EN}_{trans}	EN	RoBERTa (x5 split +x1 full)	*
S3-mono-TT-16	ES^{EN}_{trans}	EN	RoBERTa (3x5 split (15) + x1 full)	83.70
S3-multi-1	PR	EN + ES + PR	XLM-RoBERTa Base	88.88
S3-mono-ST-6	PR^{EN}_{trans}	EN + ES^{EN}_{trans} + PR^{EN}_{trans}	RoBERTa (x5 split + x1 full)	92.04
S3-mono-TT-6	PR^{EN}_{trans}	EN	RoBERTa (x5 split +x1 full)	91.21
S3-mono-TT-16	PR^{EN}_{trans}	EN	RoBERTa (3x5 split (15) + x1 full)	**93.00**

Table 8: Our submitted models for **Subtask 3 (S3), Event Sentence Coreference Identification**. All methods are based on hierarchical clustering with single linkage. $L1^{L_2}_{trans}$ means that language L_1 is translated to language L_2. Split models are trained with randomly selected 80% of the train data and full models with all train data. Highest CoNLL-2012 average (Pradhan et al., 2014) scores are given in bold. (*) means that the submission score is not produced by the leaderboard system.

Lang.	Methods	Our Score	Best Competitor Score 2021	2022	Rank 2021	2022
EN	S3-mono-TT-16	**85.11**	84.44 (Awasthy et al., 2021)	-	1	1
ES	S3-mono-ST-6	**85.25**	84.23 (Awasthy et al., 2021)	-	1	1
PR	S3-mono-TT-16	93.00	**93.03** (Tan et al., 2021)	-	2	1

Table 9: The 2021 and 2022 leaderboard scores for **Subtask 3, Event Sentence Coreference Identification**. Highest CoNLL-2012 average (Pradhan et al., 2014) scores are given in bold.

method.

We train five *split* RoBERTa models, each with 80% of the training data randomly selected from the entire training data with replacement. Furthermore, we train a single *full* RoBERTa model using the entire training data. **S3-mono-TT-6** in Table 8 uses the predictions of the five split models and one full model together. Besides, we construct a bigger ensemble to reflect more aspects from different models, such that we repeat five splits three times to get 15 different models and one full model together (**S3-mono-TT-16**). We apply the same approach to ensemble the models' predictions into final test labels as in the previous method.

4.3 Leaderboard Results

In Subtask 3, the scoring metric is CoNLL-2012 average score (Pradhan et al., 2014). The leaderboard and our ranking among 2021 and 2022 submissions can be seen in Table 9. In 2022, we accomplished the first place in all languages. In 2021 leaderboard, we get the first place in English and Spanish and we get the second place in Portuguese.

5 Subtask 4: Protest Event Extraction

5.1 Dataset

The dataset in Subtask 4 consists of entity spans in news sequences for three languages (English, Spanish, and Portuguese). Event entity types are event time, facility name, organizer, participant, place, target, and trigger. The number of sequences are highly imbalanced for English compared to Spanish and Portuguese. We provide a detailed statistics of the dataset in Table 10.

	Language	English		Spanish		Portuguese	
	Data split	Train	Test	Train	Test	Train	Test
Entity	Facility	1,201	-	49	-	48	-
	Organizer	1,261	-	25	-	19	-
	Participant	2,663	-	88	-	73	-
	Target	1,470	-	64	-	32	-
	Trigger	4,595	-	157	-	122	-
	Place	1,570	-	15	-	61	-
	Time	1,209	-	40	-	41	-
Total	Sequences	808	88	30	50	33	50
	Word count	103,327	11,334	3,712	7,852	2,780	6,280
	Vocab. size	12,841	3,160	1,379	2,424	1,034	2,046

Table 10: The number of instances and entity types in **Subtask 4**.

5.2 Methods

We utilize monolingual and multilingual models in ensemble learning of token classification with a specific focus on post-processing predictions. We preprocess the input data since there are very long sequences that do not fit the input layer of the models, where the maximum sequence length is 512. We, therefore, split sequences, whose sequence

Method	Target Lang.	Train data	Backbone Models	Majority	Post-Proc	Score
S4-multi-10	EN	EN	XLM-R (x5) + XLM-R-CRF (x5)	✓	✗	75.70
S4-multi-PP-10			XLM-R (x5) + XLM-R-CRF (x5)	✓	✓	75.90
S4-mono-PP-10-v2			DeBERTa (x5) + DeBERTa-CRF (x5)	✓	✓	77.46
S4-mono-PP-10-v3			DeBERTa-CRF (x10)	✓	✓	**77.84**
S4-multi-10	PR	EN+ES+PR	XLM-R (x5) + XLM-R-CRF (x5)	✓	✗	70.89
S4-multi-PP-10			XLM-R (x5) + XLM-R-CRF (x5)	✓	✓	71.50
S4-multi-PP-10-v2			mDeBERTa (x5) + mDeBERTa-CRF (x5)	✓	✓	**73.84**
S4-multi-PP-10-v3			mDeBERTa-CRF (x10)	✓	✓	**73.84**
S4-multi-10	ES	EN+ES+PR	XLM-R (x5) + XLM-R-CRF (x5)	✓	✗	66.08
S4-multi-PP-10			XLM-R (x5) + XLM-R-CRF (x5)	✓	✓	66.46
S4-multi-PP-10-v2			mDeBERTa (x5) + mDeBERTa-CRF (x5)	✓	✓	**68.00**
S4-multi-PP-10-v3			mDeBERTa-CRF (x10)	✓	✓	67.91

Table 11: Our submitted models for **Subtask 4 (S4), Event Extraction**. Highest CoNLL (Tjong Kim Sang and De Meulder, 2003) macro F1 scores are given in bold.

length is greater than 512 tokens, with a window size of 200. For instance, we split a sequence having 654 words as four groups having 200, 200, 200, and 54 words. We do not use data translation due to the granularity of classification (i.e. translated word spans may not match the original sequence). In Table 11, we share our best performing three submissions for each language for Subtask 4 (S4), which are based on four methods[7]:

Ensemble of multilingual language models (S4-multi): We have more number of instances in English compared to Spanish and Portuguese. Having less data in a language complicates our task, since the granularity of the task is word span-level. We use a multilingual model, XLM-R (Conneau et al., 2020). We also use XLM-R-CRF, which is a hybrid model of Transformer-based language model and Conditional Random Fields (CRF) (Lafferty et al., 2001). The motivation behind using the CRF on top of Transformer-based language model is that the hybrid model can achieve promising results for the long named entities (Ozcelik and Toraman, 2022). In Subtask 4, we use the XLM-R base cased model that has 12 layers and a hidden size of 768. We use the HuggingFace's Pytorch implementation of this model (He et al., 2021b), the corresponding tokenizer with max length 512, extra padding and truncation. We set epoch number to 20 and use constant learning rate $5e-5$.

We train five XLM-R and five XLM-R-CRF models, fine-tuned with different seeds on full train data (**S4-multi-10** in Table 11). Majority voting is applied after training of 10 models. During majority voting, instead of choosing the most frequent classes, we use a task-specific algorithm to choose best label. We first create a label transition dictionary, where possible transitions have positive weights while transition errors have negative weights. For instance, `B-etime` → `I-etime` have positive weight, but `O` → `I-{entity type}` have negative weights since `O` label cannot be followed by any type of `I-{entity type}`.

Ensemble of multilingual language models with Post-Processing (S4-multi-PP): In this method, we apply the same approach and ensemble models as in the previous method. The only differences are that we use an additional multilingual language model, mDeBERTa (He et al., 2021c) (**S4-multi-PP-10-v2** and **S4-multi-PP-10-v3** in Table 11), and we apply a post-processing step on the prediction labels of ensemble members as follows. Post-processing is applied after the majority voting step, since there still occurs transition errors for the predictions, e.g., prediction of `O` label just before `I-{entity type}`. We, thereby, automatically fill the entity chunks when transition error occurs. For instance, an entity chunk having three labels `B-target I-target I-target` is corrected if it is predicted as `B-target O I-target`.

Ensemble of monolingual language models with Post-Processing (S4-mono-PP): In this method, we apply the same approach, ensemble models, and post-processing method as in the previous method. The only difference is that we use a monolingual language model on English, namely DeBERTa (He et al., 2021a) (**S4-mono-PP-10-v2** and **S4-mono-PP-10-v3**). This method is not applied for Spanish and Portuguese since the number of training instances are very small and we do not have translations.

[7]We did not submit all versions of the following methods for each language. Instead, we submitted best performing models in our internal experiments for each language.

Language	Model	Our score	Best Competitor Score 2021	2022	Our Rank 2021	2022
EN	S4-mono-PP-10-v3	**77.84**	78.11 (Awasthy et al., 2021)	76.49	2	1
PR	S4-multi-PP-10-v3	73.84	73.24 (Awasthy et al., 2021)	**74.57**	1	2
ES	S4-multi-PP-10-v2	68.00	66.20 (Awasthy et al., 2021)	**69.87**	1	2

Table 12: The 2021 and 2022 leaderboard scores for **Subtask 4, Event Extraction**.

5.3 Leaderboard Results

In Subtask 4, the evaluation metric is CoNLL (Tjong Kim Sang and De Meulder, 2003) macro F1 score. The leaderboard and our ranking among 2021 and 2022 submissions can be seen in Table 12. We get the first place in Portuguese and Spanish in 2021, and English in 2022. We achieve promising improvement in our scores for all languages when majority and post-processing are applied. Thus, we believe that our methods can generalize to many languages in token classification tasks.

6 Discussion and Conclusion

In this study, we summarize our solutions for multilingual protest event detection under four subtasks that have different granularities from document to word span-level. Our overall approach is based on ensemble learning and post-processing, which places the first place in 6 out of 16 leaderboards organized in seven languages including English, Mandarin, and Turkish.

Based on the experiments and leaderboard results, we have the following observations.

- We argue that post-processing predictions benefit the predictions of ensemble models due to the fact that large language models are stochastic (Bender et al., 2021). Specifically, post-processing predictions have significant benefits in the performances of our ensemble models in Subtask 3 and Subtask 4.
- When zero-shot evaluation (i.e. no available training data) is considered such as Turkish in this task, we observe that Transformer-based language models pretrained on a target language perform better in ensemble learning compared to multilingual models. Furthermore, we observe that for languages such as Spanish, Mandarin, and Urdu, monolingual Transformer-based language models pretrained on English perform better than multilingual language models. For fine-tuning, we translate the training data in source languages, such as English, to a target language, such as Turkish.

We plan to extend our experiments to different data collections, such as tweets, in different languages, specifically the languages used in Eastern Europe and Middle East countries.

References

Parul Awasthy, Jian Ni, Ken Barker, and Radu Florian. 2021. IBM MNLP IE at CASE 2021 task 1: Multi-granular and multilingual event detection on protest news. In *Proceedings of the 4th Workshop on Challenges and Applications of Automated Extraction of Socio-political Events from Text (CASE 2021)*, pages 138–146, Online. Association for Computational Linguistics.

Emily M. Bender, Timnit Gebru, Angelina McMillan-Major, and Shmargaret Shmitchell. 2021. On the dangers of stochastic parrots: Can language models be too big? In *Proceedings of the 2021 ACM Conference on Fairness, Accountability, and Transparency*, FAccT '21, page 610–623, New York, NY, USA. Association for Computing Machinery.

José Cañete, Gabriel Chaperon, Rodrigo Fuentes, Jou-Hui Ho, Hojin Kang, and Jorge Pérez. 2020. Spanish pre-trained bert model and evaluation data. In *PML4DC at ICLR 2020*.

Alexis Conneau, Kartikay Khandelwal, Naman Goyal, Vishrav Chaudhary, Guillaume Wenzek, Francisco Guzmán, Edouard Grave, Myle Ott, Luke Zettlemoyer, and Veselin Stoyanov. 2020. Unsupervised cross-lingual representation learning at scale. In *Proceedings of the 58th Annual Meeting of the Association for Computational Linguistics*, pages 8440–8451, Online. Association for Computational Linguistics.

Maarten Grootendorst. 2022. Bertopic: Neural topic modeling with a class-based tf-idf procedure.

Pengcheng He, Jianfeng Gao, and Weizhu Chen. 2021a. Debertav3: Improving deberta using electra-style pre-training with gradient-disentangled embedding sharing.

Pengcheng He, Jianfeng Gao, and Weizhu Chen. 2021b. Debertav3: Improving deberta using electra-style pre-training with gradient-disentangled embedding sharing.

Pengcheng He, Xiaodong Liu, Jianfeng Gao, and Weizhu Chen. 2021c. Deberta: Decoding-enhanced bert with disentangled attention. In *International Conference on Learning Representations*.

Tiancheng Hu and Niklas Stoehr. 2021. Team "noconflict" at case 2021 task 1: Pretraining for sentence-level protest event detection. In *Proceedings of the 4th Workshop on Challenges and Applications of Automated Extraction of Socio-political Events from Text (CASE 2021)*, pages 152–160. Association for Computational Linguistics.

Ali Hürriyetoğlu, Osman Mutlu, Fırat Duruşan, Onur Uca, Alaeddin Selçuk Gürel, Benjamin Radford, Yaoyao Dai, Hansi Hettiarachchi, Niklas Stoehr, Tadashi Nomoto, Milena Slavcheva, Francielle Vargas, Aaqib Javid, Fatih Beyhan, and Erdem Yörük. 2022. Extended multilingual protest news detection - shared task 1, case 2021 and 2022. In *Proceedings of the 5th Workshop on Challenges and Applications of Automated Extraction of Socio-political Events from Text (CASE 2022)*, online. Association for Computational Linguistics (ACL).

Ali Hürriyetoğlu, Osman Mutlu, Erdem Yörük, Farhana Ferdousi Liza, Ritesh Kumar, and Shyam Ratan. 2021. Multilingual protest news detection - shared task 1, CASE 2021. In *Proceedings of the 4th Workshop on Challenges and Applications of Automated Extraction of Socio-political Events from Text (CASE 2021)*, pages 79–91, Online. Association for Computational Linguistics.

Ali Hürriyetoğlu, Erdem Yörük, Deniz Yüret, Osman Mutlu, Çağrı Yoltar, Fırat Duruşan, and Burak Gürel. 2020. Cross-context news corpus for protest events related knowledge base construction.

John D. Lafferty, Andrew McCallum, and Fernando C. N. Pereira. 2001. Conditional random fields: Probabilistic models for segmenting and labeling sequence data. In *Proceedings of the Eighteenth International Conference on Machine Learning (ICML 2001), Williams College, Williamstown, MA, USA, June 28 - July 1, 2001*, pages 282–289. Morgan Kaufmann.

Yinhan Liu, Myle Ott, Naman Goyal, Jingfei Du, Mandar Joshi, Danqi Chen, Omer Levy, Mike Lewis, Luke Zettlemoyer, and Veselin Stoyanov. 2019. Roberta: A robustly optimized BERT pretraining approach. *CoRR*, abs/1907.11692.

Oguzhan Ozcelik and Cagri Toraman. 2022. Named entity recognition in turkish: A comparative study with detailed error analysis. *Information Processing & Management*, 59(6):103065.

Sameer Pradhan, Xiaoqiang Luo, Marta Recasens, Eduard Hovy, Vincent Ng, and Michael Strube. 2014. Scoring coreference partitions of predicted mentions: A reference implementation. In *Proceedings of the 52nd Annual Meeting of the Association for Computational Linguistics (Volume 2: Short Papers)*, pages 30–35, Baltimore, Maryland. Association for Computational Linguistics.

Nils Reimers and Iryna Gurevych. 2019. Sentence-bert: Sentence embeddings using siamese bert-networks. In *Proceedings of the 2019 Conference on Empirical Methods in Natural Language Processing*. Association for Computational Linguistics.

Fábio Souza, Rodrigo Nogueira, and Roberto Lotufo. 2020. BERTimbau: pretrained BERT models for Brazilian Portuguese. In *9th Brazilian Conference on Intelligent Systems, BRACIS, Rio Grande do Sul, Brazil, October 20-23 (to appear)*.

Fiona Anting Tan, Sujatha Das Gollapalli, and See-Kiong Ng. 2021. NUS-IDS at CASE 2021 task 1: Improving multilingual event sentence coreference identification with linguistic information. In *Proceedings of the 4th Workshop on Challenges and Applications of Automated Extraction of Socio-political Events from Text (CASE 2021)*, pages 105–112, Online. Association for Computational Linguistics.

Erik F. Tjong Kim Sang and Fien De Meulder. 2003. Introduction to the CoNLL-2003 shared task: Language-independent named entity recognition. In *Proceedings of the Seventh Conference on Natural Language Learning at HLT-NAACL 2003*, pages 142–147.

CEIA-NLP at CASE 2022 Task 1: Protest News Detection for Portuguese

Diogo Fernandes Costa Silva, Adalberto Junior, Gabriel da Mata Marques, Anderson da Silva Soares and Arlindo Rodrigues Galvao Filho
Federal University of Goiás
Goiânia, Goiás
diogo_fernandes@discente.ufg.br

Abstract

This paper summarizes our work on the document classification subtask of Multilingual protest news detection of the CASE @ ACL-IJCNLP 2022 workshop. In this context, we investigate the performance of monolingual and multilingual transformer-based models in low data resources, taking Portuguese as an example and evaluating language models on document classification. Our approach became the winning solution in Portuguese document classification achieving 0.8007 F1 Score on Test set. The experimental results demonstrate that multilingual models achieves best results than monolingual models in scenarios with few dataset samples of specific language, because we can train models using datasets from other languages of the same task and domain.

1 Introduction

Observing the prominent ease of use and variety of virtual media, such as social networks in general, and the exponential use of these for the organizational purpose of various manifestations, protests and social movements (McKeon and Gitomer, 2019), a large amount of information is stored in databases of applications that are not properly analyzed for a socially beneficial purpose. Therefore, it is important to explore alternatives for an analysis capable of classifying and even predicting the organization of social movements such as those mentioned above.

Considering the importance of detecting crises and sociopolitical events present in social networks (Hürriyetoğlu et al., 2022). The practical application of extracting and classifying information and its importance in the field of collective social manifestations, in order to obtain several useful results for important political and economic decisions (Duruşan et al., 2022).

In this paper, we investigate the performance of monolingual and multilingual language models for classification of documents in Portuguese. The experiments are conducted on Socio-political datasets and all models are transformer-based models. Our submission achieved the 1st place in document level predictions for the Portuguese language at first shared task of the CASE @ ACL-IJCNLP 2022 workshop (Hürriyetoğlu, Ali and Mutlu, Osman and Duruşan, Fırat and Uca, Onur and Gürel, Alaeddin Selçuk et al., 2022), the Multilingual protest news detection subtask (Hürriyetoğlu et al., 2021a,b).

This article is organized as follows. In Section 2, reviews the related work. Section 3 details of subtask and data. Section 4 describes the methodology, while experiments results are discussed in Section 5. Section 6 brings the conclusions.

2 Related Work

Kalyan et al. (2021) proposed applying LSTM layers on top of 3 different models and combining the probabilities of each model in a soft voting manner. The models used were mBERT (Devlin et al., 2018), DistilmBERT (Sanh et al., 2019) and RoBERTa (Liu et al., 2019). They achieved a Macro F1 score of 0.7951 for the Portuguese.

Hettiarachchi et al. (2021) studied the use of long-range models such as big-bird and longformer as well as monolingual and multilingual models. They found that low-resource languages benefited from multilingual learning, but high-resource languages such as English will get better results from monolingual models. Their approach is similar to ours regarding the monolingual versus multilingual paradigm and their results demonstrated that multilingual models perfomance better than monolingual models in low data scenarios. Awasthy et al. (2021) work also agrees with the benefit from training with multilingual data on low-resource language cases.

Francesco Ignazio Re (2021) presented a disruptive perspective with the exploratory analysis of the dataset. Their conclusions approached differences in the use of state versus non-state conflict

Proceedings of the 5th Workshop on Challenges and Applications of Automated Extraction of Socio-political Events from Text (CASE), pages 184 - 188
December 7-8, 2022

actors based on conditional probabilities, and also identified an outlier in the English corpus via the Tf-Idf-weighted principal component analysis (PCA).

3 Subtask and Data

The dataset was provided by the organization of CASE 2022's first multilingual protest news detection shared task. Table 1 show some examples of dataset. The CASE 2022's a combination of CASE 2021 with new test data for Document classification subtask. These subtask focus on predicting whether a document contains information about some event related to protests. The dataset are composed of three languages: English, Spanish and Portuguese (Hürriyetoğlu et al., 2019a,b) for Socio-political Events in text domain. Table 2 shows the dataset distribution for each language. We random split the dataset in the ratio of 80% for the training and 20% validation set.

4 Methodology

We used pretrained transformer-based models for portuguese to investigate the classification performance of monolingual across multilingual models in scenario with low dataset resources. For this study, we selected two models and their multilingual versions:

- *BERT:* BERT (Devlin et al., 2018) is a pretrained language model trained using a masked language modeling and next sentence prediction objectives. The model has about 30k tokens in its vocabulary. Our version is the BERTimbau (Souza et al., 2020), trained on portuguese with the BRWAC dataset (Wagner Filho et al., 2018).

- *mBERT:* The multilingual cased version of BERT. It was trained on top of 104 languages using the wikipedia dataset. The training procedure was masked language modeling and next sentence prediction as in the original BERT, the main difference being the vocabulary size 110k tokens instead of 30k and the multilingual dataset.

- *RoBERTa:* The original RoBERTa (Liu et al., 2019) showed that increasing the vocabulary from around 30k to around 50k tokens and dropping the next sentence prediction training objective was beneficial for the model. Our version, trained on Portuguese, has a vocabulary size of 128k tokens and was trained on the Portuguese portion of OSCAR dataset and BRWAC dataset (Wagner Filho et al., 2018) for 100k steps.

- *xlm-RoBERTa:* the xlm-RoBERTa (Conneau et al., 2019) is a multilingual pretrained version of RoBERTa, which showed better performance than mBERT on NLI. It was pretrained similarly to Roberta but the training was done with 2.5TB of filtered CommonCrawl data containing 100 languages. The model has as vocabulary of about 250k tokens.

These models were optimized with a grid search optimization on held-out development set with a combination of finetuning hyperparameters provided by Table 3. We selected the best hyperparameter values based on 5 random seeds.

5 Results and Evaluation

All experiments were conducted on the Hugging's Face transformer library using one Nvidia A100 GPU (Choquette et al., 2021) for classify whether a document in Portuguese mentions an event or not. The models performance was evaluated by the macro F1-Scores on the validation set, which were created by splitting the dataset. The dataset for multilingual models was created by combining training data from each languages into one dataset. Table 5 shows the results of Portuguese document classification experiments on validation set using different sequence lengths and models. We can observe that increasing the max sequence length improves the performance on all tested models. Both multilingual versions of the models were better than their monolingual versions, showing that learning representations of other languages in the same task and domain can improve the model performance. The best result is shown in bold using the xlm-RoBERTa Large model achieving 0.8818 F1 score.

The results for the test set are shown in Table 4 with all models tested and the two best results submitted in the competition. According to the results, our best model became the best system for the document classification for Portuguese language. The xlm-RoBERTa model achieves the best result reaching 1st place with 0.8007 F1 score at Task 1 SubTask 1 Portuguese competition.

Table 1: Dataset examples for each language indicating the event mentions

Sentence	Language	Label
Publicidade Nessa propaganda dos		0
Explosão de carro-bomba deixa vários feridos em Israel Publi	Portuguese	1
Nos começos de 1964, instalara-se no cenário nacional a mesma divisão		0
OTHER STATES Kashmir unrest Protestors indulge in stone		1
Mass disconnection driv	English	0
403 Forbidden You don't have p		0
Las autoridades egipcias perdieron e		0
33 son los basquetbolistas argentino	Spanish	0
Un nuevo atentado sacudió al continente asiático. Do		1

Table 2: Dataset distribution

Language	Class 0	Class 1
Portuguese	1290	197
English	869	131
Spanish	869	131

Table 3: Hyperparameters for finetuning

Hyperparameter	CASE 2022
Max Epochs	{10, 20}
BatchSize	{8, 16, 32, 64}
Learning Rate	{2e-5, 3e-5, 4e-5, 5e-5}
Max Sequence Length	{128, 256, 512}
Learning Rate Decay	Linear
Warmup Ratio	0.1
Weight Decay	{0.1, 0.01}

6 Conclusion

In this paper, we have explored the capabilities of multilingual and monolingual language models on document classification of the CASE 2022 Task 1: Multilingual protest news detection. We demonstrate that multilingual transformer-based approach could be more competitive that monolingual transformer-based model in scenarios that have low data resources of a specific language and more data of other languages can help achieve a best performance. The proposed xlm-RoBERTa model achieved the 1st place for the Portuguese language with 0.8007 F1 Score on Test set.

These results illustrate the importance of increasing the maximum sequence length for document classification. As future work, it would be interesting to extend the study to architectures with much longer input sequences. We also investigate other methodologies based on ensemble approach, data augmentation and few shot models.

Limitations

Recent works demonstrated that monolingual language models achieves better performance than multilingual models in NLP downstream task. The dataset size for a specific language task can be an issue (scenarios with low amount of data resource). Our experimental results demonstrate that using a multilingual model with more data from other languages achieves a better result than a monolingual model trained only in a specific language. The low amount of data for non-English language be a difficult for training monolingual language models. Finally, in this case, the size of maximum sequence length has a big impact in performance and transformers-based models size resulting a requirement of large GPU resources to processing long texts.

Ethics Statement

Most of the recent work on language models rely on vast amount of unannotated data to achieve good results, which means that these models are very likely to be training on harmful content to some degree. It is possible that the bias present in the pretraining continues to play a role after the fine-tuning of the model. The amount of bias influencing the model is yet to be quantified and future work should try to measure this before and after fine-tuning on specific data.

Table 4: Document classification results for Portuguese test data set. Best results is in Bold.

Model	Training data	Macro F1
team1	-	0.7985
team2	-	0.7922
BERT	pt	0.7372
mBERT	pt + en + es	0.7525
RoBERTa	pt	0.7732
xlm-RoBERTa	pt + en + es	**0.8007**

Table 5: Macro F1 results of document classification experiments for Portuguese using different sequence lengths and models on dev set. Best results is in Bold.

Model	Training data	Seq. Length	Accuracy	Macro F1
BERT	pt	128	0.9142	0.8443
		256	0.9199	0.8491
		512	0.9261	0.8533
mBERT	pt + en + es	128	0.9076	0.8528
		256	0.9086	0.8542
		512	0.9136	0.8600
RoBERTa	pt	128	**0.9328**	0.8641
		256	0.9327	0.8696
		512	0.9362	0.8721
xlm-RoBERTa	pt + en + es	128	0.9246	0.8727
		256	0.9293	0.8781
		512	0.9310	**0.8818**

Acknowledgements

Authors thank Center of Excellence in Artificial Intelligence (CEIA) of Federal University of Goiás for their support in conducting this study.

References

Parul Awasthy, Jian Ni, Ken Barker, and Radu Florian. 2021. Ibm mnlp ie at case 2021 task 1: Multigranular and multilingual event detection on protest news. pages 138–146.

Jack Choquette, Wishwesh Gandhi, Olivier Giroux, Nick Stam, and Ronny Krashinsky. 2021. Nvidia a100 tensor core gpu: Performance and innovation. *IEEE Micro*, 41(2):29–35.

Alexis Conneau, Kartikay Khandelwal, Naman Goyal, Vishrav Chaudhary, Guillaume Wenzek, Francisco Guzmán, Edouard Grave, Myle Ott, Luke Zettlemoyer, and Veselin Stoyanov. 2019. Unsupervised cross-lingual representation learning at scale. *CoRR*, abs/1911.02116.

Jacob Devlin, Ming-Wei Chang, Kenton Lee, and Kristina Toutanova. 2018. BERT: pre-training of deep bidirectional transformers for language understanding. *CoRR*, abs/1810.04805.

Fırat Duruşan, Ali Hürriyetoğlu, Erdem Yörük, Osman Mutlu, Çağrı Yoltar, Burak Gürel, and Alvaro Comin. 2022. Global contentious politics database (glocon) annotation manuals.

Dennis Atzenhofer Niklas Stoehr Francesco Ignazio Re, Daniel Véegh. 2021. Team "dadefrni" at case 2021 task 1: Document and sentence classification for protest event detection. pages 138–146.

Hansi Hettiarachchi, Mariam Adedoyin-Olowe, Jagdev Bhogal, and Mohamed Gaber. 2021. Daai at case 2021 task 1: Transformer-based multilingual socio-political and crisis event detection. pages 120–130.

Ali Hürriyetoğlu, Osman Mutlu, Farhana Ferdousi Liza, Erdem Yörük, Ritesh Kumar, and Shyam Ratan. 2021a. Multilingual protest news detection - shared task 1, case 2021. In *Proceedings of the 4th Workshop on Challenges and Applications of Automated Extraction of Socio-political Events from Text (CASE*

2021), online. Association for Computational Linguistics (ACL).

Ali Hürriyetoğlu, Hristo Tanev, Vanni Zavarella, Jakub Piskorski, Reyyan Yeniterzi, Erdem Yörük, Osman Mutlu, Deniz Yüret, and Aline Villavicencio. 2021b. Challenges and applications of automated extraction of socio-political events from text (case 2021): Workshop and shared task report. In *Proceedings of the 4th Workshop on Challenges and Applications of Automated Extraction of Socio-political Events from Text (CASE 2021)*, online. Association for Computational Linguistics (ACL).

Ali Hürriyetoğlu, Hristo Tanev, Vanni Zavarella, Reyyan Yeniterzi, Osman Mutlu, and Erdem Yörük. 2022. Challenges and applications of automated extraction of socio-political events from text (case 2022): Workshop and shared task report. In *Proceedings of the 4th Workshop on Challenges and Applications of Automated Extraction of Socio-political Events from Text (CASE 2022)*, online. Association for Computational Linguistics (ACL).

Ali Hürriyetoğlu, Erdem Yörük, Deniz Yüret, Çağrı Yoltar, Burak Gürel, Fırat Duruşan, and Osman Mutlu. 2019a. A task set proposal for automatic protest information collection across multiple countries. In *Advances in Information Retrieval*, pages 316–323, Cham. Springer International Publishing.

Ali Hürriyetoğlu, Erdem Yörük, Deniz Yüret, Çağrı Yoltar, Burak Gürel, Fırat Duruşan, Osman Mutlu, and Arda Akdemir. 2019b. Overview of clef 2019 lab protestnews: Extracting protests from news in a cross-context setting. In *Experimental IR Meets Multilinguality, Multimodality, and Interaction*, pages 425–432, Cham. Springer International Publishing.

Hürriyetoğlu, Ali and Mutlu, Osman and Duruşan, Fırat and Uca, Onur and Gürel, Alaeddin Selçuk, Benjamin Radford, Yaoyao Dai, Hansi Hettiarachchi, Niklas Stoehr, Tadashi Nomoto, Milena Slavcheva, Francielle Vargas, Aaqib Javid, Fatih Beyhan, and Erdem Yörük. 2022. Extended multilingual protest news detection - shared task 1, case 2021 and 2022. In *Proceedings of the 5th Workshop on Challenges and Applications of Automated Extraction of Socio-political Events from Text (CASE 2022)*, online. Association for Computational Linguistics (ACL).

Pawan Kalyan, Duddukunta Reddy, Adeep Hande, Ruba Priyadharshini, Sakuntharaj Ratnasingam, and Bharathi Chakravarthi. 2021. Iiitt at case 2021 task 1: Leveraging pretrained language models for multilingual protest detection. pages 98–104.

Yinhan Liu, Myle Ott, Naman Goyal, Jingfei Du, Mandar Joshi, Danqi Chen, Omer Levy, Mike Lewis, Luke Zettlemoyer, and Veselin Stoyanov. 2019. Roberta: A robustly optimized BERT pretraining approach. *CoRR*, abs/1907.11692.

Robin Tamarelli McKeon and Drew H. Gitomer. 2019. Social media, political mobilization, and high-stakes testing. *Frontiers in Education*, 0. [Online; accessed 2022-09-25].

Victor Sanh, Lysandre Debut, Julien Chaumond, and Thomas Wolf. 2019. Distilbert, a distilled version of bert: smaller, faster, cheaper and lighter. *ArXiv*, abs/1910.01108.

Fábio Souza, Rodrigo Nogueira, and Roberto Lotufo. 2020. BERTimbau: pretrained BERT models for Brazilian Portuguese. In *9th Brazilian Conference on Intelligent Systems, BRACIS, Rio Grande do Sul, Brazil, October 20-23 (to appear)*.

Jorge A Wagner Filho, Rodrigo Wilkens, Marco Idiart, and Aline Villavicencio. 2018. The brwac corpus: A new open resource for brazilian portuguese. In *Proceedings of the Eleventh International Conference on Language Resources and Evaluation (LREC 2018)*.

SPARTA at CASE 2021 Task 1: Evaluating Different Techniques to Improve Event Extraction

Arthur Müller
University of the Bundeswehr Munich
85577 Neubiberg, Germany
arthur.mueller@unibw.de

Andreas Dafnos
University of the Bundeswehr Munich
85577 Neubiberg, Germany
andreas.dafnos@unibw.de

Abstract

We participated in the Shared Task 1 at CASE 2021, Subtask 4 on protest event extraction from news articles (Hürriyetoğlu et al., 2022) and examined different techniques aimed at improving the performance of the winning system from the last competition round (Hürriyetoğlu et al., 2021). We evaluated in-domain pre-training, task-specific pre-fine-tuning, alternative loss function, translation of the English training dataset into other target languages (i.e., Portuguese, Spanish, and Hindi) for the token classification task, and a simple data augmentation technique by random sentence reordering. This paper summarizes the results, showing that random sentence reordering leads to a consistent improvement of the model performance.

1 Introduction

The generation of protest event datasets over the last decades has allowed social movement scholars to study the dynamics and evolution of collective action in contemporary societies. The collection of relevant events is usually based on the systematic, manual analysis of news articles, which provide information about the variables of interest such as the location, date, and main protagonists of protest demonstrations (Hutter, 2014).

It has been noted, however, that the manual coding of news articles is time and labor-consuming, and, as a result, comparative and longitudinal studies that rely on multiple news sources may not be feasible (Lorenzini et al., 2022). Recent work on approaches that automatically retrieve protest information is promising and may address this challenge.

CASE 2021 Task 1: Multilingual protest news detection (Hürriyetoğlu et al., 2021) constitutes a collaborative project that attempts to map the features of political contention through the automated analysis of news articles at different data levels. We participate in Subtask 4, which focuses on identifying event triggers and their arguments and involves detecting protest events in three languages: English, Portuguese, and Spanish.

The paper proceeds as follows: Section 2 discusses related work in the field of computational social science, whereas section 3 defines the task of event extraction. Section 4 describes the architecture of our approach. Section 5 provides details about the experiments we conducted. Finally, in section 6, we summarize and discuss the results.

2 Related Work

The use of automated tools for the identification and coding of political event data spans a period of more than 30 years (Hanna, 2017), and, for this task, several methodological approaches have been developed and tested. Initial attempts to automatically parse text and produce structured data were based on the Kansas Event Data System (KEDS) (Schrodt et al., 1994), which, along with its successors programs such as TABARI (Schrodt, 2009) and PETRARCH (Norris, 2016), was designed to provide information about different types of political action and also their source and target actors.

In the field of contentious politics, that is mainly interested in the activities of social movements and protest groups, the standard approach involved for a long time the manual coding of text. However, half-automated techniques have also been introduced. For instance, Lorenzini et al. (2022) have developed several filters (e.g., a location-based filter) and document and event-trigger classifiers to select newspaper articles that contain protest-related information. In the final step of their procedure, the authors create samples of relevant articles and manually extract the features of protest events.

Taking advantage of recent advances in machine learning methods, other scholars have turned their attention to approaches that automatically detect and classify protest information. However, unlike coding systems such as KEDS and its successors programs that make use of actor and verb dictio-

Proceedings of the 5th Workshop on Challenges and Applications of Automated Extraction of Socio-political Events from Text (CASE), pages 189 - 194
December 7-8, 2022

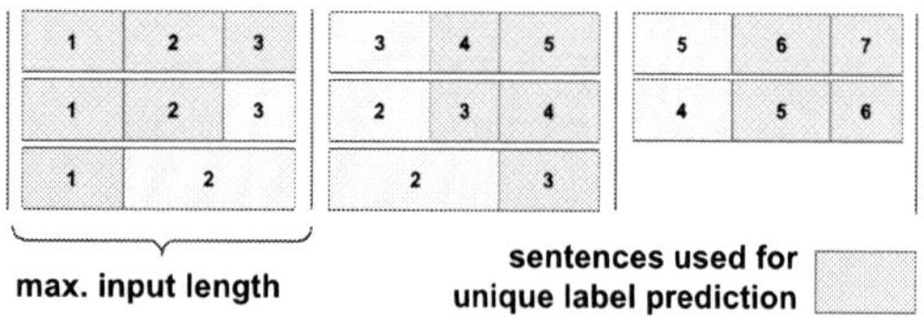

Figure 1: Sentence splitting into overlapping sequences.

naries, the new techniques primarily rely on pre-trained transformer-based language models (Liu et al., 2021), such as BERT (Devlin et al., 2018). CASE 2021 and 2022 Task 1 (Hürriyetoğlu et al., 2021, 2022) are such research projects—organized as shared tasks—that focus on the generation of multilingual protest event data and involve four subtasks: 1. Document classification; 2. Sentence classification; 3. Event sentence coreference identification; and 4. Event extraction.

In the following sections, we focus on subtask 4 and discuss techniques that improve over the baseline multilingual model XLM-RoBERTa (Conneau et al., 2019).

3 Event Extraction Task

The event extraction task consists of identifying text spans in given news article sentences and classifying them into entity types such as *trigger*, *participant*, *place* etc. Given $S = (w_1, .., w_n)$ a sentence and $T = \{t_1, .., t_m\}$ a set of entity types, the task consists of identifying spans $s = (w_b, .., w_e)$ such that $typeof(s) \in T$. This task can be reformulated as the token classification task, where IOB2 labels (Sang and Veenstra, 1999) are assigned to tokens in sentences to form spans. Hereby, the first token w_b within the span s is assigned the label B_{type} and the rest of the tokens the label I_{type}, where $type \in T$. All tokens outside of any identified spans are assigned the token O.

4 Architecture

The objective of the conducted evaluations was to show possible improvement compared to the winning system from last year's participation at CASE 2021 (Hürriyetoğlu et al., 2021) by the *IBM* team (Awasthy et al., 2021). The authors trained variants of the multilingual model XLM-RoBERTa$_{\text{large}}$ (Conneau et al., 2019) on news article sentences to predict IOB2 labels for event extraction. Therefore, all experiments in our paper used the same base model and similar training settings.

In contrast to *IBM* team's approach, we did not provide an ensemble variant of the model but relied only on a single multilingual model. Another significant architectural difference was how the inputs were provided to the model; instead of splitting the news articles into single sentences, we used the maximum possible input length of 512 tokens and fed as many full sentences as possible to the model, providing as a result more context. If the news article exceeded the maximum input length, it was split into overlapping sentence sequences as shown in Figure 1. Thus, some sentences were presented to the model multiple times during the fine-tuning procedure with different preceding or following contexts. However, the final predicted token labels during the test procedure were derived only from the reconstructed non-overlapping sequence of sentences, leading to unique predictions. In both procedures, we removed the concatenating separator token `[SEP]` from the input. We should also note that the predicted token labels correspond to the IOB2 labels.

5 Experiments

Starting from the base model, several techniques were evaluated after fine-tuning the model on the provided dataset for Subtask 4 (Hürriyetoğlu et al., 2021). Similar to the *IBM* team, we used only 10% of the English dataset as a development set. Thus, the influence of the employed techniques on other languages was mainly inferred from the testing results in the provided Codalab page. The best models for submission were selected according to the highest CoNLL F1 score and lowest mean validation loss on the development set. The best values of F1 achieved 80.06% and 80.86%. Models were fine-tuned for 20 epochs using hyperparameters as shown in Table 1. The fine-tuning was conducted on four NVIDIA A100 GPUs each with 40GB RAM leveraging the Distributed Data Parallel (DP) paradigm (Li et al., 2020).

5.1 Further Pre-Training

The current literature suggests that further pre-training of models on in-domain data can produce promising results, especially when the target language has a different—and yet unknown—token distribution for the pre-trained model. For instance, in the case of the language used on Twitter, further pre-training of the XLM-R models led to significant improvements in the task of stance detection

Parameter	Pre-Training	Fine-Tuning
Input Length	512	512
Batch Size	1280	20
$AdamW_{lr}$	1e-5	2e-5
$AdamW_{beta}$	(0.9, 0.999)	(0.9, 0.999)
$AdamW_{eps}$	1e-6	1e-8
Weight Decay	0	0.001
Linear Warmup	0	0.1
Dice Loss Parameter		**Fine-Tuning**
Smooth		0.5
Square Denominator		true
Using Logits		true
Ohem Ratio		0.0
Alpha		0.0
Reduction		mean
Index Label Position		true

Table 1: Parameters for pre-training and fine-tuning.

Datasets	en	es	pr	hi
Count Love	38k			
Count Love_t		38k	38k	38k
POLUSA	21k			
POLUSA_t		21k	21k	21k
GDELT 2.0	177k	40k	8.3k	0.5k
GDELT 2.0_t		177k	177k	177k
Sum per lang	236k	276k	244.3k	236.5k
Sum total				992.8k

Table 2: Sizes of collected, filtered, and translated datasets for further pre-training. The index t indicates the datasets translated from English.

(Müller et al., 2022). *NoConflict* team used further pre-training for subtasks 1 and 2 at CASE 2021 (Hu and Stöhr, 2021). It was also employed with success for the task of event extraction on a dataset that was based on online news archives from India (Caselli et al., 2021). The approach used BERT (Devlin et al., 2018) as the base model.

In this paper, our objective was to evaluate whether further pre-training on protest-specific news articles can integrate more—yet unknown—token distributions into the model. Therefore, we collected, filtered, and translated multiple datasets for four languages: English, Portuguese, Spanish, and Hindi. We used the Hindi language for pre-training, although a dataset for Hindi is not provided for subtask 4.

The Count Love dataset (Leung and Perkins, 2021) consists of semi-automated collected protest news articles in English. We used the provided crawler to recollect data and removed missing articles collecting 81,500 articles, of which ca. 38,000 were labeled as protest-related news. To filter missing articles, we used the content length of 150 characters and expressions that indicated missing or restricted web pages during the crawling process, such as *"Unfortunately, our website is currently unavailable"* and *"Please whitelist us to continue reading"*. Some web pages were not accessible due to necessary subscriptions or legal geographic restrictions. The collected English dataset was translated into Portuguese, Spanish, and Hindi using the Argos Translate library. We reused the provided labels in order to train a binary classifier based on the $\text{XLM-RoBERTa}_{base}$ (Conneau et al., 2019) and identify protest-related news for each of the four languages with an F1 score of ca. 85%, which was used to filter articles in the following datasets:

The POLUSA dataset (Gebhard and Hamborg, 2020) consists of ca. 0.9 mio political news articles in English. It was also used by the previously mentioned *NoConflict* team at CASE 2021 for Subtasks 1 and 2 (Hu and Stöhr, 2021). The authors provided us with the full dataset, and we used the previously trained binary English-based classifier to filter protest-related news; a process which resulted in ca. 21,000 articles. We translated them into the three languages mentioned above.

GDELT 2.0 Event Database is a large-scale news database that monitors different types of events in 65 languages. We downloaded the files containing links to articles beginning from February 2015 to July 2022 and filtered them to obtain protest-related news using codes 140–149 according to the CAMEO codebook. Additionally, we applied the binary classifier to filter protest-related articles. Those consisted of ca. 4% for Hindi and ca. 11% for English, Spanish, and Portuguese. Finally, we translated English texts into these three languages.

As can be seen from the overview of collected and translated dataset sizes in Table 2, even the originally multilingual GDELT dataset resulted in very low amounts of items for non-English languages. Therefore, the translation procedure we employed was driven by the idea that translated texts could create more diversity in the token distribution regarding the different ways protests are described.

The pre-training of the base model was conducted using the full multilingual collected dataset with hyperparameters according to Table 1. It was repeated up to 7 epochs on the same but randomly ordered articles. In contrast to the fine-tuning procedure, we did not split sentences. Instead, the first 512 tokens were fed into the model, assuming that the most important information is available at the beginning of the article. All pre-trained models for each epoch and parameter combination were fine-tuned and the best model was selected for evaluation on the Codalab page. The pre-training was conducted on an NVIDIA DGX V100 machine with 16 GPUs each with 32 GB RAM. We used the Fully Shared Data Parallel (FSDP) paradigm (Baines et al., 2021). To achieve the high batch size of 1280, the technique of gradient accumulation was additionally leveraged.

5.2 Pre-Fine-Tuning on Similar Tasks

Learning similar or related tasks is known to be beneficial for model performance (Ruder, 2017). Therefore, we evaluated fine-tuned models that were trained on the Spanish part of the CoNLL 2002 dataset (Tjong Kim Sang, 2002) and are available on HuggingFace (Wolf et al., 2020):

1. *xlm-roberta-large-finetuned-conll02-spanish*
2. *MMG/xlm-roberta-large-ner-spanish*

5.3 Dice Loss Function

As an alternative to classic cross-entropy loss for fine-tuning, we used the Dice Loss (Li et al., 2019), which has been shown to be beneficial for tasks with imbalanced class distributions. This is true for token classification tasks, where most tokens are labeled using the IOB2 label *O*. Also, other annotated entity types are highly imbalanced in the data provided for Subtask 4.

5.4 Translating the Training Dataset

Translating the training dataset for the token classification task and transferring corresponding IOB2 labels to translated tokens has already been explored by the *Handshakes* team at CASE 2021 (Kalyan et al., 2021). Their approach was based on translating sentences word-by-word using auxiliary embedding mapping. Here we explored an alternative technique suggested for Named Entity Entity Recognition in the clinical domain (Schäfer et al., 2022). We used a trained model for Neural Machine Translation, the multilingual $BART_{50}$

Model	**Loss**	**en**	**pr**	**es**
IBM's S1	cross	75.95	73.24	66.20
PT_1	dice	75.70	**74.57**	69.08
PT_2	cross	**76.49**	73.11	69.58
$FT_{es\text{-}1}$	cross	75.72	74.45	**69.87**
$FT_{es\text{-}2}$	cross	75.28	73.33	69.35

Table 3: Summary of the best models as CoNLL F1 score. *PT* indicates models with further pre-training on the multilingual dataset. *FT* models were previously fine-tuned on the Spanish part of the CoNNL 2002 task. The loss functions *dice* and *cross* correspond to Dice Loss and Cross-Entropy. The underlined numbers are the best results from the previous competition round at CASE 2021. The bold numbers show our best values.

Model	**Data**	**en**	**pr**	**es**
$TR_{en+es+pr}$	en+pr+es +pr-pseudo +es-pseudo	75.66	67.23	62.18
TR_{es}	pr+es +es-pseudo		71.59	63.94
TR_{pr}	pr+es +pr-pseudo		69.68	66.01

Table 4: Summary of the best models as CoNLL F1 score for dataset translation. The data labels *en*, *pr*, *es* indicate the usage of original parts of the training dataset. The parts *pr-pseudo* and *es-pseudo* are translated from the English dataset into Portuguese and Spanish.

model (Tang et al., 2020), to first translate the original English text into the target languages. Next, embeddings from an auxiliary model were used to map every word of the source sentence to one or multiple tokens in the translated sentence. For this task, we employed the multilingual $BERT_{base\text{-}cased}$ model (Devlin et al., 2018).

5.5 Augmentation by Sentence Reordering

Since we used sentence sequences as the input to our models, it was possible to randomly reorder them as a simple data augmentation technique. For every article with more than one sentence, we added up to three random combinations to the training fold. This technique was initially employed by default for all experiments.

6 Final Results and Discussion

The final results on testing datasets for the approaches of pre-training and pre-fine-tuning are summarized in Table 3. We compare the results to IBM's S1 multilingual model as the baseline, which was trained on the same multilingual dataset. IBM's S1 achieved the best results for Portuguese and Spanish languages in the last CASE 2021 competition. At least one of our models achieved better results for each of the three languages; however, the most pronounced difference is for Spanish—between 2.88 and 3.67 points. The further pre-trained model PT_1 and the pre-fine-tuned model $FT_{es\text{-}1}$ achieved nearly the same results for Portuguese.

The numbers indicate that conducting an expensive pre-training procedure on additional protest-related data does not have the expected boosting effect for the model performance. This suggests that the XLM-R models already integrate sufficient knowledge about the type of language used to describe protests. Comparable results can be achieved using a pre-fine-tuned model on a similar task. Furthermore, the usage of the Dice Loss does not lead either to very different results compared to the classical Cross-Entropy loss on this task.

It is important to mention that models in Table 3 were trained using the simple data augmentation technique. We argue that at least part of the performance increase was caused by this technique. To evaluate its influence, we retrained 10 models using different parameters but without augmentation, including the best models. There was a consistent increase measured on the English development set due to data augmentation on average by 0.70 points. On testing datasets, the average improvement resulted in 0.73 points for English, 1.03 for Portuguese, and 0.70 for Spanish.

Finally, we evaluated the translation technique, which resulted in performance drops. Table 4 summarizes the results of these three models. In the first model, the original dataset parts for the three languages were used, and the English part was further translated into Portuguese and Spanish. The following two models used the Portuguese and Spanish datasets and a translated part into one of these languages. Compared to IBM's S1, the performance dropped especially for those target languages in which datasets were extended by additional translated parts. Apparently, this approach introduced lots of noise. Manual evaluation of the Spanish translation showed that in many cases the conjunctions and articles within entity spans—such as *de, del, la, etc.*—were missing the appropriate labels.

7 Conclusion

In this paper, we presented the models developed for the Shared Task 1 Subtask 4 at CASE 2021. We explored different techniques to improve the baseline multilingual model. The best result was achieved by improving on the Spanish test data by 3.67 points of CoNLL F1 score over the winner of the previous competition round. Our submissions ranked 1st for Portuguese and Spanish and 2nd for English in the current competition round.

Acknowledgments

This research is funded by dtec.bw—Digitalization and Technology Research Center of the Bundeswehr [project SPARTA]. Furthermore, the authors gratefully acknowledge the computing time granted by the Institute for Distributed Intelligent Systems and provided on the GPU cluster Monacum One at the Bundeswehr University Munich.

References

Parul Awasthy, Jian Ni, Ken Barker, and Radu Florian. 2021. IBM MNLP IE at CASE 2021 Task 1: Multigranular and multilingual event detection on protest news. In *Proceedings of the 4th Workshop on Challenges and Applications of Automated Extraction of Socio-political Events from Text (CASE 2021)*, pages 138–146.

Mandeep Baines, Shruti Bhosale, Vittorio Caggiano, Naman Goyal, Siddharth Goyal, Myle Ott, Benjamin Lefaudeux, Vitaliy Liptchinsky, Mike Rabbat, Sam Sheiffer, et al. 2021. Fairscale: A general purpose modular pytorch library for high performance and large scale training.

Tommaso Caselli, Osman Mutlu, Angelo Basile, and Ali Hürriyetoğlu. 2021. PROTEST-ER: Retraining BERT for Protest Event Extraction. In *Proceedings of the 4th Workshop on Challenges and Applications of Automated Extraction of Socio-political Events from Text (CASE 2021)*, pages 12–19.

Alexis Conneau, Kartikay Khandelwal, Naman Goyal, Vishrav Chaudhary, Guillaume Wenzek, Francisco Guzmán, Edouard Grave, Myle Ott, Luke Zettlemoyer, and Veselin Stoyanov. 2019. Unsupervised cross-lingual representation learning at scale. *arXiv preprint arXiv:1911.02116*.

Jacob Devlin, Ming-Wei Chang, Kenton Lee, and Kristina Toutanova. 2018. BERT: pre-training of deep bidirectional transformers for language understanding. *CoRR*, abs/1810.04805.

Lukas Gebhard and Felix Hamborg. 2020. The POLUSA dataset: 0.9 M political news articles balanced by time and outlet popularity. In *Proceedings of the ACM/IEEE Joint Conference on Digital Libraries in 2020*, pages 467–468.

Alex Hanna. 2017. MPEDS: Automating the generation of protest event data.

Tiancheng Hu and Niklas Werner Stöhr. 2021. Team "NoConflict" at CASE 2021 Task 1: Pretraining for Sentence-Level Protest Event Detection. In *Proceedings of the 4th Workshop on Challenges and Applications of Automated Extraction of Socio-political Events from Text (CASE 2021)*, pages 152–160. Association for Computational Linguistics.

Ali Hürriyetoğlu, Osman Mutlu, Fırat Duruşan, Onur Uca, Alaeddin Selçuk Gürel, Benjamin Radford, Yaoyao Dai, Hansi Hettiarachchi, Niklas Stoehr, Tadashi Nomoto, Milena Slavcheva, Francielle Vargas, Aaqib Javid, Fatih Beyhan, and Erdem Yörük. 2022. Extended Multilingual protest news detection - Shared Task 1, CASE 2021 and 2022. In *Proceedings of the 5th Workshop on Challenges and Applications of Automated Extraction of Socio-political Events from Text (CASE 2022)*, online. Association for Computational Linguistics (ACL).

Ali Hürriyetoğlu, Osman Mutlu, Erdem Yörük, Farhana Ferdousi Liza, Ritesh Kumar, and Shyam Ratan. 2021. Multilingual protest news detection-shared Task 1, CASE 2021. In *Proceedings of the 4th Workshop on Challenges and Applications of Automated Extraction of Socio-political Events from Text (CASE 2021)*, pages 79–91.

Swen Hutter. 2014. Protest event analysis and its offspring. In *Methodological practices in social movement research*, edited by Donatella Della Porta, pages 33–67. OUP Oxford.

Ali Hürriyetoğlu, Erdem Yörük, Osman Mutlu, Fırat Duruşan, Çağrı Yoltar, Deniz Yüret, and Burak Gürel. 2021. Cross-Context News Corpus for Protest Event-Related Knowledge Base Construction. *Data Intelligence*, pages 1–28.

Vivek Kalyan, Paul Tan, Shaun Tan, and Martin Andrews. 2021. Handshakes AI Research at CASSE 2021 Task 1: Exploring different approaches for multilingual tasks. *arXiv preprint arXiv:2110.15599*.

Tommy Leung and L Nathan Perkins. 2021. Counting Protests in News Articles: A Dataset and Semi-Automated Data Collection Pipeline. *arXiv preprint arXiv:2102.00917*.

Shen Li, Yanli Zhao, Rohan Varma, Omkar Salpekar, Pieter Noordhuis, Teng Li, Adam Paszke, Jeff Smith, Brian Vaughan, Pritam Damania, et al. 2020. Pytorch distributed: Experiences on accelerating data parallel training. *arXiv preprint arXiv:2006.15704*.

Xiaoya Li, Xiaofei Sun, Yuxian Meng, Junjun Liang, Fei Wu, and Jiwei Li. 2019. Dice loss for data-imbalanced NLP tasks. *arXiv preprint arXiv:1911.02855*.

Jiangwei Liu, Liangyu Min, and Xiaohong Huang. 2021. An overview of event extraction and its applications. *arXiv preprint arXiv:2111.03212*.

Jasmine Lorenzini, Hanspeter Kriesi, Peter Makarov, and Bruno Wüest. 2022. Protest event analysis: Developing a semiautomated NLP approach. *American Behavioral Scientist*, 66(5):555–577.

Arthur Müller, Jasmin Riedl, and Wiebke Drews. 2022. Real-Time Stance Detection and Issue Analysis of the 2021 German Federal Election Campaign on Twitter. In *International Conference on Electronic Government*, pages 125–146. Springer.

Clayton Norris. 2016. PETRARCH 2: PETRARCHer. *arXiv preprint arXiv:1602.07236*.

Sebastian Ruder. 2017. An overview of multi-task learning in deep neural networks. *arXiv preprint arXiv:1706.05098*.

Erik F Sang and Jorn Veenstra. 1999. Representing text chunks. *arXiv preprint cs/9907006*.

Henning Schäfer, Ahmad Idrissi-Yaghir, Peter Horn, and Christoph Friedrich. 2022. Cross-Language Transfer of High-Quality Annotations: Combining Neural Machine Translation with Cross-Linguistic Span Alignment to Apply NER to Clinical Texts in a Low-Resource Language. In *Proceedings of the 4th Clinical Natural Language Processing Workshop*, pages 53–62.

Philip A Schrodt. 2009. TABARI: Textual analysis by augmented replacement instructions. *Dept. of Political Science, University of Kansas, Blake Hall, Version 0.7. 3B3*, pages 1–137.

Philip A Schrodt, Shannon G Davis, and Judith L Weddle. 1994. Political science: KEDS—a program for the machine coding of event data. *Social Science Computer Review*, 12(4):561–587.

Yuqing Tang, Chau Tran, Xian Li, Peng-Jen Chen, Naman Goyal, Vishrav Chaudhary, Jiatao Gu, and Angela Fan. 2020. Multilingual Translation with Extensible Multilingual Pretraining and Finetuning.

Erik F. Tjong Kim Sang. 2002. Introduction to the CoNLL-2002 shared task: Language-independent named entity recognition. In *COLING-02: The 6th Conference on Natural Language Learning 2002 (CoNLL-2002)*.

Thomas Wolf, Lysandre Debut, Victor Sanh, Julien Chaumond, Clement Delangue, Anthony Moi, Pierric Cistac, Tim Rault, Rémi Louf, Morgan Funtowicz, et al. 2020. Transformers: State-of-the-art natural language processing. In *Proceedings of the 2020 conference on empirical methods in natural language processing: system demonstrations*, pages 38–45.

Event Causality Identification with Causal News Corpus - Shared Task 3, CASE 2022

Fiona Anting Tan
Institute of Data Science, National University of Singapore, Singapore
tan.f@u.nus.edu

Hansi Hettiarachchi
School of Computing and Digital Technology, Birmingham City University, United Kingdom
hansi.hettiarachchi@mail.bcu.ac.uk

Ali Hürriyetoğlu
KNAW Humanities Cluster DHLab, The Netherlands
ali.hurriyetoglu@dh.huc.knaw.nl

Tommaso Caselli
CLCG, University of Groningen, The Netherlands
t.caselli@rug.nl

Onur Uca
Department of Sociology, Mersin University, Turkey
onuruca@mersin.edu.tr

Farhana Ferdousi Liza
School of Computing Sciences, University of East Anglia, United Kingdom
F.Liza@uea.ac.uk

Nelleke Oostdijk
Centre for Language Studies, Radboud University, The Netherlands
nelleke.oostdijk@ru.nl

Abstract

The Event Causality Identification Shared Task of CASE 2022 involved two subtasks working on the Causal News Corpus. Subtask 1 required participants to predict if a sentence contains a causal relation or not. This is a supervised binary classification task. Subtask 2 required participants to identify the Cause, Effect and Signal spans per causal sentence. This could be seen as a supervised sequence labeling task. For both subtasks, participants uploaded their predictions for a held-out test set, and ranking was done based on binary F1 and macro F1 scores for Subtask 1 and 2, respectively. This paper summarizes the work of the 17 teams that submitted their results to our competition and 12 system description papers that were received. The best F1 scores achieved for Subtask 1 and 2 were 86.19% and 54.15%, respectively. All the top-performing approaches involved pre-trained language models fine-tuned to the targeted task. We further discuss these approaches and analyze errors across participants' systems in this paper.

1 Introduction

A causal relation represents a semantic relationship between a Cause argument and an Effect argument, in which the occurrence of the Cause leads to the occurrence of the Effect (Barik et al., 2016). Extracting causal information from text has many downstream natural language processing (NLP) applications, for summarization and prediction (Radinsky et al., 2012; Radinsky and Horvitz, 2013; Izumi et al., 2021; Hashimoto et al., 2014), question answering (Dalal et al., 2021; Hassanzadeh et al., 2019; Stasaski et al., 2021), inference and understanding (Jo et al., 2021; Dunietz et al., 2020).

However, data for causal text mining is limited (Asghar, 2016; Xu et al., 2020; Yang et al., 2022; Tan et al., 2021, 2022a). There are also not many benchmarks to allow for fair model comparisons (Asghar, 2016). Therefore, in this paper, we continue our efforts with the creation of the Causal News Corpus (CNC). CNC is a corpus of news articles annotated with causal information suitable for causal text mining. Additionally, we introduce a shared task to promote modelling for two causal text mining tasks: (1) Causal Event Classification and (2) Cause-Effect-Signal Span Detection. Figure 1 provides examples from the CNC in this shared task. To our knowledge, we are the first dedicated causal text mining dataset and benchmark to include signal span detection as an objective.

The rest of the paper is organized as follows: Section 2 presents literature on event causality datasets. Section 3 describes the dataset and annotation of the corpus. Section 4 formally introduces the two subtasks for the shared task. Section 5 describes the evaluation metrics and competition set-up. Subsequently, Section 6 summarizes the methods used by

Proceedings of the 5th Workshop on Challenges and Applications of Automated Extraction of Socio-political Events from Text (CASE), pages 195 - 208
December 7-8, 2022

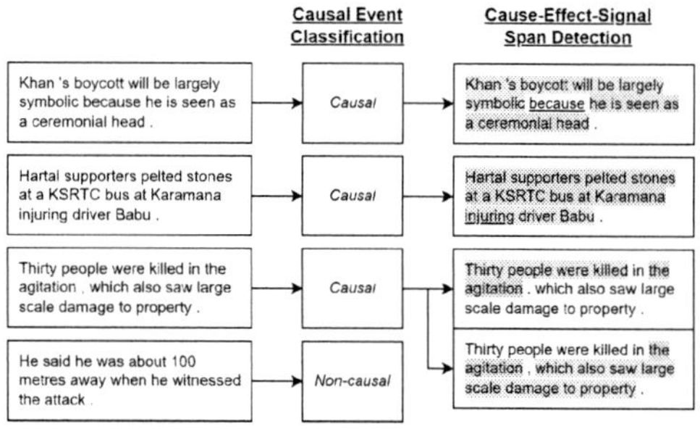

Figure 1: Examples from the CNC for the two subtasks. Cause spans are indicated by Pink, while Effect spans are indicated by Green. Signals, if present, are underlined.

participants during the competition, while Section 7 analyzes the participants' submissions. Finally, Section 8 concludes this paper.

2 Related Work

In many papers about Event Causality Identification (ECI) (Gao et al., 2019; Zuo et al., 2021b; Cao et al., 2021; Zuo et al., 2021a, 2020), the two datasets used for benchmarking are CausalTimeBank (Mirza et al., 2014; Mirza and Tonelli, 2014) and EventStoryLine (Caselli and Vossen, 2017). These datasets are unsuitable for span detection since their arguments are event headwords only.

There are two other efforts that intentionally introduce datasets for benchmarking causal text mining systems. FinCausal (Mariko et al., 2021, 2020) is a recurring shared task held within the FinNLP workshop focusing on financial news. In the first subtask, participants also aim to identify if sentences contain causal relations. In the second subtask, participants to identify the Cause and Effect spans in the causal sentences. UniCausal (Tan et al., 2022b)[1] is an open-source repository for causal text mining that has consolidated six corpora for three causal text mining tasks. The six corpora included in UniCausal are: AltLex (Hidey and McKeown, 2016), BECAUSE 2.0 (Dunietz et al., 2017), CausalTimeBank (Mirza et al., 2014; Mirza and Tonelli, 2014), EventStoryLine V1.0 (Caselli and Vossen, 2017), Penn Discourse Treebank V3.0 (Webber et al., 2019), and SemEval 2010 Task 8 (Hendrickx et al., 2010). The three tasks are: Causal Sentence Classification, Causal Pair Classification and Cause-Effect Span Detection.

[1]`https://github.com/tanfiona/UniCausal`

Similar to FinCausal and UniCausal, we included a signal span detection objective. Our annotation guidelines differ slightly, in that our arguments must contain events, and the spans are annotated in a manner that is minimally sufficient. In general, we notice that spans from FinCausal are much longer. Spans from UniCausal depend on the original data source.

Additionally, for Cause-Effect Span Detection in FinCausal, their approach to handle multiple causal relations per unique sentence was to include index numbers at the start of each sentence to differentiate the Cause-Effect predictions. This approach is problematic because (1) it leaks information that the sentence contains multiple causal relations to the model, and (2) predictions that are submitted in a different order from the true labels are unnecessarily penalised. Therefore, we differ from FinCausal when evaluating multiple causal relations in span detection since we group relations by its sentence index. This is described further in Section 5.1.

3 Dataset

3.1 Data Collection

Our shared task worked with the Causal News Corpus (CNC) (Tan et al., 2022a)[2], which consists of 869 news documents and 3,559 English sentences, annotated with causal information. CNC builds on the randomly sampled articles (Yörük et al., 2021) from multiple sources and periods featured (Hürriyetoğlu et al., 2021) in a series of workshops directed at mining socio-political events from news articles (Hürriyetoğlu et al., 2020b,a, 2021a,b; Hürriyetoğlu, 2021). CNC follows the train-test split of the original data source, with 3,248 training and 311 test examples. Later, we further split and randomly sampled 10% of the original training set to obtain the development set. Later, Table 3 presents the sentence counts per data split.

3.2 Annotation

3.2.1 Guidelines

For more information on our annotation guidelines, please refer to our annotation manual[3].

Subtask 1 In CNC, sentences were labeled as *Causal* or *Non-causal*, where the presence of causality indicates that "one argument provides the

[2]`https://github.com/tanfiona/CausalNewsCorpus`

[3]Available under the "documentation" folder of CNC's Github repository.

reason, explanation or justification for the situation described by the other" (Webber et al., 2019). Our sentences had to contain at least a pair of events, defined as "things that happen or occur, or states that are valid" (Saurı et al., 2006). These annotations correspond to the target labels for Subtask 1, Causal Event Classification.

Subtask 2 For *Causal* sentences, the words corresponding to the Cause-Effect-Signal spans of a causal relation were also marked. These annotations correspond to the target labels for Subtask 2, Cause-Effect-Signal Span Detection. However, at the current stage of writing, only a small subset of our data contains annotated spans. Span annotations are an on-going effort.

A Cause is a reason, explanation or justification that led to an Effect. We defined a Cause or Effect span as a continuous set of words sufficient for the interpretation of the causal relation meaning. This means that any context modifying or describing the argument relevant to the causal relation was included. Each Cause or Effect span must contain an event, where an event is defined as a situation that 'happen or occur', or predicates that 'describe states or circumstances in which something obtains or holds true' (Pustejovsky et al., 2003).

Signals are words that help to identify the structure of the discourse. In our case, signals highlight the relationship between the Cause and Effect.

3.2.2 Annotation Tool

We used the WebAnno tool (Eckart de Castilho et al., 2016) to conduct our annotation process.

Subtask 1 Annotation at the sequence level was relatively straightforward, where annotators selected "Yes" or "No" labels for each sentence.

Subtask 2 Annotators first marked the Cause span, Effect span, and Signal span. Subsequently, they linked the spans together by pointing Cause to Effect and Signal to Effect. An illustration is provided in Figure 2. Annotations were then downloaded and sent through checking scripts on Python to identify if there were any avoidable human errors. For example, if missing links (E.g. An Effect has no Cause) or invalid links (E.g. An Effect points to Effect) were present, and an error report was then sent to annotators for them to consider correcting their annotations.

	Train	Dev	Test	Total
K-Alpha	34.42	29.77	48.55	34.99

Table 1: Subtask 1 Inter-annotator Agreement Scores. Reported in percentages.

Metric	Span	Train+Dev	Test	Total
Exact Match	Cause	30.57	15.11	23.88
	Effect	36.30	19.86	29.19
	Signal	27.92	29.21	28.48
	Total	7.84	5.81	6.96
One-Side Bound	Cause	57.55	39.86	49.90
	Effect	60.90	45.42	54.21
	Signal	31.93	32.96	32.37
	Total	24.05	22.25	23.27
Token Overlap	Cause	63.65	49.18	57.39
	Effect	64.66	49.88	58.27
	Signal	32.09	33.15	32.55
	Total	26.94	27.78	27.31
K-Alpha	Cause	46.36	42.51	44.32
	Effect	57.18	41.89	49.89
	Signal	29.30	23.42	27.08
	Total	50.90	41.54	46.27

Table 2: Subtask 2 Inter-annotator Agreement Scores. Reported in percentages (%).

3.2.3 Annotation Process & Curation

Five annotators were involved and independently annotated for both subtasks across the span of a few months. For each round of annotations, annotators were presented with a subset of the dataset. After each round, the curator consolidated the final annotations as follows:

Subtask 1 The majority voted label was retained as the final label. Every example in the final corpus was annotated by at least two annotators. The curator has the final vote if there are ties, or if only one annotation is present. Further details are available in the CNC paper (Tan et al., 2022a).

Subtask 2 There was no straightforward way to take a majority label for span annotations. Therefore, our approach was that the curator took into account the spans highlighted by the annotators and decided on the final selection.

After each annotation round, the final span annotations were made available for annotators to review and discuss.

3.2.4 Summary Statistics

Inter-annotator Agreement For Subtask 1, scores are reflected in Table 1. Also reported in

Figure 2: Screenshot of the annotation tool used to mark Cause-Effect-Signal spans.

Stat.	Label	Train	Dev	Test	Total
#	*Causal*	1603	178	176	1957
Sent-	*Non-causal*	1322	145	135	1602
ences	Total	2925	323	311	3559
Avg.	*Causal*	35.48	36.86	41.27	36.13
#	*Non-causal*	27.34	27.35	30.25	27.59
words	Total	31.80	32.59	36.49	32.28

Table 3: Subtask 1 Data Summary Statistics.

Stat.	Train	Dev	Test	Total
# Sentences	160	15	89	264
# Relations	183	18	119	320
Avg. rels/sent	1.14	1.20	1.34	1.21
Avg. # words	17.21	16.13	28.45	20.94
Cause	6.52	7.28	12.76	8.89
Effect	7.80	6.44	10.20	8.62
Signal	1.55	1.60	1.36	1.47
Avg # signals/rel	0.67	0.56	0.82	0.72
Prop. of rels w/ signals	0.64	0.56	0.76	0.68

Table 4: Subtask 2 Data Summary Statistics.

Tan et al. (2022a), overall, the dataset has a Krippendorff's Alpha (K-Alpha) agreement score of 34.99%.

For Subtask 2, the agreement metrics used were Exact Match (EM), Token Overlap (TO), One-Side Bound (OSB), and K-Alpha. Scores are presented in Table 2. Overall, the dataset had agreement scores of 6.96% EM, 23.27% OSB, 27.31% TO, and 46.27% K-Alpha. Since OSB and TO are relaxed span evaluation metrics (Lee and Sun, 2019), they are naturally much higher than EM, which is a strict metric. How the metrics were calculated is described in the Appendix Section A.1.

Shared Task Data The summary statistics for Subtask 1 and 2 are available in Tables 3 and 4 respectively.

It is worth noting that for Subtask 2, the test set contained sentences that were much longer than those in the training sets. This is because we were annotating the shorter sentences first based on annotators' feedback that working with shorter sentences at the beginning helps them to familiarise themselves with the annotation rules. Since there were more sentences in the training set, the training set naturally also had more short sentences for us to annotate first. Once we are done with span annotations, the average number of words for Subtask 2 should tally with the causal sentences of Subtask 1, shown earlier in Table 3.

4 Task Description

The shared task is comprised of two subtasks related to Event Causality Identification. The objective of each task is described in detail as follows:

4.1 Subtask 1: Causal Event Classification

The objective of this task is to classify whether an event sentence contains any cause-effect meaning. Systems had to predict *Causal* or *Non-causal* labels per test sentence. An event sentence was defined to be *Causal* if it contains at least one causal relation.

4.2 Subtask 2: Cause-Effect-Signal Span Detection

The objective of this task is the detection of the consecutive spans relevant to a *Causal* relation. There are three types of spans involved in a *Causal* relation: The *Cause* span refers to words that describe the event that triggers another *Effect* event. The *Effect* span refers to words that describe the resulting event arising from a *Cause* event. *Signals* are optionally present, and are words that explicitly indicate a *Causal* relation is present. In our dataset, multiple *Causal* relations can exist in a sentence, and participants have to identify all of them.

5 Evaluation & Competition

5.1 Evaluation Metrics

5.1.1 Subtask 1

We evaluated participants' predictions using Accuracy (Acc), Precision (P), Recall (R), F1, and Matthews Correlation Coefficient (MCC) scores.

5.1.2 Subtask 2

Following previous evaluation metrics for Cause-Effect Span Detection (Mariko et al., 2020, 2021) and text chunking (Tjong Kim Sang and Buchholz,

2000), we assessed predictions using Macro P, R and F1 metrics.

Participants uploaded sentences with Cause-Effect-Signal spans marked directly in the text using `ARG0`, `ARG1` and `SIG` start and end boundary markers. We converted these marked sentences into two white-space tokenized sequences, one corresponding to the token labels for Cause and Effect, and another corresponding to the token labels for Signals. We used the token classification evaluation scheme from `seqeval` (Nakayama, 2018; Ramshaw and Marcus, 1995)[4] provided through Huggingface (Wolf et al., 2020)[5].

Evaluation was conducted at the relation level. In other words, examples with multiple causal relations were unpacked and each relation contributed equally to the final score.

Handling multiple relations Since one input sequence can return multiple causal relations, we adjusted the evaluation code to automatically extract the combination that results in the best F1 score. As such, participants could submit multiple Cause-Effect-Signal span predictions per input sequence in any order. An illustration is provided in Figure 5.1.2.

In evaluation, we only compare with the number of causal relations that the true label has. Let the number of predicted relations be n_p, and the number of actual relations be n_a. Our evaluation script does the following:

- If the number of predicted relations exceeds the number of actual relations ($n_p > n_a$), we kept only the first n_a predictions.
- If the number of predicted relations is less than the number of actual relations ($n_p < n_a$), the missing $n_a - n_p, n_a - n_p + 1, ..., n_a$ relation predictions were represented by tokens that all correspond to the Other (`O`) label.

5.2 Baseline

For Subtask 1, we duplicated the BERT (Devlin et al., 2019) and LSTM (Hochreiter and Schmidhuber, 1997) baselines from our previous work (Tan et al., 2022a) that achieved F1 scores of 81.20% and 78.22% respectively.

For Subtask 2, a random baseline[6] was created for reference. This baseline first randomly identifies start positions for Cause and Effect spans, and then identifies end positions for these spans with a linearly increasing probability as we move away from the start location in order to reflect our preference for longer spans. We also randomly predicted words to be signals with a 10% chance. The baseline F1 score was 0.45%.

5.3 Competition Set-up

We used the Codalab website to host our competition.[7]

Registration 37 participants requested to participate on the Codalab page. However, we required participants to email us some personal details (Name, Institution and Email) to avoid teams from creating multiple accounts to cheat. Subsequently, 29 participants were successfully registered, but only 17 accounts participated by uploading predictions.

Trial and Test Periods The trial period started on April 15, 2022 and the validation labels were released on August 01, 2022. Participants could upload any number of submissions against the validation set, and they could also submit predictions for the validation set at any point in time. The main purpose of this setting is for participants to familiarise themselves with the Codalab platform.

The test period started on August 01, 2022 and ended on August 31, 2022. Each participant was allowed only 5 submissions to prevent participants from over-fitting to the test set. After the competition ended, an additional scoring page was created,[8] where participants could upload one prediction a day to generate more scores for their description papers. Any scores from this additional scoring page is not included into the final leaderboard.

For both subtasks, models were ranked based on F1 performance on the competition test set.

[4]`https://github.com/chakki-works/seqeval`

[5]`https://huggingface.co/spaces/evaluate-metric/seqeval`

[6]`https://github.com/tanfiona/CausalNewsCorpus/blob/master/random_st2.py`

[7]The competition page is at `https://codalab.lisn.upsaclay.fr/competitions/2299`. The additional scoring page is at `https://codalab.lisn.upsaclay.fr/competitions/7046`.

[8]The additional scoring page is at `https://codalab.lisn.upsaclay.fr/competitions/7046`.

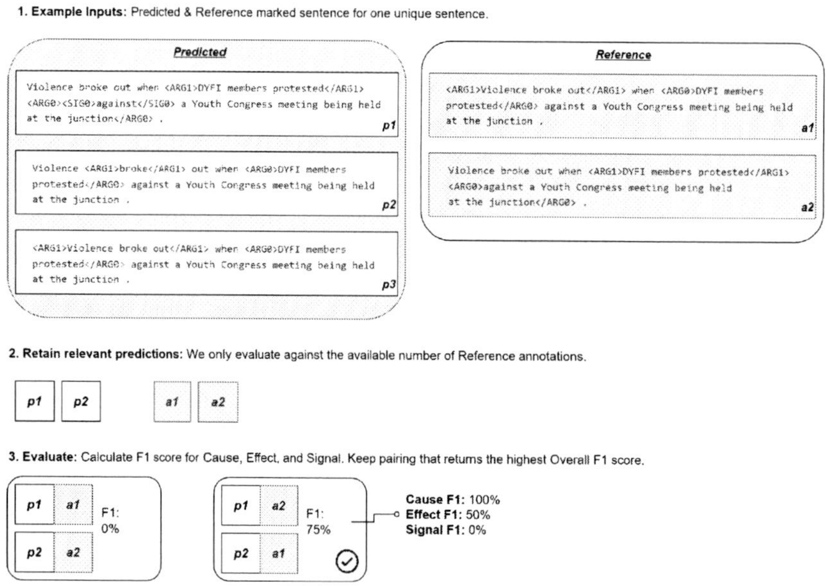

Figure 3: Illustration of how we process multi-relation examples for sequence evaluation.

6 Participant Systems

6.1 Overview

13 participants successfully submitted scores to Subtask 1 while only 4 successfully submitted scores to Subtask 2 during test period. Table 5 and 6 reflects the leaderboard for Subtask 1 and 2 respectively for evaluation metrics described earlier in Section 5.1. For Subtask 2, we further provided the performance for each span type (i.e., Cause, Effect and Signal).

For Subtask 1, the top performing team was CSECU-DSG (Aziz et al., 2022), scoring 86.19% F1. CSECU-DSG also topped the charts for P, Acc, and MCC scores. Team ARGUABLY (Kohli et al., 2022) followed closely after, with 86.10% F1 score and a high recall score of 91.48%. Both methods fine-tuned SOTA pre-trained BERT variants (RoBERTA (Liu et al., 2019) and DeBERTa (He et al., 2021)) to the classification task.

For Subtask 2, the top performing team was 1Cademy (Chen et al., 2022), scoring 54.15% F1. Team IDIAPers (Fajcik et al., 2022) and SPOCK (Saha et al., 2022) followed closely after, with 48.75% and 47.48% F1 scores respectively. Each team approached the span detection task in a different way: 1Cademy treated the task as a reading comprehension challenge and predicted start and end boundaries of the spans. IDIAPers treated the task as a decoding challenge, while SPOCK generated and classified candidate spans. All participants used pre-trained models in their frameworks.

6.2 Methods

Each teams' systems are summarized below, sorted according to their leaderboard ranking.

6.2.1 Subtask 1

CSECU-DSG (Aziz et al., 2022) proposed a way to unify predictions obtained from two neural network models, by combining the prediction scores generated from each model using a weighted arithmetic mean. The two models used were, Twitter RoBERTa and RoBERTa-base, and each was attached to a linear layer to predict the causal labels. The weights per model were 0.4 and 0.6 respectively, selected through experiments on training data. Their findings on the test set showed that the fused model achieves higher P, R, and F1 score than each model alone, and their approach clinched the top place during the competition.

ARGUABLY (Kohli et al., 2022) proposed using sentence-level data augmentation to fine-tune language models (LMs). They involved contextualised word embeddings of DistilBERT (Sanh et al., 2019) to construct new data. As for the LMs, DeBERTa and dual cross attention RoBERTa models have been experimented with. According to the results, the DeBERTa model fine-tuned on augmented data

Rank	Team Name	Codalab Username	R	P	F1	Acc	MCC
1	CSECU-DSG (Aziz et al., 2022)	csecudsg	88.64	**83.87**	**86.19**	**83.92**	**67.14**
2	ARGUABLY (Kohli et al., 2022)	guneetsk99	**91.48**	81.31	86.10	83.28	66.02
3	LTRC (Adibhatla and Shrivastava, 2022)	hiranmai	88.64	82.11	85.25	82.64	64.51
4	NLP4ITF (Krumbiegel and Decher, 2022)	pogs2022	88.07	82.45	85.16	82.64	64.49
5	IDIAPers (Burdisso et al., 2022)	msingh	87.50	82.80	85.08	82.64	64.49
6	NoisyAnnot (Nguyen and Mitra, 2022)	thearkamitra	88.07	82.01	84.93	82.32	63.83
7	SNU-Causality Lab (Kim et al., 2022)	JuHyeon_Kim	90.34	79.50	84.57	81.35	62.04
8	LXPER AI Research	brucewlee	86.36	82.61	84.44	81.99	63.18
9	1Cademy (Nik et al., 2022)	nika	86.36	81.72	83.98	81.35	61.85
10	-	quynhanh	85.80	79.06	82.29	79.10	57.19
11	BERT Baseline (Tan et al., 2022a)	tanfiona	84.66	78.01	81.20	77.81	54.52
12	GGNN (Trust et al., 2022)	PaulTrust	88.07	74.88	80.94	76.53	52.05
13	LSTM Basline (Tan et al., 2022a)	hansih	84.66	72.68	78.22	73.31	45.15
14	Innovators	lapardnemihk9989	78.98	72.02	75.34	70.74	39.81
15	-	necva	81.25	59.09	68.42	57.56	9.44

Table 5: Subtask 1 Leaderboard. Ranked by Binary F1. All scores are reported in percentages (%). Highest score per column is in bold.

Ra-nk	Team Name	Codalab Username	Overall				Cause (n=119)			Effect (n=119)			Signal (n=98)		
			R	P	F1	Acc	R	P	F1	R	P	F1	R	P	F1
1	1Cademy (Chen et al., 2022)	gezhang	**53.87**	55.09	**54.15**	**43.15**	**55.46**	**57.98**	**56.47**	**55.46**	57.14	**56.13**	50.00	49.09	48.92
2	IDIAPers (Fajcik et al., 2022)	msingh	47.62	51.21	48.75	40.83	45.38	45.38	45.38	42.86	42.86	42.86	**56.12**	**68.44**	**60.01**
3	SPOCK (Saha et al., 2022)	spock	43.75	**57.62**	47.48	36.87	37.82	49.19	41.40	39.50	**59.66**	46.29	56.12	65.39	56.32
4	LTRC (Adibhatla and Shrivastava, 2022)	hiranmai	5.65	2.34	3.23	33.03	2.52	1.10	1.53	13.45	5.51	7.60	0.00	0.00	0.00
5	Random Baseline	tanfiona	0.30	0.89	0.45	21.94	0.84	2.52	1.26	0.00	0.00	0.00	0.00	0.00	0.00

Table 6: Subtask 2 Leaderboard. Ranked by Overall Macro F1. All scores are reported in percentages (%). Highest score per column is in bold.

outperformed the unaugmented DeBERTa model and RoBERTa models.

LTRC (Adibhatla and Shrivastava, 2022) used various transformers-based language models followed by a classification head. The pre-trained models explored by them were: BART-large (Lewis et al., 2020), RoBERTa-base+Linear Layer, RoBERTa-large+Linear Layer, RoBERTa-base+Adapter and RoBERTa-large+Adapter. Their best model slightly beats the baseline scores on the development set.

NLP4ITF (Krumbiegel and Decher, 2022) proposed building a RoBERTa model with linguistic features. They mainly involved named entities (NE) and cause-effect-signal (CES) spans from Subtask 2 to incorporate linguistic features with the input text. Based on their findings, the model trained with the PER (person) NE class with CES, achieved the best results, outperforming the RoBERTa baseline (model trained on data with no linguistic features).

IDIAPers (Burdisso et al., 2022) proposed a prompt-based approach for fine-tuning LMs in which the classification task is modeled as a masked language modeling problem (MLM). This approach allows LMs natively pre-trained on MLM problems, like RoBERTa, to directly generate textual responses to domain-specific prompts. This approach allow the model to be trained in a few-shot configuration, keeping most of available data for measuring the generalization power the model. The best-performing model was trained with only 256 instances per class and yet was able to obtain the second-best precision and third-best accuracy.

NoisyAnnot (Nguyen and Mitra, 2022) proposed fine-tuning different LMs with customised cross-entropy loss functions that exploit annotation information such as the number of annotators and their agreement. They used several language models including BERT, RoBERTa and XLNET models and showed that the involvement of annotation information improves the model performance.

SNU-Causality Lab (Kim et al., 2022) proposed fine-tuning an ELECTRA model using the CNC dataset and augmented data. They followed two approaches for data augmentation: (1) concatenating SemEval-2010 to CNC and (2) generating new samples using POS tagging. With the POS tagging-based approach they mainly targeted replacing causality irrelevant words with POS tags, to generate more data while preserving the causality relevant information in the original dataset.

1Cademy (Nik et al., 2022) experimented with self-training to generate more sequence classification examples from unlabeled Wikipedia sentences. They experimented with three pretrained models (BERT, RoBERTa and ELECTRA), and also experimented with three ratios of positive to negative self-labeled examples (1:3, 1:1, 3:1). Their experiments showed that including self-labeled data during training always returns higher F1 scores. Their best model during test time was the RoBERTa-based model with 1:1 self-training ratio, which surpassed the competition baseline scores.

GGNN (Trust et al., 2022) injected word embeddings into a Gated Graph Neural Network (GGNN), which were attached to a RNN decoder to predict the sequence label. Two word embeddings were explored: Word2Vec and BERT. Their BERT+GGNN combination outperforms the BERT baseline provided during the competition for both the development and test sets for P, F1 and Acc.

6.2.2 Subtask 2

1Cademy (Chen et al., 2022) approached this task in a reading comprehension manner, and created a baseline BERT-based neural network that predicted the start and end positions of each Cause, Effect, and Signal span. They introduced beam-search methods (BSS) as post-processing constraints suited to the task. They also introduced a signal classifier that detects if a Signal exists in the sequence or not via a joint model (JS) or a separate model (ES). Additionally, BART was fine-tuned for paraphrasing to re-write Cause and Effect phrases within each sentence for data augmentation (DA). In the end, their best model is a combination of Baseline+BSS+ES+DA method, where the DA generated 3 new phrases per span. This model achieved F1 score of 54.15% on the test set, clinching the top place during the competition.

IDIAPers (Fajcik et al., 2022) approached the task in an encoder-decoder framework. They conditioned the T5 language model three times per example to generate up to four causal relations per example. In each round, given the history of a sentence, the model generates Cause, followed by Effect, and then Signal. This model is their vanilla model known as T5-CES. History refers to the input sequence with any annotated spans from the previous round, if applicable. In experiments, they also explored (1) variants involving a version without historical annotations, (2) T5-large pre-trained model, and (3) changing the order of generation to be Effect, Cause then Signal. Their best model on the test set (T5-CES) achieved 48.8 F1 score, coming in second in the competition.

SPOCK (Saha et al., 2022) designed two separate frameworks for the span detection task, span-based modelling and token classification. Both approaches far exceed the random baseline provided by the organizers during the competition period. Their span-based modelling approach achieved an F1 score of 47.48%, ranking third in the competition. This model classifies a list of candidate spans to a Cause, Effect, Signal or None label. The candidate spans are generated by considering all possible spans up to a maximum length. The model receives inputs comprising a CLS token embedding, concatenated with a width embedding, plus the span embedding representation itself. To select the final Cause-Effect-Signal span, spans below a certain threshold are removed, and then the span with the highest probability for that label is retained.

LTRC (Adibhatla and Shrivastava, 2022) approached the task as a token classification task, and designed a BERT-based IOB predicting model alongside some heuristics adjusted for the task. Their approach slightly beats the baseline scores on the development set.

7 Analysis & Discussion

7.1 Trends

Consistent with NLP trends, pre-trained language models are popular and employed by all teams and for both subtasks.

For Subtask 1, teams found novel ways to improve from the BERT and LSTM baseline by combining multiple models, adding linguistic features, incorporating additional neural network layers, and working with augmented data.

For Subtask 2, there is a wide variation in framing the task. Teams approached it as a reading comprehension, encoder-decoder, candidate span classification and token classification task. Additionally, there are two constraints that models had to accommodate: (1) The task involves predicting multiple causal relations per input sentence, and (2) Not all causal relations have a signal span. The top three teams carefully adjust their models to work with the two constraints. For (1), IDIAPers predicted different relations using rounds while incorporating the predicted annotations of

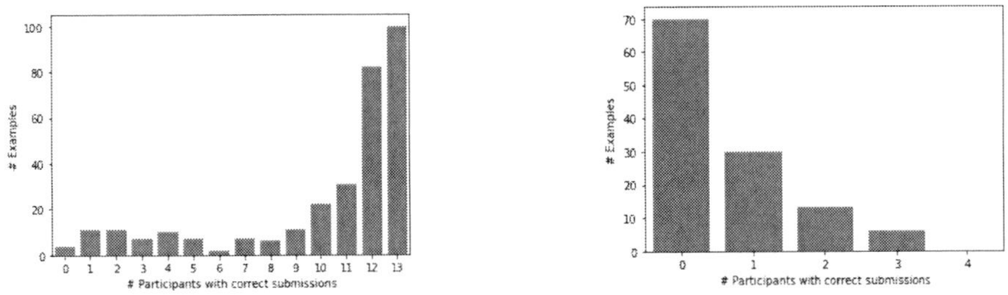

(a) Subtask 1

(b) Subtask 2

Figure 4: Histogram of exact matches.

Subtask	Finished	Failed	Total
Subtask 1	58	8	66
Subtask 2	12	24	36

Table 7: Number of submissions received for test set.

the previous round. For (2), 1Cademy included a separate classification task, while IDIAPers and SPOCK permitted "empty" or "None" span predictions. Interestingly, the F1 score for signals is highest for IDIAPers, suggesting merits to predict signal spans in a manner that includes Cause and Effect predictions as inputs.

7.2 Participation

More submissions were received for Subtask 1 than for Subtask 2, as shown in Table 7. Unsurprisingly, there is a high proportion of failed submissions in Subtask 2. Since Subtask 2 requires specific formatting of argument markings and compiling of multiple predictions into a list, it is easy to face formatting errors. For Subtask 2, although 12 participants did try to submit for the competition, only 4 managed to submit predictions of the right format. A closer look at the submission files suggests that most of the time, these participants intended to upload predictions for Subtask 1. However, because the default Codalab tab falls on Subtask 2, they make submissions to the wrong task. Nevertheless, we are aware of 1 participant who reached out to try and resolve formatting issues and did not manage to resubmit their predictions in the right format in time. This team ran into issues trying to match the spacing of the original input text.

7.3 Error Analysis

For Subtask 1, we had 13 participants while for Subtask 2, we had 4 participants. For Subtask 1, we counted the number of teams that matched the true labels exactly per example. For Subtask 2, if any predicted span exactly match the true Cause-Effect-Signal span, we considered there to be an accurate count. A histogram per subtask reflecting the accuracy counts are reflected in Figure 4.

For Subtask 1, 100 examples were predicted correctly, while 4 examples were predicted wrongly by all participants. There is a total of 52 examples that are challenging, where less than half of the participants were able to get a correct prediction.

For Subtask 2, no examples were predicted correctly by all participants. This is because LTRC's submission was very close to the Random Baseline and had no exactly correct predictions. 6 causal relations were predicted correctly by the remaining three participants. Nevertheless, most examples were predicted wrongly by all participants (i.e., 70 examples received all wrong predictions). Clearly, Subtask 2 is a challenging task and has a lot of room for growth.

8 Conclusion

In conclusion, our shared task investigated two important tasks in causal text mining, namely: (1) Causal Event Classification, and (2) Cause-Effect-Signal Span Detection. Our shared task attracted 29 registered participants and 17 active participants who made over 100 submissions on the test set. Based on the 12 description papers received, many novel methods that exceeded our initial baseline were proposed. The best F1 scores achieved for Subtask 1 and 2 were 86.19% and 54.15% respectively.

We intend to re-launch this shared task next year with even more data for Subtask 2. Additionally, we will also investigate the challenging examples in Subtask 1 that are predicted wrongly by many teams.

References

Hiranmai Sri Adibhatla and Manish Shrivastava. 2022. LTRC @ Causal News Corpus 2022: Extracting and identifying causal elements using adapters. In *Proceedings of the 5th Workshop on Challenges and Applications of Automated Extraction of Socio-political Events from Text (CASE 2022)*, Online. Association for Computational Linguistics.

Nabiha Asghar. 2016. Automatic extraction of causal relations from natural language texts: a comprehensive survey. *arXiv preprint arXiv:1605.07895*.

Abdul Aziz, Md. Akram Hossain, and Abu Nowshed Chy. 2022. CSECU-DSG @ Causal News Corpus 2022: Fusion of RoBERTa transformer variants for causal event classification. In *Proceedings of the 5th Workshop on Challenges and Applications of Automated Extraction of Socio-political Events from Text (CASE 2022)*, Online. Association for Computational Linguistics.

Biswanath Barik, Erwin Marsi, and Pinar Öztürk. 2016. Event causality extraction from natural science literature. *Res. Comput. Sci.*, 117:97–107.

Sergio Burdisso, Juan Zuluaga-Gomez, Martin Fajcik, Esaú Villatoro-Tello, Muskaan Singh, Petr Motlicek, and Pavel Smrz. 2022. IDIAPers @ Causal News Corpus 2022: Causal relation identification using a few-shot and prompt-based fine-tuning of language models. In *The 5th Workshop on Challenges and Applications of Automated Extraction of Socio-political Events from Text (CASE @ EMNLP 2022)*, Online. Association for Computational Linguistics.

Pengfei Cao, Xinyu Zuo, Yubo Chen, Kang Liu, Jun Zhao, Yuguang Chen, and Weihua Peng. 2021. Knowledge-enriched event causality identification via latent structure induction networks. In *Proceedings of the 59th Annual Meeting of the Association for Computational Linguistics and the 11th International Joint Conference on Natural Language Processing (Volume 1: Long Papers)*, pages 4862–4872, Online. Association for Computational Linguistics.

Tommaso Caselli and Piek Vossen. 2017. The event StoryLine corpus: A new benchmark for causal and temporal relation extraction. In *Proceedings of the Events and Stories in the News Workshop*, pages 77–86, Vancouver, Canada. Association for Computational Linguistics.

Xingran Chen, Ge Zhang, Adam Nik, Mingyu Li, and Jie Fu. 2022. 1Cademy @ Causal News Corpus 2022: Enhance causal span detection via beam-search-based position selector. In *Proceedings of the 5th Workshop on Challenges and Applications of Automated Extraction of Socio-political Events from Text (CASE 2022)*, Online. Association for Computational Linguistics.

Dhairya Dalal, Mihael Arcan, and Paul Buitelaar. 2021. Enhancing multiple-choice question answering with causal knowledge. In *Proceedings of Deep Learning Inside Out (DeeLIO): The 2nd Workshop on Knowledge Extraction and Integration for Deep Learning Architectures*, pages 70–80, Online. Association for Computational Linguistics.

Jacob Devlin, Ming-Wei Chang, Kenton Lee, and Kristina Toutanova. 2019. BERT: Pre-training of deep bidirectional transformers for language understanding. In *Proceedings of the 2019 Conference of the North American Chapter of the Association for Computational Linguistics: Human Language Technologies, Volume 1 (Long and Short Papers)*, pages 4171–4186, Minneapolis, Minnesota. Association for Computational Linguistics.

Jesse Dunietz, Greg Burnham, Akash Bharadwaj, Owen Rambow, Jennifer Chu-Carroll, and Dave Ferrucci. 2020. To test machine comprehension, start by defining comprehension. In *Proceedings of the 58th Annual Meeting of the Association for Computational Linguistics*, pages 7839–7859, Online. Association for Computational Linguistics.

Jesse Dunietz, Lori Levin, and Jaime Carbonell. 2017. The BECauSE corpus 2.0: Annotating causality and overlapping relations. In *Proceedings of the 11th Linguistic Annotation Workshop*, pages 95–104, Valencia, Spain. Association for Computational Linguistics.

Richard Eckart de Castilho, Éva Mújdricza-Maydt, Seid Muhie Yimam, Silvana Hartmann, Iryna Gurevych, Anette Frank, and Chris Biemann. 2016. A web-based tool for the integrated annotation of semantic and syntactic structures. In *Proceedings of the Workshop on Language Technology Resources and Tools for Digital Humanities (LT4DH)*, pages 76–84, Osaka, Japan. The COLING 2016 Organizing Committee.

Martin Fajcik, Muskaan Singh, Juan Zuluaga-Gomez, Esaú Villatoro-Tello, Sergio Burdisso, Petr Motlicek, and Pavel Smrz. 2022. IDIAPers @ Causal News Corpus 2022: Extracting cause-effect-signal triplets via pre-trained autoregressive language model. In *The 5th Workshop on Challenges and Applications of Automated Extraction of Socio-political Events from Text (CASE @ EMNLP 2022)*, Online. Association for Computational Linguistics.

Lei Gao, Prafulla Kumar Choubey, and Ruihong Huang. 2019. Modeling document-level causal structures for event causal relation identification. In *Proceedings of the 2019 Conference of the North American Chapter of the Association for Computational Linguistics: Human Language Technologies, Volume 1 (Long and Short Papers)*, pages 1808–1817, Minneapolis, Minnesota. Association for Computational Linguistics.

Chikara Hashimoto, Kentaro Torisawa, Julien Kloetzer, Motoki Sano, István Varga, Jong-Hoon Oh, and Yutaka Kidawara. 2014. Toward future scenario generation: Extracting event causality exploiting semantic relation, context, and association features. In

Proceedings of the 52nd Annual Meeting of the Association for Computational Linguistics (Volume 1: Long Papers), pages 987–997, Baltimore, Maryland. Association for Computational Linguistics.

Oktie Hassanzadeh, Debarun Bhattacharjya, Mark Feblowitz, Kavitha Srinivas, Michael Perrone, Shirin Sohrabi, and Michael Katz. 2019. Answering binary causal questions through large-scale text mining: An evaluation using cause-effect pairs from human experts. In *Proceedings of the Twenty-Eighth International Joint Conference on Artificial Intelligence, IJCAI-19*, pages 5003–5009. International Joint Conferences on Artificial Intelligence Organization.

Pengcheng He, Xiaodong Liu, Jianfeng Gao, and Weizhu Chen. 2021. Deberta: decoding-enhanced bert with disentangled attention. In *9th International Conference on Learning Representations, ICLR 2021, Virtual Event, Austria, May 3-7, 2021*. OpenReview.net.

Iris Hendrickx, Su Nam Kim, Zornitsa Kozareva, Preslav Nakov, Diarmuid Ó Séaghdha, Sebastian Padó, Marco Pennacchiotti, Lorenza Romano, and Stan Szpakowicz. 2010. SemEval-2010 task 8: Multi-way classification of semantic relations between pairs of nominals. In *Proceedings of the 5th International Workshop on Semantic Evaluation*, pages 33–38, Uppsala, Sweden. Association for Computational Linguistics.

Christopher Hidey and Kathy McKeown. 2016. Identifying causal relations using parallel Wikipedia articles. In *Proceedings of the 54th Annual Meeting of the Association for Computational Linguistics (Volume 1: Long Papers)*, pages 1424–1433, Berlin, Germany. Association for Computational Linguistics.

Sepp Hochreiter and Jürgen Schmidhuber. 1997. Long Short-Term Memory. *Neural Computation*, 9(8):1735–1780.

Ali Hürriyetoğlu, editor. 2021. *Proceedings of the 4th Workshop on Challenges and Applications of Automated Extraction of Socio-political Events from Text (CASE 2021)*. Association for Computational Linguistics, Online.

Ali Hürriyetoğlu, Osman Mutlu, Erdem Yörük, Farhana Ferdousi Liza, Ritesh Kumar, and Shyam Ratan. 2021a. Multilingual protest news detection - shared task 1, CASE 2021. In *Proceedings of the 4th Workshop on Challenges and Applications of Automated Extraction of Socio-political Events from Text (CASE 2021)*, pages 79–91, Online. Association for Computational Linguistics.

Ali Hürriyetoğlu, Hristo Tanev, Vanni Zavarella, Jakub Piskorski, Reyyan Yeniterzi, Osman Mutlu, Deniz Yuret, and Aline Villavicencio. 2021b. Challenges and applications of automated extraction of socio-political events from text (CASE 2021): Workshop and shared task report. In *Proceedings of the 4th Workshop on Challenges and Applications of Automated Extraction of Socio-political Events from Text (CASE 2021)*, pages 1–9, Online. Association for Computational Linguistics.

Ali Hürriyetoğlu, Erdem Yörük, Vanni Zavarella, and Hristo Tanev, editors. 2020a. *Proceedings of the Workshop on Automated Extraction of Socio-political Events from News 2020*. European Language Resources Association (ELRA), Marseille, France.

Ali Hürriyetoğlu, Vanni Zavarella, Hristo Tanev, Erdem Yörük, Ali Safaya, and Osman Mutlu. 2020b. Automated extraction of socio-political events from news (AESPEN): Workshop and shared task report. In *Proceedings of the Workshop on Automated Extraction of Socio-political Events from News 2020*, pages 1–6, Marseille, France. European Language Resources Association (ELRA).

Ali Hürriyetoğlu, Erdem Yörük, Osman Mutlu, Fırat Duruşan, Çağrı Yoltar, Deniz Yüret, and Burak Gürel. 2021. Cross-Context News Corpus for Protest Event-Related Knowledge Base Construction. *Data Intelligence*, 3(2):308–335.

Kiyoshi Izumi, Hitomi Sano, and Hiroki Sakaji. 2021. Economic causal-chain search and economic indicator prediction using textual data. In *Proceedings of the 3rd Financial Narrative Processing Workshop*, pages 19–25, Lancaster, United Kingdom. Association for Computational Linguistics.

Yohan Jo, Seojin Bang, Chris Reed, and Eduard H. Hovy. 2021. Classifying argumentative relations using logical mechanisms and argumentation schemes. *Trans. Assoc. Comput. Linguistics*, 9:721–739.

Juhyeon Kim, Yesong Choe, and Sanghack Lee. 2022. SNU-Causality Lab @ Causal News Corpus 2022: Detecting causality by data augmentation via part-of-speech tagging. In *Proceedings of the 5th Workshop on Challenges and Applications of Automated Extraction of Socio-political Events from Text (CASE 2022)*, Online. Association for Computational Linguistics.

Guneet Kohli, Prabsimran Kaur, and Jatin Bedi. 2022. ARGUABLY @ Causal News Corpus 2022: Contextually augmented language models for event causality identification. In *Proceedings of the 5th Workshop on Challenges and Applications of Automated Extraction of Socio-political Events from Text (CASE 2022)*, Online. Association for Computational Linguistics.

Theresa Krumbiegel and Sophie Decher. 2022. NLP4ITF @ Causal News Corpus 2022: Leveraging linguistic information for event causality classification. In *Proceedings of the 5th Workshop on Challenges and Applications of Automated Extraction of Socio-political Events from Text (CASE 2022)*, Online. Association for Computational Linguistics.

Grace E. Lee and Aixin Sun. 2019. A study on agreement in PICO span annotations. In *Proceedings of the 42nd International ACM SIGIR Conference on Research and Development in Information Retrieval, SIGIR 2019, Paris, France, July 21-25, 2019*, pages 1149–1152. ACM.

Mike Lewis, Yinhan Liu, Naman Goyal, Marjan Ghazvininejad, Abdelrahman Mohamed, Omer Levy, Veselin Stoyanov, and Luke Zettlemoyer. 2020. BART: denoising sequence-to-sequence pre-training for natural language generation, translation, and comprehension. In *Proceedings of the 58th Annual Meeting of the Association for Computational Linguistics, ACL 2020, Online, July 5-10, 2020*, pages 7871–7880. Association for Computational Linguistics.

Yinhan Liu, Myle Ott, Naman Goyal, Jingfei Du, Mandar Joshi, Danqi Chen, Omer Levy, Mike Lewis, Luke Zettlemoyer, and Veselin Stoyanov. 2019. Roberta: A robustly optimized BERT pretraining approach. *CoRR*, abs/1907.11692.

Dominique Mariko, Hanna Abi-Akl, Estelle Labidurie, Stephane Durfort, Hugues De Mazancourt, and Mahmoud El-Haj. 2020. The financial document causality detection shared task (FinCausal 2020). In *Proceedings of the 1st Joint Workshop on Financial Narrative Processing and MultiLing Financial Summarisation*, pages 23–32, Barcelona, Spain (Online). COLING.

Dominique Mariko, Hanna Abi Akl, Estelle Labidurie, Stephane Durfort, Hugues de Mazancourt, and Mahmoud El-Haj. 2021. The financial document causality detection shared task (FinCausal 2021). In *Proceedings of the 3rd Financial Narrative Processing Workshop*, pages 58–60, Lancaster, United Kingdom. Association for Computational Linguistics.

Paramita Mirza, Rachele Sprugnoli, Sara Tonelli, and Manuela Speranza. 2014. Annotating causality in the TempEval-3 corpus. In *Proceedings of the EACL 2014 Workshop on Computational Approaches to Causality in Language (CAtoCL)*, pages 10–19, Gothenburg, Sweden. Association for Computational Linguistics.

Paramita Mirza and Sara Tonelli. 2014. An analysis of causality between events and its relation to temporal information. In *Proceedings of COLING 2014, the 25th International Conference on Computational Linguistics: Technical Papers*, pages 2097–2106, Dublin, Ireland. Dublin City University and Association for Computational Linguistics.

Hiroki Nakayama. 2018. seqeval: A python framework for sequence labeling evaluation. Software available from https://github.com/chakki-works/seqeval.

Quynh Anh Nguyen and Arka Mitra. 2022. NoisyAnnot @ Causal News Corpus 2022: Causality detection using multiple annotation decision. In *Proceedings of the 5th Workshop on Challenges and Applications of Automated Extraction of Socio-political Events from Text (CASE 2022)*, Online. Association for Computational Linguistics.

Adam Nik, Ge Zhang, Xingran Chen, Mingyu Li, and Jie Fu. 2022. 1Cademy @ Causal News Corpus 2022: Leveraging self-training in causality classification of socio-political event data. In *Proceedings of the 5th Workshop on Challenges and Applications of Automated Extraction of Socio-political Events from Text (CASE 2022)*, Online. Association for Computational Linguistics.

James Pustejovsky, José M. Castaño, Robert Ingria, Roser Saurí, Robert J. Gaizauskas, Andrea Setzer, Graham Katz, and Dragomir R. Radev. 2003. Timeml: Robust specification of event and temporal expressions in text. In *New Directions in Question Answering, Papers from 2003 AAAI Spring Symposium, Stanford University, Stanford, CA, USA*, pages 28–34. AAAI Press.

Kira Radinsky, Sagie Davidovich, and Shaul Markovitch. 2012. Learning causality for news events prediction. In *Proceedings of the 21st World Wide Web Conference 2012, WWW 2012, Lyon, France, April 16-20, 2012*, pages 909–918. ACM.

Kira Radinsky and Eric Horvitz. 2013. Mining the web to predict future events. In *Sixth ACM International Conference on Web Search and Data Mining, WSDM 2013, Rome, Italy, February 4-8, 2013*, pages 255–264. ACM.

Lance Ramshaw and Mitch Marcus. 1995. Text chunking using transformation-based learning. In *Third Workshop on Very Large Corpora*.

Anik Saha, Alex Gittens, Jian Ni, Oktie Hassanzadeh, Bulent Yener, and Kavitha Srinivas. 2022. SPOCK @ Causal News Corpus 2022: Cause-effect-signal span detection using span-based and sequence tagging models. In *Proceedings of the 5th Workshop on Challenges and Applications of Automated Extraction of Socio-political Events from Text (CASE 2022)*, Online. Association for Computational Linguistics.

Victor Sanh, Lysandre Debut, Julien Chaumond, and Thomas Wolf. 2019. Distilbert, a distilled version of BERT: smaller, faster, cheaper and lighter. *CoRR*, abs/1910.01108.

Roser Saurı, Jessica Littman, Bob Knippen, Robert Gaizauskas, Andrea Setzer, and James Pustejovsky. 2006. Timeml annotation guidelines version 1.2.1.

Katherine Stasaski, Manav Rathod, Tony Tu, Yunfang Xiao, and Marti A. Hearst. 2021. Automatically generating cause-and-effect questions from passages. In *Proceedings of the 16th Workshop on Innovative Use of NLP for Building Educational Applications*, pages 158–170, Online. Association for Computational Linguistics.

Fiona Anting Tan, Devamanyu Hazarika, See-Kiong Ng, Soujanya Poria, and Roger Zimmermann. 2021. Causal augmentation for causal sentence classification. In *Proceedings of the First Workshop on Causal Inference and NLP*, pages 1–20, Punta Cana, Dominican Republic. Association for Computational Linguistics.

Fiona Anting Tan, Ali Hürriyetoğlu, Tommaso Caselli, Nelleke Oostdijk, Tadashi Nomoto, Hansi Hettiarachchi, Iqra Ameer, Onur Uca, Farhana Ferdousi Liza, and Tiancheng Hu. 2022a. The causal news corpus: Annotating causal relations in event sentences from news. In *Proceedings of the Language Resources and Evaluation Conference*, pages 2298–2310, Marseille, France. European Language Resources Association.

Fiona Anting Tan, Xinyu Zuo, and See-Kiong Ng. 2022b. Unicausal: Unified benchmark and model for causal text mining.

Erik F. Tjong Kim Sang and Sabine Buchholz. 2000. Introduction to the CoNLL-2000 shared task chunking. In *Fourth Conference on Computational Natural Language Learning and the Second Learning Language in Logic Workshop*.

Paul Trust, Provia Kadusabe, Rosane Minghim, Ahmed Zahran, Evangelos Milos, Kizito Omala, and Haseeb Yonais. 2022. GGNN @ Causal News Corpus 2022: Gated graph neural networks for causal event classification from social-political news articles. In *Proceedings of the 5th Workshop on Challenges and Applications of Automated Extraction of Socio-political Events from Text (CASE 2022)*, Online. Association for Computational Linguistics.

Bonnie Webber, Rashmi Prasad, Alan Lee, and Aravind Joshi. 2019. The penn discourse treebank 3.0 annotation manual. *Philadelphia, University of Pennsylvania*.

Thomas Wolf, Lysandre Debut, Victor Sanh, Julien Chaumond, Clement Delangue, Anthony Moi, Pierric Cistac, Tim Rault, Remi Louf, Morgan Funtowicz, Joe Davison, Sam Shleifer, Patrick von Platen, Clara Ma, Yacine Jernite, Julien Plu, Canwen Xu, Teven Le Scao, Sylvain Gugger, Mariama Drame, Quentin Lhoest, and Alexander Rush. 2020. Transformers: State-of-the-art natural language processing. In *Proceedings of the 2020 Conference on Empirical Methods in Natural Language Processing: System Demonstrations*, pages 38–45, Online. Association for Computational Linguistics.

Jinghang Xu, Wanli Zuo, Shining Liang, and Xianglin Zuo. 2020. A review of dataset and labeling methods for causality extraction. In *Proceedings of the 28th International Conference on Computational Linguistics*, pages 1519–1531, Barcelona, Spain (Online). International Committee on Computational Linguistics.

Jie Yang, Soyeon Caren Han, and Josiah Poon. 2022. A survey on extraction of causal relations from natural language text. *Knowl. Inf. Syst.*, 64(5):1161–1186.

Erdem Yörük, Ali Hürriyetoğlu, Fırat Duruşan, and Çağrı Yoltar. 2021. Random sampling in corpus design: Cross-context generalizability in automated multicountry protest event collection. *American Behavioral Scientist*, 0(0):00027642211021630.

Xinyu Zuo, Pengfei Cao, Yubo Chen, Kang Liu, Jun Zhao, Weihua Peng, and Yuguang Chen. 2021a. Improving event causality identification via self-supervised representation learning on external causal statement. In *Findings of the Association for Computational Linguistics: ACL-IJCNLP 2021*, pages 2162–2172, Online. Association for Computational Linguistics.

Xinyu Zuo, Pengfei Cao, Yubo Chen, Kang Liu, Jun Zhao, Weihua Peng, and Yuguang Chen. 2021b. LearnDA: Learnable knowledge-guided data augmentation for event causality identification. In *Proceedings of the 59th Annual Meeting of the Association for Computational Linguistics and the 11th International Joint Conference on Natural Language Processing (Volume 1: Long Papers)*, pages 3558–3571, Online. Association for Computational Linguistics.

Xinyu Zuo, Yubo Chen, Kang Liu, and Jun Zhao. 2020. KnowDis: Knowledge enhanced data augmentation for event causality detection via distant supervision. In *Proceedings of the 28th International Conference on Computational Linguistics*, pages 1544–1550, Barcelona, Spain (Online). International Committee on Computational Linguistics.

A Appendix

A.1 Subtask 2 Agreement Score Calculations

For span annotations, the agreement scores were calculated by taking a weighted average of the subset level agreement scores that takes into account the example counts per subset.

We split the training plus development set into 8 subsets and the test set into 2 subsets. While conducting the annotations, the agreement scores were evaluated at a subset level so that we can consistently assess the annotators' performance. The subset level scores takes the average scores between each pair of annotators. For example, if there were three annotators (Annotator A, B, and C) for the subset, then we took the average agreement score when comparing (A,B), (B,C) and (A,C) annotator pairs. Each pair was weighted equally.

The annotator pair level scores were computed by taking the average scores across the sentences. Each sentence was weighted equally.

At the sentence level, agreement scores were obtained by taking the average scores of each causal relation pair. Each causal relation pair was weighted equally.

Since annotators might annotate multiple spans per example, there are many ways to match the annotated relations between two annotators. We approached this conflict by considering every possible combination pair, after which, we retained the match that returned the highest possible sum of EM, OSB and TO scores. If one annotator identified more causal relations than the other, then EM, OSB and TO scores for that relation is automatically zero.

The KAlpha script was an open-source code[9]. The other three metrics were coded based on previous work (Lee and Sun, 2019).

[9]`https://github.com/emerging-welfare/kAlpha`

Tracking COVID-19 protest events in the United States. Shared Task 2: Event Database Replication, CASE 2022

Vanni Zavarella
University of Cagliari
v.zavarella@unica.it

Hristo Tanev
European Commission
hristo.tanev@ec.europa.eu

Ali Hürriyetoğlu
KNAW Humanities
Cluster DHLab
ali.hurriyetoglu@dh.huc.knaw.nl

Peratham Wiriyathammabhum
peratham.bkk@gmail.com

Bertrand De Longueville
European Commission
bertrand.de-longueville@ec.europa.eu

Abstract

The goal of Shared Task 2 is evaluating state-of-the-art event detection systems by comparing the spatio-temporal distribution of the events they detect with existing event databases.

The task focuses on some usability requirements of event detection systems in real world scenarios. Namely, it aims to measure the ability of such a system to: (i) detect socio-political event mentions in news and social media, (ii) properly find their geographical locations, (iii) de-duplicate reports extracted from multiple sources referring to the same actual event. Building an annotated corpus for training and evaluating jointly these sub-tasks is highly time consuming. One possible way to indirectly evaluate a system's output without an annotated corpus available is to measure its correlation with human-curated event data sets.

In the last three years, the COVID-19 pandemic became motivation for restrictions and anti-pandemic measures on a world scale. This has triggered a wave of reactions and citizen actions in many countries. Shared Task 2 challenges participants to identify COVID-19 related protest actions from large unstructured data sources both from mainstream and social media. We assess each system's ability to model the evolution of protest events both temporally and spatially by using a number of correlation metrics with respect to a comprehensive and validated data set of COVID-related protest events (Raleigh et al., 2010).

1 Introduction

State-of-the-art evaluation methods for event detection are based on manually coded corpora with annotated document and sub-document units, including annotation of syntactic fragments, such as event reporting verbal phrases, as well as entities having specific semantic roles, such as *victim, perpetrator, weapons*, etc., see (Hürriyetoğlu et al., 2021) and (Atkinson et al., 2017) among the others. While this type of benchmarks provide accurate means for measuring the performance of event detection approaches, their development implies significant efforts: many person-hours of annotations by journalists or linguists, which make such annotated corpora limited in number and size and generally developed for the English language only, with a few exceptions (Hürriyetoğlu et al., 2021). Moreover, such evaluation methods do not assess the overall usability of machine-coded event data sets for micro-level modelling of social processes. Also, in the domain of socio-political and armed conflicts, spatio-temporal analysis has become standard and state-of-the-art evaluation methods come short in evaluating exhaustively the spatial and temporal aspects of event detection systems.

Extracting spatio-temporal information from online text sources has developed in the late 2000's, with the advent of the so-called 'Web 2.0' and Social Networks (Pultar et al., 2008), (De Longueville et al., 2009). Since then, applications have been developed in fields as diverse as disaster management (De Longueville et al., 2010), traffic monitoring (D'Andrea et al., 2015), or fight against crime (Kounadi et al., 2015). Detecting socio-political events (and in particular, protests) emerged as an important use case (Zhang, 2019), as many applications in this field need to rely on comprehensive, timely and high-quality data that is often not available (e.g. high quality commercial data is produced on a weekly, or even monthly basis, while applications need near-real-time data). This is a gap that CASE workshops, and this shared task in particular, are aiming to address.

The dynamics of the COVID-19 protests and

Proceedings of the 5th Workshop on Challenges and Applications of Automated Extraction of Socio-political Events from Text (CASE), pages 209 - 216
December 7-8, 2022 ©2022 Association for Computational Linguistics

their varied media coverage by news outlets and social media makes it a particularly relevant use case for assessing the capability of automated event extraction systems to analyse socio-political processes. The database replicability Shared Task 2 aims at doing so by challenging event extraction systems to extract a collection of protest events from two heterogeneous text collections (i.e., news and social media). The task's evaluation is done by measuring a number of spatio-temporal correlation coefficients against a gold standard data set of protest incidents, provided by the the Armed Conflict Location and Event Data (ACLED) project (Raleigh et al., 2010).

This task is the second in a series of shared tasks at the CASE 2022 workshop (Hürriyetoğlu et al., 2022b). The first task is concerned with protest news detection at multiple text resolutions (e.g., the document and sentence level) and in multiple languages: English, Hindi, Portuguese, and Spanish (Hürriyetoğlu et al., 2021, 2022a). Task 3 is about detecting event causality in a corpus of sentence pairs that have been annotated with labels on whether there is a causal relations or not between them (Tan et al., 2022a,b).

Teams which participated in Task 1 were invited to participate in this second task. This is an evaluation only task, where all models are (i) trained on the data provided in Task 1, (ii) applied to raw news and social media data, specifically gathered for the task (i.e, news collection crawled from the Web from various news sources, as well as Twitter data), and (iii) evaluated on a manually curated, COVID-19 protest event list, gathered from the Web page of the ACLED project (Raleigh et al., 2010).

2 Related Work

Some recent studies show that performance measures such as precision, recall, and F1 are limited in their capacity to asses the efficiency of an NLP system (Derczynski, 2016; Yacouby and Axman, 2020). Moreover, evaluating a system on detecting socio-political events from text requires additional metrics such as spatio-temporal correlation of the system output and the actual distribution of the events (Wang et al., 2016; Althaus et al., 2021).

In a detailed study Cook and Weidmann (2019) demonstrates the usefulness of disaggregating event reports when considering data from event coding. Several approaches deal with assessing the correlation of automatically generated event data sets with gold standards based on disaggregated event counts, see example Ward et al. (2013) and Schrodt and Analytics (2015) among the others.

Hammond and Weidmann (2014) applied disaggregation of events across PRIO-GRID geographical cells (Tollefsen et al., 2012) to assess the spatio-temporal pattern of conflicts in the Global Database of Events, Language and Tone (GDELT) (Leetaru and Schrodt, 2013). In a later work Zavarella et al. (2020) adapted the aforementioned approach to administrative units for measuring the impact of event de-duplication on increasing correlation with ACLED event data sets.

3 Data

The goal of this task is to evaluate the performance of automatic event detection systems on modeling the spatial and temporal pattern of a social protest movement. We evaluate the capability of participant systems to reproduce a manually curated COVID-19 related protest event data set, by detecting protest event reports, enriched with location and date attributes, from a news corpus collection, a Twitter collection (both pre-filtered for COVID-19 topic occurrence) and from the union of the two.

3.1 Training Data

As a usability analysis, no training data were provided for this Task. Namely, the event definition applied for coding the reference event data set is the same as the one adopted for Shared Task 1 (Hürriyetoğlu et al., 2021) and any data utilized for Task 1 and Task 2, such as the one from Hürriyetoğlu et al. (2021); Duruşan et al. (2022); Yörük et al. (2021), or any additional data could be used to build a system/model run on the input data.

3.2 Input Data

We provide three collections of input data:

- an English language news corpus comprising a large selection of COVID-related articles from US news sources;
- an English language tweet collection comprising daily samples of COVID-related tweets with some geographical metadata referring to U.S.;
- a Spanish language tweet collection comprising daily samples of COVID-related tweets

with some geographical metadata referring to U.S.

News Collection The news corpus used in this Task is a collection of articles in English language spanning the time range July 27, 2020 through October 26,2020 from a large set of news sources from U.S. We used public APIs when available and scraped the newspaper web pages otherwise. For example, we used the New York Times Archive API [1]. The articles are filtered by checking the occurrence of keywords ["covid","coronavirus"] in the top two sentences of the articles. Overall the collection contains around 122k articles. We harmonized the news item metadata from the different collections so as to have the attributes: Publication Date of the article, Title and a Snippet from the article text, comprising the 2 lead sentences.

Twitter The corpus used in this Task is based on a large-size multilingual collection of tweets sampled from the Twitter public streaming API using the set of keywords [*"COVID19"*, *"CoronavirusPandemic"*, *"COVID-19"*, *"2019nCoV"*, *"CoronaOutbreak"*, *"coronavirus"*, *"WuhanVirus"*], described in (Banda et al., 2021). The source data of this collection, together with documentation on how to process the data, can be found on `https://github.com/thepanacealab/covid19_twitter`.

We used the clean version of this dataset that was already filtered for retweets. The collection of tweets is language tagged since July 27 2020. We further filter the data from July 27, 2020 through October 26, 2020 and produce two monolingual tweet collections for English and Spanish. Namely, in order to restrict the sample to content from the US context, we filter for tweets which have a *Place* metadata with *Place*'s *country_code="us"* or (if *Place* is None) with a *User* location specified as one of the US States. For each day, we filter up to reaching a sampling cap ratio of 0.1 and 0.5 of the original tweet collections for English and Spanish, respectively. The overall size of the tweet collections are about 2.8M and 46k for English and Spanish, respectively, with an average of 30k and 503 tweets per day. We distributed the numeric tweet ids and participants were allowed to process any of the tweet's meta-data for their system runs.

[1] `https://developer.nytimes.com/get-started`

3.3 Gold Standard Data

We challenge the participant systems to reproduce a Gold Standard data set from the ACLED project's COVID-19 Disorder Tracker[2], comprising curated disorder events directly related to the coronavirus pandemic.

These include: a.targeting of healthcare workers responding to the coronavirus, b.violent mobs attacking individuals arbitrarily viewed as linked to the coronavirus and c. demonstrations against response measures to coronavirus (government's lock-downs, etc). On the other hand, changes in already existing demonstration patterns as a result of coronavirus-related restrictions, or disorder events driven by already existing armed or political group capitalizing on the coronavirus-induced instability are not included in the data set. From the whole data set, we select events tagged with ACLED types *Protest* and *Riot* and with a US country code location, for the time range from July 27, 2020 through October 26, 2020, resulting with a set of 1449 events, with event date, city, state, country-level information and geographical coordinates.

Notice that while ACLED data come with both hierarchical, string-like location information (i.e. place names at different administrative levels) and coordinate pairs, for the sake of consistency with system output results we re-processed string-like location descriptions of Gold Standard events using the method described in 4.1 and re-generated event coordinate pairs before joining with PRIO-GRID shapefiles.

The U.S. map in Figure 1 shows the spatial distribution of these events (blue dots).

4 Evaluation

System performance is evaluated by computing correlation coefficients on event counts aggregated on cell-days, using uniform grid cells of approximately 55 kilometers sides from the PRIO-GRID data set (Tollefsen et al., 2012). We use these analytical measures as a proxy to the spatio-temporal pattern of the coronavirus-related protest events.

4.1 Data Normalization

In order to be joined with PRIO-GRID shapefiles, string-like location information of system output data had to be normalized to coordinate pairs. To do this we used the OpenStreetMap Nominatim

[2] `https://acleddata.com/analysis/covid-19-disorder-tracker/`

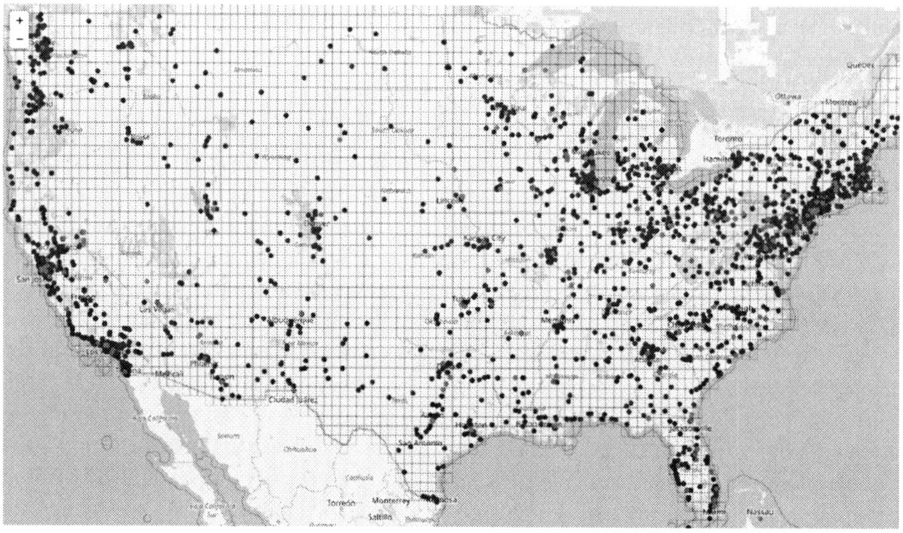

Figure 1: The geo-referenced COVID-19 protest event records from ACLED (blue dots) and the events automatically detected by the *Classbases* system (red dots), overlaid with the PRIO-GRID cells over the US.

search API[3]. For structured location name representations (i.e., *city*, *state*, *country*) we used a parametric search: if this fails, we back off to free-form query strings.

We note that geographical coordinate conversion from Nominatim places the event at the geographical centroid of the polygon of the assigned administrative unit. In our evaluation, we discarded the system output event records with no source location information or whose string-like location attribute returned *Null* results through the Nominatim API.

4.2 Metrics

We use the cell-days counts for two different types of analysis: the correlation with the total daily "protest cell" counts (i.e., time trends alone) and the event counts for each cell-day (i.e., spatial and temporal trends together).

Temporal Trends The first analysis only considers the correlation between the total number of "activated" cells (i.e., for which at least one Protest event was recorded), in the system output and the Gold Standard data set.

This time series analysis is sufficient to estimate how well the automatic system captures the development in time of the protest movement, without considering the geo-location accuracy. So, it evaluates on the task of detecting or not an event in the document collection.

Spatial and Temporal Trends To this purpose, we also measure the correlation coefficients on the absolute event counts with respect to Gold Standard, over each single cell-day. In this way also the geolocation capabilities of the system are considered.

For both analyses, we use two types of correlation coefficients to assess variable's relationship: Pearson coefficient r and Spearman's rank correlation coefficient ρ. Moreover, we used Root Mean Squared Error (RMSE) to measure the absolute value of the error on estimating cell/event counts from the Gold Standard.

4.3 Team Systems

Only one team participated in this edition of the Shared Task: *Classbases*. We briefly describe the system below and ask the reader to refer to their system paper for additional details (Wiriyathammabhum, 2022).

Classbases The *Classbases* system used the trained XLM-RoBERTa large model from subtask1 to classify the news using a concatenation of its news title and news abstract to guess whether it contains any protest events or not. If the classifier outputs positive (logits were thresholded at 0.9), we ran a SpaCy named entity recognizer (Honnibal et al., 2020) on the textual concatenation to get spans with location tags ('GPE'). Then, those spans were

[3] https://nominatim.org/release-docs/develop/api/Search/#parameters

	Data	r	ρ	RMSE
Classbases	News	-0.330	-0.331	193.60

Table 1: Correlation coefficients and error rates for daily protest cell counts: r represents Pearson correlation coefficient, ρ is Spearman's rank correlation coefficient, and RMSE is the Root Mean Squared Error computed on day-cell units.

concatenated into a query string which we used a geocoder library2 to geocode using the Bing Maps REST Services API3. We used the provided dates from the date column as outputs given the filtered ids. Finally, we outputted a row for each filtered id containing five tuples, which are the id, the date, the city, the region or state, and the country.

5 Results

Table 1 shows the Pearson r, Spearman correlation coefficient ρ, and Root Mean Squared Error (RMSE) for the total daily protest cell counts over the 92 days target time range of the only participant system,*Classbases*, run on the news data (denoted as *Classbases_new_1* in the plot.

Here, the correlations are between the total number of cells per day where the system found an event vs. the number of cells where at least one event occurred according to the Gold Standard.

The figures show no correlation between the automatically detected conflict cells and the gold standard over time. This is evident from Figure 2, where we plot the time series of total daily protest cells of the participant system against Gold Standard. We see the system evaluated on news data failing to pick up both temporal variation (i.e., the gradually declining weekly picks of protests from early August through October) and the overall magnitude of the protest movement (e.g., it detects a maximum of less then 10 protest cells per day).

While this correlation analysis is overall more tolerant to errors in geocoding[4], a more in-depth error analysis showed that geocoding inaccuracy caused: a. several detected events to wrongly activate the same cells in system output, causing the geographical spread to be significantly lower than Gold Standard; b. some highly recurrent place names to be wrongly resolved to multiple homonym locations, activating additional cells.

Table 2 reports Pearson r, Spearman correlation coefficient ρ, and Root Mean Squared Error (RMSE) over cell-day event counts of the *Classbases* system with respect to Gold Standard for the 92 days time range

Here the variables range over the whole set of PRIO-GRID cells included in the US territory and, thus, show the correlation of event numbers across geo-cells, thus better evaluating the system's fine-grained geolocation capabilities. As expected, no significant correlation with Gold Standard is found here either.

A more lenient representation of the agreement with Gold Standard is shown in Table 3. Here we report the confusion matrix between grid cells that Gold Standard and system runs code as experiencing at least a protest event. It can be observed that only few of the cells classified as Protest by Gold Standard are detected by the automatic system, which on the other hand incorrectly classified as Protest several additional cells.

6 Conclusions

The goal of the "Covid protest events" Shared Task was to explore novel performance evaluations of pre-trained event detection systems. These systems are applied to large noisy, heterogeneous text data sets (i.e., news articles and social media data) related to a specific protest movement or, as in this case, a wave of protests induced by the coronavirus crisis. Thus, the systems are being evaluated out-of-domain in terms of both data type (i.e., the systems are trained on news data and evaluated on both news and social media) and protest movement context (i.e., the training data are not necessarily related to covid-19 pandemic). Systems are evaluated on their ability to identify both events across time as well as their distribution across space. This evaluation scenario proved challenging for the system participating in the shared task, confirming the finding from the previous edition(Giorgi et al., 2021). A major problem, as shown on Table 3, is the systems' low recall.

The low recall at this years shared task may be due to the pre-filtering of the news data for the presence of covid-19 mentions. Differently than for an organized protest movement (like Black Lives

	Data	r	ρ	RMSE
**Classbases*	News	0.0247	0.0342	0.0101

Table 2: Correlation coefficients and error rates for *cell-day* event counts of the participant systems with respect to Gold Standard.

[4]Indeed, as long as the events are located in U.S., a systematic misplacement of the events might not potentially affect its geographical 'spread' in terms of number of activated cells.

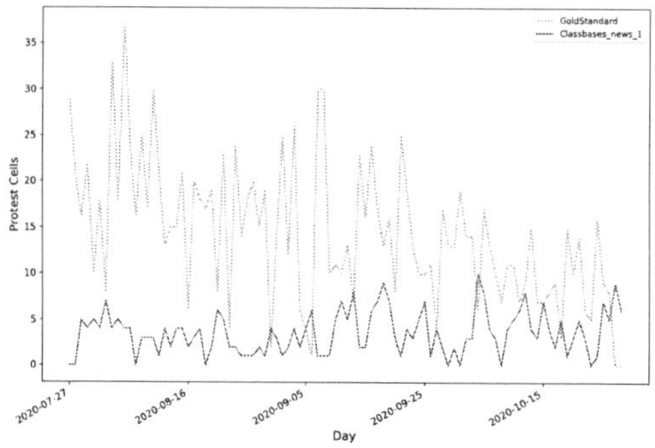

Figure 2: Time series of total daily protest cells from the Gold Standard (in orange), against the *Classbases* system run on news data.

		Gold Standard		Precision	Recall	F1
		1	0			
Classbases	1	24	312	7.14	1.76	2.83
	0	1333	478765			

Table 3: Confusion matrix of grid cells experiencing at least one Protest event (true) versus inactive cells (false), for the Gold Standard and participant systems. Given the high negative class imbalance of the data, we report Precision,Recall figures for the positive class only.

Matter), inferring a relationship of single protest events to the pandemic might not be trivial and thus explicitly stated in the protest news report: therefore, filtering for covid-19 keywords might remove relevant protest reports. However, absolute low recall does not necessarily affect correlation measures as much as inaccurate geocoding of the detected events, as shown.

Overall, this year's edition of the Task was compromised by the low attendance and it is not possible to draw further significant conclusions. We therefore decided to re-open the evaluation window open and welcome further system run submissions. Researchers interested to have their models run and evaluated on the input data provided can check the GitHub `https://github.com/zavavan/case2022_task2` or contact the authors.

Acknowledgments

The author from Koc University was funded by the European Research Council (ERC) Starting Grant 714868 awarded to Dr. Erdem Yörük for his project Emerging Welfare.

References

Scott Althaus, Buddy Peyton, and Dan Shalmon. 2021. A total error approach for validating event data. *American Behavioral Scientist*, 3(2).

Martin Atkinson, Jakub Piskorski, Hristo Tanev, and Vanni Zavarella. 2017. On the creation of a security-related event corpus. In *Proceedings of the Events and Stories in the News Workshop*, pages 59–65.

Juan M. Banda, Ramya Tekumalla, Guanyu Wang, Jingyuan Yu, Tuo Liu, Yuning Ding, Ekaterina Artemova, Elena Tutubalina, and Gerardo Chowell. 2021. A large-scale covid-19 twitter chatter dataset for open scientific research—an international collaboration. *Epidemiologia*, 2(3):315–324.

Scott J Cook and Nils B Weidmann. 2019. Lost in aggregation: Improving event analysis with report-level data. *American Journal of Political Science*, 63(1):250–264.

Eleonora D'Andrea, Pietro Ducange, Beatrice Lazzerini, and Francesco Marcelloni. 2015. Real-time detection of traffic from twitter stream analysis. *IEEE transactions on intelligent transportation systems*, 16(4):2269–2283.

Bertrand De Longueville, Gianluca Luraschi, Paul Smits, Stephen Peedell, and Tom De Groeve. 2010. Citizens as sensors for natural hazards: A vgi integration workflow. *Geomatica*, 64(1):41–59.

Bertrand De Longueville, Robin S Smith, and Gianluca Luraschi. 2009. " omg, from here, i can see the flames!" a use case of mining location based social networks to acquire spatio-temporal data on forest fires. In *Proceedings of the 2009 international workshop on location based social networks*, pages 73–80.

Leon Derczynski. 2016. Complementarity, F-score, and NLP evaluation. In *Proceedings of the Tenth International Conference on Language Resources and Evaluation (LREC'16)*, pages 261–266, Portorož, Slovenia. European Language Resources Association (ELRA).

Fırat Duruşan, Ali Hürriyetoğlu, Erdem Yörük, Osman Mutlu, Çağrı Yoltar, Burak Gürel, and Alvaro Comin. 2022. Global contentious politics database (glocon) annotation manuals.

Salvatore Giorgi, Vanni Zavarella, Hristo Tanev, Nicolas Stefanovitch, Sy Hwang, Hansi Hettiarachchi, Tharindu Ranasinghe, Vivek Kalyan, Paul Tan, Shaun Tan, Martin Andrews, Tiancheng Hu, Niklas Stoehr, Francesco Ignazio Re, Daniel Vegh, Dennis Atzenhofer, Brenda Curtis, and Ali Hürriyetoğlu. 2021. Discovering black lives matter events in the United States: Shared task 3, CASE 2021. In *Proceedings of the 4th Workshop on Challenges and Applications of Automated Extraction of Socio-political Events from Text (CASE 2021)*, pages 218–227, Online. Association for Computational Linguistics.

Jesse Hammond and Nils B Weidmann. 2014. Using machine-coded event data for the micro-level study of political violence. *Research & Politics*, 1(2):2053168014539924.

Ali Hürriyetoğlu, Osman Mutlu, Fırat Duruşan, Onur Uca, Alaeddin Selçuk Gürel, Benjamin Radford, Yaoyao Dai, Hansi Hettiarachchi, Niklas Stoehr, Tadashi Nomoto, Milena Slavcheva, Francielle Vargas, Aaqib Javid, Fatih Beyhan, and Erdem Yörük. 2022a. Extended Multilingual protest news detection - Shared Task 1, CASE 2021 and 2022. In *Proceedings of the 5th Workshop on Challenges and Applications of Automated Extraction of Socio-political Events from Text (CASE 2022)*, online. Association for Computational Linguistics (ACL).

Ali Hürriyetoğlu, Osman Mutlu, Farhana Ferdousi Liza, Erdem Yörük, Ritesh Kumar, and Shyam Ratan. 2021. Multilingual protest news detection - Shared Task 1, CASE 2021. In *Proceedings of the 4th Workshop on Challenges and Applications of Automated Extraction of Socio-political Events from Text (CASE 2021)*, online. Association for Computational Linguistics (ACL).

Ali Hürriyetoğlu, Hristo Tanev, Vanni Zavarella, Reyyan Yeniterzi, Osman Mutlu, and Erdem Yörük. 2022b. Challenges and Applications of Automated Extraction of Socio-political Events from Text (CASE 2022): Workshop and Shared Task Report. In *Proceedings of the 5th Workshop on Challenges and Applications of Automated Extraction of Socio-political Events from Text (CASE 2022)*, online. Association for Computational Linguistics (ACL).

Ali Hürriyetoğlu, Erdem Yörük, Osman Mutlu, Fırat Duruşan, Çağrı Yoltar, Deniz Yüret, and Burak Gürel. 2021. Cross-Context News Corpus for Protest Event-Related Knowledge Base Construction. *Data Intelligence*, 3(2):308–335.

Ourania Kounadi, Thomas J Lampoltshammer, Elizabeth Groff, Izabela Sitko, and Michael Leitner. 2015. Exploring twitter to analyze the public's reaction patterns to recently reported homicides in london. *PloS one*, 10(3):e0121848.

Kalev Leetaru and Philip A Schrodt. 2013. GDELT: Global data on events, location, and tone, 1979–2012. In *ISA annual convention*, volume 2, pages 1–49. Citeseer.

Edward Pultar, Martin Raubal, and Michael F Goodchild. 2008. Gedmwa: Geospatial exploratory data mining web agent. In *Proceedings of the 16th ACM SIGSPATIAL international conference on Advances in geographic information systems*, pages 1–4.

Clionadh Raleigh, Andrew Linke, Håvard Hegre, and Joakim Karlsen. 2010. Introducing acled: an armed conflict location and event dataset: special data feature. *Journal of peace research*, 47(5):651–660.

Philip A Schrodt and Parus Analytics. 2015. Comparing methods for generating large scale political event data sets. In *Text as Data meetings, New York University, 16–17, 2015*, pages 1–32.

Fiona Anting Tan, Ali Hürriyetoğlu, Tommaso Caselli, Nelleke Oostdijk, Hansi Hettiarachchi, Tadashi Nomoto, Onur Uca, and Farhana Ferdousi Liza. 2022a. Event Causality Identification with Causal News Corpus - Shared Task 3, CASE 2022. In *Proceedings of the 5th Workshop on Challenges and Applications of Automated Extraction of Socio-political Events from Text (CASE 2022)*, Online. Association for Computational Linguistics.

Fiona Anting Tan, Ali Hürriyetoğlu, Tommaso Caselli, Nelleke Oostdijk, Tadashi Nomoto, Hansi Hettiarachchi, Iqra Ameer, Onur Uca, Farhana Ferdousi Liza, and Tiancheng Hu. 2022b. The causal news corpus: Annotating causal relations in event sentences from news. In *Proceedings of the Language Resources and Evaluation Conference*, pages 2298–2310, Marseille, France. European Language Resources Association.

Andreas Forø Tollefsen, Håvard Strand, and Halvard Buhaug. 2012. Prio-grid: A unified spatial data structure. *Journal of Peace Research*, 49(2):363–374.

Wei Wang, Ryan Kennedy, David Lazer, and Naren Ramakrishnan. 2016. Growing pains for global monitoring of societal events. *Science*, 353(6307):1502–1503.

Michael D Ward, Andreas Beger, Josh Cutler, Matthew Dickenson, Cassy Dorff, and Ben Radford. 2013. Comparing gdelt and icews event data. *Event Data Analysis*, 21(1):267–297.

Peratham Wiriyathammabhum. 2022. ClassBases at CASE-2022 Multilingual Protest Event Detection Tasks: Multilingual Protest News Detection and Automatically Replicating Manually Created Event Datasets. In *Proceedings of the 5th Workshop on Challenges and Applications of Automated Extraction of Socio-political Events from Text (CASE 2022)*, online. Association for Computational Linguistics (ACL).

Reda Yacouby and Dustin Axman. 2020. Probabilistic extension of precision, recall, and f1 score for more thorough evaluation of classification models. In *Proceedings of the First Workshop on Evaluation and Comparison of NLP Systems*, pages 79–91, Online. Association for Computational Linguistics.

Erdem Yörük, Ali Hürriyetoğlu, Fırat Duruşan, and Çağrı Yoltar. 2021. Random sampling in corpus design: Cross-context generalizability in automated multicountry protest event collection. *American Behavioral Scientist*, 0(0):00027642211021630.

Vanni Zavarella, Jakub Piskorski, Camelia Ignat, Hristo Tanev, and Martin Atkinson. 2020. Mastering the media hype: Methods for deduplication of conflict events from news reports. In *Proceedings of AI4Narratives — Workshop on Artificial Intelligence for Narratives*.

Shuo Zhang. 2019. Data mining Mandarin tone contour shapes. In *Proceedings of the 16th Workshop on Computational Research in Phonetics, Phonology, and Morphology*, pages 144–153, Florence, Italy. Association for Computational Linguistics.

Challenges and Applications of Automated Extraction of Socio-political Events from Text (CASE 2022): Workshop and Shared Task Report

Ali Hürriyetoğlu
KNAW Humanities Cluster DHLab
ali.hurriyetoglu@dh.huc.knaw.nl

Hristo Tanev
European Commission
hristo.tanev@ec.europa.eu

Vanni Zavarella
University of Cagliari
v.zavarella@unica.it

Reyyan Yeniterzi
Sabanci University
reyyan.yeniterzi@sabanciuniv.edu

Osman Mutlu
Koc University
omutlu@ku.edu.tr

Erdem Yörük
Koc University
eryoruk@ku.edu.tr

Abstract

We provide a summary of the fifth edition of the CASE workshop that is held in the scope of EMNLP 2022. The workshop consists of regular papers, two keynotes, working papers of shared task participants, and task overview papers. This workshop has been bringing together all aspects of event information collection across technical and social science fields. In addition to the progress in depth, the submission and acceptance of multimodal approaches show the widening of this interdisciplinary research topic.

1 Introduction

The workshop on Challenges and Applications of Automated Extraction of Socio-political Events from Text (CASE) has become a significant venue where all technical and social science aspects of event information collection can be discussed in its fifth edition.[1] The 2022 Conference on Empirical Methods in Natural Language Processing (EMNLP 2022) hosts the edition this year between December 7 and 11 in Abu Dhabi .[2]

Socio-political event extraction (SPE) has long been a challenge for the natural language processing (NLP) community as it requires sophisticated methods in defining event ontologies, creating language resources, and developing algorithmic approaches (Pustejovsky et al., 2003; Boroş, 2018; Chen et al., 2021). Social and political scientists have been working to create socio-political event (SPE) databases such as ACLED, EMBERS, GDELT, ICEWS, MMAD, PHOENIX, POLDEM, SPEED, TERRIER, and UCDP following similar steps for decades. These projects and the new ones increasingly rely on machine learning (ML), deep learning (DL), and NLP methods to deal better with the vast amount and variety of data in this domain (Hürriyetoğlu et al., 2020; Hürriyetoğlu et al., 2021b). Automation offers scholars not only the opportunity to improve existing practices but also to vastly expand the scope of data that can be collected and studied, thus potentially opening up new research frontiers within the field of SPEs, such as political violence and social movements. But automated approaches suffer from major issues like bias, generalizability, class imbalance, training data limitations, and ethical issues that have the potential to affect the results of automated text processing systems and their use drastically (Leins et al., 2020; Bhatia et al., 2020; Chang et al., 2019). Moreover, the results of the automated systems for SPE information collection have neither been comparable to each other nor been of sufficient quality (Wang et al., 2016; Schrodt, 2020).

Setting a clear path toward addressing these challenges is our main focus. We are confident that the program we put together for this year's event after rigorous and thorough reviews, would bring us closer to that goal and beyond.

We provide a summary of the accepted papers in the following Section, which is Section 2. Next, the shared tasks that are organized in the scope of this workshop are described in Section 3. The keynote abstracts and invited talks are provided in sections 4 and 5. Finally, Section 6 conclude this report with a brief summary and future outlook.

2 Accepted papers

This year, out of 12 submissions 8 were accepted by the program committee. A quick summary of these papers are provided below.

- Thapa et al. (2022) releases a multimodal dataset that consists of of 5,680 text-image pairs of tweets and a baseline for hate speech detection in the context of Russia-Ukraine war.

[1] https://emw.ku.edu.tr/case-2022/, accessed on November 14, 2022.

[2] https://2022.emnlp.org/, accessed on November 14, 2022.

Proceedings of the 5th Workshop on Challenges and Applications of Automated Extraction of Socio-political Events from Text (CASE), pages 217 - 222
December 7-8, 2022 ©2022 Association for Computational Linguistics

- You et al. (2022) propose Event-Graph, a joint framework for event extraction, which encodes events as graphs. They represent event triggers and arguments as nodes in a semantic graph. Event extraction therefore becomes a graph parsing problem.
- Desot et al. (2022) suggests event and argument role detection as one task in a hybrid event detection approach and a novel method for automatic self-attention threshold selection.
- Mehta et al. (2022) cast socio-political conflict event extraction as a machine reading comprehension (MRC) task. In this approach, extraction of socio-political actors and targets from a sentence is framed as an extractive question answering problem conditioned on event type.
- Raj et al. (2022) propose a method that utilizes existing annotated unimodal data to perform event detection in another data modality using a zero-shot setting. They focus on protest detection in text and images, and show that a pretrained vision-and-language alignment model (CLIP) can be leveraged towards this end.
- Sticha and Brenner (2022) release a comprehensive, consolidated, and cohesive assassination dataset that is prepared utilizing a robust ML framework that prioritizes understandability through visualizations and generalizability through the ability to implement different ML algorithms.
- Yaoyao et al. (2022) train a model that can produce structured political event records at the sentence level. This approach is based on text-to-text sequence generation. They also describe a method for generating synthetic text and event record pairs that we use to fit a model.
- Kiymet Akdemir and Hürriyetoğlu (2022) approach the classification problem as an entailment problem and apply zero-shot ranking to socio-political texts. Documents that are ranked at the top can be considered positively classified documents and this reduces the close reading time for the information extraction process.

3 Shared tasks

Three tasks were organized in the scope of CASE 2022. Each one of these tasks shed light on a different aspect of event information collection. These are zero-shot and detailed multilingual event information, evaluation of state-of-the-art systems in replicating manually curated event datasets, and event causality detection.

3.1 Task 1: Extended Multilingual Protest Event Detection

The extended multilingual protest news detection is the same shared task organized at CASE 2021 (Hürriyetoğlu et al., 2021a). This year we introduced additional data and languages at the evaluation stage.[3] This year, the Task 1 focused on evaluating the zero-shot prediction performance of the state-of-the-art systems for Subtask 1, document classification. The training set is the same with CASE 2021 data that is in English, Portuguese, and Spanish. But the evaluation data consists of the union of CASE 2021 test data and new data in both available and new languages. The new languages are Mandarin, Urdu, and Turkish. Details of CASE 2022 Task 1 is reported by Hürriyetoğlu et al. (2022).

3.2 Task 2: Tracking COVID-19 protest events in the United States

This task aims at automatically replicating manually created event datasets. The participants of Task 1 are invited to run the systems they develop to tackle Task 1 on a news and a Twitter archive. This is a similar setting with the edition performed last year in the scope of CASE 2021 and reported by Giorgi et al. (2021). This year's results [4] are reported by Zavarella et al. (2022).

3.3 Task 3: Event Causality identification

Causality is a core cognitive concept and appears in many natural language processing (NLP) works that aim to tackle inference and understanding. This task focuses on the study of event causality in news, and therefore, introduces the Causal News Corpus (Tan et al., 2022b). The Causal News Corpus consists of 3,559 event sentences from CASE 2021 data, extracted from protest event

[3] https://github.com/emerging-welfare/case-2022-multilingual-event, accessed on November 15, 2022.

[4] https://github.com/zavavan/case2022_task2, accessed on November 14, 2022.

news, that have been annotated with sequence labels on whether it contains causal relations or not. Subsequently, causal sentences are also annotated with Cause, Effect, and Signal spans. The two subtasks (Sequence Classification and Span Detection) work on the Causal News Corpus, and accurate, automated solutions are proposed for the detection and extraction of causal events in news. The detailed report of the task is provided in Tan et al. (2022a). [5]

4 Keynotes

Three scholars delivered two keynote speeches that are one on event extraction system development and one for error analysis of event information collection systems. The speakers were invited according to our tradition of having one keynote with technical and another one with social and political sciences, background. We provide abstracts of the keynote speeches as they are provided by the keynote speakers in the following subsections. Section 4.1 and Section 4.2 are contributions of Prof. Thien Huu Nguyen [6] and Prof. Scott Althaus[7] and Prof. J. Craig Jenkins[8] respectively.[9]

4.1 Event Extraction in the Era of Large Language Models: Structure Induction and Multilingual Learning

Events such as protests, disease outbreaks, and natural disasters are prevalent in text from different languages and domains. Event Extraction (EE) is an important task of Information Extraction that aims to identify events and their structures in unstructured text. The last decade has witnessed significant progress for EE research, featuring deep learning and large language models as the state-of-the-art technologies. However, a key issue of existing EE methods involves modeling input text sequentially to solve each EE tasks separately, thus limiting the abilities to encode long text and capture various types of dependencies to improve EE performance. In this talk, I will present some of our recent efforts to address this issue where text structures are explicitly learned to realize important objects and their interactions to facilitate the predictions for EE.

In addition, current EE research still mainly focuses on a few popular languages, e.g., English, Chinese, Arabic, and Spanish, leaving many other languages unexplored for EE. In this talk, I will also introduce our current research focus on developing evaluation benchmarks and models to extend EE systems to multiple new languages, i.e., multilingual and cross-lingual learning for EE. Finally, I will highlight some research challenges that can be studied in future work for EE.

4.2 A total error approach to validating event data that is transparent, scalable, and practical to implement

There are at least two reasonable ways to make your way toward where you want to go: looking down to carefully place one foot in front of the other, and looking up to focus on where you hope to arrive. Looking up beats looking down if there's a particular destination in mind, and for constructing valid event data that destination usually takes the form of high-quality human judgment. Yet many approaches to generating event data on protests and acts of political violence using fully-automated systems implicitly adopt a "looking down" approach by benchmarking validity as a series of incremental improvements over prior algorithmic efforts. And even those efforts that adopt a "looking up" approach often treat human-generated gold standard data as if it was prima facie valid, without ever testing or confirming the accuracy of this assumption. It stands to reason that if we want to automatically produce valid event data that approaches the validity of human judgment, then we also need to validate the human judgment tasks that provide the point of comparison. But because of obvious difficulties in implementing such a rigorous assessment within the time and budget constraints of typical research projects, this more rigorous double-validation approach is rarely attempted.

This presentation outlines a "looking up" approach for double-validating fully-automated event data developed by the Cline Center for Advanced Social Research at the University of Illinois Urbana-Champaign (USA), illustrates that approach with a test of the precision and recall for two widely-used event classification systems (the

[5] https://github.com/tanfiona/CausalNewsCorpus, accessed on November 14, 2022.

[6] https://ix.cs.uoregon.edu/~thien/, accessed on November 14, 2022.

[7] https://ix.cs.uoregon.edu/~thien/, accessed on November 14, 2022.

[8] https://sociology.osu.edu/people/jenkins.12, accessed on November 15, 2022.

[9] The personal pronoun usege such as 'I' and 'we' in the following subsections indicate the keynote speakers and not the authors of this report.

PETRARCH-2 coder used in Phoenix and TERRIER, as well as the BBN ACCENT coder used in W-ICEWS), and demonstrates the utility of the approach for developing fully-automated event data algorithms with levels of validity that approach the quality of human judgment.

The first part of the talk reviews the Cline Center's total error framework for identifying 19 types of error that can affect the validity of event data and addresses the challenge of applying a total error framework when authoritative ground truth about the actual distribution of relevant events is lacking (Althaus et al., 2022). We argue that carefully constructed gold standard datasets can effectively benchmark validity problems even in the absence of ground truth data about event populations. We propose that a strong validity assessment for event data should, at a minimum, possess three characteristics. First, there should be a standard describing ideal data; a gold standard that, in the best case, takes the form of ground truth. Second, there should be a direct "apples to apples" comparison of outputs from competing methods given identical input. Third, the test should use appropriate metrics for measuring agreement between the gold standard and data produced by competing approaches.

The second part of the talk presents the results of a validation exercise meeting all three criteria that is applied to two algorithmic event data pipelines: the Python Engine for Text Resolution and Related Coding Hierarchy (PETRARCH-2) and the BBN ACCENT event coder. It then reviews a recent Cline Center project that has built a fully-automated event coder which produces dramatic improvements in validity over both PETRARCH-2 and BBN ACCENT by leveraging the total error framework and a reliance on the double-validation approach using high-quality gold standard benchmark datasets.

5 Invited talks

Papers that are accepted to be published in the Findings of EMNLP 2022 and related to our workshop theme were invited to be presented during our workshop. The authors of the following papers were invited for presenting their papers:

- Jiao et al. (2022) define the task open-vocabulary argument role prediction. The goal of this task is to infer a set of argument roles for a given event type. They propose a novel unsupervised framework, ROLEPRED for this task and release a new human-annotated event extraction dataset including 139 customized argument roles with rich semantics.
- Faghihi et al. (2022) presents CrisisLTLSum, the largest dataset of local crisis event timelines about wildfires, local fires, traffic, and storms available to date. CrisisLTLSum was built using a semi-automated cluster-then-refine approach to collect data from the public Twitter stream.
- Ding et al. (2022) design a neural model that they refer to as the Explicit Role Interaction Network (ERIN) which allows for dynamically capturing the correlations between different argument roles within an event.
- Gao et al. (2022) present Mask-then-Fill, a flexible and effective data augmentation framework for event extraction. This approach allows for more flexible manipulation of text and thus can generate more diverse data while keeping the original event structure unchanged.

6 Conclusion

The CASE workshop series has been contributing to both technical advancement in terms of shared task organization and being a venue for scholars working at the intersection of social sciences and event extraction. This role become more significant as these series are known to a wider community. Following steps of this series should serve the community by preserving its inderdisciplinary setting, welcoming new methodologies, and promoting responsible development and utilization of the results of this scholarship.

References

Scott Althaus, Buddy Peyton, and Dan Shalmon. 2022. A total error approach for validating event data. *American Behavioral Scientist*, 66(5):603–624.

Shraey Bhatia, Jey Han Lau, and Timothy Baldwin. 2020. You are right. i am alarmed–but by climate change counter movement. *arXiv preprint arXiv:2004.14907*.

Emanuela Boroş. 2018. *Neural Methods for Event Extraction*. Ph.D. thesis, Université Paris-Saclay.

Kai-Wei Chang, Vinod Prabhakaran, and Vicente Ordonez. 2019. Bias and fairness in natural language processing. In *Proceedings of the 2019 Conference on Empirical Methods in Natural Language Processing and the 9th International Joint Conference on Natural Language Processing (EMNLP-IJCNLP): Tutorial Abstracts*, Hong Kong, China. Association for Computational Linguistics.

Muhao Chen, Hongming Zhang, Qiang Ning, Manling Li, Heng Ji, Kathleen McKeown, and Dan Roth. 2021. Event-centric natural language understanding.

Thierry Desot, Orphee De Clercq, and Veronique Hoste. 2022. A hybrid knowledge and transformer-based model for event detection with automatic self-attention threshold, layer and head selection. In *Proceedings of the 5th Workshop on Challenges and Applications of Automated Extraction of Socio-political Events from Text (CASE 2022)*, online. Association for Computational Linguistics (ACL).

Nan Ding, Chunming Hu, Kai Sun, Samuel Mensah, and Richong Zhang. 2022. Explicit role interaction network for event argument extraction. In *Findings of the Association for Computational Linguistics: EMNLP 2022*, Online. Association for Computational Linguistics.

Hossein Rajaby Faghihi Faghihi, Bashar Alhafni, Ke Zhang, Shihao Ran, Joel Tetreault, and Alejandro Jaimes. 2022. Crisisltlsum. A benchmark for local crisis event timeline extraction and summarization. In *Findings of the Association for Computational Linguistics: EMNLP 2022*, Online. Association for Computational Linguistics.

Jun Gao, Changlong Yu, Wei Wang, and Ruifeng Zhao, Huan Xu. 2022. Mask-then-fill: A flexible and effective data augmentation framework for event extraction. In *Findings of the Association for Computational Linguistics: EMNLP 2022*, Online. Association for Computational Linguistics.

Salvatore Giorgi, Vanni Zavarella, Hristo Tanev, Nicolas Stefanovitch, Sy Hwang, Hansi Hettiarachchi, Tharindu Ranasinghe, Vivek Kalyan, Paul Tan, Shaun Tan, Martin Andrews, Tiancheng Hu, Niklas Stoehr, Francesco Ignazio Re, Daniel Vegh, Dennis Atzenhofer, Brenda Curtis, and Ali Hürriyetoğlu. 2021. Discovering black lives matter events in the United States: Shared task 3, CASE 2021. In *Proceedings of the 4th Workshop on Challenges and Applications of Automated Extraction of Socio-political Events from Text (CASE 2021)*, pages 218–227, Online. Association for Computational Linguistics.

Ali Hürriyetoğlu, Osman Mutlu, Fırat Duruşan, Onur Uca, Alaeddin Selçuk Gürel, Benjamin Radford, Yaoyao Dai, Hansi Hettiarachchi, Niklas Stoehr, Tadashi Nomoto, Milena Slavcheva, Francielle Vargas, Aaqib Javid, Fatih Beyhan, and Erdem Yörük. 2022. Extended multilingual protest news detection - shared task 1, case 2021 and 2022. In *Proceedings of the 5th Workshop on Challenges and Applications of Automated Extraction of Socio-political Events from Text (CASE 2022)*, online. Association for Computational Linguistics (ACL).

Ali Hürriyetoğlu, Osman Mutlu, Erdem Yörük, Farhana Ferdousi Liza, Ritesh Kumar, and Shyam Ratan. 2021a. Multilingual protest news detection - shared task 1, CASE 2021. In *Proceedings of the 4th Workshop on Challenges and Applications of Automated Extraction of Socio-political Events from Text (CASE 2021)*, pages 79–91, Online. Association for Computational Linguistics.

Ali Hürriyetoğlu, Hristo Tanev, Vanni Zavarella, Jakub Piskorski, Reyyan Yeniterzi, Osman Mutlu, Deniz Yuret, and Aline Villavicencio. 2021b. Challenges and applications of automated extraction of socio-political events from text (CASE 2021): Workshop and shared task report. In *Proceedings of the 4th Workshop on Challenges and Applications of Automated Extraction of Socio-political Events from Text (CASE 2021)*, pages 1–9, Online. Association for Computational Linguistics.

Ali Hürriyetoğlu, Vanni Zavarella, Hristo Tanev, Erdem Yörük, Ali Safaya, and Osman Mutlu. 2020. Automated extraction of socio-political events from news (AESPEN): Workshop and shared task report. In *Proceedings of the Workshop on Automated Extraction of Socio-political Events from News 2020*, pages 1–6, Marseille, France. European Language Resources Association (ELRA).

Yizhu Jiao, Sha Li, Yiqing Xie, Ming Zhong, Heng Ji, and Jiawei Han. 2022. Open-vocabulary argument role prediction for event extraction. In *Findings of the Association for Computational Linguistics: EMNLP 2022*, Online. Association for Computational Linguistics.

Kıymet Kiymet Akdemir and Ali Hürriyetoğlu. 2022. Zero-shot ranking socio-political texts with transformer language models to reduce close reading time. In *Proceedings of the 5th Workshop on Challenges and Applications of Automated Extraction of Socio-political Events from Text (CASE 2022)*, online. Association for Computational Linguistics (ACL).

Kobi Leins, Jey Han Lau, and Timothy Baldwin. 2020. Give me convenience and give her death: Who should decide what uses of NLP are appropriate, and on what basis? In *Proceedings of the 58th Annual Meeting of the Association for Computational Linguistics*, pages 2908–2913, Online. Association for Computational Linguistics.

Sneha Mehta, Huzefa Rangwala, and Naren Ramakrishnan. 2022. Improving zero-shot event extraction via sentence simplification. In *Proceedings of the 5th Workshop on Challenges and Applications of Automated Extraction of Socio-political Events from Text (CASE 2022)*, online. Association for Computational Linguistics (ACL).

James Pustejovsky, José M Castano, Robert Ingria, Roser Sauri, Robert J Gaizauskas, Andrea Setzer, Graham Katz, and Dragomir R Radev. 2003. Timeml: Robust specification of event and temporal expressions in text. *New directions in question answering*, 3:28–34.

Ria Raj, Kajsa Andreasson, and Tobias Norlund. 2022. Cross-modal transfer between vision and language for protest detection. In *Proceedings of the 5th Workshop on Challenges and Applications of Automated Extraction of Socio-political Events from Text (CASE 2022)*, online. Association for Computational Linguistics (ACL).

Philip A. Schrodt. 2020. Keynote abstract: Current open questions for operational event data. In *Proceedings of the Workshop on Automated Extraction of Socio-political Events from News 2020*, page 8, Marseille, France. European Language Resources Association (ELRA).

Abigail Sticha and Paul R. Brenner. 2022. Hybrid knowledge engineering leveraging a robust ml framework to produce an assassination dataset. In *Proceedings of the 5th Workshop on Challenges and Applications of Automated Extraction of Socio-political Events from Text (CASE 2022)*, online. Association for Computational Linguistics (ACL).

Fiona Anting Tan, Ali Hürriyetoğlu, Tommaso Caselli, Nelleke Oostdijk, Hansi Hettiarachchi, Tadashi Nomoto, Onur Uca, and Farhana Ferdousi Liza. 2022a. Event causality identification with causal news corpus - shared task 3, CASE 2022. In *Proceedings of the 5th Workshop on Challenges and Applications of Automated Extraction of Socio-political Events from Text (CASE 2022)*, Online. Association for Computational Linguistics.

Fiona Anting Tan, Ali Hürriyetoğlu, Tommaso Caselli, Nelleke Oostdijk, Tadashi Nomoto, Hansi Hettiarachchi, Iqra Ameer, Onur Uca, Farhana Ferdousi Liza, and Tiancheng Hu. 2022b. The causal news corpus: Annotating causal relations in event sentences from news. In *Proceedings of the Language Resources and Evaluation Conference*, pages 2298–2310, Marseille, France. European Language Resources Association.

Surendrabikram Thapa, Aditya Shah, Farhan Ahmad Jafri, Usman Naseem, and Imran Razzak. 2022. A multi-modal dataset for hate speech detection on social media: Case-study of russia-ukraine conflict. In *Proceedings of the 5th Workshop on Challenges and Applications of Automated Extraction of Socio-political Events from Text (CASE 2022)*, online. Association for Computational Linguistics (ACL).

Wei Wang, Ryan Kennedy, David Lazer, and Naren Ramakrishnan. 2016. Growing pains for global monitoring of societal events. *Science*, 353(6307):1502–1503.

Dai Yaoyao, Benjamin Radford, and Andrew Halterman. 2022. Political event coding as text-to-text sequence generation. In *Proceedings of the 5th Workshop on Challenges and Applications of Automated Extraction of Socio-political Events from Text (CASE 2022)*, online. Association for Computational Linguistics (ACL).

Huiling You, David Samuel, Samia Touileb, and Lilja Øvrelid. 2022. Eventgraph: Event extraction as semantic graph parsing. In *Proceedings of the 5th Workshop on Challenges and Applications of Automated Extraction of Socio-political Events from Text (CASE 2022)*, online. Association for Computational Linguistics (ACL).

Vanni Zavarella, Hristo Tanev, Ali Hürriyetoğlu, Peratham Wiriyathammabhum, and Bertrand De Longueville. 2022. Tracking COVID-19 protest events in the United States. Shared Task 2: Event Database Replication, CASE 2022. In *Proceedings of the 5th Workshop on Challenges and Applications of Automated Extraction of Socio-political Events from Text (CASE 2022)*, online. Association for Computational Linguistics (ACL).

Extended Multilingual Protest News Detection - Shared Task 1, CASE 2021 and 2022

Ali Hürriyetoğlu
KNAW Humanities Cluster DHLab
ali.hurriyetoglu@dh.huc.knaw.nl

Osman Mutlu
Koc University
omutlu@ku.edu.tr

Fırat Duruşan
Koc University
fdurusan@ku.edu.tr

Onur Uca
Mersin University
onuruca@mersin.edu.tr

Alaeddin Selçuk Gürel
Huawei
alaeddinselcukgurel@gmail.com

Benjamin Radford
UNC Charlotte
benjamin.radford@uncc.edu

Yaoyao Dai
UNC Charlotte
yaoyao.dai@uncc.edu

Hansi Hettiarachchi
Birmingham City University
hansi.hettiarachchi@mail.bcu.ac.uk

Niklas Stoehr
ETH Zurich
niklas.stoehr@inf.ethz.ch

Tadashi Nomoto
National Institute of Japanese Literature
nomoto@acm.org

Milena Slavcheva
Bulgarian Academy of Sciences
milena@lml.bas.bg

Francielle Vargas
University of São Paulo
francielleavargas@usp.br

Aaqib Javid
Koc University
ajavid20@ku.edu.tr

Fatih Beyhan
Sabanci University
fatihbeyhan@sabanciuniv.edu

Erdem Yörük
Koc University
eryoruk@ku.edu.tr

Abstract

We report results of the CASE 2022 Shared Task 1 on Multilingual Protest Event Detection. This task is a continuation of CASE 2021 that consists of four subtasks that are i) document classification, ii) sentence classification, iii) event sentence coreference identification, and iv) event extraction. The CASE 2022 extension consists of expanding the test data with more data in previously available languages, namely, English, Hindi, Portuguese, and Spanish, and adding new test data in Mandarin, Turkish, and Urdu for Sub-task 1, document classification. The training data from CASE 2021 in English, Portuguese and Spanish were utilized. Therefore, predicting document labels in Hindi, Mandarin, Turkish, and Urdu occurs in a zero-shot setting. The CASE 2022 workshop accepts reports on systems developed for predicting test data of CASE 2021 as well. We observe that the best systems submitted by CASE 2022 participants achieve between 79.71 and 84.06 F1-macro for new languages in a zero-shot setting. The winning approaches are mainly ensembling models and merging data in multiple languages. The best two submissions on CASE 2021 data outperform submissions from last year for Subtask 1 and Subtask 2 in all languages. Only the following scenarios were not outperformed by new submissions on CASE 2021: Subtask 3 Portuguese & Subtask 4 English.

1 Introduction

We aim at determining event trigger and its arguments in a text snippet in the scope of an event extraction task. The performance of an automated system depends on the target event type as it may be broad or potentially the event trigger(s) can be ambiguous. The context of the trigger occurrence may need to be handled as well. For instance, the 'protest' event type may be synonymous with 'demonstration' or not in a specific context. Moreover, the hypothetical cases such as future protest plans may need to be excluded from the results. Finally, the relevance of a protest depends on the actors as in a contentious political event only citizen-led events are in the scope. This challenge is even harder in a cross-lingual and zero-shot setting in case training data are not available in new languages.

We provide a benchmark that consists of four subtasks and multiple languages in the scope of the 5th Workshop on Challenges and Applications of Automated Extraction of Socio-political Events from Text at The 2022 Conference on Empirical Methods in Natural Language Processing (CASE @ EMNLP 2022) (Hürriyetoğlu et al., 2022).[1] bgenfrhumil: To paraphrase: The work presented

[1] https://emw.ku.edu.tr/case-2022/, accessed on November 13, 2022.

Proceedings of the 5th Workshop on Challenges and Applications of Automated Extraction of Socio-political Events from Text (CASE), pages 223 - 228
December 7-8, 2022 ©2022 Association for Computational Linguistics

in this paper is a continuation of the work initiated in CASE 2021 Task 1 (Hürriyetoğlu et al., 2021) and consists in adding new documents in already available languages, as well as adding new languages to the evaluation data.

Task 1 consists of the following subtasks that ensure the task is tackled incrementally: i) Document classification, ii) Sentence classification, iii) event sentence coreference identification, and iv) event extraction. The training data consist of documents in English, Portuguese, and Spanish, while the evaluation texts are in English, Hindi, Mandarin, Portuguese, Spanish, Turkish, and Urdu. Subtask 1 ensures documents with relevant senses of event triggers are selected. Next, Subtask 2 focuses on identifying event sentences in a document. Discriminating sentences that are about separate events and grouping them is done in Subtask 3 (Hürriyetoğlu et al., 2020, 2022). Finally, the sentences that are about the same events are processed to identify the event trigger and its arguments in Subtask 4. In addition to accomplishing the event extraction task, the subtask division improves significantly the annotation quality, as the annotation team can focus on a specific part of the task and errors in previous levels are corrected during the preparation of the following subtask (Hürriyetoğlu et al., 2021). The significance of this specific task division is twofold: i) facilitating the work with a random sample of documents by first identifying relevant documents and sentences before annotating or processing a sample or a complete archive of documents respectively; ii) increasing the generalizability of the automated systems that may be developed using this data (Yörük et al., 2021; Mutlu, 2022).

The current report is about Task 1 in the scope of CASE 2022. Task 2 (Zavarella et al., 2022) and Task 3 (Tan et al., 2022b,a) complement Task 1 by evaluating Task 1 systems on events related to COVID-19 and detecting causality respectively.

The following section, which is Section 2 describes the data we use for the shared task. Next we describe the evaluation setting in Section 3. The results are provided in Section 4. Finally, the Section 5 conclude this report.

2 Data

We used the CASE 2021 training data as those for CASE 2022.[2] The CASE 2022 test data are the union of CASE 2021 test data and additional new documents in both available and new languages. The new languages are Mandarin, Turkish, and Urdu.

The new document level data, which are used to extend CASE 2021 data, were randomly sampled from MOT v1.2 (Palen-Michel et al., 2022) [3] and were annotated by co-authors of this report. Documents were annotated by native speakers of the respective language. A single label was attached to each document. The annotation manual followed in the annotation process (Duruşan et al., 2022) was the same as that used in CASE 2021.

The total number of CASE 2022 documents with labels is 3,870 for English, 267 for Hindi, 300 for Mandarin, 670 for Portuguese, 399 for Spanish, 300 for Turkish, and 299 for Urdu.

Teams that developed systems for Subtasks 2, 3, and 4 evaluated their systems on CASE 2021 test data.

3 Evaluation setting

We utilized Codalab for evaluation of Task 1 for CASE 2022.[4] The evaluation for CASE 2021 was performed on an additional scoring page[5] of the original[6] CASE 2021 Codalab page. Moreover, we launched an additional scoring page for CASE 2022 after completion of the official evaluation period.[7]

Five submissions per subtask and language pair could be submitted in total for CASE 2022. The additional scoring phase of both CASE 2021 and CASE 2022 allow only one submission per subtask and language combination per day. The test data of CASE 2021 were shared with participants at the same time with the training data. But the CASE 2022 evaluation data were shared around two weeks before the deadline for submission.

The same evaluation scores that are F1-macro for Subtasks 1 and 2, CoNLL-2012[8] for Subtask

[2] https://github.com/emerging-welfare/case-2021-shared-task for CASE 2021 and https://github.com/emerging-welfare/case-2022-multilingual-event for CASE 2022.

[3] https://github.com/bltlab/mot

[4] https://codalab.lisn.upsaclay.fr/competitions/7438, accessed on November 13, 2022.

[5] https://codalab.lisn.upsaclay.fr/competitions/7126, accessed on November 13, 2022.

[6] https://competitions.codalab.org/competitions/31247, which is not accessible due to change of the servers of Codalab.

[7] https://codalab.lisn.upsaclay.fr/competitions/7768, accessed on November 13, 2022.

[8] https://github.com/LoicGrobol/scorch, accessed on November 13, 2022.

3, and CoNLL-2000[9] script for Subtask 4 were utilized.

4 Results

Eighteen teams were registered for the task and obtained the training and test data for both CASE 2022 and CASE 2021. Ten and seven teams submitted their results for CASE 2021 and CASE 2022 respectively. Seven papers were submitted as system description papers to the CASE 2022 workshop in total. The scores of the submissions are calculated on two different Codalab pages for CASE 2021[10] and CASE 2022[11]. The teams that have participated are ARC-NLP (Sahin et al., 2022), CamPros (Kumari et al., 2022), CEIA-NLP (Fernandes et al., 2022), ClassBases (Wiriyathammabhum, 2022), EventGraph (You et al., 2022), NSUT-NLP (Suri et al., 2022), SPARTA (Müller and Dafnos, 2022). We provide details of the results and submissions of the participating teams for each subtask in the following subsections.[12]

4.1 CASE 2022 Subtask 1

The results for CASE 2022 subtask 1 are provided in Table 1. ARC-NLP finetune an ensemble of transformer-based language models and use ensemble learning, varying training data for each target language. They also perform tests with automatic translation of both training and test sets. They achieve 1st place both in Turkish and Mandarin, 2nd place in Portuguese and 3rd to 5th place in other languages. CEIA-NLP finetune XLM-Roberta-base transformers model with all the training data to achieve 1st place in Portuguese, 3rd or 4th places in other languages. ClassBases achieve 1st place in Hindi test data finetuning XLM-Roberta-large model, 5th or 6th places in other languages.

CamPros finetune XLM-Roberta-base model with all training data, and NSUT-NLP finetune mBERT while augmenting the data by translating different languages into each other.

4.2 CASE 2021 Subtask 1

The extended results for CASE 2021 subtask 1 are provided in Table 2. The boldness indicates CASE 2022 entries. ClassBases finetune XLM-Roberta-large transformers model to perform 1st in Hindi and 2nd in Portuguese test data. They also achieve 5th and 6th places in Spanish and English respectively. Another team that submitted their model to CASE 2021 test data is ARC-NLP, taking 5th, 8th and 9th places in Portuguese, Spanish and English.

4.3 Subtask 2

The extended results for CASE 2021 subtask 2 are provided in Table 3. The boldness indicates CASE 2022 entries. ARC-NLP train an ensemble of transformers models using all training data to achieve 4th, 5th and 7th places in Spanish, English and Portuguese respectively. ClassBases finetune mLUKE-base for Portuguese and Spanish placing 5th in both, XLM-Roberta-large for English taking 8th place.[13]

4.4 Subtask 3

The extended results for CASE 2021 subtask 3 are provided in Table 4. The boldness indicates CASE 2022 entries. ARC-NLP achieve 1st place in both English and Spanish, 2nd place in Portuguese. They use an ensemble of English transformers models for English, Portuguese and Spanish test data. They train with only English data and translating Portuguese test data into English during model prediction. For Spanish test data, they train with English, translated Portuguese and translated Spanish, and test on translated Spanish data.

4.5 Subtask 4

The extended results for CASE 2021 subtask 4 are provided in Table 5. The boldness indicates CASE 2022 entries. SPARTA employ two methods. Both of these methods build on pretrained XLM-Roberta-large and use a data augmentation technique (sentence reordering). For English and Portuguese, they gather articles that contain protest events from outside sources and use them for further pretraining. For Spanish, they use an XLM-Roberta-large model that was further pretrained on

[9] `https://github.com/sighsmile/conlleval`, accessed on November 13, 2022.

[10] `https://codalab.lisn.upsaclay.fr/competitions/7126#results`, accessed on Nov 14, 2022.

[11] `https://codalab.lisn.upsaclay.fr/competitions/7438#results`, accessed on Nov 14, 2022.

[12] The results and system descriptions from participants that did not submit a system description paper are provided as well. This shows the capacity of the state-of-the-art systems on our benchmark. These systems are provided with their codalab names that are colabhero, fine_sunny_day, gauravsingh, lapardnemihk9989, lizhuoqun2021_iscas.

[13] CamPros do not describe their model for subtask 2.

Team	English	Portuguese	Spanish	Hindi	Turkish	Urdu	Mandarin
ARC-NLP	80.74_{4}	79.85_{2}	69.44_{5}	80.08_{4}	84.06_{1}	77.99_{3}	83.39_{1}
CEIA-NLP	80.77_{3}	80.07_{1}	73.19_{3}	78.17_{6}	82.43_{4}	77.65_{4}	77.63_{4}
CamPros	76.52_{7}	77.11_{6}	69.55_{4}	80.49_{2}	74.75_{6}	73.77_{6}	75.90_{6}
ClassBases	78.50_{6}	77.11_{5}	69.25_{6}	80.78_{1}	78.57_{5}	75.72_{5}	77.16_{5}
NSUT-NLP	80.62_{5}	73.02_{7}	64.45_{7}	56.71_{7}	67.02_{7}	65.55_{7}	75.45_{7}
fine_sunny_day	82.22_{2}	79.05_{4}	73.84_{2}	80.11_{3}	82.91_{2}	79.71_{1}	80.99_{3}
lizhuoqun2021_iscas	82.49_{1}	79.22_{3}	74.96_{1}	80.01_{5}	82.89_{3}	78.67_{2}	83.06_{2}

Table 1: The performance of the submissions in terms of F1-macro and their ranks as a subscript for each language and each team participating in CASE 2022 subtask 1.

Team	English	Hindi	Portuguese	Spanish
ALEM	80.82_{10}	N/A	72.98_{11}	46.47_{13}
AMU-EuraNova	53.46_{15}	29.66_{11}	46.47_{14}	46.47_{13}
DAAI	84.55_{3}	77.07_{6}	82.43_{4}	69.31_{10}
DaDeFrTi	80.69_{11}	78.77_{3}	77.22_{10}	73.01_{7}
FKIE_itf_2021	73.90_{13}	54.24_{10}	62.39_{12}	68.20_{11}
HSAIR	77.58_{12}	59.55_{9}	81.21_{7}	69.84_{9}
IBM MNLP IE	83.93_{4}	78.53_{5}	84.00_{3}	77.27_{3}
SU-NLP	81.75_{8}	N/A	N/A	N/A
NoConflict	51.94_{16}	N/A	N/A	N/A
jitin	67.39_{14}	70.49_{8}	52.23_{13}	62.05_{12}
ARC-NLP	81.35_{9}	N/A	81.73_{5}	72.42_{8}
ClassBases	82.30_{6}	80.78_{1}	85.39_{2}	73.48_{5}
colabhero	82.34_{5}	74.21_{7}	81.73_{5}	73.27_{6}
fine_sunny_day	85.00_{2}	N/A	80.74_{8}	82.45_{1}
gauravsingh	82.28_{7}	78.60_{4}	79.41_{9}	73.86_{4}
lizhuoqun2021_iscas	85.12_{1}	80.01_{2}	85.87_{1}	81.19_{2}

Table 2: The performance of the submissions in terms of F1-macro and their ranks as a subscript for each language and each team participating in CASE 2021 subtask 1. Bold teams indicate CASE 2022 entries.

Team	English	Portuguese	Spanish
ALEM	79.67_{9}	42.79_{15}	45.30_{15}
AMU-EuraNova	75.64_{14}	81.61_{11}	76.39_{11}
DaDeFrTi	79.28_{10}	86.62_{6}	85.17_{6}
FKIE_itf_2021	64.96_{16}	75.81_{13}	70.49_{14}
HSAIR	78.50_{11}	85.06_{8}	83.25_{8}
IBM MNLP IE	84.56_{4}	88.47_{3}	88.61_{2}
IIITT	82.91_{7}	79.51_{12}	75.78_{12}
SU-NLP	83.05_{6}	N/A	N/A
NoConflict	85.32_{3}	87.00_{4}	79.97_{10}
jiawei1998	76.14_{13}	84.67_{9}	83.05_{9}
jitin	66.96_{15}	69.02_{14}	72.94_{13}
ARC-NLP	83.77_{5}	86.53_{7}	87.20_{4}
CamPros	77.94_{12}	81.63_{10}	83.69_{7}
ClassBases	81.12_{8}	86.83_{5}	87.10_{5}
fine_sunny_day	85.75_{2}	89.67_{1}	88.78_{1}
lizhuoqun2021_iscas	85.93_{1}	88.86_{2}	88.61_{2}

Table 3: The performance of the submissions in terms of F1-macro and their ranks as a subscript for each language and each team participating in subtask 2. Bold teams indicate CASE 2022 entries.

CoNLL 2002 Spanish data. They take 1st place both in Portuguese and Spanish, 3rd place in English.

ARC-NLP finetune an ensemble of transformers models for each language. They use all training data for Portuguese and Spanish, and only English for English test data. They achieve 2nd place in all languages. EventGraph aim to solve event extraction as semantic graph parsing. They use a graph encoding method where the labels for triggers and arguments are represented as node labels, also splitting multiple triggers. They use the pretrained XLM-Roberta-large as their encoder. They achieve 4th place both in English and Portuguese, 5th place in Spanish. ClassBases take 9th place in all languages finetuning XLM-Roberta-base transformers model.

Team	English	Portuguese	Spanish
DAAI	80.40_{4}	90.23_{6}	81.83_{6}
FKIE_itf_2021	77.05_{7}	91.33_{4}	82.52_{4}
Handshakes AI Research	79.01_{5}	90.61_{5}	81.95_{5}
IBM MNLP IE	84.44_{2}	92.84_{3}	84.23_{2}
NUS-IDS	81.20_{3}	93.03_{1}	83.15_{3}
SU-NLP	78.67_{6}	N/A	N/A
ARC-NLP	85.11_{1}	93.00_{2}	85.25_{1}

Table 4: The performance of the submissions in terms of CoNLL-2012 average score Pradhan et al. (2014) and their ranks as a subscript for each language and each team participating in subtask 3. Bold teams indicate CASE 2022 entries.

	Scores		
Team	English	Portuguese	Spanish
AMU-EuraNova	69.96_{7}	61.87_{8}	56.64_{8}
Handshakes AI Research	73.53_{5}	68.15_{6}	62.21_{6}
IBM MNLP IE	78.11_{1}	73.24_{3}	66.20_{3}
SU-NLP	2.58_{10}	N/A	N/A
jitin	66.43_{8}	64.19_{7}	58.35_{7}
ARC-NLP	77.83_{2}	73.84_{2}	67.99_{2}
ClassBases	46.88_{9}	12.52_{9}	37.09_{9}
EventGraph	74.76_{4}	71.72_{4}	64.48_{5}
SPARTA	76.60_{3}	74.56_{1}	69.86_{1}
lapardnemihk9989	72.18_{6}	70.98_{5}	64.83_{4}

Table 5: The performance of the submissions in terms of F1 score based on CoNLL-2003 (Tjong Kim Sang and De Meulder, 2003) and their ranks as a subscript for each language and each team participating in subtask 4. Bold teams indicate CASE 2022 entries.

5 Conclusion

The CASE 2022 extension consists of expanding the test data with more data in previously available languages, namely, English, Hindi, Portuguese, and Spanish, and adding new test data in Mandarin, Turkish, and Urdu for Sub-task 1, document classification. The training data from CASE 2021 in English, Portuguese and Spanish were utilized. Therefore, predicting document labels in Hindi, Mandarin, Turkish, and Urdu occurs in a zero-shot setting.

The CASE 2022 workshop accepts reports on systems developed for predicting test data of CASE 2021 as well. We observe that the best systems submitted by CASE 2022 participants achieve between 79.71 and 84.06 F1-macro for new languages in a zero-shot setting. The winning approaches are mainly ensembling models and merging data in multiple languages. The best two submissions on CASE 2021 data outperform submissions from last year for Subtask 1 and Subtask 2 in all languages. Only the following scenarios were not outperformed by new submissions on CASE 2021: Subtask 3 Portuguese & Subtask 4 English.

We aim at increasing number of languages and subtasks such as event coreference resolution (Hürriyetoğlu et al., 2022) and event type classification(Hürriyetoğlu et al., 2021) in the scope of following edition of this shared task.

References

Fırat Duruşan, Ali Hürriyetoğlu, Erdem Yörük, Osman Mutlu, Çağrı Yoltar, Burak Gürel, and Alvaro Comin. 2022. Global contentious politics database (glocon) annotation manuals.

Diogo Fernandes, Adalberto Junior, Gabriel da Mata Marques, Anderson da Silva Soares, and Arlindo Rodrigues Galvao Filho. 2022. CEIA-NLP at CASE 2022 Task 1: Protest News Detection for Portuguese. In *Proceedings of the 5th Workshop on Challenges and Applications of Automated Extraction of Socio-political Events from Text (CASE 2022)*, online. Association for Computational Linguistics (ACL).

Ali Hürriyetoğlu, Osman Mutlu, Erdem Yörük, Farhana Ferdousi Liza, Ritesh Kumar, and Shyam Ratan. 2021. Multilingual protest news detection - shared task 1, CASE 2021. In *Proceedings of the 4th Workshop on Challenges and Applications of Automated Extraction of Socio-political Events from Text (CASE 2021)*, pages 79–91, Online. Association for Computational Linguistics.

Ali Hürriyetoğlu, Hristo Tanev, Vanni Zavarella, Reyyan Yeniterzi, Osman Mutlu, and Erdem Yörük. 2022. Challenges and applications of automated extraction of socio-political events from text (case 2022): Workshop and shared task report. In *Proceedings of the 5th Workshop on Challenges and Applications of Automated Extraction of Socio-political Events from Text (CASE 2022)*, online. Association for Computational Linguistics (ACL).

Ali Hürriyetoğlu, Osman Mutlu, Fatih Beyhan, Fırat Duruşan, Ali Safaya, Reyyan Yeniterzi, and Erdem Yörük. 2022. Event coreference resolution for contentious politics events.

Ali Hürriyetoğlu, Erdem Yörük, Osman Mutlu, Fırat Duruşan, Çağrı Yoltar, Deniz Yüret, and Burak Gürel. 2021. Cross-Context News Corpus for Protest Event-Related Knowledge Base Construction. *Data Intelligence*, 3(2):308–335.

Ali Hürriyetoğlu, Vanni Zavarella, Hristo Tanev, Erdem Yörük, Ali Safaya, and Osman Mutlu. 2020. Automated extraction of socio-political events from news (AESPEN): Workshop and shared task report. In *Proceedings of the Workshop on Automated Extraction of Socio-political Events from News 2020*, pages 1–6, Marseille, France. European Language Resources Association (ELRA).

Neha Kumari, Mrinal Anand, Tushar Mohan, and Ponnurangam Kumaraguru. 2022. CamPros at CASE 2022 Task 1: Transformer-based Multilingual Protest News Detection. In *Proceedings of the 5th Workshop on Challenges and Applications of Automated Extraction of Socio-political Events from Text (CASE 2022)*, online. Association for Computational Linguistics (ACL).

Osman Mutlu. 2022. Utilizing coarse-grained data in low-data settings for event extraction.

Arthur Müller and Andreas Dafnos. 2022. SPARTA at CASE 2021 Task 1: Evaluating Different Techniques to Improve Event Extraction. In *Proceedings of the 5th Workshop on Challenges and Applications of Automated Extraction of Socio-political Events from Text (CASE 2022)*, online. Association for Computational Linguistics (ACL).

Chester Palen-Michel, June Kim, and Constantine Lignos. 2022. Multilingual open text release 1: Public domain news in 44 languages. In *Proceedings of the Thirteenth Language Resources and Evaluation Conference*, pages 2080–2089, Marseille, France. European Language Resources Association.

Sameer Pradhan, Xiaoqiang Luo, Marta Recasens, Eduard Hovy, Vincent Ng, and Michael Strube. 2014. Scoring coreference partitions of predicted mentions: A reference implementation. In *Proceedings of the 52nd Annual Meeting of the Association for Computational Linguistics (Volume 2: Short Papers)*, pages 30–35, Baltimore, Maryland. Association for Computational Linguistics.

Umitcan Sahin, Oguzhan Ozcelik, Izzet Emre Kucukkaya, and Cagri Toraman. 2022. ARC-NLP at CASE 2022 Task 1: Ensemble Learning for Multilingual Protest Event Detection. In *Proceedings of the 5th Workshop on Challenges and Applications of Automated Extraction of Socio-political Events from Text (CASE 2022)*, online. Association for Computational Linguistics (ACL).

Manan Suri, Krish Chopra, and Adwita Arora. 2022. NSUT-NLP at CASE 2022 Task 1: Multilingual Protest Event Detection using Transformer-based Models. In *Proceedings of the 5th Workshop on Challenges and Applications of Automated Extraction of Socio-political Events from Text (CASE 2022)*, online. Association for Computational Linguistics (ACL).

Fiona Anting Tan, Ali Hürriyetoğlu, Tommaso Caselli, Nelleke Oostdijk, Hansi Hettiarachchi, Tadashi Nomoto, Onur Uca, and Farhana Ferdousi Liza. 2022a. Event causality identification with causal news corpus - shared task 3, CASE 2022. In *Proceedings of the 5th Workshop on Challenges and Applications of Automated Extraction of Socio-political Events from Text (CASE 2022)*, Online. Association for Computational Linguistics.

Fiona Anting Tan, Ali Hürrriyetoğlu, Tommaso Caselli, Nelleke Oostdijk, Tadashi Nomoto, Hansi Hettiarachchi, Iqra Ameer, Onur Uca, Farhana Ferdousi Liza, and Tiancheng Hu. 2022b. The causal news corpus: Annotating causal relations in event sentences from news. In *Proceedings of the Language Resources and Evaluation Conference*, pages 2298–2310, Marseille, France. European Language Resources Association.

Erik F. Tjong Kim Sang and Fien De Meulder. 2003. Introduction to the conll-2003 shared task: Language-independent named entity recognition. In *Proceedings of the Seventh Conference on Natural Language Learning at HLT-NAACL 2003 - Volume 4*, CONLL '03, page 142–147, USA. Association for Computational Linguistics.

Peratham Wiriyathammabhum. 2022. ClassBases at the CASE-2022 Multilingual Protest Event Detection Task: Multilingual Protest News Detection and Automatically Replicating Manually Created Event Datasets. In *Proceedings of the 5th Workshop on Challenges and Applications of Automated Extraction of Socio-political Events from Text (CASE 2022)*, online. Association for Computational Linguistics (ACL).

Huiling You, David Samuel, Samia Touileb, and Lilja Øvrelid. 2022. EventGraph at CASE 2021 Task 1: A General Graph-based Approach to Protest Event Extraction. In *Proceedings of the 5th Workshop on Challenges and Applications of Automated Extraction of Socio-political Events from Text (CASE 2022)*, online. Association for Computational Linguistics (ACL).

Erdem Yörük, Ali Hürriyetoğlu, Fırat Duruşan, and Çağrı Yoltar. 2021. Random sampling in corpus design: Cross-context generalizability in automated multicountry protest event collection. *American Behavioral Scientist*, 0(0):00027642211021630.

Vanni Zavarella, Hristo Tanev, Ali Hürriyetoğlu, Peratham Wiriyathammabhum, and Bertrand De Longueville. 2022. Tracking COVID-19 protest events in the United States. Shared Task 2: Event Database Replication, CASE 2022. In *Proceedings of the 5th Workshop on Challenges and Applications of Automated Extraction of Socio-political Events from Text (CASE 2022)*, online. Association for Computational Linguistics (ACL).

Author Index

Association for Computational Linguistics
209 N. Eighth Street
Stroudsburg, Pennsylvania 18360

ISBN 978-1-7138-9105-5

CURRAN ASSOCIATES INC.
proceedings
.com